Strained Relations

**A National Bureau
of Economic Research
Monograph**

Strained Relations
US Foreign-Exchange Operations and Monetary Policy in the Twentieth Century

Michael D. Bordo, Owen F. Humpage, and Anna J. Schwartz

The University of Chicago Press

Chicago and London

MICHAEL D. BORDO is a Board of Governors Professor of Economics at Rutgers University, the State University of New Jersey; a research associate of the National Bureau of Economic Research; and a Distinguished Visiting Fellow at the Hoover Institution, Stanford University. OWEN F. HUMPAGE is a senior economic advisor in the Research Department of the Federal Reserve Bank of Cleveland. ANNA J. SCHWARTZ (1915–2012) was a research associate of the National Bureau of Economic Research for more than seventy years.

The University of Chicago Press, Chicago 60637
The University of Chicago Press, Ltd., London
© 2015 by The University of Chicago
All rights reserved. Published 2015.
Printed in the United States of America

24 23 22 21 20 19 18 17 16 15   1 2 3 4 5

ISBN-13: 978-0-226-05148-2 (cloth)
ISBN-13: 978-0-226-05151-2 (e-book)
DOI: 10.7208/chicago/9780226051512.001.0001

Library of Congress Cataloging-in-Publication Data

Bordo, Michael D., author.
    Strained relations : US foreign-exchange operations and monetary policy in the twentieth century / Michael D. Bordo, Owen F. Humpage, and Anna J. Schwartz.
    pages cm. — (A National Bureau of Economic Research monograph)
    Includes bibliographical references and index.
    ISBN 978-0-226-05148-2 (cloth : alkaline paper) — ISBN 978-0-226-05151-2 (e-book)
    1. Foreign exchange—Law and legislation—United States—History—20th century.
2. Foreign exchange market—History—20th century. 3. United States—Economic policy—20th century. I. Humpage, Owen F., author. II. Schwartz, Anna J. (Anna Jacobson), 1915–2012, author. III. Title. IV. Series: National Bureau of Economic Research monograph.
HG3903.B67 2015
332.4′509730904—dc23

2014014046

⊚ This paper meets the requirements of ANSI/NISO Z39.48–1992 (Permanence of Paper).

Relation of the Directors to the
Work and Publications of the
National Bureau of Economic Research

1. The object of the NBER is to ascertain and present to the economics profession, and to the public more generally, important economic facts and their interpretation in a scientific manner without policy recommendations. The Board of Directors is charged with the responsibility of ensuring that the work of the NBER is carried on in strict conformity with this object.

2. The President shall establish an internal review process to ensure that book manuscripts proposed for publication DO NOT contain policy recommendations. This shall apply both to the proceedings of conferences and to manuscripts by a single author or by one or more co-authors but shall not apply to authors of comments at NBER conferences who are not NBER affiliates.

3. No book manuscript reporting research shall be published by the NBER until the President has sent to each member of the Board a notice that a manuscript is recommended for publication and that in the President's opinion it is suitable for publication in accordance with the above principles of the NBER. Such notification will include a table of contents and an abstract or summary of the manuscript's content, a list of contributors if applicable, and a response form for use by Directors who desire a copy of the manuscript for review. Each manuscript shall contain a summary drawing attention to the nature and treatment of the problem studied and the main conclusions reached.

4. No volume shall be published until forty-five days have elapsed from the above notification of intention to publish it. During this period a copy shall be sent to any Director requesting it, and if any Director objects to publication on the grounds that the manuscript contains policy recommendations, the objection will be presented to the author(s) or editor(s). In case of dispute, all members of the Board shall be notified, and the President shall appoint an ad hoc committee of the Board to decide the matter; thirty days additional shall be granted for this purpose.

5. The President shall present annually to the Board a report describing the internal manuscript review process, any objections made by Directors before publication or by anyone after publication, any disputes about such matters, and how they were handled.

6. Publications of the NBER issued for informational purposes concerning the work of the Bureau, or issued to inform the public of the activities at the Bureau, including but not limited to the NBER Digest and Reporter, shall be consistent with the object stated in paragraph 1. They shall contain a specific disclaimer noting that they have not passed through the review procedures required in this resolution. The Executive Committee of the Board is charged with the review of all such publications from time to time.

7. NBER working papers and manuscripts distributed on the Bureau's web site are not deemed to be publications for the purpose of this resolution, but they shall be consistent with the object stated in paragraph 1. Working papers shall contain a specific disclaimer noting that they have not passed through the review procedures required in this resolution. The NBER's web site shall contain a similar disclaimer. The President shall establish an internal review process to ensure that the working papers and the web site do not contain policy recommendations, and shall report annually to the Board on this process and any concerns raised in connection with it.

8. Unless otherwise determined by the Board or exempted by the terms of paragraphs 6 and 7, a copy of this resolution shall be printed in each NBER publication as described in paragraph 2 above.

Contents

Preface

This book has been in preparation for a long time. Michael Bordo and Anna Schwartz conceived of the idea for a history of US exchange-market intervention and began collaborating on the research in 1990. Owen Humpage joined the project in 2000. We are deeply indebted to many individuals and organizations for help and encouragement over the years.

Much of our research relied heavily on a unique, heretofore confidential, data set consisting of all official US foreign-exchange transactions conducted through the Federal Reserve Bank of New York between 1962 and 1995. We are very grateful to Dino Kos and Laura Weir at the Federal Reserve Bank of New York, Michael Leahy at the Board of Governors of the Federal Reserve System, and Timothy D. DuLaney at the US Treasury for providing us with these data. We owe a huge debt to Zebo Zakir, a former research assistant at the Federal Reserve Bank of Cleveland, for painstakingly entering these data into computer files from various printed documents. Likewise, we extend our sincere appreciation to Michael Shenk, who, as we learned more about the operations, helped us reorganize a large part of the data. We also sincerely thank Norman Bernard at the Board of Governors of the Federal Reserve System for providing us with many unpublished documents that explained US foreign-exchange operations.

We wish to express our sincere gratitude to the Federal Reserve Bank of Cleveland, especially Jerry Jordan, Sandra Pianalto, and Mark Sniderman, which provided generous support for the project, and to the Sarah Scaife Foundation which generously funded the research. We also thank the National Bureau of Economic Research for its financial support. Martin Feldstein, past president of the NBER, offered encouragement from the start. Marinella Moscheni, at the NBER's New York office, provided very valuable administrative assistance.

Our thanks to Will Melick at Kenyon College, Allan Meltzer at Carnegie Mellon University, and Christopher Neely at the Federal Reserve Bank of St. Louis for their comments on some of the chapters, to Michele Lachman at the Federal Reserve Bank of Cleveland for her editorial recommendations on some of the chapters, and to Monica Crabtree-Reusser for her assistance with the figures.

We are grateful to David Wheelock for giving us a copy of W. A. Brown's unpublished 1942 manuscript on the Exchange Stabilization Fund and to Sarah Millard at the Bank of England who provided materials from the Bank of England archives related to that bank's interactions with the Federal Reserve Bank of New York and the US Treasury in the 1930s. Finally, we thank Michael Leahy at the Board of Governors for graciously enduring many questions and requests related to this and similar projects over the years and for his comments on chapters 4, 5, and 6.

Our coauthor, Anna J. Schwartz, passed away on 21 June 2012. Anna wrote chapter 3 before we completed most of the other chapters and before we settled on the main organizing theme of the book. We decided not to alter Anna's chapter, since it is her last professional contribution to economic history.

The views expressed in this book are the authors' and not necessarily those of the Federal Reserve Bank of Cleveland, the Board of Governors of the Federal Reserve System, the board staff, or the NBER.

For acknowledgments, sources of research support, and disclosure of the authors' material financial relationships, if any, please see www.nber.org /chapters/c12908.ack.

1

On the Evolution of US Foreign-Exchange-Market Intervention
Thesis, Theory, and Institutions

1.1 Introduction

Today, most of the advanced economies—Australia, Canada, Japan, the euro area, Sweden, the United Kingdom, and the United States—allow market forces to determine their exchange rates. Policymakers in these economies understand that if they want to focus their monetary policies on independently determined domestic objectives—low inflation and growth at potential—and to continue to enjoy the substantial benefit of free cross-border financial flows, they must allow their exchange rates to float.

Nevertheless, these same monetary authorities recognize that, from time to time, the normally smooth operation of foreign-exchange markets can become impaired, and they maintain the capacity to influence key nominal exchange rates. Usually, they do so through official purchases or sales of foreign exchange. The effectiveness, the limitations, and the costs of these policies, however, have been and remain the subject of debate. Over the last twenty years or so, reflecting the modern tenor of this debate, the monetary authorities in most of the large advanced economies have come to regard foreign-exchange-market intervention as a tool that they should deploy sparingly, if at all.

This has not always been the prevailing view. Throughout most of the twentieth century, monetary authorities considered exchange-rate stability an important, if not the sole, objective of monetary policy. Even after the adoption of generalized floating in 1973, policymakers hoped that foreign-exchange-market intervention offered a means of influencing exchange rates independent of their monetary policies. Traditional instruments of monetary policy, they believed, could focus on price stability or growth at potential, while intervention could influence the path of key exchange rates. This view was never constant, and it seldom went unchallenged.

This book explores the evolution of exchange-market policy—primarily foreign-exchange intervention—in the United States. It is fundamentally a study of institutional learning and adaptation as the monetary-policy regime changed following the collapse of the classical gold standard. As such, this study explains the economic developments, the political environment, and the bureaucratic issues that nurtured those changes. Although we reference many of the econometric studies of foreign-exchange-market intervention, ours is not a survey of the voluminous literature.[1] While we introduce some empirical analysis, ours is primarily a historical narrative.

We observe this evolutionary process primarily through the lens of Federal Reserve documents and a unique data set consisting of all official US foreign-exchange transactions executed through the foreign exchange desk at the Federal Reserve Bank of New York between 1961 and 1997. Although we discuss operations of the US Treasury, particularly as they dovetail with the Federal Reserve's policies, we lacked detailed documentation of Treasury attitudes about intervention. Hence the scope of our analysis is somewhat restricted to the Federal Reserve. We also refer to other advanced countries in our narrative, but again, we only consider them insofar as they relate to US policies. For the most part, we do not discuss how foreign governments formulated policies in an open economy.

This introductory chapter starts with an overview of the major theme of this book: Attitudes about foreign-exchange intervention and monetary policy have changed over the decades and have come to embrace a monetary policy focused on price stability, freely floating exchange rates, and global openness. It then discusses the economics of exchange-market intervention, offers a brief interpretation of existing empirical research, and provides an overview of the institutional arrangements for intervention in the United States. In subsequent chapters, our historical narrative explores all of the topics in much greater detail. The final section of this introduction offers a road map to the subsequent chapters.

1.2   Monetary-Policy Evolution and the Development of Foreign-Exchange-Market Intervention

The same evolutionary process that forged modern views about monetary policy has shaped contemporary attitudes about foreign-exchange-market intervention. Over the past century, monetary authorities have grappled with the basic problem of having more economic policy objectives than independent instruments with which to attain them. Standard monetary-policy tools, which alter bank reserves and interest rates, cannot continuously maintain fixed exchange rates and independent domestic policy objectives unless a monetary authority also restricts financial flows. This is the well-known trilemma of international finance.[2] Modern foreign-exchange intervention resulted from attempts to find an additional instrument with which to affect exchange rates while allowing monetary authorities to set independent domestic inflation objectives without sacrificing the gains from unfettered cross-border financial flows. Intervention was an attempt to skirt the trilemma.

By the end of the twentieth century, monetary authorities saw a credible commitment to price stability as the key contribution that central banks can make in maintaining economic growth at potential—or along a full-employment path of output—and in fostering exchange-rate stability.[3] In this view, an activist intervention policy is worse than superfluous. To be effective monetary policy must be credible, and foreign-exchange intervention—even interventions that leave the money stock unaltered—can threaten that credibility. This is especially true for a central bank, like the Federal Reserve, that operates without a legislative mandate for price stability and is subservient in its intervention operations to fiscal authorities (Broaddus and Goodfriend 1996).

Intervention—the key focus of this book—refers to official purchases and sales of foreign exchange that monetary officials undertake to influence exchange rates. This definition describes intervention in terms of a type of transaction and a motive guiding that transaction. The distinction among various types of transactions is important because countries have many policy levers affecting the exchange value of their currencies. This broader set of operations constitutes exchange-rate policy, of which intervention is a subset, and it includes other things such as commercial policies, restraints of financial flows, or even monetary-policy actions targeted at exchange rates. An understanding of the motive for buying and selling foreign exchange is also a necessary component of the definition of intervention because governments often transact in foreign-exchange markets for purposes other than altering their exchange rates. Central banks sometimes buy or sell foreign exchange to manage the currency composition of their reserve portfolios or to undertake transactions for customers, such as their own fiscal authorities and other monetary authorities, or even to conduct domestically focused monetary policy. While these transactions may well affect exchange rates, this is not their purpose, and hence, they do not constitute intervention.[4]

Intervention, and exchange-rate policies more broadly, derive from a desire to limit exchange-rate variability—a policy objective that the classical gold standard most completely reached. Under the classical gold standard (1880–1914) countries did not maintain domestic monetary-policy objectives as such; they effectively focused on preserving fixed exchange rates. Countries set an official price of gold and promised to buy and sell unlimited quantities of gold to maintain that price. They also allowed individuals to freely import and export gold. Exchange-rate parities were derivatives of official gold prices and were contained within gold export and import points, which the cost of arbitrage in gold determined. Forms of money other than gold coins, such as bank notes and national currencies, circulated but were ultimately convertible into gold. With these arrangements, the gold standard limited monetary authorities' abilities to undertake discretionary policy actions and anchored expectations about the long-run internal and external values of money. The classical gold standard solved the trilemma at the expense of domestic monetary-policy independence.

The gold standard, however, did not completely eliminate discretionary monetary-policy actions to protect the domestic economy and banking sector from disruptive gold flows.[5] The ideal view of quick and automatic gold-standard adjustment rests on a frictionless world, but real and financial frictions did exist and encouraged discretionary governmental actions.[6] Central banks, of course, could operate with some latitude within the gold points. They could, for example, alter the ratio of gold reserves to currency or change their discount rates. If, however, a substantial amount of gold flowed in or out of a country, pushing its exchange rate to one or the other gold point, central banks were generally expected to reinforce the domestic monetary effects of these gold flows through their discount-rate policies. Many monetary authorities did not conform to these so-called rules of the game. If the ratio of their gold reserves to currency remained sufficiently high, they could either not act at the gold point or attempt to offset the effects of gold flows on their monetary bases. Some countries resorted to gold devices—policies that effectively altered the gold points—such as artificial impediments to the export or import of gold. Some central banks even acquired foreign-exchange reserves and intervened both to smooth exchange-rate fluctuations and to keep exchange rates within the gold points. These operations at the gold points served to soften the trilemma's constraints. Still, maintaining the official gold price and fixed exchange rates with free cross-border financial flows was sacrosanct.

The classical gold standard collapsed at the onset of World War I, along with the view that monetary policy should focus on maintaining a fixed exchange rate to the near-complete exclusion of domestic-policy objectives. To be sure, the gold-exchange standard (1925–1931) remained a strong commitment to fixed exchange rates, but not one for which countries would long sacrifice internal economic conditions. When necessary, countries sterilized gold flows, devalued their currencies, and erected trade barriers and capital controls. Countries also intervened in foreign-currency markets. They were trying to escape the strictures of the trilemma.

The Great Depression saw the collapse of the gold-exchange standard as countries focused monetary policy on domestic objectives. Still, exchange-rate stability remained a desirable objective. The United Kingdom established the Exchange Equalisation Account (1932) and the United States followed with its own Exchange Stabilization Fund (1934). Both funds sought to promote exchange-rate stability through interventions in the gold and foreign-exchange markets, while monetary and fiscal policies pursued macroeconomic objectives. The Tripartite Agreement of 1936 introduced a degree of international cooperation into attempts at exchange-rate management, which would persist thereafter. The funds and the agreement sought to offer policymakers an additional means to meet their expanding set of objectives.

The disconnection between discretionary monetary policy and adherence to rigidly fixed exchange rates, which grew as the classical gold standard collapsed, progressed through the Bretton Woods era. The Federal Reserve System—the dominant central bank under Bretton Woods—focused monetary policy almost exclusively on domestic economic objectives, notably full employment or growth at potential. Other countries bore the burden of intervening to defend their currencies. Constraints on financial flows often proliferated. By 1960, the fundamental weakness of the Bretton Woods system, which Triffin's paradox described, began to appear. The US Treasury's Exchange Stabilization Fund (ESF) and the Federal Reserve System adopted myriad stopgap mechanisms, notably temporary facilities offering cover for foreign central banks' dollar exposures and funding for deficit countries' interventions. These mechanisms lengthened the Bretton Woods system's tenure, but offered no solution to the trilemma. Bretton Woods collapsed because neither the Federal Reserve nor other central banks would indefinitely subvert domestic economic conditions to the rigors of maintaining fixed exchange rates. Generalized floating began in 1973.

Although Bretton Woods imposed few, if any, constraints on US monetary policy, the Federal Reserve failed to maintain price stability after 1965. By the late 1970s, inflation in the United States reached double-digit levels through a combination of bad economic theory, a blinkered focus on full employment, poor measurement, and at times political pressure. People no longer believed that the Federal Reserve would continue to accept the real output and employment costs of eliminating inflation. Inflation expectations became imbedded in economic decisions with adverse consequences for potential growth. The near crisis atmosphere that emerged in the late 1970s prompted a dramatic change in monetary policy under Chairman Paul Volcker. The Federal Reserve, thereafter, embarked on a long process of rebuilding its credibility. Monetary policy increasingly focused on an inflation objective, and the Federal Open Market Committee (FOMC) eventually accepted that low and stable inflation expectations were necessary for maintaining the economy's growth at potential.

A similar learning process occurred with respect to foreign-exchange operations after the collapse of Bretton Woods. Monetary authorities reluctantly accepted floating exchange rates, and, despite their desire for a greater degree of policy independence, they initially feared giving exchange rates free reign. Policymakers believed that foreign-exchange-market inefficiencies created unnecessary volatility and caused rates to deviate from fundamental values.

Intervention—particularly on the part of the United States—was necessary to provide guidance and to calm market disorder. Moreover, the early-on, predominant explanation for the effectiveness of sterilized intervention— the portfolio-balance channel—supported exchange-market activism by suggesting that intervention solved the instrument-versus-objectives problem. In this view, monetary policy could focus on domestic objectives, and intervention could manage exchange rates. Intervention offered a solution to the trilemma.

Views about exchange-market efficiency changed more slowly than attitudes about effectiveness of intervention. By the early 1980s, policymakers in the United States were questioning whether sterilized intervention did indeed provide a means of systematically affecting exchange rates independent of monetary policy. Reflecting this uncertainty, the United States, from 1981 through 1985, adopted a minimalist approach to exchange-market operations, but as the dollar dramatically appreciated under a mix of tight monetary and loose fiscal policies and seemed to overshoot a value consistent with fundamentals, pressure for intervention reemerged. The Plaza and Louvre Accords were attempts to reemphasize exchange rates as objectives of policy. Unfortunately, by then the now prevailing view of intervention— that it signaled future monetary-policy changes—left advocates of coordinated exchange-market operations short one policy instrument.

That intervention did not solve the trilemma was one thing; that it made the situation even worse was something altogether intolerable. In the late 1980s and early 1990s, as the FOMC worked to strengthen its policy credibility, the thrust of foreign-exchange intervention—now usually undertaken at the Treasury's behest—often conflicted with the motivation for monetary policy. The FOMC believed that such interventions created uncertainty about its commitment to price stability. Moreover, the committee feared that the related institutional connections between the US Treasury and the Federal Reserve—chiefly swap lines and warehousing privileges—also threatened the Federal Reserve's independence and, therefore, its credibility. These concerns—not questions about intervention's effectiveness—curtailed the operations. By the late 1990s, central banks in the advanced economies accepted that a commitment of price stability also removed uncertainty about monetary policy as a source of volatility in foreign-exchange markets. Most large developed economies ended their activist approach to intervention. The large developed economies solved the trilemma in favor of monetary policy independence, floating exchange rates, and free cross-border financial flows.

Nevertheless, the large developed economies have not completely forsaken foreign exchange-market intervention. While policymakers now generally view foreign-exchange markets as highly efficient, they still see the potential for occasional bouts of disorder. One might dismiss intervention as an independent instrument with which to routinely—or frequently—manage exchange rates, but one cannot deny that intervention sometimes affects exchange rates.

1.3   Intervention as Distinct from Monetary Policy

Economists have offered two broad channels through which intervention, as distinct from monetary policy, might affect exchange rates. Each channel has different implications for what intervention might achieve and how it should be conducted. To understand these channels, one must first understand the important distinction between sterilized and nonsterilized intervention, since only the former could possibly give monetary authorities an additional instrument with which to pursue an exchange-rate objective independent of their monetary policy.

When a central bank buys or sells foreign exchange, it typically makes or accepts payment in domestic currency by crediting or debiting the reserve accounts of the appropriate commercial banks. Except for the instruments involved, the mechanics of the transactions are similar to those of an open-market operation, and like an open-market operation, foreign-exchange interventions have the potential to drain or add bank reserves.

Central banks in large developed economies typically offset, or sterilize, any unwanted impacts from their foreign-exchange interventions on bank reserves (see Lecourt and Raymond 2006; Neely 2001, 2007). They can do so through offsetting open-market operations. Any central bank that conducts its monetary policy through an interest-rate or reserve-aggregate target— as many usually do—will automatically offset all transactions, including foreign-exchange interventions, that threaten the attainment of its operating objective.

Sterilization prevents foreign-exchange transactions from interfering with the domestic objectives of monetary policy. The potential for conflict between the two depends on the nature of the underlying disturbance to the exchange market. In general, only if the underlying disturbance is domestic in origin and monetary in nature, will pursuing an exchange-rate objective through nonsterilized intervention *not* conflict with a central bank's inflation objective. A central bank, for example, whose currency appreciates in the face of a domestic deflation, can prevent both a deflation and a currency appreciation through faster money growth produced either by nonsterilized intervention or traditional monetary policy. If the underlying shock is either foreign or real in nature, a nonsterilized intervention will inevitably interfere with a central bank's inflation objective (Craig and Humpage 2003; Bordo and Schwartz 1989).[7]

Sterilization is also important in countries whose central banks are independent, but whose fiscal authorities maintain primary responsibility for intervention, because in the absence of sterilization, the fiscal authorities would maintain some direct control over monetary policy. In Japan, for example, the Ministry of Finance maintains authority for foreign-exchange intervention, and the otherwise independent Bank of Japan acts as its agent. A similar relationship exists in the United States where the US Treasury and the Federal Reserve share responsibility for intervention. If these central banks did not routinely sterilize foreign-exchange operations, their independence and the credibility of their monetary policies might come under question. A loss of credibility could increase the speed with which monetary impulses translate into inflation and adversely skew any short-term inflation-output tradeoff.

To be sure, central banks sometimes factor nominal exchange-rate objectives into their monetary-policy decisions. The Federal Reserve, for example, has occasionally altered its federal-funds-rate target while undertaking compatible foreign-exchange operations. One might expect that implementing the appropriate monetary-policy change through the purchase or sale of foreign currency could have a bigger impact on the exchange rate than implementing the move through open-market operations in government securities, and thereby justify official nonsterilized foreign-exchange operations. Bonser-Neal, Roley, and Sellon (1998) and Humpage (1999) show that US interventions undertaken in conjunction with changes in the federal funds rate have no apparent effect on exchange rates; both studies attribute observed exchange-rate responses solely to the federal funds rate.[8]

Under the best of circumstances, nonsterilized interventions seem redundant to conventional open-market operations.[9] Under the worst of circumstances, nonsterilized interventions can conflict with domestic monetary policy objectives. Sterilized intervention, on the other hand, holds open the prospect of providing central banks with the means of affecting exchange rates independent of their domestic monetary policy objectives. How sterilized intervention might actually do this has been the focus of research over at least the last thirty-five years.

1.4   Theoretical Underpinnings

The asset-market approach to exchange-rate determination provides a useful framework for conceptualizing the channels through which sterilized intervention might influence exchange rates (see Dominguez 1992; Aguilar and Nydahl 2000). The asset-market approach, which emphasizes the importance of expectations, describes current exchange rates in terms of existing fundamentals and expectations about their future paths. Within this framework, sterilized intervention can affect current exchange rates if it alters fundamental determinants of exchange rates (other than the monetary base), if it affects expectations about these fundamentals, or even if it impacts expectations that are unrelated to fundamentals.

1.4.1 Portfolio-Balance Channel

Although sterilized intervention has no effect on the monetary base, sterilization alters the currency composition of publicly held government securities. The associated rebalancing of private-sector portfolios, however, offers central banks a potential channel through which to routinely and fundamentally affect exchange rates without interfering with their domestic monetary-policy objectives. Economists refer to this as the portfolio-balance channel.

The very act of sterilizing an intervention increases outstanding government securities denominated in the currency that central banks are selling relative to government securities denominated in the currency that central banks are buying. If risk-averse asset holders view securities in different currency denominations as imperfect substitutes, they will only hold the relatively more abundant asset in their portfolios if the expected rate of return on that asset compensates them for the perceived risk of doing so.[10] Their initial reluctance to hold the relatively more abundant security forces a spot depreciation of the currency that central banks are selling relative to the currency that they are buying. The spot depreciation relative to the exchange rate's longer-term expected value then raises the anticipated rate of return on the now more-abundant securities, and compensates asset holders for the perceived increase in risk.[11]

Unfortunately, most empirical studies find the relevant elasticities to be either statistically insignificant or quantitatively negligible (Edison 1993). Central banks also do not put much stock in the portfolio-balance channel (Neely 2007, 11). Dominguez and Frankel (1993a) is a notable, often-cited exception to the standard conclusion; they find a statistically and economically significant relationship. The reason offered for the absence of a portfolio effect is that the typical intervention transaction is miniscule relative to the stock of outstanding government assets.

If, however, US intervention did operate through a portfolio-balance channel, then intervention should exert a fairly robust influence on exchange rates. A number of papers find some connection between intervention and uncovered interest parity, but the relationship is not very robust across either time periods or currencies, suggesting that the finding does not stem from a portfolio-balance effect (see, e.g., Humpage and Osterberg 1992).

Recently, proponents of the microstructure approach to exchange-rate determination have renewed interest in the portfolio-balance approach (Evans and Lyons 2001; Lyons 2001). These models focus on the role of foreign-exchange dealers who, as market makers, stand ready to buy and sell foreign exchange. These same dealers typically do not hold sizable open positions in a foreign currency, especially overnight (Cheung and Chinn 2001). They will try to distribute their unwanted currency holdings among other dealers and eventually among their commercial customers. Since different currencies are not perfect substitutes in the dealers' portfolio, this inventory-adjustment process resembles a portfolio-balance-like mechanism at the microlevel. Evans and Lyons (2001, 2005) claim evidence of both temporary (dealer to dealer inventory reshuffling) and permanent (dealer to customer) portfolio-balance effects. The permanent component of this model, however, is at odds with the macroliterature. The microstructure model measures only currency flows in the foreign-exchange market. It does not account for the fact that the sterilization process leaves the total amount of bank reserves for each currency unchanged, while changing the relative stock of domestic- and foreign-currency-denominated government securities in the hands of the public.

1.4.2   Expectations Channel

Exchange markets are highly efficient processors of information, but not perfectly so. If information is costly, at any point in time, market participants either will not have complete information or will not fully understand its implications. In such cases, market exchange rates cannot continuously reflect all available information.

The volume of foreign-exchange trading, estimated at approximately $4 trillion equivalent per day, seems large relative to the volume of cross-border commercial transactions (BIS 2010). Approximately 80 percent of trades occur among traditional market-making dealers or between these dealers and other financial customers, rather than between dealers and nonfinancial customers (BIS 2010). Much of this seemingly excessive dealer trading undoubtedly results from heterogeneous information among market participants and is vital to price discovery.

Survey evidence does indeed suggest that access to private information differentiates market participants (Cheung and Chinn 2001). Large foreign-exchange players have better information derived from a broader customer base and market network, which gives them a keener insight about order flow and the activities of other trading banks. In such a market, exchange rates perform a dual role of describing the terms of trade and of transferring this information. In markets characterized by information asymmetries, however, nonfundamental forces like bandwagon effects, overreaction to news, technical trading, and excessive speculation may affect short-term exchange-rate dynamics. Any trader whom others suspect of having superior information, including a monetary authority, could affect price if market participants observed his or her trades.

Research into foreign exchange market intervention then is largely predicated on the assumption that monetary authorities possess a significant informational advantage over other market participants, and that intervention can serve as a conduit for transferring that information. Is this a reasonable assumption for any player—let alone a central bank—in a highly efficient market? If so, is this advantage routine or episodic?

Mussa (1981) suggested that central banks might signal future, unanticipated changes in monetary policy through their sterilized interventions, with sales or purchases of foreign exchange implying, respectively, domestic monetary tightening or ease. Such trades would have direct implications for future fundamentals, and forward-looking traders would immediately adjust their spot exchange-rate quotations. Mussa suggested that such signals could be particularly potent—more so than a mere announcement of monetary-policy intentions—because the intervention gives monetary authorities open positions (i.e., exposures) in foreign currencies that would result in losses if they failed to validate their signal. Reeves (1997) formalized Mussa's approach and demonstrated that if the signal is not fully credible, or if the market does not use all available information, then the response of the exchange rate to intervention will be muted. In Reeves's model, the amount of intervention influences the market's response.

When Mussa proposed this signaling effect, the Federal Reserve—and other central banks—had lost much of their integrity for price stability. If, however, central banks are credible, signaling future monetary policy through intervention would seem unnecessary. Markets can easily anticipate the future monetary policies of credible central banks. Carlson, McIntire, and Thomson (1995) showed that federal-funds futures anticipated monetary-policy changes fairly accurately within a two-month horizon, while Fatum and Hutchison (1999) found that intervention added noise to the federal-funds-futures market. These findings suggest that a credible central bank simply may not routinely have private information even about its own future monetary policies.[12]

Even central banks with private information about monetary policy are not likely to actively employ intervention as a signal. For one thing, when a central bank eventually validates its signals, the interventions are no longer sterilized. Consequently, such intervention does not ultimately provide central banks with an independent influence over exchange rates and, as we explained above, it can interfere with monetary-policy credibility.[13] Moreover, most large central banks do not intervene for profit, and although central banks do not like to sustain huge losses on their foreign-exchange portfolios, the fear of losses does not strongly motivate their near-term actions. Finally, as noted above, in countries like Japan and the United States where intervention falls under the purview of the fiscal authorities, central banks could lose their independence if they altered monetary policy in response to the interventions of the fiscal authorities.

Intervention, of course, may offer a *passive* signal of future monetary policy; that is, purchases and sales of foreign exchange may simply be correlated with a future easing or tightening in monetary policy, with no signal intended. In this case, one might find episodic evidence of signaling. Specifically, when the original shock to the exchange market resulted from an excessive easing or tightening in monetary policy, intervention might predict future policy corrections. One would then only find a consistent correlation between intervention and future changes in monetary policy if the underlying shock to the exchange rate was persistently associated with domestic monetary policies. If the underlying shock to the exchange market was not of that type, one might not find evidence of signaling. Kaminsky and Lewis (1996), who investigate the signaling hypothesis, find that when consistent monetary policy supports intervention, exchange rates tend to respond in the expected direction, but when inconsistent monetary policy accompanies intervention, exchange rates tend to move in the opposite direction.

The connection between intervention and compatible monetary policy highlights the essential ambiguity in the monetary-policy signaling story: If intervention only works when it is consistent with imminent monetary-policy changes, that implies that prior and current monetary policy created the exchange-rate disturbance in the first place. Why then intervene? Why not just alter monetary policy? The usefulness would seem to depend on central-bank credibility. This narrow interpretation of signaling seems passé.

Monetary authorities often claim to intervene when they view current exchange rates as being inconsistent with market fundamentals defined more broadly than monetary-policy variables. They have large research staffs that gather and interpret statistics on current economic conditions. If central banks have useful private information about market fundamentals, providing that information to the market through intervention can alter market expectations. Bhattacharya and Weller (1997) and Vitale (1999) present theoretical models in which central banks maintain an informational advantage and disseminate their information to the market. Popper and Montgomery (2001) provide a particularly interesting model in which a central bank aggregates the private information of individual traders and disseminates this information through intervention. Central banks typically maintain an ongoing informational relationship with a select group of major banks (domestic and foreign) and use these banks as counterparties for their foreign exchange transactions.[14] In exchange for their exclusivity, these dealers provide the central banks with interpretations of general market conditions, perceived reasons for market movements, and order flows. If monetary authorities routinely have better broad-based information than other market participants, as Popper and Montgomery (2001) argue, then their interventions should accurately predict future exchange-rate movements; that is, researchers should be able to uncover a statistically valid relationship between the two.

1.4.3   Coordination

In extreme cases of information imperfections, when a substantial portion of market participants base trades on extrapolations of past exchange-rate movements, exchange rates might remain misaligned vis-à-vis their fundamentals, even if the more-informed private traders believed that the current exchange rate is inappropriate in terms of economic fundamentals.[15] As Reitz and Taylor (2008, 57–59) explain, if the exchange rate has moved beyond a range consistent with market fundamentals, those traders who base their trades on fundamental analysis may have suffered recent losses and drained their liquidity. If so, they may have lost confidence in their judgment as well as their credibility with their managers. This can deter them from trading on fundamentals, even though each knows that if they acted in concert, the exchange rate would return to a level consistent with market fundamentals. The misalignment persists.

In such a situation, a central bank could intervene openly and offer a coordinating signal to those traders who react to fundamentals. This signal bolsters those traders' confidence about their exchange-rate expectations and encourages them to take positions in the market. Monetary authorities need not have better information than the private sector to provide a coordination role, but they must be able to take a long-term position without fear of incurring temporary losses (Reitz and Taylor 2008, 58). As noted, central banks do not intervene for profits.

The coordination channel is distinct from the expectation channel because it does not require that the central bank necessarily have better information than the market. It does, like the signaling channel, seem to require that the monetary authorities lack credibility. A credible central bank could simply announce that the exchange rate is misaligned, and get a reaction from the market. A central bank lacking credibility may need to "put its money where its mouth is" (Reitz and Taylor 2008, 59).

1.5   Does Intervention Work?

Over the years, empirical research on the effectiveness of sterilized intervention has grown sharply. The myriad studies are almost all empirical, and they incorporate a broad range of experimental strategies and techniques. The results clearly demonstrate a high frequency—daily or intradaily—connection between foreign-exchange-market intervention and exchange rates. The results, however, are often not robust across currencies, time periods, and empirical techniques. Intervention often seems more like a hit-or-miss proposition than a sure thing.[16]

Even though most empirical studies do not provide a fully articulated theoretical model of intervention, economists typically interpret the results from such studies as evidence of a broad expectation or a coordination channel. We do not know much about the duration of these effects, but given the near martingale nature of exchange-rate changes, it seems reasonable to interpret them as highly persistent, if not permanent. A successful sterilized intervention would seem to set an exchange rate off along an alternative path, but one that is still consistent with preexisting, unaltered fundamentals.

The lack of robustness in the empirical literature suggests that if intervention does indeed operate through a general expectations channel, monetary authorities do not always possess an information advantage over the market. Large interventions, especially those undertaken in concert with other central banks, seem more likely to affect exchange rates in the desired direction than small, unilateral operations.[17] From an expectations perspective, large interventions may demonstrate a higher conviction on the part of the monetary authorities, in the same manner that a speculator who is very certain about his or her private information will take a larger position in the market. Coordinated interventions suggest that more than one monetary authority share a particular view about the market.[18]

Somewhat more controversial is the relative importance of secrecy to an intervention's effectiveness. Prior to the late 1970s, the Federal Reserve usually operated covertly. Thereafter, the Federal Reserve usually operated openly. Given that intervention often operates through an expectations channel, secrecy may seem counterproductive, but Bhattacharya and Weller (1997) and Vitale (1999) present theoretical models in which secrecy contributes to an intervention's success. Dominguez and Frankel (1993a), Hung (1997), Chiu (2003), and Beine and Bernal (2007) also discuss various reasons for maintaining secrecy.

In the end, however, if sterilized intervention does not affect market fundamentals, it does not afford monetary authorities a means of routinely guiding their exchange rates along a path that they determine independent of their monetary policies. It can instead conflict with monetary policy. That, we argue, is why the Federal Reserve stopped intervening.

1.6   The Mechanics of US Intervention

In the United States, both the Treasury and the Federal Reserve System have separate legal authority for intervention, but the Gold Reserve Act of 1934 made the Treasury first among equals in this arrangement. The Treasury and the Federal Reserve have always coordinated their operations and, depending on their exact nature, have often acted in close concert. Since 1980, for example, each agency has usually financed an equal share of every intervention operation. The Federal Reserve Bank of New York executes all foreign exchange transactions for the accounts of both the Federal Reserve and the Treasury.

At various times over the years, each agency has lobbied the other for or against initiating an intervention, depending on its individual assessment of the operation's overall appropriateness and its likelihood for success. At times, the Treasury has basically delegated intervention operations completely to the Federal Reserve, and at other times the Treasury has closely monitored and controlled minor details of the operations (Task Force 1990c, Paper no. 6, 12). In any event, the Treasury and the Federal Reserve have always ironed out differences over the operating strategies and the best techniques to follow (Task Force 1990c, Paper no. 6, 14). The Federal Reserve, however, has never intervened for its own account without the Treasury's authorization, but the Treasury, presumably, cannot direct the Federal Reserve to intervene for its own account against the latter's will. Still, the Federal Reserve has at times unwillingly participated in Treasury-initiated interventions because appearing not to cooperate in a legitimate policy action of the administration would raise market uncertainty and could sabotage the operation's chances for success. Congress has repeatedly cautioned that the Federal Reserve should conform to the Treasury's foreign financial policies (Task Force 1990c, Paper no. 6). By the mid-1990s, however, the Federal Open Market Committee (FOMC) stopped intervening with the tacit approval of the Treasury because it feared that intervention—especially when directed by the Treasury—threatened its independence and weakened the credibility of US monetary policy.

1.6.1   Exchange Stabilization Fund

The Treasury conducts intervention through the Exchange Stabilization Fund (ESF), which Congress established at the urging of the Roosevelt administration under the Gold Act of 1934 (see chapter 3).[19] The ESF's primary objective was to stabilize the exchange value of the dollar by buying or selling foreign currencies and gold. In addition to foreign-exchange intervention, the ESF has provided temporary stabilization loans to select developing countries. Most of these have been Latin American countries, with Mexico being the most persistent recipient. While these operations conform broadly to the ESF's directive of stabilizing dollar exchange rates—many of these countries pegged their currencies to the dollar—the recipients need not use these funds directly in their exchange markets. Some, for example, have dressed up their foreign exchange reserves on reporting dates. Consequently, the loans often have a distinct foreign-aid and foreign-policy flavor.[20]

Congress initially capitalized the fund with $2.0 billion acquired from the devaluation of the dollar against gold, but later used $1.8 billion of the ESF's funds to make an initial quota payment to the International Monetary Fund (IMF). Besides its initial capitalization, Congress allowed the ESF to retain all of the earnings from its operations and to remain outside of the annual appropriations process. Doing so guarded the agency's secrecy, a precious commodity when attempting to stabilize exchange rates. In a similar vein, Congress gave the secretary of the Treasury—who ultimately reports to the US president—exclusive control over ESF operations. The secretary's decisions are final and not subject to the review of any other officer of the US government.[21] Responding quickly is also essential for successful foreign-exchange operations.

Still the ESF's ability to expand its balance sheet is fairly inelastic. Its capacity to acquire foreign exchange through intervention or to extend loans is limited by the amount of dollar denominated assets in its portfolio. Absent a congressional appropriation, the ESF can acquire additional dollars through two mechanisms: First, the fund can monetize special drawing rights (SDRs) with the Federal Reserve System. With the authorization of the Treasury secretary, the ESF creates "SDR certificates," a liability on its balance sheet, and sells them to the Federal Reserve, which is legally obliged to accept them. The ESF can also obtain dollars by warehousing foreign exchange with the Federal Reserve. Warehousing is a currency swap in which the Federal Reserve buys foreign currency from the ESF in a spot transaction and immediately sells it back—typically for delivery within twelve months—in a forward transaction. At times, the Treasury has also augmented the ESF's foreign-currency reserves directly by issuing foreign-currency-denominated securities—Roosa and Carter bonds. The Treasury can also draw on the US quota with the International Monetary Fund (IMF) and turn the proceeds over to the ESF. Still, the ESF's balance sheet is inelastic. The need to quickly augment the ESF's resources in the early 1960s was a key reason that the Federal Reserve decided to participate in US foreign exchange operations, as chapter 4 explains.

1.6.2   The Federal Reserve System

The FOMC has derived its legal authority for intervention from various sections of the Federal Reserve Act (see chapter 4). Under this authority, Federal Reserve banks—chiefly the Federal Reserve Bank of New York—first undertook some limited exchange-market operations during World War I and extended stabilization credits to European central banks in the mid-1920s (see chapter 2). These operations were controversial, and Congress amended the Federal Reserve Act in 1933 to prevent Federal Reserve banks from operating without the Board of Governors' direct oversight (Task Force 1990a, Paper no. 2, 2). After a long hiatus, the Federal Reserve reestablished its own portfolio of foreign-exchange in 1962 and began intervening to forestall gold losses and to stabilize the dollar. The Federal Reserve remained a fairly active participant in the foreign-exchange market from 1962 through the mid-1990s. Since 1995, it has intervened on only three occasions, but it maintains a portfolio of foreign exchange for that purpose. Although some FOMC participants argued that the Federal Reserve lacked clear legal authority for intervention after 1933, Congress has never attempted to prevent the Federal Reserve's activities in the foreign-exchange market. The FOMC, moreover, interprets Congress's passage of the Monetary Control Act of 1980, which expanded the Federal Reserve's authority for investing its foreign-exchange portfolio, as tacit congressional recognition of the FOMC's authority for foreign-exchange operations.

Within the Federal Reserve System, the FOMC maintains authority over intervention operations because intervention involves a type of open-market transaction. A subcommittee consisting of the chairman and vice-chairman of the FOMC, the vice-chairman of the Board of Governors, and one other member of the Board of Governors, whom the chairman appoints and who has responsibility for international matters, is accountable for intervention decisions when the full FOMC is not immediately available to render vital judgments.

The FOMC's guidelines for intervention operations consist of three documents. The first, *Authorization for Foreign Currency Operations*, sanctions the desk's purchases of foreign exchange, permits holding of specific foreign-currency balances, and establishes overall limits on the Federal Reserve's net-open position—its foreign-exchange exposure. The second, *Foreign Currency Directive*, focuses more on the objectives of intervention and on the manner in which the desk at the Federal Reserve Bank of New York should undertake foreign-exchange transactions. Finally, the *Procedural Instructions* clarify the relationship among the FOMC, the Foreign Exchange Subcommittee, and the manager of the desk at the Federal Reserve Bank of New York. From time to time, the FOMC established informal agreements, such as limits on the amounts of intervention the desk can take in specific currencies.

The Federal Reserve—in stark contrast to the ESF—finances its purchases of foreign exchange by creating reserves. Consequently, its capacity to acquire foreign exchange is ultimately limited only by the FOMC's willingness to acquire foreign-exchange risk. The Federal Reserve finances sales of foreign exchange either from its portfolio of foreign exchange assets or via its capacity to borrow or buy foreign exchange from other central banks or from the US Treasury. As noted, the Federal Reserve undertakes intervention "in close and continuous consultation and cooperation with the United States Treasury" (Task Force 1990c, Paper no. 6, 1).

The United States also closely coordinates its intervention operations with foreign central banks. In the broad sense, this means that the United States seeks permission to buy and sell a particular foreign currency from the issuing central bank. More narrowly, however, the United States and the relevant foreign central bank have often operated in concert, both to signal agreement with the operation's objectives and to increase the amount of intervention.

The oft-stated objective of US foreign exchange operations is to counter disorderly market conditions—a very amorphous concept. Greene (1984c, 12–13) described the desk's perception of market disorder:

> In making judgments about conditions in the exchange market and the need for orderly market intervention, US authorities considered many dimensions of trading. They evaluated the variability of the exchange rate itself as indicated, for example, by the magnitude and speed of rate changes within a day, day to day, cumulatively over several days or longer, and relative to perceived or known changes in the underlying economic fundamentals. They also evaluated market participants' perceptions of

the risk of dealing as indicated, for instance, by the width of bid-asked spreads, the existence of large gaps between successive rate quotations, or an unwillingness on the part of market professionals to take currency into position even temporarily, and thereby cushion the impact on the market of their customers' currency needs.

Ultimately, however, market disorder was largely in the eyes of the beholder (see chapters 5 and 6).

1.6.3   Swap Lines

Both the US Treasury and the Federal Reserve have from time to time set up swap lines either as a means of acquiring foreign exchange or as a method of supplying dollar reserves temporarily to a foreign government or central bank in need of dollars. In a swap, the United States and a foreign government exchange currencies spot and simultaneously reverse the transaction at a known forward exchange rate on a specific date in the future. The Federal Reserve maintained an extensive network of swap lines during the 1960s and 1970s and commonly relied on them for intervention purposes. Use of swap lines to finance intervention dropped off by the early 1980s, but the Federal Reserve resurrected an extensive swap network during the Great Recession as a mean of providing dollar liquidity to foreign central banks, which offered it to commercial banks in their jurisdictions (see epilogue). The Federal Reserve continues to maintain liquidity swap lines with the Bank of Canada, Bank of England, the European Central Bank, the Bank of Japan, and the Swiss National Bank. In addition, the Federal Reserve maintains two swap lines with the Bank of Canada and the Bank of Mexico as part of the North American Free Trade Agreement (NAFTA).

As noted, warehousing refers to a swap transaction between the US Treasury and the Federal Reserve System in which the Federal Reserve temporarily acquires foreign exchange from the Treasury and the Treasury acquires dollars from the Federal Reserve. Once the loan is extended, the Federal Reserve has absolutely no control over how the Treasury uses the funds. Warehousing is controversial because it resembles a temporary collateralized loan from the Federal Reserve to the ESF, outside of the congressional appropriations process (see chapters 5 and 6). FOMC members have worried that such loans could impede the Federal Reserve's independence and its monetary policy credibility.

1.6.4   Investments and Profits

Prior to 1980, the United States did not hold large balances of foreign exchange. Moreover, its foreign-exchange liabilities (swap drawings, Roosa and Carter bonds, or IMF drawings) exceeded its foreign-exchange assets, giving the Federal Reserve a small negative net-open position. The decision in the early 1980s to expand its portfolio and to hold an open position in foreign exchange stemmed from concerns that foreign governments could place conditions on the Federal Reserve's ability to borrow foreign exchange and that these conditions could delay or otherwise hamper US intervention operations (see chapter 5). After 1980, the Federal Reserve acquired a substantial net-open position in foreign exchange and a corresponding exposure to exchange-rate-revaluation risk. At the end of 2010, US monetary authorities held nearly $52 billion equivalent in foreign-exchange reserves split equally between the Federal Reserve System's and the US Treasury's accounts. Each portfolio contains slightly more euro assets (55 percent) than yen assets (45 percent).

Outside of small working balances, the United States currently holds its foreign exchange in highly liquid and safe interest-earning assets. Prior to 1980, the desk invested its foreign exchange holdings in deposit accounts with foreign central banks, some of which could not legally pay interest on the balances, or with the Bank for International Settlements (BIS). When interest was available, the underlying rates were generally administered rates—discount or other policy rates—or set by swap arrangements. Safe and liquid alternatives were often not available. The Monetary Control Act allowed the Federal Reserve to earn a higher (market-related) rate of return on its balances by investing them in the obligations of foreign governments and official institutions (see Task Force 1990h, Paper no. 8).

The Federal Reserve earns profits and losses on its portfolio—a realized profit or loss when the desk sells foreign exchange from the portfolio and an unrealized profit or loss each month when it marks the portfolio to market. When the Federal Reserve buys or sells foreign exchange, whether for its own account or for the ESF's account, it books the transactions at current exchange rates. Foreign-currency-denominated interest receipts on the account are treated similarly. Over time, the Federal Reserve books increments to the portfolio at different exchange rates. When it calculates the profit or loss associated with a subsequent foreign exchange sale, the desk must decide which of the exchange rates used to book the foreign-exchange acquisitions is the appropriate base for the transaction. The choice can make a substantial difference to the profit calculation when exchange rates fluctuate day to day.

The Federal Reserve resolves this problem by using a weighted-average exchange rate based on the entire portfolio. This rate equals the cumulative book value in a particular foreign currency divided by its cumulative book value in dollars. Realized profits compare the exchange rate at which currency is sold to this weighted-average rate. The Fed also calculates the valuation, or unrealized profits, on the entire portfolio using an end-of-month exchange rate and compares this valuation with the aforementioned weighted average. Essentially, this reveals the profits from selling off the entire portfolio at a particular time. On this basis, the Federal Reserve has generally profited (realized and unrealized) from intervention, but not

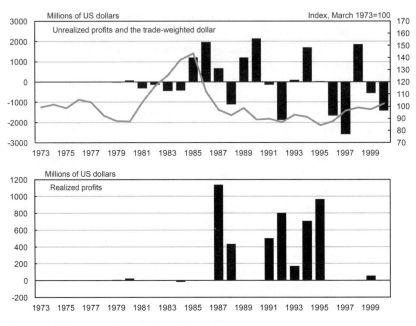

Fig. 1.1   US intervention profits, 1979–2000
Note: No data available on realize profit or loss for 1982 and 1983. Data are from the Federal Reserve.

always. Between 1979 and 1997, the years for which data are readily available, these profits were small, but their year-to-year variance has been large (see figure 1.1).[22]

During the Bretton Woods era, 1962 through 1971, exchange rates did not change much, the gold price remained fixed, and many of the mechanisms used for interventions—swap lines and Roosa bonds—contained protections against exchange-rate changes. Interest-rate differentials were largely inconsequential to profit calculations. Consequently, the United States' relatively small exposures did not generate large profits or losses (Task Force 1990e, Paper no. 10, 14–19).

The closing of the gold window on 15 August 1971 meant that the United States could not sell gold to meet outstanding foreign-currency obligations, and had to look for an alternative means of repaying the debt. The United States had nearly $5 billion in outstanding obligations, primarily in Swiss francs, British pounds, Belgian francs, and German marks. Estimates of the profit or loss associated with repayment range widely from a loss of about $2 1/2 billion to a small gain, depending on the counterfactual assumptions that one makes about the Treasury's ability to sell gold (Task Force 1990e, Paper no. 10, 24–27).

While the Federal Reserve, out of its fiduciary responsibility to Congress and the American people, hopes to avoid losses on its foreign-exchange portfolio, a desire for profits has never motivated US intervention operations. As noted, the desk intervenes to calm market disorder. In holding a net open position in foreign exchange, however, the Federal Reserve and the US Treasury are acting much like speculators, and they earn profits or incur losses at the expense of the private sector. If, for example, the Federal Reserve acquires Japanese yen through its market interventions, and the yen subsequently appreciates against the dollar, the Federal Reserve's net worth rises while the private sector's net worth falls relative to what it would have been in the absence of the intervention (Task Force 1990e, Paper no. 10, 6–7).

Friedman (1953) suggested that profits contained information about the effectiveness of official interventions. Destabilizing foreign-exchange speculators necessarily incur losses that quickly drive them from the market.[23] Only stabilizing speculators remain in the market. He warned, however, that central banks do not face hard budget constraints and, therefore, could undertake more persistent unprofitable and destabilizing transactions. Subsequent work, however, indicated that Friedman's correspondence between profitable and stabilizing speculation need not hold, especially if the underlying equilibrium exchange rate is not constant. Profitable intervention can sometimes be destabilizing, and unprofitable intervention can sometimes be stabilizing (Task Force 1990e, Paper no. 10, 2). Consequently, one cannot infer much about the ability of central banks to stabilize exchange rates from the profitability of the foreign-exchange operations.

Perhaps the most interesting way to think about central-bank profits, particular valuation gains or losses, is in terms of their connection to profits or losses generated in the private market. A substantial number of studies, for example, have found that fairly simple technical trading rules—including ex ante rules, as in Neely, Weller, and Ditmar (1997)—generate profits that are difficult to explain in terms of standard risk measures.[24] Recent surveys suggest that technical trading rules seem to account for a large segment of foreign-exchange trading.

Quite a few studies have shown that technical trading rules generate excess returns during periods of central-bank intervention (LeBaron 1999). This seems especially likely if central banks adopt a "leaning-against-the-wind" intervention strategy. If central banks slow, but do not reverse, exchange-rate movements, they will inevitably sustain valuation losses, at least in the short run. By taking a position opposite that of the central bank, technical traders apparently stand to profit. In contrast to these findings, however, many other studies conclude that central banks have earned small profits from their intervention operations since the collapse of Bretton Woods.

Neely (1998) reconciles the technical trading results with the apparent overall profitability of intervention by showing that intervention profits occur over a longer time horizon than technical trading profits. In the short run, intervention often generates losses, a point that Goodhart and Hesse

(1993) also illustrate. Hence, it is possible that technical traders profit against central banks in the short run while central banks profit in the long term. This raises questions about the effect that sustained intervention might have on the functioning of private foreign-exchange markets.[25]

1.7   Road Map

This chapter has presented background material on foreign-exchange intervention and on the US institutional framework for that intervention. The remainder of this book explains how theories of intervention and institutional arrangements evolved in the United States, primarily during the twentieth century. The key concern is how these developments interacted with monetary policy.

As chapter 2 explains, precedents for modern foreign-exchange-market operations are found in European experience with the classical gold standard, but they quickly grew and developed after World War I as countries first attempted to return to the gold standard and then reacted to the Great Depression. European central banks under the classical gold standard often bent the "rules of the game" through discount policies and gold devices. These were early exchange-market operations. Some European central banks held foreign-exchange reserves and stabilized their exchange rates within the gold points through intervention. Chapter 2 illustrates early uses of secrecy, sterilization, and forward transactions—all of which become important characteristics of modern interventions. The chapter also discusses the establishment of the British Exchange Equalisation Account, which directly intervened in the foreign-exchange market.

American antecedents also aided the development of foreign-exchange operations in the United States. Chapter 2 explains the rise of private firms that specialized in the spatial and temporal arbitrage of sterling bills and related instruments. The Second Bank of the United States under Nicholas Biddle extended these operations, buying and selling foreign exchange to stabilize exchange rates and to insulate the domestic economy from external shocks. Biddle conducted foreign-exchange-market intervention, or at least a prototype of it. The Civil War saw the issuance of greenbacks and floating exchange rates. After the war, the Treasury contracted the money supply to return to the gold standard and avoided exchange-market operations until World War I. Both the issuance of greenbacks and the return to the gold standard were decisions on how to deal with the trilemma.

In 1914, Congress established the Federal Reserve System and gave it powers consistent with foreign-exchange operations. World War I turned the potential for such operations into an actuality. As chapter 2 shows, by the end of the war, the machinery for future exchange-market operations was clearly in place. With the war as a precedent, the Federal Reserve Bank of New York participated in a number of stabilization programs for other countries and engaged in several direct foreign-exchange-market interventions during the 1920s and early 1930s. As the chapter also illustrates, these operations saw the beginnings of central-bank cooperation in gold and foreign-exchange operations, which would become the hallmark of Bretton Woods and, later, the Plaza and Louvre accords. The object of most of the activities in the 1920s and 1930s was to preserve the gold standard—a pillar of monetary stability and a solution to the trilemma.

Chapter 3 introduces the US Exchange Stabilization Fund, chronicling its establishment, structure, and operations from its inception through 1961. In the depth of the Great Depression, Britain devalued the pound and established the Exchange Equalisation Account. President Roosevelt saw the Exchange Equalisation Account as a protectionist device, and as a countermove, he devalued the dollar and established the Exchange Stabilization Fund in January 1934. The Exchange Stabilization Fund (ESF), which is the primary vehicle for foreign-exchange-market intervention in the United States, has a structure conducive to intervention, but one that is unlike most other government agencies: It is under exclusive control of the US Secretary of the Treasury and has always been self-financing, meaning it is outside of the congressional appropriations process.

The ESF first intervened in dollars and gold against French francs, British pounds, Belgian francs, and Netherlands guilders. Chapter 3 details these early operations. Information about many of the transactions during the 1930s, including data on their dollar amounts come from William Brown's (1942) rare, unpublished manuscript. In addition, chapter 3 draws on newly available material from the Morgenthau Diaries to construct the narrative.

In 1936, Britain, France, and the United States signed the Tripartite Agreement—a cooperative effort to stabilize exchange rates through intervention in gold and foreign exchange. (Belgium, the Netherlands, and Switzerland also accepted the principles of the Tripartite Agreement.) The Tripartite Agreement enabled France to devalue the franc without foreign offsets and reestablished mechanisms for gold settlements. (Belgium also soon devalued.) Intervention in currency and gold—mostly the latter—occurred through 1939 with the objective of stabilizing exchange rates. While the Tripartite intervention between 1934 and the outbreak of World War II may have helped stabilize short-term exchange-rate movements, it did not address the fundamental misalignment among key currencies. The Tripartite Agreement did not solve the trilemma. World War II, with its exchange controls and disruptions, ended the Great Depression and the problems that it posed for exchange markets in the 1930s.

Because the ESF holds substantial assets, is self-financing, and is solely under the direction of the Treasury, it can also undertake myriad operations only tangentially related to its original objective. Chapter 3 explains three such operations of the ESF. First, the ESF has often made loans to developing countries, especially Mexico and other Latin American nations. Second, under the Silver Purchase Act of 1934, the ESF purchased silver and lifted its price. It, therefore, intervened in the silver market. Third, the ESF had authority to invest in government securities, and therefore could support the market and potentially interfere with monetary policy.

Chapter 4 discusses US foreign-exchange operations during the Bretton Woods era. Bretton Woods—established in 1944—became fully functional in 1958 when key European countries made their currencies convertible for current-account transactions. By 1961, however, the total external dollar liabilities of the United States exceeded the US gold stock, implying that the United States could not fulfill its commitment to exchange dollars for gold at $35 per ounce. This development encouraged central banks to convert unwanted dollars for gold, heightened uncertainty about the exchange rates, and fostered speculation. A rising US inflation rate in the late 1960s and early 1970s only aggravated the situation.

To protect the US gold stock and to neutralize speculative activities, the US Treasury began intervening in 1961. The Federal Reserve System joined a year later after a debate about its legal authority to do so. As illustrated in chapter 4, the Treasury and Federal Reserve cooperated closely, but a clear division of labor emerged. The Federal Reserve formed the first line of defense primarily through its reciprocal currency arrangements or swap lines—a key focus of the chapter. The swap lines provided the central banks of surplus countries with cover for their temporary acquisitions of unwanted dollars and offered the central banks of deficit countries dollar liquidity to defend their pegs. The US Treasury, with its clearer authority for intervention, focused on longer-term operations. If, for example, market conditions prevented the desk from acquiring enough foreign exchange to reverse a swap drawing, the Treasury could acquire the necessary foreign exchange by issuing foreign-currency-denominated securities, drawing foreign exchange from the IMF, or selling gold.

United States foreign-exchange-market operations from 1961 through 1973 may have successfully delayed the disintegration of the Bretton Woods system, but by allowing monetary authorities to postpone more fundamental and necessary adjustments, they only delayed the inevitable. Bretton Woods ultimately failed because countries would not subvert their domestic economic objectives to the maintenance of fixed exchange rates. Floating rates offered a viable solution to the trilemma.

Still, monetary authorities would not allow exchange rates free reign, as chapter 5 explains. During the early float period (1973–1981), policymakers viewed exchange markets as inherently prone to bouts of disorder in which information imperfections caused exchange rates to deviate from their fundamental values, fostered excessive volatility, and encouraged destabilizing speculation. Many thought that intervention was necessary to maintain order. United States policymakers, however, never clearly articulated the transmission mechanism through which intervention worked. Early on, economists viewed intervention as affecting exchange rates through a portfolio-balance mechanism. Oddly, the foreign exchange desk at the Federal Reserve Bank of New York did not seem to espouse this view. They described intervention as having a vague "psychological" impact on exchange markets, which came about because the desk demonstrated concern for the dollar.

Between 1973 and 1981, as chapter 5 details, the desk operated on both sides of the market. Typically, the desk sold foreign exchange to bolster the dollar. Because these operations were usually financed through swap drawing, the desk then quickly looked for opportunities to buy back the dollars and to repay the swaps. In 1977, the dollar began to depreciate sharply as confidence in the United States' willingness to deal decisively with inflation was rapidly evaporating. Over the next two years, US intervention operations increased in amount, frequency, and openness.

The record of US operations between 1973 and 1981 was at best equivocal. During nearly every operation, the dollar continued to depreciate, although intervention often seemed to moderate the pace. Only after the United States changed monetary policy on 6 October 1979 and convinced markets that it would pursue disinflation despite a recession and rising unemployment, did the dollar start to strengthen. Intervention's lackluster record during the early float led the Reagan administration to adopt a minimalist approach in 1981.

By the late 1970s, foreign central banks, impatient with the US response to inflation, threatened to attach conditions to continued swap drawings. In response, as chapter 5 explains, the FOMC began to acquire a portfolio of foreign-exchange reserves. Drawing on the swap lines to finance intervention soon ended. In contrast, the Federal Reserve's swap lines with the US Treasury—its warehousing facility—continued and grew. Chapter 5 also looks backward to explain the evolution of warehousing.

Chapter 6 discusses intervention during the Volcker and Greenspan eras. By the early 1980s, most economists concluded that intervention did not work through a portfolio-balance channel. The Jurgensen Report (1983)—a multinational pronouncement about intervention's effectiveness—suggested that if intervention were to be effective, monetary policy had to support it. This implied that intervention did not provide a means of affecting exchange rates independent of monetary policy. Intervention could not solve the trilemma.

The dollar appreciated sharply on both a nominal and a real basis between 1980 and early 1985 under tight monetary and loose fiscal policies. Facing pressure from myriad directions, the administration abandoned its minimalist strategy. Coordinated interventions, highlighted by the Plaza and Louvre accords, followed. Many believe this period offers clear support for concerted foreign-exchange intervention and macroeconomic policy coordination, but our narrative and statistical evidence in chapter 6 are less supportive.

A lack of unequivocal statistical support for intervention was never key to its demise. The FOMC stopped intervening primarily because FOMC participants believed that intervention, and the institutional arrangements associated with it, undermined their ability to establish and to maintain a credible commitment to price stability. As chapter 6 explains, the FOMC's objections were threefold. First, while legally independent, the Federal Reserve had little choice but to participate with the Treasury in major foreign-exchange operations. This undermined the Federal Reserve's independence. Second, FOMC participants—recalling the Jurgensen Report—feared that if markets interpreted sterilized intervention as a signal of future monetary-policy changes, intervention created uncertainty about the FOMC's commitment to price stability. Third, losses on its now substantial portfolio of foreign exchange and large commitments to warehouse funds for the Treasury could result in congressional actions to limit the Federal Reserve's independence.

Our conclusion, chapter 7, summarizes our main argument: Official attitudes about intervention and monetary policy evolved in tandem. Frequent intervention ended because it did not offer monetary authorities an independent instrument with which to pursue an additional policy goal. Intervention did not solve the trilemma. Instead, intervention and its associated institutions weakened the Federal Reserve's credibility for price stability.

The United States essentially stopped intervening by the mid-1990s, but US policymakers never dismissed intervention as completely ineffectual. Since then, the Federal Reserve has intervened on three occasions: on 17 June 1997, the Federal Reserve purchased $833 million worth of Japanese yen in concert with the Japanese Ministry of Finance; on 22 September 2000, the Federal Reserve bought $1.3 billion equivalent euros in concert with the European Central Bank, and on 17 March 2011, the United States intervened in concert with the Japanese Ministry of Finance and other governments to buy yen following Japan's earthquake and tsunami. Our epilogue briefly discusses modern intervention operations in Japan, Switzerland, China, and among the many emerging market and developing countries. We also explain the use of swap lines during the recent financial crisis.

2

Exchange Market Policy in the United States
Precedents and Antecedents

2.1 Introduction

Exchange market operations had considerable precedent in policies followed in Europe during the classical gold standard era from 1870–1913 and in the gold exchange standard between 1925–1933. It also had antecedents in US history going back at least to the first decade of the nineteenth century.

Under the classical gold standard, the trilemma as outlined in chapter 1 was solved (at least in theory) with perfectly fixed exchange rates, open capital markets, and no role for monetary policy. However in practice, in the classical era from 1870 to 1913, the assumptions needed to make this work did not hold completely. The classical Humean adjustment mechanism did not work perfectly because wages and prices were not perfectly flexible, labor was not perfectly mobile, and there were real and financial frictions and shocks. These real world complications created leeway for central banks to influence financial activity and the real economy. They also provided a limited role for exchange market policy.

Under the interwar gold exchange standard, a change in the political climate which expanded the suffrage and the power of labor unions, as well as greatly reduced price and wage flexibility (O'Rourke and Taylor 2013), led to increased pressure to use monetary policy to stabilize the real economy and smooth financial markets. It also made the case for an expanded role for exchange market policies.

The exchange market policies followed before 1934, as we discuss in this chapter, were not quite the same as modern exchange market intervention, but we believe that an understanding of the historical evolution of current arrangements can yield important insights for modern practices.

Modern exchange market intervention involves operations to influence the exchange rate independent of other instruments of monetary policy. This has been interpreted during some episodes as pertaining to the level of the exchange rates and in other episodes to its volatility. The techniques used include direct purchases and sales of foreign currencies (both spot and forward) as well as swaps (a simultaneous spot and forward transaction). In addition, most interventions today are sterilized (accompanied by offsetting open-market operations in domestic assets).

Exchange market policies followed before 1934 operated under a different exchange rate regime environment than in the post-1934 period. It was dominated by universal adherence to the gold standard (classical up to 1914, gold exchange 1925–1933).

Under the classical gold standard, the basic rule that all adherents followed was to fix the price of domestic currency in terms of gold. This meant officially defining the currency (e.g., the dollar) as a fixed weight of gold. From 1834 to 1933 (with the exception of the greenback era from 1861 to 1878) it was defined as 24.75 grams of gold or .052 ounces. This translated into the price of $20.67 per ounce. In the United Kingdom from 1821 to 1914, the fixed price of gold was £3, 17s, 10 1/2 d. The monetary authority had to be willing to freely buy and sell gold to maintain the official parity. The rule also meant that central banks had to make their notes fully convertible into gold.

In the United States before the establishment of the Federal Reserve System in 1914, the monetary authority was the US Treasury. In the United Kingdom and other European countries the monetary authority was the central bank. Under the gold standard, each country chose its official parity. The ratios of the official parities represented the exchange rate (e.g., the official exchange rate between the dollar and the pound sterling was 4.867). By each country fixing the price of their currencies, the gold standard represented a fixed exchange rate system.

Although in theory exchange rates were supposed to be perfectly rigid, in practice the rate of exchange was bound by upper and lower limits—the gold points—within which the exchange rate floated. The gold points were determined by the costs of shipping gold between countries. These costs included freight, insurance, and foregone interest (Officer 1996). In the classical gold standard era, the gold points between major financial centers was one percent or less on either side of parity.

Under the classical gold standard, disturbances to the balance of payments were automatically equilibrated by the Humean price specie flow mechanism. Under the mechanism, arbitrage in gold kept nations' price levels in line. Gold would flow from countries with balance of payment deficits to those with surpluses keeping their domestic money supplies and prices in line. Adjustment was greatly facilitated by short-term capital flows. Capital would quickly flow between countries to rectify interest differentials.

In this regime the primary objective of exchange market policy then was to preserve adherence to the gold standard (i.e., to maintain the fixed gold parity by influencing gold flows). The three principal approaches were used for this end: gold policy, that is, policies to influence the position of the gold export and import points such as restrictions on the time available and location of offices where domestic fiduciary currency could be exchanged for gold; monetary policy actions (changes in discount rates and open-market operations) targeted to influence the market exchange rate by altering interest rates to affect expenditure or to influence capital movement; and direct antecedents to modern exchange market operations such as the purchase and sale of foreign exchange (unsterilized and sterilized).

In what follows we document other countries' experiences (the precedents) and the earlier US experience of exchange market policy (the antecedents).

Section 2.2 focuses on foreign precedents to exchange market policy. Many of the modern tools were well developed by European central banks under the classical gold standard and perfected under the interwar gold exchange standard. Section 2.2.1 covers the pre–World War I gold standard, treating separately the gold policy undertaken by the Bank of England (section 2.2.2), and gold policy and exchange market intervention undertaken by other European central banks (section 2.2.3). Section 2.2.4 examines the interwar period, focusing on innovations in exchange market policy by the Bank of England.

We then document US historical experience. Section 2.3 describes the background of the nascent foreign exchange market under the bimetallic specie standard and exchange market operations in the pre–Civil War era 1810–1860. The narrative covers operations by private exchange dealers whose objective was to make profits from currency arbitrage. This differed from official intervention. We focus primarily on the House of Brown which dominated the market for much of the nineteenth century (section 2.3.2), and on the Second Bank of the United States, a protocentral bank, according to leading authorities. Under the leadership of Nicholas Biddle it was the key player from 1826 to 1836 (section 2.3.3). Section 2.3.4 discusses the exchange market in the Civil War and greenback periods and operations by the US Treasury and private banks. Section 2.3.5 details operations by the Treasury and the newly formed Federal Reserve System during World War I, when much of the modern machinery of exchange rate policy followed today was established. Section 2.3.6 then describes the exchange market operations and other international financial interventions undertaken by the Federal Reserve under the direction of Benjamin Strong, governor of the Federal Reserve Bank of New York from 1914 until his death in 1928, and then from 1928 to the collapse of sterling in 1931 by his successor in New York, George Harrison. They, on occasion, acted independently of the Federal Reserve System as a whole, though notifying the board.

Finally section 2.4 provides an overview and evaluates the legacy of this earlier experience for the post-1934 era.

2.2   European Precedents

In this section we examine the experience of the Bank of England and other European central banks with exchange market policies both in the classical gold standard period and the interwar gold exchange standard. Many of the techniques later used by the Federal Reserve were first developed by the Europeans.

2.2.1   The Classical Gold Standard and the Rules of the Game, 1870–1914

The basic rule followed by central banks under the classical gold standard was to maintain convertibility of their currencies (notes) into gold. This meant that external convertibility would dominate any other objectives the central bank might have, such as offsetting cyclical and seasonal shocks to the economy. The way in which central banks were supposed to pursue monetary policy, as described in the massive literature on the subject that has developed since 1914 (Bordo 1984), was to follow "the rules of the game" a phrase usually attributed to Keynes (1930).

According to the rules a central bank was supposed to use its policy tools, the discount rate and open-market operations to speed up balance of payments adjustment. Thus when faced with a deficit, the central bank, observing a decline in its gold reserves (its gold reserve ratio relative to the statutory minimum ratio) would tighten its policy, raise its discount rate, or sell government securities. The tight policy in turn would raise domestic short-term interest rates and encourage a short-term capital inflow. It would also depress domestic aggregate demand, reduce prices and incomes, and hence reduce the demand for imports and stimulate the demand for exports. Both channels would attenuate the gold outflow and restore external balance. In the face of a balance of payments surplus, manifest in rising gold reserves, the rule of thumb was to loosen money.

An extensive literature developed to ascertain whether central banks actually followed the rules (see Bordo [1984]; Bordo and MacDonald [2005] for surveys). In a classic article written in 1959, Arthur Bloomfield reached conclusions based on his evidence, which revealed the absence of a positive correlation between changes in central bank international reserves and central bank credit as postulated by the "rules," that the rules (with the possible exception of the Bank of England) were generally violated. Subsequent studies for a number of countries confirmed Bloomfield's basic finding (Jonung 1984; Fratianni and Spinelli 1984; McGouldrick 1984). A more recent literature has refined the meaning of the rules. In addition, the rules included the sterilization of reserve flows, reaction to domestic goals such as the level of output, the price level, and interest rate stability (Dutton 1984; Giovannini 1986; Jeanne 1995; Davatyan and Parke 1995). This literature concludes that the rules were often violated by the Bank of

England, the Reichsbank, and other central banks in the sense that some short-run sterilization occurred and that they responded to domestic goals, but that they attached primary importance to preserving convertibility; this objective became more important the longer the time period that was under consideration.

The combination of short run violations of the "rules" and long-run adherence to convertibility may be explained by private agents' beliefs that the commitment to maintain convertibility was credible. This gave the monetary authorities the breathing room to satisfy other objectives. According to Bordo and MacDonald (2005), the gold points served as a target zone within which the credible central banks of the United Kingdom, France, and Germany had some leeway to allow their discount rates to depart from world rates in order to satisfy domestic objectives without immediately provoking offsetting capital and gold flows. Thus these central banks had the ability to perform, and sometimes engaged in, monetary policy actions of a very modern sort. They also developed various techniques to alter the gold points and to influence gold flows over and above the leeway given by the target zone which we describe below.

2.2.2 Gold Policy

The Bank of England and the other principal central banks engaged in "gold policy" or used "gold devices" to alter the gold export and import points. These policies were used to complement discount rate policy and sometimes served as a substitute. Sayers (1936, 1957) described how the Bank of England before 1890 had manipulated the gold points to "make Bank rate effective." The policies followed by virtually all central banks included altering the prices for gold bars or foreign gold coin, granting interest-free advances to gold importers during periods of gold transit, only redeeming notes at the head office, and placing physical impediments to the export of gold (Bloomfield 1959, 1963).

According to Sayers (1976), the Bank of England preferred the use of gold policy as a tool of monetary policy between 1852 and 1908. The bank was constrained in the price it could use to buy and sell gold sovereigns but not in the prices it could offer for bar gold or foreign coin. Thus

> to check for example an export of gold to the U.S.A. it would raise the selling price for American gold eagles or else refuse to sell them at all, forcing diversion to gold bars; and the Bank might raise its buying price for these coins when this little encouragement would tip the balance in favor of reinforcement, from that uncomfortably low reserve.[1] (Sayers 1976, vol. I, 49–50)

Sayers then described how the use of the full panoply of gold devices aided the bank in the crises of 1890, 1893, and 1906–07. After 1908, the gold devices were seldom used because by then

London's foreign lending was on such a scale that a trifling disturbance by Bank rate of the timing of loan remittances could make immediate impression on the gold position; the growth of the internationally mobile supply of bills market in the same direction. (Sayers, 53)

2.2.3   Foreign Exchange Market Intervention

The Bank of England never used official purchases and sales of foreign exchange as a policy to keep the exchange rate within the gold points because it did not hold reserves other than gold. The Banque de France and the Reichsbank rarely used such operations. However, Bloomfield (1963) describes how other European central banks which held reserves in both gold and foreign exchange (sterling, francs, and reichsmarks) as well as the monetary authorities of the colonies operating on a gold exchange standard, did engage in such policies. According to Bloomfield (1963, 21) many European central banks including those of Belgium, Holland, Sweden, Switzerland, and Russia engaged in exchange market intervention to smooth seasonal and erratic fluctuations in the exchange rate, as well as to arrest movements to the gold export point.

Two countries which extensively relied on exchange market intervention before 1914 were Finland and Austria-Hungary. In the case of Finland, after it adopted the gold standard in 1877, "the exchange rate was kept within the gold points exclusively by purchases and sales of foreign exchange by the Bank of Finland." (Bloomfield 1963, 23). Chart 2 in Bloomfield shows that the Bank of Finland's gold holdings were virtually unchanged between 1880 and 1904 while its foreign exchange reserves varied considerably.

From 1896 to 1914, after the empire adopted a gold currency in 1897,[2] the Austro-Hungarian Bank was able to maintain parity between the crown and gold by its foreign exchange policy. Bloomfield (1963, 24) describes how the bank would sell foreign exchange just before the theoretical gold export point was reached and buy foreign exchange just before reaching the gold import point. The Austro-Hungarian Bank was also an early pioneer in the use of official operations in the forward market.[3]

Thus exchange rate policy, both gold policy and exchange market interventions, were well developed before 1914 in Europe. These policies were further developed in the interwar gold exchange standard. However we must keep in mind that the omnipresence of the gold standard rule limited the extent of these operations in comparison to the regimes which followed.

2.2.4   Exchange Market Operations in the Interwar

Background—The Restoration of the Gold Exchange Standard

The gold standard dissolved during World War I as all major countries, with the exception of the United States, suspended gold convertibility de facto, if not de jure. The United States imposed an embargo on gold exports from 1917 to 1919. After the war, the United Kingdom and other countries expressed a strong preference to return to gold at the original parity (United Kingdom, 1979).

Plans for reconstructing the international gold standard were laid at the Genoa Conference of 1922, where the financial commission, under British leadership, urged that the world return to a gold exchange standard under which member countries would make their currencies convertible into gold, but to use foreign exchange—the currencies of key reserve countries, the United Kingdom and the United States—as a substitute for gold.

The gold exchange standard was restored worldwide in the period 1924–27 on the basis of the recommendations of Genoa. Central bank statutes typically required a cover ratio for currencies of between 30 and 40 percent, divided between gold and foreign exchange. Central reserve countries (the United States and the United Kingdom) were to hold reserves only in the form of gold.

The key event which restored the system was the United Kingdom's return to its original gold parity on 28 April 1925. The United Kingdom was quickly followed by the British Commonwealth and other nations so that by the end of 1928, thirty-five countries had their currencies officially convertible to gold. Restoration was virtually completed when France declared de facto convertibility (at a parity which depreciated the franc by 80 percent) in July 1926. De jure French convertibility occurred in June 1928.

In 1919 there were five nations in the world on the gold standard: the United States, Canada, Nicaragua, Panama, and the Philippines. Notably, the latter four were closely linked to the United States. At the peak of the interwar gold standard in 1929, forty-six nations were on a gold exchange standard.

When the gold standard was restored in the 1920s it usually involved several states, with national fiscal and currency stabilization first, often accompanied by the creation or reform of the central bank. Then the nation might have de facto exchange rate stabilization, in terms of gold, with de jure stabilization somewhat later. The speed and character of the process of gold standard restoration was frequently and importantly affected by foreign missions. The League of Nations sent financial missions to advise central and Eastern Europe. British, American, and French central bankers officially and unofficially offered advice and financial help. The American economist Kemmerer and other private financial experts were widely used in Latin America and elsewhere.

Most important, the return to the gold standard in the financially troubled principal European economies in the 1920s was also generally supported by international advice and cooperation by the principal financial powers. Indeed American involvement was crucial in the 1923 international commission to help Germany deal with her reparations obligations and get beyond the national and international logjam that produced its disastrous postwar hyperinflation. In addition, Britain's own return to gold in April 1925 was sharply supported by Benjamin Strong and the New York capital markets.

Many believe that the gold exchange standard was established based on incorrect parities. It is widely held that sterling returned to gold at an overvalued rate of between 5 and 15 percent depending on the price index used (Keynes, 1925; Redmond, 1984). Consequently, Britain suffered a competitive disadvantage with her trading partners and a chronic balance of payments deficit which forced the Bank of England to continuously follow contractionary monetary policies to maintain gold convertibility. The United Kingdom's weak position threatened the stability of one of the key reserve countries and hence the system itself. At the same time, France restored gold at a vastly undervalued parity. Hence, she ran persistent balance of payments surpluses and gold inflows.

This maladjustment involving two key members was greatly aggravated by inappropriate monetary policies pursued by France and the United States (see Eichengreen 1992; Meltzer 2003; Friedman and Schwartz 1963). Each nation as well as other countries (Nurkse 1944), consistently sterilized gold inflows which reduced gold reserves available to the rest of the world and enhanced deflationary pressure.

The global gold exchange standard lasted until the United Kingdom abandoned it in September 1931. It collapsed in the face of the shocks of the Great Depression. Tight monetary policy by the Federal Reserve in 1928 to deflate the stock market boom and France's progold policies precipitated a downturn in the United States and the rest of the world in 1929. Subsequent monetary collapse in the United States following a series of banking panics transmitted deflationary and contractionary pressure to the rest of the world on the gold standard.

As soon as doubts began to surface about the stability of the reserve currencies, central banks scrambled to liquidate their exchange reserves and replace them with gold. The share of foreign exchange in global central bank reserves plummeted from 37 percent at the end of 1930 to 13 percent at the end of 1931 and 11 percent at the end of 1932 (Nurkse 1944, appendix II). The implosion of the foreign-exchange component of the global reserve base exerted strong deflationary pressure on the world economy. Although there was only so much gold to go around, central banks around the world wanted more. To attract it, they jacked up interest rates in the face of an unprecedented slump.

Exchange Market Operation in the Interwar

The European central banks and especially the Bank of England engaged in extensive exchange market operations once the gold standard was fully restored in 1926. The Bank of England engaged in gold policies similar to those before 1914 and it also operated directly on the exchange rate.[4]

Active policy began after the July 1927 Long Island meeting between

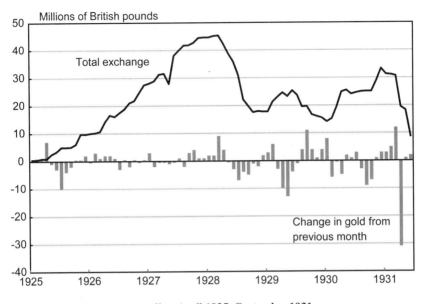

Fig. 2.1   British monetary policy, April 1925–September 1931
Note: Data are in Moggridge (1972) and are from the Bank of England.

Bank of England Governor Montagu Norman and Federal Reserve Bank of New York Governor Benjamin Strong. The object of the policy was to divert gold withdrawals by the Banque de France and other continental central banks away from London and to New York, despite the fact that gold prices were, as a rule, cheaper in London.[5] The bank began paying higher than its 77s 9d (the standard ounce of gold) buying price in the summer of 1928 and followed similar (pre-1914) policies as well as moral suasion until September 1931 (Moggridge 1972, 173). Einzig (1931) estimated that these measures could affect the London-New York gold export point by as much as 1 percent. The Bank of England was also aided on occasion in its attempt to influence gold movements by concerted efforts by the Reichsbank and other central banks (Moggridge 1972, 176)

The Bank of England and the other central banks also pursued vigorous exchange market interventions in the interwar period. Moggridge details the largely secret operations undertaken by the Bank of England. Figure 2.1 provides a monthly summary of the bank's major holdings of dollars and francs, as total exchange. The bank's operations developed from policies it used to peg sterling to the dollar in World War I.

The bank operated directly in the foreign exchange market through a number of correspondent banks and through dealings with other central banks. The bank's operations until 1931 (and subsequently) were done in the strictest secrecy and the transactions were buried under the item *Other*

Securities in the banking department's balance sheet. The bank feared that if the public knew it held hidden reserves as large as its published reserves that it would have great difficulty in pursuing its deflationary policies.[6] The bank also automatically sterilized its operations by compensating security purchases or sales. According to Moggridge (1972, 185), this policy of automatic complete offsetting represented an innovation.

The most active period of intervention was September 1926–September 1929, when, to prevent gold exports, the bank sold dollars in the open market spot for ten months when the sterling dollar rate was below the average gold export point (Moggridge 1972, 185). It also, on occasion (March 1928 and in 1930), sold foreign exchange to reduce funds in the domestic market (a form of monetary policy; Moggridge [1972], 186), and it used its foreign exchange holdings to shift asset conversions to other central banks (Moggridge 1972, 188).

The bank engaged in forward transactions to influence spot rates beginning in November 1926,

> when spot Sterling was near the gold export point the Bank instructed the New York Fed to sell spot dollars for sterling and to repurchase any dollars sold to or three months forward. (Moggridge 1972, 191).

As discussed in section 2.2.6 above, the Bank of England in its perennial defense of sterling was also supported using foreign exchange market intervention by the New York Fed, the Banque de France, and other central banks. The Fed purchased sterling on three occasions between June 1927 and December 1930, and the Banque de France supported sterling in late 1930 and 1931.

Finally the bank engaged in massive interventions in the 1931 sterling crisis. Between July and September, the bank sold $381 million spot and $125 forward as well as £53 million in francs and 83 percent of its reserve losses came from both operations (Moggridge 1972).

Despite the disaster at the end, the bank's exchange market policies enabled it to raise its gold reserves in the majority of quarters from 1926 to 1931. It also allowed the bank to follow an easier policy than otherwise, to violate the gold points on numerous occasions, and to insulate the British economy from external shocks (Moggridge 1972, 196–97). A key problem with the success of its secret intervention is that the bank's international reserves did not serve as a good signal of the state of the British economy. This in turn prevented the normal price specie flow adjustment mechanism of the gold standard from working and thus creating the conditions for a later adjustment through a crisis.

2.2.5   The Exchange Equalisation Account

The final European precedent to US institutions was the British Exchange Equalisation Account (EEA) established 1 June 1932. After Britain left the gold standard in September 1931, sterling depreciated to $3.25 by the end of December, a development which was applauded. However in early 1932, the pound strengthened, leading to concern by the monetary authorities that reflation would be derailed (Sayers 1976, ch. 18; Bank of England 1968; Howson 1980). This led leading officials to make the case for massive exchange market intervention.

The British government decided to set up a new account in the Treasury rather than keeping it with the Bank of England because of concern that the size of the operations imagined would impair the bank's ability to conduct its domestic monetary policy; that exchange market operations would be easy to detect; and that the bank as a private institution would not be able to absorb political losses (Sayers 1976, 426).

The new account was established with initial reserves of £150 million plus £20 million from an old Treasury exchange account. Funds not used to purchase foreign exchange would be invested in Treasury bills.

Once in operation the EEA actively attempted to influence the dollar exchange rate until 1935, and thereafter, the franc and the price of gold, buying foreign exchange or gold and selling sterling spot. The EEA also used forward operations to supplement its spot operations (Howson 1980, 34–39).

EEA operation tended to be automatically sterilized. According to Howson (1980, 9) an EEA purchase of foreign exchange would both increase the currency in the hands of the public and reduce the EEA's holding of Treasury bills. If the government then issued the same amount of bills, the cash supplied to the public by the EEA would be offset by the withdrawal of cash in payment for bills.[7]

The EEA was used successfully throughout the 1930s and then again in the Bretton Woods era. It was disbanded only in 1979.

2.3   Pre–Civil War Antecedents: The House of Brown and Nicholas Biddle and the Second Bank of the United States

2.3.1   Background

The United States in the first half of the nineteenth century was what today would be described as an emerging market economy. It was small relative to the advanced countries of Europe but with a level of per capita income not far behind England, France, and the Netherlands. Its financial institutions and banking system of unit state-chartered banks were still undeveloped compared to those of the western European countries but undergoing rapid transformation.[8] The United States also could be characterized as a small open economy on a fixed exchange rate, the international specie standard.[9] Most of its international trade was with England and involved staple exports of cotton and tobacco from the South and imports by the North of manufactured goods and commodities.

The US monetary standard was bimetallic. The official mint ratio of the price of gold to silver was fixed at 15:1 by the Coinage Act of 1792. By the early nineteenth century silver was relatively abundant while gold was undervalued at the Mint so that domestic transactions were undertaken largely in silver coins. International transactions, however, were conducted in gold, which sold at a premium.[10] In 1834, the bimetallic ratio was raised to 16:1, which put the United States on a de facto gold standard—with the exception of the greenback episode of fiat issue from 1861 to 1879. It became de jure in 1900 and lasted until 1933.

Under the gold standard, at least in theory, payments imbalances were settled by gold flows. For example, a US trade deficit with England when it imported more than it exported created an excess demand for sterling. This raised the price of sterling to the gold export point so that gold (coins or bars) would be exported to England. In the case of a US surplus, the price of sterling fell. Gold would be imported from England.

In reality, international payments in the nineteenth century involved much more than the textbook example indicates. Most payments were settled in the form of bills of exchange rather than in specie. Sterling bills were drawn by merchant banks and other financial institutions in England. A bill of exchange, first developed in England in the seventeenth century, was a form of credit or promissory note in which a buyer of commodities promised to pay the seller at a fixed date in the future, facilitating trade across distances and over time.[11]

In the United States before the Civil War, the supply of sterling bills was generated by staple exports, so for example, a cotton exporter (factor) in New Orleans who wished to arrange to ship cotton to Liverpool would obtain an advance on consignment from an English merchant bank up to 90 percent of the sale value of the cotton to be shipped. When the English importer received the cotton in Liverpool and sold it for sterling, the proceeds would then be used to settle the bill drawn in New Orleans. The bill could then be transferred to a third party for cash, thus creating a liquid financial instrument. On the other side of the market, an importer of British goods in the North would obtain a letter of credit (a guarantee of payment) from a merchant bank allowing him to purchase a bill of exchange which could then be remitted to England in exchange for the goods.

Two problems complicated this market: distance and the seasons. The supply of bills was generated in the summer and fall when southern staples were exported to Europe, and the demand for bills by northern importers generally arose in winter. To fill the temporal and spatial gaps, a new financial intermediary, the exchange dealer, evolved after the turn of the nineteenth century.[12] These firms would sell sterling bills to the northern merchants in winter when the price of foreign exchange was generally high, and invest the proceeds in short-term commercial paper. Then when the cotton crop moved in the fall, they would sell the commercial bills and use the proceeds to buy sterling bills of exchange at seasonally low prices from the cotton factors and then remit the proceeds to their correspondents/branches in England.

In the second decade of the century several prominent private firms such as the House of Brown; Prime, Ward, and King; Fitch Bowen and Co.; and also the Second Bank of the United States possessed sufficient capital, an interregional branch network, and correspondents or branches in England, to develop this market. Their operations served to create a national sterling bills market and to efficiently allocate resources across regions and over the seasons. Their operations also helped achieve greater internal exchange market integration (moving the exchange rates closer to parity), external integration (narrowing the gold points), and arbitrage between exchange rates in different locations. Over time they reduced the variation in exchange rates (Officer 1992).

2.3.2 The House of Brown

The premier foreign exchange dealer in the first three quarters of the nineteenth century was the House of Brown, which began operations in Baltimore at the turn of the century. Brown Bros. dominated the sterling bill market from 1810 to 1825 until it was eclipsed for a decade by the Second Bank of the United States under the direction of Nicholas Biddle, and then rose again to prominence from 1836 to 1879 (Perkins 1975). The firm evolved from being a linen importer in Baltimore to becoming a foreign exchange broker between exporters in the Chesapeake and importers in Baltimore, to becoming a dealer, buying and selling foreign exchange on its own account and trading with other dealers.

The firm expanded by setting up a branch in Liverpool in 1810, and then branches in Philadelphia in 1818, New York in 1825, New Orleans in 1823, and other port cities in subsequent years. Through its English branches it was able to obtain sterling bills, and by shifting funds between its various branches in key US ports, it was able to take advantage of arbitrage opportunities, in turn helping to integrate the market. This activity was greatly enhanced in the 1840s once the telegraph began linking major centers.

Its operations were both covered and uncovered. Much of its seasonal arbitrage was covered. In the spring northern branches of Brown sold foreign exchange to importers. The cash was invested in short-term commercial paper. Then in the fall when the cotton crop moved, Brown's would sell off its commercial bills and shift the proceeds to its southern branches. These branches then purchased bills and remitted them to Liverpool, which would use them to cover overdrawn sterling accounts of the northern branches (Perkins 1975). The firm engaged in uncovered transactions when the dealers sold sterling bills in amounts in excess of the volume of bills purchased and remittances. Such transactions took advantage of a future expected decline in prices. During the interval when the firm's account remained uncovered, payments were financed by the Liverpool branch (Perkins 1975, 151). The firm also shipped specie between the United States and England when informed by its English branches to do so (Perkins 1975, 28).

Brown Bros. was not an official monetary authority and it did not conduct anything like the exchange market operations undertaken by European central banks or even some of the operations attributed to Nicholas Biddle and the Second Bank of the United States. But its operations did help integrate the US domestic market for sterling bills. It also aided in the international integration of the exchange market. It helped to reduce the volatility of exchange rates by smoothing seasonal variations and by international arbitrage operations. This was a stated purpose of modern exchange rate policy.

2.3.3   Nicholas Biddle and the Second Bank of the United States

The Second Bank of the United States was established in 1816. Its mandate was similar to that of the First Bank of the United States (1791–1811). Its charter had not been renewed because of strong populist and states' rights opposition to its federal enactment and its market power (Timberlake 1978). The mandate of the Second Bank was to serve as the federal government's fiscal agent, to create a uniform national currency, and to promote economic development. The bank established twenty-eight branches across the country and was heavily capitalized at $35 million (ten times the size of the largest private bank).

It became involved in the foreign exchange market through operations designed to create a uniform national currency, that is, to reduce the discounts on bank notes in the West and the South and to equalize exchange rates on domestic bills. In its early years, the Second Bank, like its predecessor the First Bank of the United States, sought to create a uniform currency by requiring its correspondent state banks in the interior to redeem their notes in specie on demand in order to deal with a perennial internal balance of trade deficit. It also remitted specie from its western to its eastern branches. These policies, in addition to being unpopular, also created economic distress in the West. Nicholas Biddle, upon becoming president of the bank in 1821, substituted the use of domestic bills of exchange for specie in settling interregional branch imbalances. He instructed his local branch managers to replace local discounts, payable in local currency, with domestic bills payable at commercial centers (Knodell 2003). Consequently bills became the main means of long distance remittances. The Second Bank's large size and extensive branch networks enabled it to quickly dominate the domestic bill market.

The bank began operations in foreign exchange in 1825 in competition with Brown Bros. and the other private banks. Because of its size, extensive branch networks, connection, and line of credit of £250 million with Barings, the leading British merchant bank, the Second Bank quickly dominated the market for sterling bills.

Like Brown's, Biddle engaged in the profitable activity of interregional arbitrage.[13] Thus in the winter and spring, when cotton moved to market and sterling fell to a discount, the southern branches of the bank bought bills on London. Then in the summer and fall, when imports were purchased and sterling rose to a premium, the northern branches sold the bills in London. Access to its extensive line of credit with Barings allowed the Second Bank of the United States to take an uncovered position and to undertake these counterseasonal exchange rate operations since bills drawn on Barings might exceed current remittances to the Second Bank's account (Knodell 2003).

However, the Second Bank under Nicholas Biddle went much further than Brown's in its exchange market operations. Nicholas Biddle, according to Redlich (1951), in addition to understanding well the effects of seasonal exchange market operations on the variance of the exchange rate, also had a clear understanding of the linkages earlier postulated by Thornton (1802), between the balance of trade, specie flows, the deviations of the exchange rate from parity on the one hand and the domestic money supply and the real economy on the other hand. Consequently he favored operations to both reduce the variability of exchange rates and to insulate the domestic economy from external shocks.

> A participation also in the foreign exchanges forms an essential part of the system, not merely as auxiliary to the transfer of funds by which the circulating medium is accompanied and protected, but as the best defense of the currency from external influences . . . . It belongs then to the conservative power over the circulating medium which devolves on the Bank, not to be a passive observer of these movements, but to take an ample share in all that concerns the foreign exchanges (Redlich 1951, fn. 209, ch. VI).

Although Redlich (1951) claimed that Biddle engaged in deliberate exchange market intervention action, "Biddle entered the field of foreign exchange in order to protect the currency from foreign influences and to counteract possible disturbances of business" (131). The same claim is made by Smith (1953), Hammond (1957), Myers (1970, 88) and most recently by Officer (1992) who states,

> Biddle was concerned whenever the exchange rate went beyond the gold-point spread . . . . In such circumstances he would take steps to return the exchange rate to within the spread either through direct exchange transactions or through GTF/GPA (gold-effected transfer of funds/gold point arbitrage). (204)

Yet we could find no actual empirical evidence of such operations.[14] However, Smith's (1953) chart V, which we reproduce as figure 2.2, shows an inverse relationship between the sterling exchange rate (sixty day bills on London) and the foreign position of the Second Bank. According to Smith

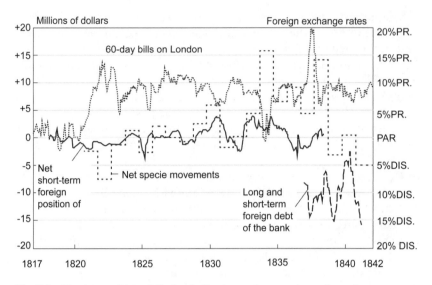

Fig. 2.2   Foreign position of the bank, foreign exchange rates and specie movements, United States, 1817–1842

Note: Figure is reproduced from Smith (1953, 45).

> Up to 1836, the Bank built up its foreign balances in the periods when foreign exchange rates were low and went into debt when the rates were high, a process not only stabilizing in its effects, but profitable to the banks."
> (Smith 1953, 46)

thereby stabilizing the exchange rate.

Nicholas Biddle's understanding of the foreign exchange market and of the potential intervention role of the monetary authority was way ahead of his time. However, the counter seasonal operation of the Second Bank, done largely for commercial reasons, and its influence on the exchange rate, also predated the deliberate exchange market policies pursued later in the nineteenth century by European central banks. Without further evidence, however, the jury is out on whether Biddle actually engaged in exchange market intervention in the modern sense.

2.3.4   The Post–Civil War Period

After the demise of the Second Bank of the United States in 1836, the House of Brown again became the dominant player in the US sterling bill market. It followed the spatial and temporal arbitrage strategies that it had applied before 1825 and expanded its branch network (Perkins 1975, 157). The market became more integrated, thanks to the innovations introduced by Biddle and the national spread of the telegraph in the 1840s. Brown's dominated the sterling exchange market through the 1870s but faced increasing competition from other dealers, especially Prime, Ward, and King, and Fitch Brothers, and after 1871 by Drexel Morgan, which eclipsed it by 1879. Private bankers dominated the market until the end of the nineteenth century when the major New York money center banks took over (Officer 1996, 211). None of these institutions engaged in operations other than those described above.

In 1862 during the Civil War and for fourteen years afterward, specie convertibility was suspended and the United States was on the greenback floating exchange rate standard. In that era, the dollar-pound exchange rate floated, measured by the premium on gold (the price of a gold dollar in terms of greenbacks). An active gold market developed in New York, which operated virtually without government interference (Friedman and Schwartz 1963). International payments were still settled by sterling bills. Brown's and the other two dominant dealers strengthened their position in the sterling bill market. Because they had the experience and the resources to deal with the added risk of a floating exchange rate, they eliminated most of their competition (Perkins 1975, 207).

Before the Civil War, the US Treasury had virtually no connection with the foreign exchange market. With the establishment of the independent Treasury in 1847, the Treasury's role was restricted to receiving tax and other revenues in specie to finance very limited government expenditures and to manage the government debt. From the 1840s onward, the United States ran a budget surplus and the national debt was virtually paid off by the eve of the Civil War (Timberlake 1978).

After the Civil War ended, the Treasury became actively involved in issues of the monetary standard and the exchange rate. A significant fraction of Union wartime expenditures had been financed by the issue of greenbacks (noninterest bearing notes denominated in dollars and declared to be legal tender) and the money supply doubled. Under the Legal Tender Act, the dates and provisions for convertibility of greenbacks were not specified. In January 1862 the commercial banks suspended specie convertibility and the dollar began a rapid depreciation against sterling, peaking in 1862 at slightly over double the prewar parity. Shortly after the war, Secretary of the Treasury Hugh McCulloch made clear his intention to resume payments and restore the prewar sterling parity of $4.86. This resulted in passage of the Contraction Act of 12 April 1866, which provided for the limited withdrawal of US notes. The act was successful in reducing prices (and the premium on gold) raising the dollar pound exchange rate (see figure 2.3) from 1866 to 1868, but widespread perceptions of a declining economy,[15] led to a public outcry and the repeal of the Act in February 1868. Over the next seven years, a fierce debate raged between the hard money factions—advocates of rapid resumption—and soft money factions, some of whom were opposed to restoring the gold standard. While others favored resumption at a devalued parity, others opposed undue deflation and favored allowing the economy

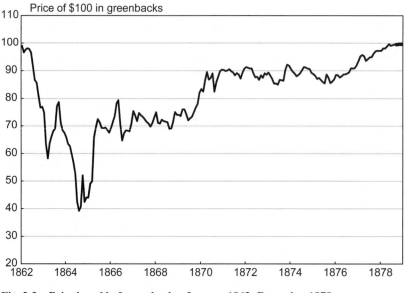

Fig. 2.3   Price in gold of greenbacks, January 1862–December 1878
Note: Data are from Mitchell (1908).

to grow up to its money supply (Unger 1964; Sharkey 1959). Triumphs of the conflicting factions were manifest in legislation—the Public Credit Act of 1869 contracting the greenback issue, the reissue of $26 million of retired greenbacks in 1873 expanding it—and in Supreme Court decisions, initially declaring the Legal Tender Acts unconstitutional (Hepburn vs. Griswold, February 1870), and then reversing the decision (Knox vs. Lee, May 1871). Finally, the decision to resume convertibility on 1 January 1879 was made in the Resumption Act of 14 January 1875, which can be interpreted as a form of exchange rate policy.[16]

In addition to proclaiming the date of resumption and the original parity, the act authorized the Treasury to use its surplus revenues and the proceeds of bond sales to accumulate a gold reserve.[17] According to Friedman and Schwartz (1963) the achievement of successful resumption in 1879 had little to do with Treasury policies.[18] Restoration of prewar purchasing power parity in 1878 was achieved by the real economy growing up to a relatively constant money supply.[19]

Once the gold standard was restored in 1879, the Treasury rarely was involved in any form of exchange market operations until the outbreak of World War I. Two episodes stand out, however.

The first was a rescue operation of the US Treasury arranged by a private consortium headed by J. P. Morgan and August Belmont in 1895 at the apex of the struggle over free silver.[20] A US budget deficit after 1890 and the issue of legal tender Treasury notes of 1890, redeemable in coin that the Sherman Silver Purchase Act of 1890 mandated, created uncertainty about the convertibility of the US dollar, despite the repeal of the Sherman Act in 1893. To finance the deficit, the Treasury ran down the stock of gold and legal tenders. Presentation of the legal tenders outstanding for redemption threatened the gold reserve. The Treasury attempted, in January and November 1894, to restore its gold reserve at a minimum to $100 million by offering for public subscription $50 million 10-year 5 percent bonds. The subscribers, however, used legal tenders to obtain gold to pay for the bonds, with no increment to the gold reserve. In January 1895, a run on gold in exchange for legal tenders reduced the reserve to $45 million.

Stymied in February 1895, the Treasury secretary contracted with the Belmont-Morgan banking syndicate under an 1862 law which authorized him to purchase coin on terms he negotiated, to market a 4 percent bond issue, and provide the Treasury with a six-month short-term interest-free gold credit line to restore the gold reserve. One half of the 3.5 million ounces of gold delivered was to be shipped from Europe at a rate not exceeding 300,000 ounces a month. The syndicate agreed to protect the Treasury against gold withdrawals paid out to redeem legal tenders or sold to obtain exchange. It delivered an additional $25 million in gold in exchange for legal tenders, and borrowed exchange in London to sell in New York, effectively controlling the exchange market. The syndicate marketed the bonds for a total of $68.8 million.

During the five months after the contract was signed, no gold was withdrawn from the Treasury. At the end of August 1895, when agricultural exports and associated gold imports rose, the syndicate was dissolved.

The second episode was an attempt in 1906 by Secretary Shaw to raise the gold import point. On several occasions in the national banking era (1865–1914), the US Treasury, although not a formal central bank, used several of the tools of monetary policy to allay banking panics, following policies such as shifting deposits between the independent Treasury and the New York money market banks.[21]

On at least one occasion in March 1906, to reduce pressure on the New York commercial banks, Secretary Shaw reduced the interest cost on gold imports and thereby reduced the gold import point by a few cents. According to Beckhart, Smith, and Brown (1932, vol. IV), he "allowed the New York banks to count gold in transit as part of their reserves."

Then according to Myers (1931),

> he discarded this plan for another which was more nearly in line with the law. He permitted banks which had engaged gold for imports to secure government deposits to 110% of the amount of gold, by depositing with the Treasury securities of the classes acceptable to the New York savings banks. The deposits made against this collateral were returned to the Treasury when the gold arrived. As a result of this scheme the banks had

the use of the amount imported while it was on its way to New York, and the interest cost for the ten days in transit was thus eliminated. (Myers 1931, vol. I, 343)[22]

Shaw was following the type of gold policies which had already been perfected by the Bank of England and other European central banks. Although there had been pressure on the Treasury to support sterling exchange in New York on earlier occasions (Beckhart, Smith, and Brown 1932, vol. IV, 190) such as during the panic of 1873, these seem to be the only episodes when such operations were actually followed.

2.3.5   World War I and the Establishment of the Federal Reserve

The Federal Reserve Act was passed in 1913 and the system began operations in 1914. Its mandate was to provide monetary stability (interpreted as both price level and output stability) and to serve as a lender of last resort. It was also given a limited role in the operation of the foreign exchange market. The Federal Reserve Board was given the power

> to permit the acceptance of drafts drawn to create dollar exchange, to pass upon applications for and to regulate foreign trade banks and foreign branches of member banks and to regulate direct dealings by the Federal Reserve banks in gold, cable transfers and bills of exchange." (Beckhart, Smith, and Brown 1932, vol. IV, 216)

As holders of gold reserves backing Federal Reserve deposits and notes, the system had considerable power over specie payments, but the ultimate responsibility for maintaining adherence to the gold standard rested with the US Treasury under the Gold Standard Act of 1900. This was done through purchases of gold at the Mints and Assay offices and redemption of currency in Washington (Beckhart, Smith, and Brown 1932, 217).

Between 1915 and 1917 arrangements were made to coordinate gold transactions between the Federal Reserve and the Treasury. For example in 1915, the Treasury

> began to accept deposits of gold in [the Reserve Banks of] San Francisco and Philadelphia and to make payments against them by telegraphic transfer in New York (217) . . . . In 1916, the Secretary of the Treasury deposited the government's working balance in the Federal Reserve banks, [and] the Assay Office began to pay for gold in treasurer's checks payable to the Federal Reserve Bank. (Beckhart, Smith, and Brown 1932, 218)

Thus a machinery was created and founded in an amendment in June 1917 to the Federal Reserve Act

> whereby gold imports were reflected directly in changes in the holdings of the Federal Reserve Banks in gold, and in the reserve accounts of the member banks. . . . Gold for export instead of being withdrawn from the individual reserves of banks, or from the sub-treasuries in exchange for

legal tender was provided by the Federal Reserve Banks, chiefly the New York Bank, from their accumulated stock, and charged to the reserve account of the withdrawing bank. (Bekhart, Smith, and Brown 1932, 218)

The outbreak of World War I in Europe created a crisis in the foreign exchange market in New York which led to significant policy interventions by the monetary authorities. The outbreak of hostilities led British acceptance houses to cut off the normal supply of sterling bills to exporters just at the height of the crop moving season. At the same time European investors rushed to liquidate their US securities and equities and to remit the proceeds in gold back home. This put extreme upward pressure on sterling exchange. The crisis also led to a sell-off on the New York Stock Exchange which was closed 31 July 1914 (and not reopened until November) and to an incipient banking panic as the rush to remit gold drained the reserves of the New York banks.

Treasury Secretary William G. McAdoo intervened on 2 August by imposing an informal embargo on further gold shipments and permitting the issue of close to $300 million in emergency currency under the Aldrich Vreeland Act of 1908 (Beckhart, Smith, and Brown 1932, ch. XI). Further Treasury actions to alleviate the pressure included obtaining legislation (the Ship Registry Act), which permitted foreign ships to be transferred to American Registry, hence providing ships to move the staple exports (which had been frozen by the cutoff of finance and the heightened state of uncertainty), and through the provision of war risk insurance by the Treasury's Bureau of War Risk Insurance, the creation of a gold fund of $100 million by the commercial banks under the auspices of the Federal Reserve Bank of New York to provide gold for export, and on 20 August 1914, by placing public deposits in the New York banks to help the foreign exchange markets (Beckhart, Smith, and Brown 1932, 207).

After the initial crisis eased, sterling and the franc had sunk well below parity. Stabilization of sterling at $4.76 1/2 was accomplished by the British through the suspension of gold shipments to the United States for British account, by the sale of British owned securities in New York, and by direct loans arranged by J. P. Morgan. Stabilization of the franc was achieved in 1916 by an agreement between Great Britain and France. With the United States' entry into the war in April 1917, the monetary authorities began active involvement in stabilizing exchange rates.

Once the United States entered the war in April 1917, credits were given to the allies to help peg their currencies, and arrangements were made so that the allies could pay for exports directly (Beckhart, Smith, and Brown 1932, 238). A growing problem facing the monetary expansion policies of the US authorities arose from a gold drain to neutral countries—because US exports to them had been diverted to the allies. It led to the imposition of an embargo on gold exports in June 1917 and the institution of strict exchange controls beginning in February 1918. The controls which were administered by the Federal Reserve Board required licenses for anyone seeking access to foreign exchange and a division of foreign exchange was set up in Washington and New York (Beckhart, Smith, and Brown 1932, 243).

In September 1918, to address the continuing discount on the dollar in neutral countries, the secretary of the Treasury negotiated special credit arrangements to provide a supply of neutral foreign exchange from these countries. Finally in September 1918, the Treasury was given the power to cooperate with other countries to stabilize their currencies (Beckhart, Smith, and Brown 1932, 248).

Once the war ended exchange controls were quickly removed in December 1918, support of the pound and the franc ended in March 1919, the gold embargo was terminated in June 1919. Export credits to the allies were ended in May 1920.

The panoply of controls over the foreign exchange markets and stabilization credits to the allies established the machinery for future exchange market operations by the US monetary authorities.

Based on this precedent the Federal Reserve in the subsequent decade participated in a number of stabilization programs for other countries. It also engaged in several direct interventions in the foreign exchange markets.

2.3.6   Exchange Market Policies, 1919–1931

US Exchange Market Policies

After the war, Benjamin Strong, governor of the Federal Reserve Bank of New York, emerged as the dominant player in the development of US monetary policy. Strong had a deep interest in international monetary affairs and he wanted the Federal Reserve to follow policies similar to those the European central banks had developed before the war. He also was a keen advocate for a return by the Europeans to gold convertibility and for the Fed to pursue policies in cooperation with the central banks of the core countries to secure that aim. Although an advocate of international cooperation, according to Chandler (1958), Strong never followed international policies that conflicted with domestic needs.

Strong began a series of international arrangements with an agreement in 1916 with the Bank of England (and later with the Bank of France) for the New York Fed to maintain an account with the Bank of England in earmarked gold and for the Bank of England to purchase prime sterling bills for the Fed.

Beginning in late 1919, the Federal Reserve, concerned over declining gold reserves, switched to a tight monetary policy, in an attempt to reverse five years of wartime and postwar inflation (Meltzer 2003). The policy was successful in restoring US gold reserves and in rolling back prices to their

1917 level but at the cost of a very serious recession and, according to Friedman and Schwartz (1963, ch. 4), the Fed's first serious policy mistake. In the subsequent years concern switched from declining gold reserves to rising reserves which were perceived as inflationary. Beginning in 1921, the Fed began sterilizing gold flows by leaving gold in earmark at the Bank of England.[23]

2.3.7   The Resumption of Sterling

The heyday of Federal Reserve international policies and the use of various types of exchange market operations began in 1924 when the New York Fed followed policies designed to help Britain restore convertibility for sterling at the prewar parity of $4.86. Strong had developed a good rapport with Montagu Norman of the Bank of England over the years after his first visit in 1916. Both had similar views on restoring and maintaining the gold standard and in pursuing cooperative policies. Both agreed that for a successful resumption, countries had to balance their budgets, establish independent central banks, have balance in their trade accounts, accumulate sufficient gold reserves, and finally restore their price levels as closely as possible to prewar purchasing parities (Clarke 1967). It was also believed that the stabilization of sterling would be the catalyst for other countries to restore convertibility.

By 1924 several important developments, including the Dawes loan and stabilization of the German mark, settlement of British war debts to the United States, and the convergence of British prices toward those of the United States, created conditions favorable to resumption. A decline in interest rates in New York below those in London, a US balance of payments deficit, and capital outflows persuaded Norman and Strong to act (Chandler 1958; Clarke 1967). A cooperative strategy to reduce the price gap, calculated by Strong at 10 percent, by lowering US interest rates, and providing credits to the Bank of England was followed. In May 1924, the New York Fed established a $200 million two-year line of credit for the Bank of England in gold or dollars with interest to be charged only on amounts actually drawn, with the rate set at 1 percent above the New York Fed's discount rate on ninety-day bills. At the same time a private line of credit for the British government with J. P. Morgan for $150 million was arranged.

In addition the Federal Reserve began easing its monetary policy in the spring of 1924 to deal with a recession which had begun in the fall of 1923. The New York Fed cut its discount rate three times between May and August (from 4 1/2 percent to 3 percent and kept it at that level until February 1925). The Fed also conducted significant open market purchases of securities and bills (Clarke 1967). At the same time, the Bank of England kept interest rates firm at 4 percent despite high unemployment. The coordinated policy was considered a success, sterling rose toward parity from May 1924 to April 1925, British gold reserves increased, and the price differential between the two countries dropped to within 2 1/2 percent of parity, allowing Britain to resume convertibility in April 1925 (Clarke 1967).

Once sterling was stabilized, the New York Fed participated in a number of stabilization packages to restore convertibility to the Belgian franc in 1926, the French franc in 1926, the Italian lira in 1927, and a number of lesser currencies in the rest of the decade. All of these packages involved lines of credit supplied by the Federal Reserve as well as private credits to the governments (Chandler 1958).

2.3.8   Preserving Sterling and Central Bank Cooperation, 1927–1931

Once the gold standard was reinstated it was faced with ongoing pressures especially on sterling which had, it turned out, returned to parity at a significantly overvalued rate. The key source of pressure on the British gold reserves came from France which stabilized its currency in December 1926 at an undervalued parity and which began following a pro-gold policy, that is, sterilizing reserve inflows and converting foreign exchange (both sterling and dollars) into gold. Germany also kept running payments surpluses in the mid to late 1920s with Britain. Finally the United States, beginning in 1926, faced continuous gold inflows reflecting bouyant economic conditions and a booming stock market.

Clarke (1967) discusses in detail the extensive cooperation between Benjamin Strong, Montagu Norman, Emile Moreau, president of the Banque de France, and Hjalmar Schact, president of the Reichsbank. Strong was instrumental in persuading the French and the Germans to pursue policies which would ease the gold drain in Britain and in helping the Federal Reserve facilitate some of these operations. For example, in April 1927 when the Banque de France repaid a 1923 debt to the Bank of England and

> recovered more than $80 million of gold formally pledged as security for the loan and then sold the gold to Irving Trust Company in New York . . . Strong then purchased $60 million and held it under earmark at the Bank of England. (Chandler, 375)

The policy prevented

> a rise in the gold reserve of the New York Bank, avoided the psychological effects that might have arisen from a large gold shipment, and provided Strong with a gold balance in London that later proved useful. (Ibid., 375)

Later in June

> when Moreau was taking gold from London, Strong sold him the $60 million of earmarked gold thereby easing the drain from the Bank of England. He also purchased some sterling bills to ease the British position and to prevent gold flows to the United States. (Ibid., 378)

The most important episode of coordinated exchange market policy then took place beginning in July 1927 when Strong invited Norman, Moreau, and Schacht to a conference at the Long Island estate of Ogden Mills, under-secretary of the Treasury. The conference led to a number of significant policy actions. First, the Federal Reserve engaged in expansionary open market purchases from June to November of about $200 million and lowered the discount rate from 4 to 3 1/2 percent from 29 July to mid-September. The expansionary policy reflected both concerns over a domestic recession which had begun in October 1926 and the international situation. Second, both the Banque de France and the Reichsbank shifted their gold purchases from London to New York. Third, the Reichsbank also reduced its discount rate (Chandler 1958, 275–77; Clarke 1967).

These policy moves were utilized successfully in easing the US recession and temporarily taking pressure off sterling. In 1928–29, the strains in the international monetary system continued to build up. In response to the Wall Street stock market boom the Federal Reserve began tightening monetary policy, conducting open market sales, and raising the discount rate from 3 1/2 to 4 1/2 percent. This encouraged capital flows from Europe. Additional strain on sterling came from the Banque de France which after the de jure stabilization of the franc on 25 June 1928, began a strong pro-gold policy of absorbing gold inflows and converting its foreign exchange reserves into gold (Clarke 1967). Attempts at further cooperation came to naught until the summer of 1929, when Harrison at the New York Fed (Strong's successor) engaged in market operations to support sterling. The New York Fed purchased $41 million in sterling in August and September after the Fed had raised its discount rate from 5 percent to 6 percent.

The Great Depression began with a recession starting in the United States in August 1929, exacerbated by the Wall Street crash in October. The depression spread from the United States to the rest of the world via the fixed exchange rate links of the gold standard. In 1930–31, the Federal Reserve was involved in a number of exchange market operations to initially help shore up and later save the British pound as well as the Austrian schilling and the German mark. In September 1930, to prevent a gold drain from London to New York, Norman asked Harrison to help support sterling. Between October 14 and October 30 the New York Fed acquired £4.7 million. Then in November, New York bought another £2.5 million. The operation was deemed successful (Clarke, 1967 175).

The final episode in US exchange market operations occurred during the 1931 crisis. The collapse of the Credit Anstalt Bank in May 1931 led to a banking crisis, a bailout by the Austrian National Bank, and a speculative attack on the schilling. A coordinated rescue engineered by the Bank of International Settlement provided a credit of $14 million (of which the US share was $3 million) which was too little and too late to stem the crisis. The crisis spread to Germany. A speculative attack on the Reichsbank's reserves threatened to breach its statutory gold reserve requirements in June. The Reichsbank then sought and obtained an international loan of $100 million

($25 million each from the Bank of England, Banque de France, Federal Reserve Bank of New York, and the BIS) on 25 June. The loan proved insufficient to stem the speculative attack. A second loan request by Hans Luther, the President of the Reichsbank, for $1 billion foundered in the face of opposition by both the Banque de France and the Federal Reserve. The external drain was finally halted by the announcement of a standstill agreement on 20 July and the imposition of exchange controls (Bordo and Schwartz 1999).

The crisis then spread to Great Britain and a speculative attack on the Bank of England's gold reserves in the late summer of 1931 triggered by the freezing of British deposits and assets in Austria and Germany but ultimately reflecting a seriously deteriorating fiscal problem. In the final week of July 1931, the Bank of England obtained matching credits for £25 million from the Federal Reserve Bank of New York and the Banque de France. The amount was inadequate to halt the run. Further loans to Britain of $200 million each from a syndicate formed by J. P. Morgan with the help of Harrison in New York and the syndicate in Paris also proved inadequate.

The Federal Reserve was heavily involved in various types of exchange market policies from 1924 to 1931. These interventions and credits were all done for the expressed purpose of strengthening and protecting the currencies of other countries, and in particular Great Britain. The object was to preserve the gold (exchange) standard which was believed to be the key pillar of monetary stability. Until 1931, many of these operations were successful in achieving their aims. Ultimately the gold exchange standard collapsed but debate still continues as to whether it could have survived absent the shock of the Great Depression. The traditional view is that it would have collapsed sooner or later because of an ultimate gold shortage, because of the strain on the system placed by French and US pro-gold and sterilization policies, and because of the overvaluation of sterling and the undervaluation of the franc. However its successful operation up to 1929, aided by the policies described above, suggest that it might have survived much longer, although whether central bank cooperation was the sine qua non for its survival is an open question.[24]

2.4   Precedents and Antecedents: The Lessons

The Exchange Stabilization Fund, established by the United States in 1934, and later the Federal Reserve when it began interventions in 1962, had available a wealth of techniques and experiences drawn from Treasury and Fed wartime and interwar operations as well as from the pre-1914 experiences of the Second Bank and private institutions like the House of Brown. United States' policies and institutions may also have been influenced by those developed by the Bank of England and other European central banks.

Yet while the Federal Reserve did engage in exchange market intervention in the 1920s, its legacy for future US policy was limited at best. First it was only used sporadically and then only at the behest of the Bank of England. Second, the international monetary policies followed by Benjamin Strong and the New York Federal Reserve to help restore and preserve the international gold standard, and especially the actions taken to alleviate threats to Britain's continued adherence to gold in 1927, were later viewed as key causes of the Wall Street crash in October 1929 and the Great Depression.

The view critical of the international policy of Strong and later Harrison was propounded by Adolph Miller of the Federal Reserve Board, Parker B. Willis of Columbia University, and Carter Glass, chairman of the House Banking Committee. Later in his memoirs, Herbert Hoover also blamed the New York Fed for the 1929–33 debacle (Chandler 1958, 255). According to Miller (1935) the open market purchases and discount rate cuts undertaken in the spring and summer of 1927 to both offset domestic recession and to ease strain on the Bank of England added considerable fuel to the Stock Market boom that was already underway. The subsequent New York Fed directed tightening policy in the second half of 1928 was insufficiently tight to prevent stock prices from rising to unsustainable heights, making the crash and all that followed inevitable.[25] According to Miller (1931, 134), "It was the greatest and boldest operation ever by the Federal Reserve System, and in my judgment resulted in one of the most costly errors committed by it or any banking system in the last 75 years."

The posthumous case against Strong made by Willis and Glass was that he had violated the intent of the Federal Reserve Act by acting on behalf of the New York Federal Reserve banks alone and not on behalf of the system in engaging in international monetary policy.

> For several years it had been the practice of the Federal Reserve Bank of New York to take upon itself authority to represent the entire system in foreign negotiations, and this assumption, usually "winked at" or tolerated by the Federal Reserve Board, largely through a desire of the latter not to have to assume responsibility in foreign markets, had grown into a practice of representing the Federal Reserve of New York in other countries as practically the manager or head of the system—the other Reserve Banks being thought of as "interior banks or branches or auxiliaries of the Federal Reserve Bank of New York." (Willis and Chapman 1934, 82–83)

As a consequence "in order to correct this misunderstanding the 1933 Banking Act carried a section providing that no negotiations with other central banks be conducted except with the knowledge and consent of the Federal Reserve Board" (Willis and Chapman 1934, 83).

Thus in the face of this withering attack, it is likely that there was little interest in the Federal Reserve in again pursuing the type of international cooperation and exchange market policies associated with Benjamin Strong and the 1920s, and that when the Federal Reserve again began pursuing such policies in the 1960s, it started with a clean slate. At the same time the perception in the Roosevelt administration that the crash and the Depression was caused by the inappropriate policies of the New York Fed and by the greed of bankers, Wall Street and finance capitalism in general led to the shift in monetary policy making away from the Federal Reserve and toward the Treasury.[26] International economic policy in general and exchange market intervention in particular was to be conducted by the Exchange Stabilization Fund as is discussed in chapter 3. The ESF in turn used some of the policy tools that were surveyed in this chapter.

Moreover when we consider the legacy of earlier experience we need to keep in mind that the earlier exchange market policies took place in an environment of very different exchange rate regimes. The pre-1914 gold standard was very different from the interwar, Bretton Woods, and today's managed floats. The gold standard regime was based on a high degree of credibility of commitment to maintaining gold parity while domestic considerations (except in wartime) were very limited. In this environment, the intervention which took place was very successful because the objectives were very limited—to marginally influence the gold points.

Many of the techniques and policies developed under the gold standard were used again in the subsequent regimes with very different results. In the interwar gold exchange, standard credibility of commitment to convertibility was weakened by greater importance placed on domestic objectives. This meant that the classical adjustment was deliberately impeded through sterilization, gold policy, exchange market operations, and central bank cooperation. Many of these operations were successful at the tactical level but did not prevent the system from collapsing under the shocks of the Great Depression—an event largely brought about by the major countries following incorrect and inconsistent policies and the basic misalignment of exchange rates. (Friedman and Schwartz 1963; Eichengreen 1992; Meltzer 2003).

Many of the techniques developed in the interwar period were used again in the Bretton Woods period—an adjustable peg exchange rate regime in which the US dollar was pegged to gold and the currencies of other member countries were pegged to the dollar. Various techniques of exchange market intervention were used to support sterling and other currencies and ultimately the dollar peg to gold. Like the gold exchange standard, at the tactical level these operations, as we shall see in chapter 4, were successful but the system ultimately collapsed reflecting monetary policies inconsistent with the fundamentals of the regime.

Today's environment of managed floating is very different from the gold-based pegged exchange rate regimes of the past. The object of policy is no longer to influence gold points or to preserve the peg. It is to create orderly markets or possibly to influence the level of the exchange rate. Yet while the stakes involved with exchange market policy are less today than in the past and the criteria for success or failure are different, it is still regarded as an important supplement to the monetary policy tool kit and often as monetary policy in a different guise.

Introducing the Exchange
Stabilization Fund, 1934–1961

3.1 Introduction

The first formal US institution designed to conduct official intervention in the foreign exchange market dates from 1934. In earlier years, as the preceding chapter has shown, makeshift arrangements for intervention prevailed. Why the Exchange Stabilization Fund (ESF) was created and how it performed in the period ending in 1961 are the subject of this chapter. After thriving in the prewar years from 1934 to 1939, little opportunity for intervention arose thereafter through the closing years of this period, so it is a natural dividing point in ESF history. The change in the fund's operations occurred as a result of the Federal Reserve's decision in 1962 to become its partner in official intervention. A subsequent chapter takes up the evolution of the fund thereafter.

3.2 Background

We first provide some information about the background to the legislation that established the ESF. The chronology of action with respect to gold by the Roosevelt administration begins on 6 March 1933. On that date a banking holiday was declared by proclamation of the president. Banks were prohibited from paying out or exporting gold. Government offices were prohibited from paying out gold except under license. On 9 March the Emergency Banking Act extended authority to regulate transactions in gold, silver, and foreign exchange. On 10 March, by executive order, the export of gold was prohibited except under regulations or license. On 5 April, gold and gold certificates were required by executive order to be surrendered. On

19 April, for the purpose of supporting the dollar in the foreign exchange market, the issuance of licenses to export gold from the United States was suspended. On 20 April, by executive order, the authority of the secretary of the Treasury to issue licenses to export or earmark gold was defined. On 5 June, by a joint resolution of Congress, so-called gold clauses in many government and private obligations, requiring payment either in gold or in a nominal amount of currency equal to the value of a specified weight of gold, were declared invalid in all public or private contracts, past or future. On 29 August, by executive order, the sale of domestic newly mined gold was authorized to industry at home and abroad. On 25 October, by executive order, the Reconstruction Finance Corporation (RFC) was authorized to acquire newly mined domestic gold. On 30 January 1934, the Gold Reserve Act transferred title to all gold of the Federal Reserve System to the United States, established the Exchange Stabilization Fund (ESF), and provided that the weight of the gold dollar should be fixed at no more than 60 percent of its existing weight.

It was at the president's initiative, not that of Congress, that the legislation establishing the ESF was shaped. Within a few days of his request, Congress complied, speeding the process whereby each House acted. The president revealed a motive for the creation of the new fund by proclamation the day after the enactment.

As is well known, the Roosevelt administration took office in March 1933 with the express intention to permit the dollar to depreciate in terms of foreign currencies as a means of achieving a rise in domestic prices. To further this aim, it initiated a gold purchase program to increase both the number of ounces and the price per ounce of the US gold stock. Had gold clauses been honored to protect lenders against currency depreciation, the gold purchase program could not have been implemented, since the lenders would have multiplied the nominal obligations of the federal government and private borrowers for interest and principal of debt by the ratio of the new price of gold to the old price. Accordingly, the abrogation of gold clauses by congressional resolution seemed to eliminate this problem. As we shall see at a later point, the lawsuits challenging the resolution roiled the foreign exchange value of the dollar until the Supreme Court ruled in its favor in February 1935. The gold purchase program thus went forward in September 1933, when the Treasury agreed to buy gold at an official gold price to be fixed daily, and in October, when the RFC was enlisted to buy newly mined domestic gold, and the Federal Reserve Banks to buy gold abroad at a purchase price that was raised almost daily.

The period of a variable price of gold came to an end on 31 January 1934, when the president, under the authority of the Gold Reserve Act passed the day before, specified a fixed buying and selling price of $35 an ounce for gold (formerly $20.67), thereby devaluing the gold dollar to 59.06 percent of its former weight. Since the Act authorized the president to fix the weight of the gold dollar at any level between 50 and 60 percent of its prior legal weight, the devaluation in January 1934 thus did not fully exhaust the president's authority to lower the gold weight of the dollar and increase the buying and selling price of an ounce of gold. The exercise of this residual authority to devalue was proposed in 1937 as a measure to combat the recession that began that year. The proposal was never adopted.

On 31 January, regulations were also issued governing transactions in gold, and authorizing purchase of certain types of gold at the rate of $35 per ounce less one quarter of 1 percent. The secretary of the Treasury, in addition, announced that he would sell gold for export to foreign central banks whenever our exchange rate with gold standard currencies reached the gold export point.

3.2.1   US Gold Accounts before the Gold Reserve Act Changes

Before the enactment of the Gold Reserve Act, the US monetary gold stock of $4.2 billion was held in the Treasury, at Federal Reserve banks, and in circulation. The Treasury's gold holdings were liabilities of its general fund for the gold redemption fund against Federal Reserve notes, for gold held against Federal Reserve Bank notes and National Bank notes, and liabilities of the Treasury's gold account. The monetary gold stock was valued at $20.67 an ounce. The Treasury and the Reconstruction Finance Corporation (RFC) also held gold purchased at more than $20.67 an ounce in three phases under the New Deal gold purchase program. The first phase lasted from 8 September to 24 October 1933, during which the Treasury bought newly mined gold at the Mints and Assay Offices for sale to licensed purchasers for nonmonetary purposes and for sale to foreign purchasers. The sale was at world prices. The second phase began on 25 October when the RFC purchased gold at home and abroad at $31.36 per fine ounce and at higher prices on subsequent days until 1 December when the price paid was $34.01. The gold was bought by the Guaranty Trust Company in Paris and London either from the Bank of France or the Bank of England or in the open market at prices set by the Federal Reserve Bank of New York (FRBNY), fiscal agent for the RFC. The RFC bought the gold from the Guaranty Trust with its own notes payable in gold. On 23 November 1933 Guaranty Trust was instructed to transfer the gold it had purchased from its Paris and London offices to the Bank of France and the Bank of England. The third phase ran from December until the end of January.

On 1 February 1934, the Treasury took over the RFC gold. That day the gold purchase program was transferred from the RFC to the Treasury, which was authorized to issue $250 million US bonds dated 16 January 1934 maturing 18 April 1934, to pay for purchases of gold coin. The reason the bond proceeds had to be used to purchase coin rather than gold bars was that the Treasury's legal authority to buy gold at more than $20.67 an ounce was limited to coins, as stipulated by the Civil War Act of 17 March 1862. This was accomplished by an arrangement with Guaranty Trust to exchange gold coin at the Assay Office in New York for gold bullion abroad at $20.67 an ounce and the repurchase of the gold coin at prices the Treasury fixed.

This was the situation before the Gold Reserve Act was passed. The Act made a momentous change in Treasury operations. The bookkeeping accounts that before 1934 showed how the Treasury kept track of the gold it held had to be replaced by a new set of accounts showing its liability for the gold transferred to it by the provisions of the Act.

On 30 January 1934 the Treasury took title to all the gold the Federal Reserve System owned in exchange for inconvertible gold certificates specifying that there was gold on deposit in the Treasury payable to the bearer. (Previously a $20 gold certificate stated that twenty dollars in gold coin payable to the bearer was on deposit in the Treasury.) The gold transferred from the Federal Reserve System was listed in the Treasury daily statement as gold certificate fund (Federal Reserve Board). The gold that the Treasury general fund held in custody for the redemption of Federal Reserve notes was transferred to the Treasury's gold account, and the liability was listed as redemption fund (Federal Reserve notes). A separate liability for the Gold reserve (US notes) was also listed, as was the liability for gold in the general fund.

The Treasury also was the recipient of gold coin, gold bullion, and gold certificates that individuals, partnerships, and corporations were required by executive order to deliver. They were paid in dollars at face value for the amounts they transferred.

3.2.2   Gold as of 31 January 1934

On 31 January, the reduction of the gold content of the dollar went into effect. The Treasury took over the gold from the RFC and revalued it at $35 an ounce along with the gold it itself had acquired under the gold purchase program, as well as the gold in the Treasurer's gold account. The final result increased the value of the gold from $4.2 billion to $7.0 billion, for a profit of $2.8 billion.

The contents of the act with respect to the ESF that the president desired Congress to pass, as described in the message by him delivered to Congress on 15 January, included the following paragraph (*Board* February 1934, 62–63):

That we may be further prepared to bring some greater degree of stability to foreign exchange rates in the interests of our people, there should be added to the present power of the Secretary of the Treasury to buy and sell gold at home and abroad, express power to deal in foreign exchange as such. As a part of this power, I suggest that, out of the profits from any devaluation, there should be set up a fund of $2,000,000,000 for such purchases and sales of gold, foreign exchange, and Government securities as the regulation of the currency, the maintenance of the credit of the Government and the general welfare of the United States may require.

In response to the president's message, a bill (H.R. 6976) was introduced in the House and passed the next day, referred to the Committee on Coinage, Weights, and Measures, which held public hearings, and reported the bill to the House with amendments on 18 January (Report no. 202). A minority report (Report no. 202, pt. 2) was presented on 19 January. House Resolution 6976 was passed 20 January, and sent to the Senate on 22 January. A similar bill was introduced in the Senate, referred to the Committee on Banking and Currency, which held hearings. The House bill was reported to the Senate (Report no. 201) with amendments, and the Senate passed the bill 27 January. The House agreed to the Senate amendments. The act (PL 87, 73d Cong.) was signed by the president 30 January 1934 (idem. 72–73).

The president's proclamation the next day fixed the weight of the gold dollar at 15 5/21 grains nine tenths fine (formerly 25.8 grains nine tenths fine), and justified the change as follows:

> Whereas, I find upon investigation, that the foreign commerce of the United States is adversely affected by reason of the depreciation in the value of the currencies of other governments in relation to the present standard value of gold . . . . and . . . Whereas, I find, from my investigation, that, in order to stabilize domestic prices and to protect the foreign commerce against the adverse effect of depreciated foreign currencies, it is necessary to fix the weight of the gold dollar at 15 5/21, grains nine tenths fine. (idem. 69)

There was only one major foreign currency in 1934 that did not have a fixed foreign exchange rate relative to the dollar—the British pound. Britain suspended the gold standard in September 1931, and decided to use foreign exchange policy to control sterling exchange. The Bank of England formed an exchange committee when it suspended, intervening in close association with the Treasury. It had a dollar exchange account with limited resources, and determined that a new government account with larger resources was desirable. Thus the Exchange Equalisation Account (EEA) came into existence on 24 June and officially began operations on 1 July 1932. The bank transferred its foreign exchange holdings to the account. The announced purpose of the EEA was to stabilize sterling exchange rates, not to determine their level. But in its operations it clearly sought to influence their level. A motive for establishing the ESF was US suspicion that the EEA was created to keep sterling from appreciating relative to the dollar. To make depreciation of the dollar that devaluation had achieved effective, the administration concluded required establishment of a fund comparable to the one the British had.

Roosevelt's comments in the proclamation on currency depreciation by other governments referred to the EEA. We note at a later point that the two funds differed in some crucial features, although they shared a common purpose.

3.2.3   ESF Legislation

Section 10 of the Gold Reserve Act, providing for the ESF, reads as follows:

> SEC. 10. (a) For the purpose of stabilizing the exchange value of the dollar, the Secretary of the Treasury, with the approval of the President, directly or through such agencies as he may designate, is authorized, for the account of the fund established in this section, to deal in gold and foreign exchange and such other instruments of credit and securities as he may deem necessary to carry out the purpose of this section. An annual audit of such fund shall be made and a report thereof submitted to the President.
>
> (b) To enable the Secretary of the Treasury to carry out the provisions of this section there is hereby appropriated, out of the receipts which are directed to be covered into the Treasury under section 7 hereof, the sum of $2,000,000,000, which sum when available shall be deposited with the Treasurer of the United States in a stabilization fund (hereinafter called the "fund") under the exclusive control of the Secretary of the Treasury, with the approval of the President, whose decisions shall be final and not subject to review by any other officer of the United States. The fund shall be available for expenditure, under the direction of the Secretary of the Treasury and in his discretion, for any purpose in connection with carrying out the provisions of this section, including the investment and reinvestment in direct obligations of the United States of any portions of the fund which the Secretary of the Treasury, with the approval of the President, may from time to time determine are not currently required for stabilizing the exchange value of the dollar. The proceeds of all sales and investments and all earnings and interest accruing under the operations of this section shall be paid into the fund and shall be available for the purposes of the fund.
>
> (c) All the powers conferred by this section shall expire two years after the date of enactment of this Act, unless the President shall sooner declare the existing emergency ended and the operation of the stabilization fund terminated; but the President may extend such period for not more than one additional year after such date by proclamation recognizing the continuance of such emergency. (idem. 65–66)

The sunset provision for the ESF was not part of the president's message requesting the legislation. It was an insertion in the reports by the House and Senate committees on their respective bills that appeared in the final version of the act. The sunset provision, however, did not take effect. In 1936 the president renewed the ESF for one year by proclamation. From 1937 on, Congress renewed the fund every two years until it was made permanent by the Bretton Woods Agreement Act of 1945.

3.2.4   Establishing the ESF

On 17 March 1934 $2 billion of the profit appropriated under the Gold Reserve Act for the establishment of the ESF was made available to the secretary of the Treasury by a check issued by the treasurer of the United States, and on 27 April the ESF was formally set up. The $2 billion was divided into three parts: an account of $100 million with the FRBNY, a disbursing account of $100 million, and an inactive deposit of $1.8 billion, both with the treasurer. The setup effectively provided secrecy for the ESF's transactions. Its dollar assets were divided between "Deposits of Government Officers, Postmasters, Clerks of Courts, etc. in the General Fund" and "Other Deposits" at the FRBNY—through which many other transactions were reported—and the gold, silver, or government securities that it might acquire would not appear in published statements until it made public its own balance sheet.

3.3   What the Fund's Design Was Intended to Accomplish

Based on the background information, we can now describe the salient features of the ESF. Foremost among these was that it was intentionally excluded from the congressional appropriation process once its initial capitalization was in place. It was to be self-financing, and was not required to seek congressional funding for its operations.[1] The virtue of the self-financing arrangement was that it contributed to the secrecy of ESF actions, since the fund did not have to justify its expenditures during annual appeals to Congress for appropriations.

The fund was conceived to operate in secrecy under the exclusive control of the president, "whose decisions shall be final and not subject to review by any other officer of the United States." The intention was to cloak foreign exchange market intervention.

The secrecy promoted two objectives. One was to conceal from the public and Congress the exchange rates at which foreign currencies were bought and sold, particularly if they involved losses. A second objective was to permit the Treasury, if it so desired, to conceal information about any other operations the ESF might undertake.

No change has occurred in the status of the secretary of the Treasury's decisions as final, with approval of the president, and not subject to review. In more recent years, Congress has required the president to give it information about ESF transactions, but the constitutionality of the ESF has not been challenged. The ESF in its original design as a creature of the executive branch, immune to legislative oversight, despite later modifications, breaches the separation of powers. It is hard to believe that a fund with similar powers would win legislative approval currently. As shown in section 3.2 above, the legislation in 1934 was initiated by the administration, Congress largely rubber-stamping what was put before it. Ordinary citizens have no standing to mount a challenge to the constitutionality of the ESF, and seventy-odd years after its creation, it is unlikely to happen.[2]

3.3.1   Comparing the ESF and EEA

The ESF and EEA shared a common purpose: to ward off appreciation of its national currency relative to the rival currency. The operations of both the American and British stabilization funds were intended to be conducted in secrecy.[3] The EEA was described as "an anonymous and secret body whose actions are not open to continuous scrutiny and criticism" (Hall 1935, 81). The House of Commons did not know and could not be told what the EEA was doing (Drummond 1981, 188). Of course, each fund would have liked to know what the other's intentions and actions were. However, the adversarial attitude of the funds, as we note below, did not last beyond the initial months after the ESF's establishment.

One respect in which the two funds differed was their financing. To operate the EEA, Parliament appropriated £175 million in Treasury bills, an amount that in later years was sizably increased (Sayers 1976, 427, 487–88). The ESF was programmed to be self-financing.

3.3.2   Problem for Empirical Research of ESF Secrecy

An empirical study is seriously limited when the agency under investigation chooses to maintain secrecy about its operations. This situation applies to the ESF with respect to intervention before 1962. For post-1962 developments, however, our study is much better situated, since the Federal Reserve System has given us the data on Treasury and Federal Reserve intervention activities, even if not the full documentary record.

Accordingly, the content of this chapter is essentially based on the information that the authorities have chosen to reveal. The published primary sources are the reports of the Treasury Department on the ESF, and of the Federal Reserve. The Treasury Department has more information than it has made available to the market and, with one exception, which we describe below, to scholars. Another source that includes some indirect references to ESF operations among a host of other topics is available in the microfilm of documents that Treasury Secretary Morgenthau deposited in the FDR Library in Hyde Park, New York. The microfilm, in 60 reels, covers the period 1934–45. The material in the FDR Library contains transcripts of every telephone conversation that the secretary held with Treasury representatives at US embassies abroad; every meeting with Treasury staff, representatives of other departments, or visiting foreign officials; and of particular interest, telephone conversations with George Harrison, governor, later president of the FRBNY, and with the manager of the foreign exchange desk at the bank, to whom the secretary conveyed instructions regarding purchases and sales. We refer to these documents as the Morgenthau Papers. They are not Morgenthau's diaries, the title the FDR Library assigns to the microfilm collection. The diaries are separate from the Morgenthau Papers.

The microfilm does not contain copies of the original documents with instructions related to specific intervention measures, so it does not explain why the archives of the Treasury Department in College Park, Maryland, that we examined, are woefully lacking in such documentary information on ESF foreign exchange intervention.

The main source we have drawn on, based on ESF documents from 1934 to 1939, is an unpublished 200-page study by W. A. Brown, Jr., written in 1942. Our efforts to learn how he was allowed to have access to Treasury files that are generally closed to nonofficial users long after the date of their creation have been fruitless. Brown listed what needed to be checked in his manuscript and left blank pages for charts. He did not resume work on the manuscript. Despite its unfinished form, it has added to our knowledge.

In the main, Brown simply reported without his own comment or interpretation the intervention actions taken by the Treasury and the ESF as recorded in the documents to which he had access. In a few other sources to which we refer, the authors may reflect on the relationships between the dollar and other currencies during 1934–39 but with no information on the factual record of intervention.

Brown was the author of the two-volume *The International Gold Standard Reinterpreted 1914–1934*, published in 1940 by the National Bureau of Economic Research, as well as of the chapter on exchange stabilization funds (chapter VI) in the 1944 League of Nations study, *International Currency Experience,* of which Ragnar Nurkse was the main author. We also make use of Brown's reflections on the ESF in his chapter in the League of Nations work.

3.4   Core Mission of the ESF

The statute authorized the ESF to deal in gold and foreign exchange. As Brown (League of Nations 1944, 160), however, observed, "Since an Exchange Fund is a large collection of assets in official hands, it may be used for many purposes not directly connected with exchange stabilization." He then noted examples of the type of operations in which the ESF engaged that were unrelated to its core mission. We discuss these examples in section 3.5. Here we deal with what we know about ESF foreign exchange market intervention.

The ESF could support the dollar exchange rate by exporting gold and acquiring foreign exchange for resale for dollars. It could support other currencies by buying foreign exchange and importing gold.

The period between the date of the Gold Reserve Act and 27 April, when the ESF began operations, and 5 September, when it first intervened in the foreign exchange market, afforded the Treasury the time to invent the details of the way the new agency would function. It also had to put into effect the framework of the new monetary system centralizing gold in the Treasury that the Gold Reserve Act set up. Accordingly, the Treasury issued regulations affecting gold market participants and foreign central banks and communicated its wishes to the FRBNY, which was its designated fiscal agent as well as that of the RFC, but had not yet been named the fiscal agent of the ESF. The main regulation the Treasury imposed was that in order to obtain gold from the Treasury, the only legal source, it would issue a license to qualifying applicants, mainly commercial banks whose customers needed gold. Even the FRBNY required a license.

The Morgenthau Papers contain no statement expressing the Treasury's views on the gold standard either before sterling began to float against the dollar and other currencies or after the dollar was devalued. We know, however, from the Treasury's announcement on 31 January 1934 that it would sell gold to foreign central banks whenever US exchange rates with gold standard currencies reached the gold export point and that the Treasury was familiar with a crucial feature of the gold standard—old style or new—the gold export and import points that defined the range within which exchange rates could fluctuate. It was the responsibility of a monetary authority in a gold standard regime to keep the level of exchange rates of their national currency within boundaries set between the fixed gold import and the fixed gold export points. In 1934 the only currencies with such fixed points were the French franc, the currencies of the gold bloc countries, and the US dollar. Sterling, by contrast, had no mint parity from which to calculate import and export points. As we shall see, transactions in both gold and foreign exchange kept a currency that was on the gold standard and one that floated within a given range. A floating currency's value oscillated between a high and a low value. The spread was not fixed as was the distance between the gold points, but the spreads were comparable. Operating within the gold points or between high and low values of a floating currency used the same techniques. At the gold export point and at the peak floating rate value, the monetary authority bought gold to counter appreciation. How did that work? In order to buy gold, say, from the United States, it had to buy dollars, thereby lowering the relative foreign exchange rate of the national currency. At the gold import point and at the low floating rate value, it sold gold, which it might have held as reserves, or borrowed, to strengthen its currency. In selling gold, say, to the US Treasury and receiving dollars in payment, a foreign monetary authority could buy its own currency, thereby strengthening it.

In addition to gold operations, another channel that was used to reduce fluctuations in the exchange value of a currency was the purchase and sale of that currency to bolster or to rein in its value.

The monetary authority was not the sole participant in gold minimizing exchange rate fluctuations. Commercial banks were active in seeking profitable arbitrage opportunities and also in transferring funds. Each involved buying gold in one country and shipping it across the Atlantic to be sold in another country. When it was cheaper to transfer funds from one country to another by shipping gold than by buying and selling foreign exchange, the gold transaction was obviously preferred.[4]

What was different in the way intervention was conducted before the dollar was devalued was that the FRBNY was the central institution, and market participants were unregulated. After devaluation, the Treasury was the central institution and it regulated market participants by limiting their operations to those it licensed.

The Treasury was very much aware of one difference between the post-1934 international monetary order and its predecessor. The earlier gold standard was a central bank responsibility. The Treasury sought to make finance ministers the responsible officials for stabilizing exchange rates. Central banks in the Treasury's view were privately owned institutions that did not operate in their countries' interests. It was not until 25 September 1936, when the Tripartite Agreement was announced, that the Treasury was able to impose its views on other countries. Central banks were to be demoted to fiscal agency status, executing instructions that finance ministers issued. Stabilization funds established by the terms of the new arrangement had the resources to intervene in the foreign exchange market.

In a broader context, the Treasury view of the difference between the earlier gold standard and the fractured one in which it would participate from April 1934 until the Tripartite was formed was too limited. The big difference was the change in the role of short-term capital flows. They were highly stabilizing earlier because the commitment to back national currencies with gold at a fixed rate of exchange gave investors confidence to move funds to whatever destination promised the best return. Short-term interest rates rose modestly to encourage capital inflows. Outflows were not disruptive. In the 1930s short-term capital movements often were generated by political uncertainty, fiscal improvidence, and revolving ineffective governments. Capital flight from the unstable country to the relatively more stable one weakened exchange rates in the former and strengthened exchange rates in the other, with harmful effects in both. When temporary improvements occurred in the political situation of the country that suffered capital flight, it might experience a return flow of that capital, again impacting the country that had provided a temporary abode. The Treasury was cognizant of these short-term capital flows when they occurred, but we know of no discussion by its staff of their relation to the way the gold standard operated.

We now turn to the details of Treasury intervention, first in support of the French franc, and then in a more adversarial role with respect to sterling. The Treasury was less concerned with the gold bloc currencies, but we also report measures affecting them. We cover the pre-Tripartite period and then the different arrangements that followed.

3.4.1   Dollar-Franc Rate Intervention before the Tripartite Agreement

Even before the ESF had engaged in its first intervention, the FRBNY had been authorized by a 23 March letter from the Treasury secretary to acquire gold bullion for sale directly or through intermediaries to foreign central banks that bought gold at a fixed price.[5] The sales were authorized when exchange rates were below the gold export point from New York. A letter of 15 August expanded the bank's authority to acquire gold from the Treasury at any time for sale by it to such central banks to replace exchange previously sold at a rate at or above the gold export point. The FRBNY was thus permitted to help foreign central banks in gold standard countries prevent their exchange rates from actually reaching the gold export point.

It is useful to preface this section on US intervention in the French franc exchange rate with facts about the French economy. In the second half of 1933 recovery was under way in the world economy, but France began to experience a deepening depression. Earlier, it had been insulated against the worldwide economic decline by its massive gold reserves. However, by 1933, the situation in France had changed. The government budget was in deficit, as it had been since 1931. To preserve the parity of the franc, it was believed necessary to lower prices and control the budget deficit.

Predating the grant of authority to the FRBNY to sell gold to gold standard countries in the last quarter of 1933, the Bank of France regarded with equanimity domestic and foreign gold withdrawals, given the size of the reserves—amounting to 55 billion francs ($216 million)—that it had accumulated since 1928. In January 1934, however, publicity about the Stavisky scandal—a municipal bond scandal in Bayonne—in which ministers of the radical government of Camille Chautemps were implicated, became a parliamentary crisis. At the end of January, Edouard Daladier replaced Chautemps as premier. After street riots and an attempt to attack the Chamber of Deputies, Daladier was forced to resign on 6 February. He was replaced by Gaston Doumergue as the head of a government of National Union. The aim of that government was to restore public order after the riots, not to balance the budget.

By the end of January 1934, the gold outflow amounted to 195 million francs (Mouré 1991, 146). Clement Moret, governor of the Bank of France, believed the US devaluation of the gold content of the dollar on 31 January accounted for the French gold loss. He waited until 6 February to raise the discount rate by 1/2 percent to 3 percent. He opposed tighter monetary policy because it would harm the Treasury in issuing bills and *bons* (national defense bonds).

The Treasury's situation worsened as the Stavisky scandal unfolded. It had to discount expected receipts of a medium-term bond issue in late January at the main Paris banks. To make payments, it had to rely on sales of Treasury bills only at higher interest rates than it was content to pay. The three largest Paris banks refused a request in early March to buy Treasury bills in the amount of 1,500 million francs because their deposits had been depleted by withdrawals, and the Bank of France would not rediscount Treasury bills. The bank, however, agreed to buy more Treasury bonds, if necessary. The Treasury, however, was fortunate to obtain a loan of 1,350 million francs from a Dutch bank, and in April its situation eased. By decrees that month, budget expenditures were reduced through cuts in civil service employment, salaries, and pensions. The finance minister attempted to reduce interest rates to stimulate recovery, and asked the Bank of France to reduce the discount rate. Moret was uncooperative and refused to do so until the rate on Treasury bills was further lowered.

At the end of May 1934, the Bank of France lowered the discount rate to its former value at 2 1/2 percent, where it remained for the next year. The bank was wary of open market purchases that other central banks engaged in. In the bank's view, they were inflationary and the cause of the world depression. A central bank's proper role was to be passive, leaving it to the credit market to approach the discount window if it needed liquidity. Traditionally, the Bank of France was opposed to a varying discount rate. It believed the discount rate should be stable.

The letter of 15 August 1934 from the Treasury to the FRBNY (referred to in the first paragraph of section 3.4.1) was sent on a day when the Paris telegraph transfer rate on New York was above the gold export point. On that day the FRBNY acquired 38.5 thousand ounces of gold ($1.28 million) from the Treasury. It sold $1 million to Guaranty Trust for shipment to the Bank of France to replace 15 million francs that the bank had sold at a rate above the gold export point (Brown 1942, 23–24).[6] The balance was sold to Bankers Trust Company for shipment to the National Bank of Belgium. Shipments of gold to the Bank of France continued on 25 August and on later dates up to 4 September and also to the Bank of the Netherlands.

Thus the Treasury was in a position to intervene during the weeks before arrangements for the ESF to take over intervention operations were completed. We have no information from a French source on the reason gold was wanted at the Bank of France in August and September. We know that the bank's gold reserves had increased from 76 billion francs in the spring of 1934 to 82 billion in September (Mouré 1991, 171). The minister of finance then urged Moret to lower the rate on discounts and advances to reduce gold imports and stimulate the economy. Moret answered that a lower interest rate would have little influence on gold imports, but would lower bank profits and invite speculation. The gold inflow, he held, testified to the strength of the franc. It also provided the occasion for the first ESF intervention.

The first intervention by the ESF on 5 September 1934 occurred the day after the FRBNY was appointed by a Treasury letter to deal in foreign exchange for the account of the ESF for present or future delivery. The letter noted that the kinds and rates of exchange to be dealt in within designated times and at designated places, and the maximum amounts to be bought or sold would be prescribed by the Treasury, which would provide the FRBNY the dollars and foreign exchange to implement authorized contracts. The agents employed by the FRBNY were to be paid a commission of 1/8 of one cent per French franc and one-half of 1 cent per Dutch guilder and Belgian franc on purchases and sales made through them. The commission was to be added to the customary charges made by brokers, both outlays to be paid by the Treasury. Chase National Bank, National City Bank, Guaranty Trust, and Bankers Trust were among the appointed agents.

The circumstance that impelled the large-scale intervention by the ESF on 5 September was the strength of the franc relative to the dollar and relative to sterling (from mid-August on). Gold from the London market moved to Paris, not to New York. The market believed that a further devaluation of the dollar or a substantial US inflation was likely, and that sterling depreciation would accompany the dollar's movement. Speculators sold dollars.

At this time the French government was legally obliged to reduce its outstanding French Treasury bills to limit this means of borrowing, and French banks were moving funds from London to add to their balances at the Bank of France. Because there was a demand for sterling to pay for US Treasury purchases of silver under the Silver Purchase Act, sterling was stronger in New York than in Paris. It was profitable to sell sterling for dollars, dollars for francs, and francs for sterling, further weakening the dollar relative to the franc. On several days the dollar-franc rate rose above the gold export point from New York to Paris, and gold exports to France from the United States followed. ESF intervention halted this movement.

On 5 September the ESF acquired 134.4 million spot francs by selling 140.0 million francs three months forward against spot. It sold 85.2 million of the spot francs plus 3.7 million francs three months forward. Guaranty Trust as the FRBNY agent executed these transactions, forcing the dollar-franc rate below the gold export point. Brown (1942, 47) is aware of problems with his description of the intervention. It seems to state that a forward sale of francs for dollars on 5 September financed the purchase that same day of spot francs. The ESF, however, could not have collected the dollars from the forward sale until three months later. In a footnote Brown writes, "If the order in which the individual transactions could be safely assumed to be the order in which the specific authorizations appear in the files, an account could be given of the details of this ('trapping' of the short interest) maneuver." The order of the transactions is thus not clear from the files that Brown examined.

It is possible that what might have occurred was a swap, whereby the ESF bought 134.4 million francs with dollars spot from the Bank of France, and entered an agreement to sell them forward again to the Bank of France at a known exchange rate. The ESF then used the francs to intervene with the market, selling 85.2 million spot and 1.2 million forward. The fund ended with a net uncovered forward position of $6 million equivalent francs. From 5 to 25 September it sold spot francs at a price above the dollar-franc parity but below the gold export point to Paris. The dollar strengthened in Paris during 22–28 September and the ESF was able to buy spot francs at a profitable rate to cover its forward position. Brown (1942, 50) credits the ESF with imposing a check on an outward movement of gold to Paris because of purely temporary causes, thus contributing to stability in the dollar-franc rate. Shipments of gold in both directions were avoided and as a by-product, the ESF had a profit of $335 thousand.

There is no mention in the Treasury's 1934 annual report of either the franc intervention conducted first under the Treasury's and then under the ESF's auspices. The information comes from Brown's unpublished manuscript based on documents in files he was able to consult, we believe, at the FRBNY.

The Doumergue government fell in November 1934, when the fiscal condition was much improved. Pierre-Etienne Flandin replaced that government, hoping that cheap money would bring economic recovery and bigger government receipts to balance the budget. In January 1935 the minister of finance dismissed Moret and appointed Jean Tannery as governor of the Bank of France. The minister's efforts to obtain greater accommodation at the bank under Tannery than under Moret were disappointed. The bank's regents, while agreeing to accept short-term government securities, so restricted the amounts and terms that the effect on credit conditions for the French treasury was negligible. Instead the bank resumed indirect advances to the state by discounting Treasury bills for commercial banks in its commercial portfolio.

Weakening of the franc in January 1935 was occasioned by uncertainty about the outcome of the case before the Supreme Court on the constitutionality of the Congressional resolution abrogating the gold clause in all public and private contracts. The dollar-franc rate fell from 6.59 cents to 6.47, which under normal conditions would have made gold imports highly profitable. The market was concerned, however, that an unfavorable decision resulting in a downward revision of the price of gold would impose losses while gold was in transit to Paris. Foreign currencies were dumped to buy dollars that would be expected to appreciate.

From 15 to 28 January the ESF intervened to support the franc. On 15 January the FRBNY was authorized to buy 28.25 million francs at New York market price, but not over 6.58 3/4 cents. The Bank of France was immediately to convert the francs to gold to be held under earmark for the FRBNY as an ESF fiscal agent. The next day the FRBNY instructed the Bank of France to buy $4 million worth of francs in Paris at 6.57 1/4 cents to be converted into gold and also held under earmark. On the same day, the

FRBNY made a second authorization for the purchase of $5 million worth of francs by the Bank of France at 6.59 cents or better. The ESF was in the market daily from 17 to 28 January in amounts from $5 million to $3 million per day as a seller of dollars for francs at any rate up to 6.59 cents. During that period the ESF spent $38.1 million for francs bought in New York and dollar sales to buy francs in Paris (Brown 1942, 65).

Between 24 January and 14 February the Treasury imported the gold acquired in the Paris market by the sale of dollars. By 4 February $4 million of this gold had reached the United States and had been sold by the ESF to the treasurer and credited to its special account at the FRBNY. The gold acquired by the initial purchase of francs in New York may have been transferred to the Bank of England (Brown 1942, 57). (We discuss ESF support of sterling in section 3.4.2 below.)

Despite the ESF's intervention, the franc rate, nevertheless, remained below the gold export point to New York until 11 February. On that day in a Treasury press release that also appeared in the 1935 Annual Report (Exhibit 40, 235), Secretary Morgenthau stated:

> 1. Since January 14th banks and dealers in foreign exchange and gold have practically stopped buying and selling gold, within gold import and export points—which means that the International Gold Standard as between foreign countries and the United States has ceased its automatic operation.
> 2. Thanks to the foresight of 73rd Congress, we have a Stabilization Fund.
> 3. When we saw that the external value of the dollar was rapidly going out of control, we put the Stabilization Fund to work on a moment's notice, with the result that for the past four weeks we have successfully managed the value of the dollar in terms of foreign currencies. The country can go about its business with *assurance* that we are prepared to manage the external value of the dollar as long as it may be necessary.

Seventy years after it was issued, the statement strikes a fatuous note. It revealed nothing of what the ESF and the Treasury were actually doing.

On 18 February the decision of the Supreme Court upholding the abrogation of the gold clause ended the scare that a reduction in the $35 dollar gold price was possible. Immediately following the decision, the ESF briefly continued supporting the franc, buying 15 1/2 million francs for $1 million in New York, Paris, and London, but shortly reversed itself in response to a stronger franc. It sold 3.5 million francs in New York at 6.64 cents. It had an open position in francs that had to be liquidated. On 6 March the Treasury authorized the FRBNY to transfer $11 million in gold held under earmark at the Bank of England for sale to the Bank of France. On 6 March the franc proceeds were sold by the ESF at 6.68 1/2 cents. The ESF then withdrew from the franc market until 18 May 1935, when pronounced weakness of the franc again developed.

In the meantime, in March 1935, a crisis developed for gold bloc countries, each of which had an overvalued currency. Belgium, a member of the gold bloc that had endured the greatest deflation, was the first driven to devalue. Of the group, Belgium was the most export-oriented, with trade focused on the sterling area, so it was the hardest hit by sterling depreciation in the first three months of 1935. Gold losses zoomed, a banking crisis occurred, and Belgium appealed to France for help on trade, which quotas France imposed in 1931 impeded, but without success. The Belgian government resigned on 18 March. A new government on 25 March devalued the Belgian franc five days later. Efforts to strengthen trade with gold-bloc countries were unacceptable to France, holding that commercial relations with non-gold-bloc countries were more important.

The French franc's weakness in May 1935 was produced by political agitation for its devaluation, unsolved budget difficulties, and loss of gold by the Bank of France. The French government that was formed in November 1934 led by Pierre-Etienne Flandin, as noted above, sought economic growth as a way to avoid devaluation. He was unable, however, to win emergency powers to deal with the budget deficit, and instead increased short-term government borrowing. Confidence in the franc fell, and a flight from the currency that ensued led to a heavy loss of gold reserves in May and June.

The US Treasury determined once more to use the ESF to support the French franc in the following manner. By telephone, it arranged for the FRBNY to buy up to $5 million in gold to be earmarked at the Bank of France in the name of the FRBNY, guaranteed for export under all circumstances. Unlike other examples of earmarking guarantees, which were provided not only by the central bank but also by the government, in this case the French government guarantee was not required. The Bank of France was authorized to sell dollars for francs at 6.58 or better up to $5 million. The sale of the dollars provided francs to the Bank of France, which was authorized to earmark the equivalent gold for the FRBNY.

The authorization was good for each day from 18 to 23 May. However, no transactions occurred under the authorizations, and the Bank of France continued to lose gold. So on 23 May it raised the discount rate from 2 1/2 percent to 3 percent. As a result, the franc-dollar rate did not fall below the gold export point of 6.58 cents. American official support of the market did not arise until the rate had fallen below the export point.

Whereas US intervention in support of the franc in January 1935 was unilateral, in May the ESF offered a cooperative arrangement with the Bank of France, which could exercise discretion subject to limits to the rate and total amount. On 24 May the FRBNY altered the form in which assistance was offered to the Bank of France, while renewing the bank's authority to sell $5 million for francs at 6.56 cents or better. Two conditions were set. One required the bank, if it sold dollars, to advance the franc equivalent value as of 25 May and convert the francs into gold to be earmarked in the FRBNY name on 25 May, guaranteed free for export to the FRB by the first available steamer. The FRBNY, on receipt of cable advice of the amount of dollar sale and conversion of francs into gold earmarked in its name, would give the Bank of France credit on its books for the value of such dollars on 25 May.

The FRB also offered to buy up to $5 million in gold earmarked at the bank to be shipped to the US Assay Office in New York by the first available direct steamer, settlement to be provided by the Treasury. On receipt of advice that the gold had been earmarked, the FRB would credit the bank with dollars to dispose of as it wished. The dollars this offer extended to the bank enabled it to purchase francs at a rate of its choice, and it immediately accepted the offer.

The ESF then bought $5 million in gold from the bank. The offer was renewed and the ESF bought another $5 million in gold. No improvement was registered in the exchange market. To halt gold losses, beginning 23 May, the Bank of France raised the discount rate in steps from 2 1/2 percent until 28 May, when it raised the discount rate to 6 percent.

The ESF again came to the rescue. The FRBNY on 27 May offered to buy $25 million in gold on 28 May on the same terms as earlier. The amount was bought in two tenders on 27 and 28 May. On 31 May the ESF bought $33.8 million in gold of the $150 million purchase from the Bank of France that the Treasury authorized.

In the last week of May the Flandin government asked for powers to raise taxes and cut public spending that it had previously shunned. Parliament denied the government the powers it sought. Flandin's government then fell and for three days the franc rose above the gold export point. The successor coalition government had no better success in obtaining deflationary powers and also fell. It was succeeded on 7 June by the Pierre Laval government, which obtained the emergency powers that eluded its predecessors. The Treasury then renewed its offer to have the ESF buy gold from the Bank of France for the balance of the $150 million.

By 17 June $68.8 million in gold the ESF had purchased had been imported and sold to the treasurer. The fund's assets at this date were predominantly in dollars.

Laval replaced Flandin's expansionary policies with deflationary measures, reducing all types of public spending. In addition, nominal debts were reduced by decree. The budget deficit, however, was not eliminated. Government debt then ballooned, and the Bank of France continued to lose gold. From 16 to 23 November 1935, the ESF offered to buy up to $25 million in gold from the Bank of France, but the offer was not accepted.

Laval was forced to resign in January 1936. The Popular Front government of left-wing parties led by Leon Blum then took office and adopted the Flandin dash for growth program while hoping to preserve convertibility. No salvation was possible for the Popular Front with the two irreconcilable policies.[7]

French governments since 1931 sought economic recovery, preservation of the franc's parity, and elimination of budget deficits. To achieve the latter, it was believed to be necessary to raise taxes and cut expenditures, but parliament declined to approve deflationary measures, and even when implemented by decree, they were contradicted by agricultural subsidies and price supports. Governments resorted to borrowing as revenues declined. Interest rates rose and confidence fell.

The renewal of the French financial crisis in June 1936 was marked by a drain of gold from the Bank of France to the United States. Gold losses persisted through September. Popular discontent with deflation mounted. France finally had to confront the prospect of devaluation, which it had firmly rejected in the years since the franc's parity was established in 1928. It had come to believe that it was not the franc that was out of line, but the dollar and sterling that were out of line with the franc. The reality could no longer be denied.

The reversal of course by the decision to devalue, however, was an embarrassment for French policymakers. To explain the new tactic to the French public, it was convenient for them to portray acquiescence to the devaluation by the Americans and the British as international stabilization (Mouré 1991, 257).

Foreign observers of the deterioration of the French economy in 1936 were positive that devaluation was the proper measure to alleviate the problem. Their assessment that devaluation was the correct policy to deal with French deflation agreed with their approval both of the British departure from the gold standard in 1931 and the US decision in 1933 to raise the price of gold in order to reflate. What was different in the case of France was that the French public believed their politicians' sworn determination never to devalue. Hence political difficulties delayed and obfuscated the devaluation imperative.

The chronic French financial problem was temporarily solved by the Tripartite Agreement adopted on 25 September by the United States, Britain, and France to allow the French to devalue the franc with no retaliation by the others. On 26 September the government agreed to back suspension of the gold standard by the Bank of France.

We discuss the changes in international exchange rate policy as a result of the Tripartite Agreement in section 3.4.4. Here we simply note that the Americans and British believed that the alternatives for them, had they not proceeded as they did, were far worse. France might have adopted exchange controls or allowed the franc to depreciate or to devalue it unilaterally, so they chose the path of cooperation. Given that the franc was misaligned, it is not obvious to us that the Americans and British would have been worse off had the French devalued the franc unilaterally, and there had been no Tripartite Agreement.

3.4.2   Dollar-Sterling Rate Intervention before the Tripartite Agreement

The initial aim of the ESF was to defend the dollar against competitive exchange depreciation, in particular movements in sterling that the United States regarded with suspicion. The United States was willing to buy and sell gold at a fixed price but only for currencies convertible into gold at a fixed price. Since sterling was not convertible into gold at a fixed price, the ESF in principle would not sell gold in London for which it would be paid in inconvertible sterling. It did not sell gold to the EEA from April 1934, when the ESF was established, until October 1936, when agreement was reached among the Tripartite principals for reciprocity with respect to sales of gold to each other (League of Nations 1944, 158). For that period the EEA in turn did not deal in dollar exchange. The Treasury, however, had no objection to buying gold either from the Bank of England or the London gold market.

Brown (League of Nations 1944, 147) refers to this "non-intercourse between the British Fund and the American Treasury." Exceptions to the nonintercourse rule, as we shall see, were American initiatives. The British for their part did not seek rapprochement with the Americans. No regular channel of communication with respect to foreign exchange moves during this interval existed between the United States and Britain. The documents from the Bank of England archives, dealing with US intervention in the British gold market in 1935, however, demonstrate that informal contacts between the FRBNY and the bank were commonplace.[8] The documents also intimate that Secretary Morgenthau sought to establish a link with the representative of the British Treasury in Washington, DC.[9]

The Treasury was wary of a high price for gold fixed unilaterally by the EEA and a consequent depreciation of sterling in terms of dollars. Yet the price of gold in London was basically determined by the dollar-sterling rate and the fixed buying price for gold with which the Treasury operated. The influence on the London price of gold was transmitted indirectly through the stable franc-dollar rate that gold standard arrangements were responsible for (League of Nations 1944, 147).

The EEA for its part could not manage the sterling rate with operations in New York, but it could achieve its ends through operations in francs. To prevent an appreciation of sterling, it would buy francs that it sold immediately for gold from the Bank of France. In the opposite case, if the EEA wanted to stem excessive sterling depreciation, it could sell gold to the Bank of France for francs to support sterling. Since the dollar-franc rate was kept within narrow margins by gold standard arrangements, arbitrage between London, Paris, and New York tended to make the sterling-dollar rate a reflection of the sterling-franc rate (Clarke 1977, 6). Had France, like the United States, chosen to deal only with countries on the gold standard, the EEA could not have stabilized sterling by operating on the exchange market; it would have had to operate on the gold market.

Apart from the Treasury's refusal to sell gold to the Bank of England, it was under no obligation to intervene in the exchange market to narrow the range of the fluctuations in the dollar-sterling exchange rate, but it did have an obligation to support the parity of the dollar-franc exchange rate. Whenever the franc exchange rate rose to the gold export point, the Treasury would release gold to France or any other gold standard country under the same circumstances. Whenever the franc exchange rate fell to the gold import point, the Bank of France would release gold to the United States. The upper and lower gold points differed by 1 percent.

In practice, however, both the market and the US Treasury treated sterling just as it treated the franc. The franc exchange rate fluctuated within the spread between the fixed gold export point and the fixed gold import point. The dollar-sterling exchange rate fluctuated between a shifting high market value and a shifting low market value of the dollar-sterling exchange rate. Whenever sterling rose to a peak value, the market and the Treasury sold sterling. Gold would also move to London. Whenever sterling fell to its low values, the Treasury bought sterling and gold in London. It was in the interest of the United States to keep sterling within its market boundaries.

Britain's economic situation at the time the ESF began to intervene in sterling can be briefly described. By abandoning the gold standard in September 1931, it gained the flexibility to lower interest rates (after a delay) in June 1932, expand high-powered money and yet augment its reserves, with the result that its exports grew, unemployment declined, and national income rose in each year from 1933 to the outbreak of the war.[10]

On 15 January 1935, when the market was roiled by worry that the Supreme Court might rule that the abrogation of the gold clause was unconstitutional and both the franc and sterling were weak, the ESF bought francs in Paris, and also bought 14,300 ounces of gold in London at $34.60 per ounce, and an additional 30,100 ounces at $35.65 the next day. For the next 10 days the sterling rate moved between $4.875 and $4.882, but on 24 January, the ESF resumed buying gold in London. On 26 January, when the sterling rate fell to $4.86, it bought sterling in New York at $4.8510 and sold $5 million for sterling in London on 28 January, despite the fact that sterling was not convertible. The sterling purchases were accompanied by further gold purchases in London: $1.54 million during 15–21 January, $9.95 million the following week, and $16.83 million during 28 January–4 February.[11]

Presumably, the motive for supporting sterling was to prevent a fall in US trade receipts that might result from cheaper sterling prices for goods than dollar prices.

During the three weeks that the ESF actively entered the exchange market, it had spent $21 million for gold in London, sold $36 million for francs and gold in Paris, and bought $14 million in sterling. The ESF paid for these outlays by drawing on both its checking account with the treasurer and the secretary's account with the FRBNY. It replenished the account with the treasurer by selling Treasury notes from its assets, and the account at the FRBNY by selling gold it acquired in Paris from the sale of dollars and that it subsequently imported. These inflows to the two accounts were supplemented by imports of gold from London that roughly matched its purchases in January and February. The gold was sold to the treasurer to build up the ESF's dollar balances.

During the period of intervention from 16 January to 18 February, the ESF's outlay in support of sterling totaled $85.8 million (Brown 1942, 65). After the Supreme Court decision on 18 February upholding the abrogation of the gold clause, sterling strengthened, and the fund sold $2.81 million in sterling in New York at $4.8842. An open position in sterling remained to be liquidated, but intervention was at an end.

The ESF disposed of some sterling between 4 and 25 March for the purchase of silver under the Silver Purchase Program (see section 3.5) for which the Treasury reimbursed it in dollars. Beginning 4 April, it sold sterling in New York directly for dollars, continuing to do so daily from 8 to 17 April. It then withdrew from the market.

The ESF reentered the market as a seller of sterling when sterling rose to $4.88 1/2 on 10 May. The position of sterling reflected the movement of funds from Paris to London as the franc's exchange rate deteriorated. (This was the period when French governments had only brief tenures as their efforts to control budget deficits failed.) The ESF sold sterling daily in large amounts from 10 to 20 May at rates that rose steadily to $4.91 5/8. The ESF also took advantage of the strength of sterling from 27 to 31 May to sell 225,600 ounces of gold it held at the Bank of England at $34.98, transferring the proceeds first to Guaranty Trust Company, and then to the secretary's account at the FRBNY. The price at which the gold was sold was lower than the price at which the ESF would sell gold to gold standard central banks—$35 plus 1/4 per ounce—but even below the official gold value of the dollar (Brown 1942, 73).

The advantage of selling sterling when its proceeds in dollars were high is obvious, as is also the advantage of selling gold for sterling at a high price. It does not, however, explain sales of gold for dollars at less than the official price. We do not know the reason the ESF did so. The gold that was sold was held at the Bank of England and probably was acquired by London gold market brokers. Were supply conditions in that market such that ESF sales were possible only at the reported low price? In May 1935 gold was deserting Paris for London, as noted above, likely destined for the Bank of England. If the conjecture about the London gold market is not valid, the ESF transaction remains an enigma. In any event, the ESF must have desired the dollar proceeds that the gold sales provided for its FRBNY account.

On the instruction of the US Treasury, President George Harrison of the

FRBNY on 15 November telephoned Montagu Norman to discuss "the possibility of the Federal Reserve Bank bidding for gold in the London market at a price slightly above that offered by commercial banks, such gold to be earmarked at the Bank of England for account of the Federal Reserve Bank and the attendant expenses of shipment of gold to New York to be thus avoided. Such gold would subsequently be sold to the Bank of England or some other central bank, or repatriated to New York as circumstances might dictate. He said that the price at which the commercial banks can buy gold is $34.76 per ounce and he would propose that the Federal Reserve Bank should offer such price between that figure and $34.77 as might be necessary to secure the gold" (Bank of England archive, note of a telephone conversation). Norman told Harrison that the bank would gladly act for the FRBNY in the matter.

To anticipate details of the plan that Harrison outlined, the Treasury's objective in buying gold in London that the FRBNY, as its agent was furthering, was not to accumulate gold there, but to offer arbitrageurs in that market (who would sell the gold) a price per ounce that would match or exceed the amount they could collect by selling the gold to the US Assay Office in New York, so there would be nothing to gain from shipping gold to New York. The gold would remain in London. The Treasury's objective was to deter gold shipments to New York. The stated reason was to reduce unnecessary gold movements in and out of the United States. In 1935 the motive would not have been to moderate growth of the monetary base produced by massive gold inflows to the United States in response to the rise in the price to $35 an ounce. At that time, growth of the monetary base was still desired to raise the price level. It was not until December 1936 that the Treasury first began sterilizing gold inflows.

The problem the FRBNY encountered was that the Bank of England did not agree with the price per ounce of gold that the former believed would elicit sales. How did that happen?

H. A. Siepmann (adviser to the Bank of England and member of the committee of Treasury), in a comment on Harrison's proposal, on 15 November wrote to E. M. Harvey, the deputy governor, that theoretically a shipper of gold to New York would collect $34.7722 per ounce. If the bank bid $34.77 per ounce for gold in London for the account of the FRBNY, normally an arbitrageur would accept this price instead of shipping gold to New York. However, at the moment there was a freight war in the North Atlantic and a small "premium" on forward dollars that would affect the amount a shipper would collect in New York. To retain gold in London, it would be advisable to bid up to $34.77 1/2 per ounce. This arrangement would allow the FRB to sell the bank gold at a reasonable price when it needed sterling to pay for silver. It was likely that Rothschilds (the brokers who managed the London gold market) would not cover the whole gold market (some gold arrived in

London that was not disposed of in the gold market), so the bank would need to undertake special arrangements (Archives of the Bank of England).

The price at which Harrison suggested that the Bank of England buy gold for the US Treasury—$34.77 per ounce of gold—was based on a calculation of the London-New York shipping parity.

The London-New York shipping parity was the price for gold (which varied daily) bought with sterling in the London market at which it would be profitable, at the ruling sterling-dollar exchange rate, to ship gold to New York, when sold for the statutory $35 per ounce, less the expense incurred in London for brokerage, packing, insurance, freight, and interest, and the expense in New York for handling charge, assaying, and the US commission of 1/4 percent (Waight 1939, 88–90).[12]

The shipping parity could be reached if the sterling- dollar rate was unchanged, provided there was a fall in the London price of gold, or the dollar appreciated in terms of sterling while the London price of gold was unchanged, or by a combination of a fall in the London price of gold and decline in the sterling-dollar exchange rate.

The EEA regulated the sterling price of gold. It was able to determine by how much the sterling price of gold exceeded the London-New York shipping parity (the "premium") or by how much it fell short of the parity (the "discount"). (A premium raised the dollar expense incurred in shipping gold; a discount lowered the dollar expense.) The EEA monopoly over supply and demand in the gold market enabled it to decide whether it was profitable for arbitrageurs to buy and ship gold to New York, and whether the sterling-dollar exchange rate rose or fell, the main reason for the EEA's establishment (Waight 1939, 25). It was possible for the FRBNY and the Bank of England to arrive at different figures for the shipping parity and the sterling equivalent price of an ounce of gold.

Commercial banks normally took advantage of arbitrage opportunities by shipping gold to New York. The "discount" on the sterling price that made shipments of gold to New York profitable could not be sizable. If it were, demand for gold for shipment would increase, and the EEA would have had the option to cut off sales of gold and eliminate the "discount." However, gold arbitrage for the exporting country increased the demand for sterling, and for the importing country, it increased the supply of dollars on offer. The EEA might have desired the consequent improvement in the sterling-dollar exchange rate.

Following Harrison's 15 November 1935 telephone conversation with Montagu Norman, internal memoranda by Bank of England officials commented on the substance of Harrison's proposal (Bank of England archives). In appendix 1, we summarize some of the documents that discuss the proposal and subsequently its implementation. British Treasury officials also reviewed Bank of England memoranda.

A confirmation of the motive for the Harrison proposal is provided by a telegram (no. 379) to the Bank of England from Sir Ronald Lindsay (British Ambassador to the United States) on 17 November, reporting a conversation of Secretary Morgenthau with T. Bewley, British Treasury representative in Washington. Morgenthau referred to Harrison's proposal as a plan "which would do something towards reducing pressure on gold flow to" the United States.

Cable (no. 283/35) from Harrison to Deputy Governor E. M. Harvey on 19 November, changed the proposal from a possibility to an actuality. It requested the bank to buy on or before 23 November for the FRBNY as fiscal agent of the United States up to 700,000 fine troy ounces refined gold bars at not more than $34.77 per fine troy ounce exclusive of brokerage, and to earmark the purchase in the bank's vaults in the FRB name. The US Treasury would deposit to the bank's account at the FRB the dollar equivalent of the cost of the gold as of the date purchased and earmarked in accordance with the cable.[13]

In a note of a telephone conversation between the deputy governor and Harrison, 19 November (before the cable was sent), Harrison suggested that the bank should sell sufficient dollars to provide the sterling necessary for any gold purchased. The deputy governor stated the theoretical result to a shipment of gold, according to the bank's exchange department (as explained by Siepmann in his communication to the deputy governor), and the department thought it would be necessary for the bank to be given discretion to pay somewhat more than $34.77. Harrison put the dollar amount that would be attractive to the arbitrageur at about $34.76, but said his figure would be checked.

Despite Bank of England's doubts that the American price was high enough to obtain gold from sellers in London, sales at that price were made. Between 27 November and 6 December some 37,000 ounces of gold was purchased under the standing offer and held by the fund under earmark at the Bank of England until sold in London on 26 January 1936. The fund then reentered the sterling market.

At the beginning of January 1936 the ESF had sold a small remaining sterling balance at $4.93. By the end of that month, the sterling rate approached $5.00, when it began to sell sterling one month forward to check the appreciation. Between 24 January and 27 February the ESF sold forward in New York $14.4 million in sterling, most of the sales at just over $5 and the bulk for end-of-February delivery. To cover this position the Fund purchased spot beginning on 14 February both in New York and London from $4.97 3/4 to $4.99 3/4. At the end of February it sold additional sterling forward for end-of-March delivery, so that its net forward position on 2 March was $8.2 million. The March position closed at gradually declining rates to $4.99. A still smaller forward position taken at the end of April was carried forward to the end of May at $4.93 1/2 and the whole of the May position was closed out by the purchase of sterling for delivery 29 May at rates from $4.95 to $4.97. On 8 May the ESF retired from the sterling market until 26 September, the day following the announcement of the Tripartite Agreement.

Retirement from the sterling market did not preclude operations in the gold market. On 29 March 1936 the Treasury renewed its standing offer to buy up to 700,000 ounces of gold in London at $34.77 per ounce at the New York shipping parity. According to Siepmann, writing to Sproul on 2 May 1936, there were three sales (apparently on 28 and 30 April and 2 May). Siepmann does not mention the number of ounces that were acquired. The Treasury offer to buy was repeated until 16 May when the amount was reduced to 500,000 ounces, and again repeated until 8 August when the amount was further reduced to 350,000 ounces. The offer was maintained at that amount until 26 September. For the first time since 19 December 1935 the offer became effective from 28 April to 22 October 1936 at $34.77 per ounce. (There is no reference in the documents to the amounts bought between 6 and 19 December 1935, nor between 2 May and 22 October 1936.) The total amount the ESF paid for the gold it bought in 1936 was $13.8 million, all of which was held under earmark at the Bank of England.

Did the US Treasury regard the outcome of the standing offer as effective in deflecting gold shipments to New York? We have seen no evidence that would answer the question. Sproul apparently was skeptical. He wrote to Siepmann, "This little business of ours is not of itself of great importance" (handwritten, 20 April 1936, archives, Bank of England).

The Bank of England continued to buy gold for the Treasury under the Tripartite Agreement whenever the price was operative until the war, but no longer was the justification to bar shipments across the Atlantic. The gold purchases were shipped to New York and sold by the ESF to the Treasury. Gold flows were not, however, limited to movements westward. Gold was also sold by the Treasury to European nations.

In June 1936, when the Popular Front took office in France, not only was French adherence to a fixed gold standard dollar-franc rate threatened, the US regulatory policy to sell gold at $35 plus 1/4 to central banks of countries on the gold standard also appeared to be shaken. On 8 June the secretary of the Treasury obtained authority from the president to sell gold through the ESF to all or any foreign governments or central banks as he might deem advantageous to the public interest. The authority concerning the sale of gold did not refer to the Bank of England in particular but Brown (1942, 112) reports that an ESF principal conveyed the information to him orally that the change in gold policy that the president authorized was intended for the sake of gold sales to England.

Why did the Treasury want to change its original regulation on enactment of the 1934 Gold Reserve Act that it would sell gold only to gold standard countries? That excluded England. The Treasury obtained FDR's permission to change the regulation in order to authorize it to sell gold to any country or central bank. By 1936 the United States and Secretary Morgenthau in particular had a political motive to support democracies in view of mounting concern about the German military threat. The explanation for the change in the regulation is that it enabled the Treasury to sell gold to any democracy whether or not it adhered to the gold standard.

The following arrangements were made in view of a prospective sale of gold to the Bank of England. The FRBNY was authorized on 8 June by the secretary to acquire up to $51 million of gold from that which the New York Assay Office acquired from abroad between 8 and 16 June. Payment was to be made at the usual price of $35 per ounce less 1/4 less mint charges, the FRB to pay to the consignee $34.9125 per ounce, and the Assay Office to be credited as a miscellaneous receipt of the Treasury .0875 per ounce. The Assay Office was to hold the gold imported in a special account subject to the order of the FRBNY, the gold to be in bars equivalent to the gold imported. The Assay Office was instructed to waive its bar charges, so the mint charges would cover only minting and refining costs.

The advantage of ESF taking gold coming from abroad upon arrival was that it prevented the gold from appearing among Treasury assets as an addition to the monetary gold stock. Accordingly, when the ESF disposed of the gold to the Bank of England the transaction would not reduce the gold stock and the operations of the ESF would not be revealed to the public.

Under this arrangement the ESF acquired $48.6 million in gold by 22 June. The amount grew to $50.3 million by 13 July. On that day the total amount held by the ESF was $59.1 million. Under a further authorization on 15 September for the ESF to acquire an additional $51 million in gold from gold received from abroad at the Assay Office, from 15 September to 12 October 1936, when the Tripartite Agreement became operative, $29.6 million had been obtained. On that day the total gold held by the ESF was $93.7 million.

The transfer of this gold to the Bank of England, however, did not take place. The gold that the ESF had been accumulating since June 1936 was part of a plan to forge an Anglo-American understanding. The plan was finally developed in the course of the negotiations in September that assured France that Britain and the United States would not retaliate to a French devaluation. The original US policy of 1934 that excluded the Bank of England from buying gold in the United States because England was not on the gold standard was superseded by the provisions of the Tripartite Agreement, which we discuss in section 3.4.4.

Brown's account of ESF intervention at various dates to weaken or strengthen sterling would obviously have greater value if we had access to a parallel account from the British perspective of the American operations. To a limited extent, our access to Bank of England archives dealing with British reaction to the Treasury standing offer to the Bank of England to buy gold for it serves this purpose. We do not have EEA data as the counterparty to

ESF data. Howson's (1980) study of the operations of the EEA, 1932–39, unfortunately contains no information on particular transactions the agency conducted and no references to EEA reactions to ESF actions that affected the sterling rate. We are well aware that our report on intervention by the ESF vis-à-vis the pound is consequently one-sided.

3.4.3   ESF Exchange Rate Policy with Respect to Minor Currencies

Even after the ESF came into existence, the FRBNY continued its familiar practice of earmarking gold abroad against an advance of dollars in New York or by the purchase of gold abroad against immediate payment in dollars. Thus in November 1934 it had an arrangement, made on the initiative of the National Bank of Belgium, to advance dollars to it against gold earmarked in its name in Brussels, guaranteed free for export under all circumstances and to be shipped by the first available steamer to New York. On arrival in New York the gold was sold to the US treasurer at the price of $35 per ounce less 1/4. The term of the dollar advance was reckoned from the moment of earmarking up to the delivery of the gold. Interest was charged at the FRBNY discount rate. The limit of the advance was set at $25 million. The arrangement was not activated even when Belgium devalued the Belgian franc by 28 percent on 31 March 1935.

On 10 April, the Netherlands Bank inquired of the FRBNY whether it would be willing to advance dollars against gold earmarked in Amsterdam for the account of the FRB. The latter discussed the request with the secretary of the Treasury. The Netherlands Bank was advised that, when it wanted dollars, the Treasury would buy up to $10 million in gold for immediate payment in dollars. The gold was to be earmarked in the vaults of the Netherlands Bank in the name of the FRBNY and shipped to the US Assay Office in New York on the first available steamer at the former's expense and risk. The gold was to be guaranteed by the Dutch government to be free for export under any circumstances and to be settled for on the basis of the Assay Office's findings at $35 per ounce less 1/4.

The Netherlands Bank consented to the proposed arrangement, interpreting the first available steamer to mean the first available Dutch steamer in regular service with the United States. It then obtained the guarantee of the Dutch minister of finance. On 17 April it notified the United States of its formal acceptance of the arrangement, indicating that it would avail itself of the facility only in the case of erratic exchange movements above the gold export point.

Brown (1942, 76) comments that, whereas the FRBNY-National Bank of Belgium understanding was an informal type of intercentral bank cooperation, by requiring a guarantee from the Dutch government that the gold would be free for export under all circumstances, Morgenthau changed the character of the arrangement to an agreement between governments.

Both the earlier intercentral bank cooperation set up and the later arrangement involving governments seemed to be similar in not specifying a date of termination. It turned out, however, that the Netherlands Bank was not the recipient of a standing facility available at any time up to the amount specified. On 4 September 1935 the FRBNY proposed that the 10–11 April arrangement with the Bank of Netherlands should terminate at the end of December. On 2 December the Netherlands Bank asked for an extension of one year. The request was refused on 7 January 1936. On instructions from the Treasury, the FRBNY advised the Netherlands Bank to cable when it needed dollars, and that the request would be given prompt attention. The latter responded that it would wish to sell dollars in case erratic movements of the dollar rate should occur, which could happen suddenly. Intervention would be delayed and ineffective if it first had to make an arrangement with the FRBNY. The Netherlands Bank therefore asked to obtain the facility for half a year or even three months on the understanding that a renewal would be granted. The answer to this appeal that the FRBNY gave on the Treasury's instruction was that there was no obvious need at this time for the arrangement, as there had been in April of the past year. Then it appeared that the free movement of gold at the gold export point might be interrupted by the hesitancy of commercial banks to assume the risk involved. Steamer facilities or insurance coverage at times and in amounts necessary to take care of a large shipment were then in doubt. Since then any necessary gold shipments had been made in the normal manner. Unless conditions arose that prevent commercial banks from conducting these transactions in the normal way, the Treasury did not consider it expedient to grant the Netherlands Bank its request.

The arrangement with the Netherlands Bank was not renewed until the end of May 1936 when the guilder was weak following the Popular Front victory in the French elections of 26 April and 3 May 1936. Early in May, Dutch funds began to move to London and New York. The Treasury this time did not wait for the Dutch to ask for the facility for support of the guilder. On 26 May it instructed the FRBNY to cable the Netherlands Bank that to aid in the prevention of erratic exchange fluctuations, the secretary of the Treasury was willing for the Netherlands Bank to draw on the FRBNY on or before 2 June up to $10 million against an equivalent amount of gold earmarked in Amsterdam at $34.77 per ounce, the gold to be guaranteed free for export under any circumstances. The Treasury offered to make the dollars immediately available on receipt of a cable from the Netherlands Bank signifying its agreement. The FRBNY was informed that the ESF would carry out this transaction.

The Netherlands Bank accepted the terms of the Treasury offer but on 26 May, when the guilder dropped below the gold export point from Amsterdam to New York, it cabled that it would not need the facility immediately and asked for an extension beyond 2 June. The extension was granted until 6 June and extended weekly until 11 July. The Netherlands Bank then informed the FRBNY that, if a longer extension was not possible, it would give up the arrangement on the understanding that it might ask for a renewal at any time. The Treasury agreed and the arrangement then lapsed until 26 September, the day Holland suspended the gold standard. Three weekly renewals from 28 September to 17 October were then negotiated. The arrangement that the Netherlands Bank never actually used became obsolete on 24 November when the Dutch adhered to the Tripartite Agreement.

3.4.4   Tripartite Agreement

This section is in two parts. The first one describes the formation of the Tripartite system of foreign exchange market intervention. The second part tracks exchange rates between the dollar and the currency of each of the other members of the system from September–October 1936 until the outbreak of the war in August 1939.

Ground Rules of the Agreement

After protracted negotiations over a period of months conducted by Secretary Morgenthau (through intermediaries in Washington and Paris) with British Chancellor of the Exchequer Neville Chamberlain and French Minister of Finance Vincent Auriol, to draft a common declaration, the British, French, and Americans finally agreed on a text that each country issued on 25 September 1936, pledging to cooperate in stabilizing international economic relations.[14] The agreement was between governments, not central banks, although central banks were clearly crucial in fixing the technical arrangements.

These government statements of intent became effective in October and November with a series of bilateral agreements. A new international gold settlements system was thereupon established including sterling, the French franc, the dollar, the belga, the Swiss franc, and the guilder. No change, however, had been made in the official gold policy of the Treasury of 31 January 1934, according to which the Treasury would sell gold for export only to central banks of countries on the gold standard when their exchange rates reached the gold export point of their currencies. This was so, even though the secretary of the Treasury had obtained the president's approval on 8 June 1936 for the sale of gold by the ESF to all central banks. The official gold policy would not allow the Treasury to sell gold to the French, Swiss, and Dutch after their devaluations, or to the British and the Dutch, since neither country was on the gold standard, and the French and Swiss had no fixed gold parities from which to calculate the gold export points. The EEA could not buy foreign exchange that was inconvertible into gold at a fixed price, so for the time being it could not operate in either the continental or American foreign exchange markets.

To deal with this problem the secretary of the Treasury sent a letter to the president on 27 September requesting authority to purchase gold through the ESF by the use of dollars, foreign exchange or other obligations, currency or securities, from all or any foreign governments, foreign central banks, or the Bank for International Settlements. The president approved the request the same day.[15]

Accordingly, the secretary of the Treasury on 27 September announced that, in addition to certain countries designated in the 31 January 1934 statement from whom the Treasury would buy gold and to whom it would sell gold for export, it would thereafter, on twenty-four hours notice, "also sell gold for immediate export to, or earmark for the account of, the exchange equalization or stabilization funds of those countries whose funds likewise are offering to sell gold to the United States, provided such offerings of gold are at such rates and upon such terms and conditions as the Secretary may deem most advantageous to the public interest" (Board of Governors 1922, 852). On 13 October a press release informed the world that the Treasury under new regulations would exchange gold for dollars and dollars for gold at a fixed rate with any country that gave reciprocal facilities to the United States. It also noted that the British government would provide facilities in London to the United States for the exchange of sterling for gold and gold for sterling, as would the Bank of France in Paris for the exchange of francs for gold and gold for francs. A later statement (23 November) also included "treasuries or any fiscal agencies" of foreign countries guaranteeing reciprocal transactions in gold (idem. [12]: 940).

On 1 October French legislation authorized devaluation of the franc between 25.19 and 34.35 percent of the old gold parity. The Bank of France was authorized to revalue its gold stock at the upper end of these limits. The law also authorized the creation of an exchange stabilization fund, to which 10 billion of the 17 billion franc devaluation profit was assigned.

Following the French announcement, the British and Americans stated their support for the French decision. The Swiss franc was also devalued. The Netherlands Bank did not devalue the guilder but allowed it to depreciate 20 percent in dollars and maintained it at that level.[16] Greece, Latvia, Turkey, Italy, and Czechoslovakia also made currency changes. The Belgians, who, as noted above, had devalued the Belgian franc by 28 percent on 31 March 1935 and renamed it the belga, returned to the gold standard at the lower parity in March 1936. After the 13 October announcement, they declared their willingness to take part in consultations with other governments and institutions of the Tripartite system. On 21 November the Swiss and Dutch governments accepted the principles of the Tripartite Agreement.

In addition, the powers of the FRBNY under the monetary policy of 31 January 1934 were modified to conform to the arrangements under the Tripartite Agreement. As fiscal agent of the ESF, the FRBNY negotiated the details of the operation of the Tripartite Agreement with the Bank of England and the Bank of France, as follows. Each central bank would convert into gold the balances in its own currency accumulated each day by the other central bank as a result of its foreign exchange dealings, and release from earmark the gold that would match the obligations incurred by the foreign central bank.

The central banks also agreed to notify each other each day of transactions as a result of which gold was to be earmarked or released. Since the gold value of the franc fluctuated within stipulated limits and there was no official gold price at all for sterling, both the Bank of France and the Bank of England agreed to quote buying and selling prices for gold to the FRBNY that would hold for each day for the settlement of transactions. Only the United States had a fixed buying price for an ounce of gold: $35 less one quarter of 1 percent handling charge.[17] These arrangements were subject to modification or cancellation by either party on twenty-four hour notice.

At a press conference on 13 October 1936, Morgenthau remarked that as he saw it, "we are not returning to the old gold standard, we are not seeking stabilization, merely stabilizing foreign exchange rates. Nor do we seek a stability that is fixed in amount or perpetual in duration. The needs of foreign trade and commerce are met, although exchange rates vary, if the fluctuation is not too wide, and even such stability need be sought only for the relatively short period of time, or when the needs of foreign forward commitment in foreign trade are customarily made" (Morgenthau Papers, reel 11, book 39, 175). Morgenthau's intent clearly was to disavow any resemblance to the "old" gold standard of the Tripartite system.

The details of the new system follow. Two separate accounts were instituted by the three central banks, one for currency, and one for gold through which the transactions of the stabilization funds would be recorded. The sterling and franc accounts opened for the FRBNY at the Bank of England and the Bank of France were labeled no. 3 accounts. The gold accounts were labeled account B (Brown 1942, 131). At a later point in his unpublished study, Brown (1942, 170) introduces two additional accounts: no. 2, apparently covering sterling transactions that were not part of the Tripartite control system, and account A, gold bought under the ESF's standing authority at London-New York shipping parity and held under earmark. Brown does not explain the reason for establishing two sets of accounts for sterling, one set as part of the Tripartite control system, the other set separate from the Tripartite control system. It appears, based on a discussion in Sayers (1976), noted below, that the second set was useful for transactions undertaken on behalf of central banks that were not members of the Tripartite system and their customers.

The second set of accounts was needed because London was involved in transactions, as we shall see, unrelated to the Tripartite system. The fact that the sterling exchange rate floated was irrelevant.

Upon the completion of these arrangements, on 13 October the Treasury named Britain and France as countries complying with the conditions of Tripartite participation. By the middle of November similar understandings were reached between the Belgian, Swiss, and Dutch treasuries and the US Treasury, and on 24 November these countries were named by the Treasury as complying with those conditions.

The conditions the Belgian and Swiss National Banks agreed to, to sell gold to and buy gold from the FRBNY for delivery in Brussels and Berne, respectively, were identical except for each country's buying and selling prices. These were fixed prices that each agreed to, as were the US Treasury's buying and selling prices. As a result, these agreements stabilized the belga-dollar and Swiss franc-dollar rates as they would have been in a gold standard system except that the gold points were wide apart and the agreements were for twenty-four hours. The stabilizing mechanism was official gold transactions and not private gold arbitrage.

Since the Dutch stabilization fund had no legal requirement to buy or sell gold within fixed limits, the agreement with the Netherlands Bank was like that with the Bank of France. The bank agreed to consult with the FRBNY as to the amounts of dollars to be purchased or sold in Amsterdam, the amounts of guilders to be purchased or sold in New York, and the rates at which purchases or sales of the currencies would be made. Any dollars acquired by the Dutch stabilization fund would be converted into gold by the FRBNY at the rate of $35 per ounce fine plus 1/4 of 1 percent handling charges, and any guilders acquired for the account of the FRBNY as fiscal agent of the United States would be converted by the Dutch fund into gold at $35 per ounce fine less 1/4 of 1 percent handling charge. The gold that was acquired would be earmarked for the account of the owner in the country of the other partner and at the request of the owner, shipped to the country of the owner by the first available steamer of his country, the cost of shipment including insurance, melting charges, and any loss in weight through melting to be borne by the Dutch stabilization fund.

All three banks were advised to establish accounts of the same sort as those set up at the Bank of England and Bank of France.

The three countries that joined the Tripartite Agreement in November 1936 were former gold bloc countries. No similar success in attracting sterling area members was on record.[18]

Reciprocity in gold dealings was a key condition of the Tripartite Agreement. The US Treasury, however, had a complicated system of gold regulations, according to which foreign governments and central banks were confronted with six different procedures for gold transactions in this country, depending on which US agency was involved in the purchase or sale, and whether a special license was required.

The restrictions in force on the transfer of gold earmarked at the FRBNY for the account of other Tripartite members and the BIS seemed inconsistent with reciprocity, since such transfers were freely allowed by central banks of other country members of the Tripartite group. On 27 January 1937 the Treasury yielded to the general opposition to its procedures in this matter, and agreed to the free transfer of earmarked gold between members of the Tripartite group. The FRBNY on 22 March was given the necessary authority to make transfers of gold earmarks in accordance with this change.

One further clarification of the Tripartite Agreement, in response to a query by a member, was that stabilization operations within the twenty-four hour provision excluded from the scope of the Agreement open positions in the currencies of other members.

Meltzer (2003, 544) sees two basic flaws in the agreement. One was the emphasis on cooperation as if it were an alternative to exchange rate adjustment, when the problem in the mid-thirties was misalignment of exchange rates and prices. A second flaw was the failure of the agreement to distinguish between nominal and real exchange rate adjustment. The discussions that preceded it overlooked the crucial fact that fixing nominal exchange rates meant that price changes would be the channel through which adjustment would have to occur. Meltzer shows that the real dollar-sterling and dollar-franc exchange rates in October 1936 did not correct the misalignment beginning in 1929.[19]

We now report on the gold and foreign exchange operations of the ESF under the Tripartite Agreement until the outbreak of the war.

Fourth Quarter 1936

Following the French devaluation, sterling declined from $5.03 in September 1936 to $4.89 in October (monthly averages of daily quotations for cable transfers of funds) (Board of Governors, December 1936, 1028). During this interval, the ESF provided some support for sterling. It bought $2.25 million at rates from $4.96 to $4.89 1/2. Under the standing order it bought $1 million in gold at $34.77. On 12 October it held $10.83 million in sterling and $13.76 million in gold under earmark at the Bank of England. The motive for the sterling and gold purchases during the initial Tripartite experience was to keep sterling within a narrow band around $4.89. We learn from Sayers that the EEA operated "to funnel dollars to continental buyers" (Sayers 1976, 488). By 1936–37, fluctuations in exchange rates had "retreated" in all ordinary weeks "almost to the range of the old gold points." The ESF was not a passive observer of a less volatile dollar-sterling exchange rate; it was actively engaged in maintaining that stability.

After that date the principal means the ESF used to stabilize the foreign exchanges was earmarked gold or gold released from earmark under the twenty-four hour rule. These transactions were recorded in the new control accounts established with each participating central bank on behalf of their respective governments or exchange funds. The ESF, however, did not take open positions in foreign currencies as it previously had sometimes done in francs and sterling.

The way the ESF operated in the new system was that its purchase of sterling was credited to its no. 3 account at the Bank of England, and then immediately debited as the sterling was converted into gold by the bank and earmarked in account B. Sterling could also be held in a no. 2 account which was separate from the Tripartite control system. Sterling sold by the ESF was charged to its no. 2 account, and replenished by the release of gold under earmark at the bank.

The ESF held a long position in sterling when the Tripartite system took effect. It kept this sterling in the no. 2 account at the bank until 2 December, when 2 million pounds was invested by the bank for the ESF at 7/16 percent and appeared in a "Money Employed" account. The rate of interest fluctuated with the changes in short-term interest rates in London. Most of the ESF'S open sterling position that was held in the no. 2 account was transferred to the "Money Employed" account. The balance in the no. 2 account varied from trifling on 25 January 1937 to $64,000 on 12 July 1937, when the "Money Employed" account was zero.[20]

The ESF made active use of the no. 3 sterling account until the outbreak of the war.[21]

From October 1936 to June 1937 the new system of exchange rates remained as stable as it would have been under the international gold standard, except for the effect of the franc's second devaluation in June to the lower limit set by the law of 1 October 1936. As Meltzer (2003, 543) points out, lauding stability of exchange rates as a virtue of the agreement misses its central problem: real exchange rates were not stable, as differences in price levels and economic policies in the member countries attest. France pursued policies that raised prices, necessitating devaluation. The policies were inconsistent with the agreement.

During this period the ESF bought sterling for conversion into gold in account B at the Bank of England at the price the bank quoted to it daily.

For account A earmark it also bought gold at $34.77, increasing its standing offer on 30 October from 700,000 to 2.859 million ounces, subsequently reduced in two steps to 1.450 million ounces on 23 November. This amount was regularly renewed until 29 October 1937, when it lapsed. The bank requested renewal of the original order of purchases up to 700,000 ounces in March 1938. These purchases were motivated by the relation between the London gold price and the sterling-dollar rate, and not by the level of the sterling-dollar rate. By 30 November gold in account A peaked at $72.55 million. The purchases continued after a Treasury decision to sell gold acquired in account B as a stabilization operation.

The circumstance that prompted the Treasury's decision was an appreciation in sterling that appeared to reflect badly on the Tripartite's stabilization mechanism.[22] So the decision was made for the ESF to sell some of its gold in London. The sales from account B occurred on 23–25 November and 8 December 1936, continuing through 8–12 March 1937. The sterling proceeds were credited to account no. 2 at the Bank of England. The gold sales helped to limit fluctuations in the sterling-dollar rate for the duration of the Tripartite Agreement.

Why did gold sales for sterling by the ESF in London limit sterling appreciation? According to Johnson (1939,154), the sterling-dollar relationship depended on (a) the US gold price, (b) the London gold price, and (c) the pound-dollar exchange rate. Before 1933, the first two were fixed. The third was the only variable, and its movements were restricted to the gold points. Gold movements occurred only when the rate moved beyond those points. From 1934 on, not one, but two variables existed: the London gold price was not fixed, but was established by the London world gold market, based on demand and supply. The relation of the fluctuating London gold price to the fixed US gold price of $35 per ounce reflected the third variable, the pound-dollar rate. The London gold price and the pound-dollar rate tended to move together. A change in either one could initiate gold movements. Equilibrium in gold movements could be established at any level of the pound-dollar rate. Thus a fall in the London gold price (say, because the EEA reduced its gold purchases) could lead simultaneously to a flow of gold to New York and a weakening of the dollar exchange rate. The dollar weakened in Johnson's explanation because he focused on the period of gold sterilization by the Treasury (December 1936–April 1938) . The Treasury then paid for gold by borrowing instead of using the cash balances it could create by depositing gold certificates at the Reserve banks that increased its cash and Reserve bank deposits. The dollar weakened during the period of gold sterilization because Treasury indebtedness rose. The United States was the largest official gold buyer with a fixed price, so the entire current supply of gold in the London gold market flowed to the United States unless there were other buyers on the London market, and the London price of gold in relation to the dollar exchange rate was maintained from sources other than American buying. The only other significant buyer was the EEA, which was under no necessity to do so. The EEA had reason to share the burden of absorbing the flow of gold to London with the United States because otherwise the dollar would weaken in terms of the pound as a result of American arbitrage buying made profitable by the fall in the London gold price.

The Treasury's actions to limit sterling appreciation began with sales of gold it held in London, with the sterling proceeds credited to account no. 2 at the Bank of England. By increasing the supply of gold in the London market, its sales of gold there reduced the London price of gold, which lowered the pound-dollar rate.

Tripartite members also were involved in transactions with nonparticipating central banks. In November 1936 the ESF and EEA collaborated to enable Argentina to pay off a loan in New York without disturbing the foreign exchange market. The Central Bank of Argentina cabled the FRBNY that it would sell sterling in New York and buy dollars in London to cover in part its requirement. On 19 November the ESF bought 200,000 pounds worth of sterling at $4.88 7/8 from the Central Bank of Argentina, most of which it converted into gold. On 23 November it sold in the market from its no. 2 account 175,000 pounds of sterling that it obtained by the release of gold from earmark.

There were many buyers of sterling on that day in London and no apparent offers, and the presumption was that the sterling rate would therefore run up. The ESF, however, could supply sterling by release of gold from earmark at the price the EEA quoted to the fund daily each morning.

The ESF bought another 1 1/2 million pounds of sterling on 25 November from the Argentine central bank at $4.895 that was credited to the no. 3 account. A little less than half this amount was sold at the same rate and the balance was converted into gold.

On 8 December $2 million in gold was released of which the ESF sold about $404,000 that day at $4.91. The next day it bought $450,000 at $4.90, which it converted into gold. On 28 December it sold 165,000 pounds sterling for account no. 2 and bought 100,000 pounds the next day for conversion into gold. These were routine interventions to steady the markets.

First Quarter 1937

In January 1937 Argentina had to negotiate substantial transfers of funds. From 19 to 21 January the ESF bought from the Central Bank 2 million pounds for delivery on the twenty-sixth.[23] It immediately sold 950,000 pounds to the market in small lots and 400,000 pounds to the Bank of England from its "Money Employed" account, which it later replenished.

The ESF was a net purchaser of sterling in the market amounting to $1,600,000, and gold under earmark in its account B increased by that amount. From 7 January to 1 February it bought $15 million to pay for gold at $34.77 an ounce. Sterling, however, remained weak and it bought $14 million in small lots from 27 January to 5 March at rates from $4.89 to $4.87. These purchases were converted into gold. In the last two weeks of February and the first week of March, it bought $10 1/5 million in gold in continued support of sterling.

The ESF four days later switched to sales of sterling at $4. 88 to $4.88 4/8 in the amount of $6.6 million, which was available in part from a release of gold from earmark and a withdrawal of $2 million from the "Money Employed" account. On 10 March it repurchased $1.055 million sterling which it converted into gold. On 12 March, however, it released $867, 000 in gold from its earmarked account B and sold the sterling equivalent in the market.

The ESF continued to sell sterling to the market in March, 250,000 pounds by reducing the "Money Employed" account and an additional 2 million pounds bought from the Central Bank of Argentina for delivery 25 March. Of the latter amount it sold $1.740 million to the Bank of England. Sales up to 29 March exceeded the sterling bought from the Argentine bank. The "Money Employed" account rather than the release of gold made up the difference. By the end of March sterling reached $4.89 and $34.77 was no longer an effective price for the purchase of gold in the London bullion market.

To summarize the ESF's activities in the sterling market from 13 October 1936, when the sterling-dollar rate was just over $4.89, to 30 March 1937, when it was at the same level, the low and high between the two dates ranged only from $4.87 3/4 to $4.91 3/4, a stability that the fund's operations assisted. By 29 March 1937 it held $59.5 million in account B and $1.043 million in account A at the Bank of England. The "Money Employed" account had been reduced from $9.83 million on 7 December, the opening date, to $6 million on 29 March. In December 1936 the ESF imported $20 million in gold from its A account, which it sold to the Treasury in early January 1937, and imported to the United States all the rest of the gold in account A for its own use.

We next report on the transactions the ESF conducted with the Bank of France and the Netherlands Bank during the period 13 October 1936 and 29 March 1937. On the initial date it sold on behalf of the Bank of France 3.2 million francs in New York at 4.66 1/2 cents per franc. It converted the proceeds into gold earmarked for the Bank of France at the FRBNY.

On 21 October the fund bought 1 million francs at 4.647 cents, bringing its deposit with the Bank of France to $6,000. On 21 October it bought 35 kilos of gold in Paris at 24.056 francs per kilo for earmark in its account B with the Bank of France. At approximately the same prices the ESF on 9 December bought an additional 1 million francs and 45 kilos of gold. It had no further dealings in francs until after the second French devaluation. On 8 November 1937 it sold 82 kilos of gold in Paris at 33.074 francs per kilo and 2.74 million francs at 3.41 1/4 cents, getting rid of its balance in francs and gold holding at the Bank of France.

The cessation of ESF operations in France did not preclude operations on behalf of the Bank of France in New York during the period of stability following the first French devaluation. The fund sold gold from its own holdings to the bank at $35 plus 1/4 for immediate export or to be held under earmark and bought gold at $35 less 1/4 that the bank delivered from gold earmarked at the FRBNY. The bank placed the gold bought from the fund under earmark at the FRBNY. However, the bank was a net seller of gold under the Tripartite Agreement in the last quarter of 1936. Brown (1942, 179) comments that there does not appear to have been "strong pressure on the franc in any direction" during the period.

The Netherlands Bank arranged on 17 December with the FRBNY to have dollars up to the equivalent of 10 million guilders in exchange for gold to be placed under earmark. The ESF sold gold daily in small amounts to the Netherlands Bank from 21 December 1936 to 10 February 1937 in response to the bank's wish. The Netherlands Bank bought gold in New York on its own on 15 February. On 31 December 1936 it increased its request to 25 million guilders for conversion into dollars. Purchase of dollars and gold served to prevent a rise in the Dutch currency.

Not only the guilder but also the Swiss franc and the dollar were strong currencies at this time.[24] The movement of gold to all of these countries made domestic credit overly expansionary. The flow of $500 million of gold to the United States during the last five months of 1936 led the Treasury on 22 December to announce that it would sterilize further gold imports to segregate the monetary base from their effect.[25] Instead, on and after 23 December the US treasurer showed as inactive gold in the general fund all gold received daily. Until April 1938, the Treasury paid for the gold it bought by borrowing rather than by using the cash balances it could create by depositing gold certificates at the Reserve banks that increased its cash and Reserve bank deposits. Instead, the gold sterilization program increased the Treasury's indebtedness.

Second Quarter 1937

During the second quarter of 1937 several participating Tripartite countries experienced disturbances to their currencies; in addition, two nonmember countries shipped large quantities of gold that member countries had to absorb.

The franc was weak throughout the quarter. The ESF bought francs in the New York market for the account of the Bank of France. It bought 25.6 million francs at rates between 4.45 and 4.46 cents per franc from 9 to 26 June. At the end of June, 9 million of these francs were sold at 4.46. The franc rate, however, at the lower limit fixed by the 1 October 1936 Devaluation Law was unsustainable. The Blum government fell in June, as French industry languished under the costs social legislation had imposed. The new government devalued the franc by 15 percent but vowed to keep the franc within the range 3.80 to 3.96 cents. The French agreed to announce a daily buying and selling rate for gold. The ESF thereupon was notified by the Bank of France when it desired francs to be bought and sold for its account in the New York market. During the quarter, the Bank of France was a net seller to the ESF in its gold transactions under the Tripartite Agreement.

The dollar-belga exchange rate was subject to disturbance as the rate rose above the gold export point from Brussels to New York. For this reason the National Bank of Belgium inquired whether the FRBNY would buy gold from it. The latter agreed to buy up to $10 million in Belgium at $35 less 1/4 less mint charges, the gold to be shipped by an American vessel guaranteed free for export. Belgium did not act on this offer until 5 June. The ESF then bought a series of shipments of gold in Belgium amounting to $5.227 million for sale to the general treasurer.

The Netherlands Bank, which had been a seller of gold in small amounts to the ESF in April 1937, became a substantial buyer in June. However, its net sales of gold during the second quarter amounting to $17.8 million, were second only in amount to that acquired from the Bank of England.

Early in April gold shipments to the United States, large in relation to exchange transactions, began to arrive from Russia and Japan. The Russian gold, apparently new production, was imported on a dollar basis by New

York banks that had Russian accounts or were of Russian origin. Who the actual seller was is not known. By 11 April $25 million had arrived, Russian balances having increased by that amount.

At the same time large gold shipments were en route from Japan; the Japanese advised the Treasury about this through diplomatic channels. Inquiries were made about the purpose of the shipments, amounting to a total of 250 million yen. The agent of the Bank of Japan told Allan Sproul, president of the FRBNY, that the reason for sending gold was to settle international accounts. The answer did not set aside American doubts that they had been told the truth.

The great gold inflows, which were almost entirely placed in the inactive account, led to the rumor in April that the Treasury would lower its buying price to discourage further shipments. Enormous gold flows to the United States from all quarters generated rumors in April 1937 that to reduce the gold inflow, the United States would lower the buying price of gold.[26] As a result the market shifted from holding assets in gold to holding currency assets. The appreciation of sterling proceeded to a level that the market believed would not persist. Consequently, the discount on sterling for future delivery rose. A better return could be realized by London banks placing funds in New York and buying future sterling back at a discount than could be made by lending the same funds in the London open market. The weakening dollar in turn stimulated a flow of funds and gold to the United States. British authorities could have prevented the gold scare and undue gold movements to the United States by being prepared to buy an unlimited amount of gold at the London-American shipping parity.

The rumor sparked a discount from New York shipping parity in the London price of gold that lasted until June when the discount was 7 1/2 percent.[27]

Sterling was strong in the second quarter, rising to $4.94 on 30 April, but the relationship of the sterling-dollar rate to the London market price of gold made the ESF's standing offer of $34.77 per ounce again effective. At this price it bought $23 million in gold, placed under earmark in account A at the Bank of England. This gold was imported and sold to the General Treasurer.

The fallout from the rumor of a reduction in the Treasury's buying price for gold caused serious difficulties. Gold flowed strongly to London, so the EEA had to absorb large amounts. If it acquired enough gold from the London bullion market that otherwise would move to the United States, it might have pushed the London gold price back to New York shipping parity. But that would have meant that sterling would lose dollar support, which kept the sterling-dollar rate at prevailing levels.

The British instead did not forgo the opportunity provided by the ESF's standing offer to buy gold from them at $34.77 per ounce. The British sold $63 million in June. On 24 June the ESF began to buy sterling for conversion into gold in the London bullion market. The sterling purchases at $4.93

to \$4.94 amounting to nearly £1 million were entered into the fund's no. 3 account at the Bank of England, but the gold that was bought with the sterling apparently was purchased in the market, and not from the Bank of England at its daily quoted price under the Tripartite Agreement.

The ESF purchase of gold from the Bank of England, part for account A and part for account B, as well as from the London market, made only a partial offset to the sizable gold inflow to England in the first half of 1937. On 28 June the EEA received £200 million in additional Treasury bills to enable it to continue gold purchases.[28]

The ESF imported the greater part of the gold it had accumulated abroad under earmark, much of which it sold to the general treasurer. In general the ESF would buy gold only from members of the Tripartite Agreement. Exceptions occurred, however, when a non-Tripartite member wanted to sell gold on a Saturday when the Assay Office was closed, or when the FRBNY received instructions late in the day to make delivery to the Assay Office.

Foreign gold markings at the FRBNY, which had sharply declined while rumors were current of a likely reduction in the US Treasury buying price, resumed once the rumors were stamped out.

Third Quarter 1937

During the third quarter of 1937 the ESF conducted routine operations in several currencies of Tripartite members. Its purchases and sales of francs for the account of the Bank of France did not overcome the underlying market trend of franc weakness. The franc rate tended to fall during each transaction over the three-month period.

On 13 July the Netherlands Bank instructed the FRBNY to sell 1.225 million guilders in New York for its account at 55.07 and two smaller orders at 55.22 and 55.30. There were no further operations through the ESF until 24 September, when the bank sold 1.936 million guilders at 55.30, which was the gold export point from New York. At this rate the ESF carried out sales starting 1 October and ending in the fourth quarter on 3 November.

To support the belga the National Bank of Belgium sold gold, and on three dates in June and July renewed the arrangement of the preceding April with the ESF for it to purchase up to \$10 million in gold in Belgium. The FRBNY, however, inquired why gold bars could not be imported at \$35 per ounce less mint charges less 1/4 percent, since the gold market had become practically normal. The Belgian central bank replied that the rumors of a dollar revaluation had not died down in Europe. Therefore arbitrageurs declined to sell gold to the US Treasury for dollars when the rate would permit it once the gold export point had been reached. As a result the central bank had to supply dollars to the market through the arrangement with the ESF. The reply convinced the Americans. The ESF between 16 July and 3 August bought \$29.479 million in gold in Brussels that it imported for sale to the general treasurer.

Sterling, on the other hand, needed no support. The dollar-sterling rate in August 1937 was over \$4.98 and never below \$4.95. At these rates the ESF sold sterling and released gold from earmark at the Bank of England at selected dates from 9 July through 1 October, all within the Tripartite framework. A special sterling transaction on 12 August involved the ESF in the purchase of £300,000 from its no. 2 account at the Bank of England for sale to the Central Bank of China. It also sold \$30 million in gold to the Central Bank that it acquired from the inactive gold account that the general treasurer sold.

In addition mostly in September, the ESF added to its account A gold at the Bank of England at \$34.77 per ounce, at this price \$64 million in total. On 9 September it made a £45,000 purchase of sterling for conversion into gold in the bullion market.

As was usual, the ESF sold to the general treasurer the gold accumulated abroad that it gradually imported. Nevertheless, on 4 October, ESF assets totaled \$175 million in gold and its dollar balance was only \$7 million.

Fourth Quarter 1937

The ESF's asset structure during the following quarter was transformed. By the end of 1937, the fund held only \$30 million in unpledged gold and a dollar balance of \$129 million. A number of factors contributed to this result. The Treasury for one gave up some of the gold in the inactive account. In response to the Federal Reserve's request in September, the Treasury released \$300 million in gold from the inactive gold account in its general fund to its working balance at the FRBNY in which it deposited gold certificates. In addition, \$44 million of the fund's gold was not available since it served as collateral for Chinese yuan that it had purchased from the Central Bank of China (see section 3.5).

In addition, in November the United States began to export gold, for a reason discussed below. Under these circumstances in October the FRBNY was instructed by the ESF to sell in London from its A account all the gold held under earmark at the Bank of England at \$34.79 per ounce. Then gold from account B was sold still at that price until 8 November when the sale was made at \$35.09 per ounce. On 22 November the only gold under earmark at the Bank of England was \$3.4 million in account B. The 82 kilos in account B at the Bank of France were sold as well.

During the last quarter of 1937 the dollar came under attack. A large-scale withdrawal of foreign short-term balances from the United States occurred as rumors, opposite to those that spread in the second quarter, that this time foresaw further devaluation of the dollar as a possible measure to counter the cyclical downturn that began in May. This was feasible because the devaluation in January 1934 still left the president with authority to increase the purchase price of gold and lower the gold weight of the dollar (see section 3.2 above).[29]

The downward movement of the franc for the time being was halted and sterling was strong in New York. The London gold price rose enough for a premium to appear over the New York shipping parity.

The ESF was also a seller of gold: $1.5 million to the Bank of England at dates in October and November to obtain sterling that the fund sold at $4.95–96; again to the Bank of England, $4.6 million in gold on a dollar basis ($35 less 1/4), which it took from its own holdings in New York. From 11 October to 6 December, it sold gold almost daily to the Bank of France on a dollar basis in the amount of $60.5 million, with delivery in New York. At this time the ESF withdrew the 82 kilos of gold that it held in account B at the Bank of France.

Despite the drain of dollars from the Bank of France, the exchange rate of the franc was stationary at 3.35 cents. The bank operated in the New York market as both seller and buyer of francs in small amounts.

After small purchases in October and November, the Netherlands Bank became a purchaser on 2 December of 1.425 million ounces ($49,875,000) of gold from the ESF. The Swiss National Bank bought $27,978,000 in gold on 6 and 9 November and $79.8 million on 20 December. The selling price was $35 per ounce less 1/4.

To meet the demands on the ESF by foreign central banks for gold and to provide it with gold for support of the dollar, the FRBNY was instructed to purchase for the ESF's account all incoming gold received at the Assay Office in New York beginning 27 October at the flat rate of $35 per ounce. Japan was the source of the gold inflow, so the San Francisco Mint was requested to send telegraphic advice to the FRB of gold received from Japan to be paid for at the Assay Office in New York. The instruction was broadened on 4 November to include gold purchased daily at all US Mints and Assay Offices. The FRB was to be informed how much to purchase from the New York Assay Office for the account of the ESF. The payment was to be charged to the secretary's special account and credited to the treasurer's general account with the FRB—a wash. The FRB was not required in this case to pay the Treasury through the gold certificate fund. In this way the ESF during the last quarter of 1937 acquired $170 million in gold but it was not enough to match its foreign sales. As noted above, at year end the ESF was mainly a dollar fund.

First Quarter 1938

By 14 February 1938 the ESF gold assets amounted to $48.4 million compared to a total of $30 million at the close of 1937. Its acquisitions included gold bought from the inactive account, and gold bought from Mexico and the Bank of France. The next day the ESF sold to the general treasurer all the gold it had bought since the end of 1937 with the exception of the $5 million bought from the inactive account to replace gold sold for export on 2 January.

On 15 February the ESF bought an additional $9 million from the inactive account to replace sales of that amount to Mexico (see section 3.5). Except for the forgoing transactions with Mexico and the Bank of France the ESF did not operate in the foreign exchange market while the program for the desterilization of the inactive gold account was set beginning 1 January (it was completed 19 April). No sterling transactions were executed. However, the ESF continued to buy and sell francs for the Bank of France from 10 January to 15 February. The transactions were at declining prices, portending the end of the Bonnet franc.[30] The Daladier franc replaced it in May.[31] The deliberate weakening of the franc below its market level made it difficult for the EEA, which lost gold and foreign exchange, to hold the sterling-dollar rate at about $4.98. Sayers (1976, 562) notes, "the Americans were ready to complain at any depreciation of sterling."

Transactions involving the ESF during the six-week period from 14 February on behalf of the Bank of France were devoted to the support of the franc. Purchases totaled $6.8 million francs, sales only $150,000, with the rate declining from 3.29 1/16 to 3.02 1/2 cents. The bank was a net buyer of over $3 million in gold.

The ESF sold $20.55 million in gold to the Swiss National Bank from 17 to 20 February, and $0.975 million on two dates in February and March to the Swedish National Bank.

On 14 February the ESF made its transaction in sterling that month, selling £455,000 at 5.02 1/2, which it obtained by the release of earmarked gold in account B at the Bank of England.

The outbreak of the Czech crisis in March affected the foreign exchange market. On 15 March, when sterling fell to $4.96, the Bank of England cabled the FRBNY to renew its offer of November 1935 to buy up to 700,000 ounces of gold at $34.77 per ounce. The ESF renewed the offer on 17 March for 1,400,000 ounces, but on 28 March reduced it to 700,000 ounces, where it remained until the Munich Pact on 29 September.

Before 21 March the ESF under this authority bought $26 million in gold earmarked in account A at the Bank of England. The ESF also bought sterling in New York for conversion into gold in the London market. It bought £1.179 million at $4.96 5/8 on 16 March and £812,000 at $4.95 1/2 on 18 March as well as small amounts on 21 and 25 March. Sterling recovered and the ESF thereupon sold £561,000 at $4.96 1/8 on 19 March. The gold was immediately exported to the United States except for small balances left in both account A and B at the Bank of England. No further transactions in sterling were executed until 11 April when a new series of sales at $4.97 7/16 began.

There was little change in the ESF's gold account from its dealings with foreign governments and central banks.[32] It continued to buy from the general treasurer the equivalent of gold imports into the United States and bought by the US Mints and Assay Offices. By 31 March net purchases amounted to $28 million. Thereafter until the outbreak of the war, the ESF bought no more gold from the general treasurer. This change in part was a consequence of the 14 April end of the sterilization policy, with the transfer of the gold in the inactive account to the working fund of the Treasury and then deposited in the Federal Reserve gold certificate fund.[33]

Second Quarter 1938

Until 1 August ESF transactions were exclusively with the Bank of England and the Bank of France. Sterling and the franc were both firm in April. From 12 to 27 April the ESF sold 28.750 million francs and bought 5.1 million francs for the account of the Bank of France at rates generally above 3.11 1/2 cents. The rate then fell and by 5 May, despite further support in New York, was down to 2.29 cents.[34] The French then again devalued to 175 francs to the pound and 2.8 cents per franc (Meltzer 2003, 543). The real exchange rate was 3.6 cents per franc, 12 percent lower than in October 1936.

During this quarter transactions by the ESF with the Bank of England were on a small scale. The ESF bought £1 million sterling from the Swedish National Bank for conversion into gold on 21 May. The only other sterling transactions were sales in April and June at rates from $4.97 to $5.01. The sterling for these sales was obtained by release of gold from account A, all gold in account B having been imported. On 14 June the ESF bought $5 million in gold in London that was immediately imported. This was its last purchase from the Bank of England at the sterling-gold price quoted to it daily until the war began.

Third Quarter 1938

The Bank of France actively supported the franc in New York throughout August and September. Through the ESF it bought 321 million francs. It made a few small sales on 4 September. The condition of the franc during the summer was in fact robust, thanks to a record tourist season. The franc-sterling rate was fairly stable not only through September but through the rest of 1938 (Sayers 1976, vol. 2, 562). The stability of the franc in terms of sterling meant that sterling was depreciating somewhat in terms of the dollar. American concern centered on sterling depreciation, which, it was believed, would also bring down the franc.

In July the ESF bought a small amount of gold from the Bank of England at $34.77. In August it reentered the sterling market in New York for conversion into gold in the bullion market. By August political tension in Europe led to a capital movement to the United States. The ESF then bought sterling in New York in support of the pound. From 2 to 30 August it bought 974,000 pounds at rates from $4.90 1/8 to $4.86 1/16 for conversion into gold in the bullion market.

The Bank of England realized that the flight of funds from London to New York would continue so there was no rate at which a sterling peg could be maintained. Its policy therefore was not to resist pressure on the rate to fall somewhat, but to push the rate up a little whenever pressure diminished. For this reason, in June and up to 23 July the EEA lost £10 million of its reserves , and sterling lost 3 cents falling from $4.95 to $4.92 (Sayers 1976, vol. 2, 563). During the next 4 weeks, EEA lost £21½ million and the rate fell to $4.88, and in the 4 weeks to 17 September, the decline was £75 million and $4.80 for the rate.

The demands by Hitler for the union of predominantly German districts in Czechoslovakia with Germany intensified pressure on sterling. By 20 September the ESF bought an additional £7.567 million in New York at rates that declined to $4.73 3/8. Nearly half of this amount was bought on 9 and 13 September at the height of the crisis. The morning of the Munich Pact, 28 September, the rate fell to $4.60, but by the afternoon, a rebound began, the rate rising above $4.80 in the first few days of October. It did not last, as we note in the narrative of the final quarter of 1938.

The ESF also bought gold from the Bank of England under its standing offer at $34.77 per ounce until it reached 4.2 million ounces from 12 to 17 September. The price was gradually reduced from 15 September, falling to $34.60 by 28 September, reflecting higher war risk insurance rates. Total gold purchases from the beginning of August until 26 September reached $237 million, the amount earmarked in account A.

During this quarter the ESF bought gold from other central banks as well: $7.460 million from the Bank of France, $33.306 million from the Netherlands Bank, and $5.628 million from the Swiss Bank. On instructions from the Treasury, the FRBNY advised the Netherlands Bank that it would be a good idea to earmark gold against dollars that could be sold to support the guilder. A $25 million limit was set, the gold to be held for the account of the ESF pending shipment to the United States.

The ESF had acquired more gold than it could pay for. Its purchases also taxed the capacity of the shipping companies and of the insurance companies. To facilitate the import of the gold, the ESF began to use foreign ships and to insure a part of the gold under the government's self-insurance arrangement. In September it sold gold to the Treasury in large amounts, but the instructions issued to the FRBNY to import gold specified that the Treasury was aware that the FRB would insure against marine risk only for a portion of the value of the shipment at rates the government proposed, and that risks of war, strike, riot, or civil commotions were uninsurable. The FRBNY was told to record the shipment under the Government Losses in Shipment Act for the amount not privately insured.

Four shipments of gold from the Bank of England's account A to the United States were by US naval vessels. Another solution to the problem was tried. On 8 September the FRBNY was instructed to sell to the general fund of the Treasury at a flat $35 per ounce gold originally purchased for the ESF. Such gold was to be held by the FRB in a special custody account. In addition, some of the gold transferred by the ESF to the treasurer was placed in a special custody account for the US treasurer. In this way, although the ESF on 25 September was credited with gold assets of $391 million, it had a liability of about half that amount that was owed to the treasurer.

Fourth Quarter 1938

Sales of gold to the US treasurer by the ESF extended to 21 November from the preceding quarter. On that date for the first time there was a substantial reduction in its gold holdings.

In October the Netherlands Bank sold $16.188 million in gold to the ESF and the Swiss bank sold a little more than half that amount.

The ESF bought $172.350 million in gold in New York from the Bank of England in October from gold earmarked for the bank at the FRBNY. From 14 to 21 November a further $42.284 million in gold was bought in this way. On 5 December the price per ounce of gold was set at $34.7625. On 28 December the ESF bought $25 million in gold from the Bank of England's earmark at the FRBNY.

Heavy purchases of sterling continued in October at rates between $4.73 and $4.80, the sterling for conversion into gold. On 21 November for the first time sterling fell below $4.70, and at the end of that month the rate was $4.62.[35] The ESF continued to buy at declining rates. Total sterling purchases from 22 November to early January amounted to $20 million.

The Bank of England took advantage of a transitory opportunity in December to produce a scramble for sterling that enabled it to hold the sterling rate stable at $4.65, with only a small loss of reserves by the EEA. The occasion was the expiration of three-months contracts for forward sales of sterling, entered into in London during the Munich crisis, especially in the middle of September, by many foreign banks and others. The contracts for delivery of sterling for which dollars would be paid fell due in December. The bank estimated the short position in the exchange market at £70–80. To execute its plot, the bank informed the American authorities of what was afoot and seven of the big banks, who agreed not to use any of their own funds in the forward market. The squeeze worked, but it was only temporary. In January, with no change in the international political situation, the drain of reserves from the EEA and pressure on sterling resumed (Sayers 1976, vol. 1, 363–64).

On 3 December the ESF bought $8 million in gold from the Bank of France. From 5 December onward the bank became a steady buyer of gold from the ESF in small amounts.

First Quarter 1939

Until this quarter British authorities did not seek to restrict ordinary business. They managed foreign exchange rates by trading in the market as buyers and sellers of gold and exchange. By 1938 they knew that war was imminent and that ordinary operations suitable for peacetime would no longer be useful.

In preparation for the actual outbreak of war, in January the British adopted a four-part program to be implemented when needed. To resist pressure against sterling, the following measures were planned: (a) a complete embargo on foreign lending; (b) a complete embargo on forward gold operations; (c) supervision of exchange transactions; and (d) transfer of gold from the Bank of England to the EEA.

In the meantime, in this quarter, despite a heavy movement of hoarded gold from London to New York, the bank was able to hold the sterling rate between $4.65 1/2 and $4.69, with not much loss of EEA reserves. In March, however, when Prague was occupied, and as the political situation worsened, so did the loss of reserves.

In January the Bank of England began to support sterling actively in the New York market. It instructed the FRBNY to purchase sterling with gold released from earmark at the FRB. Beginning 11 January, it bought sterling regularly in New York for the account of the bank at just over $4.67 and from 16 March, $4.68 1/8. The bank acquired dollars for the purchase by releasing gold from earmark at the FRBNY, and by ESF purchase of gold in London from the bank in accordance with its standing offer. In February the ESF bought gold from the Bank of England at $34.7625 per ounce. It also bought gold from the bank's New York holding on a large scale and in March, in addition to these purchases, it bought sterling in New York amounting to £1.731 million on behalf of the Bank of England.

From January until 24 August, when support was withdrawn, the sterling rate was pegged at $4.68.

The ESF purchased sterling in the amount of £877,000 at $4.67 3/16 on 9 January for its own account after selling on 5 and 6 January £170,000 in gold from gold released from its account B at the Bank of England.

On 3 January, the ESF bought $25.893 million in gold from the Bank of France, for delivery to the Assay Office and sale to the general treasurer at $35 per ounce. The Bank of France made no further sales of gold to the ESF before the war. It became a steady buyer of gold from the ESF in small amounts from 5 December 1938. For long periods it was almost a daily purchaser. In all, the Bank of France bought back nearly $8 million of the gold it had sold to the ESF in December 1938 and January 1939. In trading operations in francs in New York through the ESF, it bought 44.15 million and sold 22.985 million at rates ranging from 3.61 7/8 to 2.53 7/8 cents. It also made one purchase of 13.25 million francs for the Bank of France

On 30 January the ESF bought gold from the Netherlands Bank, and continued to do so until by 22 March; the purchases amounted to $40.885 million, of which part was for sale to the Treasury.

In March the ESF bought gold, first $20 million from the Swiss National Bank from its earmark in New York, and then $40.471 million. On 30 March

Paris and London offered Swiss francs in New York with no buyers and the ESF stepped in and bought 250,000 Swiss francs at 22.42 cents, advising the Swiss National Bank through the FRBNY to convert the francs into gold for shipment at an early date. The bank informed the FRB that it would not welcome intervention without instructions from it. The bank offered to buy the francs from the FRB rather than converting them to gold, and the francs were sold at the purchase price. The FRB advised the bank that in the future it would be guided by its wishes, but reserved the right to intervene under the Tripartite if unexpected developments made action compelling. This was the ESF's only intervention in the Swiss franc market.

The ESF also bought belgas for conversion into gold in Brussels in the month from 3 March. In total 15 million belgas at 16.43 cents were earmarked for the ESF's account.

The Bank of France, however, continued its gold purchases from the ESF, buying in the first quarter over $93 million. The ESF's operations in New York for the bank were limited to the purchase of 28.25 million francs in the last two weeks of March.

ESF operations in the first quarter, except for gold purchases from the Bank of England in London, transactions either with the Bank of Belgium or the Bank of France, and the single transaction in Swiss francs, were confined to New York. The procedure by which gold bought from foreign central banks was placed in ESF's custody and then sold to the treasurer lost importance. Only $18 million was transferred to the treasurer from the ESF's gold during this interval.

3 April to 31 July 1939

The ESF bought £9 million in gold for the account of the Bank of England in New York at $4.68 1/8, mostly in April. It bought 15 million francs in April and 13.75 million in June at 2.65 cents for the account of the Bank of France. It bought 6.19 million guilders for the account of the Netherlands Bank at 53.08 cents. Between 10 and 28 April the ESF bought $135 million in gold from the Bank of England ($95 million in London $40 million in New York); $20 million from the Swiss National Bank; $15 million each from the Netherlands and the Belgium banks. During this period of pressure on the franc the Bank of France sold gold to the ESF, but became a large purchaser ($57 million) during the following three months.

The Bank of England sterling peg at $4.68 held, but gold losses of the EEA mounted. The bank considered lowering the peg to $4.50, but decided that the reduction would not stem the losses and might suggest that reserves were near exhaustion (Sayers 1976, 566–67).

The War Crisis, August–September 1939

One difference between the summer of 1914 and the summer of 1939 was that until the assassination of the heir to the Austrian throne on 29 June, there had been no war fears, whereas in 1939, people had been living with the specter of war from the time Hitler revealed his plans to dominate Europe. There were no plans on hand in 1914 to deal with a war crisis. They were improvised to meet the collapse of international credit. In 1939, authorities could adapt the measures that were useful in 1914 to the existing circumstances. A basic difference between the preludes to the two wars was that in 1914 the gold standard was intact in the core Allied countries, whereas in 1939, the international monetary system was a pale shadow of its former incarnation; exchange stabilization funds of each of the adherents to the Tripartite Agreement were intervening in foreign exchange markets.

On 1 August the ESF reentered the sterling market as a purchaser in New York of £7.432 million on behalf of the Bank of England and continued to buy until 24 August. It also bought $185.24 million in gold from the bank in New York. In addition, it bought $88.095 million in gold in London at $34.76 per ounce, increasing its standing offer from 700,000 to 2,100,000 ounces for the period 21 to 26 August. On 23 August gold under earmark for the ESF was shown in account A at the Bank of England, and was immediately imported.

The sterling transactions on 24 August, which were used to buy over 2 million ounces of gold (over $71 million), were the last at $4.64 1/8. The pegged $4.68 rate did not hold, and EEA gold losses were huge. The British then decided to remove the peg from sterling and let it depreciate. On 25 August the Bank of England cabled the FRBNY that it would not give gold dealing prices. And on 6 September the Treasury was informed of the transfer of the Bank of England's gold to the EEA. On 12 September the ESF was authorized to sell £8,000 sterling at the wartime rate of $4.03 5/8. On that day the Bank of England transferred the balance of £1,676 held by the bank in the FRBNY account 3 to account no. 2, closing the control account under the Tripartite Agreement.

The Bank of France continued to buy gold from the ESF in small amounts until 8 September. On 23–24 August it instructed the fund to buy 8.2 million francs for its account at 2.65 cents, but reversed its position once sterling was allowed to depreciate. It became a seller of francs in New York at rates that declined to 2.31 cents on 6 September. On 8–9 September the last of these transactions were sales for the account of the bank of 3.1 million francs at from 2.27 1/4 to 2.28 5/8 cents. On 8 September the ESF bought francs for its own account for the first time in two years. It instructed the FRB to buy 3.7 million francs at 2.25 3/8 cents, to transfer them to the Bank of France to be converted into gold along with the small balance in its no. 3 account, and to place the gold under earmark. The ESF's control account B was also closed.

On 9 September the FRBNY did not receive the daily cable from the Bank of France fixing the French gold price. The Treasury was informed when it phoned Paris that French monetary policy was under review. The secretary of the Treasury was advised that the French government had set up a system of exchange control.

On 31 August the National Bank of Belgium repurchased about one-third of the $6.861 million in gold which it had just sold to the ESF. At the same time the ESF sold substantial amounts of gold to non-European countries: $949 million to the Royal Thai Treasury, $2 million to the State Bank of the USSR, and $11 million to the Central Bank of Argentina.

This concludes Brown's (1942) report on ESF foreign exchange market intervention up to the eve of the outbreak of the Second World War. Free exchange markets were replaced by various measures of exchange control. Convertibility of the dollar and foreign currencies ended.

In retrospect, of the ESF's foreign exchange market intervention activities over the entire period ending 1961, the years 1934–39 were the zenith of its exercise of the mandate it was established to fulfill.

3.4.5   ESF Intervention Activity, 1940–1961

During the war the ESF held Swiss francs and balances in foreign currencies at depositories abroad. It made the Swiss francs "available for government and humanitarian purposes," according to the Treasury's statement (Treasury 1945, *Annual Report* , 95). Little official intervention by the ESF occurred in the years after the war ended. Most foreign currencies were not convertible. In addition, the US stock of gold reserves was ample, the US balance of payments was in surplus, and there was an excess demand by the world for dollars.

The US Bretton Woods Agreement Act (PL 171,79th Cong.) of 31 July 1945 made a great change with long-term effects on ESF operations. Before that date, the ESF may not have had access to the bulk of the funds that the Gold Reserve Act had set aside for it, but they were a prospective resource. After that date, ESF resources were permanently limited.

That change was the consequence of the provision in section 7 of the agreement that amended the Gold Reserve Act. The amendment directed the secretary of the Treasury to use $1.8 billion of the ESF capital (shown on the balance sheet as cash in the form of gold held by the US treasurer) to pay part of the $2,750 million US subscription to the IMF.

By June 1946, the United States had paid $275,000 of its subscription (Treasury 1946, *Annual Report*, 83). It completed payment of its subscription on 26 February 1947, in the form of $687.5 million in gold, $280.5 million in cash, the remaining $1,782 million in nonnegotiable noninterest-bearing notes, payable on demand in dollars when needed by the IMF (Treasury 1947, *Annual Report* , 48).

From 1946 until 1961 the ESF held no foreign exchange of the industrialized countries. A role for an exchange stabilization fund would seem to have been obviated, since the IMF was in place to manage exchange rates, but the ESF regarded the IMF as needing its support.

The conditions that prevailed when the war ended were markedly different from the mid-1950s on. The economies of Western European nations had recovered, world trade had grown, and demand for US goods and services and dollars to pay for them became less pronounced. By 1958 the currencies of most of these countries achieved convertibility on current account.

Speculation against the dollar arose as the balance of payments weakened and rumors of dollar devaluation spread. Sterling was also under pressure. At the same time the exchange values of the currencies of Germany, the Netherlands, and Switzerland, (the countries in surplus), were rising above par as private holders of dollars and sterling sold them for Deutsche marks (D-marks), guilders, and Swiss francs.

By January 1961, when the Kennedy administration took office, the US balance of payments as measured by outflows of gold and dollars to countries in surplus had substantially deteriorated. The loss of gold to foreigners in that month was seen as an expression of a lack of confidence in the administration's commitment to a dollar convertible into gold at a fixed price. The twin goals became to eliminate the balance-of-payments deficit and to check speculation against the dollar. The first goal was elusive. To achieve the second goal the Treasury wanted to be in the same position as other countries that influenced the exchange value of their currencies. That required resources to buy and sell other currencies or, in official parlance, sales and purchases of dollars.

To that end the ESF began to operate directly in the foreign exchange market. By June 1961 it had bought spot $25.4 million sterling and $20.1 million D-marks, and $65 million Swiss francs to counter threats against the dollar.

In March 1961, after revaluations of the D-mark and the Dutch guilder, the ESF made forward sales of D-marks to drive down the forward premium on the mark (discount on the dollar). The Treasury's forward mark commitments were liquidated by early December; it used marks it had acquired in April 1961 from a German debt repayment to the United States to settle in part forward contracts that were maturing in the fall of 1961.

There were similar forward operations by the Treasury in Swiss francs and Dutch guilders to bring down the premium on these currencies. As a response to the rise in the exchange value of the Italian lira in 1961 to its upper limit against the dollar, the Treasury took over forward lire contracts from the Italian foreign exchange office and drew on a $250 million line of credit in lire it obtained by issuing three-month certificates of indebtedness to support spot and forward operations in lire. As a result dollar accumulations in Italy were lessened.

Even these limited operations strained the resources of the ESF. In June 1961 it had $200 million in capital plus $136 million in net earnings accumulated over its twenty-seven-year life. Average annual net earnings approximated $5 million, from income on gold bullion sales, gold and exchange transactions, and interest on its government securities portfolio. To finance its foreign exchange purchases of roughly $100 million in 1961, the ESF had reduced its account at the FRBNY by $91 million and sold US government securities (Schwartz 1997, 144).

The Treasury's immediate aim was to find ways to supplement ESF foreign currency balances. It did so, first by persuading the G10 countries to create a facility that would expand the IMF's ability to lend. The IMF held only about $1.5 billion in currencies other than dollars. The new facility, established in December 1961, was the General Arrangements to Borrow (GAB), which provided the IMF with a $6 billion line of credit from central banks of countries with balance of payments in surplus to assist countries with balance of payments in deficit, in particular, the United States. The US quota in the IMF was nearly $6 billion. The IMF held far less in convertible currency assets, so the United States could not draw enough from the IMF to meet its reserve needs. The GAB was intended to serve as a supplementary source of liquidity for the United States. The IMF would sell to the United States for dollars foreign convertible currencies borrowed from other countries. These currencies would enable the United States to buy up dollars offered in the market and to redeem dollars foreign central banks did not want to hold, thus maintaining US monetary gold reserves.

The Treasury next persuaded the Federal Reserve to serve as its partner in exchange market intervention. So began the second period of ESF intervention operation (see chap. 4).

3.5 ESF Nonintervention Activities

The ESF has been used by the Treasury for at least three purposes not directly related to the stabilization of the exchange value of the dollar. The chief activity of the ESF other than dollar exchange stabilization has been extending loans to governments of political importance to US national interests (section 3.5.1). A second use of the ESF during the period covered by this chapter was the purchase of silver in connection with the Silver Purchase Act of 19 June 1934 (PL 438, 73rd Cong.) that directed the secretary of the Treasury to purchase silver at home and abroad until the market price reached $1.29+ an ounce, or until the monetary value of the silver stock held by the Treasury reached one-third of the monetary value of the gold stock (section 3.5.2). A third use of the ESF was related to the statutory authorization to deal in government securities with assets that it did not need for exchange stabilization (section 3.5.3).

3.5.1 ESF as Lender

There was no explicit authority in section 10 of the Gold Reserve Act for the president or secretary of the Treasury to make a loan to a foreign country instead of intervening in its currency or debt instruments. Nevertheless, the ESF has lent dollars to low-income countries, clearly a form of foreign aid.[36]

Before 1961 ten Latin American countries at one time or another had loans, often with renewals. The countries in this group were Argentina, Bolivia, Brazil, Chile, Cuba, Ecuador, Mexico, Nicaragua, Paraguay, and Peru.

Mexico had the longest record of loan agreements with the ESF. The first one was extended in January 1936 with stringent conditions. The FRBNY was instructed by the Treasury to advance $5 million to the Banco de Mexico against the purchase by the ESF of an equivalent amount of Mexican pesos (see Bordo and Schwartz 2001). The Mexican bank agreed to repurchase the pesos in dollars on the demand of the US Treasury at any time at the rate at which they had been acquired. The Mexican bank also agreed to deposit silver collateral. Brown (1942, 98ff.) gives the text of the letter of the agreement that the FRBNY sent the Mexican bank, noting that the Mexican agreement was the model for later ESF loans.[37] The bank paid 3 percent interest on the peso deposit on its books credited to the FRBNY, and the FRBNY credited the bank with a dollar amount equal to the amount in pesos at the then prevailing exchange rate. The collateral was silver held for the account of the bank under earmark, one half at the FRBNY, the other half at the FRB of San Francisco. Pledged as security for the performance of the agreement, the silver was the dollar equivalent of the pesos the United States purchased. The agreement continued in effect until 1 February 1936 and from month to month thereafter, but was to be discontinued if the FRBNY advised the bank on or before the fifteenth day of any month. The bank repurchased the pesos under the terms of the agreement in May and June 1936. A somewhat similar arrangement with Mexico was reached in January 1938; subsequent loans to Mexico were made in November 1941, July 1945, July 1947, June 1949, July 1951, July 1953, and January 1958. Loans to Mexico after 1961 were just as frequent as in the earlier period.

An agreement identical in all important respects with the Mexican agreement was concluded on 25 May 1936 for the purchase of Chinese yuan against dollars secured by silver collateral. The arrangements which the FRBNY made with the Central Bank of China provided for the purchase of up to $20 million of Chinese yuan. The collateral the Central Bank provided was to bear the same proportion to 50,000 ounces of silver as the amount of dollars used in the purchase of yuan bore to $20 million. The dollars provided by the ESF were to be credited to the Central Bank of China in a special account at the FRBNY. A requirement was added that the yuan credited to the FRBNY as fiscal agent and interest should be repurchased at the same rate of exchange at which the yuan earning the interest had been bought. The silver pledged as collateral was not to be set aside as in the Mexican agreement from silver already under earmark by the FRBNY, but was to be held by the Central Bank of China in depositaries in New York or San Francisco, designated by the Treasury for the account of the FRBNY as fiscal agent or to be placed onboard a US steamer in Shanghai consigned to the FRBNY at such depositaries. The agreement detailed the shipping and insurance provisions.

As in the Mexican agreement, in the event of failure on the part of the Central Bank of China to repurchase the yuan including interest, the FRB was safeguarded in taking over the collateral from any loss as a result of the failure. The Chinese agreement differed from the Mexican one in that the Central Bank of China had to arrange to have the collateral converted into silver bars for delivery in New York. Any purchase of yuan by the FRBNY as fiscal agent was subject to prior fulfillment by the Central Bank of China of the pledge of collateral.

The termination date of the agreement was 15 December 1936; notice of a desired renewal had to reach the FRBNY thirty days before.

The first Chinese agreement did not take effect. The ESF listed on its balance sheet of 3 August a liability to the Central Bank of China of $138,000, and from 14 September to 19 October of $312,000. There is no explanation accompanying the balance sheet of the reason a liability to China is listed, although China did not take up the loan the ESF offered.

During World War II the scope of ESF loans was broadened to include provision of dollars to countries deemed worthy of such assistance for their importance in the war effort. In Europe, only Iceland had a loan agreement, but the ESF provided the USSR with dollars in exchange for gold. In Asia the 1936 loan agreement with China for yuan with silver collateral was repeated in April 1941, but again not used. The ESF had wartime agreements with India, Iran, and Egypt to sell gold in exchange for local currencies for use by US personnel stationed there. It provided Liberia with US currency when it converted its monetary system from British coins.

During the postwar years ESF loan programs were combined with IMF standby arrangements, Export-Import Bank (EXIM Bank) foreign currency credits, and assistance from the International Cooperation Administration and the Agency for International Development that was established in 1961. These overlapping authorities represented different executive departments including commerce and state. The ESF contribution to these credit packages was small. One advantage of combining the ESF loan with others was that the latter often provided the less developed country (LDC) recipient with the means to repay the ESF.

3.5.2   The ESF in the Silver Market

Neither section 9 or 10 of the Gold Reserve Act mentions silver as one of the items the secretary of the Treasury is authorized to deal in. The Treasury, however, wanted to dispose of gold the FRBNY held under earmark at the Bank of England to acquire silver instead. For this reason on 24 April 1934, Secretary Morgenthau inquired of US Attorney General Cummings whether he was empowered to do so. Treasury Attorney General Oliphant supported a broad interpretation of the secretary's powers. Cummings' opinion was broad enough to cover not only ESF purchase of silver with the proceeds of gold sold abroad and to sell the silver so acquired, but also to authorize its purchase of additional silver with the secretary's special account at the FRBNY.

The ESF thus became a useful means for carrying out some of the purposes of the Silver Purchase Act of 19 June 1934, and the original plan of exchanging gold held in London for silver was adapted to the requirements of the Silver Purchase Act. It was enacted because of the political clout of senators from western states who represented silver mining interests. The price deflation of 1929–33 created a political movement in the United States to buy silver and raise its price in order to check deflation. Key Pittman of Nevada was chairman of the Senate Foreign Relations Committee. Roosevelt needed Pittman's support to repeal the arms embargo act. The quid pro quo was Roosevelt's promise to get the Silver Purchase Act passed.

Before the ESF was actually in operation on 27 April, and before the legislation was signed on 19 June, the Treasury made the necessary fiscal arrangements. It sent instructions to the FRBNY (a) to purchase spot silver in London in amounts and at prices to be specified from time to time; (b) to sell as much of the $44.6 million in gold held abroad under earmark for the Treasury to make these purchases; (c) to select silver depositories in London and pay the cost of transportation into the United States when so directed by the Treasury; (d) to deposit, as fiscal agent of the United States, sterling balances accruing from the sale of gold, not immediately needed to purchase silver, in London banks designated as depositories of the United States.[38]

Instructions were then extended to cover the purchase of spot silver in New York. The FRBNY and its agents were authorized to advance sums needed to cover the cost of silver in New York, at current rates of interest, and to reimburse themselves from the proceeds of sales of gold sold in London at the market rate of exchange. The Treasury also authorized the purchase of forward as well as spot silver in carrying out the exchange of silver for gold.

The fiscal agency and depository arrangements were made to take care of the sale of gold for silver, but were further expanded as the US silver purchase program got underway. On 5 June, just before the enactment of the Silver Purchase law, the secretary authorized the FRBNY as fiscal agent to purchase silver not only with the proceeds of gold sold abroad but also with the ESF's dollar assets in the secretary's special account at the FRBNY.

On 26 October the secretary authorized the FRBNY to purchase silver in markets other than New York and London, and to pay a commission of 2 cents per ounce on such silver. The bank was instructed to write to agents it selected to carry out silver purchases under various letters of authority.[39]

The ESF at the end of 1934 was able to buy spot or forward silver in any market through the FRB or its agents, the Guaranty Trust Company, Chase Bank, and National City Bank, and to deposit this silver in any one of fourteen depositories, seven in London, seven in New York. No specific arrangements, however, were in place for disposing of silver in the market and no banks had been appointed to carry out such sales.

Only part of the gold held abroad by the ESF was actually disposed of for silver. The balance of ESF gold remained under earmark at the Bank of England, and the silver bought with the proceeds of the gold that had been sold was in various depositories. Proceeds of gold sales were not used for the purchase of 67 million ounces of silver at an average cost of 44.8 cents, in accordance with the secretary's instructions, but were paid for instead by debits to his special account at the FRBNY. In June the silver was imported into the United States and held by the Assay Office in a special account for the secretary.

The ESF's gold and silver assets were unchanged between 16 June and 22 October 1934. From 26 October, however, the ESF began buying silver abroad and its sale to the US treasurer under the Silver Purchase Act. In addition, the Mint was authorized to sell to the Treasurer at 50.01 cents an ounce, 50 million of the 67 million ounces held in the name of the ESF. [40] The proceeds were credited to the ESF's checking account with the treasurer. The remaining 17 million ounces were transferred to the ESF which sold them directly to the treasurer.

The transactions involving ESF sale of gold, purchase of silver abroad, and sale of silver to the treasurer at 50.01 cents per ounce were followed by a series of ESF purchases of silver in London under the Silver Purchase Act, held in London for short periods, sold to the treasurer, and replaced by fresh purchases.

During February 1935, when the ESF was supporting sterling by purchases of both sterling and gold (and without drawing on its sterling balances), it also bought under the Silver Purchase Act 7.2 million ounces of silver at about 24 pence an ounce through the agents of the FRBNY. The silver was imported into the United States and sold to the treasurer.

In addition, the ESF bought silver in London with sterling. This was the equivalent of a transfer of sterling by the ESF to the treasurer for the purchase of silver under the Silver Purchase Act. From 19 February to 4 March 1935, the ESF through its agents bought 1.4 million ounces of silver in London at about 25 pence per ounce. From 18 February to 10 June 1935 it also transferred $3.63 million in sterling to the treasurer for the purchase of silver under the Silver Purchase Act.

In the week of 4 March the ESF took delivery of 2 million ounces of silver from the Central Bank of China. This was part of a purchase of 10 million ounces at about 54 cents an ounce that the Chase National Bank had negotiated for the ESF in November 1934 for delivery to the Chase branch in Shanghai. Because of delivery problems, a schedule of partial deliveries in March, April, and May 1935 was set.[41] Under this arrangement the Central Bank could elect to make delivery in London subject to a small reduction in the price it was paid and it did so, with deliveries early in March and early in May. By the end of May, 7.25 million ounces had been delivered, and the balance postponed to September and November 1935.

In all, the ESF conducted four operations in silver in the eight months following the passage of the Silver Purchase Act: (a) between 17 December 1934 and 2 January 1935, it bought 10 million ounces in London on a dollar basis ranging from 53.08 to 54.75 per ounce; (b) it bought 10 million ounces from the Central Bank of China at just over 54 cents per ounce; (c) it bought melted down old silver piastres in Saigon, Indochina; (d) it bought in London on a sterling basis, while supporting sterling, 7.2 million ounces at prices just under 25 pence per ounce.

In the course of the four ESF purchases the price per ounce of silver rose from 45 cents in June 1934 close to 55 cents a year later.

After 18 February 1935 the world price of silver rose rapidly as speculators entered the market in the expectation that the ESF would purchase at increasing prices. As market prices rose, the Treasury purchase price of 64.5 cents per ounce of newly mined domestic silver was clearly out of line. On 10 April the domestic price at which the United States bought silver was raised to 71.1 cents by presidential proclamation. By 26 April the world price reached 81 cents. The domestic price again was raised, this time to 77.57 cents.

The world price in London in fact was a price that the Treasury alone set as it was the only buyer. When it stopped buying, the price fell. It did not completely withdraw from the market on 26 April but bought moderate amounts of silver through 17 June. Through 9 May it bought on a sterling basis in London by which date it was left with only enough sterling balances to pay for silver purchased in Saigon. Thereafter ESF purchases in London were on a dollar basis at prices that declined from 74.47 to 72.36 per ounce. Its total acquisition in the two and a half months from 29 April was 9 million ounces. This silver was regularly imported to the United States and sold to the treasurer. On 9 July through its agents the ESF bought 350,000 ounces at 67.21 cents per ounce.

In the middle of July 1935 the ESF began accumulating large hoards of silver for its own custody, the purchases in New York at slightly over 65 cents per ounce becoming virtually its exclusive business. It also sold sterling to the Treasury that it had acquired at from $4.96 to $4.98 for purchases under the Silver Purchase Act. From 8 July to 5 December it bought sterling in London for the purchase of about 170 million ounces for its own account. It transferred sterling to the Treasury for the purchase of 28 million more ounces. By September 1935 the ESF held about 126 million ounces.

From 16 July to 10 August 1935 the ESF pegged the silver price at 30 3/16 pence, equivalent at a sterling rate of $4.96 1/4 or 67.33 cents per ounce. The ESF was almost a daily buyer at this price, acquiring 45 million ounces at a cost of $30 million. The FRBNY as the ESF's fiscal agent was given the option in executing these purchases of charging the secretary's special account in dollars or its account with the Bank of England in sterling. The ESF therefore was in the market for sterling and for silver while the designated agents were in the market as well for sterling to pay for silver in London.

At the fixed pence price for silver, great amounts of silver were offered by China in particular from 7 to 10 August. On 12 August the ESF lowered the pence price slightly and on 15 August pegged it at 19 pence per ounce. In the four days from 12 to 15 August the ESF bought 43.75 million ounces at a cost of $25.275 million. The ESF also bought £473.6 million, which it transferred to the treasurer for silver purchases on 12–14 August. This sterling support raised its rate to $4.98 1/4 .

For the rest of August sterling remained at about $4.98, and the pegged London price of silver at 29 pence. The dollar price of silver the ESF bought, which ranged between 65 to 64.9 cents per ounce, was steady until 5 December.

From 15 July to 9 September the ESF bought 136 million ounces, of which only 16 million ounces had been sold to the treasurer. Of the 120 million, 90 million ounces were held in London. Thereafter silver purchases were on a smaller scale, but silver imported from abroad and sold to the treasurer exceeded purchases.

Silver bought after 10 September was priced at 29 3/16 to 15/16 pence and on 11 October the ESF began to buy silver regularly at a pegged 29 15/16 pence price. The ESF bought sterling at $4.91 1/2 to $4.94 for the treasurer to buy silver in London at the pegged price. From 30 October to 6 December the FRBNY was instructed regularly to purchase and transfer to the treasurer sufficient sterling to pay for a specified number of ounces of silver, in all, 12.27 million ounces. The ESF bought 29.275 million ounces through the FRBNY agents for its own account at the pegged price. Its London holdings were all imported by 23 December and sold to the treasurer. By the end of the year, however, the ESF acquired substantial amounts by purchases in China.

In addition to support of the silver market in London, as indicated above, the ESF also acquired silver in the Far East. The first one was the purchase in November 1934 of 10 million ounces from the Central Bank of China at about 54 cents an ounce. The second one was the purchase in May 1935 of 4.66 million ounces of demonetized Indo-Chinese piastres in Saigon, Indochina. The Banque de Paris et des Pays Bas, as agent for the French Indo-Chinese government in Saigon, submitted the offer to sell to the Bankers Trust Company in New York. The piastres were to be delivered onboard the American steamer *Golden Dragon* scheduled to sail for San Francisco on 3 June. On that date the ESF paid for the purchase from its sterling balance in London. We alluded above to the difficulties the Central Bank of China experienced in delivering the 10 million ounces the ESF had purchased, as well as 25 million ounces directly bought by the Treasury. The Central Bank on 24 May offered to deliver the silver to the Chase Bank in Shanghai but not to export it. The Treasury notified the Chase Bank on 22 July that, if it regarded the arrangement as safe, the Treasury would accept the undelivered silver in Shanghai in monthly lots of 500,000 ounces. It also inquired whether the arrangement would lead Chinese officials to express less hostility to the US silver purchase program.[42] The proposed arrangement, however, was not adopted. On 30 September 1935, 2 million ounces of the arrears of the direct Treasury purchase was delivered in London and delivery of 2 million ounces still owed to the ESF was extended to 30 November 1935.

A third ESF Asian purchase was made on 22 August 1935 of 286.9 thousand ounces in Bombay in bar form known as "broken bill smelters." Priced at 24 3/4 pence and shipped to the United States on the American steamer *President Adams*, the cost was paid in sterling from the fund's account at the Bank of England.

China's abandonment of the silver standard in November 1935 led to a changed silver purchase policy of direct purchases by the Treasury wherever available: the entire Mexican 1935 silver production of 76 million ounces at the current New York price; a bid for 25 million ounces to the Central Bank of China freight on board (FOB) American steamer in Shanghai not later than 11 February 1936 at 65.17 cents. The bank could not supply all the silver in fine bars, so the Treasury made a lower bid for bars of lesser fineness shipped to San Francisco but not via Suez or New York. The terms were accepted and another 25 million ounces was bought. The silver was shipped in January 1936.

On 5 December 1935 the ESF discontinued silver purchases at 65 cents per ounce. The London market found no bidders for 25 million ounces on offer. By 20 December the price fell to 51.75 cents in New York and 48.29 in London. The ESF bought 1.25 million ounces in London in January 1936 at prices in the 44–45 cent range. The silver was sold to the treasurer. On 19 October the ESF through its agents bought 2.458 million ounces in the range of 43–44 cents per ounce. Thereafter the ESF operated on a small scale in the silver market. The major ESF silver transactions in 1936 involved use of silver as collateral for its loans to Mexico and China.

The silver purchase program accomplished neither objective of the Silver Purchase Act. It did not achieve a market price equal to the monetary value of $1.29+ or a 1:3 ratio of the monetary stocks of silver to gold. In June 1963 the Act was repealed.

3.5.3   The ESF in the Government Securities Market

Section 10 of the Gold Reserve Act authorized the ESF to use the part of its assets not needed for exchange market intervention to deal in direct obligations of the US government. The proceeds of sales and investments and all earnings and interest were to be paid to the fund for its use. This authorization made it possible for the ESF to influence the state of the government bond market as well as monetary policy if it engaged in open-market operations. These considerations are quite apart from the matter of whether intervention in the foreign exchanges had an impact on the domestic credit structure.

With respect to the power of the Treasury to conduct open-market operations in government bonds through the ESF, Secretary Morgenthau in hearings before the Senate Committee on Banking and Currency in June 1941 held that the power should not be lodged exclusively with the Federal Reserve but there was no conflict between the Treasury and the Federal Reserve. But he explicitly stated that the ESF bought and held government securities only as earning assets (US Senate 1941, 20–21). Initially, the ESF bought government bonds from other government agencies that sought to sell them. Shortly after its establishment the ESF bought $19.5 million of 2 percent consols (held to secure the notes of insolvent national banks) from the comptroller of the currency. The ESF drew on its account with the treasurer to pay for the purchase. On 18 May 1934 the FRBNY for the ESF bought $10 million Treasury bonds issued to secure the circulation of insolvent banks. This purchase was paid for by drawing on the secretary's special account with the FRBNY.

On 21 and 22 May the ESF bought $5 million treasuries in the open market through the FRBNY. On 23 May the secretary bought directly for the ESF $2.815 million of various Treasury issues offered by the Farm Credit Association. In total between 18 and 23 May $13 million in Treasury bonds were kept off the market by ESF purchases from government agencies. In addition, through the FRBNY the fund bought $5 million in the market. These transactions may account for the comment by Brown (League of Nations 1944, 160), "It is probable that it did on at least one occasion offer support to the government bond market."

By the end of 1934 the ESF had bought $44.5 million par value of government securities, all but $5 million from other government agencies. On 11 January 1935 the FRBNY was instructed to sell all the securities held by the ESF except for 2 percent consols and Panama Canal bonds. The Treasury bond market then was firm and the ESF made a profit on the sale. ESF government securities assets from 1934 to 1961 ranged between $10 and $60 million.[43]

3.6   Conclusion

The ESF is an arm of the Treasury Department. Sometimes during the ESF's formative years the Treasury chose to conduct the varied operations it was responsible for through its singular agency, and other times reserved for itself the execution of similar operations. What determined the decision is not obvious to us.

The chapter covered many aspects of the ESF from its establishment, its similarities to and differences from the British EEA, the ESF mission, intervention before and after the Tripartite Agreement, ESF nonintervention activities as a lender to mainly Third World foreign governments, as the purchaser of silver at home and abroad in fulfillment of the June 1934 Silver Purchase Act, and as an investor in the government securities market.

We limit our attention in this concluding section to official foreign exchange market activities, the central concern of this book, whether conducted by the ESF or the Treasury, covering three related topics: (a) What were the objectives of US policymakers in a world divided between a floating exchange rate for sterling, controlled exchanges in central European countries, and a rear guard of gold standard adherents? Whose interests were promoted by US forays into the foreign exchange market? (section 3.6.1); (b) Why were exchange rates emphasized as the means of achieving expanded trade rather than policies to remove barriers to trade? (section 3.6.2); (c) What was US monetary policy during the period covered by chapter 3, and did intervention affect monetary policy? (section 3.6.3)

3.6.1 Objectives of Intervention and Were They Successful?

The initial motive for intervention was to imitate the British invention of its EEA, believed by the Roosevelt administration to be depressing the exchange value of sterling at the expense of American foreign trade. By contrast, the attitude to currencies of gold standard countries was supportive, selling them gold and buying their currencies when weak, providing them with dollars when needed.

Suspicion that Britain was an adversary with respect to exchange rate policy probably persisted even when the Treasury in 1935 first persuaded the Bank of England to buy gold on its behalf in the London gold market at a price the Treasury set, an arrangement that was renewed until the outbreak of the Second World War. The price did not vary in the intervening years until war risks forced changes. Originally the Treasury believed the price it set would produce a profit to arbitrageurs equivalent to what shipping the gold to New York and selling it there would have yielded, and hence obviated the need for them to ship gold. Eventually, the standing order by the Treasury to the Bank of England to buy gold on its behalf had less to do with checking the profit incentive of arbitrageurs to ship gold to New York. Instead, it became the means for the orderly transfer of gold to the Treasury from the London entrepot for the enlarged output of international gold mines. The gold would in any case have poured into the Treasury since it offered a fixed price of $35 an ounce to all sellers, including gold hoarders (who sought a safe haven as war neared). But for the standing offer, the market, not the Treasury would have determined the rate of inflow.

Neither before nor after the Tripartite Agreement was the fact of misalignment of currencies recognized. No effort was made in all the flurry of intervention to address the fundamental exchange rate problem, revealed by differences in domestic government spending, taxes, labor market policies, inflation, and monetary policy. The Tripartite Agreement was not a solution since it simply preserved the preexisting misalignment despite devaluations of the gold bloc currencies. Intervention by the ESF and each of the countries the ESF dealt with, even if it alleviated an immediate problem, did not contribute to improved economic or trade stability.

3.6.2   If Expanded Trade Was Sought, Why Not Trade Liberalization rather than Exchange Rate Forays?

If expanded foreign trade was an objective of exchange rate policy, it would be useful to know whether it had such an effect and, whether or not it did, the response of foreign trade to the contemporaneous reduction in trade barriers. Unfortunately, there are no quantitative measures of the contribution of either factor.

The United States was the target of higher foreign trade barriers imposed by countries worldwide experiencing the depression from 1929 to 1933, possibly in retaliation for the Smoot-Hawley Tariff. In March 1934, to increase American exports and also imports, the president asked Congress to pass legislation authorizing him to reduce US tariffs in trade agreements not requiring congressional approval. The result was the Reciprocal Trade Agreements Act passed as an amendment to the Smoot-Hawley Tariff Act. Congress also endorsed unconditional most favored nation clauses that automatically extended to other countries a tariff reduction negotiated with one country. By 1936 trade agreements had been reached with three countries only: Canada (the largest of America's trading partners), France, and the Netherlands. Britain, at first, was cool to the idea of a trade agreement. Since its exports to the United States constituted just 6 percent of its total exports, although it was America's second largest trading partner, Britain saw no advantage in signing an agreement until war loomed, when it reconsidered. It was finally signed in 1938, but lasted only until August 1939, when Britain declared war. Irwin (1997) reported that the agreements made only a modest contribution to trade recovery during 1934–39, although trade may have shifted to the few countries with trade agreements. Net exports in any case had a minor effect on real economic growth. So if boosting foreign trade was the driving force behind both trade liberalization and intervention, one must conclude that neither served that purpose.

3.6.3   US Monetary and Intervention Policies

We have found no evidence that the issue of the relation of intervention policy to monetary policy was raised before or after the ESF was established. This statement also applies to the subsequent Bretton Woods period predating the Federal Reserve's decision to intervene on its own account. When the Treasury inaugurated the program of gold sterilization in December 1936 to offset the increase in the monetary base that its gold purchases produced, it did so without recognition of the fact that intervention purchases of foreign currencies increased the base, and sales of foreign currencies reduced it. Central banks engaged in foreign exchange market intervention since the demise of Bretton Woods routinely sterilize their operations. The growth of the monetary base before December 1936, thanks to gold and silver purchases and intervention, was welcomed by the Treasury for raising the price level. To sterilize this effect would have been deemed obtuse.

United States monetary policy following the Great Depression was marked by Federal Reserve passivity from 1933 to 1941, during which it kept its bond portfolio unchanged. It was gold purchases by the Treasury, as already noted, that was correlated with movements in the monetary base. Relative to the size of gold inflows, the amounts of purchases and sales of foreign currencies by the ESF and Treasury were minor.

From 1941 to 1947 the Federal Reserve pegged the price of government securities, maintaining a pattern of rates of different maturities by buying or selling any amounts offered or demanded at these rates. The only difference in 1946–47 was that the short-term rate was raised slightly with no change in long-term rates.

In 1951 the Federal Reserve was released by the Federal Reserve–Treasury Accord from its commitment to peg government bond prices, but it was not until 1953 that it actually did so, largely in response to an inflationary threat unleashed by the Korean War. The introduction of the Bretton Woods system in 1946 did not influence domestic monetary policy in the United States. That changed in 1961 at the conclusion of the period covered by this chapter.

4

US Intervention during the Bretton Woods Era, 1962–1973

There is little evidence . . . of any systematic effort by the
Federal Reserve to conduct monetary policy in a manner
consistent with the requirements of a fixed exchange rate system. And, there is no evidence that any of the administrations
objected to this neglect.
—Allan H. Meltzer (1991, 55)

4.1 Introduction

The Bretton Woods fixed-exchange-rate system attempted to maintain
par values and promoted free cross-border financial flows while still allowing countries to promote domestic macroeconomic objectives, notably full
employment. It hoped to do so by allowing countries to alter parities in the
face of fundamental disequilibria and to temporarily impose restraints on
financial flows. Whether such a system ever offered a long-term, viable solution to the fundamental trilemma of international finance seems unlikely,
but more immediate flaws shortened whatever longevity Bretton Woods may
have had.

By the early 1960s, as Bretton Woods became fully functional, the amount
of US dollar claims held abroad began to exceed the US government's stock
of gold. This situation implied that the United States could not fully keep
its pledge to convert dollars into gold at the official price and raised fears of
a dollar devaluation. These dollars, once necessary to maintain the system,
were becoming a source of instability. By the late 1960s, a rising US inflation
rate and speculative flows in anticipation of cross exchange-rate adjustments were adding even more unwanted dollars to many foreign central-
bank portfolios.

Hoping to neutralize the growing speculative activity, the US Treasury
began intervening in the foreign exchange market in March 1961. A year
later, the Federal Reserve also began foreign-exchange-market operations
primarily aimed at forestalling foreign central-bank claims on the US gold
stock. These operations were stopgap, which seemed appropriate in the early
1960s. United States administrations blamed transitional factors, largely
associated with the postwar global recovery and military needs, for much

of the pressure on the US balance of payments, so mechanisms designed to buy time for an inevitable adjustment seemed suitable.

By the late 1960s, however, US inflation aggravated the structural weaknesses of Bretton Woods. Increasingly the situation appeared to be a dollar problem. Within the Bretton Woods framework, either the United States had to forgo its domestic growth and employment goals or the other developed countries had to sacrifice their inflation objectives. Ultimately, elected officials were unwilling to do so and jettisoned the fixed-parity framework. The United States closed its gold window in August 1971, and generalized floating commenced in March 1973. As a solution to the fundamental trilemma, Bretton Woods failed.

The US foreign-exchange operations between 1961 and 1973 were paradoxically both a short-term success and a long-term failure. By raising the costs of speculation and by providing cover for unwanted, temporary, and ultimately reversible dollar flows, these operations forestalled US gold losses and boosted credibility in the Bretton Woods system, but to the extent that these operations substituted for more fundamental adjustments, they only postponed and heightened the inevitable collapse of Bretton Woods. In addition, the institutional arrangements girding these foreign-exchange operations raised important issues about the Federal Reserve's independence, which would often resurface over the next twenty-five years or so.

4.2   Bretton Woods: Prospects and Problems

The officials who signed the International Monetary Fund (IMF) *Articles of Agreement* at Bretton Woods, New Hampshire, in July 1944 envisioned an international financial system based on close cooperation that would foster stability, promote full employment, and prevent a return to the beggar-thy-neighbor policies of the early 1930s.[1] Under the agreement, the United States pegged the dollar to gold at $35 per ounce and pledged to buy and sell the metal freely at this price. Other nations established parities for their currencies relative to the dollar and were obliged to keep their exchange rates within a 1 percent band around the central value through foreign-exchange interventions, restraints on financial flows, and presumably the adoption of compatible macroeconomic policies.[2] When faced with a transitory balance-of-payments problem, a country with insufficient reserves to finance its intervention could borrow from the IMF instead of quickly instituting deflationary macroeconomic programs. The ability to borrow reserves would also lessen the deficit country's incentive to impose trade restraints or exchange controls on current-account transactions.

Exchange rates were not immutable under the Bretton Woods system. After IMF consultation and approval, countries facing a "fundamental disequilibrium" in their balance of payments could adjust their parities. In principle, the IMF could also insist that the country adopt macroeconomic policies consistent with any exchange-rate realignment, but the IMF lacked a credible enforcement mechanism. Deficit countries, which felt pressures to adjust more immediately than surplus countries, postponed devaluation to avoid the stigma—one of "failed economic policies"—that devaluation carried.

Although the Bretton Woods system began operating in 1946, European currencies remained inconvertible for current-account transactions until late 1958, and the Japanese yen stayed similarly inconvertible until 1964. Initially, these war-ravaged countries maintained inconvertible currencies as a means of limiting their current-account deficits. Most lacked sufficient international reserves to sustain growing deficits for long, even after allowing for IMF credits. In 1949, the situation compelled many European countries to devalue their currencies relative to the dollar. France devalued in 1957 and again as late as 1959.[3]

During the 1950s, however, the international position of the war-torn industrialized countries greatly improved. Foreign productivity and competitiveness recovered. Government grants and long-term financial outflows from the United States helped the recovery process. The resulting US balance-of-payments deficits provided a source of much needed international reserves to accommodate expanding international trade. A general quota increase in 1959 also augmented IMF funds that were available for temporary balance-of-payments assistance. By the late 1950s, more than a decade after its beginning, the Bretton Woods exchange-rate system became fully functional.

At about the same time, however, markets and central banks were quickly losing confidence in the viability of the official dollar gold price, the keystone of the entire Bretton Woods structure. Two interrelated developments proved particularly problematic: Triffin's paradox, which describes a fundamental defect in gold-exchange standards like Bretton Woods, and an accelerating US inflation rate after 1965. A third factor, which acquired importance only in conjunction with the previous two, stemmed from inevitable cross-rate adjustment problems among participating countries other than the United States. We describe each of these factors in turn.

4.2.1   Triffin's Paradox

The framers of Bretton Woods set the official price of gold at $35 per ounce, the same price that the US Gold Reserve Act of 1934 had established. Because of inflation during World War II and shortly thereafter, this official price became too low in real terms to induce sufficient gold production for expanding reserve needs (see Bordo 1993; James 1996; Meltzer 1991). By the early 1950s, the real price of gold was only half of its 1934 value (see figure 4.1).[4] Between 1948 and 1958, the free world's gold stock increased only 16 percent while its imports rose 68 percent (Triffin 1960, table 14, 72–73).

The United States, as noted, provided needed liquidity by running per-

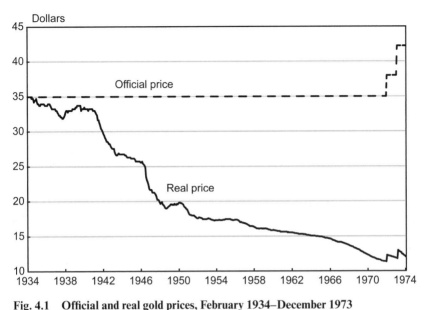

Fig. 4.1   Official and real gold prices, February 1934–December 1973

Note: Real gold price constructed with US Consumer Price Index (CPI) from the US Bureau of Labor Statistics.

sistent balance-of-payments deficits. Between 1950 and 1957, these deficits averaged $1.3 billion per year, as government grants, private remittances, and long-term financial outflows typically exceeded surpluses elsewhere in the accounts (figure 4.2).[5] Neither the United States nor the international financial community seemed to view these deficits with much concern because they stemmed from postwar redevelopment efforts and from the provision of military security. Without the international reserves that these deficits provided, the postwar recovery of global trade and world economic activity would have proceeded more slowly, because countries facing even temporary balance-of-payments deficits would quickly need to deflate, devalue, or impose disruptive trade and financial restraints.

By the early 1960s, however, the total external dollar liabilities associated with the persistent US balance-of-payments deficits began to exceed the US gold stock, implying that the United States could not completely fulfill its obligation to sell gold at the official price (see figure 4.3).[6] The very act of providing needed liquidity was itself creating uncertainty about the long-term viability of the parity structure. This was Triffin's paradox (Triffin, 1960). At the time, however, few interpreted the situation as inevitably leading to the demise of the Bretton Woods system.[7]

An outflow of gold accompanied the US balance-of-payments deficits during the 1950s, but it seemed a reasonable reversal of the substantial—

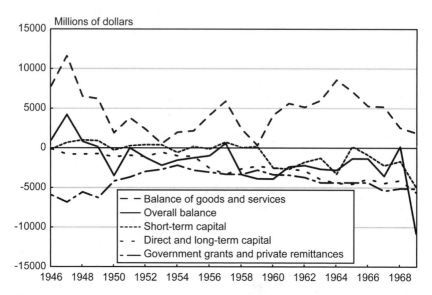

Fig. 4.2   US balance of payments trends, 1946–1969

Note: Data are from the US Department of Commerce.

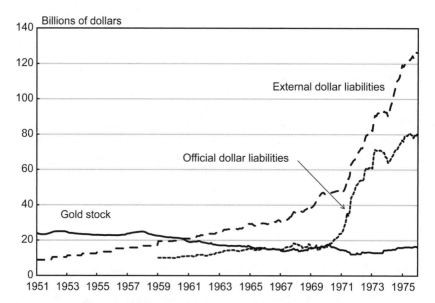

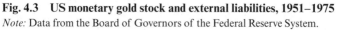

Fig. 4.3   US monetary gold stock and external liabilities, 1951–1975

Note: Data from the Board of Governors of the Federal Reserve System.

Fig. 4.4   US monetary gold stock, 1951–1975
Note: Data are from the Board of Governors of the Federal Reserve System.

largely safe-haven—gold acquisitions that the United States experienced in the 1930s and 1940s. The United States, which held 60 percent of the world's gold reserves in 1950, lost only $213 million worth of gold on average each year between 1950 and 1957 (see figure 4.4).[8] During that time, foreign countries increased their gold reserves mainly out of free-world gold production and through small purchases from the Soviet Union. In addition, the IMF sold the United States $800 million worth of gold between 1951 and 1957 (Board of Governors 1963, 422).

Between 1958 and 1960, however, US balance-of-payments deficits widened to $3.7 billion per year on average as surpluses on US goods and services trade narrowed slightly and as long-term financial outflows increased sharply. The most disturbing aspect of the expanding US balance-of-payments deficits, however, occurred with respect to short-term financial flows beginning in 1960. Heretofore, the United States had typically experienced small short-term financial inflows (including unrecorded items), but in 1960 the country witnessed a large outflow of nearly $2.5 billion. Although US balance-of-payments deficits narrowed somewhat in 1961 and 1962, substantial outflows of short-term financial capital, often motivated by exchange-rate concerns, generally persisted.

Between 1958 and 1962, the average US gold loss increased sixfold to nearly $1.4 billion per year. The US gold stock declined by $6.8 billion or 30 percent as foreign countries converted dollar reserves into gold.[9] The heavy gold losses would not have been so disturbing to US policymakers if they had not been accompanied by evidence of a run on the dollar. Foreign monetary authorities were not only converting new acquisitions of dollars into gold, but they were also converting—or planning to convert—a substantial portion of their existing dollar balances (FOMC *Minutes*, 10 January 1961, 10).

Between 1957 and 1962, the proportion of international reserves held in gold by noncommunist countries increased from 45 percent to 49 percent (Board of Governors 1963, 423). European countries, particularly France, Italy, and Germany, accounted for almost all of this gain; most other countries kept the share of their gold reserves fairly constant (Board of Governors 1963, 424). Despite the accelerated gold losses, the United States still held $16 billion worth of gold reserves in 1962, approximately two-fifths of the world's gold stock.[10]

On 20 October 1960, the price of gold on the London market shot above the official US gold price to $40 per ounce, as private demand for gold reached record levels. This was a critical juncture in the Bretton Woods era. Given the inelastic supply of gold at the official price, Bretton Woods was unworkable without dollar reserves, but with additional dollar reserves, Bretton Woods became increasing unstable. Henceforth, as we will document, both gold and foreign-exchange markets would remain vulnerable to speculative pressures as suggested by Triffin's paradox.

4.2.2   US Inflation after 1965

The corrosive inevitabilities that Triffin explained became substantially worse after 1965 as US inflation accelerated. Inflation in the United States rose from around 1 percent in late 1964 to 6 percent in mid-1970. Inflation then moderated, following a recession that year, to 4.6 percent in August 1971, when President Nixon ended convertibility, and then to a low of 2.7 percent in June 1972. Thereafter, inflation rose again, reaching 4.6 percent in March 1973 when Bretton Woods collapsed. Inflation in the United States put additional unwanted dollars in the coffers of foreign central banks that intervened to prevent their currencies from appreciating against the dollar.[11] In that way, inflation aggravated Triffin's paradox and weakened Bretton Woods. Eventually, a loss of credibility in US monetary policy and a fear of importing US inflation would be a key factor in the demise of the Bretton Woods system.

Ideally, defining the dollar in terms of gold should have constrained inflation in the United States. A higher inflation rate could worsen the US balance of payments and cause further gold losses, which eventually would undermine the official gold price. Before 1958, Bretton Woods never posed a significant restraint on US monetary policy because of the growing global demand for dollar reserves and the large US gold stock. In the first half of the 1960s, by contrast, the Bretton Woods system had some influence on

US monetary-policy decisions.[12] Thereafter, however, its influence weakened. Balance-of-payments considerations still arose within the FOMC, and during crisis periods, such as the devaluation of the British pound in 1967, they directly shaped US monetary policy. But, once the Treasury (with the Federal Reserve's help) took an active role in the area of emerging international-finance problems, the FOMC saw the balance of payments as primarily a Treasury concern and focused on domestic objectives (see Bordo and Eichengreen 2013).

While the weakening of the Bretton Woods constraint freed the Federal Reserve to pursue domestic economic objectives, it does not explain why the Federal Reserve was unable to maintain price stability. Economists have offered various explanations, which we discuss in chapter 5. Basically, however, inflation resulted because policymakers and many academic economists adopted an economic framework that deemphasized the role of money in the inflation process (see Hetzel 2008; Meltzer 2005, 2009a). For the most part, money was to support fiscal policies, which led in the management of aggregate demand. Moreover, many policymakers saw unemployment as a more critical social problem than inflation and were willing to accept higher inflation if it lowered the unemployment rate. Whatever the underlying source, US inflation worsened Triffin's paradox and accelerated the demise of Bretton Woods.

4.2.3   Cross-Rate Adjustment Problems

A third shortcoming of the Bretton Woods system that aggravated Triffin's paradox arose because cross exchange rates did not quickly adjust to balance-of-payments disequilibria. When both Germany and the United Kingdom pegged to the dollar, the mark-pound cross rate was also fixed. Although cross-rate-adjustment problems arose from economic developments within specific foreign countries, they contributed to the dollar's difficulties because of the dollar's role as the key international reserve and vehicle currency. Deficit countries defended their pegs by selling US dollars, while surplus countries defended their pegs by buying dollars. Financial funds flowed from deficit countries to surplus countries through dollars, adding to the large, often unwanted, dollar positions of surplus countries and creating inflationary pressures in these countries. Speculators (or their banks) fearing a pound devaluation, for example, would first sell pounds for dollars and then dollars for a strong currency, like Swiss francs or German marks. Dollars, not pounds, flowed into these countries. Many surplus countries, like Switzerland, strictly limited the ratio of dollar reserves to gold reserves in their portfolios and would sell unwanted dollars to the United States. The cross-rate-adjustment problem, notably among the United Kingdom, Germany, and France created uncertainty about the *entire* Bretton Woods parity structure, as we illustrate below.

4.3   The Policy Dilemma

If the emerging US balance-of-payments problems were indeed evidence of a fundamental disequilibrium, the United States had to undertake a real dollar depreciation.[13] Hemmed in by the perception of persistently weak domestic demand, constrained by the dollar's unique role in the Bretton Woods system, and still uncertain about the true underlying nature of recent balance-of-payments developments, none of the standard methods for achieving a real dollar depreciation seemed viable or even appropriate to US policymakers. Instead, policymakers in the early 1960s opted for a number of stopgap policies, of which exchange-market intervention became the most enduring.

The Eisenhower and Kennedy administrations attributed the worsening US balance-of-payments position between 1957 and 1962 to transitory factors stemming from US military and economic aid commitments, recent cyclical developments, and the reemergence of Western Europe and Japan as global competitors. In response to these developments, the United States undertook a series of policy initiatives to hasten adjustment in the US trade and long-term financial accounts and to improve the operation of the international financial system. These initiatives, however, suggest that US policymakers did not view the current situation as critical or enduring.

United States policymakers also appreciated that with the maturation of the Bretton Woods system—economic recovery abroad, growing currency convertibility, and an adequate pool of liquidity—short-term financial flows could henceforth be more sensitive to international interest-rate differentials and exchange-rate uncertainty. They seemed to believe, however, that once the transitory adjustments to the US trade and long-term financial accounts were complete, credibility in the dollar would strengthen. After all, reserve gains in France and Italy since 1957 illustrated how quickly countries' international positions could change (Board of Governors 1963, 421–28). Strengthened credibility in the dollar would lessen the problem of short-term financial flows.

Even if US policymakers had fleetingly glimpsed emerging events as evidence that the US balance-of-payments position was fundamentally unsustainable, they were unwilling to make the appropriate policy adjustments in the early 1960s. A fundamental disequilibrium would imply that the dollar was overvalued on a real basis and that a real depreciation was necessary to restore equilibrium to the US balance of payments. The United States could achieve a real depreciation only through one, or some combination, of four mechanisms: a nominal dollar devaluation, a deflation in the United States, an inflation in the rest of the world, or a general revaluation of foreign currencies. Whereas US policymakers might have welcomed a higher rate of inflation abroad, and whereas they actively encouraged the revaluation of currencies in surplus countries, they were unwilling to alter the official gold price or to dampen aggregate demand in the United States for balance-of-payments purposes.[14]

A one-time nominal dollar devaluation was simply out of the question. By imposing wealth losses on central banks and individuals that held open positions in US dollars, any dollar devaluation could forever threaten the reserve-currency status of the US dollar. Moreover, short-term financial outflows might actually increase if a one-time devaluation proved insufficient for balance-of-payments adjustment, or if other countries simultaneously devalued their currencies against the dollar. The United States also opposed an increase in the gold price because it would specifically benefit South Africa and the Soviet Union, the two major gold producers (Task Force 1990b, Paper no. 3, 10). For these reasons, the Kennedy administration went to considerable lengths to convince markets of its commitment to the official gold price.

Similarly, administration and Federal Reserve policymakers were unwilling to dampen aggregate demand for balance-of-payments purposes. The president of the Federal Reserve Bank of Atlanta, Malcolm Bryan, seems to have typified the view, at least as it prevailed among many Federal Reserve policymakers:

> the last time the [Federal Reserve] System reacted in its policy decisions primarily because of foreign developments was . . . in 1931. At that time, with unemployment constantly increasing and with every element in the domestic economy calling for ease, the System responded by tightening in order to protect the gold supply. (FOMC *Minutes*, 10 January 1961, 41)

He, like many other policymakers, feared a replay of the past. The United States had experienced back-to-back recessions from the third quarter of 1957 through the first quarter of 1958, and again from the second quarter of 1960 through the first quarter of 1961. These cost the Republicans the election in 1960. Kennedy pledged to "get the country moving again." The unemployment rate remained stubbornly high, and President Kennedy's Council of Economic Advisors expected US economic activity to remain below its potential level through 1963. Consequently, policymakers would not undertake deflationary macroeconomic programs.

While the overall thrust of macroeconomic policy was to promote the growth of aggregate demand, international considerations did exert some limited influence on the contours of both fiscal and monetary policies in the early 1960s. Under the Kennedy administration, the federal budget shifted from a surplus of $0.3 billion in 1960 to deficits of $3.4 billion in 1961, $7.2 billion in 1962, and $4.8 billion in 1963.[15] In 1962, the administration introduced an investment tax credit and liberalized depreciation allowances primarily to spur aggregate demand, but the administration also thought that these tax cuts could improve the country's international competitiveness.

For its part, the Federal Open Market Committee (FOMC) eased policy in

1960, initially by cutting the official discount rate, then by injecting reserves through open-market operations and by allowing banks to count vault cash as reserves. Thereafter, the committee held course through 1963—sometimes under pressure from the Kennedy administration—and then tacked slowly in the other direction through 1965 (figure 4.5). In 107 policy decisions between the 13 September 1960 and the 1 November 1966 FOMC meetings, the committee voted ninety-two times to maintain the current stance of policy.[16] On fifteen occasions over this period, the FOMC voted for additional restraint. Most of the decisions to tighten were undertaken for a mixture of domestic and international considerations, with the domestic situation undoubtedly holding more weight.[17] On only four occasions— three in 1963 and one in late 1964—did the committee tighten policy solely for international considerations. During the early 1960s, domestic considerations usually motivated committee member dissents for a looser policy, while international consideration usually motivated committee member dissents for a tighter policy. Nevertheless, monetary policy seemed relatively accommodative until late 1964 and 1965 (see figure 4.6).

Short-term capital outflows did affect *how* the Federal Reserve conducted monetary policy in the early 1960s, even if they did not alter the overall thrust of monetary policy very much. Since April 1953, except for brief periods of extreme market disorder, as in 1955 and 1958, the Federal Reserve had operated under a "bills only" doctrine; that is, the Federal Reserve con-

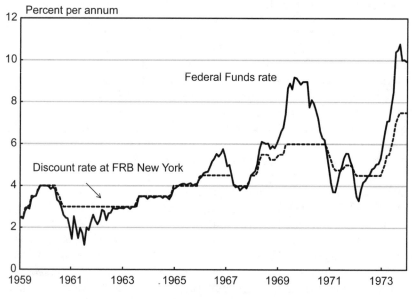

Fig. 4.5   Federal Reserve policy rates, 1959–1973
Note: Data are from the Federal Reserve System.

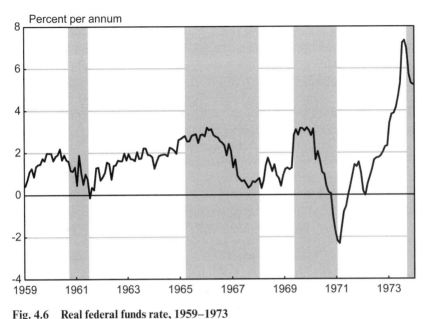

Fig. 4.6   Real federal funds rate, 1959–1973
Notes: The real federal funds rate equals the nominal federal funds rate less the year-to-year percent change in the core CPI. Shaded areas are recessions. Data are from the Federal Reserve System, the Bureau of Labor Statistics, and National Bureau of Economic Research.

fined open-market operations to the very short end of the market for US Treasury securities. Faced with a potential conflict between domestic and balance-of-payments objectives, the Federal Reserve, and later the Kennedy administration, undertook a program intended to promote domestic investment and economic growth through lower long-term interest rates and to discourage short-term financial outflows through higher short-term interest rates (Martin, 1961).[18] After October 1960, the Federal Reserve began to purchase longer-term securities, while sometimes selling Treasury bills. In addition, the Treasury began issuing more short-term securities, and government trust funds increased the portion of long-term securities in their portfolios (Yeager 1966, 448). In this way, policymakers hoped to twist the yield curve for balance-of-payments purposes while maintaining an overall accommodative policy stance.

Although US policymakers were unwilling to devalue the dollar or reduce US aggregate demand for balance-of-payments purposes, they instituted a number of ad hoc policies designed to improve the country's competitive position, and thereby improve the US balance of payments. As noted, the Eisenhower and Kennedy administrations attributed postwar balance-of-payments deficits in large part to the United States' unusual military-assistance and economic-development programs. Cutting these programs could have had severe political and military consequences in the antagonistic Cold War environment (Gavin 2004). To mitigate their effects on the US balance of payments, the Kennedy administration, often using the threat of troop redeployment, extended the requirements—initially developed under the Eisenhower administration—that tied military and development assistance to purchases of US goods and services (Gavin 2004). The United States also encouraged countries to hasten the repayment of their war debts and to contribute aid to developing nations.

After European currencies became convertible in 1958, US traded goods came under more intense competitive pressures. In response, the Eisenhower and Kennedy administrations lobbied for the removal of discriminatory trade practices, which foreign countries leveled primarily against the United States. The United States had long tolerated these restraints both as means of promoting European and Japanese development and as a way of conserving international reserves. The Kennedy administration also undertook various efforts to promote exports and reduce the duty-free allowance for US tourists. In 1961, the Kennedy administration revised the depreciation schedule, hoping to raise US manufacturing productivity, improve international competitiveness, and promote exports.

While undertaking policy initiatives to improve the United States' international competitive position, policymakers here and abroad attempted to shore up Bretton Woods institutions against short-term capital flight and reserve losses, as well as fostering closer cooperation among the major developed countries. A major initiative was the General Arrangements to Borrow. With short-term financial flows larger, more mobile, and increasingly driven by uncertainties about exchange rates, countries—notably the United States and the United Kingdom—might need to borrow foreign exchange reserves to quell temporary balance-of-payments problems. Under existing quota arrangements, however, the IMF did not have sufficient foreign exchange to supply some needed currencies. In late 1962, the major developed countries instituted a new credit mechanism, the General Arrangements to Borrow, within the IMF. These countries collectively pledged $6 billion (equivalent) of their currencies to meet borrowing requests through the IMF (James 1996, 161–65).

To address the strong private demand for gold, President Eisenhower issued an order in January 1961 forbidding US residents from holding gold abroad. More importantly, in 1961 the United States, the United Kingdom, and six continental European countries formed the Gold Pool to keep the London price of gold in line with the official price. (We discuss the Gold Pool in more detail below.)

In 1963, the United States also attempted to trim long-term financial outflows through an Interest Equalization Tax. Initially, the administration levied a 1 percent tax on interest earnings from US-held foreign bonds. In 1965, the tax was broadened to include US bank loans to foreigners with a maturity of one year or more. The tax exempted Canada and developing countries. At this time, the Commerce Department initiated a voluntary program to encourage multinationals to borrow abroad. By 1967, the administration raised the Interest Equalization Tax to 2 percent (see Meltzer 1991, 52). In 1965, the Federal Reserve System also instituted a Voluntary Foreign Credit Restrain Program, designed to reduce US financial institutions' foreign lending and investing.

All of these initiatives attempted to address important aspects of the US balance-of-payments problem. None, however, was capable of immediately offsetting speculative financial flows, which could create contagion problems and increase dollar balances in central banks already holding excess dollars. To address these short-term speculative financial flows and to protect the US gold stock, the Treasury began intervening in 1961.

4.4   The US Treasury's Decision to Intervene

In March 1961, the Exchange Stabilization Fund (ESF), with the Federal Reserve Bank of New York acting as its agent, began to intervene in the foreign exchange market for the first time since 1939.[19] Increased speculative flows prompted the action. The Treasury's operations consisted primarily of forward sales of continental currencies, which were designed to reduce forward premia on these currencies.[20] Forward premia served as barometers of market confidence in the dollar and provided a strong incentive for financial flows when they exceeded levels consistent with the existing interest-rate differential.

Forward transactions offered the Treasury a number of advantages over spot trades. For one thing, the Treasury, which had only $336 million in assets available for intervention in mid-1961, did not need to spend scarce foreign-currency reserves until the contract's maturity date, and then only if the position incurred a loss.[21] A loss, however, was unlikely. Since the ESF sold foreign currencies forward at known premia over the official spot rates, the United States could only incur a substantial loss if the foreign currencies were revalued.[22] Absent a revaluation, the ESF could buy the foreign currencies needed to repay the forward at the official price. The ESF typically covered its forward sales against a possible revaluation.

The Treasury also undertook some limited spot transactions. These were largely experimental, designed to learn how the market operated and to gauge the impact of such operations on speculative activity. In addition, the Treasury also undertook some unusual gold swaps, which temporarily improved the mix of reserve assets on foreign balance sheets.

4.4.1   German Mark Interventions

On 6 and 7 March 1961, Germany and the Netherlands, respectively, revalued their currencies by approximately 5 percent, a smaller amount than market participants anticipated. Within days, funds flowed out of British sterling and, to a lesser extent, out of dollars and into continental currencies, especially German marks and Swiss francs. In response, British authorities sold dollars to defend the pound. The speculative attack and Britain's defensive dollar sales inflated dollar holdings at continental central banks and threatened to push their dollar-to-gold reserve ratios above acceptable levels. In addition to adding to the potential demand for US gold reserves, the heavy speculative flows pushed the dollar to a substantial forward discount against many of the European currencies, which tended only to reinforce expectations of further revaluations. Moreover, the limited availability of forward cover induced many market participants with dollar receivables to borrow dollars in New York or in the Eurodollar market and use these funds to buy marks in the spot market (*Bulletin*, September 1962, 1141). This hedging strategy added further to foreign central banks' dollar reserves.

On Monday, 13 March 1961, after consultations with Bundesbank and Federal Reserve officials, the ESF began selling German marks forward in an attempt to reduce the forward premium on marks, which had reached a peak of 4 percent, and hopefully to stabilize exchange-rate fluctuations in both the spot and forward markets. A so-called "parallel" agreement covered the Treasury's risk exposure. Accordingly, the Bundesbank would supply the US Treasury with any marks that it might need to fulfill the forward contracts, and the US Treasury and the Bundesbank would split any profits. The forward sales reached $63 million per week by the second week of the operations and continued at a rate of $30 million to $40 million per week for several weeks thereafter. The operations topped $320 million in mid-June, but then fell off quickly (US Treasury 1962a, 4).

The Treasury also concluded an arrangement with the German government whereby Germany would immediately prepay $100 million of a $587 million debt that was due to the United States in April 1961.[23] Germany paid in marks. Of this amount, the ESF received $50 million equivalent German marks. The ESF used most of it as cover for the forward transactions, but made small intervention sales of German marks in the New York market during June and July to lift the dollar off its floor vis-à-vis the mark. The Treasury coordinated these operations with Bundesbank interventions. The Treasury sold the remaining $50 million worth of German marks from the debt prepayment directly to the Bundesbank for dollars on 1 September 1962, thereby reducing Germany's potential claim on US gold reserves (US Treasury 1962a, 5).

When the Soviets built the Berlin wall in August 1961, a substantial amount of funds quickly moved out of Germany. This reversal of financial flows provided a source for funding the US Treasury's forward commitments which, unlike the "parallel agreement," would not cause the Bundesbank to again acquire additional dollar reserves. By mid-December 1961, the Treasury liquidated all of the forward mark commitments, and although the ESF incurred small losses on its spot transactions, the overall operation accrued a $750 thousand profit (US Treasury 1962a, 5).

The German mark operations convinced US Treasury officials that such cooperative arrangements could provide a "first line of defense" for the dollar. With the US balance-of-payments deficit continuing, further speculative attacks seemed certain. Consequently, the ESF acquired additional German marks from the market when the Berlin crisis temporarily weakened that currency. The ESF made further forward mark sales in late December 1961 when that currency's forward premium again rose above 1 percent against the dollar. By the end of January 1962, the ESF held $55 million worth of German marks, of which $50 million (equivalent) were invested in German Treasury bills. Forward commitments amounted to $10 million worth of marks. Of these, "parallel" agreements with the Bundesbank covered $5.6 million equivalent, and ESF mark holdings covered the remainder (US Treasury 1962a, 6–7). The US Treasury liquidated its forward commitments in German marks by the end of March 1962.

4.4.2   Swiss Franc Interventions

In early 1961, dollar inflows increased liquidity in the Swiss banking system and raised the dollar-to-gold ratio at the Swiss National Bank above its legal limit. Instead of converting the excess dollar reserves immediately into gold with the US Treasury, the Swiss National Bank lent dollars to the Bank of England to finance Britain's pound-stabilization program. The Bank of England, however, was arranging financing through the IMF and intended to liquidate Swiss dollar credits (*Bulletin* September 1962, 1143). The Swiss National Bank (SNB) then sought a mechanism to reduce the excess liquidity in Switzerland stemming from these dollar inflows.

The Swiss National Bank believed that the inflows of funds were temporary and that forward sales of Swiss francs could stem or possibly reverse them by reducing the forward premium on francs. Swiss law, however, prohibited the bank from operating in the forward market. Instead, on 12 July 1961, the ESF began forward sales of Swiss francs. The ESF intended to use $15 million worth of Swiss francs, which it had acquired earlier from the Swiss National Bank, as cover for the forward operation, but the bank also offered additional Swiss francs against Treasury gold sales.

These initial foreign-exchange operations were small and mainly experimental, but after the Berlin Wall was erected, dollar flows into Switzerland increased sharply. The ESF's forward Swiss franc (SF) sales increased substantially to $152.5 million equivalent by the end of November. The Swiss National Bank had earlier provided the US Treasury with a SF 430 million ($100 million) credit line to cover the ESF's forward commitments. To draw on this line, the US Treasury issued $46 million of certificates of indebtedness denominated in Swiss francs in October 1961. This was the first time that the Treasury had issued foreign-currency-denominated debt since

World War I. The Treasury issued the certificates in two lots, at a rate of 1.25 percent with a three-month maturity. The ESF received $15 million worth of Swiss francs from the proceeds to meet Swiss franc forward commitments, and the Treasury's general fund kept the remaining $31 million worth of francs with the Swiss National Bank. The Treasury rolled over one lot of certificates and repaid the other as pressure on the Swiss franc subsided. In addition to these Treasury activities, the Swiss National Bank doubled its dollar working balances to $200 million, and thereby reduced the potential gold drain that the US Treasury faced (US Treasury 1962a, 7–8).

The Treasury viewed the Swiss franc operation, as it did the German mark interventions, as highly successful, contending that without it, the United States would have lost somewhere between $250 million and $400 million in gold reserves (US Treasury 1962a, 8). At the end of January 1962, the Treasury had $146.5 million worth of outstanding Swiss franc forward contracts. Profits on the operation amounted to $450 thousand.

In February 1962, the Swiss franc began to weaken, requiring the Swiss National Bank to support it with dollar sales. To acquire the necessary dollar balances, the Swiss National Bank sold the Treasury $73.5 million in gold and $93.2 million in Swiss francs through May 1962.[24] Part of the Swiss franc purchases ($28.1 million equivalent) were on a swap basis.[25] The Treasury used Swiss franc balances to liquidate forward commitments and the certificates of indebtedness as they matured (*Bulletin*, September 1962, 1145).

4.4.3 Netherlands Guilder Intervention

In September 1961, the US Treasury purchased $15 million worth of Netherlands guilders, most of which it invested in guilder securities. With these funds providing cover, the Treasury undertook $4.9 million (equivalent) in forward sales of guilders through the Netherlands Bank in the Dutch market beginning in January 1962. In February, the Treasury acquired an additional $15 million worth of guilders, raising its total to $30 million, and expanded its forward operations (US Treasury 1962a, 10). Treasury forward guilder sales in January and February 1962 reached $20.8 million (equivalent) (*Desk Report* 1963, B-22). In July 1962, Britain made a large drawing of guilders from the IMF, which it used to buy dollars from the Netherlands Bank. To replenish its dollar reserves, the Netherlands Bank sold $20 million guilders (equivalent) to the Treasury under a temporary swap agreement (*Bulletin*, September 1962, 1145). Hence, the Treasury's operations were more than covered, and any excessive inflow of dollars to the Netherlands had ended.

4.4.4 Italian Lira Interventions

In 1961, strong dollar inflows pushed the Italian lira to its upper parity limit and kindled rumors of a revaluation. As Italy's dollar-to-gold reserve ratio rose, Italian authorities undertook dollar swaps with domestic commercial banks that covered the latter's dollar exposure. (We discuss the mechanics of these market swaps below.) The temporary cover that these swaps provided to the Italian commercial banks encouraged them to hold dollar balances instead of converting them to lira at the Bank of Italy. The transactions could be renewed.

In January 1962, the US Treasury took over $200 million of these swaps, obligating it to deliver lira forward. The Treasury obtained some cover for its commitments through a $150 million (equivalent) credit line with Italian authorities. The Treasury acquired an additional $100 million of these swap obligations in March. In early 1962, the Treasury also undertook some experimental spot lira transactions (US Treasury 1962a, 10–11).

4.4.5 Gold Swaps

In addition to these foreign-currency transactions, the US Treasury undertook a series of three-month gold swaps with the Swiss National Bank and with the Bank of England in 1961. In March, the Treasury sold gold to the SNB for $25 million worth of Swiss francs under an agreement to reverse the transaction on June 30. At maturity, the Treasury rolled the swap over until 29 July 1961, and also undertook a second $25 million gold swap, which it reversed on 13 July 1961. The Treasury undertook a $50 million (equivalent) gold swap with the Bank of England in April 1961, which matured in equal parts in May and July of that year.

The purpose of these gold swaps is not entirely clear. The Treasury reports that: "These gold transactions were undertaken at US initiative and were designed to smooth out random short-run fluctuations in the Treasury's gold stock." (US Treasury 1962a, 11–12). That may be, but another objective—particularly in the Swiss case—may have been to keep the ratio of dollar reserves to gold below levels that may have required these countries to exchange dollars for US gold.

4.5   The Federal Reserve's Decision to Intervene

Both the Treasury and the Federal Reserve System viewed the Treasury's exchange-market interventions in 1961 and early 1962 as unmitigated successes (FOMC *Minutes*, 12 September 1961, 44).[26] The Treasury had acted against short-term speculative movements of funds and easily—and profitably—unwound its positions when those speculative pressures reversed.

The ability of the US Treasury to mount another broader dollar defense, however, was severely limited. By late 1962, the ESF had assets equal to approximately $340 million, but a large portion of this was committed to stabilization agreements with Latin American countries. This left the ESF with a paltry $100 million equivalent in European currencies and only about $20 million to $25 million available for acquiring additional foreign exchange.[27]

The Treasury welcomed and encouraged the Federal Reserve's participation in foreign-exchange-market interventions primarily because it would increase the amount of funds available for such operations.[28] Since March 1961, the Federal Reserve had sharpened its expertise in the area as the agent for the US Treasury and foreign central banks, but the Treasury already had access to the desk's expertise. What the Treasury needed was the Federal Reserve's seemingly boundless capacity to create reserves and to acquire additional foreign exchange.

On 13 February 1962, the FOMC authorized intervention in the foreign-exchange market for the Federal Reserve's own account. By participating with the Treasury, the Federal Reserve hoped to reassert, and possibly extend, its dormant influence in this area. In fact, Chairman Martin may have wanted to bring the entire foreign-exchange operation into the Federal Reserve's domain (FOMC *Minutes*, 6 March 1962, 72). Foreign-exchange transactions closely paralleled and often interacted with domestic monetary-policy operations, so much so that many countries viewed intervention as solely a central-bank function. The Federal Reserve Act did not explicitly preclude such activities, and indeed the Federal Reserve had undertaken foreign-exchange operations in the past. One way or another, US foreign-exchange operations were going forward, and the Federal Reserve wanted to shape their development.

To be sure, support for intervention within the Federal Reserve at the time was not unanimous. The debates at the FOMC meetings in late 1961 and early 1962 raised issues that would resurface periodically over the next thirty-five years, with the exception that as time went on, dissenters became more concerned about the adverse interactions between intervention and monetary policy, and less concerned about its legality than they were in the early 1960s. In any event, a clear majority of FOMC members have always favored Federal Reserve foreign-exchange operations, provided that they did not make the Federal Reserve in any way subservient to the Treasury, that they did not raise the ire of Congress, and—eventually—that they did not interfere with the domestic objectives of monetary policy.

4.5.1   Legal Authority for Federal Reserve Interventions

At their 12 September 1961 meeting, FOMC participants first formally discussed Federal Reserve participation in foreign-exchange operations. Chairman William McChesney Martin, with strong support from the New York Federal Reserve Bank, advocated the central bank's participation. To his mind, there was "no question but that this country was going to be in the business of foreign-exchange operations," and he wanted the Federal Reserve involved either alone, or in conjunction with the US Treasury (FOMC *Minutes*, 12 September 1961, 44).

Martin contended that the public did not distinguish between the Federal Reserve and the US Treasury in foreign-exchange operations. Moreover, congressmen had already asked him informally if the Fed approved of the Treasury's actions, which he interpreted as indicating that the Fed's opinion was important in these matters. To Martin, participating was imperative, even if the Fed's role was very limited. He realized, however, "that the primary direction must come from the Treasury and that everything done by the Federal Reserve must be coordinated with the Treasury." (FOMC *Minutes,* 12 September1961, 49) Martin did not think this threatened the Federal Reserve's independence. He always contended that the Federal Reserve was independent *within* the government and was not independent *of* the government. His distinction implied that the Federal Reserve must coordinate and cooperate with the Treasury as far as possible, and particularly in government actions that did not directly interfere with monetary-policy decisions (see Bremner 2004; Meltzer 2005). Intervention, he believed, was just such an action.

The FOMC's primary concern was Congress, whose opinion about Federal Reserve intervention in the foreign-exchange market had never been unequivocal and firm. In the current climate, if all went smoothly, Congress probably would acquiesce. Congress was aware of the balance-of-payments problem and sympathetic to the policy dilemma that it posed. If the Fed's operations incurred a substantial loss or appeared to interfere with foreign policy, however, the Federal Reserve's relations with Congress could deteriorate. Legislative support for the operations, which Congress never explicitly offered, would have eased the FOMC's concerns. At a minimum, however, the FOMC wanted to be sure that its actions were legal.

The Federal Reserve Act did refer to specific types of foreign-exchange transactions, and at least seven times between 1924 and 1929, the Federal Reserve Bank of New York extended credits to foreign central banks to shore up their reserves in defense of their currencies (Task Force 1990d, Paper no.1, 4–5). In 1925, for example, the Federal Reserve Bank of New York made $200 million worth of gold available to the Bank of England with the understanding that the Bank of England would place proceeds from any gold sales in a sterling investment account for the Federal Reserve Bank of New York (see chapter 2). In 1933, however, Senator Carter Glass, whom many regarded as the father of the Federal Reserve Act, criticized these transactions, indicating that such "stabilization operations" were inconsistent with the original Act. At that time, as discussed below, the Board of Governors took a position that was not inconsistent with Senator Glass's view. In 1934, Congress passed the Gold Reserve Act, establishing the ESF specifically for the purpose of intervening (see chapter 3). But in passing the Gold Reserve Act, did Congress mean to preclude the Federal Reserve from this arena?

In 1961, Howard Hackley, the Board of Governors' general counsel, provided a legal interpretation of the Federal Reserve Act that the FOMC would now adopt (Hackley 1961; Todd 1992).[29] The often-cited "Hackley Memo" argued that various sections of the Act—when considered together—authorized the Federal Reserve System to hold foreign exchange, to intervene in both the spot and forward markets, and to engage in swap transactions with foreign central banks and with the US Treasury.

Section 14 of the Act seemed to be the key. It allowed the Federal Reserve to purchase and sell both spot and forward "cable transfers" in both domestic and foreign markets. Since cable transfers were the standard means of acquiring foreign exchange in the early part of the century, section 14 seemed to sanction—according to Hackley's interpretation—both types of foreign-exchange intervention. More generally, however, section 12A(c) instructed the Federal Reserve System to undertake open-market operations—including transactions in foreign exchange—that accommodate commerce and business by promoting sound credit conditions in the United States. Defending the dollar, cooperating with foreign central banks and the IMF, and promoting trade certainly seemed consistent with this general objective. Section 12A(b) of the Act also specifically required the FOMC's authorization for all such open-market operations.

In addition, section 14(e) allowed the Federal Reserve to hold foreign exchange in the form of open accounts in foreign countries, to appoint correspondents, and to establish agencies.[30] These are necessary aspects of an intervention operation, particularly if the Federal Reserve hoped to operate through a foreign commercial bank or a central bank in a foreign market. In the 1930s, however, the Board of Governors interpreted this clause narrowly, arguing that the Act allowed the Federal Reserve to open accounts only to facilitate direct intervention transactions, but that the Act did not allow the central bank to hold foreign currency beyond what was immediately necessary for intervention. This interpretation seemed to preclude holding foreign-currency positions acquired outright or through swaps. In 1961, Hackley broadened the interpretation, arguing that the FOMC instead could construe the Act as allowing the Federal Reserve to maintain such accounts provided that it had a reasonable expectation of using them to finance intervention (Hackley 1961, 13). Accordingly, the Federal Reserve now regarded section 14(e) as authorizing it to undertake swaps with other central banks and eventually to amass a huge portfolio of foreign exchange. Hackley's interpretation was a clear change in the Board's attitude and was in agreement with the Federal Reserve Bank of New York's original actions in the 1930s.[31]

More problematic for the Federal Reserve, however, was finding legal authority for purchasing foreign exchange from the ESF on either a permanent or temporary (warehousing) basis.[32] The Banking Act of 1935 prohibited the Federal Reserve from purchasing government obligations except in the open market. Although Congress had permitted some direct purchases of government securities during World War II, and although the Fed retained some very limited authority to do so after the war, Congress clearly did not want the central bank lending resources to the Treasury "in a manner that might be inconsistent with the [Federal Reserve] System's monetary and credit responsibilities" (Hackley 1961, 18). Hackley argued that swap agreements with the Treasury did not violate the open-market provisions of the Banking Act of 1935. In contrast to government securities, foreign currency was not a liability on the US Treasury's balance sheet; therefore, that agency was part of the open market for foreign exchange. Moreover, Hackley asserted, the United States was a "domestic corporation." This was a necessary criterion because the Federal Reserve Act also limited open-market operations to domestic corporations. In Hackley's opinion, the Federal Reserve could lawfully buy and sell foreign exchange from the ESF or the Treasury.[33] Unlike most of the legal controversies associated with Federal Reserve intervention, the debate about the appropriateness of warehousing would never quite disappear (Broaddus and Goodfriend 1996; Hetzel 1996). Opponents would consistently argue that warehousing constituted a central bank loan to the ESF using foreign exchange as collateral and was, therefore, inappropriate. It contravened principles of central-bank independence and thereby impinged on the credibility of monetary policy. Proponents would eventually argue that warehousing did not constitute a loan, but instead was a straightforward and permissible asset swap between the two agencies.

4.5.2   Other FOMC Objections

Aside from the question of the Federal Reserve's legal authority for intervention, four other key issues arose during the FOMC's discussions in late 1961 and early 1962. One was political: Some members of the FOMC feared that even if the Federal Reserve Act did provide legal authority for intervention, Congress might interpret the Federal Reserve's involvement as a budgetary bailout for the Treasury. Congress established the ESF specifically for the purpose of intervening in the foreign-exchange market, and capitalized the fund with an appropriation of $2.0 billion. In 1945, Congress used $1.8 billion of ESF funds to pay the US contribution to the IMF. Karl Bopp, the president of the Federal Reserve Bank of Philadelphia, argued that these events suggested that Congress intended to limit the amount of funds that the ESF could devote to foreign-exchange operations (FOMC *Minutes*, 12 September 1961, 49–50). If so, then the Federal Reserve's unlimited participation with the ESF might appear as a method of circumventing Congress's budgetary authority. If the ESF wanted more funds for intervention, it should seek a larger Congressional appropriation.[34] Moreover, the ESF made loans to developing countries and currently had a substantial amount committed to Latin America. These were essentially foreign-policy actions related to State Department functions. Might Congress view the Federal Reserve's foreign-exchange operations as a backdoor means of financing these foreign-policy operations? Could the Federal Reserve become embroiled in a dispute among Congress, the Treasury, and the State Department about foreign policy?

A second FOMC concern focused on the bureaucratic authority for intervention and its implication for Federal Reserve independence. Congress created the ESF and vested the Treasury with primary responsibility for intervention in part because of its dissatisfaction with Fed interventions during the 1920s and 1930s. If the Treasury had primary responsibility for intervention, as Chairman Martin acknowledged, could it direct how the Federal Reserve operated for its own account? The US secretary of the Treasury, the nation's primary financial officer, is responsible to both the president and the Congress of the United States for formulating and implementing all US financial policies, and the Gold Reserve Act of 1934 gave the Treasury primary responsibility for intervention. If, as the FOMC now claimed, the Federal Reserve Act authorized the Federal Reserve to conduct foreign-exchange operations independently, the potential for conflict with the Treasury existed. At a minimum, the Federal Reserve's foreign-exchange operations cannot act in a way contrary to US international financial policies (Task Force 1990c, Paper no. 6). In subsequent testimony before the House Committee on Banking and Currency, Chairman Martin pledged to avoid conflicts with the Treasury in conducting the Federal Reserve's intervention operations, saying "the [Federal Reserve] System will, of course, coordinate its foreign-exchange operations with those of the Treasury Stabilization Fund" (Task Force 1990c, Paper no. 6, 1). Coordination would be on a day-to-day basis.

In addition, the Board staff assumed that the Treasury could not direct the Federal Reserve in operations for the central bank's account (FOMC *Minutes*, 12 September 1961, 51). Coombs (1976, 72) claims that, by agreement, the Treasury could veto Federal Reserve intervention operations with which it did not agree, and that the Federal Reserve could refuse to undertake any operations for its own account with which it did not agree. In an 18 December 1961 letter to Chairman Martin, Treasury Secretary Dillon pledged, "the Treasury on its part would naturally want to avoid impinging on the independence of the Federal Reserve System within the Government." [35] The lines of authority were not clearly defined in the early 1960s, and experience would show that the Treasury's preeminence in the area would indeed create difficulties for the Federal Reserve System, as when the central bank attempted to stop intervening in the 1990s (see chapter 6).

On the surface, the third concern focused on the ability of the Federal Reserve to respond quickly to speculative attacks against the dollar, but underlying this may have been a deeper concern about who would actually run the show within the Fed, and how it would affect the relative authority of the FOMC, the Board of Governors, and the Federal Reserve Bank of New York. Many within the Federal Reserve System thought that a special subcommittee of the FOMC was necessary to directly oversee foreign-exchange intervention because an emergency situation could quickly arise when the full committee was unavailable for consultation and reaching immediate decisions. Making a quick response time all the more crucial, the Fed needed to coordinate most operations with foreign central banks, which might be five or even twelve hours ahead. In a memorandum dated 8 February 1962, the Board's general counsel, Howard Hackley, recommended that foreign-exchange operations be put under the supervision of the Board of Governors instead of the FOMC. The board meets almost daily and has foreign-exchange experts on staff. Moreover, while Hackley contended that the law allowing the Federal Reserve to engage in foreign-exchange operations was clear, he also argued that giving control to the Board of Governors instead of the FOMC was ". . . more defensible from a legal standpoint." (FOMC *Minutes*, 13 February 1962, 64). Others, including Governor Robertson who opposed Hackley's interpretation of the Federal Reserve's authority for intervention, and the president of the Federal Reserve Bank of Cleveland, W. D. Fulton, supported Hackley by arguing that the board was more of a "public body" than the FOMC. Apparently, because elected officials appointed governors, but not Federal Reserve Bank presidents, the former had more authority to deal with issues that touched the fringe of foreign policy than the latter. The president of the San Francisco Federal Reserve Bank, Eliot Swan, however, articulated the underlying concern with Hackley's recommendation: "To shift from the Committee to the Board might give support to those who would like to change rather basically the fundamental structure of the [Federal Reserve] System." (FOMC *Minutes*, 13 February 1962, 68).

While most participants favored maintaining FOMC authority, many thought that a smaller management group was necessary to deal with emergency situations. At issue was the extent of a subcommittee's authority. A subcommittee with broad authority might not confine its activities to administration, but would instead actually make policy (FOMC *Minutes*, 5 December 1961, 71). Ultimately, the FOMC decided to authorize a committee consisting of the chairman and the vice chairman of the FOMC and the vice chairman of the board to conduct operations when the full committee was unavailable. The subcommittee, however, was to act within FOMC guidelines, which we discuss below. This subcommittee could, however, set maximum amounts of individual currency holdings, establish exchange-rate limits, review and approve any agreements between the Federal Reserve Bank of New York and foreign central banks, and take emergency actions when the full FOMC was unavailable.

Chairman Martin also wanted the special manager, who actually undertook intervention operations through the foreign exchange desk at the Federal Reserve Bank of New York, to be an employee of the FOMC and not, as currently was the case, an employee of the Federal Reserve Bank of New York. Not surprisingly, the president of the Federal Reserve Bank of New

York objected that this move would reduce the bank's authority—specifically the authority of its directors—and wanted to maintain the current setup. The FOMC, however, accepted the chairman's recommendation and the special manager became an employee of the (FOMC *Minutes*, 17 April 1962, 2–3).

A final issue focused on the exact role of intervention. Policymakers at the Federal Reserve all seemed to agree that the broad objective of intervention was to defend the dollar, thereby reducing gold outflows and bolstering confidence in the dollar's parity. But how extensive should these operations be? At one point, the Federal Reserve Bank of New York suggested undertaking seasonal and cyclical interventions to smooth out anticipated balance-of-payments flows (FOMC *Minutes*, 5 December 1961, 49). Some FOMC members, however, were concerned that prolonged intervention might actually interfere with balance-of-payments adjustment and actually prolong disequilibrium. Governor Mitchell argued that if a foreign country had a balance-of-payments surplus and wanted to acquire gold, the United States should accommodate that country. The United States, therefore, needed a policy to facilitate an orderly loss of gold. Intervention might prevent a sudden loss of gold, but the danger of prolonged operations was that, absent a fundamental policy change, the demand for gold would continue to grow and eventually worsen confidence in the official gold price. Similarly, Governor King feared that "people would be likely to put too much reliance on these operations to guard the dollar . . ." (FOMC *Minutes*, 12 September 1961, 55). Governor Roberts also feared that if the Fed repeatedly disrupted the private market's pricing process, the willingness of private market participants to make a market in foreign exchange might deteriorate (FOMC *Minutes*, 5 December 1961, 60). For these reasons, the FOMC favored only temporary interventions that would offset transitional disruptions in the foreign-exchange market and that would not attempt to avoid fundamental market adjustments. As time would tell, however, distinguishing between temporary developments and those of a more fundamental nature was extremely difficult.

4.5.3   A Cautious Approach

Most FOMC members favored intervention and were sympathetic to Hackley's interpretation of the Federal Reserve Act. Nevertheless, they wanted to proceed cautiously and to first seek, with the cooperation of the Treasury, legislative clarification from Congress (FOMC *Minutes*, 5 December 1961, 78–79). In the face of this hesitancy, Chairman Martin, Federal Reserve Bank of New York President Alfred Hayes, and First Vice President of the Federal Reserve Bank of New York Charles Coombs stressed that foreign-exchange markets were currently very sensitive to speculative pressures. They argued for going forward on an emergency basis and seeking congressional approval afterwards. (The Treasury made a similar appeal.)

The sense of urgency swayed the FOMC. While urgency was the chairman's stated motivation, he also may have hoped to avoid a full-fledged congressional review of the Federal Reserve's role in intervention, especially one that might provide an opportunity for other changes in the Federal Reserve Act.[36]

On 23 January 1962, with two members dissenting, the FOMC approved foreign-exchange operations for the Federal Reserve's account on an experimental basis (FOMC *Minutes*, 23 January 1962, 41). Governor Mitchell objected, contending that the Federal Reserve first needed Congress's explicit approval. Similarly, Governor Roberts dissented, arguing that the Federal Reserve Act did not clearly authorize these types of stabilization actions, that the FOMC was basing its decision on incidental authority in the Act, and that Congress intended to confer only limited authority for such actions to the Treasury's ESF.[37]

In late February 1962, Chairman Martin reported to the House Committee on Banking and Exchange that the Federal Reserve "had recently decided to reenter the field of foreign-exchange transactions." He reported that the general counsel for the US Treasury and the attorney general of the United States concurred with Hackley's interpretation of the legal basis for the FOMC's decision. In general, the US Congress accepted the Federal Reserve's interpretation of its authority. Representatives Henry Reuss and Wright Patman, however, did not agree. Representative Reuss contended:

> Much of the operation that you are doing . . . seems to me to duplicate the foreign exchange stabilization operation that the Secretary of the Treasury has very properly undertaken pursuant to the Gold Reserve Act of 1934. To me this is a tremendous power you have taken upon yourself, and I must serve notice on you right now that I consider this an usurpation of the powers of Congress . . . . You come in here and tell us that you propose to go off on, if I may say so, a frolic of your own, involving unspecified sums without the slightest statutory guidance. (Hetzel 1996).

The Federal Reserve has since reported on its foreign-exchange operations, and Congress has been aware of its activities. In the 1980s, under the Monetary Control Act, Congress amended section 14(B)(1) of the Federal Reserve Act to allow the Federal Reserve to invest foreign currencies acquired through its foreign-exchange operations in short-term foreign government securities.[38] The FOMC has interpreted this as tacit congressional approval of the Federal Reserve's foreign-exchange operations. Serious concern about the legal authority of the Federal Reserve's intervention activities never again arose within the FOMC. The Federal Reserve, however, continued to worry that Congress might view intervention and related activities as interfering with its appropriations power, and remained concerned about how intervention conducted in conjunction with the Treasury might interfere with its ability to conduct such operations independently. Eventually, as we detail in chapter 6, FOMC participants would worry that the operations interfered with the credibility of monetary policy (Broaddus and Goodfriend 1996; Hetzel 1996).

4.5.4   Rules of Engagement

On 13 February 1962, the FOMC approved the Authorization Regarding Open Market Transactions in Foreign Currencies, the Guidelines for System Foreign Currency Operations, and the Continuing Authority Directive on System Foreign Currency Operations.[39] These documents provided the FOMC's instructions to the subcommittee of foreign exchange, the special manager, and the foreign exchange desk of the Federal Reserve Bank of New York for undertaking foreign-exchange operations for the Federal Reserve's account.

The authorization listed the goals of the operations and sanctioned specific types of transactions. As stated in this document, the basic purposes of the operations were: (a) to safeguard the value of the dollar, (b) to improve the efficiency of payments by avoiding disorderly conditions, (c) to promote monetary cooperation among central banks and international organizations, (d) to moderate temporary international payments imbalances that might adversely affect reserves, and (e) to foster growth in international liquidity compatible with the needs of an expanding world economy. In addition to these basic purposes, the document also listed more specific aims for the Federal Reserve's transactions. These were: (a) to protect the US gold reserve from international payments flows stemming from temporary disequilibrating forces or transitional market disturbances, (b) to temper abrupt changes in spot rates and moderate forward premia and discounts judged to be disequilibrating, (c) to supplement exchange arrangements such as those made through the IMF, and (d) to provide a means whereby reciprocal holdings of foreign currencies might contribute to international liquidity needs. The Authorization allowed spot and forward transactions at prevailing rates in both US and foreign markets and allowed transactions with the ESF.

The authorization also provides guidance with respect to communications. Besides keeping the FOMC informed of the operations, the Authorization required close consultation with foreign central banks and also instructed the chairman to keep the secretary of the Treasury fully advised about Federal Reserve foreign-currency operations. The chairman was to consult with the secretary on all matters that related to Treasury responsibilities, and the Federal Reserve staff was to transmit all pertinent information about Federal Reserve foreign-currency operations to the US Treasury. A daily conference call would take place among representatives of the Federal Reserve Board, the Treasury, and the Federal Reserve Bank of New York (US Treasury 1962b, 5–6). At this call, participants would discuss current market conditions and any planned operations. At the end of the day, the Federal Reserve Bank of New York would provide to all principals a summary of the day's operations. The Authorization also instructed the chairman to report periodically to the National Advisory Council on International Monetary and Financial Problems. The FOMC also understood that the Federal Reserve and the Treasury would consult before "either entered into any agreements with foreign central banks or governments regarding possible foreign-currency operations." (FOMC *Minutes*, 13 February 1962, 93). The Authorization established the aforementioned subcommittee for foreign-exchange operations to instruct the special manager when the full FOMC was unavailable.

The guidelines are more explicit with respect to current operations. On 13 February 1962, they limited the holdings of foreign currency to an amount that would allow the foreign exchange desk to "exert a market influence," and to cover outstanding forward commitments. It also instructed the Federal Reserve Bank of New York on operating procedures. The desk was to transact at prevailing exchange rates and was not to attempt to establish rates that were inconsistent with underlying market forces. Absent explicit authorization to the contrary, the Federal Reserve Bank of New York was to purchase foreign currencies at or below their par values and was to lower the rate that it paid for any foreign currency as the amount that the bank held approached the limits that the FOMC set. The Federal Reserve Bank of New York was to follow a similar technique for sales of foreign exchange. The document also required that operations be coordinated in the sense of not acting at cross purposes with another central bank.

The guidelines indicated that spot intervention was appropriate "whenever exchange-market instability threatens to produce disorderly conditions" and listed some conditions (e.g., political tensions, wide interest-rate differentials) that might signal such developments (FOMC *Minutes*, 13 February 1962, 88). Forward operations were appropriate when forward premia or discounts were inconsistent with interest-rate differentials or when such forward operations "encourage[ed] the retention or accumulation of dollar holdings abroad." (FOMC *Minutes*, 13 February 1962, 89) This latter condition allowed for swap transactions. The Guidelines also allowed the FOMC to take over outstanding forward contracts that the ESF originated. The Federal Reserve also agreed to purchase foreign currencies that the Treasury acquired under existing credit arrangements with foreign central banks and governments and to do likewise—after consultation—in the future, and to buy foreign currencies that the Treasury acquired from the IMF (FOMC *Minutes*, 13 February 1962, 94). Moreover, the Federal Reserve agreed "to purchase currencies . . . from the Treasury either outright or under mutually satisfactory resale agreement [warehousing], in the event that exchange-market developments obliged the Fund to exhaust available resources." (FOMC *Minutes*, 13 February 1962, 94).

The initial continuing authority sanctioned transactions in British pounds, French francs, German marks, Italian lira, Netherlands guilders, and Swiss francs, with total holdings not to exceed $500 million. This limitation and listing of currencies would frequently change to accommodate broader operations.

4.5.5   Acquiring an Initial Position

With a balance-of-payments deficit and the dollar often trading at the lower end of parity bands, the Fed needed foreign exchange to mount any dollar defense, but any purchase of foreign exchange would supply more dollars to the market, put additional downward pressure on the dollar, and increase the potential drain of US gold reserves (US Treasury 1962b). The Fed looked to acquire a small amount of foreign exchange from the market or from foreign central banks whenever a fortuitous opportunity presented itself, and some occasions arose in early 1962. In addition, the Treasury sold outright to the Federal Reserve System $32 million worth of German marks in February and March, and $0.5 million worth (each) of Swiss francs, Netherlands guilder, and Italian lira (*Desk Report* 1963). The Treasury also agreed to sell to the Federal Reserve System, either outright or through repurchase agreements, currencies held by the ESF, if the ESF exhausted its available dollar funds for foreign-exchange operations. These currencies permitted the Federal Reserve to open accounts with the central banks of Germany, Switzerland, the Netherlands, and Italy. The Federal Reserve already had British sterling and French francs in accounts with the Bank of England and with the Bank of France (FOMC 1962, 1).[40] Holding large balances in a wide range of foreign currency, however, increased the Federal Reserve's risks of a valuation loss (Coombs 1976, 74).

The Federal Reserve also established a series of reciprocal currency arrangements—the swap network—with major central banks. The swap network, which provided the Federal Reserve—and foreign central banks—an off-market mechanism for financing foreign exchange operations, was the United States' first line of defense during Bretton Woods.

4.6   Mechanisms of Exchange-Rate Policy

During the Bretton Woods era, the Federal Reserve System and the US Treasury intervened using various mechanisms, which we review in this section. Although the Federal Reserve and the Treasury often worked in tandem adopting similar techniques at the same time, a clear division of responsibility existed between these agencies. The Federal Reserve focused on short-term operations, typically financed through drawings on its swap lines. Ideally, the Federal Reserve would soon reverse these transactions, so exchange-rate exposure and exchange loss generally were not big concerns. The US Treasury, as noted, often engaged in similar short-term operations, but because of its clearer authority for intervention, the Treasury also undertook operations of a longer-term nature. Most importantly, as per a

23 July 1962 understanding between Chairman Martin and Treasury Secretary Fowler, the Treasury stood ready to backstop central bank's operations if market conditions prevented the Federal Reserve from reversing a swap drawing on time. To do so, the Treasury could either issue foreign-currency-denominated securities—short-term certificates of indebtedness or long-term Roosa bonds—or draw foreign exchange from the International Monetary Fund, or sell gold for foreign exchange and then sell the proceeds to the Federal Reserve. In addition, the US government sometimes cajoled foreign governments into holding larger dollar portfolios.

4.6.1   Reciprocal Currency Agreements—Swap Lines

From 1962 until the closing of the US gold window in August 1971, the reciprocal currency arrangements, or swap lines, were the Federal Reserve System's key mechanism for defending the US gold stock, and they also became an important means for temporarily providing dollar liquidity to foreign central banks.[41] Swaps involve the simultaneous spot purchase and forward sale of one currency against another.[42] The transactions provided both the Federal Reserve and participating foreign central banks with short-term credits for dealing with temporary and unwanted changes in official dollar reserves. Temporary—the key operative word—implied reserve changes that monetary authorities expected to quickly turn around. Countries were not to use swap drawings to avoid fundamental balance-of-payments adjustments, although distinguishing between temporary and fundamental problems proved a formidable, often impossible, task.

Ideally, "the very existence of the arrangements, even when they [were] not used, [was] thought to have a stabilizing effect." (Holland 1967, 4–5; Solomon 1971) This passive influence occurred through two channels. For one thing, the swap lines signaled central-bank cooperation and thereby mitigated uncertainty that otherwise might foster speculative activity. In addition, the existence of the swap lines raised the potential costs of speculation. Central banks often increased the swap lines during tumultuous periods, but as figure 4.7 shows, they never drew on the full capacity of the lines. Swaps offered a threat to speculators.

The swap mechanism functioned as follows: The Federal Reserve System would sell US dollars spot to a foreign central bank for its own currency and immediately sell that foreign currency back to that same foreign central bank for delivery at a set future date (Task Force 1990f, Paper no. 9).[43] The repayment would terminate the swap drawing, but not the line. Central banks, in almost all cases, annually negotiated—on a bilateral basis—overall credit limits for the swap lines. Drawings initially had a term of three months, but could be renewed once if the parties agreed. (The swap line with the National Bank of Belgium had an initial six-month term.) Ideally, banks were not to seek a second renewal, and "every effort was made to prevent a facility from being in continuous use for as long as a year." (Task Force 1990f, Paper

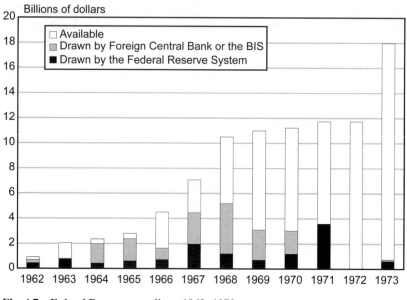

Fig. 4.7   Federal Reserve swap lines, 1962–1973
Note: Data are from the Federal Reserve System.

no. 9, 3) The Federal Reserve's lines—unlike the Treasury's—were reciprocal, meaning that either party could initiate a drawing.

Because swaps provided only temporary credits under a pegged-rate system, they were unlikely to result in large losses. Quite the contrary, when all things worked according to design, the central bank that drew on the swap line tended to profit from the operation, because it sold foreign exchange against its own currency when its own currency was trading below par and bought foreign exchange to repay the line when its currency had appreciated (Bodner 1970, 1). Because swaps were relatively safe, central banks did not apply conditions such as the adoption of macroeconomic policies or the application for funds from the IMF to their use.[44] This made them readily available. Only a two-day notice was necessary for a drawing.

Participants undertook the spot leg of the swap at prevailing market exchange rates. During the Bretton Woods era, the forward leg of any transaction was undertaken at the same exchange rate. Hence, the swap itself incurred no exchange-rate risk. The central bank that drew on a swap line and used the foreign exchange for intervention, however, was exposed to exchange-rate risk, since it did not know the precise price of obtaining foreign exchange to retire the swap drawing. To protect the debtor central bank should the creditor central bank revalue its currency during the term of a swap drawing, the lines included "revaluation clauses" allowing the borrowing central bank to obtain from the creditor central bank sufficient foreign exchange to repay its obligation at a market-based exchange rate prevailing prior to the revaluation. As we will see, revaluation clauses proved problematic in the face of a dollar devaluation, and they did not apply to the adoption of a float. The Federal Reserve exercised a revaluation clause only once, in May 1971, against the Netherlands Bank.

In all cases, the central bank initiating the swap also paid interest on its borrowings. The creditor central bank invested the foreign currency that it acquired from the debtor central bank for the term of the swap in a time deposit or in some other interest-earning asset. (The debtor would do likewise with any unused balances.) During the Bretton Woods era, both the interest rate that the creditor country received and the interest rate that the borrower received were equal to the interest rate on three-month US Treasury bills.[45] If necessary, interest effectively could be paid by adjusting the spot and forward exchange rates on the swap.

In March 1962, the Federal Reserve established its first swap line with the Bank of France.[46] The Federal Reserve drew on this line, renewed it once, and repaid the line in August 1962. The Federal Reserve did not intervene with the funds so acquired; the operation was a test of the mechanisms. The French franc swap line then existed on standby status. In May 1962, the Federal Reserve established a second line with the Bank of England. Again, the Federal Reserve drew on the line to test the "telex, investment, and other technical procedures" involved with the operations (Coombs 1976, 79). By the end of that year, the Federal Reserve had established lines with eight key European central banks and the Bank of Canada that provided up to $900 million equivalent in foreign exchange.[47] A broad set of lines was necessary because many foreign central banks acquired excess dollars, a potential claim on US gold. The network continued to grow, and it evolved from a small, very short-term credit facility in 1962 to a large, intermediate-term facility by the closing of the US gold window in 1971 (see figure 4.7). By then, the swap network totaled $11.2 billion equivalent and involved fourteen central banks, having picked up the central banks of Denmark, Japan, Mexico, Norway, and Sweden over the intervening years.[48] In addition, the term of a typical swap drawing increased from the original three months to six months. The expansion of the swap lines was a natural consequence of both the mounting threat to the US gold stock and the growing volume of international transactions, but the increasing length of swap drawings and the frequent tendency to renew them suggested that the underlying disequilibrium was of a more fundamental than temporary nature.

4.6.2   Providing Cover—the Swiss Franc Example

Between 1962 and the closing of the US gold window in 1971, the Federal Reserve borrowed $11.5 billion worth of foreign exchange through its swap lines (see figure 4.8).[49] Usually—but not exclusively—the Federal Reserve used these funds to provide foreign central banks with cover for temporary,

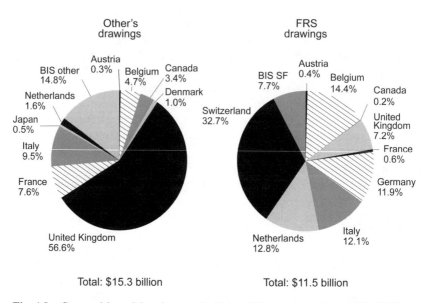

Total: $15.3 billion   Total: $11.5 billion

Fig. 4.8   Composition of drawings on the Federal Reserve swap lines, 1962–1971
Note: Data are from the Federal Reserve System.

undesirable surges in their dollar balances, and thereby to discourage these central banks from quickly converting unwanted dollars into gold with the US Treasury. To accomplish this, the Federal Reserve used the foreign exchange that it obtained in a swap drawing to acquire dollars from the same foreign central bank. This set of transactions—the swap drawing and the acquisition of dollars—left the foreign central bank holding exactly the same amount of dollars as it did before the swap took place. The dollars that the foreign central bank now held, however, were free of foreign exchange risk since the Federal Reserve contracted to buy them back via the forward leg of the swap at a set exchange rate.

By far, the Federal Reserve undertook the largest cover operations with the Swiss National Bank (SNB), and these serve as an example of the pitfalls and benefits of these types of operations. Between 1962 and 1971, the Federal Reserve drew nearly $4.7 billion equivalent Swiss francs from swap lines with the Swiss National Bank and the Bank for International Settlements (BIS).[50] The Swiss franc drawings amounted to over 40 percent of all Federal Reserve drawings during the Bretton Woods era.

At the time, the Swiss franc functioned as a key safe-haven currency, attracting funds that flowed out of British pounds, US dollars, and other overvalued currencies. As noted, these flows went through dollars and left the SNB holding unwanted dollar exposures. Absent a mechanism to provide cover, the SNB undoubtedly would have shed these dollars for gold.

In mid-1962, for example, persistent speculative inflows lifted the Swiss franc to the upper limits of its parity range against the dollar. Forced to intervene, the SNB acquired US dollars in excess of its informal limits. Special manager Charles Coombs feared that "Unless we can . . . mop up a sizable proportion of the dollars recently taken in by the Swiss National Bank we face the prospect of very large gold losses *which might easily trigger off an avalanche of demand from other quarters.*" (FOMC *Minutes,* 10 July 1962, 52–53, emphasis added). In response, the Federal Reserve opened the two aforementioned Swiss franc swap lines, each for $100 million, and immediately drew $50 million worth of Swiss francs from each line to provide cover to the SNB.

Because they matured in three months, shortly after making the drawings, the Federal Reserve looked for opportunities to acquire Swiss francs to repay the swaps. A window of opportunity presented itself from late summer until the Cuban missile crisis in mid-October 1962, during which time pressures on the Swiss franc subsided. The Federal Reserve bought Swiss francs in the market, but could not acquire enough Swiss francs to pay off all of its outstanding obligations, because, despite the relative calm, the Swiss franc often traded above its par value, and the FOMC prohibited the desk from buying foreign exchange at exchange rates above par.[51] The Federal Reserve's second option was to buy the necessary Swiss francs from the SNB, but with dollars still trickling into Switzerland, the SNB was reluctant to acquire still more dollars through such a sale. On 2 October 1962, Coombs asked the FOMC to renew for an additional three months all outstanding Swiss franc swap lines with the SNB and the BIS. This seemingly innocuous rollover, however, pointed to the fundamental problem with the swap network. How much time was necessary to distinguish between a temporary and a fundamental disequilibrium, or when should the US. Treasury settle in gold?

In early 1963, a second window of opportunity opened, and the Federal Reserve managed to liquidate $80 million worth of its $105 million equivalent Swiss franc obligation by buying Swiss francs in the market, from the US Treasury and from the SNB. The Federal Reserve, however, also took a new tack. On 28 May 1963, the FOMC authorized the desk to swap $13 million equivalent British pounds from its portfolio for Swiss francs with the BIS. Despite the limits on swap maturities and rollovers, the Federal Reserve did not repay this drawing until the end of 1964—well over one year. Using this so-called third-party swap to extinguish a bilateral swap, however, does not discharge the central bank's short position, but merely changes the currency composition of that position and extends the maturity of its liability. It also reduces the liquidity of the Federal Reserve's overall long position in foreign exchange (Board of Governors, 21 March 1966, 35).

By mid-1963, rising Swiss money market rates attracted renewed dollar inflows, and following the assassination of President Kennedy in November 1963, the Swiss francs again reached the top of the parity band. The situation led to new rounds of intervention, with the Federal Reserve providing additional cover to the SNB. By early 1964, the Federal Reserve owed the SNB $70 million worth of Swiss francs and owed the BIS $145 million worth of Swiss francs.

Once again the Swiss franc traded above par, and the Federal Reserve could not acquire sufficient Swiss francs to repay its outstanding commitments. Consequently, in May 1964, the parties involved agreed on a series of measures to reduce the Federal Reserve's outstanding debt. The Treasury issued $70 million worth of Swiss-franc-denominated Roosa bonds to the BIS and sold the proceeds outright to the Federal Reserve, which repaid an equivalent amount of Swiss-franc debt to the BIS. Through this transaction, the BIS substituted long-term dollar-denominated debt for short-term dollar-denominated debt on its books. In June 1964, the Bank of Italy swapped $100 million equivalent Italian lire for Swiss francs with SNB and sold the Swiss francs thus acquired to the Federal Reserve System for dollars to bolster Italian reserves. The central bank retired its outstanding commitments to the SNB, but to do so, the SNB had substituted lira-denominated assets for dollar-denominated assets on its books. In late June, the Federal Reserve paid down its Swiss franc debt to the BIS with francs that it obtained via the US Treasury from gold sales to the SNB.

In late 1964 and early 1965, funds again poured into Switzerland, and the Federal Reserve again drew on its Swiss franc swap lines to offer cover. This time, however, the situation quickly reversed. By spring, Swiss commercial banks began placing funds abroad, and the SNB eventually began selling dollars in support of the Swiss franc for the first time since 1962. Under these circumstances the Federal Reserve was able to acquire Swiss francs in the market, from the SNB and through transactions with other central banks to cover its outstanding obligations by midyear. The Federal Reserve's swap line reverted to standby status although the Federal Reserve still had a Swiss franc obligation with the BIS stemming from a German mark cross swap. In 1966, funds again moved out of Switzerland and into the Eurodollar market, and the Swiss National Bank sold dollars to moderate the franc's decline. To replenish its dollar reserves, the SNB sold Swiss francs to the Treasury and the Federal Reserve. In addition, the SNB sold gold to the Treasury.

Operations to provide cover persisted until the closing of the gold window in August 1971. The Federal Reserve frequently encountered problems similar to those experienced with Swiss franc swaps and resorted to similar fixes. All in all, however, the Federal Reserve's swap lines often succeeded in preventing countries from converting temporary inflows of unwanted dollar reserves into Treasury gold. Between 1962 and the end of 1969, Federal Reserve swap drawings totaled nearly $7 billion equivalent.[52] In general, reversals in flows into foreign countries—as described in the Swiss franc example—enabled the Federal Reserve to repay approximately three-fourths of its swap drawings. Repayments out of gold sales amounted to only $186 million. The issuance of US Treasury bonds denominated in foreign currencies and US drawings on the IMF financed the remainder. From the end of 1969 through 12 August 1971, the Federal Reserve drew $4.5 billion in foreign currencies through the swap lines. Suggestive of the deteriorating position of the dollar, the Treasury had to finance most of the repayments through the sale of reserve assets.

4.6.3   Temporary Liquidity

The Federal Reserve's swap lines were reciprocal, meaning that foreign central banks could initiate drawings when they needed a temporary increase in their dollar liquidity. During the Bretton Woods era, this became an important function of the swap lines. Between 1962 and 1971, foreign central banks initiated drawings of $15.3 billion dollars (figure 4.8). The Bank of England undertook over one-half of these drawings in defense of the pound's exchange rate, as we discuss below.

Canada was the first to draw on the new swap lines for liquidity purposes. In March 1962, the Canadian dollar, which had floated since September 1950, came under strong downward pressure as monetary and fiscal policies eased and speculative pressures on the Canadian dollar intensified.[53] In an effort to restore stability and confidence to the market, Canada established a par value for the dollar at US$ 0.9250 on 2 May 1962. Intense speculative pressure followed because the market anticipated a rate closer to US$ 0.90 and believed the new peg would not hold.

On 26 June 1962, the Federal Reserve System opened with the Bank of Canada a $250 million swap line—five times the size of any other line then in existence. In addition to the swap line, Canada received credits from the IMF ($300 million), the Bank of England ($100 million), and the US Export-Import Bank ($400 million). The Bank of Canada immediately drew down the entire amount of the swap line and used the proceeds to defend the newly established parity. The drawing had an initial maturity of 26 September 1962, but the Bank of Canada renewed it for another three months. Financial flows into Canada resumed by the fall of 1962, enabling Canada to repay the swap by year's end.

Despite the success of the Canadian operation, the Federal Reserve feared that the existence of temporary dollar liquidity through the swap lines might actually discourage foreign central banks from holding additional dollar balances, and indeed this seems to have happened. "Of the eleven countries with which the [Federal Reserve] System has concluded swap arrangements, five (Belgium, France, Netherlands, Switzerland, the United Kingdom) only hold necessary working balances in official dollar balances. Among the others, Germany has cut its dollar holdings in half since the end of 1961, and Austria and Canada have kept their dollar holdings at about their 1961 levels. Only Italy, Japan and Sweden have substantially increased their official dollar holdings, and only in the case of Italy has this behavior been clearly attributable to the cover given by inter-official transactions." (Board of Governors, 21 March 1966, 31).

4.6.4   Other Uses

The Federal Reserve established a second swap line—in addition to its Swiss franc line—with the BIS in 1965 to provide that bank with a means of acquiring temporary cash for routine transactions and to provide the Federal Reserve with access to additional foreign currencies. Previously if the BIS need cash, it borrowed against gold that it held at the Federal Reserve Bank of New York.

The Federal Reserve eventually began using this BIS swap line to supply funds to the Eurodollar market during times of strain when high Eurodollar rates would draw funds from the United States (Task Force 1990f, Paper no. 9, 12). The Federal Reserve asked the BIS to draw dollars on its non-Swiss franc swap line and to place the funds in the Eurodollar market.[54] Previously, the Federal Reserve had asked foreign central banks to do so during times of stress, particularly if the stress threatened to affect the foreign-exchange market, and often offered forward cover to facilitate such operations (MacLaury 1969, 10). These placements became fairly routine, but were often insufficient to the task.

Besides intervening in the Eurodollar market, the BIS drew on the line to provide support for the British pound (MacLaury 1969, 12). Almost all such drawings were repaid within a month, either at or prior to, their maturity date. The only exception occurred in a November 1967 drawing that extended for two months. After the United Kingdom, the BIS drew the largest amounts on the US swap lines, accounting for nearly 15 percent of the drawing between 1962 and 1971.

4.6.5   Sterilization

Swap drawings have the potential to affect US bank reserves, depending on what the Federal Reserve does with the foreign currency that it receives—the desk can buy dollars or hold and invest the funds—and on what the foreign central bank does with the corresponding dollars—it can buy foreign exchange, buy Treasury securities, hold a deposit at the Federal Reserve, or place the funds in the Eurodollar market. In any of these cases, the Federal Reserve could easily sterilize the transaction to any extent necessary. The manager of the domestic desk, in determining the appropriate amount of open-market operations to undertake on a particular day, regularly took account of changes in foreign accounts at the Federal Reserve, changes in Treasury cash balances, changes in float, and changes in currency in circulation. Many of these can change following a swap drawing. In addition, close communications between central banks and with the Bank for International Settlements generally kept the desk appraised of any prospective swap drawing and aware of the anticipated use of the funds. At times the Federal Reserve has requested a particular use of the dollars from a swap drawing that it initiated. The desk's ability to sterilize was further enhanced because the value date of a swap drawing occurs two business days after the transaction date. MacLaury (1969, 9) summarized the Federal Reserve's review of sterilization:

> In practice, the size of foreign drawings, large as they have been at times, has not been more than the domestic trading desk could offset—for the most part immediately—through open market operations. So long as the availability of the swap line is unconditional, the reserve consequences of foreign drawings are one of the operating factors that the Manager for domestic operations has to take into account in determining the size or direction of his own operations in any given day or week. They thus fall in the category of changes in Treasury cash balances, changes in float, and changes in currency in circulation. (MacLaury 1969, 9).

The effect of swap drawing of desk operations was no different than the normal problems that the desk faces because the dollar is a reserve and vehicle currency.

4.6.6   Spot Market Operations

Spot market interventions played a comparatively minor part in US exchange-market operations between 1962 and 1971. The Federal Reserve and the US Treasury generally did not regard spot market intervention as an effective means of preventing a persistent run on the US monetary gold stock—the key US objective.[55] At best, spot market interventions might contribute tangentially to this objective. In addition, the Board feared that spot market interventions, if they successfully alter one exchange rate, might create a "broad range" of arbitrage incentives through other currencies, requiring simultaneous interventions across a wide swath of currencies (Board of Governors, 21 March 1966, 16). Consequently, the onus of spot market intervention stayed with foreign monetary authorities who established par values for their currencies in terms of the dollar.

Although spot market transactions did not directly forestall a drain on the US monetary gold stock, US authorities occasionally intervened to calm developments that, if left unchecked, might grow to threaten the existing parity structure. The most notable occasion occurred immediately following President Kennedy's assassination on 22 November 1963.[56] At this time, trading in the New York market essentially stopped. To prevent panic selling, which seemed to afflict the stock market at the time, the foreign exchange desk placed large orders to sell all major currencies at the exchange rates that existed just prior to the assassination. By the close of business, the desk had sold $23.5 million equivalent German marks, British pounds, Netherlands guilders, Canadian dollars, and Swiss francs. On that same day, the

Bank of Canada bought $24.5 million to support the US dollar against its Canadian counterpart. The European markets were closed at the time of the assassination. When they reopened, foreign central banks intervened in their spot markets, but by then, markets had settled down.

Similarly, news of the Cuban missile crisis on 22 October 1962 generated large financial flows out of dollars and into continental currencies, especially Swiss francs. If left unchecked, the desk feared, these financial flows might raise doubts about the structure of the exchange rates. Moreover, by placing unwanted dollars in the Swiss National Bank, they contributed to a potential drain on the US gold stock. The Federal Reserve System responded by selling $8 million worth of francs into the Swiss spot market through the Swiss National Bank and $2.3 million equivalent francs into the New York spot market. The Swiss National Bank also acquired $50 million through its own intervention. (The Federal Reserve then drew $20 million equivalent Swiss francs through its swap line with the BIS on 31 October 1962 and bought dollars from the Swiss National Bank.) The Federal Reserve also sold $700 thousand equivalent Dutch guilders in the New York spot market at the onset of the Cuban missile crisis.

Interventions during international crises were relatively isolated events. Much more common between 1962 and 1971 were US efforts to moderate declines (lean against the wind) in the German mark-US dollar rate through spot transactions. These operations ultimately sought to reduce expectations of a mark revaluation (see below). The Federal Reserve often sold German marks, which it acquired through the swap drawings in the German market, and after that market closed, in the New York market.[57]

On at least one occasion, the Federal Reserve intervened to reinforce an exchange-rate movement. In September 1965, the Federal Reserve System, in conjunction with other foreign central banks, bought British pounds in the spot markets. At the time, speculators held short positions, which they needed to cover, and were consequently buying British pounds. By also buying sterling at successively higher quotes, the central bank hoped to reinforce the demand for sterling—to lean with the wind. Sterling began to appreciate.

To guard against the possibility that persistent spot market transactions might create market distortions, the FOMC's Guidelines to the Special Manager allow him to "purchase and sell authorized currencies at prevailing market rates without trying to establish rates that appear to be out of line with underlying market forces." Some opponents of intervention, for example, worried that interventions could actually encourage further speculative financial flows by signaling official concern about the seriousness of a situation.

4.6.7   Forward Market Operations

Beginning in 1964, the Federal Reserve undertook forward-market transactions—often in concert with the US Treasury—with both the private sector and foreign central banks. The transactions sought to provide counterparties with cover against dollar position and to influence forward exchange rates (Board of Governors, 21 March 1966, 24–29). As noted, the US Treasury had found forward transactions particularly successful in 1961.

The Federal Reserve System frequently sold foreign exchange forward as a means of providing forward cover to private individuals currently holding, or expecting soon to acquire, dollar balances. Often this was undertaken in conjunction with a foreign central bank's spot market sale of dollars. Sometimes it was undertaken as part of a Federal Reserve "market swap," in which the central bank bought foreign exchange spot and sold it forward into the market. Lacking the cover that such Federal Reserve forward sales generally provided, these private individuals probably would have sold their dollar balances to their respective central banks, which in turn might have converted the additional dollar balances to gold. An example of this type of forward transaction occurred in late 1964 and early 1965, when tight monetary conditions attracted funds out of British pounds, through dollars, and into Netherlands guilders. In December 1964 and January 1965, the Federal Reserve and the Exchange Stabilization Fund, in cooperation with the Netherlands Bank, sold $98.6 million and $95.4 million equivalent guilders, respectively, in the forward market.[58] This gave private individuals holding dollars the ability to sell them forward at a known exchange rate.

According to a Federal Reserve analysis, these transactions were effective in holding down the accumulation of dollars at the Netherlands Bank over the eight- to nine-month period that they were in force (Board of Governors, 21 March 1966, 25). Nevertheless, the transactions left the Federal Reserve and the Treasury carrying currency exposures for five and eight months, respectively, and raised questions about what constituted a temporary intervention. As a rule, normal Federal Reserve swap drawings with central banks at the time expired within three months and parties could not roll them over for more than a year.

In a somewhat similar type of forward transaction, US monetary authorities sometimes offered to "take over" forward commitments from foreign monetary authorities. In the fall of 1965, for example, Italian authorities were experiencing substantial dollar inflows that were creating excess liquidity in their banking system. In an effort to reduce liquidity and to shift these inflows forward, the Italian Exchange Offices (IEO) undertook swaps with Italian commercial banks. In these transactions, the IEO would sell dollars spot to commercial banks for lira, which the IEO would then use to buy dollars spot, and repurchase the lira forward. These so-called market swaps provided commercial banks with cover for their dollar exposures at a favorable rate. Moreover the IEO could roll over the market swaps if necessary until the conditions that created the inflow subsided.

Despite this maneuver, the IEO was under pressure to convert the dollars, which ultimately presented them with an exchange-risk exposure, into gold. In early 1965, the Treasury, and later the Federal Reserve, began to take technical responsibilities for the IEO swaps.[59] The Treasury started acquiring commitments in March 1965 and these rose to $1.0 billion equivalent by November 1965. The Federal Reserve—under a new authorization—acquired $500 million in forward commitments with Italian banks in November 1965. The IEO agreed to acquire the contracts at their final maturity and assumed the normal exchange-rate risks. The United States, however, guaranteed Italian authorities against any losses associated with dollar devaluation. This preferential guarantee posed a dangerous precedent for the United States (Board of Governors, 21 March 1966, 28–29).

Besides operations to provide cover, US monetary authorities frequently undertook forward transactions in an attempt to influence the premium of foreign exchange, and thereby to influence short-term financial flows. In 1964, for example, the forward discount of sterling narrowed, creating an opportunity for covered interest arbitrage. Funds began to move from New York to London. The Federal Reserve undertook a series of swaps with the market, buying sterling in the spot market and selling it forward. The operation apparently increased sterling's forward discount. These forward contracts, however, matured during a crisis in the sterling market, so that the Federal Reserve's eventual forward sterling sales conflicted with the Bank of England's objectives (Board of Governors, 21 March 1966, 26).

Although forward sales of foreign exchange typically left the Federal Reserve with an exposure, all Federal Reserve forward transactions between 1964 and 1971 proved profitable (Coombs 1971, 2). This largely stemmed from the nature of the operations under the Bretton Woods pegged-rate system. The Federal Reserve typically undertook forward transactions only when the foreign currency was selling at a substantial premium over existing spot rates, which fluctuated within 1 percent of their central parity. "In most cases" the Federal Reserve only undertook forward operations when the forward rate exceeded the spot rate's ceiling, as defined by the central parity (Coombs 1971, 2). Hence, the Federal Reserve was likely to profit, provided that the foreign country did not revalue its currency. Most countries offered the Federal Reserve revaluation guarantees similar to those that existed under the swap lines. Sometimes the Federal Reserve held sufficient foreign exchange balances to cover the operations even without a revaluation clause. On some occasions, as with German marks in 1971, the Federal Reserve drew foreign exchange on the swap lines when it sold that same foreign exchange forward (Coombs 1976, 3). The swap drawing covered the forward commitment, while the revaluation clause covered the swap repayment. Effectively, then, the revaluation clause extended to the forward commitment. On at least one occasion, to avoid supplying dollars to the Bundesbank, the Federal Reserve drew on the swap ninety days forward, a time consistent with a forward sale of German marks. The Bundesbank extended the revaluation clause to this "forward swap drawing" (Coombs 1971, 4–5).

4.6.8   IMF Drawings

The ability to draw foreign currencies from the International Monetary Fund provided the US Treasury with an additional mechanism with which to temporarily forestall the drain on the US gold stock. Countries that are members of the International Monetary Fund (IMF) can buy (borrow) foreign currencies for intervention purposes against deposits of their own currency at the fund. The amount that any country can draw on the IMF (as well as its contributions to the fund and its voting rights within the organization) depends on that country's quota subscription to the fund. Countries initially paid 75 percent of their quotas in their domestic currency and 25 percent in either gold or dollars. In February 1965, the US quota in the IMF amounted to $4.1 billion or 26 percent of the total (Yeager 1966, 348).

The IMF placed certain restrictions on countries' borrowing, although these restrictions were flexible. No members could borrow foreign currencies to such an extent that it increased the fund's holdings of the borrower's currency in excess of 200 percent of that country's quota. Since each country already paid 75 percent of its quota to the fund in its own currency, at most a country could incur foreign currency debts to the fund of 125 percent of its quota. In addition, no member's borrowings in any twelve-month period could increase the fund's holding of its currency by more than 25 percent of its quota. The rules implied that the fund could not compel a country, (i.e., a surplus country), to supply additional amounts of its currency to the fund, except in exchange for gold. Similarly, the IMF could not require a country to loan its currency to the fund to finance emergency borrowings (Yeager 1966).

The fund structured its loans to emphasize that they were intended for temporary balance-of-payments problems. The fund charged interest on borrowings in proportion to their size and duration and had myriad rules regarding repayment. Generally, however, countries had to repay loans within three to five years. In addition, regardless of the currency borrowed, all loans had to be repaid in either gold or a convertible currency. Often loans were provided under stand-by agreements that were in force for specific negotiated periods of time. The United States, for example, negotiated a one-year stand-by agreement in July 1963, on which it did not draw until February 1964. Countries could immediately borrow their "gold-tranche," an amount equal to the gold portion of their quota (normally 25 percent), and could borrow another 25 percent of their quota without much conditionality. Borrowings of additional amounts require members to undertake programs to restore balance-of-payments equilibrium.

Even though member states increased their quotas in 1959, the fund's resources were not sufficient to meet a large international crisis, particularly a speculative attack on both the US dollar and the British pound. The IMF, for example, lacked sufficient nondollar, nonsterling funds to meet the United States' notional right to borrow (James 1996, 162). On 2 October

1962, ten major industrial countries (G10) agreed to stand ready to loan the fund their own currencies up to a total of $6 billion equivalent for intervention purposes.[60] The facility was known as the General Arrangements to Borrow (GAB). Loans would be in accordance with IMF policies, but required the consent of the lending countries.

Between 1964 and 1968, the United States undertook two types of drawings from the IMF, although both ultimately sought to avoid a possible drain of the US monetary gold stock. The first, often referred to as technical, stemmed from the reserve currency role of the dollar and from IMF rules governing how many dollars the fund could hold in its portfolio. Most countries that borrowed from the IMF held their foreign-exchange reserves in dollars and repaid their IMF drawings in dollars. By 1963, however, the IMF's dollar holdings had reached 75 percent of the US quota, and IMF rules precluded borrowing countries from repaying in dollars. The US policymakers feared that if these countries could not repay their IMF obligations in dollars, they would do so with gold purchased from the US Treasury. To avoid this possibility, on 13 February 1964, the US Treasury undertook the first in a series of foreign-currency drawings from the fund. In the initial drawing, the Treasury acquired $130.5 million equivalent German marks, French francs, and Italian lira. These currencies were sold to a wide range of mostly developing countries for dollars. The Treasury undertook a second $125 million equivalent drawing of German marks and French francs on 1 June 1964. Over the course of 1964, the Treasury made five such technical drawings in seven continental European currencies, totaling $525 million equivalent. All but $75 million equivalent was disbursed. In 1965 and 1966, the United States made additional technical drawings from the IMF (*Desk Report* 1965, 1966).

The United States also drew foreign currencies from the IMF to finance more normal adjustment operations. In 1965, many countries acquired dollar reserves that the Federal Reserve covered through the swap mechanism, but because of continuing pressures on dollar exchange rates, the prospect for repaying these swaps became slim. On 30 July 1965, the United States made a $300 million equivalent, medium-term, multicurrency drawing on the IMF. The drawing consisted of $180 million equivalent Italian lira, $40 million French francs, $40 million Belgian francs, $25 million Dutch guilders, and $15 million Swedish kronor. The Treasury made the Belgian francs and most of the Italian lira available to the Federal Reserve to help retire outstanding central bank swap commitments. This was the first IMF drawing explicitly for the purpose of retiring Federal Reserve swap debts. The Treasury used the remainder of the drawing to absorb dollars at foreign central banks (*Desk Report* 1966, 39). In August 1966, the Treasury borrowed $250 million equivalent Italian lira from the fund and sold the proceeds to the Federal Reserve to refund swap obligations with the Bank of Italy and with the BIS. Because the fund was short of lira at the time of this drawing, the fund borrowed lira from the Italian government under the General Arrangements to Borrow. This was the first time that the Fund borrowed foreign currencies under the GAB. In early March 1968, the United States drew $200 million equivalent in foreign currencies under its gold tranche with the IMF and sold these currencies to the Federal Reserve to cover outstanding swap obligations.

4.6.9   Roosa Bonds

The Treasury often acquired foreign exchange to finance its intervention operations by issuing nonmarketable foreign-currency-denominated securities to foreign central banks or foreign governments. By holding such securities instead of dollars, foreign central banks were covered against the possibility of a dollar depreciation. Prior to the fall of 1962, the Treasury offered short-term debt instruments—certificates of indebtedness—to foreign central banks and governments. In November 1962, the Treasury began issuing longer-term nonmarketable securities to foreign central banks and governments, so-called Roosa bonds after Undersecretary of the Treasury, Robert Roosa. Initially the Roosa bonds were nonconvertible, but to make them more attractive to the legal and portfolio needs of foreign central banks, they became convertible on short notice into redeemable claims (Yeager 1966, 449). Often the Treasury sold the proceeds from Roosa bonds to the Federal Reserve, enabling the latter to retire outstanding swap debts. The US Treasury had $298 million worth of outstanding foreign currency denominated securities at the end of 1962. These consisted of Italian lira bonds ($200 million) and Swiss franc bonds ($98 million). The total outstanding balance of all Roosa bonds would grow to $1.7 billion by the end of 1972. Although the Treasury generally maintained a negative net open position prior to the late 1970s, the Treasury often attempted to cover the exposure associated with outstanding bonds.[61] Its early operations in Italian lira afford an example.

In 1962, the US Treasury issued a series of three-month certificates denominated in Italian lira totaling $150 million equivalent, and used the proceeds to finance forward lira sales to Italian commercial banks. Later in the year, the Treasury issued $200 million equivalent in fifteen-month lira-denominated Roosa bonds to retire the three-month certificates and to drain unwanted dollars that the Bank of Italy held. In late 1963, when the lira came under downward pressure and the Bank of Italy wanted to augment its dollar reserves, the US Treasury bought lira outright from the Bank of Italy. This purchase provided the Treasury with partial cover for its outstanding lira bonds.

In November 1963, Coombs asked the FOMC for permission to purchase foreign currency in which the Treasury had outstanding indebtedness—most immediately in Italian lira—at rates above par, if necessary, and to sell the currency forward to the Treasury to cover its outstanding indebtedness

(FOMC *Minutes*, 12 November 1963, 5–9). With the spot purchase from the market and the forward sale to the Treasury at the same exchange rate, the Federal Reserve would be "warehousing foreign currencies without capital risk until they were needed by the Treasury, whose resources for this kind of operation were limited." (FOMC *Minutes*, 12 November 1963, 7)[62] The lira that the Federal Reserve purchased and sold to the Treasury enabled the Treasury to redeem a maturing $50 million lira bond and prepay the remaining $150 million bonds outstanding.

4.7   Before the Fall: Cross-Rate Problems and the Gold Pool

Neither US macroeconomic policy nor the dollar's unique reserve currency role within the Bretton Woods system contributed directly to the devaluations of the British pound in November 1967 and French franc in August 1969, or to the revaluation of the German mark in the following October. These cross-rate adjustment problems stemmed largely from local developments—poor British macroeconomic policies, French social problems, and persistent German gains in competitiveness (Solomon 1982, 158). Nevertheless, changes in pound, franc, and mark exchange rates posed a general threat to the Bretton Woods parity structure. The associated uncertainty created speculative financial flows that caused other central banks to accumulate unwanted dollar reserves, and that affected other exchange rates and the gold market. United States operations in these markets amply illustrate the successes and failures of foreign-exchange-market operations during the Bretton Woods era. They show continuous, often complicated, back-and-forth, buy-and-sell operations, which frequently seemed to successfully delay parity changes, but in the end failed to solve the underlying problems.

4.7.1   The Devaluation of the UK Pound

In addition to protecting US gold reserves and shoring up the dollar, US intervention operations between 1962 and late 1967 aimed at providing support to the UK pound.[63] At the time, the pound was the second most widely held reserve currency, but observers increasingly questioned the viability of the pound's parity because the United Kingdom's competitive position had deteriorated since the war and its reserve position seemed low relative to its emerging balance-of-payments deficits (Cairncross and Eichengreen 2003). By 1963, the pound was subject to Triffin's paradox; the value of outstanding pound claims exceeded the United Kingdom's foreign-exchange reserves (Bordo, MacDonald, and Oliver 2010). Despite being in fundamental disequilibrium, massive amounts of foreign assistance between 1962 and 1967 helped the United Kingdom to hide its low level of reserves and maintain the pound's peg. The peg eventually collapsed when foreign governments ended their rescue efforts.

The pound's weakness presented US monetary authorities with two closely related problems. First, financial flows from the United Kingdom to Europe moved through US dollars, increasing dollar balances in European central banks and the prospects that these banks might convert the dollars into US gold. Second, US policymakers feared that if a sustained speculative run against the pound led to its devaluation, other countries would quickly follow. Pressure would then shift against the dollar's official gold price and seriously undermine, if not destroy, the credibility of the Bretton Woods system. The United States acted to support the pound (see figures 4.9 through 4.16).

After the Federal Reserve became actively involved in foreign-exchange operations in 1962, the pound experienced a series of speculative attacks.[64] The first began after French President Charles de Gaulle rejected the United Kingdom's bid for membership in the European Common Market in late January 1963. The rejection quickly put downward pressure on the pound. Largely by fortunate circumstance, the Federal Reserve was buying $5.6 million equivalent British pounds from the market to repay a January swap drawing when pressures against the pound started to build (see figures 4.9 and 4.10).[65] The Bank of England also began intervening with the dollar proceeds of the same swap drawing, but the pound continued to depreciate and fell below par. In response, the US Treasury entered the fray, purchas-

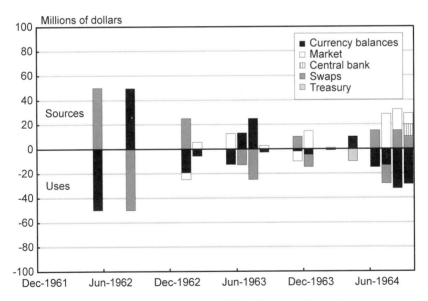

Fig. 4.9   Federal Reserve sources and uses of British pounds, December 1961–September 1964
Notes: "Central bank" contains "exceptional items." Data do not include unexplained items or profits. Data are from the Federal Reserve System.

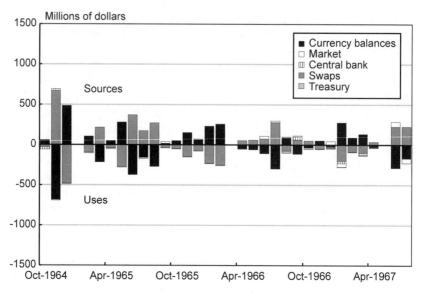

Fig. 4.10   Federal Reserve sources and uses of British pounds, October 1964–July 1967

Notes: "Central bank" contains "exceptional items." Data do not include unexplained items or profits. Data are from the Federal Reserve System.

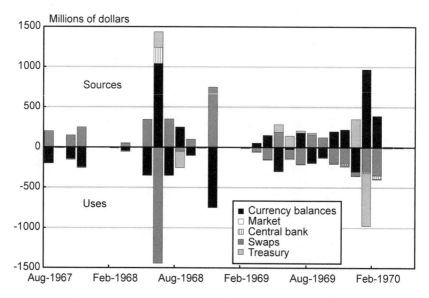

Fig. 4.11   Federal Reserve sources and uses of British pounds, August 1967–May 1970

Notes: "Central bank" contains "exceptional items." Data do not include unexplained items or profits. Data are from the Federal Reserve System.

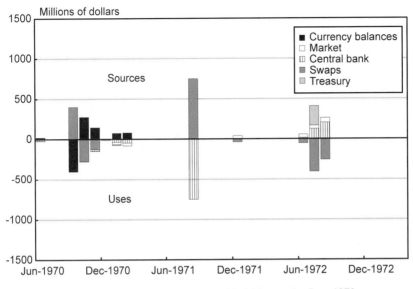

Fig. 4.12   Federal Reserve sources and uses of British pounds, June 1970–May 1973

Notes: "Central bank" contains "exceptional items." Data do not include unexplained items or profits. Data are from the Federal Reserve System.

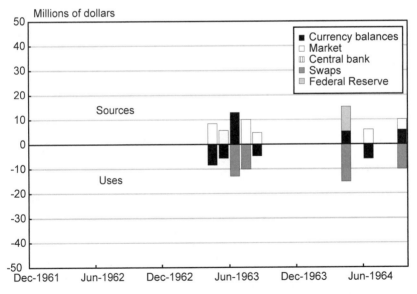

Fig. 4.13   US Treasury sources and uses of British pounds, December 1961–September 1964

Notes: "Central bank" contains "exceptional items." Data do not include unexplained items or profits. Data are from the Federal Reserve System.

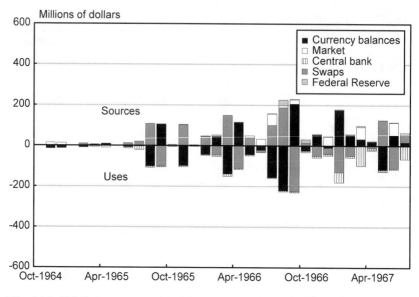

Fig. 4.14 **US Treasury sources and uses of British pounds, October 1964–July 1967**

Notes: "Central bank" contains "exceptional items." Data do not include unexplained items or profits. Data are from the Federal Reserve System.

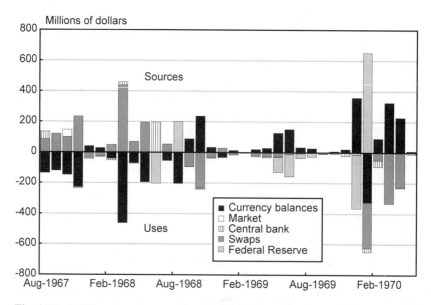

Fig. 4.15 **US Treasury sources and uses of British pounds, August 1967–May 1970**

Notes: "Central bank" contains "exceptional items." Data do not include unexplained items or profits. Data are from the Federal Reserve System.

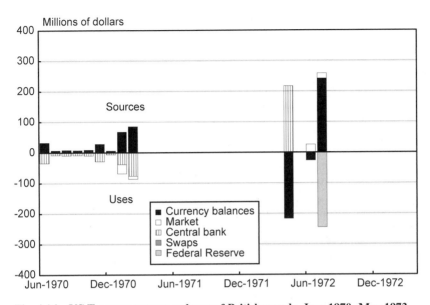

Fig. 4.16   US Treasury sources and uses of British pounds, June 1970–May 1973
Notes: "Central bank" contains "exceptional items." Data do not include unexplained items or profits. Data are from the Federal Reserve System.

ing $8.4 million worth of pounds in the market on 29 March 1963 (*Bulletin*, September 1963, 1219).

The speculative outflow from the United Kingdom caused other European central banks to acquire dollars. Consequently, instead of drawing down additional dollars from its US swap line to defend the pound, the United Kingdom negotiated $250 million worth of short-term credits with continental European central banks to shore up its potential reserves (*Bulletin*, September 1963, 1219). Britain negotiated these credits in early February, but did not make them public until April 1963. The announcement of the cooperation among central banks took much of the pressure off the rate by signaling a rise in the potential cost of speculating against a pound devaluation. The pound soon rose above par.

With pressure on sterling waning, US monetary authorities took opportunities to retire their outstanding swap debt, and in the bargain, to support the pound. On 19 May 1963, in a further move to raise the potential cost of speculation against sterling, the Federal Reserve announced an increase in its swap line with the Bank of England from $50 million to $500 million (*Bulletin*, September 1963, 1220). In considering this ten-fold increase, one FOMC member feared—quite rightly, as we have already seen—that if the Bank of England drew on the swap lines to defend the pound, the dollars thus expended might show up as unwanted dollar reserves on the books of other central banks (FOMC *Minutes*, 28 May 1963, 17). The generous swap lines with the Bank of England thus presented a prospective problem for the United States down the road.

In early 1964, the pound again came under pressure because of a deterioration in the British balance of payments, uncertainty about the timing and outcome of upcoming elections, and rumors of a possible revaluation of the German mark. Bank of England interventions, sometimes undertaken in concert with the Federal Reserve and the US Treasury, increased markedly. On 30 June, the Bank of England drew $15 million from the swap line with the Federal Reserve System, but quickly repaid the drawing in July when money-market conditions provided the pound with a respite.

In July 1964, covered interest arbitrage conditions favored a movement of funds into London. To forestall financial outflows from New York, the Federal Reserve undertook a series of swap transactions with the market designed to increase the forward discount on UK pounds by buying pounds spot against dollars and simultaneously selling them forward. These market swaps amounted to $28 million equivalent in July. In addition, the US Treasury offered $1 billion worth of Treasury bills on 22 July in an Operation Twist effort to raise short-term interest rates relative to long-term rates (*Bulletin*, September 1964, 1123). Nevertheless, covered interest arbitrage conditions continued to favor placing funds in London, and the Federal Reserve undertook additional market swaps in New York totaling $26.2 million equivalent in late August and early September (*Bulletin*, March 1965, 379). Many of these forward sales would eventually come due when speculative pressures were weighing on the pound. The Federal Reserve would then find itself making spot sales of pounds in a weak market.

In August 1964, sterling started weakening relative to other European currencies and funds again began to shift out of pounds into the Eurodollar market. Britain negotiated a $1 billion standby credit with the IMF, and in September, British monetary authorities arranged a $500 million multicountry series of swaps with several European central banks and the Bank of Canada. "By the end of September, the Bank of England had drawn $200 million of the $1 billion of [international] swap credits available" (Solomon 1982, 87). (The $1 billion credit line included the Federal Reserve's swap line.) The Bank of England embarked on a series of almost continuous swap drawings and repayments with the Federal Reserve that continued through August 1965.

Britain elected a Labour Party government on 16 October 1964 by a narrow margin. Although opinions within the government were divided, the prime minister and much of the cabinet opposed any devaluation of the pound (Cairncross and Eichengreen 2003). Nor would the Labour government deflate the economy. Prime Minister Harold Wilson's preference for renationalizing industries and expanding the welfare state instead sent financial funds flowing out of the country (Cairncross and Eichengreen 2003).

Within ten days of taking office, the new Labour government announced measures to deal with the country's growing balance-of-payments problem. These included a 15 percent import surcharge and export tax credits, which quickly resulted in threats of reprisals (*Bulletin*, March 1965, 380). The market anticipated an increase in the bank rate, but this did not immediately materialize. Finally on 20 November 1964, following another postponement of an increase in the Bank of England's discount rate, a massive selling wave began. On that same day, the United Kingdom exhausted its credit line with the Bank of Canada and with the other European central banks and drew $350 million from its swap line with the Federal Reserve (Coombs 1976, 114). On Monday, 23 November 1964, the Bank of England increased its bank rate from 5 percent to 7 percent, but with the market now anticipating a pound devaluation, selling pressures became especially heavy.

On 24 November 1964, a $3 billion short-term credit package to back up sterling began to take shape (Coombs 1976, 116–23). The FOMC approved a $250 million increase in the swap arrangement with the Bank of England to $750 million. The Bank of England had been drawing on its swap line since August, and had even sold $50 million in gold to the US Treasury. The Export-Import Bank—a frequent participant in US exchange-market intervention efforts—authorized $250 million in credit (Coombs 1976, 117). Ten other central banks and the BIS participated, creating a $2.5 billion short-term credit facility. Although France grudgingly participated, President De Gaulle claimed it would be the last time (Solomon 1982, 89). During late 1964—and throughout much of 1965—the Bank of England continued to draw on its swap line with the Federal Reserve and to make simultaneous repayments. In total, the Bank of England drew $1.4 billion between June and December 1964.[66] The multinational short-term credit lines facilitated the swap repayments. Eventually, the United Kingdom made a $1 billion multicurrency drawing from the IMF in December 1964 to help with repayments.

By late 1964, the United Kingdom was borrowing from some creditors to repay others, but the country had not addressed its fundamental underlying balance-of-payments problem. As Coombs (1976, 123) concluded: "In any event, the provision of $3 billion of new credits to the Bank of England signally failed to generate a real recovery of confidence in sterling." Although the crisis atmosphere lightened, uncertainty about the United Kingdom's trade deficit and its economic policies left the pound under downward pressure throughout December. Heavy interventions—particularly in the forward market—continued (Coombs 1976, 123; Cairncross and Eichengreen 2003, 171). The Bank of England sold an additional $75 million in gold to the US Treasury in December to acquire dollars for intervention.

Britain's balance-of-payments deficits persisted in 1965, as did speculative attacks against sterling and heavy intervention. On 25 May 1965, with reserves and credit lines nearly exhausted, the Bank of England again drew

$1.4 billion equivalent in foreign currencies from the IMF and Switzerland, and repaid $1.1 billion equivalent in outstanding short-term credits. The bank's $2 billion credit line with other central banks then terminated (Coombs 1976, 124). The Bank of England increasingly found itself attempting to defend a parity that many market participants and even official observers viewed as untenable.

After a brief midyear respite, pressure on sterling returned because of tightness in the Eurodollar market and because the Bank of England had lowered its discount rate. The Bank of England was again intervening in both spot and forward markets for sterling. These operations intensified in August following the release of unfavorable reserves figures. By August, the Bank of England had drawn the full $750 million on the Federal Reserve's swap line. On 31 August 1965, the Federal Reserve and Treasury extended a special one-day $140 million credit to the Bank of England that allowed the bank to bolster its reserves on a single day for reporting purposes (FOMC *Minutes*, 31 August 1965, 4). Henceforth, swaps would occasionally serve this function.

Following notification that the government obtained some wage and price controls, the market again settled down, but the pound remained susceptible to downward pressure. British reserves were now very low, and existing short-term credit facilities with the United States and with the IMF were fully drawn. Britain entered into new credit arrangements totaling $600 million with Canada, Japan, and the key European central banks.[67] France did not participate. For its part, the United States agreed to buy $400 million worth of pounds either on a guaranteed basis, which meant that in the event of a sterling devaluation, the Bank of England would repurchase the sterling at the initial exchange rate, or otherwise on a covered basis (Coombs 1976, 126–27; FOMC *Minutes*, 8 September 1965, 1–6). The announcement was made on 10 September 1965 at the opening of the New York market. The Bank of England in concert with US monetary authorities immediately began purchasing sterling in New York "on a substantial scale and at progressively higher rates so as to convince the market of the determination and power of the central banks in support of sterling" (*Desk Report* 1965, 13). The desk operated directly with the market, not through the brokers' market with a commercial bank as its agent, as typically had been the case (Coombs 1976, 128).[68] The Federal Reserve purchased $21.5 million worth of pounds on a "guaranteed basis." The pound rose above par, and Coombs (1976, 129, 131) viewed the operation as a successful "bear squeeze." The bears, however, did not die; they just hibernated for a while.

The enlarged international credit facility and a fortuitous improvement in Britain's balance-of-payments data checked the 1965 crisis. The Bank of England repaid $275 million of its swap debts to the Federal Reserve in October and November. By year's end, the Bank of England had liquidated $760 million of its forward market commitments and $415 million of short-term obligations to the United States. In addition, the bank managed to increase its official reserves (*Bulletin*, March 1966, 321). Nevertheless, UK fundamentals remained shaky.

When the international credit lines came up for renewal in March 1966, the foreign central banks, which had lost faith in the United Kingdom's willingness to make fundamental adjustments, placed restrictions on their use (see Coombs 1976, 132–33). By then sterling-area governments were approaching the Bank of England, looking to convert their foreign-currency reserves out of sterling. The central banks that had participated in the September 1965 credit lines were willing to offer credits against the conversion of outstanding sterling reserve balances that foreign governments held, but not against continuing British balance-of-payments deficits. Moreover, the United Kingdom's drawings at any one time were not to exceed the amount of credits that the country still had available with the IMF. Essentially, the countries wanted an IMF backstop. At best, this was an insincere vote of confidence in the pound's prospects. The United States did not participate directly, but allowed the Bank of England to earmark a portion of the current US credit lines to finance reserve losses attributable to the conversion of sterling balances.[69]

In February 1966, the pound again fell below par, prompting renewed Bank of England intervention in the spot and forward markets. By April, the Federal Reserve and the Treasury joined in, often covering their portion through simultaneous forward pound sales to the Bank of England. Pressure on sterling intensified following a British seamen's strike in mid-May, tightening credit conditions in the Eurodollar market and continuing sharp declines in British reserves. United States intervention purchases of pounds in the last half of 1966 were exceptionally large.

On 20 July 1966, the British government announced a massive austerity program that included a wage freeze, restraints on prices and dividends, additional taxes, reduced travel allowances, and further curbs on public expenditures (Coombs 1976, 136). To signal confidence in the British program, the Federal Reserve and the Treasury made huge spot purchases of sterling totaling $55.1 million equivalent and $89.6 million equivalent, respectively, in June and July. (During the same month, however, the Federal Reserve and Treasury delivered $66.6 million worth of pounds sold on a previous forward contract!) In addition, the Bank of England made a very large $100 million swap drawing during the last statement week of July, bringing its entire monthly drawing to $300 million. "In order that the [Federal Reserve] System's weekly statement would not reflect too large an increase in its 'other assets,' the System at the end of its statement week of July 27 swapped $88.2 million pounds for one day with the U.S. Treasury" (*Desk Report* 1967, 10). The Federal Reserve now sought to hide the magnitude of its sterling operations from speculators. Heavy interventions continued throughout the summer.

Although pressure on sterling began to subside in late summer, the situation remained critical. The prospects of once again getting the key central banks to provide the United Kingdom with credits to support sterling were now nil (Coombs 1976, 138–42). Consequently, the United States shouldered much of the burden.[70] On September 13, the Federal Reserve announced a substantial increase, from $2.8 billion to $4.5 billion, in its entire swap facility. The swap-line extensions included an 80 percent increase in the Federal Reserve's line with Bank of England from $750 to $1,350 million. Coombs (1976, 141) described increases in the other swap lines as a "counterbalance," a necessary part of the sterling—*and dollar*—defense. If the pound came under speculative attack, the dollars expended to support sterling very likely would end up in the portfolios of other central banks. The Federal Reserve might then need to provide these banks with cover through swap drawings to protect US gold reserves.

During the second half of September 1966, following the announced hike in the swap lines, demand for sterling increased as dealers sought to cover forward sales and to cover short positions. The Bank of England began buying dollars at each opportunity to rebuild reserves. The desk undertook market swaps totaling $36.3 million in November and $51.6 million in December, with the proceeds split evenly between the Federal Reserve's and Treasury's accounts. Britain posted its first postwar trade surplus in November 1966, further alleviating the strains on sterling. For the year as a whole, British reserves actually increased.

In early 1967, interest-rate differentials favoring pound-denominated assets continued to attract a financial inflow to Britain, despite that nation's overall weak trade performance. With its accumulated dollar reserves, by the end of March British authorities were able to repay its $510 million obligation to the United States outstanding at the end of 1966, including $350 million in swap obligations with the Federal Reserve, $50 million in special overnight credits from the Federal Reserve, and $130 million in special overnight credits with the US Treasury. In addition, the Bank of England repurchased $33 million worth of sterling from the Federal Reserve and a substantial sum from the US Treasury. This reduced the Federal Reserve System holdings of sterling balances to $101.8 million equivalent and the US Treasury's holdings to $120.9 million equivalent. In addition, the Bank of England trimmed a November 1965 sterling-for-gold swap with the US Treasury to $33.8 million. As this swap unwound, the US Treasury reduced a parallel gold-for-dollar swap with the Bundesbank. Full payment of these swaps was scheduled for June 1967 (*Desk Report* 1968, 10, fn.1). British authorities had also liquidated a substantial portion of outstanding credits from other monetary authorities.

This welcome break from speculation against sterling came to an end on 1 June 1967, when expectations of an imminent armed conflict in the Middle East caused a flight from sterling and a precautionary movement of funds out of the Eurodollar market. By 5 June, the Federal Reserve System and the US Treasury had purchased on a swap basis nearly $113 million worth of sterling in the New York market, and the Bank for International Settlements drew $143 million from the Federal Reserve's swap lines and placed the proceeds in the Eurodollar market to reduce interest-rate pressures. In early July, the Bank of England reported that it lost $120.4 million in reserves during June (*Bulletin*, March 1968, 272). This report further eroded confidence in the pound. The loss would have been larger had the Bank of England not drawn on its swap line with the Federal Reserve and on the 1966 international credit arrangements. In addition the Swiss National Bank and Swiss commercial banks shifted funds to the London market to compensate for funds moved into Switzerland during the Middle East hostilities (*Desk Report* 1968, 14, fn. 5). The closing of the Suez Canal together with a British dockworker strike helped to worsen the British trade deficit.

On 19 October 1967, the Bank of England, hoping to reverse the financial outflows, raised its discount rate. In an effort to prevent a rise in the Eurodollar rates from nullifying the discount rate hike, the Federal Reserve drew on the swap line with the BIS, which then placed the dollar proceeds in the Eurodollar market (*Bulletin*, March 1968, 273). The Bank of England intervened heavily in both the spot and forward markets. The Treasury in concert with the Bank of England purchased spot sterling in an attempt to nudge the rate higher. By the end of October, the Treasury purchased $47.1 million worth of sterling. The Treasury now held $194 million equivalent pounds under the Bank of England's guarantee against devaluation. Despite these actions, selling pressure only intensified, prompting the Bank of England to raise its discount rate again on 9 November 1967.

On Thursday, 16 November 1967, Chancellor Callaghan, responding to questions from Parliament, refused to either confirm or deny rumors of plans for a massive sterling bailout, and prompted an unprecedented rush out of sterling the next day. The Bank of England lost more than $1 billion in a single day (FOMC *Memoranda*, 27 November 1967, 8). On Saturday, 18 November 1967, the British government devalued sterling 14.3 percent to $2.40. The Bank of England raised its discount rate to 8 percent (the highest level in 58 years), placed curbs on consumer installment credit, and asked commercial banks to channel credit toward exports. In addition, the government announced plans to cut public spending and to raise the corporate income tax (*Bulletin*, March 1968, 273–74).

Contrary to the expectations of US monetary officials, no other major industrialized country followed the British devaluation. Instead, they made more than $1.5 billion in new short-term credits available to defend the new parity, and the IMF established a new $1.4 billion standby facility. The Federal Reserve System and the US Treasury contributed $500 million to this new facility (*Desk Report* 1968, 19).

The pound initially traded well above its new parity, but by the end of

1967, it weakened on news of continuing British trade deficits and because of speculative gold purchases. On 8 December 1967, the Bank of England purchased sterling when the rate moved below $2.41 (FOMC *Memoranda*, 12 December 1967, 5). By the end of 1967, the Bank of England had outstanding short-term commitments to the United States totaling $1.6 billion, and large commitments to other monetary authorities (*Desk Report* 1968, 22).

During 1968 and 1969, the British pound generally remained under downward pressure, resulting in fairly persistent reserve losses. The exchange market remained skeptical of the Labour Government's commitment to the austerity measures that accompanied the November 1967 devaluation. In addition, the devaluation imposed losses on the reserve positions of sterling area countries, and these countries sought to protect themselves from another devaluation by diversifying out the sterling. Concerns about the Gold Pool (below) and the growing prospects of a mark revaluation or a franc devaluation heightened uncertainties about the long-term viability of the new sterling peg. Consequently, the Bank of England sought major credit lines both to fund continuing support operations and to meet commitments arising from outstanding forward contracts and previous credit lines. In 1968, England did receive additional international credits, bringing England's total credit facility to $4 billion. The Federal Reserve System increased its swap line with the Bank of England by $500 million to $2 billion, and the US Treasury increased the credit facility that it extended to the Bank of England in November 1967 from $350 million to $550 million (see figures 4.9 and 4.10). In view of the severe strains on the official reserves, the United Kingdom elected to defer the year-end payment of principal and interest on postwar loans from the United States and Canada. This was the fourth postponement and left three such deferment options remaining (Cairncross and Eichengreen 2003, 193–94.)

The situation remained tenuous until late in 1969. The devaluation of the French franc on 8 August 1969 prompted heavy renewed selling pressure on the pound. The Bank of England drew on its swap line with the Federal Reserve in order to finance its support operations. Pressure on the pound continued until September, when balance-of-payments data show a surplus. Following the revaluation of the German mark, the pound began to strengthen, and the Bank of England acquired sufficient dollars to begin paying back its swap obligations. The pound traded just below parity and forward discounts narrowed. By December 1969, as Eurodollar rates dipped, the pound rose above par for the first time since April 1968. The Bank of England acquired dollars, which it used primarily to repay international credits. By early 1970, the Bank of England had fully liquidated its swap debt with the Federal Reserve and made strides at reducing other outstanding credits. On 5 March 1970, the Bank of England cut its discount rate from 7.5 percent to 7 percent. The Bank of England continued to pay down its outstanding debts throughout 1970. By April, for the first time since May 1964, the United Kingdom was free of all official debt (Cairncross and Eichengreen 2003, 194). The new exchange rate held until Bretton Woods ended.

4.7.2   The Gold Pool

Although the British devaluation did not lead to speculative attacks on other currencies, it did heighten speculative pressures in the London gold market. By March 1968, the Gold Pool disintegrated and a two-tier system of official and private gold prices replaced it.

After the United Kingdom reopened the London gold market in 1954, it rapidly reemerged as the largest, most important free market for gold in the world, and its daily fixing price became a barometer of confidence in the Bretton Woods (Bank of England 1964). Sufficiently large deviations between the London market price and the official gold price afforded central banks the potential for profitable arbitrage. The lower arbitrage point—the price at which buying gold in London and selling it to the US Treasury became advantageous—was approximately $34.80 per ounce. This equaled the official $35.00 per ounce less Treasury charges and shipping costs. The upper arbitrage point—the price at which buying gold at the official price in New York and selling it in the London market became profitable—was roughly $35.20, the official price plus the Treasury fees and shipping costs.[71] By and large, however, before 1965, the annual inflow of gold from new production and Russian sales typically accommodated private industrial, speculative, and official demands for gold, and if the London price deviated from the official price, the Bank of England could easily intervene to contain it within the arbitrage points (*Bulletin*, March 1964, 304), "by and large" here being the operative words.

This tranquillity first started to fade as the US presidential election approached in 1960. On 20 October 1960, the London gold price temporarily peaked at approximately $40 per ounce. This price spike followed a brief shortfall in gold supplies and rise in speculative demand associated with uncertainty about the Kennedy administration's commitment to the official gold price. Speculators believed that the Kennedy administration would pursue easy, inflation-prone policies that would worsen the US balance-of-payments deficit and ultimately lead to a dollar devaluation. In response, the Bank of England acted to stabilize the market, with the support of the US Treasury's gold stock, and it drove the price down to $35.60 by the end of the year (Coombs 1976, 57). The price of gold stabilized at approximately $35.08 by March 1961, following Kennedy's pledge to maintain the dollar's convertibility, and in the second quarter of 1961, a series of fortuitous, but short-lived events that added to the supply of gold in the London market. These included Russian sales, Eisenhower's limitation on private US citizens' overseas gold holdings, and British gold sales following the German and Dutch revaluations. Still, events in October 1961 "badly jolted" confidence in the dollar, and central banks "could no longer forego the privilege [of converting dollars to gold] without exposing themselves to charges of imprudent management of the national reserves entrusted to their safekeeping" (Coombs 1976, 57).

Toward the end of 1961, however, South Africa and Canada reduced supplies to the market as they sought to build up their own reserves. Consequently, when the Berlin crisis unfolded, gold in London quickly began trading around the arbitrage point, $35.20 per ounce. European central banks, concerned for the viability of the Bretton Woods system, refrained from buying US gold and selling it in London, but as demand from other central banks and from the private sector grew, the situation became extremely tenuous. Concerted action seemed necessary. The Gold Pool was the result.

The Gold Pool developed as a gentleman's agreement following the 1960 price spike in the London market (Bank of England 1964, 18). After a long period of informal discussions, mostly at the Basle meetings of central banks, in October 1961 the United States proposed the formation of an informal sales consortium to limit gold-price increases stemming from political crises or speculative activity. The governments of Belgium, France, Italy, the Netherlands, Switzerland, West Germany, and the United Kingdom accepted the proposal and formed the Gold Pool. The initial subscription amounted to $270 million worth of gold. The Bank of England acted as the consortium's agent in London and determined the appropriate amount of any sales. The United States, operating through the Federal Reserve Bank of New York, would match the gold sales of the other participating central banks. Hence, 50 percent of all Gold Pool sales involved US gold. The other central banks contracted to take set proportions of any gold sales up to their subscriptions. In addition, they agreed not to buy gold on the London market or from other sources, and they agreed not to quickly convert any excess dollars that they received from such sales into US gold. In November 1961, the Gold Pool undertook a trial run, selling a moderate amount of gold in London. When prices permitted, the Gold Pool repurchased this initial amount of gold and by the end of February 1962, redistributed it to the Pool's participants. The operations went smoothly.

In early 1962, however, gold prices began to fall, and following a proposal by the United States, the Pool began to purchase gold in the London market when the price approached the London gold export price. Now, instead of operating independently, the eight member nations bought gold in concert through the Gold Pool. By late spring 1962, the Gold Pool had purchased $80 million worth of gold (*Bulletin*, March 1964, 306).

Even before the $80 million could be distributed, a decline in US stock prices and speculative flight from Canadian dollars again pushed gold prices up. By mid-July 1962, the Gold Pool had used up its accumulated surplus, and by September 1962, the Pool had sold a net $50 million worth of gold to the market. The Cuban Missile crisis in October 1962 resulted in record demands for gold, but substantial sales from the Pool helped keep the price below $35.20. Subsequently, Russian gold sales helped drive the price down so that by the end of 1962, the Pool had recovered all of its net gold sales.

During 1963 and most of 1964, gold prices remained fairly stable. Speculative demand seemed to diminish, new production increased, and Russia sold gold to the market and to the Gold Pool. In both years, the Gold Pool acquired and distributed to its members $600 million in gold (*Bulletin*, March 1964, 307; *Bulletin*, March 1965, 389).

Up to this date, the Gold Pool generally functioned as a successful stabilizing speculator might, by buying low and selling high around what appeared to be a sustainable official price. By late 1964, however, the situation began to change, and it would only worsen hereafter in accordance with Triffin's paradox.[72] In 1965, international tensions, stemming primarily from uncertainty about the viability of sterling's parity, from France's decision to accelerate the conversion of its dollar reserves into gold, and from that country's public criticisms of the Bretton Woods system, resulted in a very heavy speculative demand for gold. In addition, communist China bought large quantities of gold during much of the year. Even though sales from South Africa ran above normal, private demand absorbed almost all of this, and the Gold Pool found its resources dwindling as it struggled to keep the gold price below $35.20. At one point early in the year, the Gold Pool operated with a $50 million gold deficit, which the Bank of England financed out of its own reserves (FOMC *Minutes*, 2 February 1965, 6). Participants agreed to continue selling gold, and by June, the Gold Pool had a deficit of $170 million (FOMC *Minutes*, 15 June 1965, 2). Nevertheless, with a good amount of "sheer luck," the Pool recouped its losses by the end of 1965 (Coombs 1976, 153).

Even though the Gold Pool was able to replenish reserves from time to time through supplies from South Africa or Russia, or through additional member contributions, demand generally continued to outpace supply through 1966. As American policymakers feared, demand for gold had become increasing tied to expectations about British sterling and, by extension, to the viability of the official gold price. Moreover, the French government, as Coombs noted, seemed intentionally to hasten the system's demise:

> The French Government continued to harass the market with a succession of announcements designed to cast doubt on the official $35 price. The latest French move in that campaign, announced on January 29, was to internationalize the hitherto domestic French gold market. Those new measures now permitted French residents to buy gold on the London market and would encourage the growth of French gold custody business for nonresidents. . . . [T]he French seemed to have deliberately put themselves on a collision course with US policy . . . (FOMC *Minutes*, 7 February 1967, 3).

Gold Pool losses increased after the 5 June 1967 outbreak of hostilities in the Middle East, requiring participating countries to contribute additional reserves to the Pool yet again. France, however, now balked at making a further commitment and withdrew, and the United States agreed to pick up their share. Other participating countries, notably Belgium and Italy, were losing confidence in the Gold Pool's viability and participants began to press the United States for a longer-term, fundamental solution to the problem.

The gold situation only worsened as the speculative attack on sterling continued. At the 14 November 1967 FOMC meeting, Coombs predicted that the Gold Pool would post a $600 million to $700 million deficit for all 1967 (FOMC *Memoranda*, 14 November 1967, 3). Since September 1966, the member countries had made eight contributions, totaling $670 million in gold to the Pool, compared with an initial contribution of $270 million. The seventh contribution had been negotiated on 8 November and had been virtually exhausted two days later. An eighth contribution was negotiated over 11 and 12 November (FOMC *Memoranda*, 14 November 1967, 3).

Coombs expected that the British Government would devalue the pound by 10 percent to 15 percent over the coming weekend unless they obtained massive support in the form of medium term credits (FOMC *Memoranda*, 14 November 1967, 4). He feared that a British devaluation would result in a run on gold, causing participants to withdraw from the Gold Pool. He expected that a financial flight from sterling would leave other European central banks with huge dollar inflows and add to the drain of US monetary gold. As the US Treasury lost gold, the market would lose confidence in the dollar.

Coombs's predictions did not immediately come true. Following the devaluation, Gold Pool members contributed a cumulative $1,370 million to the operation. The US Air Force cooperated by airlifting gold from the United States to London. The Paris newspaper *Le Monde*, however, announced that the Bank of France had withdrawn from the Pool and that two other central banks (those of Belgium and Italy) were about to do the same (FOMC *Memoranda*, 27 November 1967, 3–6).

Foreign central bank operations in the Gold Pool, however, were only contributing to their further accumulation of dollars. Increasingly, Gold Pool participants believed that the United States should absorb those dollars through an IMF drawing, rather than via swap lines, and that it should take steps to plug the ultimate source of the dollar glut, the US balance of payments deficit, through monetary and fiscal policies (FOMC *Memoranda*, 12 December 1967, 17–19). The United States promised to intervene in defense of the dollar and to pay down any such foreign currency debts arising from these operations with drawings on the IMF (Coombs 1976, 171).

Speculative gold demand remained strong in early 1968, and on 17 March 1968 the London Gold Pool suspended operations. Between the devaluation of sterling (18 November 1967) and the closing of the London gold market (17 March 1968), the Gold Pool sold $3 billion worth of gold in the London market (FOMC *Memoranda*, 2 April 1968, 4). "Of that total, the US share amounted to $2.2 billion; both Italy and Belgium had replenished their share of Pool losses during March by buying gold from the US Treasury" (FOMC *Memoranda*, 2 April 1968, 5).

The seven leading central banks agreed to replace the Gold Pool with a two-tier gold market. Ideally, the existing stock of gold presently held as official reserves would be sealed off from the market. Monetary authorities would continue to buy and sell gold among themselves at the official price of $35 per ounce, but they would refrain from transacting in the private market. With the establishment of special drawing rights (SDRs), they viewed the existing stock of official gold as sufficient for balance-of-payments purposes. All gold presently in private hands and all newly produced gold would remain outside of official reserves. Hence, the private price of gold could deviate substantially from the official price, and would become a highly visible barometer of confidence in the dollar and in the Bretton Woods system. Ironically, once the Pool dissolved, a large overhang of speculative gold reentered the market, holding the free market prices within $37 to $40 per ounce (FOMC *Memoranda*, 2 April 1968, 6).

Most other central banks and governments around the world signaled a willingness to cooperate with the two-tiered gold system. Some, of course, might not adhere strictly if the private and official prices greatly diverged. If the private market price fell below the official price, private gold producers would probably pressure their government to buy gold at the official price. Ultimately, however, the success of the venture depended on the triumphant adoption of SDRs, which could supply a nondollar reserve to satisfy future reserve needs, and on an improvement in the US balance of payments position, which could prevent a continued drain on US monetary gold stocks (Solomon 1968). These things, of course, would not happen.

4.7.3   The Devaluation of the French Franc

Between 1962 and early 1968, France became increasingly reluctant to cooperate in defense of the dollar. This reluctance stemmed from that country's fundamental displeasure with the dollar's role in the Bretton Woods system. The French government had long favored a fixed exchange-rate system that relied more heavily on gold for adjustment than did the Bretton Woods system and that did not confer unconstrained status on a single reserve currency (Bordo, Simard, and White 1996). As the provider of the reserve currency, the United States had sustained a balance-of-payments deficit, but—in accordance with Triffin's prediction—this made the system unstable. France realized this problem and believed that all countries should link their currencies directly to gold, not to the dollar, thereby making them potential reserve currencies, and that the United States should redeem dollars in gold (Coombs 1976, 174–75).

France attempted to leverage US support for its preferred revisions to the international financial system by selling dollars back to the United States and sometimes by recommending an increase in the official price of gold. Between 1960 and 1968, France continued to increase the share of its official reserves held as gold, largely via dollar sales to the US Treasury. These dollar sales accelerated between early 1965 and the ending of the Gold Pool. In 1965, for example, French purchases accounted for more than two-thirds of the Treasury's gold sales to foreign countries. After the pound's devaluation in November 1967, hints of French support for an increase in the official gold price kept downward pressure on the dollar (Bordo, Simard, and White 1996).

Between 1962 and the collapse of the Gold Pool in March 1968, the Federal Reserve System only undertook three brief exploratory operations in French francs (see figures 4.17 and 4.18). As discussed above, in March 1962, the Federal Reserve established a $50 million swap line with the Bank of France and drew $50 million equivalent francs from that line largely to "test communications, investment procedures, and other operational arrangements" (*Bulletin*, September 1962, 1148). The Federal Reserve simply held these francs in its portfolio. After one renewal, the Federal Reserve liquidated the swap drawing on 12 August 1962. In May 1963, the Federal Reserve drew $12.5 million equivalent French francs from the swap line and sold them for dollars in the Paris market. The Federal Reserve simultaneously covered this swap drawing by purchasing francs forward from the Bank of France. The desk was attempting to alter the level of the French franc-dollar exchange rate in a market that was not exhibiting compelling evidence of disorderly conditions nor under imminent threat of a speculative run. The US dollar had persistently traded at the lower parity band against the French franc, as large financial inflows contributed to a sizable French balance-of-payments surplus. The dollar rate, however, "showed no lasting sign of improvement" (Board of Governors 1966, 21). The Federal Reserve undertook a final operation in October 1963, which it financed with a $9.0 million equivalent franc swap drawing. These operations gave the Bank of France discretion to sell francs as agent for the Federal Reserve (*Bulletin*, March 1964, 303). "Again, however, the underlying strength of the franc prevailed in the market; the dollar returned to the floor"; and the desk stopped intervening (Board of Governors 1966, 21). These operations were also covered through forward purchases of French francs, and the Federal Reserve liquidated the drawing in January 1964.[73]

Over this same time period, the Treasury acquired French francs in conjunction with IMF drawings and briefly from a $25 million swap with the Bank of England in December 1964 (see figures 4.19 and 4.20). Generally, the Treasury held these French francs or sold them to third parties. In August 1965, however, the Treasury sold $40 million equivalent francs that it received from an IMF drawing to the Bank of France in order to reduce French acquisitions of US monetary gold.

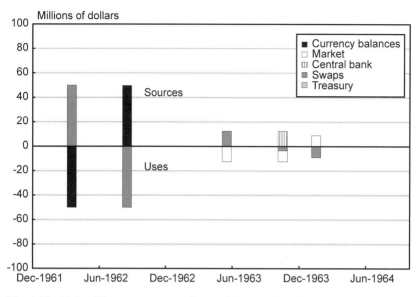

Fig. 4.17   Federal Reserve sources and uses of French francs, December 1961–September 1964

Notes: "Central bank" contains "exceptional items." Data do not include unexplained items or profits. Data are from the Federal Reserve System.

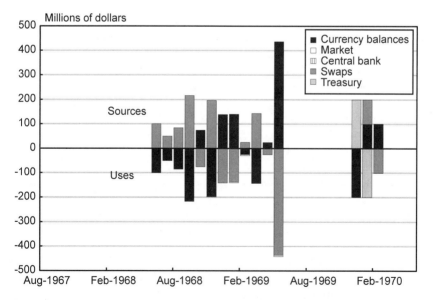

Fig. 4.18   Federal Reserve sources and uses of French francs, August 1967– July 1970

Notes: The Federal Reserve did not transact in French francs between October 1964 and May 1968 nor between March 1970 and March 1973. "Central bank" contains "exceptional items." Data do not include unexplained items or profits. Data are from the Federal Reserve System.

France's position as a strong-currency, surplus country came to an abrupt end in May 1968, when unexpected student rioting and labor strikes produced heavy financial flows out of French francs and into stronger currencies, despite the closing of most French financial institutions. The franc, which traded well above par throughout most of the 1960s, weakened precipitously. The Bank of France, whose operations were hampered by the closure of domestic financial institutions, asked the Federal Reserve System and the Bank for International Settlements to support the franc in the New York and European markets, respectively, for its account (*Bulletin*, September 1968, 728). By the end of the month, the French government imposed exchange controls on financial outflows and temporary import quotas. Export subsidies soon followed. In early June, President de Gaulle called for elections, which the Gaullists won.

Although the immediate political crisis began to subside in early June, the franc remained weak under fears that the Bank of France would accommodate the government's large wage concessions, thereby further eroding France's international competitiveness and forcing a franc devaluation. To finance a defense of the peg, the Bank of France—for the first time—drew the full $100 million from its swap line with the Federal Reserve System in June 1968 (see figure 4.18). In addition, France drew $885 million from the International Monetary Fund and sold gold from its reserves, including $220 million of gold to the US Treasury (see figure 4.20).[74] The Bank of France's net reserve losses amounted to $307 million and $203 million in May and June, respectively, but taking the various credits into consideration, the Federal Reserve estimated the total cost of supporting the franc over these two months at $1.5 billion (*Bulletin*, September 1968, 729).

France undertook additional measures in July 1968 to shore up market confidence in the franc. Early in the month, the Bank of France raised its discount rate from 3 1/2 percent to 5 percent and the French government tightened exchange controls and imposed new taxes. On 10 July 1968, the Federal Reserve System in concert with the central banks of Belgium, Germany, Italy, the Netherlands, and with the Bank for International Settlements, extended $1.3 billion in additional credits to the Bank of France. For its part, the Federal Reserve increased its swap line by $600 million to $700 million (*Bulletin*, September 1968, 729–30). During July, August, and September 1968, the Bank of France drew an additional $390 million from its swap line with the Federal Reserve, and financed the repayment of a small portion ($40 million) in August by selling $80 million of gold to the US Treasury (*Bulletin*, March 1969, 218). Despite the show of international support, speculative pressure persisted, and the Bank of France continued to lose reserves in defense of the franc.

By the fall of 1968, growing rumors of an impending mark revaluation maintained speculation against the franc as some of the earlier credits were coming due. This forced the Bank of France into the awkward position of having to acquire dollars when the franc remained weak. In October, the

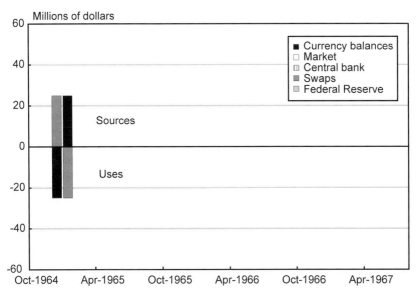

Fig. 4.19 US Treasury sources and uses of French francs, October 1964–September 1967

Notes: The US Treasury did not transact in French francs between December 1961 and September 1964. "Central bank" contains "exceptional items." Data do not include unexplained items or profits. Data are from the Federal Reserve System.

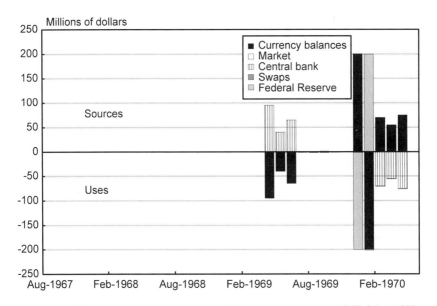

Fig. 4.20 US Treasury sources and uses of French francs, August 1967–May 1970

Notes: The US Treasury did not transact in French francs after April 1970. "Central bank" contains "exceptional items." Data do not include unexplained items or profits. Data are from the Federal Reserve System.

Bank of France undertook dollar swaps with French commercial banks, simultaneously buying dollars spot and selling them forward. The bank then used $75 million of the proceeds from these market swaps to reduce its official swap debt with the Federal Reserve System and to repay other international credits (*Desk Report* 1969, 50).

Rumors of a German mark revaluation intensified in November 1968, particularly after the Basle meeting of central bank governors, and encouraged huge movements of funds out of French francs and into German marks. The Bank of France sustained large reserve losses in support of the franc, which remained at its lower parity limit (*Bulletin*, September 1969, 706). In response, the Bank of France raised its discount rate 1 percentage point to 6 percent, tightened reserve requirements, and imposed credit controls on short-term bank lending. To keep the franc from breaching its floor value, the Bank of France intervened heavily during the first nineteen days of November 1968. In addition to drawing down its reserves, the Bank of France drew $275 million on its swap line with the Federal Reserve and $283 million from other international credits, and sold $110 million in gold to the United States and $140 million to other European countries (*Desk Report* 1969, 51–53). In all, the seven-month crisis had significantly drained French reserves (Coombs 1976, 182). On 20 November 1968, France closed the market in Paris, as the G10 nations convened in Bonn to discuss the current situation.

At the Bonn meeting, the G10 ministers persuaded France to devalue the franc by 11.1 percent, but following the Bonn conference, President de Gaulle surprised the exchange market, which widely anticipated the devaluation, by rejecting the notion (Solomon 1982, 159–60). Instead, de Gaulle outlined a series of belt-tightening policies, including much stricter exchange controls. The G10 provided France with an additional $2 billion in credits at the Bonn meeting. The United States' contribution consisted of a $300 million increase in the Federal Reserve's swap line with the Bank of France (now at $1.0 billion) and a new $200 million credit facility through the Exchange Stabilization Fund (*Bulletin*, March 1969, 218).

Governors Brimmer and Maisel worried that if the Treasury provided credits to the Bank of France through a swap mechanism and subsequently warehoused those francs with the Federal Reserve System, the central bank would in effect be financing the credit to France. Coombs said that he would resist warehousing French francs (FOMC *Memoranda*, 26 November 1968, 22–23).

Largely because of stringent exchange controls, the Bank of France gained reserves from late November 1968 and through January 1969, which it used to repay credits.[75] The Bank of France reduced its outstanding swap commitments with the Federal Reserve by $220 million and paid down international obligations.

Expectation of inflation and devaluation persisted, and by February 1969, reserve gains attributable to exchange controls were not sufficient to fully finance the franc support operations. The situation worsened in March and in April on renewed labor unrest, and the Bank of France again started to lose reserves. To finance continued interventions, the Bank of France again drew $70 million from its swap line in February and an additional $155 million in March 1969.[76] The bank also sold $50 million in gold to the US Treasury (*Bulletin*, September 1969, 707).

President de Gaulle's resignation on 28 April 1969 did not stem the reserve losses, which if continued at their current pace, would exhaust the country's reserves by year's end. Many no longer believed that the franc's parity was viable, despite a further tightening of monetary policy in mid-June and George Pompidou's solid election victory. In May, as speculation on a mark revaluation intensified, francs sold forward, "with three-month contracts quoted at discounts as wide as 32 percent per annum before the forward market temporarily dried up completely" (*Bulletin*, September 1969, 707).

In May 1969, a deadline on swap credits again compounded the Bank of France's intervention operations. The bank owed $436 million in swap debts to the Federal Reserve, as well as funds from drawings on other European credit arrangements. To service these obligations, the bank sold $275 million in gold to the US Treasury and drew the remaining $105 million available under the Treasury's swap arrangement (*Bulletin*, September 1969, 708).

Facing the prospect that its reserves would soon run out, France devalued the franc 11.1 percent on 8 August 1969 and instituted additional fiscal measures, credit restraints, and price controls to back up the new parity. The country had lost $500 million per month in reserves during the last half 1968 and $300 million per month during the first half of 1969 (*Bulletin*, September 1969, 708). The Bank of France also received additional international credits and applied for a standby credit of $985 million with the IMF (*Bulletin*, September1969, 708). Despite the devaluation, the franc remained under downward pressure, forcing France to further tighten its monetary policy.

Speculative pressures on the franc only began to unwind following the mark revaluation in October 1969. France's balance-of-payments position then began to shift from a large deficit to a surplus, and the franc moved from near its lower parity limit to near its ceiling. French authorities were able to repay $1.5 billion in short-term international indebtedness, in part by drawing $985 million from the IMF. In addition, the Bank of France removed some of its most restrictive exchange controls (*Bulletin*, September 1970, 701–03).

France continued to acquire reserves through 1971. Although the Bank of France eased monetary policy, French interest rates fell at a slower pace than US interest rates, and consequently encouraged a financial inflow. France used the additional reserves to continue to pay down its short-term international indebtedness. On 9 August 1971, the Bank of France paid off its IMF debt (*Bulletin*, March 1972, 246). Because France had to repay a portion of this debt in gold, that country bought $191 million in gold from the US Treasury.

4.7.4   The Revaluation of the German Mark

During the Bretton Woods period, Germany generally maintained a relatively tight monetary policy, ran fairly persistent trade surpluses, and experienced inflows of dollar reserves. Unlike many countries, Germany often refrained from converting dollar reserves into gold, as a means of compensating the United States for the American troops deployed on its soil. To some extent, this agreement freed US monetary authorities of the need to provide the Bundesbank with cover for excess dollar holdings. Nevertheless, the United States did undertake such cover operations from time to time with the US Treasury instead of the Federal Reserve, often playing the leading role. More often, however, US foreign-exchange operations tended to focus on influencing spot and forward mark-dollar exchange rates through direct interventions. Financing these operations through swap drawing proved difficult because the mark, which increasingly seemed undervalued, often traded above par and the FOMC's authorization precluded the desk from buying currencies above par.

To create an initial portfolio in early 1962—before the Federal Reserve established its $50 million swap line with the Bundesbank—the Federal Reserve purchased $32 million worth of German marks from the US Treasury (see figures 4.21 through 4.28). On 20 June 1962, with the German mark trading above parity, the Federal Reserve System began selling marks spot in the New York market. Between 1962 and 1966, the desk typically operated in the New York market after the European market had closed. Sometimes, however, the desk assumed all or part of the Bundesbank's intervention purchases of dollars in the European market (Board of Governors 1966, 22). This relieved the Bundesbank from holding additional dollar reserves. In late July 1962, just as the Federal Reserve began to intervene in concert with the Treasury, the mark began to ease against the dollar and afforded US monetary authorities with an opportunity to reconstitute their mark portfolios. At the end of September, the Federal Reserve and the US Treasury held open positions in marks equal to $31.2 million and $31.7 million, respectively.[77] The Federal Reserve had not drawn on its swap line.

During the first half of 1963, improvements in the German trade balance, long-term financial inflows, and relatively tight monetary policy resulted in almost continuous buying pressure on the mark. Between early April and the end of July 1963, the Bundesbank and the Federal Reserve Bank of New York undertook fairly heavy coordinated interventions to stem the mark's appreciation. This time the Federal Reserve financed nearly all of its interventions from two swap drawings. In August, buying pressure on the German mark eased somewhat along with conditions in the German money market, but with the mark often trading above par, the Federal Reserve System was unable to acquire enough German marks from the market to fully

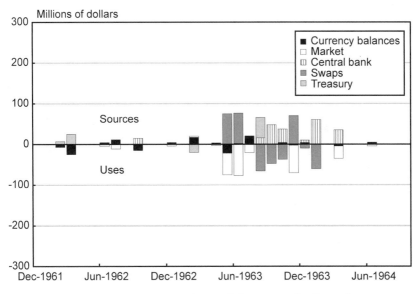

Fig. 4.21   Federal Reserve sources and uses of German marks, December 1961–September 1964

Notes: "Central bank" contains "exceptional items." Data do not include unexplained items or profits. Data are from the Federal Reserve System.

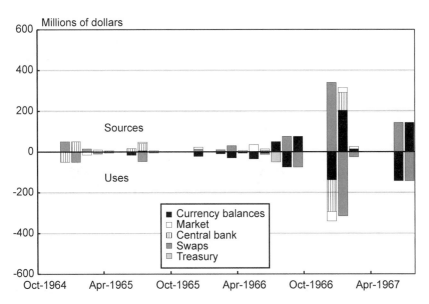

Fig. 4.22   Federal Reserve sources and uses of German marks, October 1964–July 1967

Notes: "Central bank" contains "exceptional items." Data do not include unexplained items or profits. Data are from the Federal Reserve System.

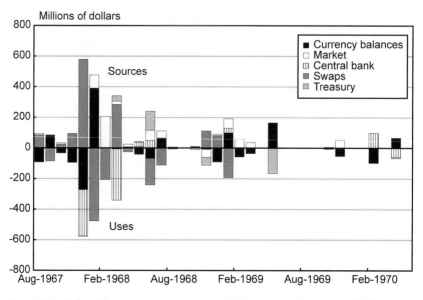

Fig. 4.23 Federal Reserve sources and uses of German marks, August 1967–May 1970

Notes: "Central bank" contains "exceptional items." Data do not include unexplained items or profits. Data are from the Federal Reserve System.

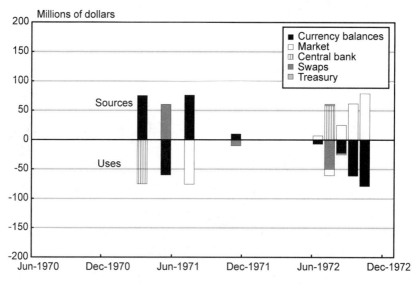

Fig. 4.24 Federal Reserve sources and uses of German marks, June 1970–December 1972

Notes: "Central bank" contains "exceptional items." Data do not include unexplained items or profits. Data are from the Federal Reserve System.

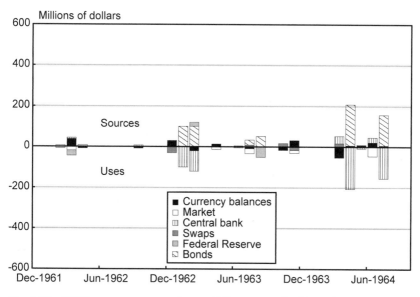

Fig. 4.25 **US Treasury sources and uses of German marks, December 1961–September 1964**

Notes: "Central bank" contains "exceptional items." Data do not include unexplained items or profits. Data are from the Federal Reserve System.

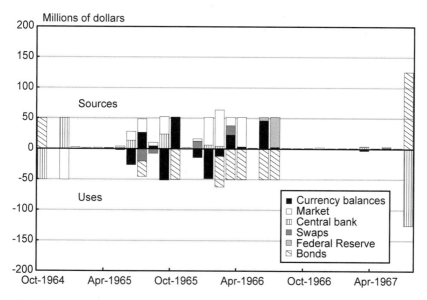

Fig. 4.26 **US Treasury sources and uses of German marks, October 1964–July 1967**

Notes: "Central bank" contains "exceptional items." Data do not include unexplained items or profits. Data are from the Federal Reserve System.

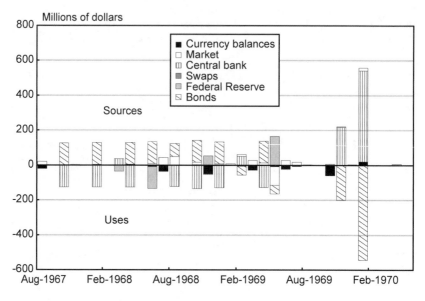

Fig. 4.27   US Treasury sources and uses of German marks, August 1967–
May 1970

Notes: "Central bank" contains "exceptional items." Data do not include unexplained items
or profits. Data are from the Federal Reserve System.

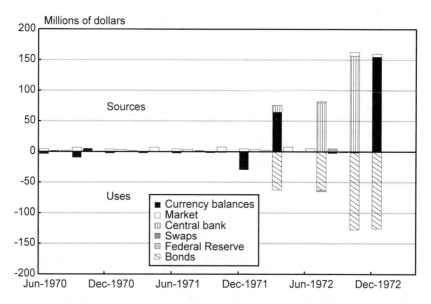

Fig. 4.28   US Treasury sources and uses of German marks, June 1970–May 1972

Notes: "Central bank" contains "exceptional items." Data do not include unexplained items
or profits. Data are from the Federal Reserve System.

repay its swap drawing. The Bundesbank offered to extend the swap line, but the Federal Reserve instead turned to the US Treasury. The Treasury issued $50 million worth of two-year, mark-denominated bonds (Roosa bonds) to the Bundesbank and sold the proceeds to the Federal Reserve System. This was the first time that the Treasury backstopped a central bank swap by issuing Roosa bonds. Over the next three months, when pressure on the mark eased, the Federal Reserve purchased marks off-market from central banks and from the German Defense Ministry, which needed dollars to buy US military equipment (*Bulletin*, March 1964, 297). On 10 October 1963, with recent swap debt repaid, the Federal Reserve System increased its swap line with the Bundesbank to $250 million.

In late 1963, short-term funds moved back into German marks, prompting the Federal Reserve to draw $70 million equivalent marks from its swap line with the Bundesbank. The Federal Reserve used part of these funds to intervene with the US Treasury in the New York market, but in contrast to earlier episodes, the Federal Reserve also used a portion of the proceeds from the swap drawing to cover excess dollar balances at the Bundesbank. Over 1963, foreign-exchange reserves in Germany—presumably all dollars—had increased substantially. In January 1964, the German government, which needed additional dollars for military expenditures, supplied the Federal Reserve with marks to repay its swap drawing in full by early 1964.

In response to rumors of a mark revaluation, the Treasury—in concert with the Bundesbank—sold $21 million equivalent marks three months forward. This was the Treasury's first outright forward sale since 1961. On 23 March 1964, Germany imposed a 25 percent withholding tax on non-residents' interest income from German fixed-interest securities (*Bulletin*, September 1964, 1124). The tax reduced long-term financial inflows and induced some liquidation of investments in German bonds. In addition, the Bundesbank undertook market swaps with German commercial banks (selling dollars spot and repurchasing them forward for delivery in 90 to 180 days) at preferential rates hoping to encourage these banks to purchase US Treasury securities—a financial outflow. Such market swaps would eventually create a problem for the Bundesbank, because the commercial banks would simply sell the dollars thus acquired back into the market. The Federal Reserve used the respite that controls afforded to buy marks and repay the swap drawings made early in March.

Although pressure on the mark-dollar rate had subsided, the US Treasury sold $200 million worth of mark-denominated bonds to the Bundesbank in April 1964 and used the proceeds to again buy excess dollar balances from the Bundesbank.[78] The excess dollars resulted from financial flows out of Italy and into Germany. The Bank of Italy required dollar reserves for support of the lira, so the US Treasury repaid a $200 million equivalent lira bond that it had issued in 1962 to the Bank of Italy. To do so, the Treasury purchased lira from the Bank of Italy with the dollars it acquired selling the bonds to the Bundesbank. In the end, the Treasury financed a lira support operation with debt issued to the Bundesbank.

The mark came under renewed upward pressure in mid-1964, and by the end of the year, US Treasury had $678 million equivalent in mark-denominated bonds outstanding. In December 1964, the Federal Reserve also drew $50 million worth of marks on the swap line to absorb dollar balances at the Bundesbank. Germany's need for dollars to finance military purchases again enabled the Federal Reserve to reverse this swap in January 1965.

From May 1965 through October 1965, Germany's trade balance deteriorated and the mark began to trade below its parity. With pressure off of the German mark, the Federal Reserve System and the US Treasury purchased German marks from central banks and from the market in order to strengthen their reserve positions and to pay down US Treasury mark-denominated bonds. This was the first liquidation of the bonds since the Treasury issued them in 1963, but at the end of 1965, the Treasury still had a total of $602 million worth of mark-denominated bonds outstanding.

The German balance-of-payments deficit that emerged in 1965 continued through the first five months of 1966, now largely because higher Euro-dollar rates attracted a short-term financial outflow from Germany. The mark generally traded below par; the Bundesbank intervened substantially, and Germany's foreign-exchange balances declined. The Treasury took this opportunity to reduce its mark indebtedness further, in part, with the Federal Reserve's help. The Federal Reserve purchased marks from the market and European central banks between April and June and sold them to the US Treasury.

In May 1966, the Bundesbank raised its discount rate (*Bulletin*, September 1966, 1322). This hike, in conjunction with the renewed wave of sterling selling, produced a financial flow into German marks that returned the spot rate to parity and resulted in the Bundesbank acquiring more reserves than it previously had lost. Eventually, the Bundesbank cut its reserve requirements, but it continued to acquire dollar reserves.

Again, the Federal Reserve used its own balances and drew on its swap line to purchase dollars from the Bundesbank. The Federal Reserve also sold marks outright and undertook swap transactions with the market involving a spot sale of German marks and a forward purchase. The Treasury, which was intent on trying to pay down outstanding mark obligations, did not participate in these interventions.

In early 1967, as the mark once again eased, the Federal Reserve easily repaid its swap drawings. The Federal Reserve then bought marks as a precaution. In November 1967, the market became unsettled following the depreciation of the pound and rumors of a mark appreciation. Demand for German marks increased. The Bundesbank acquired $357 million outright in the spot market (*Bulletin*, March 1968, 277–78). The Bundesbank then undertook market swaps, selling dollars spot against forward purchases with

German commercial banks to keep dollars in the market and to reduce a widening premium on forward marks. By 30 November 1967, the Bundesbank had outstanding market swaps totaling $600 million (*Bulletin*, March 1968, 278). The Federal Reserve increased its swap line with the Bundesbank from $400 million to $750 million. The Federal Reserve then drew $300 million equivalent marks on that line and sold them to the Bundesbank for dollars. This official swap transaction provided the Bundesbank with cover for one-half of its outstanding swap commitments with German commercial banks (*Bulletin*, March 1968, 278). In addition, as uncertainty about the official gold prices grew, the Federal Reserve sold $7.3 million worth of marks in the New York market. Late in December 1967, when dollars briefly flowed out of Germany, the Federal Reserve bought marks.

After the closing of the Gold Pool in March 1968, speculative financial flows into Germany increased and the Bundesbank quickly acquired $800 million. The Bundesbank immediately offered most of these dollars to commercial banks on an attractive swap basis. This swap offering was intended to provide dollar liquidity to the Eurodollar market, lower Eurodollar interest rates, and thereby to take pressure off of the British pound. The Federal Reserve absorbed $300 million through its swap line, thereby providing some cover for the forward leg of Bundesbank's swap transactions (*Bulletin*, September 1968, 731).

In May 1968, Bundesbank President Karl Blessing reiterated Germany's intention not to convert dollars into gold. That same month, as unrest was erupting in France, the German mark came under downward pressure following an April increase in the Federal Reserve's discount rate. At the time, the Bundesbank had announced an easing in German monetary policy. The Federal Reserve again used the opportunity afforded by the financial outflow from Germany to buy marks in the New York market and to repay its outstanding mark obligations. In May 1968, the Federal Reserve also purchased $25.2 million worth of marks from Canada, which had recently floated a bond in Germany, and in June the Federal Reserve acquired $50 million equivalent marks from the Bundesbank when the latter sought to replenish dollar reserves following a sale of dollars to France. In late June, the central bank acquired an additional $125 million equivalent marks from the US Treasury, which had just issued special mark-denominated securities to German banks as part of an agreement with Germany to absorb dollars associated with stationing troops there (*Bulletin*, September 1968, 732). By the end of August 1968, these mark acquisitions enabled the Federal Reserve to repay all of its swap obligations to the Bundesbank and to the BIS. In that same month, the Treasury issued the first of a new series of mark-denominated securities to the Bundesbank, which were designed to absorb troop dollars, in addition to the securities already issued to German commercial banks. By year's end, the Treasury had $1.3 billion equivalent mark-denominated securities outstanding.

In late August 1968, however, rumors of a mark revaluation resurfaced. After permitting an unprecedented one-day appreciation of the mark to its ceiling, the Bundesbank acquired $820 million as the Labor Day weekend approached, with half of that amount coming on Friday alone (*Desk Report* 1969, 34). Between August 27 and September 6 the Bundesbank purchased $1.6 billion (*Bulletin*, March 1969, 214). The Bundesbank also undertook market swaps to encourage German commercial banks to hold dollars. In cooperation with the Bundesbank, the Federal Reserve and the US Treasury each sold $17 million equivalent German marks forward in the New York market during August and early September, but despite the concerted actions to limit speculation, the Bundesbank acquired an additional $840 million in the three days ending 6 September 1968.

Speculation dramatically intensified in November, after a brief respite in October. At the Basle Meeting, the central bank governors recommended a 7.5 percent revaluation of the mark (Solomon 1982, 2). Instead the Bundesbank intensified its intervention efforts, making very large dollar purchases (over $1 billion in just two days ending Friday, 15 November 1968, and $2 billion since the beginning of the month) and undertaking approximately $1 billion in swaps with German commercial banks (*Desk Report* 1969, 37; *Bulletin*, March 1969, 215). Rather than invest the swap proceeds in interest-earning assets, however, these commercial banks resold the now-covered dollars in the market, thereby negating the effects of the swap and leaving the Bundesbank with a forward obligation to sell marks. The Bundesbank responded by issuing swaps only to banks that used the proceeds to acquire US Treasury securities, but it soon had to sell marks through outright forwards (*Bulletin*, March 1969, 215–16). German banks wanted outright cover for their dollar position; they did not want cover on a swap basis which eventually had to be rolled over, and therefore left them with some exposure. Bundesbank forward mark sales in late November amounted to $246 million equivalent (*Bulletin*, March 1969, 216). The Federal Reserve drew $111.3 million equivalent marks on its swap line with the Bundesbank and sold $47 million equivalent marks spot in New York. With the remaining marks from the swap drawing as partial cover, the Federal Reserve also sold $72 million equivalent marks forward in New York. In December, as the mark temporarily weakened, the Federal Reserve bought marks spot as additional cover for its forward position.

After acquiring $850 million over two days—18 and 19 November 1968—the German authorities announced that they would *not* revalue the mark.[79] They then undertook a faux revaluation by adjusting value-added tax rates to raise export prices and lower import prices (Solomon 1982, 158). In addition, the Bundesbank imposed 100 percent reserve requirements on new foreign-owned mark deposits at German banks, reinforcing the previous ban against interest payments on such deposits (*Bulletin*, March 1969, 216).

These policies were sufficient to encourage a financial outflow by the end of November 1968, enabling the Federal Reserve to acquire, once again, sufficient marks to repay its swap drawings by January 1969.[80] Nevertheless, in 1968, Germany had acquired a little more than $1 billion in foreign exchange reserves. In January, as the mark moved below par, the Bundesbank sold large amounts of dollars in the market and reduced the attractiveness of its swaps with commercial banks. The larger sales of dollars continued in February and March 1968. United States monetary authorities made heavy market purchases of German marks between December 1968 and March 1969. In addition to paying down its swap drawings, the Federal Reserve used the newly acquired marks to meet forward obligations as they matured, and to increase balances. In February 1969, the Treasury, which also had been acquiring small amounts of marks from the market and from the Bundesbank, redeemed a $50 million equivalent outstanding mark-denominated note.

The outflow of funds from Germany reversed itself in April 1969, when President de Gaulle's resignation heightened speculation of a French franc devaluation. Concurrent rumors that some members of the German cabinet favored an 8 to 10 percent mark revaluation as part of a multilateral exchange rate readjustment encouraged speculative flows into marks (*Desk Report* 1970, 9). Moreover, a tightening of monetary and fiscal policies to combat growing inflationary forces only worsened Germany's balance-of-payments situation (*Desk Report* 1970, 9–10).

Speculative flows became massive, so much so that in the three days prior to Friday, 2 May 1969, the Bundesbank acquired $860 million (*Bulletin*, September 1969, 702). On 7 May, the Bundesbank discontinued its swap operations, since commercial banks were now placing the funds into the Eurodollar market where they were recycled into the foreign exchange market and again converted into marks. On 8 May, the Bundesbank received very heavy inflows of dollars, much of it through support operations in the New York market. The Bundesbank then limited such support operations to only 400 million German marks, an amount that quickly proved inadequate. Although IMF rules oblige a country to defend its currency in its own market, a member country was not obliged to defend its currency in a foreign market. To assist in the defense of the mark, the US Treasury sold $106 million worth of marks into the New York market. It financed this defensive operation by acquiring virtually all ($165 million equivalent) of the Federal Reserve's mark balances. The following day, speculation was equally intense, "the heaviest flow in international financial history" (*Bulletin*, September 1969, 703).

"The speculative onslaught between the end of April and May 9 increased German monetary [international] reserves by some $4.1 billion—including $2.5 billion on 8 and 9 May alone—to a record level of $12.4 billion" (*Bulletin*, September 1969, 703). After Germany emphatically dismissed revaluation rumors, speculation subsided. With inflationary pressures now emerging, Germany tightened fiscal and monetary policies. Absorbing domestic liquidity in this situation, however, could only encourage additional inflows. Revaluation now seemed a certainty; only the timing remained unclear.

Speculation intensified again as the 28 September election approached. The Bundesbank acquired increasing amounts of dollars, but was simultaneously selling dollars on a swap basis. The funds were spilling into the Eurodollar market. "[O]n September 18, after such sales had reached $0.7 billion over a 10-day period, the [Bundesbank] raised its swap rate, thus bringing to a virtual halt the covered movements of German funds into the Euro-dollar market" (*Bulletin*, March 1970, 230). A further tightening of monetary policy in mid-September only intensified the financial inflows. The government closed the foreign exchange market for the two days prior to the elections and suspended official foreign-exchange operations. In New York, the mark traded above parity. When the election was inconclusive, the Bundesbank briefly returned to the market, took in $245 million in the first hour and a half of trading, and then allowed the mark to float. The mark appreciated 7 1/4 percent by mid-October, with the Bundesbank gradually raising its buying rate to keep a floor just below the market rate (*Desk Report* 1970, 20). The Federal Reserve also bought marks. The coalition government that took office on 21 October 1969 revalued the mark 9.3 percent on 24 October 1969 and eliminated the special taxes on exports and imports that created the faux revaluation of November 1968. "The revaluation was larger than had generally been anticipated, thus decisively removing the mark from the realm of speculation" (*Bulletin*, March 1970, 231).

The revaluation led to a severe outflow of funds from Germany, which depleted official reserves and drained liquidity. To stem the movement out of marks, the Bundesbank eliminated discriminatory reserve requirements on foreign deposits. The bank also raised its Lombard rate, and in December 1969, German authorities removed the prohibition on paying interest of foreign-owned deposits. The Federal Reserve took advantage of the financial outflows to rebuild its depleted mark balances. The US Treasury activated revaluation clauses covering its mark-denominated securities. This allowed the Treasury to purchase marks at a substantial discount either to hold as cover or to resell for a substantial profit. By now, the Bundesbank had depleted most of its liquid dollar holdings. To recoup these, Germany sold mark-denominated US Treasury securities back to the Treasury for dollars, sold $500 million in gold to the US Treasury, and drew $1.1 billion in credits from the IMF (*Bulletin*, March 1970, 232).

4.8   Breakdown of Bretton Woods, 1970–1973

Much of the exchange-market turmoil from 1967 through 1969 stemmed from the adjustment problems of individual currencies.[81] While these raised uncertainties about the underlying Bretton Woods parity structure and created undesirable reshufflings of dollar reserves, they did not directly reflect problems with the dollar. Inflation in the United States, however, was accelerating, and the nature of the international financial problem was changing. By 1970, the market viewed exchange-market disorder as a dollar crisis and not, as was the case earlier, a problem of unsustainable cross rates (Solomon 1982, 182).

According to Coombs (1976, 204–11), the Nixon administration, which came to office in January 1969, believed that our major trading partners were deliberately discriminating against the United States. Consequently, the administration adopted a practice of "benign neglect" about the growing balance-of-payments deficit and the United States' commitments under Bretton Woods. A subsequent US focus on domestic growth and employment and the emergence of inflation flooded foreign economies with dollar reserves, put upward pressures on their currencies and price levels, and ultimately led to the demise of the Bretton Woods system.

4.8.1 Closing the Gold Window, 1970–1971

Despite some tightening in US monetary policy, the US inflation rate continued to accelerate through 1969, reaching nearly 6 percent by year's end. The onset of a recession induced the Federal Reserve to again loosen monetary policy and to maintain an accommodative stance in 1970 and 1971 (figure 4.6). Interest rates in the United States fell, and as US banks repaid earlier borrowings from foreign affiliates, so did Eurodollar rates. Many European countries, however, were tightening monetary policy to ward off inflationary pressures by 1969. Even when European countries lowered interest rates, as they eventually had to do, their movements typically lagged those in the United States during this period. This interest-rate pattern induced heavy financial flows out of dollar-denominated assets. Initially, much of the dollar reflow went to countries like the United Kingdom and France that needed to rebuild dollar reserves and to repay debts (*Bulletin*, September 1971, 783). The dollar reflows, however, quickly became a problem for countries like Germany, Italy, Belgium, the Netherlands, and Switzerland. Dollar inflows pushed their currencies to their upper parity limits vis-à-vis the dollar, forcing their central banks to intervene. In many cases, the acquisition of dollar reserves offset domestic monetary restraint programs designed to reduce inflationary pressures. Attempts to tighten policy further only aggravated the inflow of funds. By early 1971, as Coombs (1976, 212) notes, the process developed a self-reinforcing aspect as "overt speculation further swelled the torrent of dollars flowing to foreign markets."

By the summer of 1971, confidence in US monetary policy was rapidly evaporating and a crisis atmosphere was emerging. Inflation in the United States remained around 4.4 percent, despite slow economic growth and a high unemployment rate. Moreover, the US balance-of-payments position continued to deteriorate. Expecting further revaluations, speculators began borrowing Eurodollar funds to buy foreign currencies (*Bulletin*, September

1971, 812). On 6 August 1971, a congressional subcommittee identified the dollar as overvalued and called for a realignment of currency rates, including a dollar devaluation. On that same day, the US Treasury reported a loss of gold and reserves of $1 billion, largely as Britain and France exchanged dollars to repay IMF debts. Over the next week, $3.7 billion in gold and reserve assets moved abroad (Coombs 1976, 215). Gold moved to $44 per ounce in London, and speculative flows out of dollars and into foreign central banks intensified. On 15 August 1971, President Nixon closed the gold window; that is, he suspended convertibility of officially held dollars into gold. Acting under the Economic Stabilization Act of 1970, he ordered a ninety-day freeze on wages and prices and recommended new tax measures to stimulate investment and employment. He also introduced a temporary 10 percent surcharge on dutiable imports.

Although Chairman Burns told the FOMC that suspending the dollar's convertibility would be temporary, Charles Coombs appreciated the action's real significance: "[T]he decision to close the gold window had demolished with one stroke the Bretton Woods exchange rate system" (FOMC *Memoranda*, 24 August 1971, 27). The announcement surprised the major European governments, who closed their exchange markets and sought—unsuccessfully—a joint policy response to the US measures (*Bulletin*, September 1971, 786). They reopened their markets on Monday, 23 August, and although they formally adhered to their parities—with the exception of France—they suspended their commitments to defend them. Japan had initially attempted to defend its parity, and took in $2 billion on 15 August 1971 alone. With substantial inflows of dollars continuing, Japan suspended its official intervention on 28 August. All of the major currencies appreciated against the dollar during the next two months—except the fixed French commercial franc—as speculative flows continued. At the high end was the German mark, which rose 9.5 percent above its previous ceiling. At the low end was the French financial franc, which rose only 1.7 percent (*Bulletin*, September 1971, 786).[82]

The foreign currencies appreciated despite heavy foreign interventions, and foreign central banks continued to accumulate large amounts of unwanted dollar reserves, which contributed to their inflationary pressures. As a consequence, monetary authorities began to tighten controls on financial inflows. "The exchange rate structure thus emerging after August 15 was, in most instances, the product of controlled rather than free floating" (*Bulletin*, October 1971, 786). Europeans and Latin American countries argued that the US import surcharge was also distorting exchange-rate relationships (Solomon 1982, 189). They lodged a formal complaint with the General Agreement on Tariffs and Trade (GATT).

In 1971 prior to the closing of the gold window, the Federal Reserve frequently initiated large swap drawings to forestall foreign central banks from converting excessive dollars reserves into US monetary gold. On 1 January

1971, the Federal Reserve had outstanding swap commitments of $810 million. By July 1971, the Federal Reserve had reduced this to $605 million often with the aid of US Treasury sales of gold and SDRs, borrowings from the IMF, and the issuance of foreign-currency denominated securities. As funds moved rapidly abroad, the Federal Reserve then drew $2.2 billion on its swap lines—with assurances of a Treasury backstop—to provide further cover to central bank through 13 August 1971 (Coombs 1976, 217; *Bulletin*, September 1971, 787).

After 13 August 1971, the Federal Reserve made no further drawings on its swap lines. The Federal Reserve encountered difficulties in repaying outstanding swaps because most foreign central banks did not want the Federal Reserve buying their appreciating currencies in the market. They preferred to roll over existing swaps, expecting that new parities would soon be established and a reversal of financial flows would follow (FOMC *Memoranda*, 16 November 1971, 15; *Bulletin*, September 1971, 787). In contrast, the Belgian National Bank asked the Federal Reserve to repay a $35 million swap drawing that had been outstanding for seven months. This required the Federal Reserve to purchase Belgian francs at a premium and to incur an overall loss of $1.9 million on the transaction. The US Treasury preferred that the Federal Reserve take a loss on this transaction to financing the repayment through official reserves (FOMC *Memoranda*, 19 October 1971, 18). By 14 October 1971, the Federal Reserve had outstanding swap commitments of $3.0 billion.

Despite this heavy use of swaps, the United States lost large amounts of official reserves to foreign central banks in 1971. "From January 1, through mid-August a total of $3.1 billion in such assets was paid out, including $864 million of gold, $394 million of foreign exchange, $480 million of SDRs, and $1,362 million taken down against the US IMF position" (*Bulletin*, September 1971, 789). In addition, the Treasury issued $582.7 million in new Swiss franc denominated securities between 1 January 1971 and 13 October 1971 (*Bulletin*, September 1971, 789).

4.8.2   First to Float: Canada

In stark contrast to most other key developed countries after the Second World War, Canada had allowed its currency to float freely against the dollar from September 1950 until May 1961 (see Bordo, Dib, and Schembri 2010). Rather than import inflation from the United States, Canada again floated in 1970. Its actions set a precedent for both other countries and speculators.

Following the devaluation of sterling in November 1967, the Canadian dollar came under heavy speculative attack. The market also feared that the recently announced US restraints on financial flows might adversely affect US direct investments into Canada and short-term financial flows between the two countries (*Bulletin*, August 1968, 739). Canadian reserve losses were heavy in January and February 1968, causing Canadian monetary authorities to draw $250 million on the $750 million swap facility with the Federal Reserve and $426 million from the IMF (*Bulletin*, August 1968, 740). The Bank of Canada also increased its discount rate.

Pressures on the Canadian dollar persisted and intensified in March 1968, as speculative funds moved out of Canadian dollars and into gold. Canada sought and received additional international credits amounting to $900 million from the US Export-Import Bank, the German Bundesbank, the Bank of Italy, and the Bank for International Settlements. These credits did not include the $500 million still available to Canada through the Federal Reserve swap line, which the central bank subsequently increased to $1.0 billion (*Bulletin*, August 1968, 740). In addition, the United States exempted Canada completely from the financial restraints that it imposed in January 1968. For its part, Canada agreed to invest its dollar reserves—apart from working balances—in US government securities (*Bulletin*, August 1968, 740). Canada again raised its bank lending rate when the Federal Reserve Bank hiked the discount rate.

The situation briefly improved in the spring of 1968, enabling Canada to acquire reserves and repay international credits. In 1969, however, the United States tightened monetary policy. High interest rates in the United States and in the Eurodollar market encouraged a financial outflow from Canada and prompted the Bank of Canada to tighten its monetary policy and its restrictions on financial outflows.

With the onset of a recession in early1970, the United States eased monetary policy, and the financial tide quickly reversed. Strong inflows of both long-term and short-term funds now pushed the Canadian dollar to the top of its trading range. The Bank of Canada—as agent for the federal government—bought large amounts of US dollars to keep the Canadian dollar within its parity range, adding unwanted domestic liquidity to the Canadian market at a time when the Bank of Canada was trying to contain inflationary pressures. Inflation was currently running at approximately 4 to 5 percent and wage settlements reached 9.1 percent (Powell 2005, 71, fn. 90). Although the Bank of Canada favored a new par value with wider parity bands, the government rejected the idea out of a concern that it would provide only temporary relief and would not be credible. The government also considered asking the United States to rescind its Canadian exemption under the US Interest Equalization Tax, but the exemption helped reduce the borrowing costs of provincial governments (Powell 2005, 72).

On Sunday, 31 May 1970, Finance Minister Benson announced that the Bank of Canada would no longer defend the upper limit for the Canadian dollar, effectively allowing it to appreciate. Benson intended to refix the exchange rate as soon as possible. The Bank of Canada intervened on 1 June when the Canadian market opened to smooth the increase in the rate. Over the following weeks, the Bank of Canada intervened to dampen the swings, especially excessive increases in the exchange rate (*Bulletin*, September 1970, 695). The Canadian dollar, however, was now floating.

Coombs viewed the Canadian float as a serious threat to the Bretton Woods system. He noted that the ability of central banks to defend their parities against speculative attacks was increasingly "suspect." Nevertheless, "[u]ntil the Canadian decision to let their rate float, the market had not taken seriously official discussions of rate flexibility." (FOMC *Memoranda*, 23 June 1970, 42) Reflecting his overall attitude toward floating rates, Coombs viewed financial flows under the Canadian float as destabilizing:

> . . . the rise in the rate tended to be self-reinforcing in that it encouraged an increasing tendency to cover Canadian dollar commitments. Another factor in the market, starting toward the end of July, was the appearance of professional traders, mainly European banks, who would move in and out of the Canadian dollar within a single day to take advantage of the wide fluctuations in the rate, their actions clearly aggravating those fluctuations. (*Bulletin*, September 1970, 695)

This early float, however, insulated the Canadian dollar from much of the exchange-market chaos of 1971.

4.8.3   The German Mark Example

Germany's experience in 1970 and 1971 provides the clearest example of the problem with fixed exchange rates when domestic and international objectives conflict.[83] In the spring of 1970, the Bundesbank began to tighten monetary policy to counteract growing inflationary pressures. Germany's GNP deflator increased 7.3 percent in 1970 and 7.7 percent in 1971 (IMF 1972, 7). With interest rates on dollar-denominated assets falling—the United States experienced a recession in 1970—funds began to flow into Germany. The mark, which had been trading near its floor value ever since the October 1969 revaluation, began to rise sharply. By mid-May 1970 with the mark now trading at its upper limit, the Bundesbank began acquiring substantial amounts of dollars through its interventions. The floating of the Canadian dollar in June 1970 only added to speculative pressures against the mark. On 10 June 1970, the Bundesbank, in "the most hectic day of trading since the fall of 1969," purchased $640 million at the upper parity band, but the rate moved even higher that afternoon in New York after the close of business in Frankfurt (*Bulletin*, September 1970, 697). During the whole of the second quarter of 1970, the Bundesbank acquired $1.4 billion in reserves (*Bulletin*, March 1971, 189–207).

Germany next attempted to fine-tune its monetary policy and to supplement it with other measures, like a tighter fiscal policy. The Bundesbank cut its discount and Lombard rates hoping to take pressure off market rates, but the bank also instituted heavy reserve requirements on bank liabilities. Although short-term rates fell briefly, they quickly turned around. The net effect was that inflows of reserves continued and in the third quarter of 1970, the Bundesbank acquired almost $2.5 billion (*Bulletin*, March 1971, 198). In late October 1970, the Bundesbank converted its reserve requirements into a form of capital controls by directing them to certain interest-arbitrage transactions and to dealings related to foreign borrowing. Continued pressure on the mark, however, forced the Bundesbank to lower its discount and Lombard rates again in early November 1970. Despite these maneuvers, funds continued to flow into Germany. In December, following a cut in the US discount rate, the Bundesbank again lowered its official lending rates, and German interest rates fell more closely in line with Eurodollar interest rates. Nevertheless, in the fourth quarter of 1970, the Bundesbank acquired $2.3 billion in reserves, and remained hampered in adopting an anti-inflation policy stance.

Despite these interest-rate cuts, the spread vis-à-vis Eurodollar rates continued to attract funds into Germany during early 1971. The spot rate remained at, or near, the upper parity band and the Bundesbank continued to acquire dollars. "During the period February–April 1971, German corporate borrowing abroad amounted to roughly $2.5 billion, nearly equivalent to total business lending by the entire German banking system over the same period" (*Bulletin*, October 1971, 784). In February and March 1971, the Bundesbank undertook a series of forward German mark sales through the Federal Reserve Bank of New York in an effort to offset the attractive interest-rate differential on marks and forced the mark to a substantial forward discount. The sales failed to stop the dollar inflow, however, and in mid-March 1971, after $537 million worth of forward mark sales, the Bundesbank halted these operations (*Bulletin*, October 1971, 791).

The Bundesbank again tried to fine-tune its credit conditions. On 31 March 1971, the Bundesbank cut its discount and Lombard rates a full percentage point, but simultaneously reduced banks rediscount quotas by 10 percent (*Bulletin*, October 1971, 791). Credit conditions were little changed and speculative pressures on the mark intensified. "Within three days, the Federal Bank [Bundesbank] took in more than $1.3 billion in holding the spot mark at the ceiling and swapped some $600 million of this inflow out in the market for three months' delivery" (*Bulletin*, October 1971, 792). The funds swapped out ended up back in the market.

In April, the Bundesbank reinstituted three-month forward sales of German marks. This time, however, the Bundesbank operated in the Frankfurt market, and the Federal Reserve undertook similar forward mark sales for the Federal Reserve's account in the New York market. At this time, Eurodollar interest rates began to increase, while German rates began to ease. The spot mark rate moved off its ceiling. The Federal Reserve continued concerted forward interventions nearly every day through April 1971, with the Bundesbank selling a total $1.5 billion equivalent marks and the Federal Reserve selling $75.7 million equivalent marks (*Bulletin*, October 1971, 792). The Federal Reserve covered its operations with existing mark balances and with a $60 million swap drawing on the Bundesbank (*Bulletin*, October 1971, 792). The Bundesbank ceased these operations on 28 April 1971

(Solomon 1982, 179). Although the operations "calmed" the market and may have brought the spot rate off of the ceiling, strong pressure on the mark quickly resumed. In part, reports of an European Economic Community (EEC) meeting on 16 April 1971 fanned speculative embers. At this meeting, German Minister Schiller proposed that the European currencies float or revalue together against the dollar, and Minister d'Estaing advocated a dollar devaluation (Solomon 1982, 179). During the first four months of 1971, Germany acquired $3.0 billion and at the end of April had outstanding forward commitments of $2.7 billion (*Bulletin*, October 1971, 792).

In early May 1971, leading German economic research institutes recommended floating or revaluing the mark, and many German officials gave their suggestion a sympathetic ear (Coombs 1976, 213). Speculative flows into Germany then intensified. "The German central bank was forced to buy dollars in mounting volume: more than $1 billion on May 3 and 4 and a further $1 billion in the first 40 minutes of trading on May 5, at which point it withdrew from the market." (*Bulletin*, September 1971, 784.) The Bundesbank stopped intervening. Foreign exchange trading in Frankfurt effectively ended for the next week. Austria, Belgium, the Netherlands, and Switzerland also ceased official operations. The mark began to appreciate in other markets. On 9 May 1971, Germany indicated that it would no longer defend the parity limits although formally Germany kept the parity in place. The Bundesbank would now focus policy on keeping inflation low. The mark continued to appreciate until early June.

In June, the mark started to turn around, and the Bundesbank began a series of spot dollar sales. These helped German monetary authorities to tighten monetary policy. "By mid-June the authorities had sold $1.7 billion, considerably more than they had taken in under maturing forward contracts from the operations in February and March" (*Bulletin*, October 1971, 793). With the exchange rate less of a constraint on domestic policy, the Bundesbank substantially increased reserve requirements on banks' domestic and foreign liabilities. Interest rates in Germany rose. "Overall, from June 3 through the end of July, the Federal Bank [Bundesbank] sold $4.8 billion in the spot market while it took in a total of $2.7 billion through maturing forward contracts" (*Bulletin*, September 1971, 793). This respite in foreign exchange market proved short-lived, and the Bundesbank stopped selling dollars. By early August 1971, the spot mark reached a level 7.6 percent above its previous parity ceiling.

4.8.4 The Unraveling, 1971–1973

Nixon's actions on 15 August 1971 sent shock waves through the international community. European exchange markets remained closed for a week, and when they reopened, European governments did not defend their par values. Restraints on cross-border financial flows began to emerge. Monetary officials feared a collapse of international monetary relations amid the uncertainty about exchange rates, the imminent spread of protectionism, and the looming prospects of recession. IMF officials immediately pressed for negotiations to revamp exchange-rate parities and address other perennial complaints about Bretton Woods (de Vries 1976, 531–56). With respect to any future international monetary system, leaders wanted a return to fixed exchange rates, although in a system with wider margins around parities. The central role of the dollar, the role of gold, shared responsibility for exchange rate adjustment, and measures to deal with volatile financial flows were also raised (de Vries 1976, 531–56; FOMC *Memoranda*, 21 September 1971, 5). Negotiations proceeded over the next four months.

On 17 and 18 December 1971, monetary authorities from the Group of Ten countries met at the Smithsonian Institution in Washington, DC. The participants agreed to an 8.57 percent hike in the official gold price from $35 per ounce to $38 per ounce. The Swiss franc, the Italian lira, and the Swedish krona were also devalued slightly against gold, while the German mark, Japanese yen, Dutch guilder, and Belgian franc were revalued somewhat. The British pound and the French franc remained at their previous parities, and the Canadian dollar continued to float. The net effect was roughly a 10.7 percent average devaluation of the dollar against other key currencies (de Vries 1976, 555). In addition, the Smithsonian Agreement specified wider margins for currencies around their new central parities. Any currency could move 2 1/4 percent on either side of its central parity relative to its intervention currency—typically US dollars. This implied that currencies could diverge by as much as 4 1/2 percent against most other currencies. Further discussions toward reforming Bretton Woods were promised.

The Smithsonian Agreement did little to restore confidence in the Bretton Woods system, in part because governments still had to ratify the agreement. Funds, however, did not immediately return to the United States, and other countries continued to accumulate reserves as they attempted to defend their parities (IMF 1972, 2; Coombs 1976, 233). Germany and Japan also imposed further controls on financial flows, while others threatened similar actions (*Bulletin*, September 1972, 774). Moreover, the prospects of further dollar devaluation loomed large (Silber 2012, 94, de Vries 1976, 549). Following fifteen months of near constant uncertainty and turmoil, Bretton Woods collapsed.[84]

4.9   Outstanding Obligations from Swaps and Bonds

At the end of August 1971, the Federal Reserve had outstanding swap obligations totaling approximately $3.0 billion in UK pounds, German marks, Swiss francs, and Belgian francs (Task Force 1990e, Paper no. 10, 21). The Treasury had outstanding obligations totaling nearly $1.8 billion in German marks and Swiss francs, which, with the closing of the gold window, the Treasury could not extinguish with gold sales (Task Force 1990e,

Paper no. 10, 21). The revaluation clauses that were typical in swap drawings and Roosa bonds did not apply to a move from fixed parities to floating rates, since it was hard to determine if a creditor country appreciated or if a debtor country depreciated. The revaluation clauses only pertained to situations in which the creditor country revalued its currency. In 1972, the position emerged that if all of the G10 currencies appreciated together, that would imply a dollar depreciation (FOMC *Memoranda*, 19–20 March 1973, 63). Suppose, however, that one currency appreciated by more or less than the G10 average. Should the revaluation clause apply, and how should it apply? The situation was unclear. Without the revaluation clauses or some form of risk sharing, the United States faced a substantial loss on its outstanding obligations.

The Federal Reserve did not experience much difficulty in paying down its German mark and UK pound obligations. It had acquired marks through a swap drawing in May 1971 to cover some current forward positions. The desk acquired marks both from the market and from a central bank to pay off its swap debt by July 1972. Likewise, the Federal Reserve bought sterling in the market and extinguished its debts when the pound came under strong downward pressure in July and August 1972 (FOMC *Memoranda*, 18 July 1972, 17–18).

The Federal Reserve had more difficulty in extinguishing its Belgian and Swiss franc obligations. In part, this resulted because the Belgian franc and Swiss franc were often strong in the market, and the National Bank of Belgium and the Swiss National Bank did not want market purchases that would encourage further appreciation. Some of the $600 million worth of Belgian debt was repaid in 1971 and 1972 when the Federal Reserve made small periodic franc purchases at the request of the National Bank of Belgium. In December 1973, however, the Federal Reserve halted such purchases when the Treasury sought to clarify the issue of risk sharing with both of these central banks and, therefore, the terms of debt repayment. The Treasury wanted equal sharing, but the Belgians "interpreted this request as a change in the original agreement and felt no obligation to comply" (Task Force 1990e, Paper no.10, 23).

After delaying, the Federal Reserve reached an agreement with the National Bank of Belgium. "In December 1975, the [Federal Reserve] System and the National Bank of Belgium agreed to adjust the outstanding swap debt to take into account the revaluation of the Belgian franc in 1971, and the two devaluations of the dollar in 1971 and 1973" (Task Force 1990e, Paper no. 10, 23). As a consequence, the Federal Reserve's outstanding swap debt was increased by $54.1 million. Near the end of 1975, with the Belgian franc-US dollar exchange rate at a level that made losses associated with the remaining liability small, the Federal Reserve began a series of Belgian franc purchases. By November 1976, the central bank had liquidated the Belgian franc debt.

In August 1971, the Federal Reserve had $1.0 billion in outstanding swap obligations with the Swiss National Bank, the full amount of the line, and $600 million in outstanding Swiss franc swap obligation to the BIS. Over the next four years, the Federal Reserve made periodic purchases of Swiss francs both in the market and from the Swiss National Bank to retire this debt. In December 1975, the Federal Reserve added $196 million worth of francs to its outstanding swap debt with the SNB to reflect losses associated with two dollar devaluations.[85] Shortly thereafter, the Federal Reserve and Treasury reached a loss sharing agreement with the Swiss National Bank. In February 1976, the Federal Reserve drew $600 million on the Swiss National Bank swap line to pay down the BIS Swiss franc line completely. Then in October 1976, the Federal Reserve undertook an unusual transaction to pay down the entire line with the Swiss National Bank. The Federal Reserve negotiated a new "special" swap line with the SNB that embodied the risk sharing agreement and set a three-year timetable for repayment. The Swiss National Bank also agreed to sell the Federal Reserve and the US Treasury Swiss francs if necessary. The Federal Reserve paid off the original swap with a drawing on this special swap, and paid off the special line by April 1979. The Treasury also paid off its outstanding Swiss franc obligations in April 1979.

The Federal Reserve and the Treasury took seven and a half years to pay off its pre-August 1971 swap obligations. The estimated losses to the Federal Reserve and to the Treasury on these outstanding debts were $986 million and $1.5 million, respectively (Task Force 1990e, Paper no. 10, 25).

4.10   Conclusion

The Bretton Woods system flew in the face of the fundamental trilemma of international finance, because it attempted to credibly maintain fixed exchange rates and free financial flows, but also allowed some deviations from these desired objectives to promote domestic macroeconomic goals. When these ideals came into serious conflict by the early 1970s, national governments opted to promote domestic objectives for price stability and full employment over exchange-rate stability and free financial flows.

In hindsight, that conflict seemed inevitable. Triffin's paradox fundamentally threatened the Bretton Woods system. Although efforts to repair this basic flaw—to provide a source of liquidity not based on US balance-of-payments deficits—got underway in the mid-1960s, a high US inflation rate and inevitable cross-rate adjustment problems overtook these efforts. By 1971, Bretton Woods was quickly unraveling. By 1973, it was gone. Floating exchange rates were the predictable consequence of countries' unwillingness to make domestic economic objectives—price stability and full employment—subservient to the maintenance of par values.

United States foreign-exchange-market operations during Bretton Woods often worked as designed; they regularly provided a solution to temporary, reversible balance-of-payments disequilibria. Very often, however, the operations failed to distinguish between temporary and fundamental disequilibria situations, and they did not address the system's deep-seated weaknesses. Consequently, they arguably may have prolonged and worsened the inevitable breakdown of Bretton Woods.

The US institutional mechanisms for foreign-exchange-market interventions survived the collapse of Bretton Woods and would adapt to a floating exchange-rate environment. The fundamental reservations about these operations—ultimately their potential threat to Federal Reserve independence—would also remain. Attitudes about these reservations, however, would evolve along with thoughts about the proper role of monetary policy before intervention itself was abandoned as a threat to monetary credibility.

US Intervention and the Early Dollar Float, 1973–1981

> There's an adage in the marketplace that says one should
> always go against an intervention, since any intervention
> reflects an inherent weakness in the currency being supported.
> —*Wall Street Journal* (3 August 1983, 3)

5.1 Introduction

On 12 March 1973, the Bretton Woods fixed-parity system effectively ended when eight key European industrialized countries instituted a joint float against the dollar. In doing so, they joined Canada, Italy, Japan, Switzerland, and the United Kingdom, which already had allowed their currencies to float unilaterally against the dollar. Most monetary authorities at the time grudgingly accepted floating as a necessary step to a restructured international monetary system based once again on fixed exchange rates. In the interim, they thought, floating could raise the cost of speculation, which the February 1973 dollar depreciation had greatly encouraged, and—most importantly—could limit the substantial inflows of unwanted dollar liquidity stemming from persistent US balance-of-payments deficits and, ultimately, US inflation.[1]

The international community, of course, never returned to fixed-dollar exchange rates. Initially, a persistently high US inflation rate, the disparate impact of oil price shocks, and idiosyncratic business-cycle patterns made a return to a parity system impossible. Eventually, private markets adjusted to the volatility of floating rates, and policymakers realized that floating exchange rates fostered macroeconomic stability better than fixed exchange rates and did so with no obvious cost to international trade or investment. Under floating, countries continued to cooperate on international monetary matters; they did not revert—as was often feared—to the beggar-thy-neighbor policies of the 1930s. By 1975, then, the monetary authorities in most developed countries accepted floating exchange rates and free cross-border financial flows as a sustainable solution to the fundamental trilemma.

Although monetary authorities eventually accepted floating exchange rates, they continued to view the foreign-exchange market as inherently prone to bouts of disorder. Monetary authorities never clearly articulated the market failure underlying this alleged disorder, but they seemed to believe that information imperfections could cause exchange rates to deviate from their fundamental values, create excessive volatility, and foster destabilizing speculation. Under such conditions, they contended, foreign-exchange intervention could help direct exchange rates along a path consistent with fundamentals and could do so with lower volatility than otherwise would be the case. An official presence, particularly on the part of the United States, was necessary to maintain market order.

The record of US operations between March 1973 and April 1981, however, was equivocal at best. The United States intervened almost exclusively in support of the dollar, but during nearly every operation, the dollar continued to depreciate. To be sure, US interventions at the time often sought only to smooth dollar movements, not to prevent or reverse them.[2] On this score, we offer some limited evidence of success. Still, the overall record led many observers and practitioners to question the usefulness of sterilized intervention.

United States interventions during the early floating-rate period are best understood as reflections of the monetary policy of the era. The period covers most of the Great Inflation episode, America's longest period of peacetime inflation. The renewed acceleration of US inflation in late 1977, after repeated attempts to rein it in, seriously weakened the credibility of US monetary policy. It prompted a sharp dollar depreciation, which eventually challenged beliefs about the efficacy of sterilized intervention. By August 1979, monetary policy began to change under the direction of Federal Reserve Chairman Paul Volcker, and by April 1981, US intervention operations all but stopped with the urging of the Undersecretary of the Treasury for Monetary Affairs, Beryl Sprinkel.

5.2   The Great Inflation, 1965–1980

Exchange rates are endogenous variables that respond to, and help propagate, the impact of unanticipated economic developments. In the face of a shock, exchange rates arguably may undershoot or overshoot their equilibrium values in the short run, but ultimately their steady-state paths reflect economic fundamentals. When monetary authorities intervene, particularly when they intervene over long periods of time, they are reacting to whatever economic events sent the exchange-rate along a path that they found undesirable. In that sense, prolonged sterilized intervention is often a reflection of some fundamental underlying economic occurrence, such as inappropriate monetary policy (Sprinkel 1981, 16). Any analysis of intervention requires an understanding of the basic macroeconomic developments occurring in concert with the operation. By and large, active interventions during the early floating rate period, especially after 1976, attempted to attenuate the dollar's persistent depreciation, which itself was primarily a symptom of the Great Inflation.

During the early 1960s, the Bretton Woods system constrained US monetary policy and anchored inflation expectations.[3] Under a dollar peg, inflation would worsen the US balance-of-payments position and eventually undermine the official dollar price of gold. Because the private sector understood this constraint, inflation expectations did not respond to shocks, and inflation demonstrated little inertia. This check on US monetary policy was not particularly important during the dollar-shortage period of the Bretton Woods era, roughly 1949 through 1958, since the world needed dollar reserves. As explained in chapter 4, the constraint began to bind around 1960, as the many foreign central banks that held excessive amounts of dollars increasingly demanded gold. The US Treasury and the Federal Reserve undertook many ad hoc policies to limit US gold losses, thereby weakening the constraint and allowing policymakers greater latitude to pursue expansionary policies in pursuit of domestic objectives. Eventually, however, Bretton Woods proved incompatible with these policies, and the fixed-exchange-rate regime collapsed.

America's Great Inflation began in late 1965 and lasted through 1982, when the disinflation policies of the Volcker FOMC finally began to take hold. Inflation started to accelerate in late 1965 and rose above 2 percent on a year-over-year basis in early 1966 (see figure 5.1). In contrast, between 1960 and 1965, inflation had averaged only 1.2 percent per year with relatively little variation. During the Great Inflation, inflation cycled upward in three big movements, first reaching a 6 1/2 percent annual rate in early 1970 before subsiding, then climbing above a 12 percent annual rate in 1974 before again slowing, and finally attaining a 14 1/2 percent annual rate in 1980. As with each cyclical peak, each cyclical trough was higher than its predecessor. According to contemporary accounts, inflation expectations became a problem for policymakers by 1969 (Hetzel 2008, 75). By late 1976, worldwide confidence in the ability and willingness of the Federal Reserve System to control inflation was quickly waning. By early 1977, the dollar, which had depreciated on balance since the inception of generalized floating, came under even stronger downward pressure, and by 1978, international investors were moving funds out of dollar-denominated assets.

The Great Inflation occurred because the Federal Reserve did not pursue a policy of price stability. Instead, monetary policy became exceptionally easy from 1966 through 1968, again from 1970 through 1972, and finally throughout the last half of the 1970s (see figure 5.2). Economic historians have attributed the pursuit of these policies primarily to the adoption of an economic framework that downplayed money's causal role in the inflation process, but a policy preference for low unemployment over low inflation,

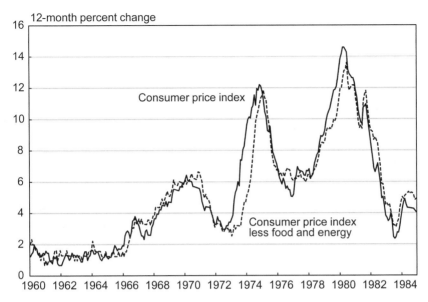

Fig. 5.1   US inflation, 1960–1984
Note: Data are from the US Bureau of Labor Statistics.

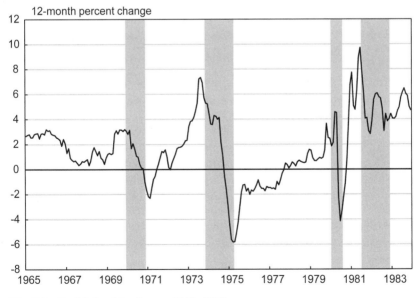

Fig. 5.2   Real federal funds rate, 1965–1983
Notes: The real federal funds rate equals the effective federal funds rate minus the percentage change in the core CPI over the past twelve months. Shaded bars are recessions. Data are from the Federal Reserve, the Bureau of Labor Statistics, and the National Bureau of Economic Research.

mismeasurement, and political pressures also contributed to the nation's policy errors.

With the ascendancy of Keynesian economics by 1960, policymakers began to distinguish between demand-pull inflation and cost-push (or structural) inflation (Hetzel 2008). Demand-pull inflation resulted when aggregate demand, as measured by actual GDP, exceeded aggregate supply, as measured by potential GDP. (Alternatively, aggregate demand exceeded aggregate supply when the unemployment rate fell below its natural rate, generally pegged at 4 percent in the 1960s and 1970s.) According to the then conventional model, if the economy were operating below potential, demand-pull inflation could not be a problem, except possibly for some lingering inertial effects that would eventually dissipate. The proper role of macroeconomic policy was to return GDP quickly to its potential growth path and to restore full employment. As Hetzel (2008) emphasizes, this framework induced a stop-go quality to policy, which decimated inflation expectations.

Mainstream Keynesian economists saw demand-pull inflation as stemming from excess aggregate demand and not from excess money growth per se. Within this framework, either a budget surplus or tight monetary policy could reduce inflation, but because tight monetary policy raised interest rates, whereas tight fiscal policy did not, fiscal policy remained the tool of choice for demand management at least until the early 1970s (Hetzel 2008, 80–81). Monetary policy was to manage interest rates either in support of fiscal policies or in actions like Operation Twist. Beginning around 1970, however, the importance of monetary policy began to rise relative to that of fiscal policy (Hetzel 2008, 79).

Within the conventional model, any inflation that existed when economic activity fell below potential must be of the cost-push variety. Chief among the causes of cost-push inflation were union wage demands, but monopoly-pricing power, commodity-price shocks, dollar depreciations, and myriad other ad hoc price pressures also contributed to cost-push inflation. Demand management—fiscal and monetary policies—could do nothing about cost-push inflation short of pushing the economy into a protracted recession, and should therefore not attempt to offset it. Eliminating cost-push inflation required some type of incomes policy. Consistent with this prescription, the Kennedy administration pursued wage and price guidelines, the Nixon administration used direct price freezes and controls, and the Carter administration attempted price guidelines.

Complicating matters, especially during the 1960s, economists believed that they could permanently lower the unemployment rate by accepting a higher inflation rate (Romer and Romer 2002, 24). According to Mayer (1999, 122–24), many economists and policymakers believed that inflation was not as socially disruptive as unemployment. He attributes this belief partly to economists' experience with the Great Depression and partly to their lack of experience with peacetime inflations. Hetzel (2008, 65, 67), sounding a similar chord, contends that the social unrest of the 1960s and 1970s had policymakers fearful about high unemployment.[4] They often regarded an unemployment rate high enough to eliminate inflation as politically infeasible (Hetzel 2008, 111).

Policymakers, of course, could only achieve a trade-off between lower unemployment and higher inflation to the extent that the public formed expectations about inflation from past experience and not from beliefs about future economic developments. Policymakers assumed this and initial evidence seemed to confirm it. Given the low and stable inflation rates of the 1960s, inflation expectations were slow to build after 1965. In the early 1970s, however, economists began to amend this view and to worry about inflation expectations.

The Great Inflation proved hard to overcome because heightened inflation expectations eventually increased the output and employment costs of any subsequent disinflationary policy, and the administration and the Federal Reserve became increasingly reluctant to incur these costs. Chari, Christiano, and Eichenbaum (1998) and Christiano and Gust (2000) refer to this as an expectations trap. The greater the concern that a central bank shows for real economic developments, the more likely it becomes that the central bank can fall into the expectations trap.

Basing policy on a split between demand-pull and cost-push inflation requires reliable measurement. Romer and Romer (2002), Orphanides (2002, 2003), and Clarida, Gali, and Gertler (2000) have argued that, in large measure, the Federal Reserve's performance during the Great Inflation was the result of policymakers consistently underestimating the natural rate of unemployment or, equivalently, consistently overestimating the level and growth rate of potential output. Such estimation errors would lead policymakers to underpredict inflation, to incorrectly attribute any observed inflation to cost-push factors, and to pursue a monetary policy that was excessively accommodative.

Two hallmark events of the 1970s undoubtedly contributed to measurement errors. First, sharp hikes in relative oil prices lowered structural productivity growth and potential output.[5] Second, unprecedented shifts in labor participation rates raised the natural rate of unemployment. Together, lower structural productivity growth and a higher natural rate of unemployment would lower potential output. According to current Congressional Budget Office (CBO) estimates, potential GDP grew at an average annual rate of 4.0 percent between 1947 and 1973, but over the next 10 years, potential grew on average at less than half this rate (1.2 percent). Moreover for most of this period, the administration put the natural rate of unemployment at 4 percent, but subsequent CBO estimates indicate that the natural rate continually rose, reaching a peak of 6.3 percent in 1978. Given the substantial relative-price shocks and structural changes taking place in the 1970s, it is not surprising that policymakers overestimated the nation's potential growth path and underestimated the natural rate of unemployment.

With the perception that the economy was often below potential or that unemployment was too high, the administration often exerted pressure on the Federal Reserve to accommodate fiscal expansions by keeping interest rates low (Meltzer 2005). Chairmen Martin and Burns viewed the Federal Reserve System as independent *within* the government, not independent *of* the government. By this, they meant that the Federal Reserve should not undertake actions that might thwart the administration's ability to achieve its policy objectives, such as low unemployment. As a consequence, the Federal Reserve often delayed tightening monetary policy in the face of rising inflation or reversed direction when the unemployment rate rose substantially to avoid administration and congressional criticism. Not until the Volcker chairmanship in 1979 would the Federal Reserve fully recognize inflation as a monetary phenomenon and clearly assert its independence to pursue price stability. In the meantime, the dollar depreciated broadly in foreign-exchange markets.

5.3   Providing Guidance: US Intervention, 1973–1977

After an initial sharp depreciation in the months immediately following the inception of generalized floating, the dollar remained fairly stable through mid-1977, despite the run-up in US inflation (see figure 5.3). Still, US policymakers regarded floating exchange rates as inherently prone to disorder. In their view, the private-sector information inefficiencies caused excessive exchange-rate volatility and prolonged disparities between observed rates and their equilibrium values as determined by economic fundamentals. Intervention, according to the official view, was necessary to provide market guidance and to calm market disorder.

Exactly how officials thought intervention achieved market calm is unclear; they never clearly articulated a theoretical channel of influence. Although many staff economists discussed intervention within the context of a portfolio-balance model, the foreign exchange desk viewed intervention as having a "psychological" effect on the market that came about because the intervention expressed an official concern for exchange rates. The desk, however, never clearly equated this view with a modern expectations channel, through which the desk might aid price discovery by signaling new private information to the market.

As we will show, the operations seemed wholly out of place with either a portfolio-balance mechanism or an expectations channel (see chapter 1). By and large, the interventions were financed through short-term swap borrowings, which the desk quickly repaid, thereby offsetting any portfolio effect. The desk also kept the transactions small and undertook them covertly out of a fear that private market participants would bet against the Federal

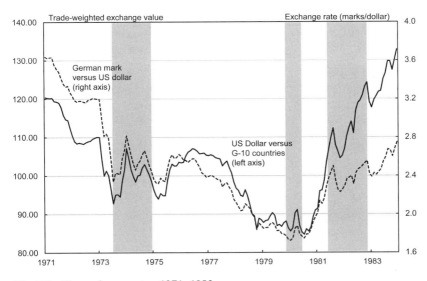

Fig. 5.3   Key exchange rates, 1971–1983
Notes: Shaded bars are recessions. Data are from the Federal Reserve and the National Bureau of Economic Research.

Reserve and possibly overwhelm an operation. If the desk had private information, undertaking small, covert operations seems an inefficient method of transmitting it. At best, the desk may have simply attempted to trick some market participants into believing that others had changed their perceptions, but this does not seem consistent with expressing official concern for exchange rates.

In any event, the operations had some limited effect on exchange-rate movements. Official purchases and sales of foreign exchange did not result in dollar depreciations or appreciations. In fact, market participants could have profitably bet against the foreign exchange desk. The interventions, however, seemed sometimes to smooth dollar movements.

5.3.1   The Advent of Floating

Despite the dollar devaluation in December 1971, the Bretton Woods system continued to unravel.[6] The US balance-of-payments position improved somewhat after the devaluation, but it continued to show large overall deficits. United States inflation had moderated somewhat in 1970 and 1971, but at 3.3 percent in mid-1972, it remained substantially higher than in the early 1960s. By 1973, the US inflation rate was again starting to rise and soon exceeded the inflation rate in Germany—the key European country (see figure 5.4). Cross-border financial flows grew and seemed increasingly sensitive to interest-rate differentials and speculative prospects. Foreign countries—notably Germany and Japan—continued to intervene heavily

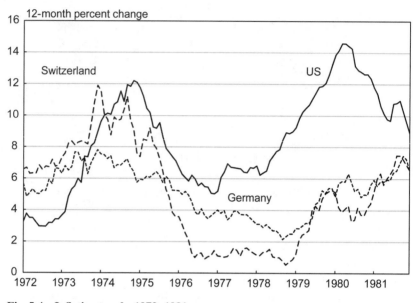

Fig. 5.4   Inflation trends, 1972–1981

Note: Data are from the Deutsche Bundesbank, Swiss Federal Statistics Office, and Bureau of Labor Statistics.

and to amass unwanted dollar reserves, which created for them excessive domestic liquidity. Inflation in Germany was around 5 percent to 6 percent in 1972 and accelerating, while inflation in Japan was quickly approaching double-digit levels.

In January and early February 1973, as speculation against the dollar intensified, the foreign exchange desk at the Federal Reserve Bank of New York sold $318.6 million worth of German marks in the New York market, with roughly 15 percent of the total from the US Treasury's account. To finance its portion, the Federal Reserve used up its entire portfolio of $167.4 million equivalent German marks and borrowed $104.6 million worth of marks from its swap line with the Bundesbank. The Federal Reserve also sold $20.4 million worth of its Netherlands guilders. Despite its size, the intervention had little effect, and the situation continued to deteriorate.

On 12 February 1973, the United States devalued the dollar for a second time by raising the official price of gold from $38 per ounce to $42 per ounce. This devaluation brought the total dollar depreciation since 1971 to 15 1/2 percent on a trade-weighted basis against the G10 currencies, an amount that many officials thought sufficient to correct the US balance-of-payments problem (de Vries 1985, 67; Silber 2012, 94). United States officials also indicated that they would phase out controls on financial flows by the end of 1974, about the time that they expected the devaluation to improve the US balance-of-payments position.[7]

Private markets were not so sanguine about the dollar's prospects and speculation against the dollar intensified. As Charles Coombs, the special manager of the Federal Reserve Bank of New York's foreign exchange desk noted, the second devaluation taught all of those holding dollars "a harsh lesson," and they were rapidly positioning themselves not to be caught off guard again (FOMC *Memoranda*, 7 March 1973, 3). Gold, already well above the new official price of $42 per ounce, rose rapidly as markets perceived a good chance for a further dollar depreciation. Adding fuel to the speculative fire, US authorities indicated that they would not intervene in defense of the new parities; they would follow the old Bretton Woods custom of leaving that task to other countries.

In response to the second dollar devaluation, Italy and Japan immediately floated their currencies. On 1 March 1973, the Bundesbank acquired $3.7 billion, the largest amount ever bought or sold by a central bank in a single day, and on 2 March, the Bank of France bought $580 million in just 90 minutes (de Vries 1985, 76). With speculation rampant, the European exchange markets quickly closed.

On 12 March 1973, Belgium, France, Germany, Luxemburg, and the Netherlands agreed to a joint float against the dollar—the snake (Solomon 1982, 218). A year earlier, the six European Economic Community countries had decided to limit fluctuations in their exchange rates to 2 1/4 percent through intervention in each other's currencies—the snake in the tunnel.[8] They would finance their operations through short-term borrowing arrangements with settlement in prescribed reserve assets. A country in the snake would intervene in dollars only when its exchange rate was at the edge of the band; otherwise all intervention was in the constituent currencies. As part of the March 1973 agreement, Germany revalued the mark by 3 percent against the SDR. On 20 March 1973, Norway and Sweden joined the joint float. Although this effectively ended the Bretton Woods system, policymakers at the time viewed the float against the dollar only as a necessary interim mechanism toward the reformation of Bretton Woods. Talks were already underway.

In July 1972, the international financial community had established the Committee of Twenty within the International Monetary Fund to reform the Bretton Woods system.[9] Although participants generally favored a system based on set parities, they knew that any new exchange-rate system would need to be more flexible than its predecessor. Greater flexibility could be achieved within a fixed-but-adjustable rate system through wider margins around the parities and more frequent central-rate adjustments. Indicators based on changes in countries' reserve holdings or on their basic balance-of-payments trends might promote greater flexibility by depoliticizing parity changes and by ensuring that surplus countries shared in the adjustment burden (de Vries 1985, 163–97; Solomon 1982, 235–66).

By early 1973, most monetary officials also expressed a tolerance for—if not an outright acceptance of—temporarily floating exchange rates.[10] In the current circumstances of heightened speculation, large international imbalances, more fluid financial movements, and excessive worldwide liquidity, fixed exchange rates were simply unworkable. A temporary reliance on floating rates was necessary.

Few, however, believed that an international monetary system based on floating exchange rates was sustainable. Many feared that the uncertainties inherent in floating rates would discourage international trade and investment and would promote the same disruptive policies—protectionism and competitive depreciations—that characterized the 1930s. Some, including Federal Reserve Chairman Arthur Burns, extrapolating these fears, believed that floating would promote the formation of currency blocs or—worse still—would lead to a complete breakdown of international monetary cooperation and financial order among nations (Burns 1973, 510–11).

Nevertheless, in the wake of the oil price shocks of December 1973 and the huge payments imbalances that they portended, the industrial countries were unwilling to commit to parities anytime soon. In January 1974, the Committee of Twenty ceased its reform efforts. With floating rates continuing for the foreseeable future, the IMF set out instead to develop procedures that might maintain a cooperative international monetary environment.

In June 1974, the IMF proposed guidelines for floating exchange rates which, despite their objective, revealed a clear preference for fixed exchange rates and presumed a heavy central bank presence in the market. The IMF guidelines recommended day-to-day or week-to-week interventions to prevent or moderate erratic fluctuations in exchange rates. The guidelines also condoned intermediate-term interventions (month to month or quarter to quarter) to moderate longer-term—but temporary—movements in rates. The IMF, however, objected to aggressive, beggar-thy-neighbor interventions. A central bank was not to buy foreign exchange when its currency was depreciating over the intermediate term nor sell foreign exchange when its currency was appreciating over the intermediate term. The guidelines also recognized that some member countries might operate floating rates within a target-zone framework and suggested that such countries consult with the IMF about the target. In addition, the IMF recommended that member states with floating rates discuss with them the broad objectives for their official-reserve policies. These guidelines, however, were never fully implemented, in part because of different views about how to do so, and in part because some executive directors of the IMF felt that the guidelines put a bigger consultation and information burden on members with floating rates than on members with fixed rates (de Vries 1985, 297–302).

Many nations, particularly France and most developing countries, still favored a return to fixed exchange rates, but events in the mid-1970s continued to overtake reform efforts. By 1975, the US position under Treasury Secretary William Simon, with prodding from the US Congress, was shifting in favor of long-term floating (Solomon 1982, 269). The Rambouillet meeting of the Group of Seven nations on 15–17 November 1975 became a compromise of sorts between the US and French views. Participants rewrote IMF Article IV, allowing countries to choose floating in the long-term, but leaving open the possibility of a return to a fixed-exchange-rate system with greater flexibility than Bretton Woods. Policymakers, moreover, were quickly eradicating the central role of gold in the international monetary system (Schwartz 1983, 34–36). Gold would not anchor any future fixed-rate system. The Rambouillet communiqué emphasized the need for exchange-rate stability but saw stability as the product of "orderly underlying economic and financial fundamentals." Supportive official actions to counter disorderly market conditions were welcome, but nations should not attempt to impose stability at a particular rate or to "manipulate" exchange rates for advantage (Volcker and Gyohten 1992, 141; Solomon 1982, 274). United States officials saw Rambouillet as requiring the United States to become more active in the foreign exchange market—especially to counter "erratic movements" in rates—and to quickly establish a mechanism for day-to-day consultation (FOMC *Memoranda*, 16 December 1975, 3–6).

5.3.2 Market Failure and the Role of Intervention

Despite their growing approval of a generalized floating regime during the 1970s, US monetary authorities were unwilling to give the private market free rein in determining exchange rates. They considered foreign-exchange markets prone to disorderly conditions, as revealed through price volatility, cumulative or self-propagating exchange-rate movements, wide bid-ask spreads, and fairly persistent exchange-rate deviations from fundamentals. The market, in their view, required official guidance. As Coombs once complained, he had "little hope that market forces can be relied upon to restore orderly markets and to maintain an appropriate exchange rate structure" (FOMC *Memoranda*, 19–20 November 1973, 31).

United States policymakers were never explicit about the exact nature of the underlying market failure. In part—at least initially—they seemed to view the market, particularly the New York market, as being underdeveloped. Greene (1984a, no. 127, 5) pointed out that in late 1974 most US multinationals conducted their exchange business abroad and that most US banks maintained their key foreign-exchange operations abroad. Under Bretton Woods, the dollar became the key international vehicle currency, easily enabling US banks to specialize in providing liquid dollar markets, not foreign-exchange facilities. Moreover, under the parity system, hedging against exchange-rate fluctuations was not the make-or-break priority that it now became under floating. The failures of both the Herstatt and Franklin National banks in 1974 because of foreign-exchange exposures dramatically illustrated to policymakers the problem of learning to operate in the new regime. The Herstatt failure led to a "marked drop in foreign exchange market activity as participants grew wary of credit risk" (Dooley and Shafer

1983, 48). These bank failures caused both bank management and governments to restrict banks' ability to take open positions, contributing—along with a general uncertainty about future monetary policies—to a lack of sufficient stabilizing private speculation (McKinnon 1976). Official guidance seemed necessary in such an underdeveloped market.

More fundamentally, however, US policymakers seemed to believe that information imperfections plagued the foreign-exchange market. In a fairly common description of market activity, the foreign exchange desk at the Federal Reserve Bank of New York observed that, "Traders ignored fundamental factors that would normally favor the dollar" (*Bulletin*, December 1977, 1049). From the desk's view, information imperfections—like traders' ignorance of fundamentals—caused exchange rates to deviate from their equilibrium values, created excessive volatility, and fostered destabilizing speculation. Tests undertaken at the Board of Governors in 1976 seemed to reject the martingale model of exchange rates, suggesting that market participants did not use information efficiently (Dooley and Shafer 1983).

Although US monetary officials believed that intervention could repair these reoccurring market failures, the FOMC never discussed a transmission mechanism in public documents like the FOMC *Minutes*, or the *Bulletin*'s reports on "Treasury and Federal Reserve Foreign-Exchange Operations." Theoretically, intervention can affect exchange rates through a monetary mechanism, a portfolio-balance channel, and an expectations effect, as explained in chapter one.

Economists have often wondered if central banks during the early floating exchange rate period completely sterilized their operations, since only then could intervention operate independently of monetary policy. In the 1970s, both the staff and the FOMC understood the important distinction between sterilized and nonsterilized intervention, and the Federal Reserve routinely sterilized all foreign-exchange operations (Morton and Truman 1979, 12; Truman 1980, 10; Adams and Henderson 1983, 1; Greene 1984a, no. 127, 16). As Truman (1980, 10) explained: "If the Federal Reserve intervenes to counteract [a] rise in the exchange value of the dollar, it will buy marks and sell dollars. The dollars sold will add to the public's holdings of US Treasury securities because the intervention's potential expansionary impact on the US money supply is automatically offset in daily open market operations." In the case that Truman describes, the desk would sell Treasury securities to the public to offset its injection of dollar reserves. "[T]he net effect of the intervention is to increase the supply of dollar-denominated assets and decrease the supply of mark-denominated assets available to private asset holders" (Truman 1980, 10). Desk foreign-exchange operations during the early dollar float did not affect reserves in the US banking system.

Complete sterilization, as Adams and Henderson (1983, 1) emphasized, "leaves the monetary liabilities of *both home and foreign authorities* unchanged" (emphasis added). Truman (1980, 10) assumes, "that the Bundesbank also takes action to keep the German money supply unchanged." But, prior to the 1980s, many industrialized countries, including Germany, did not have well-developed money markets and did not conduct monetary policy through open-market operations. They relied instead on discount-window operations. Consequently, these banks may not have been able to sterilize foreign-exchange operations on a day-to-day basis. Indeed, as our narrative indicates, foreign central banks were often worried about the excess liquidity resulting from official US intervention sales of their currencies. Consequently, some temporary or partial monetary transmission mechanism may often have been in play.

Sterilized intervention can affect exchange rates independent of monetary policy through a portfolio-balance channel. Truman (1980) and the studies accompanying the Jurgenson Report indicate that the staff recognized the possibility of a portfolio-balance mechanism during the early floating-rate period.[11] Adams and Henderson (1983), for example, offer a definition of sterilized intervention that strictly conforms to a portfolio-balance mechanism. What ultimately matters in their definition is a change in central banks' holdings of net foreign assets. Neither the specific type of foreign-currency transaction nor its motive carries much weight in their definition. The net effect of an intervention, as Truman (1980, 10) explained, is to alter the relative stocks of dollar-denominated and foreign-currency-denominated securities that the public holds. If the public views these securities as imperfect substitutes, they might only alter their portfolios if offered a risk premium for the more abundant security. This risk premium could easily come about from a change in the spot exchange rate in the desired direction (see chapter one).

Whereas the board's economic research staff seemed to describe intervention as possibly operating through at least two macroeconomic mechanisms—the monetary and portfolio-balance channels—the foreign exchange desk never mentioned them. The desk only referred to intervention's effect on market psychology. The FOMC *Memoranda* provide an example: "the basic objective, Mr. Coombs observed, would be to influence market psychology, by providing evidence of official interest and concern . . . [W]ith some good fortune, [Federal Reserve] System operations could make a very important contribution" (FOMC *Memoranda*, 9 July 1973, 8). This and similar statements seem broadly consistent with a modern expectations channel, through which monetary authorities convey private information useful to price discovery, but the desk's statements typically relied on a show of "official interest and concern," or on "evidencing a sense of responsibility for the dollar" rather than on the transmission of new information (FOMC *Memoranda*, 9 July 1973, 13). Moreover, both Coombs and Federal Reserve Bank of New York President Alfred Hayes thought intervention needed to be part of an unspecified broader program that relied heavily on direct controls over financial flows (FOMC *Memoranda*, 7, March 1973, 8–12). Consequently, why they thought sterilized US intervention offered the United States an independent policy instrument with which to affect exchange rates remains unclear.

5.3.3   The United States Returns to the Market

On 16 March 1973, the G10 finance ministers agreed that foreign-exchange intervention was useful to maintain orderly markets within a regime of floating exchange rates.[12] The Europeans thought that US participation was particularly important for the success of such efforts. For its part, the United States remained decidedly lukewarm about the prospects of intervention, but agreed in principle to such operations. The United States had not intervened since the closing of the gold window on 15 August 1971, except for a brief operation in July 1972, and the aforementioned support operations prior to the 12 February 1973 dollar devaluation. Neither of these actions was particularly successful, but the United States' current concern about intervention centered on its financing, not on misgivings about its recent effectiveness.

Holding the United States back was the lack of a clear arrangement for risk sharing under the existing swap facilities (FOMC *Memoranda*, 19–20 March 1973, 63–64). In March 1973, the United States held virtually no foreign-exchange reserves and would need to draw on its swap lines to finance its interventions (see figures 5.5 and 5.6). Given the growing magnitude of cross-border financial flows, an expansion of the swap network also seemed necessary. In March 1973, Charles Coombs recommended an increase of roughly 50 percent to the $11.7 billion network (FOMC *Memoranda*, 19–20 March 1973, 73) (see figure 5.7).

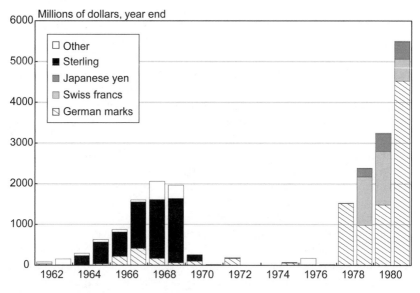

Fig. 5.5   Federal Reserve foreign currency balances, 1962–1981
Note: Data are from the Federal Reserve.

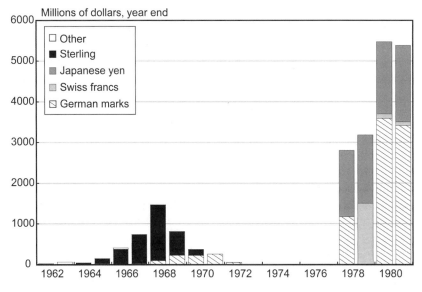

Fig. 5.6 US Treasury foreign currency balances, 1962–1981
Note: Data are from the Federal Reserve.

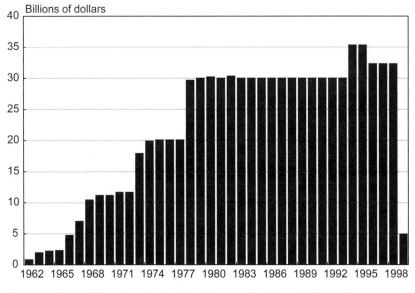

Fig. 5.7 Federal Reserve authorizations for swap drawings, 1962–1999
Note: Data are from the Federal Reserve.

For the most part, the swap lines had remained dormant because of continuing disagreements about the distribution of currency losses associated with the dollar's devaluation and with the move to floating.[13] The swap lines traditionally maintained revaluation clauses, which protected debtor countries should the creditor country revalue its currency, but the swap lines contained no clear provisions for losses resulting from a general dollar devaluation—a change in the official gold price—or from the adoption of a float. Consequently, the United States conceivably faced large losses on Belgian franc, British sterling, German mark, and Swiss franc drawings outstanding prior to 15 August 1971.

On 8 July 1973, as an inducement to undertake intervention, Belgium, France, Germany, the Netherlands, and Switzerland agreed to risk sharing arrangements with the United States (Task Force 1990f, Paper no. 9, 6).[14] Henceforth, when the Federal Reserve drew on a swap line for intervention purposes, it would share any valuation profit or loss equally with the creditor bank. With the risk-sharing issue settled, the Federal Reserve increased the swap lines on 10 July 1973 from $11.7 billion to nearly $19 billion and renewed its intervention operations.[15]

The risk sharing arrangement did not apply to foreign central bank drawings on the swap lines (Task Force 1990f, Paper no. 9, 6). When a foreign government drew on the line, it bore the entire risk.[16] In January 1974, officials at the Bank of Italy sought an increase in their swap line from $2 billion to $3 billion. Concerned about the international ramifications of the recent oil price hikes, Chairman Burns supported the increase, but he suggested that under the new line, the Bank of Italy assume all of the exchange risk. Moreover, Burns suggested—apparently with the US Treasury's approval—that the Federal Reserve announce its willingness to expand the swap lines of other countries under the same terms (FOMC *Memoranda*, January 21–22 1974, 33–51). In March 1974, Britain asked for a $1 billion increase in its swap line to $3 billion and agreed to assume all of the exchange risk associated with its subsequent drawings (FOMC *Memoranda*, 18–19 March 1974, 54–65).

As with the use of the swap lines, the objective and mechanics of US intervention under a floating exchange-rate regime would necessarily be substantially different than foreign-exchange operations had been under Bretton Woods. United States operations under the Bretton Woods system primarily sought to provide central banks with cover for their dollar exposures and thereby to dissuade them from converting unwanted dollar balances into gold with the US Treasury. The task of intervening to keep specific exchange rates within their Bretton Woods parity bounds usually fell to foreign central banks (see chapter 4). After 15 August 1971, protecting the gold stock was not an issue, and with the advent of generalized floating, calming market disorder became the oft-stated objective of intervention.

Between 12 March 1973 and 17 April 1981, the desk operated on both sides of the market, but by and large, it only *actively* intervened to alleviate downward pressure on the dollar. By actively intervened, we mean that the desk transacted with the clear intention of affecting dollar exchange rates. The desk conducted the lion's share of this intervention against German marks but occasionally undertook small operations in Belgian francs, French francs, Japanese yen, Netherlands guilders, and Swiss francs. The German mark acted as the linchpin of the snake, so an intervention that altered the mark-dollar rate might easily affect all of the European currency rates vis-à-vis the dollar.

Because the United States financed most its intervention sales of foreign exchange by borrowing via the swap lines, soon after an operation, the desk needed to repurchase foreign exchange to pay down outstanding US obligations. For the most part, the desk did not consider these purchases to be interventions: "[W]hen the Desk was acquiring currencies to repay debt, it tried to avoid having any noticeable influence on the market. Operations conducted with a view to influencing market psychology in the hope of affecting exchange rates might more properly be described as 'intervention.'" (FOMC *Memoranda*, 15 July 1975, 8) Likewise, after 1979, the desk began to buy foreign exchange explicitly to build a larger reserve portfolio. Although the desk did not undertake transactions to pay down debt or to accumulate reserves with the goal of affecting exchange rates—and therefore, did not *actively* intervene in these cases—the desk often timed these operations to minimize or maximize their impact in the market. The desk might avoid or delay transacting in the market by acquiring foreign exchange off-market with some other central bank or by rolling over the swap drawing. By timing the market transaction, the desk *passively* intervened, as Adams and Henderson (1983) explain.[17]

The foreign exchange desk operated in close consultation with the board and FOMC. Early in the day, the desk informed the board staff of any plans for intervention, and throughout the day, it maintained close communications. If the interventions were large, the desk also solicited the subcommittee's views on the operation. The subcommittee was responsible to the entire FOMC (FOMC *Memoranda*, 20 May 1975, 17–18). The FOMC, which was ultimately responsible for intervention, issued instructions to the desk. A foreign-currency authorization set overall limits on the Federal Reserve's net open position, and procedural instructions spelled out how the desk might approach its overall limits. Informal limits also governed how much of specific currencies the desk might hold within the overall authorization, and the Treasury and the desk maintained "implicit tactical day-to-day limits" (FOMC *Transcripts*, 21 October 1981, 7).

The desk also cooperated closely with other central banks, particularly after the Rambouillet agreement. Each day beginning in December 1975, a central bank from a European community country called the Federal Reserve Bank of New York at 11:00 a.m. with a summary of exchange rates, intervention, and market conditions in Europe. The desk immediately relayed that information to the Bank of Japan—through its New York office—and the Bank of Canada. At the close of the New York market, the desk sent all of these central banks a cable informing them of New York closing exchange rates, US. intervention, and market commentary (FOMC *Memoranda*, 16 December 1975, 5–6). The desk also worked out the upper limit of its intervention amounts with the appropriate central banks.

The Federal Reserve Bank of New York adopted various techniques for intervention, depending on the degree of secrecy that the desk wanted to maintain, its budget for intervention, and the market effect that the desk hoped to achieve.[18] During the 1970s, the desk appears to have conducted most of its interventions covertly (Hooper 1977, 7). This was especially true before 1979. Early on, the United States usually intervened on a relatively limited scale because of its small portfolio of foreign exchange. The operations remained secret because the desk feared that with only a limited portfolio, market participants could easily take a position against the Fed and foil the intervention operation if they knew that the Fed was in the market. If knowledge of the Federal Reserve's operations spread, the effect would be all the more intense and might actually force the desk to withdraw from the market (Hooper 1977, 8).

Ironically, however, the covert operations that Hooper describes seem inconsistent with the desk's stated view that interventions were useful to affect market psychology by demonstrating "official interest and concern" for the dollar or by "evidencing a sense of responsibility for the dollar." At best, except for their small scale, these operations seem more consistent with a portfolio-balance channel of influence. As noted, the desk and the FOMC never clearly articulated how they thought sterilized intervention worked.

In New York during the early 1970s, most foreign-exchange transactions—including interventions—went through the brokers' market. Brokers maintained direct telephone lines with the largest foreign-exchange trading banks. They did not undertake transactions for their own accounts, but matched bids and offers in a highly competitive market for small fixed commissions. Consequently, the transactions costs of operating in the brokers' market for both the Fed and private traders were significantly less than dealing on a bilateral basis.

When the Federal Reserve wanted to undertake a covert operation, it asked a trader at a commercial bank to act as the agent for the desk in the New York brokers' market. The broker arranged a trade and only afterward revealed the buying and selling parties—in this case, only two commercial traders, one of whom confidentially acted on behalf of the desk. This mode of operation not only kept the desk's identity secret, but it lent the Federal Reserve the expertise of a day-to-day commercial practitioner, and the commercial bank assumed the credit risk associated with the transaction. In return, the Federal Reserve typically paid the commercial bank a small commission (0.003 percent) on the value of the transaction (Hooper 1977, 6). Hence a typical intervention of $15 million yielded the trader $45 thousand.

In the 1970s, the Fed normally intervened through one of twenty-five major US dealing banks out of the roughly 200 banks that operated in the New York brokers' market (Hooper 1977, 3). The Federal Reserve maintained direct telephone contacts with these banks. When intervening, the central bank usually operated only with an individual bank for a single day (Hooper 1977, 4). The frequency with which the Federal Reserve called on a particular bank reflected the quality of its service, which consisted mainly of providing the desk with current market information. The desk generally felt that these correspondents offered much better information than it acquired through its more routine telephone contacts with dealers. In addition to maintaining anonymity and providing information, operating in the brokers' market through a commercial bank allowed the desk to settle in federal funds, whereas operating directly with a broker would require the desk to settle in clearinghouse funds (Hooper 1977, 7).

The apparent intent of a covert operation was simply to trick one side of the market about the intensity of private actions on the other side of the market; that is, to make one side of the market believe that the other was trading on new information. The conjecture apparently was that traders are more likely to respond favorably to a stabilizing transaction if they believe that the demand emanates from the private sector rather than from US monetary authorities. As noted in the quote at the beginning of this chapter, the market sometimes interpreted official intervention transactions as evidence of fundamental weakness in a currency. Given that the desk generally worked with individual banks for a single day, intervention lasting for a long number of days was likely to become widely known in the market—at least among the key banks (Hooper 1977, 4). Hence, to remain secret, most intervention operations needed to be of fairly short duration.

The desk often finessed its transaction amounts and its pricing strategy to get the biggest bang for its buck. Pardee (1973) discussed a number of strategies. When the dollar was depreciating, for example, the desk might probe the strength of demand for a foreign currency by placing an offer (to sell) somewhat above the typical offer rate and then observing how bidders (to buy) responded. If traders take the high offer, it suggests a stronger demand for the foreign currency than if they reject or counter the offer. The desk also varied the size of its transactions to the same end, but unusually large transactions ran the risk of tipping the Federal Reserve's hand to the market (Pardee 1973, 6). Typically the desk acted to counter market trends or "lean against the wind," but it sometimes sought to reinforce or to reverse them. The possibilities and permutations were large, as Pardee (1973) suggests. As discussed below, in early 1981, the desk even attempted to bracket the dollar's volatility by simultaneously placing bid and offer prices in the market, and it sometimes operated on both sides of the market even on a single day.[19]

On some occasions in February 1975 and frequently after 1979, the desk wanted the market to know that it was actively trading, particularly if it sought to intervene forcefully. Then, the desk placed large orders with the brokers' market or directly with particular banks. Pardee (1973, 6) reports that, "This knowledge alone can have a profound psychological effect, and could move the dollar to stronger ground without heavy intervention on our part." By late 1977, as we will see below, the desk began intervening more openly and in larger amounts. On 4 January 1978 and for a few days hence, the desk placed orders to sell marks directly with several New York commercial banks, and the mark depreciated immediately without the desk actually selling a single mark (*Bulletin*, March 1978, 166). In addition, the desk sometimes tried to enhance the operation's effects by timing the transactions to coincide with a favorable news item or economic release, or by also announcing the operation to the press. Unfortunately, as we will see, the desk's actions did not always conform to the underlying thrust of US monetary policy. So it is not always clear whether the desk added signal or noise to the market.

Commercial banks that acted as agents for the desk also could benefit in terms of their own transactions from their knowledge of the Federal Reserve's intervention (Task Force 1990g, Paper no. 5, 13). The desk expected banks that executed its transactions to do so promptly, to maintain confidentiality, and not to undertake offsetting transactions. As we will see, however, the evidence suggests that banks often seemed to interpret desk sales of foreign exchange as a signal to buy.

As noted, in addition to pure intervention, the desk undertook two other types of foreign-exchange transactions in the market. The desk bought foreign exchange to repay swap borrowing and to build foreign-exchange reserves. (Often the desk bought foreign exchange directly from foreign central banks or from other correspondents off-market for this purpose.) The desk also executed market transactions for foreign correspondents that maintained accounts with the Federal Reserve Bank of New York. When not going off-market, the desk usually dealt directly with commercial banks when undertaking these types of transactions for two reasons: Often these transactions did not occur in the standard amounts that the brokers' market handled, and if the Federal Reserve entered the brokers' market directly, it might have been forced to acknowledge and reject the credit risk associated with a specific commercial bank. The number of banks that the desk dealt with for these nonintervention transactions included the twenty-five US banks through which the Federal Reserve intervened, plus five other foreign-owned banks that resided in the United States (Hooper 1977, 8–10).

5.3.4   Were US Interventions between March 1973 and September 1977 Effective?

Although US inflation generally rose and the dollar tended to depreciate between March 1973 and September 1977, the dollar's overall downward trend was quite modest, and confidence in the dollar remained fairly firm for the most part. The October 1973 OPEC oil embargo and the associated price hikes generally seemed to bolster the dollar even though they prompted a recession and a sharp easing in US monetary policy during 1974. After rising precipitously throughout much of 1973, the real federal funds rate fell sharply in the wake of the oil shock and remained negative throughout much of 1977 (see figure 5.2). Observers, however, generally thought that the United States would be less susceptible to the adverse effects of oil-price shocks than other industrialized countries, and this perception often bolstered demand for the dollar. For one thing, OPEC priced oil in dollars. Since demand for oil was inelastic, particularly in the short term, the demand for dollars to pay for oil would rise. In addition, many thought that the dollar would likely benefit more than most other currencies from the recycling of oil revenues. The oil price increase also caused foreign central banks to hold more dollars in their portfolios, thereby reducing the dollar "overhang" that followed the August 1971 closing of the US gold window.

Despite the overall confidence in the dollar, the desk intervened fairly frequently. In addition, the period witnessed some very sharp swings in the dollar, particularly relative to the German mark, that prompted the desk to undertake four sizable intervention episodes (see figures 5.8 and 5.9). The specific events that triggered these four key intervention episodes were: a revaluation of the German mark within the European joint float in late June 1973 that led to intervention during the following month, the liberalization of barriers on financial flows in January 1974 that resulted in operations from February through April of that year, a rapid easing of US monetary policy in October 1974 that led to a subsequent six-month episode of intervention, and further European joint-float problems in early 1976 that induced intervention in January and February of that year. Table 5.1 empirically describes these operations.[20]

These first four early interventions were much smaller in scale than the active US interventions after September 1977 and not very persistent, with the exception of the operations in early 1975 (see table 5.1). The desk initiated each of these actions and undertook almost all of the interventions for the central bank's own account. While the Treasury consented to the Federal Reserve's actions, it rarely participated.[21] The desk intervened primarily against German marks, but it also transacted in Belgian francs, French francs, Swiss francs, Netherlands guilders, and, on only two occasions, Japanese yen. The desk usually undertook interventions in non-German European currencies because of developments in the European joint float. In early 1975, for example, when the German mark was at the bottom of the European joint float, the Bundesbank did not want the desk to undertake heavy mark sales, so the desk transacted primarily in Netherlands guilder and Belgian francs, which were then at the top of the joint float (FOMC *Memoranda*, 20 May 1975, 13). The Bundesbank participated in all of these operations, typically buying substantially more dollars than the Federal Reserve System.

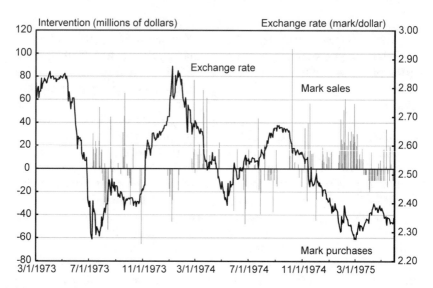

Fig. 5.8   US intervention against German marks, 1 March 1973–31 May 1975
Note: Data are from the Federal Reserve.

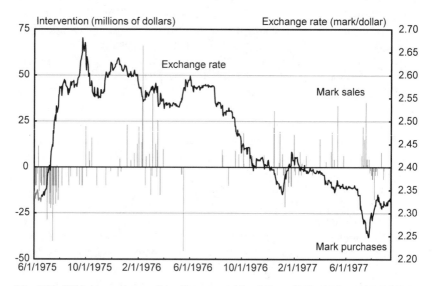

Fig. 5.9   US intervention against German marks, 1 June 1975–14 September 1977
Note: Data are from the Federal Reserve.

Table 5.1   **Intervention to support the dollar**

A.

Episodes	Total days[a] (#)	Exchange-rate change DM[b] (%)	Exchange-rate change MCI[c] (%)	US intervention against German marks Total[d] ($ mill.)	US intervention against German marks Mean[e] ($ mill.)	US intervention against German marks Count[f] (#)
1st Sub-period						
7/10/73–7/31/73	16	−0.4	1.1	220.5	18.4	12
2/1/74–4/30/74	63	−10.8	−5.7	373.4	29.0	13
10/1/74–3/31/75	122	−11.6	−3.9	978.2	21.8	52
1/5/76–2/11/76	28	−3.2	−1.0	184.7	23.1	8
2nd Sub-period						
9/30/77–10/31/78	265	−24.4	−15.9	5,203.3	55.5	97
11/1/78–12/31/78	40	3.8	4.2	5,662.5	202.4	28
6/15/79–10/5/79	79	−7.9	−2.5	9,101.1	207.3	44
4/8/80–7/11/80	68	−11.8	−10.1	3,964.8	120.7	26

B.

Episodes	US intervention against other currencies Total ($ mill.)	US intervention against other currencies Mean[d] ($ mill.)	US intervention against other currencies Count[f] (#)	Bundesbank intervention against US dollars Total[d,g] ($ mill.)	Bundesbank intervention against US dollars (DM mill.)	Ratio[h]
1st Sub-period						
7/10/73–7/31/73	52.9	8.8	6	270	630	1.2
2/1/74–4/30/74	43.5	25.3	2	222	581	0.6
10/1/74–3/31/75	291.5	12.1	26	1,246	3,028	1.1
1/5/76–2/11/76	19.6	19.6	1	200	517	1.1
2nd Sub-period						
9/30/77–10/31/78	395.2	13.2	30	1,171	2,432	0.2
11/1/78–12/31/78	914.9	47.0	20	2,791	5,282	0.5
6/15/79–10/5/79	145.1	27.0	6	2,720	4,948	0.3
4/8/80–7/11/80	370.8	33.7	11	731	1,312	0.2

Sources: Board of Governors of the Federal Reserve System, Deutsche Bundesbank, Truman (1980).
[a] Business days between first and last intervention.
[b] German marks per US dollar.
[c] Board of Governors' Major Currency Index, negative value indicates dollar depreciation.
[d] Positive and negative values are net purchases and sales of dollars, respectively.
[e] Average number of dollars purchased over days in episode.
[f] Number of days on which dollars were purchased during episode.
[g] Converted to dollars using average daily exchange rate for the period.
[h] Ratio of Bundesbank purchases of dollars to US purchases of dollars.

Because the Federal Reserve had exhausted its German mark balances in early 1973, it financed these mark sales primarily by drawing on its swap line with the Bundesbank. Consequently, as figures 8 and 9 illustrate, the desk had to quickly acquire dollars to pay down its swap obligations once market conditions improved. The desk acquired almost all of the marks for this purpose in the market, but was also able to obtain the needed currency off-market at various times from central banks (Greene 1984a, no. 127, 14–15).

Between 2 March 1973 and 14 September 1977, the United States intervened on 337 days against German marks (see table 5.2). On 161 of these intervention days, the United States sold marks, and on 176 days, the United States bought marks. By and large, the mark purchases were passive interventions. A typical (median) daily mark sale amounted to nearly $14 million equivalent, with the largest sale equal to $104 million. Roughly one-half of these operations lasted only a single day. Almost all lasted less than three consecutive days, but one operation persisted for a consecutive thirteen days. A typical mark purchase was slightly smaller than a sale. The median equaled $10 million, with the largest equal to $65.3 million. As with mark sales, most operations to buy marks lasted only a single day, with almost all persisting less than four days. The longest operation lasted fifteen consecutive days.

We evaluate the effectiveness of these US interventions in table 5.2 according to three success criteria: The first asks if US sales or purchases of German marks on a specific day were respectively associated with a same-day dollar appreciation or depreciation against the mark. The second criterion asks if US interventions moderated movements in the dollar relative to the previous day. Were, for example, official US sales of German marks on a specific day associated with a slower rate of dollar depreciation over that same day as compared with the dollar's depreciation on the previous day? The third success criterion combines the previous two into a single measure. (Appendix 2 contains mathematical descriptions of these three criteria along with a detailed discussion of our analytical methodology.)

These success criteria seem consistent with the stated objectives of intervention during the early dollar float, especially the second criterion. Managers from the Federal Reserve Bank of New York's foreign exchange desk often indicated that they did not try to defend a specific exchange rate. They instead only tried to moderate their movements or limit their fluctuations (Pardee 1973; Greene 1984a, no. 127, 8; FOMC *Memoranda*, 19–20, March 1973, 67; FOMC *Memoranda*, 17 April 1973, 58). We count the number of successes under each criterion and compare that count with the number that we would randomly anticipate given the volatile nature of day-to-day exchange-rate movements.

Only 45 (or 28 percent) of the 161 US sales of German marks prior to 14 September 1977 were associated with a same-day dollar appreciation against the mark. The observed number of successes falls well below two

Table 5.2   **Success counts for US intervention, 2 March 1973 to 14 September 1977**

German marks	Total (#)	Intervention successes (#)	(%)	Expected[a] successes (#)	Standard[a] deviation (#)
Mark sales & dollar appreciation	161	45	28.0	74	4
Mark purchases & dollar depreciation	176	67	38.1	83	5
Total	337	112	33.2		
Mark sales & smaller dollar depreciation	161	34	21.1	21	2
Mark purchases & smaller dollar appreciation	176	45	25.6	24	2
Total	337	79	23.4		
Mark sales & dollar appreciation or smaller depreciation	161	79	49.1	94	6
Mark purchases & dollar depreciation or small appreciation	176	112	63.6	107	7
Total	337	191	56.7		
Japanese Yen					
Yen sales & dollar appreciation	0	0	na	0	0
Yen purchases & dollar depreciation	2	2	100.0	1	1
Total	2	2	100.0		
Yen sales & smaller dollar depreciation	0	0	na	0	0
Yen purchases & smaller dollar appreciation	2	0	na	0	0
Total	2	0	na		
Yen sales & dollar appreciation or smaller depreciation	0	0	na	0	0
Yen purchases & dollar depreciation or small appreciation	2	2	100.0	1	1
Total	2	2	100.0		

Note: See appendix 2 for detail.
[a] Assumes that the success count is a hypergeometric random variable.

standard deviations from the expected number, suggesting that US intervention sales of German marks were a fairly reliable signal that the dollar would
depreciate against the mark, and implying—as the adage at the start of this
chapter suggests—that market participants generally could have profited
from selling dollars against marks, if they knew that the Federal Reserve was
intervening. Indeed, during each of the four active intervention episodes of
German-mark sales reported in table 5.1, the dollar depreciated against the

German mark and, with the exception of the 1973 episode, the dollar also depreciated on a trade-weighted basis against the currencies of the major developed countries.

Our analysis of the 176 official US purchases of German marks is little different than that of sales. As already noted, the desk typically undertook mark purchases over this period to repay swap loans, although US authorities timed these transactions to minimize any unwanted exchange-rate effects. Our analysis of their successes—67 or 38 percent of the transactions—suggests again that market participants who knew of the intervention could have profitably bet against the desk on average.

When we evaluate US interventions over this period in terms of moderating movements in the dollar, the picture is substantially more favorable to the idea that intervention can affect exchange rates. Of the 161 US sales of German marks prior to 14 September 1977, thirty-four (or 21 percent) were associated with a slower pace of dollar depreciation on the day of the intervention relative to the previous day. This count is more than two standard deviations above the number (twenty-one) that we expect to randomly observe. Our analysis of the largely passive forty-five US purchases of German marks produces similarly favorable results. All in all, roughly 23 percent of the interventions successfully smoothed exchange-rate movements. Still, this is a fairly small proportion of the total 337 interventions.

When we combine these two criteria into a single success count, only 49 percent of the active interventions to support the dollar and only 64 percent of the passive interventions to acquire German marks appear successful. Neither of the success counts is statistically different than random. Overall, US interventions during this period have a very limited impact on mark-dollar exchange rates.

Coombs, in a postoperation assessment of the July 1973 episode, suggested that he was limited in his activities (FOMC *Memoranda*, 21 August 1973, 14–17). He feared that interventions in excess of $50 million on any given day would weaken the Treasury's support for the Federal Reserve's operations. Indeed, as shown in table 5.1, a typical intervention in July 1973 ($18.4 million) was well below this amount. He felt that the scale of operations "on certain days" should have been $100 to $125 million. Subsequent operations before 1977 increased somewhat in their dollar amounts, but they did not approach the level Coombs thought necessary.[22]

Coombs may have been right; larger interventions—particularly open and closely coordinated ones—may have increased the chances for success. Still, the key problem with the active, dollar-support operations over this period was that they conflicted with the general tenor of US monetary policy. At the same time that the desk sold German marks and other foreign currencies to prop up the dollar, the FOMC maintained an excessively easy monetary policy that fueled the Great Inflation.

5.4   The Dollar in Crisis, October 1977 through July 1980

The years 1977 through 1981 were some of the most turbulent in the Federal Reserve's postwar history, culminating in a major change to monetary policy and in serious questions about the efficacy of foreign-exchange-market intervention. Between late 1977 and mid-1980, US intervention unsuccessfully attempted to mitigate the exchange-rate consequences of a rapidly rising US inflation rate. Inflation in the United States increased over these years, while inflation in many other key developed countries—notably Germany—moderated (see figure 5.4). In response, the Federal Reserve System raised its key policy rates beginning in 1977, but overall the Federal Reserve "remained sensitive to the possibility that a rapid firming in interest rates might prematurely put at risk the economic expansion" (Greene 1984b, no. 128, 7). Consequently, the real federal funds rate remained near zero until late in 1979 and dipped below zero again in mid-1980 when economic activity contracted (see figure 5.2). As confidence in the Federal Reserve's efforts to rein in inflation eroded, the pace of the dollar's depreciation quickened.

Over this period, the foreign-exchange market was expanding, becoming increasingly sophisticated, and more globally integrated.[23] Multinationals were centralizing their exchange-rate decisions at their headquarters, typically in the United States. Consequently, the US foreign-exchange market was growing rapidly. United States banks expanded their foreign-exchange operations and many foreign banks opened branches in the United States. Daily turnover in the global foreign-exchange market, which averaged only $5 billion in April 1977, increased more than fourfold to $23 billion by 1980 (Greene 1984b, no. 128, 12).

As the market expanded and as pressures on the dollar intensified, the desk intervened more forcefully, increasing the size, frequency, and persistence of its operations. The US Treasury began to participate with the Federal Reserve and often announced specific interventions. In addition, the desk now frequently intervened directly with commercial banks, rather than through a broker (Greene 1984b, no. 128, 12–13). Despite changing tactics, the interventions proved no more successful than in earlier years.

A lack of foreign-currency reserves continued to hinder the desk's ability to undertake large, sustained dollar-support operations. At the end of 1977, the combined foreign-currency balances of the Federal Reserve and the Treasury stood at less than $10 million equivalent—only enough for a couple of days. In addition, the United States had outstanding foreign-currency obligations, resulting from swap drawings and securities, of roughly $2 1/2 billion equivalent (Task Force 1990h, Paper no. 8, 9–10). Since the inception of floating, the United States had financed interventions primarily by borrowing on swap lines, but German authorities grew increasingly reluctant to extend further credits without changes in US macroeconomic policies

(Task Force 1990h, Paper no. 8, 10). In response, US monetary authorities decided to acquire a portfolio.

5.4.1   Dollar Free Fall, 30 September 1977–5 October 1979

In late 1977, the dollar's depreciation quickened amid persistently high US inflation and reports that OPEC was diversifying out of dollars and into German marks and Swiss francs (FOMC *Transcripts*, 17–18 October 1977, 32). By then, market participants believed that the US administration actually favored a dollar depreciation to correct the trade deficit (Greene 1984b, no. 128, 12–13; Solomon 1982, 345–46). Although the Federal Reserve had tightened monetary policy somewhat, the real federal funds rate remained near zero, and the central bank's anti-inflation credibility was quickly eroding. European governments, notably the Swiss and Germans, encouraged the Federal Reserve to intervene more forcefully (FOMC *Transcript*, 17–18 October 1977, 30). Although the desk began to intervene more frequently, at this point its tactics generally had still not changed: "the Federal Reserve's approach to the market remained covert and passive: the [Desk] worked through the agent of a different commercial bank each day that placed the Desk's offers of currency into the brokers market, and the amounts offered were no larger than those usually traded in the brokers market" (Greene 1984b, no. 128, 17).

The Federal Reserve's lack of enthusiasm may have stemmed from Arthur Burns's growing doubts about the usefulness of intervention. Burns, whose tenure as chairman was slated to end on 17 January 1978, believed that the dollar's depreciation reflected fundamentals, including the lack of a US energy policy, a stubbornly high rate of US inflation, and the absence of tax incentives for investment.[24] Without appropriate policy changes, he regarded intervention as futile. While he accepted that, at best, intervention had some "psychological benefits," Burns did not believe that it had permanent effects. He was, nevertheless, willing to intervene "for the sake of better relations with foreign countries," but Burns contended that many foreign governments actually did not favor heavy US intervention, because they could not adequately deal with the excess liquidity that such intervention created in their own markets. For these reasons, he did not want the desk to "overdo it," and he claimed to have been limiting the amount and frequency of the desk's activities.[25]

Burns's changing attitude also reflected a deeper, noneconomic concern. He suggested that if the Federal Reserve intervened on a much larger and more persistent scale, the administration and Congress would "indefinitely postpone" more permanent corrective actions (FOMC *Transcripts*, 17 January 1978, 11). He was referring to budgetary and energy policies. At the 28 February 1978 FOMC meeting, Burns said, "There are differences within the Government about steps that can and should be taken to deal with the dollar problem. The more active our intervention is, the more excuses others within this government have for not taking some of the bridging steps, or some of the more fundamental steps that need to be taken to restore the integrity of the dollar in foreign exchange markets" (FOMC *Transcripts*, 28 February 1978, 14). He recommended that the Federal Reserve cut back on the scale of intervention.[26] In addition, he did not want the desk to intervene without the Treasury taking a more active role. He seemed to have felt that without additional policy actions, intervention was doomed to failure, and he did not want the Federal Reserve held solely accountable.

Events were already moving in the direction that Burns wanted. Governor Gardner acting on behalf of the FOMC reached an understanding with the US Treasury about intervention. The Treasury, which now felt compelled to express some concern for the dollar, agreed to acknowledge that Federal Reserve operations were undertaken with the close consultation and concurrence of the Treasury. In addition, the Exchange Stabilization Fund would henceforth participate with the Federal Reserve in US operations. Assistant Treasury Secretary Solomon and Governor Gardner went to the US Congress and explained that the Treasury would establish a $1 billion swap line with the Bundesbank for the purpose of intervening (FOMC *Transcripts*, 17 January 1978, 2–3). On 4 January 1978, the Treasury and the Federal Reserve announced their intention for joint intervention "to check speculation and reestablish order in the foreign exchange markets" (*Bulletin*, January 1978, 60). The Treasury publicly announced the existence of its swap line with the Bundesbank, but not its size (Task Force 1990f, Paper no. 9, 13).

Armed with political cover against failure, the desk's operations became more forceful and open (see figures 5.10 and 5.11). Sometimes the desk even attempted to achieve a dollar appreciation, instead of moderating the dollar's depreciation. Sometimes the desk even quoted both bid and offer rates—buying and selling on the same day—to narrow spreads (Greene 1984b, no. 128, 18–22).

Prior to reactivating its swap line, the Treasury had no German mark balances. Over the first four months of 1978, the Treasury drew $1 billion worth of marks on its swap line with the Bundesbank to finance interventions (see figure 5.12). On 13 March 1978, the US Treasury also announced that it was prepared to sell $730 million of special drawing rights (SDRs) to Germany and to draw on its reserve position at the International Monetary Fund to acquire additional currencies for intervention (*Bulletin*, June 1978, 449). Between May 1978 and October 1978, the Treasury obtained $716 million equivalent marks through off-market transactions with central banks, which may have included SDR sales. In addition, the Treasury acquired $169 million worth of German marks from the Federal Reserve System. The Treasury used these funds, along with some purchases in the market, to repay part of its initial $1 billion swap drawings. Late in the period, however, the Treasury seemed to be in a particularly difficult position. With the dollar still depreciating, it was using funds acquired through swap lines

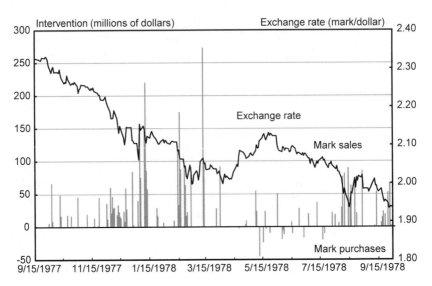

Fig. 5.10 US intervention against German marks, 15 September 1977–30 September 1978

Note: Data are from the Federal Reserve.

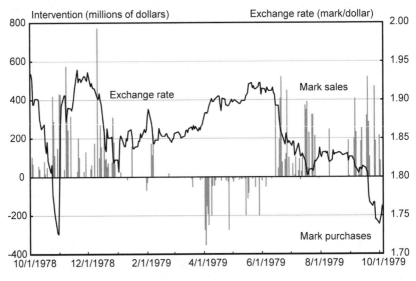

Fig. 5.11 US intervention against German marks, 1 October 1978–5 October 1979

Note: Data are from the Federal Reserve.

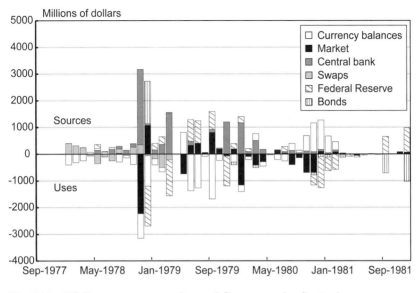

Fig. 5.12   US Treasury sources and uses of German marks, September 1977–December 1981

Notes: "Central bank" contains "exceptional items." Data do not include unexplained items or profits. Data are from the Federal Reserve System.

and through off-market transactions with central banks not only to finance further interventions, but also to repay earlier swap drawings. It was often borrowing from Peter to pay Paul.

The Federal Reserve began drawing on its own swap line in October 1977 and by the end of March 1978, the central bank had drawn $1.8 billion worth of German marks (see figure 5.13). On 13 March 1978, the Federal Reserve negotiated a $2 billion increase in the swap line with the Bundesbank, thereby doubling the facility. Initially, the additional $2 billion was not to be continuously available to the central bank. Once the Federal Reserve repaid amounts drawn on the extended line, the facility was to have reverted to $2 billion (FOMC *Transcripts*, 10 March 1978, 4–5).[27]

Over the one-year period ending on 31 October 1978, the desk intervened on ninety-seven days, purchasing on average $55 million worth of German marks on each day (see table 5.1). This average amount was substantially greater than in previous intervention episodes. Roughly one-third of these purchases were for the Treasury's account. The Federal Reserve also bought other foreign currencies on thirty days. Foreign central banks, notably the Germans, made substantial dollar purchases over this period. The Bundesbank alone bought $1.1 billion. Despite the heavy intervention, the dollar continued to depreciate, falling 24 percent against the German mark and nearly 16 percent on a trade-weighted basis.

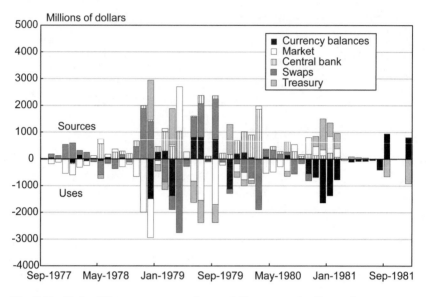

Fig. 5.13   Federal Reserve sources and uses of German marks, September 1977–December 1981

Notes: "Central bank" contains "exceptional items." Data do not include unexplained items or profits. Data are from the Federal Reserve System.

During this period, the Japanese asked the United States to intervene against the yen, which was appreciating sharply relative to the dollar (FOMC *Transcripts*, 21 March 1978, 26). Heretofore, the desk had never intervened in Japanese yen for the Federal Reserve's account.[28] The FOMC showed little support for this request in part because intervention against yen would require more resources, but also because trade restraints and other limits to foreign competition in Japanese markets bolstered that country's trade surplus. In addition, the FOMC feared that selling yen would probably result in large losses for the United States since the yen tended to appreciate (FOMC *Transcripts*, 18 July 1978, 2–3). Nevertheless, New York Federal Reserve President Volcker and Governor Wallich predicted that such interventions might happen as a concession to the Japanese on some other negotiation, as on trade or summit issues (FOMC *Transcripts*, 18 July 1978, 3).

Their prediction was accurate. In August 1978, Chairman Miller began talking about activating the Japanese swap line. The Japanese had agreed to a 50-50 risk sharing proposal and reaffirmed their $2 billion swap limit. The Federal Reserve was still negotiating interest rates on the swaps. By late October 1978, the central bank was ready. "For some time, the Federal Reserve Bank of New York had been intervening in the New York market for the account of the Japanese authorities. It was agreed that this would continue and that the U.S. authorities would join in this intervention using their own resources" (*Bulletin*, March 1979, 208).

Despite more forceful tactics in September and October 1978, the dollar's situation only worsened. Underlying the depreciation was a persistent current-account deficit, but more fundamentally, inflation in the United States was rising while inflation abroad had moderated. By mid-October, the depreciation accelerated and, in the desk's view, overshot a level consistent with fundamentals (*Bulletin*, March 1979, 201). On 24 October 1979, President Carter announced a new anti-inflation program calling for voluntary price and wage guidelines (*Bulletin*, March 1979, 202). Markets were not impressed, and "the selling of dollars reached near-panic proportions, and dollar rates plummeted to record lows against several major currencies" (Greene 1984b, no. 128, 28; Solomon 1982, 349).

On 1 November 1978, the administration in conjunction with the Federal Reserve System announced a massive dollar defense package consisting of a 1 percentage point increase in the discount rate to a historic high of 9 1/2 percent, a $30 billion increase in foreign-currency resources, and closer cooperation with Germany, Japan, and Switzerland, whose export-dependent economic growth the dollar's depreciation had crimped. The foreign currency package included a $7.6 billion increase in the Federal Reserve's swap lines with these countries. The Treasury would draw $3 billion from the US reserve position with the IMF and would sell $2 billion equivalent SDRs to acquire German marks, Japanese yen, and Swiss francs. The Treasury would also issue up to $10 billion in German mark and Swiss franc denominated securities, so-called Carter bonds (*Bulletin*, December 1978, 940–41) (see figure 5.14). The Treasury issued Carter bonds in Swiss and German securities markets, rather than to foreign central banks as was the case with Roosa bonds. Consequently, interventions financed with Carter bonds did not complicate foreign monetary policies by adding liquidity to foreign money markets. Carter bonds automatically sterilized the interventions that they financed.

The temporary, August 1978 increase in the Federal Reserve's swap line with the Bundesbank was now permanent, and the facility had jumped again to $6 billion—a $4 billion increase in less than one year. The Federal Reserve's swap line with Japan increased from $2 billion to $5 billion on 1 November 1978, and the swap line with the Swiss National Bank increased from $1.4 billion to $4 billion. This brought the Federal Reserve's entire swap facility to $29.8 billion equivalent (see figure 5.7). The Federal Reserve hoped that the increase offered a formidable warning to speculators.

The Federal Reserve quickly drew $2 billion worth of German marks from the swap line with the Bundesbank and sold nearly all of this in the market. In December, the Federal Reserve drew an additional $1.4 billion worth of German marks from the swap line and, again, sold all of these in the market. The Treasury drew $2.8 billion from the IMF and $400 million on its swap line with the Bundesbank. Most of these funds went initially into the Treasury's foreign-exchange balances, but the ESF quickly sold nearly $1 billion worth of marks into the market during November. In December,

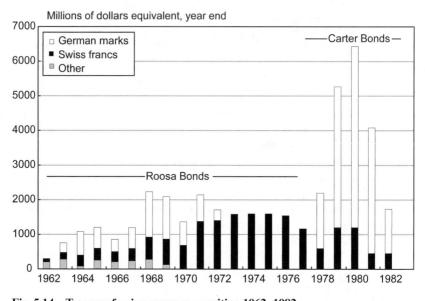

Fig. 5.14   Treasury foreign currency securities, 1962–1982

Notes: Data for 1978 include $600.4 million in Roosa bonds. Data are from the Federal Reserve System.

the Treasury drew down its balances and sold an additional $1.1 billion worth of marks. By the end of December, the United States had sold $5.7 billion worth of German marks. The Treasury accounted for approximately one-third of the total.

The dollar immediately appreciated following the 1 November 1978 announcement, especially against the German mark. Subsequent official interventions in German marks, Japanese yen, and Swiss francs were large and coordinated (*Bulletin* March 1979, 202). Over the next two months, the desk intervened on twenty-eight out of forty business days (table 5.1). The average daily amount was $202 million equivalent. The desk also intervened on twenty occasions in other foreign currencies, with an average intervention in them equal to $47 million.[29] At the end of December, the dollar was higher than at the beginning of November, a rare outcome for intervention during the early floating era.

The appreciation may have been an initial reaction to the change in intervention policy and to the temporary tightening of US monetary policy.[30] At this time, the real federal funds rate briefly started to rise. Over this period, the Bundesbank acted in concert with the United States, purchasing nearly $2.8 billion—a very substantial amount. Other central banks also intervened. In addition to signaling cooperation, which may have affected the dollar through an expectations channel, the intervention added to liquidity in European markets.

Federal Reserve Bank of St. Louis President Lawrence K. Roos wondered if the large increase in foreign-currency holdings implied a change in strategy from reacting to disorderly markets to something on the order of pegging. Holmes responded that no one was attempting to peg a rate. He said that the November 1978 program was based on the administration's, the Treasury's, and the Federal Reserve's belief that the dollar had "gone [down] too far" (FOMC *Transcripts*, 17 April 1979, 36–37). This statement suggests, however, that the Federal Reserve and Treasury were not just smoothing a decline in the dollar exchange rate, as had generally been the case in the past. United States monetary authorities were now attempting to stop the decline and hopefully reverse it (Greene 1984b, no. 128, 29).

In early 1979, pressures on the dollar subsided amid some evidence that US policymakers might focus on inflation. Those foreign central banks that intervened heavily to defend the dollar—notably the Bundesbank, the Swiss National Bank, and the Bank of Japan—used the occasion to drain liquidity (*Bulletin*, March 1979, 202). The dollar strengthened after OPEC announced another oil price hike, because market participants again believed that the United States—like the United Kingdom and Canada—was less vulnerable to oil shocks than many other countries.

With the dollar remaining firm, the Federal Reserve acquired sufficient German marks to repay outstanding swap obligations and to build balances of nearly $2.4 billion worth of marks by May 1979. The Federal Reserve purchased most of its German marks off-market from correspondents, but the desk also bought currencies in the market when the dollar was "particularly strong," suggesting passive intervention designed to stem the dollar's appreciation, or at least not encourage a depreciation (*Bulletin*, September 1979, 722).

The Treasury retired its outstanding swap debt with the Bundesbank by March 1979, when marks previously warehoused with the Federal Reserve became available.[31] The Treasury also acquired German marks through off-market transactions with a foreign central bank. In March 1979, the US Treasury held a portfolio of nearly $1.2 billion worth of German marks. The Treasury also held $1.6 billion worth of Japanese yen, which it drew from the IMF in November 1978.

The desk liquidated the Federal Reserve's yen swap debts by February 1979 and shortly acquired a portfolio of $195 million worth of yen. Throughout 1979, the yen depreciated against the dollar. By May 1979, the US Treasury, the Japanese Ministry of Finance, and the Bank of Japan were encouraging the Federal Reserve to undertake concerted and publicly announced yen purchases. The plan called for the Federal Reserve to add roughly $800 million equivalent yen to its current balances of approximately $1 billion worth of yen. The Treasury, which already held $1.6 billion equivalent yen, would acquire $200 million yen (FOMC *Transcripts*, 22 May 1979, 41). In November 1979, the Japanese wanted to draw on the swap line, even though they held a very large portfolio of reserves (presumably in dollars). They believed that a drawing would demonstrate US support for their operations (FOMC *Transcripts*, 20 November 1979, 4–5). The Federal Reserve had initiated a drawing on the yen swap line in November 1978, but no further drawings were ever undertaken. Moreover, the Federal Reserve undertook no additional yen interventions until March 1980.

By late spring 1979, attitudes toward the dollar again started to change. Inflation in the United States exceeded inflation in Germany and continued to rise. Foreign countries were tightening monetary policies faster than in the United States, and interest-rate spreads vis-à-vis short-term mark-denominated assets moved against the dollar (Greene 1984b, no. 128, 8–10). President Carter's energy speech on 15 July 1979 resulted in further dollar depreciation.

In mid-June, the desk began forcefully intervening to support the dollar, but the dollar continued to depreciate. In a telephone conference call on 17 July 1979, FOMC participants discussed the merits of intervening relative to the benefits of increasing the federal funds rate. Paul Volcker, president of the Federal Reserve Bank of New York, did not think intervention would work; he favored tightening monetary policy. Volcker worried that the "Bundesbank may well get very restive soon about the amounts of liquidity there—we're creating in their markets. I think they've been . . . quite cooperative up to now but they haven't been doing very much and we're going to be getting into complaints very soon. Gretchen [Margret Greene, assistant vice president to the desk manager] kind of had some grumbling this morning and it looks like it is pretty big. So I think it is a little bit of an illusion, if this continues, to think that we can rely on intervention" (FOMC *Transcripts*, 17 July 1979, 5).

Inflation was rising sharply and the Federal Reserve was rapidly losing credibility across the globe. As Volcker noted, "After years of failed or prematurely truncated efforts to deal with inflation, markets had developed a high degree of cynicism about the willingness of what they dismissed as 'Washington' in general, or the Federal Reserve in particular, to stand firm" (Volcker and Gyohten 1992, 165–66).

The desk intervened on forty-four of the seventy-nine business days between 15 June 1979 and 5 October 1979, selling a massive $9.1 billion worth of German marks or $207 million worth of German marks on average each intervention day (table 5.1). Slightly more than one-half of the transactions were for the Treasury's account. The desk also sold a small amount of other currencies, but it did not intervene against Japanese yen even though some transactions occurred overnight in the Far East (*Bulletin*, September 1979, 723). The Bundesbank bought $2.7 billion, on par with its previous purchases.

These interventions against German marks were, on average, the largest to date. For the first time in the early float period, foreign central banks seemed to be losing confidence in US monetary policy and becoming weary of the domestic liquidity created from buying large amounts of US dollars. Although the desk was attempting to prevent a further dollar depreciation, the dollar depreciated nearly 8 percent against the German mark and 2.5 percent on a trade-weighted average basis between 15 June 1979 and 5 October 1979.

Over this period, the Federal Reserve drew nearly $4 billion from its swap line with the Bundesbank and used these funds to finance its interventions. (The Federal Reserve did make small repayments on its swap lines in most months.) The Federal Reserve also drew down $2.4 billion from its balances and acquired another $765 million worth of German marks from central banks. The Treasury financed one-half of its interventions from marks previously warehoused with the Federal Reserve, and 38 percent by drawing down its balances of German marks. The Treasury also acquired a small amount of marks through off-market transactions with foreign central banks.

5.4.2   Were US Interventions between 15 September 1977 and 5 October 1979 Successful?

After September 1977, US interventions became more aggressive than they heretofore had been. The desk now intervened in substantially larger amounts and much more frequently than it had over the earlier floating-rate period. The Treasury became an active participant in the operations, often announcing major interventions, and the other central banks acted in closer concert with the desk. In addition, the operations were more visible, and therefore more consistent with an expectations approach. While the desk continued to operate frequently through the brokers market, it also began conducting a larger number of transactions directly with commercial banks. The strategy also changed. While the desk often strove to moderate movements in the dollar, at times it now attempted to prevent a further depreciation, to achieve a dollar appreciation, to reinforce the momentum of a dollar rise, or to moderate bid-ask spreads (Greene 1984b, no. 128, 19–20).

Despite the changes in amounts, frequency, objectives, and openness, US operations between 15 September 1977 and 5 October 1979 were no more effective than the earlier US interventions. As in the pre-1977 period, they demonstrated some tendency to moderate exchange-rate movements (see table 5.3).

Of the 175 US sales of German marks, only forty-three (or 25 percent) were associated with a same day dollar appreciation against the German mark. We would expect to find severnty-two successes purely by chance (see appendix 2). Because the observed number of successes is more than two standard deviations below the expected, the result suggests that US intervention sales of German marks were a reliable signal that the dollar would depreciate—not appreciate—against the mark. As in the earlier episode,

Table 5.3   Success counts for US intervention, 15 September 1977 to 5 October 1979

German marks	Total (#)	Intervention successes (#)	(%)	Expected[a] successes (#)	Standard[a] deviation (#)
Mark sales & dollar appreciation	175	43	24.6	72	4
Mark purchases & dollar depreciation	58	16	27.6	31	3
Total	233	59	25.3		
Mark sales & smaller dollar depreciation	175	49	28.0	31	3
Mark purchases & smaller dollar appreciation	58	12	20.7	6	1
Total	233	61	26.2		
Mark sales & dollar appreciation or smaller depreciation	175	92	52.6	103	6
Mark purchases & dollar depreciation or small appreciation	58	28	48.3	36	4
Total	233	120	51.5		
Japanese yen					
Yen sales & dollar appreciation	10	6	60.0	5	2
Yen purchases & dollar depreciation	19	5	26.3	9	2
Total	29	11	37.9		
Yen sales & smaller dollar depreciation	10	1	10.0	1	0
Yen purchases & smaller dollar appreciation	19	6	31.6	2	1
Total	29	7	24.1		
Yen sales & dollar appreciation or smaller depreciation	10	7	70.0	6	2
Yen purchases & dollar depreciation or small appreciation	19	11	57.9	11	3
Total	29	18	62.1		

Note: See appendix 2 for detail.

[a] Assumes that the success count is a hypergeometric random variable.

market participants with information about US intervention—like those banks that often operated on behalf of the desk—could have profited, on average, from selling dollars.

Our analysis of official US purchases of German marks is again no different than that for sales. As already noted, however, the desk typically undertook mark purchases over this period for the purpose of paying down outstanding mark obligations. The desk undoubtedly timed these purchases to minimize any adverse impact on the dollar. Of the fifty-eight purchases of marks, sixteen were associated with same-day dollar depreciations. Again, market participants who knew of the operations could have profited on average by selling marks for dollars.

When we evaluate US intervention over this two-year period in terms of moderating the dollar's depreciations or appreciations, the picture is again substantially more favorable to the idea that intervention affected the rate. Of the 175 sales of German marks in support of the dollar, forty-nine (or 28 percent) were associated with a slower rate of dollar depreciation on the day of the intervention as compared to the day prior to the intervention. This success count is more than two standard deviations greater than the anticipated number of successes. Of the fifty-eight purchases of German marks, twelve (or 20.7 percent) were associated with a slower pace of dollar appreciation on the day of the intervention as compared with the previous day. The number of observed successes is also more than two standard deviations larger than the expected number. The interventions tended to moderate same-day movements in the dollar.

When we combine the two criteria into a single criterion—presuming that we do not know which of them the desk was attempting to achieve on any specific day—the results suggest that intervention had no better than a random impact on exchange-rate movements. At best only about one-half of the interventions influenced the dollar-mark exchange rate in a manner consistent with the objectives of the US policymakers. This is an abysmal success rate.

Over this same period, the desk sold Japanese yen on ten days and bought yen on nineteen days. This amount seems too few to draw firm conclusions about the effectiveness of intervention against Japanese yen. Nevertheless, in no case is the actual success count statistically greater than the count we would anticipate purely by chance.

By and large over this entire period, the dollar continued to depreciate against the German mark and on a trade-weighted basis. In her detailed analysis of the operations, Greene concluded:

> Evolving U.S. efforts to provide more effective and forceful intervention support for the dollar did, at least in the first instance, help to demonstrate . . . that the U.S. government was concerned about the large and rapid decline in the dollar and was willing to try to do something about it. But when intervening actions were not soon followed up with consistent and effective measures to deal with the underlying causes of the dollar's weakness, any positive short-run impact of the intervention faded. (Greene 1984b, no. 128, 40)[32]

Her conclusion suggests that the desk viewed the effects of *sterilized* intervention to be ephemeral and ultimately not a tool with which to alter exchange rates independent of monetary policy.

5.4.3   Monetary-Policy Change

On 29 September 1979, Paul Volcker, who became the Federal Reserve chairman on 14 August 1979, went to the IMF/World Bank meeting in Belgrade, where he also conferred with German officials about the dollar's depreciation and the continuing US inflation problem. Helmut Schmidt "left no doubt that his patience with what he saw as American neglect and irresolution about the dollar had run out" (Volcker and Gyohten 1992, 165–68).[33] Volcker left the Belgrade meeting early, which raised expectations of a major change in US monetary policy. He set up a special confidential meeting of the FOMC for Saturday, 6 October 1979, ten days ahead of the scheduled meeting.

At the quickly called meeting, the Federal Reserve announced major changes in monetary policy, including a 1 percent point hike in the discount rate to 12 percent, and the imposition of an 8 percent marginal reserve requirement on increases in managed liabilities. "In addition the Federal Reserve announced that it would place greater emphasis on the supply of bank reserves in its open market procedures and less emphasis on the federal funds rate in seeking to reach its objective for the monetary aggregates." (*Bulletin*, December 1979, 954). The dollar strengthened immediately following the announced changes in policy.

The policy change initiated a temporary dollar appreciation. By mid-February, US interest rates were rising faster than foreign interest rates and the dollar moved upward. On 14 March 1980, President Carter authorized the Federal Reserve to impose credit controls (*Bulletin*, June 1980, 456; Schreft 1990). Concerns about credit controls pushed US rates higher and foreign funds moved into dollars. As the dollar appreciated, foreign central banks began selling dollars to support their currencies (*Bulletin*, June 1980, 455). "By late March [1980], the bidding for dollars had become so generalized that demand pressures, which had previously been concentrated more heavily in markets abroad, began erupting at any time during the 24-hour trading day. To counter disorderly conditions, the Desk entered the New York market in March and the first week of April [1980] as a buyer of German marks on 13 occasions, of Swiss francs on 4 occasions, and of Japanese yen on 10 occasions. In early April, the Desk also intervened on one occasion to purchase marks in the Far East" (*Bulletin*, June 1980, 456). The desk was, for the first time, *actively* intervening to limit the dollar's appreciation.

The United States used these funds, along with marks acquired through off-market transactions with other central banks, to liquidate the Federal Reserve's swap obligations with the Bundesbank and to make interest payments on outstanding foreign currency-denominated securities (*Bulletin*, June 1980, 455–56).

Despite the 6 October 1979 policy changes and the tightening of monetary policy, the nominal federal funds rate fell and the real federal funds

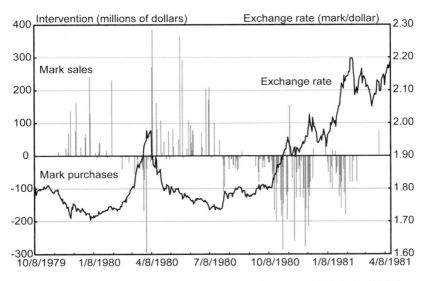

Fig. 5.15   US intervention against German marks, 8 October 1979–8 April 1981
Note: Data are from the Federal Reserve.

rate again turned negative in early 1980. Uncertainty about Volcker's prospects for reducing inflation and keeping it low with the economy now in recession and the unemployment rate rising sharply probably explains the dollar's twelve percent depreciation between 8 April 1980 and 11 July 1980. In response, the United States intervened. The desk sold German marks, but it also sold French francs to avoid aggravating the weakness of the mark relative to the franc in the EMS (*Bulletin*, June 1980, 456). The Federal Reserve sold $159.6 million worth of French francs, which it financed by drawing on its swap line with the Bank of France. The central bank continued with large periodic interventions through mid-July.

The desk intervened, buying an average of $121 million worth of German marks on each of twenty-six days during the sixty-eight-day period (see table 5.1 and figure 5.15). The average size of a transaction was smaller than in the previous two intervention episodes. On eleven days the desk bought other foreign currencies, mostly French francs ($160 million) and Swiss francs ($144 million). Despite the intervention, the dollar depreciated nearly 12 percent against the German mark and 10 percent on a trade-weighted basis.

5.4.4   Were Interventions between 8 October 1979 and 17 April 1981 Successful?

Despite the change in US monetary policy, the US interventions between 8 October 1979 and 17 April 1981 were no more successful than in earlier periods (see table 5.4). Of the fifty-five sales of German marks, only fifteen

Table 5.4   Success counts for US intervention, 8 October 1979 to 17 April 1981

German marks	Total (#)	Intervention successes (#)	(%)	Expected[a] successes (#)	Standard[a] deviation (#)
Mark sales & dollar appreciation	55	15	27.3	28	3
Mark purchases & dollar depreciation	114	41	36.0	50	4
Total	169	56	33.1		
Mark sales & smaller dollar depreciation	55	17	30.9	7	1
Mark purchases & smaller dollar appreciation	114	25	21.9	17	2
Total	169	42	24.9		
Mark sales & dollar appreciation or smaller depreciation	55	32	58.2	35	4
Mark purchases & dollar depreciation or small appreciation	114	66	57.9	68	5
Total	169	98	58.0		
Japanese yen					
Yen sales & dollar appreciation	1	1	100.0	1	1
Yen purchases & dollar depreciation	10	4	40.0	4	1
Total	11	5	45.5		
Yen sales & smaller dollar depreciation	1	0	0.0	0	0
Yen purchases & smaller dollar appreciation	10	1	10.0	1	0
Total	11	1	9.1		
Yen sales & dollar appreciation or smaller depreciation	1	1	100.0	1	0
Yen purchases & dollar depreciation or small appreciation	10	5	50.0	6	2
Total	11	6	54.5		

Note: See appendix 2 for detail.

[a] Assumes that the success count is a hypergeometric random variable.

(27.3 percent) were associated with a dollar appreciation, well below the expected number. Again, US intervention sales of German marks provided a reliable signal that the dollar would depreciate. Seventeen of these mark sales, however, were associated with a slower pace of dollar depreciation on the day of intervention than on the previous day, suggesting some tendency to dampen dollar depreciations. When we combine the two criteria into a single criterion, the number of successes was no better than random.

Between 8 October 1979 and 17 April 1981, the desk bought German marks on 114 days. As noted, sometimes the desk actively sought to slow the dollar's appreciation, but on most occasions the desk only wanted to acquire German marks to pay off debts and to accumulate a portfolio of German marks. (We discuss the acquisition of the portfolio in the next section.) Even when the desk bought German marks to pay down debts or to acquire a portfolio, it conducted passive interventions. Of these 114 purchases of German marks, forty-one (36 percent) were associated with a same-day dollar depreciation. This number was again substantially fewer than we would randomly anticipate. Twenty-five of these 114 purchases of German marks, not atypically, were associated with a smaller same-day dollar appreciation relative to the previous day. This amount was greater than anticipated and—as in previous episodes—suggests some capacity to slow the pace of a dollar appreciation. When we combine the success criteria, however, the count was no better than random.

Over this same period, the United States bought Japanese yen on 10 occasions and sold Japanese yen on only one day. While the number of interventions was too small to draw strong conclusions, the success counts were never better than the number that we would randomly anticipate, given the variable nature of day-to-day exchange-rate movements.

5.5   Foreign Currency Debt and the Decision to Increase the US Portfolio[34]

Between 1973 and 1977, the Federal Reserve never held more than $170.6 million worth of foreign exchange and never more than $51.6 million worth of German marks, its main intervention currency (figure 5.5).[35] These amounts were generally smaller than the amounts that the Federal Reserve held between 1962 and 1972. Moreover, between 1973 and 1977, the Treasury held virtually no balances of foreign exchange (figure 5.6). In large part this aversion to balances reflected the US view—a remnant of the Bretton Woods period—that foreign central banks would undertake most of the intervention (Axilrod and Holmes 1979, 1). Consistent with this view, between 1973 and 1977, the United States accounted for only about 5 percent of the total exchange-market intervention that the major central banks undertook against the dollar (Morton and Truman 1979, 3).

This lack of ready reserves forced the United States to rely heavily on borrowed funds to finance its interventions during the early dollar float. As we have shown, in order to meet their subsequent debt obligations, both the Federal Reserve and the Treasury needed to expeditiously buy back the foreign exchange that they previously sold and timed these buybacks to have the best possible effect on the market.

In early 1979, the FOMC considered increasing the Federal Reserve's portfolio of foreign exchange reserves.[36] The key reason for doing so was to avoid the growing conditions that countries—notably Germany—were attaching to swap drawings (Task Force 1990h, Paper no. 8, 11). As the amount and persistence of US interventions increased in late 1977, so did the debt obligations of the United States. At the end of 1978, for example, the Federal Reserve had a record $5.5 billion in outstanding swap obligations, and the Treasury had $890 million in swap obligations and nearly $2.2 billion in outstanding Carter bonds (Task Force1990h, Paper no. 8, table IV.b.). Any foreign-imposed conditions could limit the United States' ability to conduct future interventions quickly and efficiently.

In part, countries increasingly imposed conditions on borrowing because the nature of intervention and the risks associated with repayment had changed. Under Bretton Woods, countries presumably borrowed to finance temporary balance-of-payments shortfalls not reflecting fundamentals. Monetary authorities viewed such debts as largely self-liquidating and easily repayable when financial funds flowed back into the borrowing country (see chapter 4). Now, however, with intervention becoming larger, more persistent, and aimed at smoothing longer-term movement in exchange rates, rather than financing temporary and reversible balance-of-payments problems, the previous conceptualization of self-liquidating debt was no longer valid. Confidence in countries' ability to quickly repay their debts had ebbed (FOMC *Transcripts*, 20 April 1976, 2–4). The United States itself had occasionally placed conditions on the swap drawings of other countries to insure their timely repayment. In 1976, for example, the United States conditioned a swap loan to Britain, requiring that country to subsequently obtain foreign exchange from the International Monetary Fund (*Bulletin*, December 1976, 1005).

The conditions that countries—notably Germany—wanted to place on the United States, however, had more to do with a pessimism about US monetary policy than about the country's ability to repay. Prolonged interventions, after all, were a symptom of a US policy failure, and Germany, which was reducing its inflation at the time, wished to limit the spillover effects. As Holmes and Pardee (1979, 4) explained: "[In 1978,] the Bundesbank went so far as to limit our use of the swap lines because of its concern that the marks so created would contribute to a potentially inflationary expansion of the monetary base in Germany." If Germany and other countries limited quick access to borrowed funds, the United States needed a larger portfolio of foreign exchange to pursue a strategy of smoothing longer-term movements in the dollar (Axilrod and Holmes 1979, 1).[37]

Another important motive for increasing the portfolio centered on the Federal Reserve's relationship to the US Treasury concerning intervention. From 1973 through 1977, the Treasury rarely intervened; it essentially continued its traditional role of promising to backstop the central bank's swap borrowings. The Federal Reserve had essentially free rein in running US intervention policy. In November 1978, the Treasury expanded its role in terms of both its overall resources and its willingness to engage in day-to-day operations. By 1979, the Treasury had a substantial portfolio of $3.2 billion in foreign exchange, largely by issuing Carter bonds (Task Force 1990h, Paper no. 8, table 1).

The Federal Reserve's staff worried that if US interventions increased in size and frequency, and if the Treasury's portfolio of foreign exchange continued to expand relative to the Federal Reserve's, the FOMC would lose its influence over US intervention policies. Although the Treasury had relinquished much of its authority to the Federal Reserve in recent years, it continued to have primary responsibility over exchange-rate policies. While the central bank had legal authority for its own intervention, its exact role vis-à-vis the Treasury remained ambiguous but clearly secondary (see chapter 4). Beyond its technical expertise, the Federal Reserve acquired much of its authority through the resources that it brought to the venture. Now its relative influence seemed threatened.

The FOMC also worried about Congress's response to the acquisition of foreign exchange. In 1979, Congress did not seem to favor the accumulation of additional reserves (Morton and Truman 1979, 7). Many of the FOMC's concerns mirrored those that it had faced when it initially began intervening in 1962 (see chapter 4). Some FOMC members wanted clear congressional and Treasury approval before the Federal Reserve acquired a larger portfolio and a greater exposure to foreign-exchange risk (FOMC *Transcripts*, 17 April 1979, 35–45).

Holmes and Pardee (1979, 9) suggested that, "A good cushion to begin with would be 2 to 3 days' worth of heavy intervention." That seemed to translate into $1 billion worth of German marks, $400 million worth of Swiss francs, and $300 million worth of Japanese yen. These were the key international currencies, and the staff thought that these currencies' dollar exchange rates had wider effects on markets and sentiments than other currencies' dollar exchange rates. In addition, the staff recommended $100 million worth (each) of French francs, Netherlands guilders, and Belgian francs (Holmes and Pardee 1979, 9). These amounts would increase the Federal Reserve's informal limits on currencies from $500 million equivalent to $2 billion equivalent.

As the dollar began to stabilize in 1979, the Federal Reserve and the Treasury began to acquire foreign currencies, but they needed these funds initially to pay down outstanding debts rather than to build reserve balances. At the end of 1979, the United States had, on net, outstanding foreign currency obligations totaling nearly $2.9 billion equivalent, mostly in German marks. The Federal Reserve held nearly $2.4 billion in foreign currency assets, but it had $5.3 billion in outstanding foreign currency obligations, including warehoused funds and swap debts. The Treasury held nearly $5.3 billion in foreign currency assets, including a substantial amount warehoused with the Federal Reserve. Against these assets the Treasury had roughly an equal amount of outstanding Carter bonds.[38] On balance, the United States had net foreign currency obligations in 1979. United States monetary authorities had maintained a negative net open position in foreign currencies (net liabilities) in nearly every year since interventions began in 1962 (Task Force 1990h, Paper no. 8, table I).[39]

After October 1979, as the dollar appeared to bottom out, and especially after September 1980 as the dollar began a sustained appreciation, the desk took advantage of opportunities to buy foreign currency and pay down outstanding debts. Because the desk remained concerned about sparking another dollar depreciation through its foreign currency purchases, it operated on both sides of the market. The desk bought foreign currency when conditions permitted (passively intervened) and actively intervened when markets were disorderly.[40] It did so in close proximity, even during the same day: "On several occasions, operations of both types were conducted at different times or in different markets within a day" (Greene 1984c, no. 129, 12).

The desk also began considering commercial bank offers to sell foreign exchange directly to the United States. "In general, banks came to the Desk with offers to sell currencies when there were few other buyers—such as when the dollar was moving up sharply or after the bulk of trading had subsided for the day—or when they had an order they felt was too large for the market to absorb" (Greene 1984c, no. 129, 12).[41]

The United States began acquiring foreign exchange to pay down its debt to foreign central banks, especially the Bundesbank. The Bundesbank sold the desk marks off market and also acted as its agent in the Frankfurt market. The desk also operated in the Far East (Greene 1984c, no. 129, 13–14).

The US strategy was to pay down short-term debts—swap lines—before paying off longer-term obligations, like Carter bonds. Since all of the Federal Reserve's debts were short term, the Federal Reserve paid them off by 15 October 1980. The Treasury was debt free by 5 December 1980 (Task Force1990h, Paper no. 8, 11–12).

After paying down or covering their obligations, the Federal Reserve and the Treasury continued to take advantage of the dollar's appreciation and to acquire foreign currencies. By the end of 1980, the United States held a positive net open position of $2.5 billion equivalent, its first since 1962. When these operations ended in February 1981, the Federal Reserve held approximately $4.5 billion in German marks and roughly another $1 billion in other currencies. The Treasury held $3.5 billion in German marks and roughly $2 billion in other currencies (Task Force 1990h, Paper no. 8, 12, and tables II.b. and II.c.). At the end of 1981, the United States held a net open position equivalent to $6.8 billion.

Technically, acquiring such a portfolio was not very difficult, but investing it in earning assets posed problems for the central bank. Prior to 1980, the Federal Reserve did not have very good options for investing its foreign-currency balances. The Federal Reserve Act did not allow the desk to invest in foreign government securities; it only allowed the desk to place funds in interest-bearing deposits with other central banks and in bills of exchange. Holmes claimed, however, that the Federal Reserve lacked authority to invest in foreign government securities only because few such securities existed in 1914. The Federal Reserve Act listed things in which the central bank could invest, and if government securities existed, he claimed that they would have been included. Holmes offered that government securities were not "prohibited"; they just were not "listed" (FOMC *Transcripts*, 17 April 1979, 38–39).

Because of the legal restrictions against holding foreign government securities, the desk invested currency balances in deposit accounts at central banks or with the Bank for International Settlements prior to 1980.[42] If a central bank paid interest on Federal Reserve deposits, they based the rate on a nonmarket rate, such as the bank's discount rate. Sometimes the funds simply earned no interest. The Federal Reserve often placed funds with the BIS to gain interest earnings if a central bank paid none, or to accommodate foreign central banks' desire to keep funds in the market for monetary-policy considerations (Task Force1990h, Paper no. 8, 17–18).

As suggested, some central banks—notably the Bundesbank, whose currency constituted the bulk of the Federal Reserve's foreign-exchange holdings—were not legally allowed to pay interest on deposits or even to offer the Federal Reserve deposits. To earn a return on US holdings of German marks, the United States established a double-forward facility with the Bundesbank in 1978. Accordingly, the United States sold its mark holdings forward to the Bundesbank and simultaneously bought the marks back forward with the exchange rates structured to yield the United States a return. The instruments typically matured in three months. The Treasury also placed mark balances acquired through the sale of Carter bonds in securities that the German Finance Ministry issued. These had limited transferability and marketability (Task Force 1990h, Paper no. 8, 18–19).

The Monetary Control Act of 1980 allowed the Federal Reserve to invest foreign currency balances in securities that foreign governments issued or guaranteed (Task Force 1990h, Paper no. 8, 13). This allowed the Federal Reserve to invest in an array of instruments, some more liquid than others.

5.6 Warehousing

Warehousing refers to a foreign-currency swap between the Federal Reserve System and the US Treasury that gives the Exchange Stabilization Fund (ESF) temporary access to dollars. In a typical warehousing transaction, the ESF sells foreign currencies spot to the Federal Reserve and simultaneously buys them back for delivery at a specific future date, generally within one year. Because both the spot and forward legs of the swap occur at the same exchange rate, neither party incurs foreign-exchange risk from warehousing, but the foreign currency can still sustain valuation gains or losses vis-à-vis the market, which then fall to the ESF. The Federal Reserve places the warehoused foreign exchange into an appropriate interest-earning instrument and derives a return over the interim of the operation, while the ESF has use of the dollars so acquired. Warehousing typically has occurred at the Treasury's initiative, but unlike with the monetization of gold or special drawing rights (SDRs), the Federal Reserve is not obliged to warehouse funds for the Treasury. The FOMC must give its approval to the operations and annually sets an overall authorization for warehousing.

As with any foreign-exchange operation, the Federal Reserve stands ready to offset unwanted changes in bank reserves that may result from warehousing. Should the ESF subsequently buy foreign exchange with its newly acquired dollars, the desk will drain any unwanted increase in dollar reserves. Often, however, the ESF will not immediately purchase additional foreign exchange and instead will temporarily "lend" the funds to the Treasury by acquiring a Treasury security. In this case, the Treasury's account at the Federal Reserve Bank of New York increases. If the Treasury subsequently draws down this account, the desk can easily sterilize the resulting increase in bank reserves. Likewise, the Federal Reserve will sterilize any unwanted drain on bank reserves that might arise when the ESF repays its warehousing obligation to the Federal Reserve System.

Over the years, warehousing-type transactions have served four functions. In the main, warehousing has temporarily augmented the limited dollar resources of the ESF. As explained in chapter three, the ESF has financed its foreign-exchange operations over the years from an initial congressional appropriation and from the periodic monetization of SDRs, which the ESF acquired either through IMF allocations or from other countries (Schwartz 1997). Initially, however, warehousing-like operations served a second purpose. As detailed below, they provided the Treasury with a means of covering its foreign-currency exposure on outstanding debt obligations that did not entail selling foreign exchange to the Federal Reserve, and thereby shifting that exposure to the Federal Reserve. On a couple of occasions, warehousing functioned in reverse: The Federal Reserve initiated a warehousing operation to acquire needed foreign exchange. Last, warehousing may have occasionally provided the US Treasury with a means of acquiring temporary dollar funding that avoided the federal debt limit. When the ESF parks the dollars that it has acquired through warehousing in US Treasury securities, the Treasury can reduce the amount of debt that it sells to the public and the amount of debt subject to the Congressional debt ceiling (Stevens 1989).

5.6.1   The Evolution of Warehousing

In 1963, the FOMC gave the desk authority to buy foreign exchange in the market and to sell it to the Treasury, which then held it as cover for outstanding foreign-exchange obligations. This authorization became the basis for future warehousing. At the end of 1963, the Treasury had outstanding lira securities amounting to nearly $200 million and wanted to cover its expo-sure by buying lira, but the Treasury lacked sufficient resources to do so. At the time, the lira was trading somewhat below par, making lira purchases especially propitious (FOMC *Minutes*, 12 November 1963, 1–10). Charles Coombs, special desk manager, recommended that the Federal Reserve System acquire Italian lira spot and sell it forward to the Treasury. The forward sale eliminated the Federal Reserve's lira exposure, but still gave the desk a lira asset that became available when the forward contract expired. Coombs sought authority for $100 million equivalent.

Coombs viewed the current situation as a "rather special one" and sought authorization only for lira. The Treasury had outstanding debt obligations in other currencies, and Coombs assumed that he could seek further specific authorization should the need arise. However, the president of the Federal Reserve Bank of Boston, George H. Ellis, thought that a routine facility would help in redeeming Treasury foreign-currency securities and might also make them more saleable (FOMC *Minutes*, 12 November 1963, 7). The resulting foreign currency directive stated:

> The Federal Reserve Bank of New York is also authorized and directed to make purchases through spot transactions, *including purchases from the U.S. Stabilization Fund*, and concurrent sales through forward transactions to the U.S. Stabilization Fund, of any of the foregoing [authorized] currencies in which the U.S. Treasury has outstanding indebtedness, in accordance with the Guidelines and up to a total of $100 million equivalent. Purchases may be at rates above par, and both purchases and sales are to be made at the same rate. (FOMC *Minutes*, 12 November 1963, 10) (emphasis added)

In allowing the desk to buy foreign exchange spot from the ESF and sell it back forward to the ESF, the directive authorized warehousing. The FOMC *Minutes*, however, do not reveal how the insertion of the critical phrase "including purchases from the U.S. Stabilization Fund" came about.[43]

The mechanism of these initial lira purchases, of course, did not conform to a warehousing operation as it would eventually be understood. In January and March 1964, the desk purchased $83 million lira spot from a foreign central bank and sold it forward to the Treasury. The authorization also constrained the operations by specifying that warehousing transactions be limited to currencies in which the Treasury had an outstanding indebtedness.

In March and April 1966, the desk used such operations to provide cover against the Treasury's Swiss franc and German mark obligations and quickly began running out of authority. Coombs proposed an increase to $150 million for such operations, but " some members suggested that the limit might be removed entirely, or set at a level considerably higher than Mr. Coombs proposed, since the operations under discussion were riskless and helpful to the Treasury" (FOMC *Minutes*, 12 April 1966, 6–7). The Committee authorized $200 million, but the actual amount of marks and francs that the Treasury held under this authority never exceeded $75 million equivalent (Morton 1977, 1) (see figure 5.13).

In July and August 1966, the Federal Reserve also sold over $100 million British pounds on a "swap basis" to the US Treasury—essentially warehousing in reverse. One of these transactions was for a single day, designed to reduce the Federal Reserve's balances on a statement day, while the other extended until January 1967.[44] These were not to cover Treasury debt obligations, and hence, not subject to the November 1963 authorization. The Federal Reserve, however, had frequently transacted in foreign exchange on a spot and forward basis even prior to the 1963 authorization. The reason for the November 1963 authorization was that covering the Treasury's outstanding debt had little to do directly with exchange-market stabilization, and so might seem to require a separate FOMC approval.

In November 1967, as part of an international aid package for Britain, the United States agreed to buy $500 million in "guaranteed sterling." Afraid that the transaction would leave the ESF cash strapped and hoping to give the central bank a bigger stake in the associated policy decisions, Coombs recommended that the Federal Reserve warehouse—in the traditional sense—an additional $150 million in guaranteed sterling for the ESF.[45] The Federal Reserve had authority to warehouse up to $200 million in currencies for which the Treasury had an outstanding indebtedness, but the Treasury did not have an outstanding indebtedness in British pounds. Hence, in addition to increasing the warehousing authority to $350 million, Coombs also asked the FOMC to delete the provision in the authorization that restricted warehousing to currencies in which the Treasury had outstanding indebtedness (FOMC *Memoranda*, 14 November 1967, 18–19). After all, the desk had already engaged in such transactions without a clear authorization.

The Federal Reserve's share of the US aid package to Britain was $100 million. Coombs thought that he could explain the Federal Reserve's holding of this amount of British pounds as necessary to meet its "needs for market operations." In fact, however, the United States was trying to prevent a devaluation of the pound—not looking to defend the dollar. Policy makers viewed the $500 million as an extended credit. The Federal Reserve Act justified foreign-exchange operations "undertaken to deal with such problems as short-run disturbances in the foreign exchange market. An extension of longer-term credit by the Federal Reserve to the Bank of England—even if ultimately for the purpose of safeguarding the value of the dollar—was of a character quite different from open-market operations" (FOMC *Memoranda*, 14 November 1967, 34). Warehousing an additional $150 million worth of British pounds for the Treasury allowed the Federal Reserve to help extend credits to the Bank of England without appearing to violate its mandate for intervention and, perhaps more importantly, gave the Federal Reserve more weight in the policy decision.

The FOMC raised the authorization to $350 million at its November meeting, but the Federal Reserve did not undertake any warehousing until June 1968. Then it warehoused $200 million worth of guaranteed sterling for the Treasury until August 1968. In September 1968, the FOMC raised the authorization for warehousing to $1 billion to facilitate further credits to Britain (Morton 1977, 2). The Treasury, however, did not ask to reuse the facility, and the Federal Reserve warehoused no foreign exchange until May 1969.

Implicit in the November 1967 authorization was an understanding that the $150 million increase in the overall authorization pertained only to British pounds and that the central bank could only warehouse $200 million—the April 1966 limit—in other currencies. In mid-1969, the Treasury expected France to sell it gold. While the Treasury could monetize gold with the Federal Reserve to pay for the transaction, it preferred to wait, because the Treasury expected the IMF to exercise an outstanding claim on the US gold stock. Instead, the Treasury hoped to bridge the two possible gold transactions by warehousing foreign currencies with the Federal Reserve. In June 1969, the FOMC agreed to liberalize the "informal understanding governing use of the existing authority to warehouse" so that the ESF could use the entire facility for general purposes. The need, however, did not materialize until December 1969 when the Federal Reserve warehoused francs and lira.

In May 1969, the Federal Reserve began warehousing British pounds for the ESF. By August, the central bank held $300 million equivalent. The ESF had also undertaken a series of gold purchases that depleted its funds. By year's end, following an additional $500 million gold purchase, the Federal Reserve's warehousing operations reached $975 million, and in early January they briefly hit the $1 billion limit. At that point, the Federal Reserve had warehoused $675 million in British pounds, $200 million worth of French francs, and $125 million equivalent Italian lira. The Treasury subsequently monetized $1 billion of gold and paid off its warehousing obligations to the Federal Reserve.

After this, the warehousing facility remained dormant for the next eight years, except for one warehousing-like transaction that the Federal Reserve initiated. In July 1972, the central bank intervened in the foreign exchange market against German marks. At the time, the Federal Reserve held very few German marks, and the Treasury had suspended the swap lines. To finance its intervention, the Federal Reserve bought $2.5 million worth of marks on a swap basis from the US Treasury and sold them back forward—a Federal Reserve–initiated warehousing operation.

On 17 January 1977, at the request of Treasury Secretary William Simon, the FOMC raised the warehousing authorization to $1.5 billion, and agreed to warehouse up to one-half of this amount for twelve months and the remainder for six months. The FOMC allowed the more generous warehousing authorization to help finance the Treasury's participation in another credit facility for the Bank of England, but the Treasury never drew on the line.[46]

On 14 December 1978, the FOMC again altered its authorization, increasing the limit to $1.75 billion and now allowing the Federal Reserve to warehouse foreign currencies directly with the US Treasury as well as the ESF.[47] The committee took this action in conjunction with the 1 November 1978 dollar support program, which we previously discussed. The Federal Reserve was a strong advocate of a large active dollar-support program, and viewed warehousing as a necessary contribution to the operation. Five days later, the committee raised its warehousing limit to $5 billion with a standard twelve-month term. This would allow the Treasury to exchange foreign currencies acquired through the issuance of Carter bonds with the Federal Reserve for dollars. The Treasury issued nearly $1.6 billion German-mark-denominated bonds in December 1978 and immediately warehoused almost that entire amount.[48] The Treasury also issued $1.4 billion in Swiss franc Carter bonds in January 1979, and likewise warehoused nearly all of the proceeds with the Federal Reserve. By May 1979, the central bank had warehoused nearly $3.5 billion for the Treasury, and by June 1981, the Treasury had warehoused $4.2 billion with the Federal Reserve. The Federal Reserve continued to warehouse these currencies for the Treasury through mid-1983 (see figure 5.16).

5.6.2   Financing Public Debt

An important aspect of warehousing is that it provided the Treasury with funds that were not subject to the congressional limits on public debt. When the ESF did not immediately use the dollar proceeds from a warehousing operation to purchase foreign exchange, it placed those funds in Treasury securities. As a consequence, the Treasury issued less debt to the public—debt subject to a statutory limit. The Federal Reserve had no control over how the Treasury or the ESF used the dollar funds that it acquired through warehousing, but clearly understood the issue at hand.

In late January 1969, Holmes suggested warehousing foreign exchange for the Treasury as a way to help the Treasury avoid breaching the statutory debt ceiling. At the time, the Treasury simply needed cash. "The Treasury's current problem," according to Holmes, "is not related in any way to current developments in the international situation" (Hackley 1969, 2–3).

Board of Governors General Counsel Howard Hackley pointed out that the Federal Reserve had legal authority to warehouse since purchases of foreign exchange from the Treasury were tantamount to open-market operations and that the Federal Reserve had no control over how the Treasury used the dollar funds: "the fact that their purpose may appear to be solely to provide the Treasury with additional cash does not affect their legality" (Hackley 1969, 3). Hackley cautioned, however, that open-market opera-

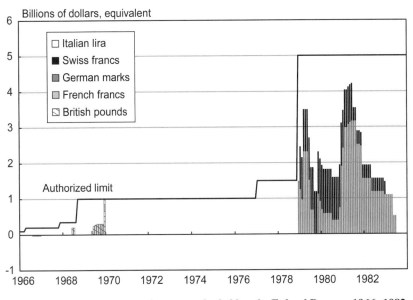

Fig. 5.16   Warehousing: Foreign currencies held at the Federal Reserve, 1966–1982
Note: Data are from the Federal Reserve.

tions should be used "to accommodate commerce and business with regard to their bearing on the general credit situation" (Hackley 1969, 3). At that time, General Counsel Hackley suggested that such a use of warehousing would be legally acceptable, because to do otherwise might affect the general credit situation of the country and the value of the dollar. This was particularly likely, Hackely reasoned, if the Treasury otherwise sought cash by selling off a substantial part of its foreign-exchange portfolio (Hackley 1969, 3–4).

Hackley, however, understood the precarious position that using warehousing to avoid the debt limit could pose for the Federal Reserve System:

It must be recognized that adoption of the proposed arrangement could subject the [Federal Reserve] System to criticism. It might be charged, for example, that the proposed warehousing transaction would constitute a direct extension of credit to the Treasury by the Federal Reserve and would be contrary to the spirit if not the letter of the law, particularly in view of the express provisions contained in section 14(b) of the Federal Reserve Act for direct borrowing by the Treasury from the Federal Reserve within prescribed statutory limits. However . . . I believe that the transactions would be legally defensible as not being designed primarily to aid the Treasury but as intended to avoid developments that would have an adverse impact upon the "credit situation of the country." (Hackley 1969, 4–5)

Until the British pound support program in May 1969, the Federal Reserve did not warehouse any foreign exchange for the Treasury. An improvement in the Treasury's cash flow relieved the immediate debt-limit problem (FOMC *Memoranda*, 4 February 1969, 16). Still the central bank understood that warehousing financed Treasury expenditures:

> During the six-month period [August 1978 to January 1979], the Federal Reserve "warehoused" foreign currencies by taking foreign exchange acquired by the Treasury that was not immediately needed to finance foreign exchange intervention in return for dollars *that were needed by the Treasury in its own domestic operations.* (*Bulletin*, March 1979, 219) (emphasis added)

Congress raised the US statutory debt limit in August 1978. By December, outstanding eligible debt was rapidly approaching the new limit. All else constant, the Treasury would have breached the debt limit in March 1979 had it not warehoused funds with the central bank.

The situation became more problematic for the Federal Reserve after December 1978, when the FOMC extended warehousing directly to the Treasury—as opposed to only the ESF. The warehousing with the Treasury was less defensible than warehousing with the ESF. Volcker seemed to appreciate the distinction:

> [warehousing] could be construed as a form of Treasury borrowing from the Federal Reserve which isn't covered by the other prohibitions on their borrowing [the debt limit]. We need the justification that it is the Exchange Stabilization Fund's lack of assets, not a general lack of funds on the part of the Treasury, that gives rise to this [warehousing]. (FOMC *Transcripts*, 18–19 December 1980, 26)

The Federal Reserve did not want to appear to finance Treasury borrowing in breach of the appropriations process and congressional limits on public debt.

As explained in chapter six, authorization for warehousing would eventually reach $20 billion. The parallels between warehousing foreign exchange for the ESF and lending directly to the Treasury, in conjunction with concerns about the Federal Reserve's independence, would be a key factor in eventually terminating US intervention.

5.7 A Minimalist Approach

By late February 1981, as the dollar continued to appreciate, the United States had effectively stopped intervening.[49] On 17 April 1981, Treasury Secretary Donald Regan announced that henceforth the United States would follow a minimalist strategy with respect to intervention. Over the next four years, the United States rarely intervened in the foreign-exchange market.

Undersecretary of the Treasury for Monetary Affairs, Beryl Sprinkel, the architect of the policy change, explained the Treasury's reasons to the US Congress Joint Economic Committee on 4 May 1981 (Sprinkel 1981). His analysis of intervention was strikingly modern for the time. Sprinkel understood that the dollar's depreciation since 1973 mainly reflected the rising US inflation rate, and he noted that the United States primarily intervened to slow the rate of the dollar's depreciation. The US inflation rate had exceeded the German inflation rate consistently since 1974. This type of intervention—particularly the heavy interventions after 1978—did not address the fundamental underlying economic problem; it only "treated the symptoms." Sprinkel pointed out that sterilized intervention did not affect the macroeconomic determinants of exchange rates. He suggested that in such cases intervention "merely encourages disarray in the exchange market" (Sprinkel 1981, 12–13).

Sprinkel did not deny that exchange markets occasionally became disorderly, but he believed that the exchange market had evolved over the years of generalized floating and had become "more efficient in evaluating and adjusting to new information." As this observation suggests, he viewed intervention as potentially operating through a broad expectations (or signaling) channel—a more modern version of the desk's "psychological" effect—and he took this interpretation to its logical, and uncomfortable, conclusion: "Significant and frequent intervention by governments assumes that relatively few officials know better where exchange rates should (or shouldn't) be than a larger number of decision makers in the market, and that public funds should be put at risk on the basis of that assumption" (Sprinkel 1981, 13).

The Undersecretary also suggested that heavy, persistent intervention could make it "more difficult to follow the correct domestic monetary policy" (Sprinkel 1981, 13). He did not elaborate, but since 1979, the desk had been acquiring foreign exchange—selling dollars—while the FOMC was attempting to tighten monetary policy. The Federal Reserve sterilized this intervention, but such contradictory activities complicates policy making and, if observed by the markets, must weaken central-bank credibility. This exact issue would arise again in the late 1980s and early 1990s and would prove the key reason for ending the United States' long involvement in intervention.

5.8   Conclusion

From the inception of generalized floating through the middle of 1980, the dollar depreciated 54 percent against the German mark, the key target of US interventions over this period. The dollar's depreciation was a symptom of the Great Inflation, which chiefly resulted from a policy framework that downplayed the role of money in the inflation process and from a policy preference for low unemployment over low inflation. During almost all of this time, the real federal funds rate was either negative or close to zero, and inflation in the United States exceeded inflation in Germany, often by a substantial margin. By 1977, confidence in the FOMC's ability and willingness to subdue inflation was rapidly evaporating. The dollar's depreciation quickened and did not reverse until mid-1980, after the FOMC substantially changed its monetary-policy approach and demonstrated a willingness to maintain a disinflationary stance despite severe economic weakness.

As one might expect in an inflation-charged atmosphere, US foreign-exchange interventions over this period were largely ineffectual in halting the dollar's decline. Overall, private market participants could have made money by following the adage at the beginning of this chapter and betting against the desk's operations. Still, on 25 percent of the days over which the desk sold German marks, the dollar experienced a smaller depreciation than on the previous day. This percentage is greater than we would anticipate given the random nature of day-to-day exchange-rate movements, and it suggests that the desk had a limited short-term capacity to lean against the wind. This narrow competency, however, could not quell a growing skepticism about the operations' effectiveness, which led to their termination in early 1981.

Besides inflation, the absence of a clear theoretical framework surely hampered the operations. Such a framework never guided the desk's actions. The desk claimed a general "psychological effect," but their interventions—covert, and small—were wholly inconsistent with the view that officials might provide the market with information useful for price discovery. Quite the contrary, a fear that the market might learn about an intervention, bet against it, or totally overwhelm it, drove the desk's operations, at least through 1977. Instead of providing new information to the market, the desk attempted to trick those market participants who were selling dollars into thinking that a market-based force was emerging to buy dollars. The desk's operations also seemed out of sync with academic thinking. At the time, most economists, including the Board's research staff, viewed intervention as operating through a portfolio-balance mechanism. A policy of borrowing foreign exchange to finance relatively small dollar support operations, but then quickly reversing course to repay the loans, would not have a significant lasting effect on the outstanding stock of dollar-, and mark-denominated assets nor on any risk premia. Hence, the operations could not affect exchange rates through a portfolio-balance channel. At best, the operations may have had an occasional temporary effect by creating unwanted liquidity in German money markets, but the Bundesbank, like the Federal Reserve System, was attempting to reduce inflation. For that reason, Germany grew increasingly reluctant to fund dollar support operations through swap lines.

In the end, as Sprinkel seemed to understand, foreign exchange intervention during the early dollar float did not provide US monetary authorities with a means of consistently affecting exchange rates independent of monetary policy. Intervention did not offer a way around—or at least a way to dampen the effects of—the fundamental trilemma of international finance. During the next fifteen years or so, FOMC participants would come to see that intervention not only failed to provide a way to evade the fundamental trilemma, but that the operations were detrimental to sound monetary policy.

6

US Foreign-Exchange-Market Intervention during the Volcker-Greenspan Era, 1981–1997

I think I have been around too long to be able to give you a precise definition of what is a disorderly market. . . . Disorder to some extent is in the eyes of the beholder.
—Edwin Truman, Director Board of Governor's International Division, 15 November 1994

I think intervention undermines the credibility of monetary policy by introducing some confusion as to what our fundamental objectives are as between domestic price stability and exchange rate objectives at particular points in time. . . . I think some foreign exchange operations could over time undermine public support for the Fed's financial independence, which is the ultimate foundation for our credibility.
—J. Alfred Broaddus, President of the Federal Reserve Bank of Richmond, 2–3 July 1996

6.1 Introduction

After 6 October 1979, through both the Volcker and Greenspan chairmanships, the Federal Reserve System underwent a long—sometimes tentative—process of rebuilding its credibility. The FOMC came to focus on an inflation objective, acknowledging an inevitable connection between achieving low, stable inflation expectations and maintaining the nation's maximum sustainable economic growth rate. Over these years, economists increasingly recognized the crucial links between central-bank independence, the integrity of monetary policy, and the Federal Reserve's ability to achieve its goals.

At the same time, the Federal Reserve underwent a similar learning process with respect to foreign-exchange operations, initially concluding that sterilized intervention was largely ineffectual—that is, it did not overcome the fundamental trilemma of international finance—but eventually deciding that intervention, even sterilized intervention, could create uncertainty about monetary policy. Between 1981 and 1985, the United States adopted a minimalist approach to intervention, but reversed course under the urging of foreign governments, US politicians, and some influential economists who continued to view floating exchange rates as excessively volatile, vulnerable to destabilizing speculation, and prone to serious departures from their fundamentals. In 1985, the Treasury again adopted an activist approach. The sterilized interventions that followed the Plaza and Louvre accords seemed no more effective than earlier operations. The movements in dollar exchange rates during these episodes appeared to reflect changes in monetary policy, not intervention. At most, intervention gave the impression of international cooperation and US concern about dollar exchange rates, but the Federal Reserve came to view that impression as very costly.

As attitudes about the proper role of monetary policy changed, monetary economists increasingly found intervention inconsistent with anchoring inflation expectations. The Federal Reserve's response to the 19 October 1987 stock-market collapse first highlighted the potential for conflict between monetary policy and intervention, but the problem became critical in 1989. At that time, the FOMC was tightening, trying to stem a rise in inflation and to consolidate long-fought gains in its credibility, but the foreign exchange desk, under strong pressure from the US Treasury, was buying huge amounts of German marks and Japanese yen and warehousing large amounts of foreign exchange for the Treasury. At the 3 October 1989 FOMC meeting, opponents of intervention went beyond perennial concerns about intervention and argued forcefully that intervention created uncertainty about the objectives of monetary policy. A central bank cannot credibly anchor inflation expectations and attempt to manage exchange rates, particularly when the fiscal authority has primary responsibility for the latter. Thereafter, the Federal Reserve began to back away from foreign-exchange intervention, and since 1995, has intervened on only three occasions: against the Japanese yen on 17 June 1998, against the euro on 22 September 2000, and against the Japanese yen on 18 March 2011.

6.2   Before Plaza, 1981–1985

Soon after the Reagan administration formally inaugurated its minimalist intervention strategy, the dollar started a sustained, broad-based appreciation on both a nominal and a real basis.[1] During this time, a tightening in US monetary policy, in conjunction with expanding federal budget deficits, raised real interest rates in the United States and attracted substantial inflows of foreign funds. While these financial inflows mitigated the traditional, interest-sensitive crowding out that economists expected from the emerging US policy mix, the resulting real dollar appreciation opened US manufacturers to intense foreign competition. Confronted with mounting protectionist threats and faced with the criticism of those policymakers and academics who still regarded intervention, particularly US intervention, as necessary to maintain orderly market conditions, the administration eased back into an activist's intervention role in early 1985, despite evidence that intervention did not offer an independent tool for affecting exchange rates, and therefore could not solve the fundamental trilemma (see figures 6.1 and 6.2).

6.2.1   Dollar Appreciation

Between July 1980 and March 1985, the US dollar appreciated nearly 55 percent on a nominal trade-weighted basis relative to the currencies of the other major developed countries. Over this same time period, the dollar appreciated 89 percent relative to the German mark, the United States' key intervention currency and the linchpin of the European exchange-rate mechanism (figure 6.1). Movements against the Japanese yen, which emerged as a second key US intervention currency around this time, were more muted. Between July 1980 and March 1985, the dollar appreciated only 17 percent against the yen (figure 6.2). Most of the dollar's appreciation was on a real basis, suggesting a significant deterioration in the competitive position of the US traded-goods sector. On a trade-weighted real basis, the dollar appreciated nearly 49 percent between the mid-1980 and early 1985.

A tightening of US monetary policy prompted the dollar's appreciation. The Federal Reserve had initially moved to tighten monetary policy and to eliminate inflation after Paul Volcker became chairman in August 1979.[2] At a secret meeting on 6 October 1979, the FOMC adopted new operating procedures that attempted to improve the Federal Reserve's credibility with respect to its monetary targets by focusing on a reserve aggregate as an operating target rather than on the federal funds rate (Hetzel 2008, 166–69).[3] The Federal Reserve also raised marginal reserve requirements and, at the Carter administration's request, imposed credit controls (Schreft 1990). The economy slipped into recession by January 1980.

The committee's initial policy steps toward eliminating inflation proved tentative. During the recession of 1980, for example, the Federal Reserve, now under its new operating procedure, allowed the federal funds rate to fall sharply, resulting in a negative real federal funds rate in mid-1980 (see figures 6.3 and 6.4). After the board removed credit controls in July 1980, economic activity improved, but high long-term bond rates suggested no improvement in inflation expectations. The Federal Reserve tightened again in 1981 and generally maintained that stance despite a serious recession that began in the middle of the year and continued through almost all of 1982. In mid-1982, the committee again allowed nominal policy rates to ease somewhat. In part, this was a response to the continuing recession and to a continuing moderation of inflation, but an emerging developing country debt crisis also contributed to the policy change.[4]

Although the federal funds rate generally fell during this pre-Plaza period, the decline conformed to the Taylor principle. As the economy recovered after the 1982 recession, Volcker acted to prevent a rise in inflation expectations by keeping the real funds rate high and by responding to increases in long-term bond rates (Hetzel 2008, 172–79). The real federal funds rate

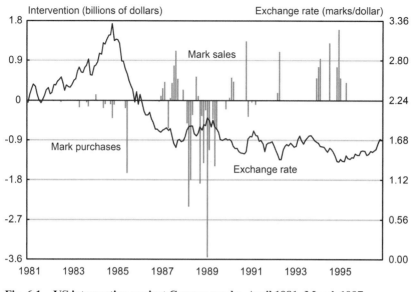

Fig. 6.1   US intervention against German marks, April 1981–March 1997
Note: Data are from the Federal Reserve.

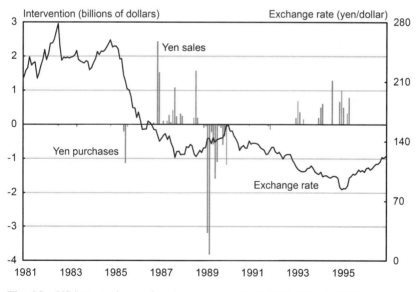

Fig. 6.2   US intervention against Japanese yen, April 1981–March 1997
Note: Data are from the Federal Reserve.

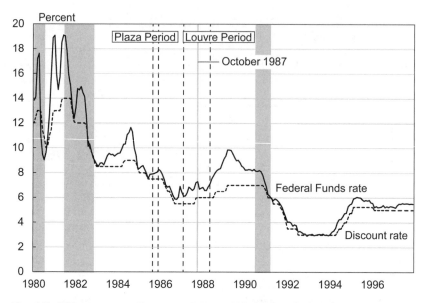

Fig. 6.3   US monetary policy rates, January 1980–December 1997

Notes: Shaded bars are recessions. Data are from the Federal Reserve and the National Bureau of Economic Research.

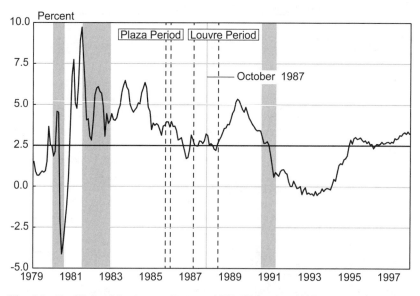

Fig. 6.4   Real federal funds rate, January 1979–December 1997

Notes: The real federal funds rate equals the effective federal funds rate minus the percentage change in the core CPI over the past twelve months. Shaded bars are recessions. Data are from the Federal Reserve, the Bureau of Labor Statistics, and the National Bureau of Economic Research.

fluctuated around 5.2 percent between 1981 and 1985, which was high by historical standards.

Against the backdrop of tight monetary policy, the Reagan administration entered the White House in January 1981, instituting substantial cuts in personal income taxes and increases in military expenditures. The Reagan administration also hoped for cuts in nondefense federal spending, but Congress was unwilling to enact these.[5] Consequently, the federal-budget deficit increased from 2 1/2 percent of GDP in FY1981 to 4 percent of GDP in FY1982, and to 6 percent of GDP in FY1983. The federal-budget deficit then remained near 5 percent of GDP over the next three fiscal years.

By 1982, the tight-money, loose-fiscal policy mix had pushed nominal interest rates in the United States above those in the other major developed countries, even though many countries tried to resist the resulting downward pressures on their own currencies by tightening monetary policy, often through nonsterilized interventions (BIS 1983, 67–68) (see figures 6.5 and 6.6). In addition, the economic recovery from the 1981–82 recession occurred sooner, and remained subsequently stronger in the United States than in most European countries. The improved business outlook, more favorable business taxes, and lower expected inflation improved the real return on capital in the United States. These conditions attracted foreign funds into dollar-denominated assets.[6]

During any period of tight monetary policy and strong economic growth, such an expansion of the federal budget deficit might have crowded out private investment and other interest-sensitive economic activity. Yet, in the early 1980s, traditional crowding out did not take place. Fixed investment in the United States fell as a percentage of GDP in 1982, but thereafter increased and was higher in 1984 and 1985 than in 1981 or in the late 1970s. Strong foreign financial inflows and the dollar's appreciation shifted fiscal crowding out from interest-sensitive sectors of the economy to the traded-goods sector.

Prior to 1985, few in the administration worried about the impact of the strong dollar on the traded-goods sector. They seemed to view crowding out in this sector as better than the traditional variety. The Council of Economic Advisors (1984, 55–57) suggested that the investment sector contributed more to potential economic growth than the traded-goods sector, and that higher potential growth eased inflationary pressures.

The administration actually took steps to encourage foreign financial inflows in the years prior to the Plaza Accord. The Treasury pressured foreign governments, notably Japan, to liberalize their financial markets, giving the United States greater access to borrowed funds. In 1984, the administration eliminated the withholding tax on interest payments to foreigners who invested in US corporate and government bonds. The Treasury also allowed US corporations to issue bearer bonds to foreigners and designed new US government bonds to be more attractive to foreigners.

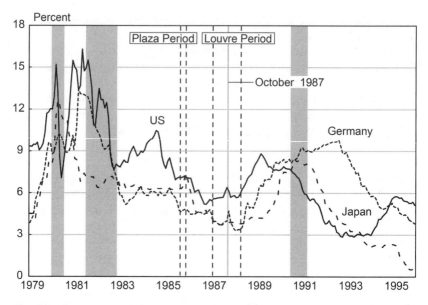

Fig. 6.5 Short-term interest rates, January 1979–December 1995

Notes: Shaded bars are US recessions. Data are from the International Monetary Fund and the National Bureau of Economic Research.

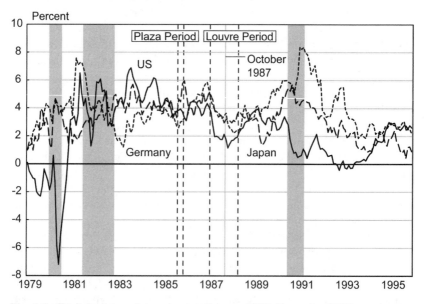

Fig. 6.6 Real short-term interest rates, January 1979–December 1995

Notes: Real rates equal the nominal interest rate minus the percentage change in each country's CPI over the past twelve months. Shaded bars are US recessions. Data are from the International Monetary Fund and the National Bureau of Economic Research.

Treasury Secretary Regan interpreted the dollar's appreciation as an international vote of confidence in the administration's policies (Feldstein 1994, 70; Volcker and Gyohten 1992, 179) and was unwilling to amend the minimalist intervention strategy that Undersecretary of the Treasury for Monetary Affairs Beryl Sprinkel had introduced in early 1981.[7] As the dollar appreciated, however, foreign central banks—notably the Bundesbank—intervened heavily and generally tightened monetary policy in attempts to limit their currencies' depreciations. They complained about the US policy mix and urged intervention (Destler and Henning 1989, 23). Foreign central banks, particularly the French, continued to believe that intervention was effective. They maintained that exchange rates frequently deviated from fundamentals and that excessive exchange-rate volatility was detrimental both to domestic economic activity and to the international adjustment process. They continued to believe, as they did back in 1973, that US intervention, in particular, had an important "psychological" effect on the market (see FOMC *Transcripts*, 29–30 March 1982, 4).

Perhaps to mollify foreign criticism of its minimalist approach, at the Versailles Economic Summit on 4–6 June 1982, the United States agreed to a French proposal for a study of the G7's experience with intervention since the inception of generalized floating. In March 1983, the working group on exchange market intervention released their findings, generally known as the Jurgensen Report after its chairman (Jurgensen 1983).

6.2.2 The Jurgensen Report and Emerging Research

With a decade of observations, the Jurgensen Report was the first official study of intervention. It confirmed that many G7 participants still had a wary attitude about freely floating exchange rates. They saw the market as inefficient, prone to disorder, and capable of serious deviations from fundamentals, which they generally considered current-account balances and inflation differentials.

As a treatise on intervention, however, the Jurgensen Report fell far short. The report did not clearly address and answer the most critical question: Did intervention enable central banks to systematically pursue an exchange-rate objective independent of their other monetary-policy goals? Its narrative often did not carefully distinguish between sterilized intervention and unsterilized intervention, or isolate intervention from other policy actions. As a result, while the conclusions may have tempered people's beliefs about the effectiveness (or ineffectiveness) of intervention, they could dispel neither an activist's, nor a nonactivist's position. The imprecision seemed, and probably was, intentional. To its credit, the Jurgensen Report did initiate some serious background studies of intervention, which addressed the critical issues more directly, and it opened the door for further academic work (see Henderson and Sampson 1983).

The Jurgensen report found that intervention—presumably both the

unsterilized and sterilized varieties—had been an effective tool for influencing exchange rates *in the short run*. The report claimed that unsterilized
intervention was more effective than sterilized intervention, but it failed to
discuss the potential conflict with domestic monetary-policy objectives that
unsterilized intervention could create. The report also indicated that, in the
face of persistent market pressures, sterilized intervention was ineffective
and that "supportive" domestic monetary-policy changes were necessary.[8]
But why then undertake sterilized intervention? Was it not redundant to
normal open-market operations? Many participants asserted that sterilized
intervention could reinforce the exchange-rate consequences of monetary-
policy changes, but the report offered no support for this important con-
tention. Bonser-Neal, Roley, and Sellon (1998) would eventually refute this
claim, at least, for the United States. If, on the other hand, domestic policies were inconsistent with exchange-rate objectives, sterilized intervention
would prove ineffectual. The Jurgensen Report gave a qualified nod to coordinated interventions over unilateral actions and eschewed capital controls,
which many countries still maintained in their arsenals of exchange-rate
policies (Jurgensen 1983, 17–21; Henderson and Sampson 1983, 830–33).

At about the time of the Jurgensen Report, academic attitudes about
foreign-exchange intervention were undergoing an important change. The
dominant paradigm for investigating sterilized intervention was still the
portfolio-balance approach. Definitions still described sterilized intervention as a change in the currency composition of outstanding interest-bearing
government debt that left the monetary base unchanged (Jurgensen 1983,
6; Rogoff 1984, 133; Loopesko 1984). Adams and Henderson (1983, 3), for
example, noted the difficulty in measuring and testing intervention: "Many
other actions of the financial authorities affect the currency composition
of net official assets in ways essentially indistinguishable from the effects
of the traditional proxies [for intervention]."[9] This, of course, is all correct, but the emphasis on asset composition is only relevant if intervention
works through a portfolio-balance channel. Today, by contrast, researchers
define sterilized intervention as not affecting the monetary base. They refer
to changes in asset compositions as the method of achieving sterilization,
not as the defining characteristic of sterilized intervention.

Despite the portfolio-balance approach's predominance and evidence of
a time-varying risk premium, the emerging empirical evidence offered little
support for an exploitable portfolio-balance channel.[10] As Obstefeld and
Rogoff (1997, 594) later concluded, "A large body of empirical research
finds very little evidence of a portfolio-balance effect on foreign exchange
risk premiums. . . . Global government debt levels simply change too slowly
and predictably . . . to explain the size and the volatility of the exchange rate
risk premium." The early work—prior to the Jurgensen Report—on the
portfolio-balance effect did not directly include intervention data, which
monetary authorities still kept confidential, but given the definition of steril-

ized intervention, this work's conclusions were germane to any assessment of intervention's effectiveness. Hutchison's (1984) investigation of Japanese intervention is a good example, and his conclusions are about as charitable to a portfolio-balance effect as anyone at the time had offered. Hutchison, while not completely rejecting a portfolio-balance mechanism, concluded that Japanese intervention would need to be massive to affect the yen-dollar exchange rate through this channel.

While the portfolio-balance framework was still dominant, a signaling channel had emerged (Mussa 1981; Genberg 1981). Most researchers in the early 1980s interpreted signaling as providing information and affecting private expectation predominately—if not *only*—about future monetary policies (Rogoff 1984, 133; Solomon 1983, 10–11). This narrow view of signaling seems odd because the desk had often referred to the "psychological" effects of intervention. Presumably this meant that when traders were misinformed about fundamentals defined more broadly than merely future monetary policies, the desk with its superior private information about market fundamentals could guide them via its interventions.

With the Jurgensen Report, studies began to emerge that used official confidential data to consider the effects of intervention on exchange rates.[11] This evidence offered mixed support for intervention. Loopesko (1984)—the most influential paper associated with the Jurgensen Report—found that in most of her tests, cumulative sterilized intervention affected unexploited profits from an uncovered-interest-parity condition through *either* a portfolio-balance effect or a signaling channel. Moreover, she found support explicitly for the portfolio-balance model in about half of currencies pairs that she considered. She did not, however, report coefficients, which in previous work had often proved wrong-signed in portfolio models. Rogoff (1984), in contrast, found no evidence that Canadian intervention operated through a portfolio-balance channel. Humpage (1984) using time-series techniques and focusing on exchange rates instead of unexploited profits, found that the heavy US intervention in 1978 and 1979 had no obvious effect on daily exchange-rate movements. Micossi and Rebecchini (1984), in contrast, found some evidence that official Italian intervention affected the lira.

While inconclusive, the weight of the evidence did not rule out sterilized intervention, but it appeared to shift against a portfolio-balance channel and toward a narrowly defined signaling channel; that is, intervention as a signal of future monetary-policy changes. If intervention operated through a signaling mechanism, however, it was not completely independent of monetary policy, which economists at the time understood. To keep the signal credible, monetary policy would have to eventually respond in the appropriate manner. Moreover, for narrowly interpreted signaling to work, monetary authorities probably should not undertake intervention secretively, as the United States heretofore had often done (Genberg 1981, 6–8). The amount of an intervention did not seem to matter as much for a signaling mechanism as it did for a portfolio-balance effect. Infrequent, announced, and coordinated operations might heighten the intended signal. If, on the other hand, intervention might still work predominately through a portfolio-balance mechanism, the operations should be massive and could remain secretive. Coordination would only contribute by increasing the dollar amount of intervention.

6.2.3 Pressure, Politics, and Monetary Policy

Academic studies, however, never had much of an impact on intervention policy. By 1983 and 1984, calls for US intervention were widespread and growing. In addition to many G7 countries, Federal Reserve officials, notably Chairman Paul Volcker and Federal Reserve Bank of New York President Anthony Solomon, pressed the Treasury to undertake intervention during the years of the dollar's appreciation. Volcker feared that the prolonged real dollar appreciation, even though it tended to lower the relative dollar price of traded goods, might actually undermine the Federal Reserve's anti-inflation policies. He observed that the real dollar appreciation was having serious structural effects on US manufacturers by eroding their competitiveness. He worried that if business activity began to slow, the Federal Reserve would come under heavy administration and congressional pressures to back away from its tough monetary-policy stance and to offset the dollar's appreciation through lower interest rates. He did not want monetary policy to pursue an exchange-rate objective at the expense of an inflation goal (Volcker and Gyohten 1992, 179–80; Destler and Henning 1989, 30–31). Sterilized intervention might at least buy him some cover.

As early as March 1983, Solomon wanted to approach the Treasury about automatically intervening when the dollar moved "quickly" (that is, disorderly), and he complained that intervention opportunities were routinely lost because the Treasury typically hesitated (FOMC *Transcripts*, 28–29 March 1983, 18). Later, out of frustration with the minimalist approach, he suggested that the small amounts of funds devoted to intervention stemmed from the Treasury's desire to discredit the operations entirely (FOMC *Transcripts*, 19–20 December 1983, 52).

While Paul Volcker's argument for intervention in 1984 did not stem from a fear that the US current-account position was unsustainable, by that time others within the Federal Reserve held such a view (*Bulletin*, September 1984, 694). At some point, they feared, foreign investors would become reluctant to hold additional dollar-denominated assets in their portfolios without compensation for the risks of doing so. The dollar's appreciation prolonged and worsened the problem. When the inevitable portfolio adjustment took place, the dollar could come under intense downward pressure.

After the Treasury continually rebuffed Federal Reserve suggestions for a more active intervention policy, Volcker briefly considered, but rejected, intervening without the Treasury's participation. He feared that asserting the Federal Reserve's independent authority for intervention would create political problems for the central bank and dissension within the FOMC, particularly given the lingering doubts about the efficacy of intervention (Volcker and Gyohten 1992, 180–81). Emblematic of the difference of opinion about intervention within the FOMC at the time was the following exchange: During a discussion of intervention, Governor Roberts asked if the desk knew better than the market where the dollar should be. Chairman Volcker responded, "At times"; Governor Wallich stated, "Yes"; but Governor Partee quipped, "I doubt it" (FOMC *Transcripts*, 28–29 March 1983, 18).

By mid-1983, the manufacturing sector was starting to pressure the administration and Congress for relief from the competitive effects of the strong dollar. Between 1981 and 1985, their petitions for trade policy almost doubled from the late-1970s average and seemed to follow business-cycle conditions and the dollar's appreciation (Richardson 1994, 636–37). Manufacturers directed their ire particularly against Japan. Increasingly, manufacturers blamed persistent US trade deficits with Japan on unfair Japanese trading practices such as dumping, limiting market access, and industrial policies. United States manufacturers saw domestic trade restrictions as justified retaliation.

When complaints about the dollar's appreciation fell on deaf ears within the administration, Congress began to apply leverage by introducing a wide range of protectionist legislation. In October 1984, the administration attempted to head off complaints about the strong dollar and widening trade deficits by reaching an agreement with Japan to remove capital controls and the so-called administrative guidance that discouraged foreign financial flows into Japan. Stronger financial flows from the United States to Japan would encourage a yen appreciation vis-à-vis the dollar and, presumably, improve the United States' competitive position. These efforts had little effect, and by 1985, prior to the Plaza Accord, Congress generated "a veritable explosion of trade legislation" (Destler and Henning 1989, 39).

Adding to the mix of pressures on the administration and the Federal Reserve, some academic economists began to contend that the dollar's appreciation in late 1984 and early 1985 was inconsistent with market fundaments and started to question the allocative efficacy of floating exchange rates (Frankel 1994, 301). To be sure, Meese and Rogoff (1981, 1982, 1983) had already cast serious doubt on the profession's ability to accurately describe equilibrium exchange rates. Still, many economists maintained that exchange rates ultimately must respond to relative inflation differentials or current-account imbalances. Dornbusch (1976) had demonstrated that exchange rates could overshoot a purchasing-power-parity equilibrium, and many economists understood that trading rules generated profits, suggesting that exchange markets were not perfectly efficient. To these economists, the dollar was clearly overshooting its equilibrium, implying that any resulting changes in output, prices, or trading patterns were temporary, reversible, and a misallocation of resources.[12] They called for a policy response.[13]

If the monetary authorities would not respond, Congress would. Just prior to August 1985, Senators Bradley, Moynihan, and Baucus submitted legislation that would require the Treasury and the Federal Reserve to intervene in the foreign-exchange market in specific amounts when the United States ran a large current-account deficit (Destler and Henning 1989, 36–39).[14]

6.2.4   Ending the Minimalist Strategy

In late 1984, the Federal Reserve began to lower its policy rates, but the central bank's actions remained limited until early 1986. Real rates remained relatively high throughout both years (see figures 6.5 and 6.6). Initially foreign countries—notably Germany and Japan—were reluctant to cut interest rates, but they eventually followed suit. By mid-1984, interest-rate spreads that favored the dollar began to narrow, suggesting a dollar depreciation. These cautious and limited monetary-policy changes set an important guiding tone for the dollar over the subsequent two years.

On 17 January 1985, the G5 met in Washington. Treasury Secretary Regan announced that the G5 countries had reaffirmed their commitment to macroeconomic convergence, but the G5's recent discussions focused more on exchange markets than in the past. The G5 "reaffirmed" their 1983 Williamsburg Summit commitment to concerted intervention and agreed to sell dollars. The heavier emphasis on intervention evolved because the large industrial countries resented tightening their domestic monetary policies as a counterweight to the dollar's strength. (They seem to have already forgotten the conclusions reached in the Jurgensen Report.) Their recent economic recovery had been sluggish. Any intervention would be undertaken when all parties to an operation agreed, and it would be concerted with each central bank acting in its own market.[15]

The objective of the intervention was a lower dollar, but—as Chairman Volcker indicated—the United States was not undertaking "drive-the-dollar-down operations" (FOMC *Transcripts*, 18 January 1985, 5). Consistent with Volcker's characterization, US operations remained fairly limited. Between 22 January 1985 and 1 March 1985, the United States only bought German marks on eight days. The transactions ranged from $46 million equivalent in January to $100 million by the end of February. The United States also bought $48 million equivalent Japanese yen on 1 February 1985. The Bundesbank and other monetary authorities also intervened. Germany intervened more frequently than the United States (nineteen days), and typically on a much larger scale ($200 million equivalent).

During this period, the United States intervened primarily in German marks because of the mark's importance within the European monetary system. By buying and selling German marks, the United States could potentially affect the relationship of the dollar vis-à-vis all European currencies. In addition, the United States bought $48.8 million worth of Japanese yen on 1 February 1985.[16] The yen was quickly acquiring international status (FOMC *Transcripts*, 18 January 1985, 4). Typically in G5 communiqués, the United States mentioned a willingness to intervene in G5 currencies, and the United States continued to maintain the system of swap lines that it established in the 1960s to finance interventions, but after 1980 the United States never intervened in any other currency besides the mark and yen—with one exception.

The United States undertook an unusual intervention in British pounds in February 1985 for political reasons. At the time, sterling was under strong downward pressure, and Prime Minister Thatcher was scheduled to visit the United States. The United States bought $16.4 million worth of British pounds, split between the Federal Reserve's and the US Treasury's accounts, sometime in February.[17] When Governor Rice questioned the political nature of this intervention, Sam Cross responded (FOMC *Transcripts*, 26 March 1985, 3): "Well, I think it had some implication of being done in light of those political circumstances, yes."

Economically, this transaction was inconsequential, but it highlighted an important problem that intervention always posed for central-bank independence when the political authorities had some control over the operations. Consistent with fears expressed by the FOMC in the early 1960s, by undertaking this intervention, the Federal Reserve seemed to act as a foreign-policy appendage of the State Department and outside of the appropriations process (see chapter 3).

The dollar peaked in late February 1985, and thereafter generally depreciated throughout the next three years. In late August and early September 1985, however, it seemed like the depreciation had stalled. At this time, the dollar began to appreciate as market participants temporarily lowered their expectations for further interest-rate cuts in the United States. Economic activity seemed robust, money growth was strong, and foreign investors were not rebalancing their portfolios away from US securities as some had feared (*Bulletin*, February 1986, 109–10).

6.2.5   An Analysis of Pre-Plaza Interventions

The Regan-Sprinkel minimalist approach did not entirely preclude foreign-exchange intervention (see figures 6.1 and 6.2 and table 6.1). Under this regime, the United States intervened "only when necessary to counter conditions of clear and manifest disorder in exchange markets" (*Desk Report*, 1982, 2). "Clear" and "manifest" seemed to be the new operative words. Between 20 April 1981 and 29 March 1985, a period consisting of 1,030 business days, the United States intervened on twenty-five occasions against German marks. On eight of these occasions, the desk also bought Japanese yen. The desk bought *only* yen on three days. As can be seen in

Table 6.1   Interventions during the minimalist period

	All	1981	1982	1983	1984	1985
German marks	25	0	4	5	8	8
purchases	24	0	4	5	7	8
sales	1	0	0	0	1	0
Japanese yen	11	0	5	5	0	1
purchases	11	0	5	5	0	1
sales	0	0	0	0	0	0

Note: Purchases or sales of foreign currencies against US dollars between 20 April 1981 and 29 March 1985.

table 6.1, the frequency of these transactions grew as the dollar continued to appreciate relative to the German mark. Most transactions were split equally between the Treasury's and the Federal Reserve's accounts.

While the number of interventions during this pre-Plaza period is too small to draw strong conclusions, our analysis, which we explain in the empirical appendix, suggests that although US purchases of marks and yen did not foster dollar depreciations, they did seem to moderate the pace of the dollar's appreciation (see table 6.2). Only six of the twenty-four US purchases of German marks were associated with a same-day dollar depreciation against the German mark, and only four of the eleven US purchases of Japanese yen were associated with a same-day dollar depreciation against the Japanese yen. In both cases, the observed number of successes is smaller, but not statistically different, than the number that we would randomly anticipate, given the variable pattern of day-to-day exchange-rate movements. The evidence of success is somewhat more favorable when judged on a leaning-against-the-wind criterion. During seven of the twenty-four days on which the United States bought German marks, the pace of the dollar's appreciation slowed relative to the previous day. This number is two standard deviations greater than the expected number of successes. Similarly, during five of the eleven days on which the United States purchased Japanese yen, the pace of the dollar's appreciation slowed relative to the previous day. This number was also greater than two standard deviations above the expected number of successes. While our observations during this period are too few to offer strong evidence on the overall effectiveness of US intervention, this result persists through most other intervention episodes during the Volcker-Greenspan chairmanships.

Figure 6.7 isolates the eight US interventions against German marks that the United States undertook between 22 January 1985 and 1 March 1985, and allows a different perspective on the operations than the analysis in table 6.2.[18] In concert with each of these US transactions, the Bundesbank bought dollars. Of the eight interventions shown in figure 6.7, only three (38 percent) proved successful. The dollar, which had generally been

Table 6.2   **Success counts for US intervention, 20 April 1981 to 29 March 1985**

German marks	Total (#)	Intervention successes (#)	(%)	Expected[a] successes (#)	Standard[a] deviation (#)
Mark sales & dollar appreciation	1	0	0.0	1	0
Mark purchases & dollar depreciation	24	6	25.0	11	2
Total	25	6	24.0		
Mark sales & smaller dollar depreciation	1	0	0.0	0	0
Mark purchases & smaller dollar appreciation	24	7	29.2	3	1
Total	25	7	28.0		
Mark sales & dollar appreciation or smaller depreciation	1	0	0.0	1	0
Mark purchases & dollar depreciation or small appreciation	24	13	54.2	14	3
Total	25	13	52.0		
Japanese yen					
Yen sales & dollar appreciation	0	0	na	0	0
Yen purchases & dollar depreciation	11	4	36.4	5	1
Total	11	4	36.4		
Yen sales & smaller dollar depreciation	0	0	na	0	0
Yen purchases & smaller dollar appreciation	11	5	45.5	2	1
Total	11	5	45.5		
Yen sales & dollar appreciation or smaller depreciation	0	0	na	0	0
Yen purchases & dollar depreciation or small appreciation	11	9	81.8	6	2
Total	11	9	81.8		

Note: See appendix 2 for detail.
[a] Assumes that the success count is a hypergeometric random variable.

strengthening against the German mark, appreciates from 25 January 1985 through 26 February 1985. Of the first five interventions, only one seems to successfully slow the pace of this appreciation. The dollar depreciates sharply between the opening quote on 26 February and the opening quote on 27 February; during these twenty-four hours the Bundesbank undertook a very large $1.1 billion intervention. The first US intervention on 27 February is associated with a further depreciation. The second, however,

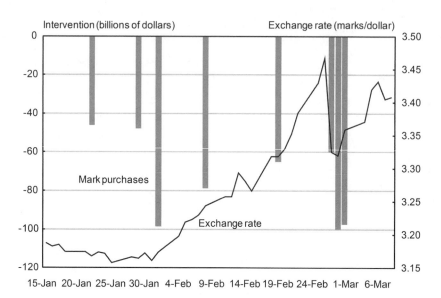

Fig. 6.7   US intervention against German marks, 15 January 1981–8 March 1981
Note: Data are from the Federal Reserve.

has no apparent effect. The third, again preceded by a massive German sale of $1.1 billion, briefly slows the pace of the dollar's appreciation. Overall, however, these interventions had little effect.

Bagshaw and Humpage (1986), using an entirely different statistical technique, likewise found that intervention during the minimalist period had little effect. They compared exchange-rate volatility during a subsample of the minimalist-intervention period from 1 April 1981 to 31 March 1982, with a period of heavy intervention from 1 March 1980 to 28 February 1981. They found virtually no evidence of a change in volatility over the two periods, except some tendency for relatively large exchange-rate changes to be more common during the minimalist period.[19] In addition, they found that exchange rates generally were no more volatile than other asset prices over the two periods.

6.3   From the Plaza to the Louvre, 1985–1987

On 3 February 1985, James Baker replaced Donald Regan as US Secretary of the Treasury. Over the next three years, he pursued macroeconomic-policy coordination to resolve perceived global imbalances much more vigorously than his predecessor had. Like many in the United States, Baker believed that Germany and Japan relied too heavily on their export sectors and, by extension, US economic growth to drive their economies. Both countries maintained sizable and persistent trade surpluses with the United States. Baker wanted Germany and Japan to spur economic growth internally through the adoption of expansionary fiscal and monetary policies. Both countries had experienced relatively sluggish economic growth since the last recession and, hence, had ample room to expand. Not only would faster growth in Germany and Japan help alleviate global current-account imbalances, but it would reinforce the world economic expansion at a time when the US economy showed signs of slowing (Volcker and Gyohten, 1992).

Baker was also free to toss foreign-exchange-market intervention into the policy-coordination mix since, unlike his predecessor, he had never objected to such operations. The Plaza interventions in late 1985 sought to lower the dollar and to avoid protectionist threats emanating from the US Congress. By 1987, with the dollar now depreciated, the Louvre interventions attempted to stabilize the dollar-yen and dollar-mark exchange rates. The administration then used the threat of backing away from the Louvre agreement and letting the dollar depreciate anew to gain leverage over Germany and Japan for macroeconomic-policy coordination.

6.3.1 The Plaza Accord

The dollar began to depreciate in late February 1985, shortly after Baker took office, but well before the September Plaza Accord. The Federal Reserve had tentatively started to ease monetary policy in late 1984 and continued to do so through 1986 (see figures 6.3 and 6.4). By August, the dollar had depreciated 9 percent on a trade-weighted basis against the currencies of the major developed countries, but late in that month the dollar's depreciation began to reverse as interest-rate spreads moved temporarily in favor of dollar assets.[20] Money growth had exceeded its target, and many Fed watchers thought that the FOMC would act to rein it back into its target range. By mid-September, the dollar had appreciated 8 percent against the German mark and 3 percent against the Japanese yen. Although the dollar subsequently began to depreciate, even prior to the G5 meeting in New York, this "pause" lent support to those who thought the dollar had lost touch with fundamentals and favored coordinated intervention.[21]

The 22 September 1985 (or Plaza) communiqué of the G5 noted that, although some progress toward macroeconomic convergence had been made, exchange rates had not responded fully. The Plaza Accord said that "exchange rates should better reflect fundamental economic conditions than has been the case," that "some further orderly appreciation of the main nondollar currencies is desirable," and that the G5 "stand ready to cooperate more closely to encourage this when to do so would be helpful."[22] In other words, the G5 would intervene to depreciate the dollar.

Funabashi (1988, 17–18) and Frankel (1994, 304) contend that the G5 agreed to specifics about intervention as spelled out in a "nonpaper," which was never released. The paper targeted a 10 to 12 percent depreciation of the dollar over the near term.[23] This would place the dollar in a range of roughly 214 to 218 against the yen and 2.54 to 2.59 against the mark. Once key exchange rates reached these levels, countries would be relieved of their obligation to intervene, but the agreement did not preclude further collective or individual interventions.

Following the Plaza meeting, the dollar fell sharply, even before any intervention had taken place. On Monday morning, 23 September 1985, the dollar had fallen 5 percent against the German mark and 2.6 percent against the Japanese yen since the previous Friday. The Bundesbank began intervening on Monday in the European markets, selling $8 million. Later in the day, when the New York market opened, the United States began buying German marks and Japanese yen. With Japanese markets closed on that Monday, the Bank of Japan did not begin intervening until Tuesday, 24 September 1985. Over these first three days, the United States and the other G5 central banks collectively intervened in "massive" amounts (*Bulletin*, February 1986, 110).

The dollar depreciated sharply against both the mark and the yen until 4 October 1985, as the United States sold $199 million against German marks and $262 million against Japanese yen. As the dollar began to firm somewhat after 4 October, the United States intensified its intervention efforts, selling nearly $1.6 billion against marks and nearly $618 million against Japanese yen during the middle two weeks of October. Central banks in other large developed countries continued to intervene (*Bulletin*, February 1986, 110–11). After this, intervention efforts rapidly tapered off and by 8 November the Plaza efforts ended. Overall, the United States sold nearly $1.9 billion against German marks and just over $1.4 billion against Japanese yen. The US Treasury's and the Federal Reserve's accounts shared equally in the operations. The interventions also were closely coordinated with the Bank of Japan and the European G5 countries (*Bulletin*, February 1986, 111). Germany sold $1.2 billion. All of the operations were highly visible to the market, suggesting that the operations sought to influence expectations.

During this period, the desk sometimes intervened in the Far East, which it had not done in quite a while, but the desk did not buy Japanese yen.[24] When the Japanese were operating in their own market against dollars, the United States transacted in the Far East in German marks to show evidence of a coordinated approach. These operations also were typically visible to the market (FOMC *Transcripts*, 4–5 November 1985, 1).

Although the operations were intended to encourage the dollar depreciation that was already under way, the desk did not generally lean *with* the wind in a traditional sense. That is, the desk did not buy foreign exchange when the dollar was depreciating. Instead, the desk usually bought foreign exchange when the dollar was rising as a way of resisting appreciations. According to Cross (FOMC *Transcripts*, 1 October 1985, 2), "US authorities did not want to push the dollar down in a way that could start an uncontrolled fall." Volcker's concern about the dollar had shifted; he now worried about a hard-landing scenario—a dollar free fall, as he called it—that would put upward pressure on interest rates and prices in the United States and, thereby, complicate monetary policy.

The hard-landing scenario envisioned international investors shifting quickly out of dollar-denominated assets to avoid capital losses associated with a dollar depreciation. The US net international investment position was shrinking because of persistent US current-account deficits, and it would become negative by 1986, implying that the rest of the world held net claims against the United States. If US current-account deficits continued, at some point, international investors would become increasingly reluctant to add additional dollar-denominated assets to their portfolios without compensation for the growing risks of doing so. Then, as their reluctance grew, the dollar would depreciate in the spot market relative to its forward rates and US real interest rates would rise relative to rates abroad. These adjustments would proceed until they raised the foreign-currency return on dollar-denominated assets and provided investors with ample compensation for the perceived risk of holding them.

At question was the speed with which such a development might play out. A smooth adjustment would have few adverse economic consequences for the United States, but a very rapid adjustment could be cataclysmic, and any attempt to push the dollar down, Volcker feared, might trigger a rush out of dollar-denominated assets. The concern that Volcker voiced helps explain why US intervention operations, even during this cooperative period, remained fairly limited (Volcker and Gyohten 1992, 244–47).

The primary effect of the Plaza Accord was to induce an immediate, short-lived depreciation of the dollar against both the German mark and the Japanese yen through a narrow expectations channel (see figures 6.8 and 6.9). According to the Federal Reserve's review of the episode (*Bulletin*, February 1986, 110), market participants interpreted the accord's announcement, which was unanticipated and the product of a US initiative, as signaling a change in the administration's regard for a strong dollar. For one thing, the minimalist approach seemed to have ended. Under its minimalist strategy, the administration intervened only to "counter conditions of clear and manifest disorder." Now, the administration was actively trying to push the dollar down and to bring exchange rates back in line with perceived fundamentals. Most important for exchange rates, however, the Plaza Accord reduced the chances that the Federal Reserve would tighten reserve conditions even though aggregates exceed their target range. Many market participants expected US monetary authorities to lower interest rates, possibly in conjunction with interest-rate cuts among the other G5 countries, but in a manner that reduced the incentive for investing in dollar-denominated assets, and that thereby fostered a dollar depreciation (*Bulletin*, May 1986,

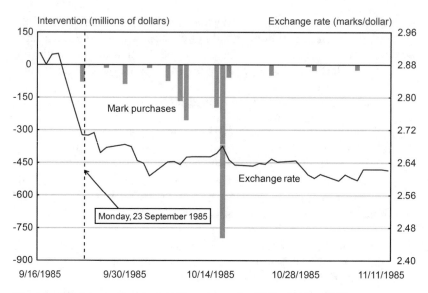

Fig. 6.8   US intervention against German marks, 16 September 1985–12 November 1985

Note: Data are from the Federal Reserve.

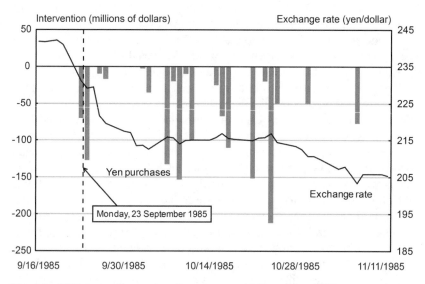

Fig. 6.9   US intervention against Japanese yen, 16 September 1985–12 November 1985

Note: Data are from the Federal Reserve.

299). During the Plaza episode, as figures 6.5 and 6.6 indicate, both nominal and real Japanese short-term interest rates rose sharply, while nominal and real German short-term rates also drifted up. Consequently, nominal and real interest-rate spreads tended to move in a direction that fostered a dollar depreciation.

The dollar's sharp depreciation against both the German mark and Japanese yen seems, for the most part, associated with the Plaza announcement and not with the subsequent intervention. The dollar opened lower in New York against both the mark and yen on that Monday compared with Friday, even before the United States intervened. (Of course, this depreciation—at least against the German mark—could have been a response to the German intervention, which was already underway.)

Between 23 September and 8 November 1985, the United States sold German marks on fourteen days, of which nine (64 percent) seemed successful according to our criteria (figure 6.8). The Bundesbank intervened on all but five days through 24 October 1985. Thereafter, its operations tapered off. Nine US interventions occurred on the same day as the Bundesbank sold dollars, and two-thirds of these were successful. Over this same time period, the United States sold Japanese yen on twenty days, of which twelve (60 percent) were successful (figure 6.9). The patterns depicted in figures 6.8 and 6.9 do not clearly suggest that the Plaza interventions drove the dollar lower.[25]

Humpage (1988), using simple regression techniques, found no systematic relationship between intervention and subsequent day-to-day exchange rate movements during the Plaza period. Feldstein (1986), using exchange-rate data at both a monthly and a weekly frequency, concluded that Plaza interventions essentially produced a one-time downward shift in key exchange-rates, but did not otherwise alter their trend movements.[26] Whereas intervention itself seems to have had no clearly discernible, persistent effects on exchange rates, monetary policies between the United States and Germany, and especially between the United States and Japan, changed in manners consistent with dollar depreciations. Subsequent policy validated the expectations that the Plaza Accord created, at least for a while.

The effects of the Plaza agreement began to wear off by early October because policy makers in the G5 countries were no longer reinforcing or substantiating expectations of additional policy initiatives to drive the dollar lower. The dollar actually appreciated 3 percent against the mark between 4 October and 16 October 1985. The market, which anticipated additional policy initiatives on the part of the G5 countries, began to lose confidence when the recent IMF and International Bank for Reconstruction and Development meetings focused on the international-debt situation rather than on macroeconomic convergence. Moreover, Bundesbank President Pöhl quickly expressed satisfaction with the extent of the dollar depreciation. According to Destler and Henning (1989, 50), Pöhl announced that the dollar had reached an acceptable level in a little more than two weeks after the Plaza declaration, when the dollar had depreciated only about 7 percent against the German mark. Funabashi (1988, 30–31) notes that the United States criticized Germany for not intervening more following the Plaza agreement. He maintains that in part, the Europeans saw the dollar chiefly overvalued against the yen. In addition, Funabashi notes that the EMS constrained German actions. If the Germans had undertaken much larger dollar sales, the mark risked appreciating within the EMS, since the Bundesbank could not quickly sterilize the intervention. In Germany's view, other European countries needed to sell more dollars in order to maintain the EMS (Funabashi 1988, 30–31).

This criticism of Pöhl's announcement may be justified, but nevertheless, the Bundesbank sold nearly as many dollars as the United States. Between 23 September 1985 and 8 November 1985, the Bundesbank sold approximately $1.2 billion, while the United States bought nearly $1.9 billion equivalent German marks. Moreover, by late October, Federal Reserve officials, like their German counterparts, were busy denying the existence of any agreement to encourage a dollar depreciation by manipulating international interest-rate spreads (*Bulletin*, February 1986, 111).

While the intervention may have had a signaling effect—causing market participants to anticipate further reductions in interest rates—Volcker suggests that, within the Federal Reserve, the dollar's depreciation dampened the FOMC's ardor for monetary ease. To be sure, monetary policy in the United States eased as growth slowed and inflation moderated. Many Federal Reserve banks were requesting a discount-rate reduction, which forecasted their intended policy stance at the next FOMC meeting. "But with the dollar already declining so sharply, the balance of the argument to me [Volcker] and most of my colleagues was the other way. Without clearer evidence that the expansion had petered out, easing money in the face of a rapid decline in the dollar seemed too much like pouring Federal Reserve oil on a fire already burning that I wanted to keep under control" (Volcker and Gyohten 1992, 247).

Overall during the Plaza episode (20 September to 8 November 1985) the dollar depreciated nearly 8 percent against the German mark and 14 percent against the Japanese yen. The dollar stood at 2.62 marks per dollar on 8 November 1985, not quite in the 2.54 to 2.56 range that Funabashi suggested was an implicit target. The dollar did, however, slide beyond the 214–218 yen per dollar implicit target that Funabashi mentioned, to 205.6 on 8 November 1985.

The slight variation between the Japanese yen and German mark might have resulted because the Japanese monetary authorities were not as quick as their West German counterparts to disavow their currency's appreciation. The dollar continued to depreciate against the Japanese yen through early November 1985. Officials at the Bank of Japan and at the Japanese

Finance Ministry had announced on 15 October additional policy changes to encourage a yen appreciation. Yen interest rates rose, especially short-term interest rates.

6.3.2   Between Plaza and Louvre

Throughout 1986, the dollar depreciated on balance in an orderly manner against all major currencies, particularly the Japanese yen. The overall dollar depreciation seemed consistent with the continuing worldwide trade imbalances and with general trends in interest-rate differentials. With the dollar now consistent with the perceived fundamentals, the United States saw no need to intervene. Between mid-November 1985 and the Louvre accord in February 1987, the United States intervened on only two occasions, and in very small amounts.[27]

Other key central banks, however, bought substantial amounts of dollars throughout 1986 and January 1987. As early as March 1986, the Japanese started to view the Plaza Accord as a mistake, because they believed that it kicked off a persistent yen appreciation, which continued through 1988. Japanese exporters, particularly small- to medium-sized firms, complained (Volcker and Gyohten 1992, 256).

United States Treasury Secretary Baker, who had been trying to get Germany and Japan to stimulate their economies, wanted the G5 to undertake coordinated interest-rate cuts in part to offset the global effects of a projected slowing in US real economic growth, in part to help developing countries with their debt problems, and in part to alleviate global current-account imbalances. The G7 ministers and central-bank governors began meeting regularly to promote policy coordination, specifically a convergence among their monetary policies. Baker threatened that if the G7 did not participate, unilaterally lower US interest rates would cause further dollar depreciation. Volcker, who continued to worry about a hard-landing scenario for the dollar, was not in favor of unilateral interest-rate cuts, particularly when dictated by the US Treasury. The Reagan appointees on the Board of Governors, however, advocated monetary ease.

Volcker had already discussed the need for coordinated interest-rate cuts with the Bank of Japan and with the Bundesbank, but to no avail. On 24 February 1986, the Federal Reserve Board voted four to three to cut the discount rate over Volcker's objection. After Volcker threatened ViceChairman Preston Martin and Governor Wayne Angell with his resignation, the board agreed to wait. Volcker and Pöhl subsequently agreed to undertake coordinated rate cuts in March after the Bundesbank's next policy meeting. On 6 and 7 March 1986, Germany, France, Japan, and the United States cut rates in concert (see figure 6.10). Vice-Chairman Preston Martin resigned on 31 March 1986. On 21 April 1986, the board undertook another rate cut that was coordinated with the Bank of Japan.[28]

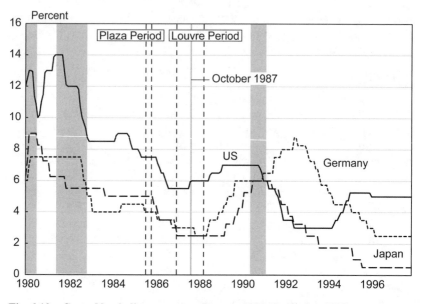

Fig. 6.10   Central bank discount rates, January 1980–December 1997

Notes: Shaded bars are US recessions. Data are from the International Monetary Fund and National Bureau of Economic Research.

The Federal Reserve undertook two unilateral discount rate cuts on 11 July 1986 and 21 August 1986 and may have been trying to encourage Germany and Japan to take further steps to stimulate their economies. According to Funabashi (1988, 53), when Volcker pressed, "Pöhl responded that he and his colleagues would consider a rate cut, but only with the stipulation that Baker announce publicly after the next G5 meeting that the United States was prepared to stabilize the dollar. Volcker promised to discuss the proposal with Baker." Baker, however, rejected the idea.

With Germany and Japan now concerned about further dollar depreciation, Baker continued with his strategy of trying to persuade countries to adopt expansionary policies under the threat of a dollar depreciation. At the Tokyo Summit in May 1986, the G7 avoided discussion of exchange rates, but agreed with a US proposal for adopting a wide array of economic indicators and quantitative objectives by which to judge countries' economic performances.

In September 1986, Baker met secretly with Japanese Finance Minister Kiichi Miyazawa in San Francisco. The United States reaffirmed its commitment to the Gramm-Rudman-Hollings Deficit Reduction Act, and the Japanese agreed to an expansionary supplemental fiscal package. Both countries claimed that the dollar was consistent with fundamentals—after allowances for these fiscal proposals—and agreed to stabilize the dollar. By the time that the deal was announced in October 1986, however, the yen had depreciated sharply, albeit temporarily, and US officials suspected that the Japanese had deliberately engineered the depreciation to take advantage of the agreement (Frankel 1994, 306).

6.3.3   Louvre Period, 1987

By early 1987, the dollar had reversed nearly all of the real and nominal appreciation that it had experienced between 1981 and 1985, but global trade imbalances had not yet shown any improvement and remained a contentious political issue. The US current-account deficit remained around 3 1/2 percent of GDP; the net international investment position had now become negative, and both Germany and Japan continued to post substantial current-account surpluses. Private foreign investors seemed increasingly reluctant to acquire dollar-denominated assets. The dollar continued to depreciate, but at a more modest pace, and interest-rate spreads widened to attract private financial flows. Germany and Japan became even more reluctant to stimulate their economies since both were concerned about money growth and inflationary pressures. At the same time, neither wanted to encourage a further dollar depreciation. Many believed that a pause in exchange-rate realignments was needed to allow the recent adjustments to feed through and to prevent an overshoot on the downside (Dobson 1991, 61).

In January 1987, the dollar came under heavy selling pressure that contributed to a realignment of central rates within the European monetary system. Despite the problems in the EMS, much of the dollar's movement in January occurred relative to the Japanese yen, and it prompted heavy Japanese intervention (*Bulletin*, May 1987, 333). On 28 January, the United States intervened in an uncertain market, selling a small amount ($50 million equivalent) of yen (*Bulletin*, May 1987, 333). The intervention followed statements reaffirming cooperation among the major central banks. A 1.2 percent appreciation of the dollar relative to the yen followed, and the yen-dollar rate remained relatively stable through mid-March.

The dollar seemed to stabilize in February following the release of more favorable trade data in late January 1987. At the 22 February 1987, Louvre meeting of the G6—the G5 plus Canada (Italy abstained)—the United States pledged to stabilize the dollar in return for a Japanese and German commitment to additional economic stimulus. Japan agreed to cut its discount rate and to submit a supplemental budget to stimulate domestic demand, and Germany agreed to increase planned 1988 tax cuts. For its part, the United States also reiterated its Gramm-Rudman-Hollings targets for deficit reduction (Destler and Henning 1989, 60). With respect to exchange rates, the Louvre communiqué (paragraph 10) stated that:

the substantial exchange rate changes since the Plaza Agreement will increasingly contribute to reducing external imbalances and have now brought their [the G6 countries'] currencies within ranges broadly consistent with underlying economic fundamentals . . . . Further substantial exchange rate shifts among their currencies could damage growth and adjustment prospects in their countries. In current circumstances, therefore, they agreed to cooperate closely to foster stability of exchange rates around current levels.[29]

Funabashi (1988, 185–87) claims that the G6 agreed to secret targets for the mark-dollar and yen-dollar exchange rates at their Louvre meeting.[30] His narrative, however, is not clear about how seriously the delegates actually took any targets. They were not widely favored, and any obligation seemed vague and open to interpretation.[31] Indeed, Treasury Secretary Baker said on 23 March 1987 that the G6 did not set target zones for dollar exchange rates. We can find no statement of the targets in published Federal Reserve documents, but Volcker and Gyohten (1992) contend that target ranges had been discussed within the US Treasury for some time prior to the Louvre. According to Funabashi (1988, 186):

> In the final hour of the Louvre dinner, de Larosiére and Darman worked together to give final shape to a joint proposal. Two specified midpoint rates were agreed: 1.8250 deutsche marks to the dollar and 153.50 yen to the dollar; plus or minus 2.5 percent was determined as a first line of defense for mutual intervention on a voluntary basis, while at 5 percent consultation on policy adjustment was to be obligatory; between these limits of 2.5 percent to 5 percent, intervention efforts were expected to intensify. All the agreements were to be kept strictly confidential and were provisional until the Washington G-5 meeting in April.

The French seemed to favor target zones, and the US Treasury was receptive to the idea, but the Germans and the British did not want target ranges (Funabashi 1988, 183–86).

The 2.5 percent range for the yen was 149.75 to 157.33 and the 5 percent range was 146.19 to 161.7. The 2.5 percent range for the German mark was 1.7804 to 1.8706, and the 5 percent range for the German mark was 1.73809 to 1.9262. The targets suggested that mandatory intervention against the Japanese yen would take place when the dollar depreciated below 146.19 or appreciated above 161.17, but official sales of yen might start as early as 149.75, and official purchases of yen might start at a rate of 157.33. The Japanese, however, did not want the yen-dollar rate to fall below 150. Similarly, mandatory intervention against German marks would take place when the dollar depreciated below 1.7389 or appreciated beyond 1.9262, but official sales of marks might start as early as 1.7804, and official purchases of marks might start at 1.8706.

The United States, Germany, Japan, and other key central banks did not immediately intervene following the Louvre communiqué. On 11 March 1987, as the dollar rose above 1.8600 marks, the United States bought

$30 million equivalent German marks, but would not intervene again against marks until late April (see figure 6.11). The dollar continued to appreciate on 11 March, suggesting that the intervention had not been successful, but the dollar began a sustained depreciation on the next day. Less than two weeks later, however, the United States began to intervene frequently and very heavily in Japanese yen as heightened trade tensions with Japan sent the dollar below 150 yen (see figure 6.12). The desk sold roughly $3.0 billion worth of Japanese yen on 11 consecutive days between 23 March and 6 April 1987, often in concert with the Bank of Japan (*Bulletin*, July 1987, 552–53). The FOMC subcommittee on foreign exchange allowed the desk to exceed daily intervention limits on yen (*Desk Report* 1988, 7). On 6 April, according to Funabashi (1988, 6), the G6 rebased the yen. They set a new central rate of 146, a 2.5 percent range of 142.43 to 149.65 and a 5 percent range of 139.04 to 153.30. Then, through the end of April 1987, the desk sold an additional $1.0 billion worth of yen, often in concert with the Bank of Japan and several European banks (*Bulletin*, July 1987, 555). The Bundesbank, however, did not participate in these interventions. The operations had little obvious effect on exchange rates (see figure 6.12).

Baker was upset with the Germans for not acting in concert. The Bundesbank did not intervene until late in April because it "feared that massive interventions to prop up the dollar would swell West Germany's currency reserves and create excessive liquidity" (Funabashi 1988, 191). In 1979, the Bundesbank—like the Federal Reserve—had begun to pursue a goal of price stability, and it had adopted monetary targets to improve the credibility of its commitment. The Bundesbank overshot its monetary targets in 1986, and it would do so again in 1987 and 1988, in part because of attempts to resist an appreciation of the mark (Hetzel 2002, 50–51; Kole and Meade 1995, 917–31). Because of these persistent monetary overshoots, the Bundesbank was unenthusiastic about any policy coordination, or intervention that ascribed to Germany an expansionary obligation.

Neumann and von Hagen (1991) show that the German Bundesbank has often permitted deviations between actual money growth and targeted money growth because of exchange-rate considerations. Von Hagen (1989) also argues that when the market was strong against both the dollar and the exchange rate mechanism (ERM) currencies, the Bundesbank did not permanently sterilize its interventions.[32]

The situation was similar for Japan. Hutchison (1984) indicates that the Bank of Japan factored an exchange-rate objective into its monetary-policy decisions between 1978 and 1985, and Takagi (1991) claimed that after late 1985, the Bank of Japan allowed intervention to affect its monetary base.

In late April and early May 1987, US interest rates continued to firm, and "market participants became impressed by the Federal Reserve's willingness to adjust monetary policy to support the dollar, as well as by the complementary policy adjustments taken in other countries. Market observers particu-

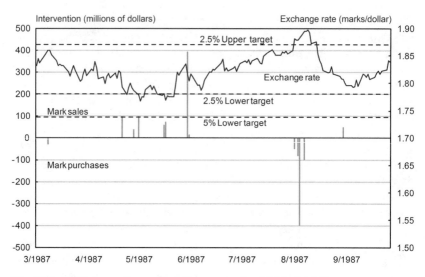

**Fig. 6.11   US intervention against German marks, 1 March 1987–
30 September 1987**

Note: Data are from the Federal Reserve.

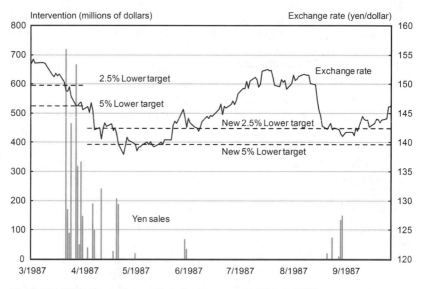

**Fig. 6.12   US intervention against Japanese yen, 1 March 1987–
30 September 1987**

Note: Data are from the Federal Reserve.

larly noted comments made in late April by Chairman Volcker that the Federal Reserve had adjusted monetary policy—'snugged up' interest rates—to counter exchange-market pressures as well as comments by Japanese Prime Minister Nakasone that the Bank of Japan would ease short-term interest rates" (*Desk Report* 1988, 9–10). The German Bundesbank also seemed to cooperate in the efforts to stabilize the exchange rate by reducing the rates at which it provided liquidity to its banking system. Interest-rate differentials vis-à-vis German mark and Japanese yen denominated assets stood at their widest point since the dollar's peak and began to attract funds into dollars (*Desk Report* 1988, 10). An improvement in US net exports and tensions in the Middle East also buoyed the dollar. As the dollar rose above 1.89 marks, the desk began to buy German marks.

By May 1987, however, the FOMC began to question the appropriateness of heavy intervention (FOMC *Transcripts*, 19 May 1987, 3–5). Intervention continued very intermittently throughout May and June, with the United States selling a relatively small $123 million equivalent yen and relatively moderate $680 million equivalent German marks, often in concert with other central banks (*Bulletin*, October 1987, 780–81).

The dollar continued to firm until early August. Then, the dollar rose above 1.85 marks, prompting the United States to intervene again against marks. Between 4 and 10 August 1987, the desk bought $631 million worth of marks to resist the appreciation of the dollar (see figure 6.11). The Bundesbank sold $227 million and other G6 monetary authorities participated as well (*Bulletin*, January 1988, 14–15). These interventions had no net effect; on 10 August 1987 the exchange rate was 1.8953 marks per dollar compared with 1.8817 on 4 August 1987.

By 11 August, following the release of poor trade numbers, the dollar turned about and began to depreciate, especially against the Japanese yen. Between 24 August 1987 and 2 September 1987, the desk sold $390 million equivalent yen in concert with the Japanese Ministry of Finance (*Bulletin*, January 1988, 14–15). Between 28 August 1987 and 18 September 1987, the Bundesbank bought $414 million; other central banks intervened to support the dollar (*Bulletin*, January 1988, 15). On 2 September 1987, the desk sold $50 million against German marks. Despite the interventions, the dollar continued to depreciate. On 4 September, the Federal Reserve increased the discount rate to deal with mounting inflationary pressures. Interest rates in the United States subsequently began to rise.

Although US monetary authorities sometimes bought foreign exchange, the Louvre operations consisted mostly of sales of foreign exchange in an attempt to support the dollar. The Federal Reserve System financed most of the German mark operations during the Louvre period, while the Treasury financed most of the Japanese yen intervention. The operations failed to keep the targeted dollar exchange rates within the envisioned ranges.

The perception of international cooperation started to erode in mid-October 1987. Market participants believed that the Bank of Japan, and particularly the Bundesbank might raise policy rates and adopt less accommodative monetary policies. Money growth in both countries exceeded targets and contributed to concerns over mounting inflation. Interest rates rose in Germany and Japan, although interest-rate differentials continued to support dollar assets (*Desk Report* 1988, 14).

In September and early October 1987, Secretary of the Treasury Baker publicly criticized foreign interest rate increases as not being in compliance with the Louvre accord. He reportedly threatened Germany with a still weaker dollar, although the administration later denied the reports (*New York Times* 16 October 1987, A1). He also suggested that US interest rates would not follow German interest rates higher.

On 19 October 1987, the stock market crashed and the Federal Reserve provided sufficient liquidity to the market to lower interest rates. The dollar depreciated sharply against both the German mark and Japanese yen. Baker then met with German Finance Minister Stoltenberg to set aside recent criticisms and to reaffirm their Louvre commitments. They agreed to renewed cooperation on monetary policies and on stabilizing dollar exchange rates. German interest rates subsequently moved substantially lower. By 27 October 1987, the United States began selling German marks and Japanese yen to stem the dollar's depreciation (see figures 6.13 and 6.14). Between 27 October 1987 and 11 November 1987, the desk sold $1.1 billion equivalent German marks and $443 million equivalent Japanese yen. Over roughly the same days, the Bundesbank bought $1.4 billion. The Bank of Japan and other central banks also bought dollars in concert with US authorities (*Bulletin*, January 1988, 17). The Bundesbank subsequently cut its key policy rates.

Following the stock-market crash, as concerns about a possible recession grew, public support for exchange-rate stabilization efforts began to wane. "Widespread press commentary questioned the priority for the United States of stabilizing exchange rates in view of concerns about the possible impact of the stock market decline on US economic activity." (*Desk Report* 1988, 16) Likewise, "on December 22 [1987] when the Group of Seven nations issued a statement reaffirming economic policy coordination and stating that a further decline of the dollar could be counterproductive, market participants remained unconvinced that decisive action would be taken to halt the dollar's decline" (*Desk Report* 1988, 18). The market seemed to understand that intervening to support the dollar was inconsistent with the need for monetary ease in the United States.

The dollar continued to depreciate and the desk continued operations to support the dollar. Between 27 November 1987 and 21 January 1988, the desk sold $1.7 billion worth of marks and $1.4 billion equivalent yen often in concert with other central banks (*Bulletin*, April 1988, 209–11).

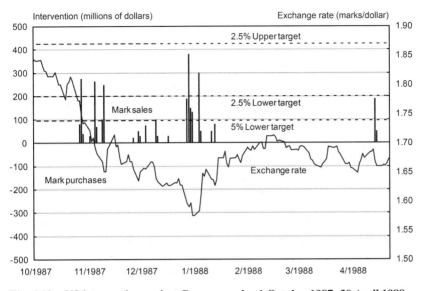

Fig. 6.13   US intervention against German marks, 1 October 1987–30 April 1988
Note: Data are from the Federal Reserve.

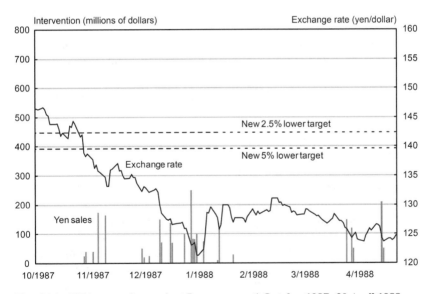

Fig. 6.14   US intervention against Japanese yen, 1 October 1987–30 April 1988
Note: Data are from the Federal Reserve.

The Bundesbank, for example, bought $1.7 billion. As Volcker (Volcker and Gyohten 1992, 269) recalled:

> The [December 1987 G7 communiqué] marked the end of a somewhat confused three-year process, the results of which were not very satisfactory, at least at the time, because all our efforts in aligning exchange rates and coordinating macroeconomic policy had failed to produce tangible, clear results. The external imbalance among major countries—especially the Japanese trade surplus and the American deficit, the two-sided political irritant that has started the whole exercise—did not improve despite the major changes in exchange rate relationships.

6.3.4   Why Policy Coordination Fails

By the late 1980s, many economists seemed to share Volcker's observations about the recent failures of macroeconomic-policy coordination. Myriad empirical papers appeared and concluded that the gains from the types of policies that Treasury Secretaries Baker and Brady had been pursuing within the G5 and G7 were small and asymmetrically distributed, with the United States often benefiting least (Humpage 1990; Hamada and Kawai 1997; McKibbin 1997). These studies showed that the theoretical gleam of ongoing macroeconomic policy coordination tarnished quickly when exposed to empirical verification.

In a world where markets are closely integrated, the policy actions of any one nation, particularly those of a large developed country, are certain to affect the well-being of other nations. Sometimes these policy spillovers are positive; sometimes they are negative. The existence of such policy interdependencies offers a theoretical justification for macroeconomic policy coordination.

Countries understand these external policy effects, but they evaluate them unevenly. They consider the implications of foreign-policy actions on their own economic well-being, and they set their own policy instruments after taking foreign policies into account. When all countries react in this way to the actions of others, they achieve a Nash equilibrium. Still, better outcomes are conceivably possible, if each country also considers the direct implications of its own policies for the economic welfare of the other countries. Ideally, coordination forces such a consideration and achieves a better outcome.

In most theoretical applications, however, the welfare improving effect of coordination is fragile. Countries often have strong incentives to renege on the coordinated policy once they believe that other countries have adopted it. Consequently, the world tends to gravitate back to the Nash equilibrium of each country only reacting to the actions of every other country. Absent some sort of strict enforcement mechanism, macroeconomic policy coordination may not be sustainable, even in theory.

The emerging empirical studies went beyond this theoretical fragility and suggested at least three conditions under which macroeconomic policy coordination could be welfare reducing: First, for macroeconomic policy coordination to enhance welfare relative to noncooperative policies, policymakers—even different policymakers within a single country—must have similar preferences for such economic goals as price stability, real economic growth (or full employment), exchange-rate volatility, and current-account positions. If fiscal policymakers coordinate across countries on economic growth, but monetary policymakers have different objectives (e.g., a primacy of price stability) and do not coordinate with their fiscal counterparts, the outcome need not be Pareto superior to the noncooperative outcome. Second, macroeconomic policy coordination requires that policymakers coordinate under the true economic model. Coordinating macroeconomic policies internationally under an incorrect model may leave nations worse off relative to no coordination (Frankel and Rockett 1988; Holthan and Hallet 1987; Ghosh and Masson 1988). The gains to a single country from discovering the true economic model and moving to it are often greater than any gains from policy coordination. To be sure, this information problem occurs in a purely autarkic setting, but then policy multipliers under both the true and false model typically differ only by degree. In large, open-economy models, multipliers often differ in terms of sign, hence coordinating under the wrong model can be destructive. Third—and most important—macroeconomic policy coordination can affect government credibility relative to the private sector with important implications for welfare. Rogoff (1985) constructs an example in which coordination eliminates the exchange rate as a constraint on fiscal authorities' inflation bias, thereby adversely affecting inflation expectations.

By the late 1980s, concerns similar to those expressed in this literature began to influence many FOMC participants. International macroeconomic policy coordination, like foreign-exchange operations, fell primarily under the auspices of the US Treasury. At a minimum, efforts to coordinate macroeconomic policies could give the impression of administration pressure on US monetary policy. As such, policy coordination could weaken the credibility of monetary policy and increase the difficulty of achieving price stability.

6.3.5   An Analysis of the Plaza and Louvre Interventions

Many analysts seem to regard both the Plaza and the Louvre operations as clear examples of successful macroeconomic coordination and sterilized intervention, but our narrative and statistical evidence are much less supportive. At most, we find some evidence that official US sales of German marks moderated dollar depreciations against the mark, but we find no support for the view that intervention influences exchange rates in a manner that might force the dollar lower, as under the Plaza Accord, or maintain target zones, as under the Louvre accord.

As suggested throughout our previous narrative, most of the movements in exchange rates over the Plaza and Louvre period seem attributable to policy changes, not intervention. On this point, Obstfeld (1990, 199) seems to agree:

> The conclusion reached is that monetary and fiscal policies, and not intervention per se, have been the main policy determinants of exchange rates in recent years [1985–88]. Pure intervention seems to have played an effective signaling role, in the sense of speeding desired exchange rate movements or impeding undesired ones, when promptly backed up by other, more substantive policy adjustments. But the portfolio effects of pure intervention have generally been elusive enough that interventions cannot be regarded as a macroeconomic policy tool in their own right, with an impact somehow independent of short-term decision on monetary and fiscal policy.

By the mid-1980s, as Obstfeld's comment suggests, academic explanations for how intervention might affect exchange rates largely relied on a narrow signaling channel, which held that interventions signaled unanticipated changes in future monetary policy to the market.[33] The Jurgensen Report, after all, concluded that sterilized intervention was largely ineffective if not accompanied by supporting monetary-policy changes. Empirical studies undertaken in the late 1980s and early 1990s, however, offered little evidence that interventions signaled monetary-policy changes.[34] Soon a broader interpretation of an expectations channel would emerge and would, henceforth, guide most empirical work. According to this view, if central banks had better information about fundamentals in general, they might still affect exchange rates through their intervention (see chapter 1; Baillie, Humpage, and Osterberg 2000; Humpage 1991).

Our empirical evidence, however, suggests that US interventions between 1 April 1985 and 29 April 1988, a period that encompasses both the Plaza and Louvre accords, had very limited effects on expectations. Over this time period, the United States sold German marks on thirty-three days and bought German marks on nineteen days (see table 6.3). Only eleven of the mark sales were associated with a same-day dollar appreciation and only eight of the mark purchases were associated with a same-day dollar depreciation. Given the variable nature of day-to-day exchange-rate changes, however, we expect that fourteen of the mark sales and ten of the mark purchases will be associated with dollar appreciations or depreciations purely by chance. Because the observed number of such successes is within one standard deviation of the expected number, the outcome seems random. (The empirical appendix explains our analytical technique.)

Likewise over this same period, the United States sold Japanese yen on fifty-two days and bought Japanese yen on twenty days. Only twenty-five of the Japanese yen sales and ten of the yen purchases were associated with a same-day dollar appreciation or depreciation against the yen. Although the twenty-five successes out of fifty-two yen sales is two more than we would

Table 6.3   **Success counts for US intervention, 1 April 1985 to 29 April 1988**

German marks	Total (#)	Intervention successes (#)	(%)	Expected[a] successes (#)	Standard[a] deviation (#)
Mark sales & dollar appreciation	33	11	33.3	14	2
Mark purchases & dollar depreciation	19	8	42.1	10	2
Total	52	19	36.5		
Mark sales & smaller dollar depreciation	33	11	33.3	5	1
Mark purchases & smaller dollar appreciation	19	4	21.1	2	1
Total	52	15	28.8		
Mark sales & dollar appreciation or smaller depreciation	33	22	66.7	20	4
Mark purchases & dollar depreciation or small appreciation	19	12	63.2	12	3
Total	52	34	65.4		
Japanese yen					
Yen sales & dollar appreciation	52	25	48.1	23	3
Yen purchases & dollar depreciation	20	10	50.0	10	2
Total	72	35	48.6		
Yen sales & smaller dollar depreciation	52	10	19.2	7	1
Yen purchases & smaller dollar appreciation	20	2	10.0	2	0
Total	72	12	16.7		
Yen sales & dollar appreciation or smaller depreciation	52	35	67.3	30	4
Yen purchases & dollar depreciation or small appreciation	20	12	60.0	12	3
Total	72	47	65.3		

Note: See appendix 2 for detail.
[a] Assumes that the success count is a hypergeometric random variable.

anticipate, the count still falls within one standard deviation of the expected number of successes and, therefore, seems no better than random. Likewise, the ten successful purchases of Japanese yen appear no greater than the number we would randomly anticipate.

Still, intervention had some limited exchange-rate effects: Eleven of the thirty-three US sales of German marks were associated with a smaller dollar depreciation against the mark on the day of the intervention than occurred on the previous day. This count exceeds the expected number of successes by more than two standard deviations, suggesting that the outcome is not a random event. A similar outcome is evident for US purchases of German marks. The four successes exceed the expected number by more than two standard deviations.

The results for intervention against Japanese yen are weaker than those for the German mark. Ten of the fifty-two US sales of Japanese yen were associated with smaller dollar depreciations on days of intervention as compared with the previous day. While greater than the expected number of successes, ten is still one shy of two standard deviations greater. Two of the twenty US purchases of yen were associated with a smaller same-day dollar appreciation relative to the previous day. Two is equal to the number of successes that we would randomly anticipate given the volatile nature of daily exchange-rate movements.

Altogether, approximately 65 percent of the US interventions against either of these currencies appeared successful under one or the other of our success criteria. The observed overall success counts—both criteria combined—were never more than two standard deviations above the expected number of successes, suggesting that the Plaza and Louvre periods did not offer strong support for an active approach to intervention.

6.4   The End of the Activist Agenda, 1988–1995

Ever since the Federal Reserve System began intervening in the foreign-exchange market, FOMC participants had frequently questioned the effectiveness of the transactions, the appropriateness of the Federal Reserve's involvement with the US Treasury, and the operation's potential for raising congressional ire. After the 1987 stock-market collapse, these questions arose anew, but now they took on a new distinctive tone: FOMC participants criticized intervention because they worried that the operations interfered with the credibility of the Federal Reserve's commitment to price stability.

By the late 1980s, the FOMC was trying to consolidate gains from its prolonged fight against inflation. Discussions of monetary policy focused on building credibility and included such issues as rules versus discretion, central-bank independence, and inflation targeting. Many FOMC participants felt that in the absence of a legislated numerical mandate for price stability, anything that even suggested behavior inconsistent with that goal could damage the central bank's integrity. Intervention was just such a thing and attitudes soon reached a tipping point.

Three aspects of US intervention operations conflicted with FOMC's drive for credibility. First, although legally independent, the Federal Reserve System had little choice but to participate with the US Treasury in major foreign-exchange operations. This connection proved especially challenging to the Federal Reserve's credibility when the Treasury decided exchange-rate policies within G5 or G7 forums and commented on monetary policy. Consequently, intervention gave the fiscal authority leverage over an independent Federal Reserve and weakened the FOMC'S commitment to price stability. Second, FOMC participants—recalling the Jurgensen Report—feared that if markets interpreted sterilized intervention as a signal of future monetary-policy changes, intervention would create uncertainty about the Federal Reserve's commitment to price stability.[35] The dollar often appreciated when the FOMC tightened. Consequently, the desk could find itself buying foreign exchange, ostensibly adding reserves to the banking system, while at the same time it drained reserves through open-market operations in pursuit of price stability. A third argument against intervention noted that operations to offset dollar appreciations and warehousing with the US Treasury left the Federal Reserve holding foreign-currency assets on its books. Losses on the foreign-exchange portfolio could lead Congress to accuse the central bank of mismanagement or, in the case of warehousing, of interfering with the appropriations process. Such criticisms could lead to policies that might impinge on the Federal Reserve's independence.

6.4.1   Stock-Market Collapse

Frictions between US monetary policy and foreign-exchange intervention first heated up within the FOMC shortly after the 19 October 1987 stock-market crash. On the following day, the Federal Reserve provided liquidity to the market and moved quickly to lower the federal-funds-rate target by 50 basis points to 7 percent (see figure 6.3). Over the next few weeks, the Federal Reserve used high-profile techniques to inject liquidity into the banking system (Carlson 2006). As interest rates in the United States fell faster than rates abroad, the dollar dropped below 1.76 marks and 141 yen, prompting heavy concerted intervention to support the dollar, which we previously explained.

Although the desk automatically sterilized interventions that were incompatible with its federal-funds-rate target, its sales of foreign exchange after the stock-market collapse seemed inconsistent with the FOMC's efforts to inject liquidity into the banking system. At the 3 November 1987 FOMC meeting, Robert Forrestal, President of the Federal Reserve Bank of Atlanta, and not a vociferous opponent of intervention, noted the incompatibility of the desk's operations: "I find it a little anomalous that we are draining reserves to defend the dollar while, at the same time, we are adding reserves to add liquidity to the domestic economy" (FOMC *Transcripts*, 3 November 1987, 2).

The discussions that followed suggested that many FOMC participants wanted to focus on price stability and to ease out of frequent foreign-exchange interventions, but Sam Cross, an advocate of an activist approach, argued that the Federal Reserve had no choice but to intervene at the Treasury's behest. Although the Federal Reserve had independent authority for intervention, it was obliged to cooperate with the Treasury on international financial matters, according to Cross. He described a failure to do so as a major event, one requiring prior consultation with Congress. Barring congressional approval, Cross claimed, the Federal Reserve's only option was to attempt to influence the Treasury's decisions about intervention from a cooperative and accommodating position (FOMC *Transcripts*, 3 November 1987, 6). Cross seemed to echo Chairman Martin's interpretation of Federal Reserve independence: The Federal Reserve is independent within—not of—government. This view, however, appeared inconsistent with price stability to many on the committee.

To be sure, the conflict between monetary policy and intervention from late October 1987 through mid-January 1988 did not seriously jeopardize the FOMC's commitment to price stability. The Federal Reserve eased policy to avoid a financial crisis. The federal-funds-rate target declined, but the real federal funds rate remained little changed (see figures 6.3 and 6.4). The desk's intervention sales of German marks and Japanese yen were at least consistent with the FOMC's longer-term inflation fight.

During early 1988, intervention and monetary policy became compatible (see figure 6.15). The US economy proved more resilient than many thought at the time of the stock-market crash, allowing the FOMC to renew an anti-inflation policy thrust by March 1988. The desk sold moderate amounts of Japanese yen and German marks in brief interventions in late March and mid-April 1988. So the desk's foreign operations appeared broadly consistent with its domestic objective of draining reserves.

In late June 1988, however, the situation changed. The FOMC remained concerned about prospective inflation and raised the federal funds rate. The dollar began to appreciate sharply, especially relative to the German mark. To moderate the dollar's rise, the United States began a series of very large, very persistent purchases of German marks. In all, between 27 June and 26 September 1988, the Desk bought $5.1 billion equivalent German marks, a massive amount (see figure 6.16). The Bundesbank sold $8.8 billion and increased its policy rates.

Initially, FOMC participants attributed the dollar's appreciation largely to temporary speculative activity, implying that the intervention would be limited and not prejudicial to the committee's inflation fight (FOMC *Transcripts*, 29 & 30 June 1988, 1–7). As official purchases of marks persisted, however, the FOMC discarded this view, and its tone began to change. At the 16 August 1988 FOMC meeting, Vice-Chairman Corrigan unwittingly initiated a renewed debate about intervention when he applauded the recent interventions for curtailing the dollar's rise. This was an argument that he could not empirically substantiate.[36] Corrigan argued that the nature of the foreign-exchange market had changed over the last few years. The volume of trading had grown enormously, and program trading strategies increased the likelihood of one-way markets and of overshooting. He argued that

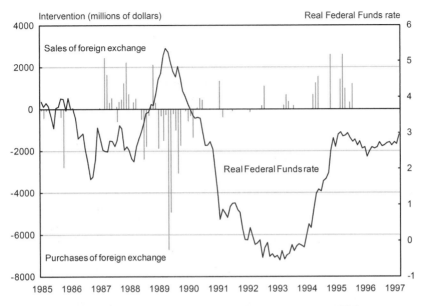

Fig. 6.15 US intervention and the real federal funds rate, January 1985–March 1997

Notes: US intervention is the sum of transactions against German marks and Japanese yen. The real federal funds rate equals the effective federal funds rate minus the percentage change in the core CPI over the past twelve months. Data are from the Federal Reserve and Bureau of Labor Statistics.

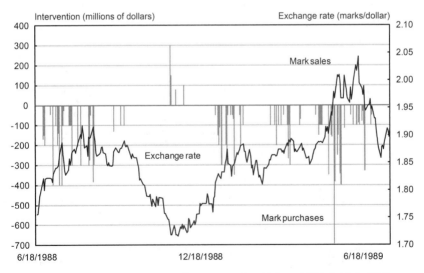

Fig. 6.16 US intervention against German marks, 18 June 1988–20 July 1989

Note: Data are from the Federal Reserve.

intervention "does play a useful role in reaffirming the fact that there are two-way markets" (FOMC *Transcripts*, 16 August 1988, 2).

Other FOMC members, notably Governors Wayne Angell, Robert Heller, Manuel Johnson, and Federal Reserve Bank of Cleveland President Lee Hoskins, argued that markets generally functioned well. Governor Heller, for example, agreed that a large intervention hitting a one-way market potentially could have an effect, but he worried that such an intervention created uncertainty, which could reduce the incentives for taking positions and could actually raise volatility (FOMC *Transcripts*, 16 August 1988, 3).[37] President Hoskins questioned what a one-way market really was, other than a sustained bidding up of the price. Why was this necessarily evidence of a market failure? Hoskins allowed that markets might occasionally be disorderly, as in a panic or crash, but these were very infrequent events, and intervention should be equally infrequent. A disorderly market argument in no way justified intervention at the frequency he had recently observed (FOMC *Transcripts*, 16 August 1988, 4). Governor Johnson, echoing to some extent Governor Angell, argued that intervention interfered with monetary policy: "When we are doing consistent interventions and it's working in the other direction from our open market operations, it does run the risk . . . of confusing the federal funds market as to what our reserve needs may be. . . . Maybe we want the two-way risk on the foreign exchange market, but we don't want this uncertainty in the open market operations" (FOMC *Transcripts*, 16 August 1988, 5).

The United States continued to buy German marks through September 1988, but shortly thereafter the dollar depreciated. From 31 October 1988 through 2 December 1988, the desk shifted operations and sold nearly $2.0 billion worth of Japanese yen and $0.6 billion worth of German marks (figures 6.16 and 6.17). At the 1 November 1988 FOMC meeting, President Hoskins pointed out that intervening over a fairly short period of time on both sides of the market suggested that the desk knew the "right" exchange rate, which seemed unlikely. This, of course, was not a new criticism, but emblematic of the changing views among many FOMC participants. Hoskins continued: "by doing this I think we continue to confuse the public as to what our [monetary] policy is all about and divert attention from our long-term objective of stable prices. And secondly, I think we run the risk of confusing ourselves as to our abilities to influence exchange rates in an appropriate fashion" (FOMC *Transcripts*, 1 November 1988, 13). Indicative of changing attitudes, Hoskins worried first of all that intervention interfered with monetary policy; his secondary concern was about its effectiveness.

During the first half of 1989, the dollar once again appreciated, and the United States undertook an unprecedented amount of intervention—so much so, that the desk had to request two intermeeting increases in its limits on intervention (FOMC *Transcripts*, July 1989, appendix 5, 3). The autho-

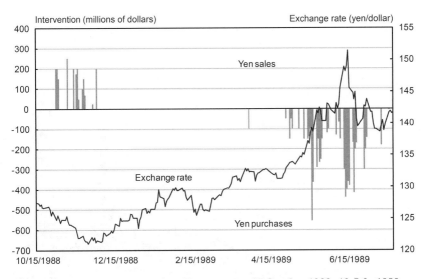

Fig. 6.17   US intervention against Japanese yen, 15 October 1988–19 July 1989
Note: Data are from the Federal Reserve.

rizations for the net-open position increased from $12 billion to $18 billion. The desk bought $8.5 billion worth of German marks and nearly $7.2 billion worth of Japanese yen during the first half of the year. Germany, which had been selling dollars since mid-December 1988, sold $7.2 billion. The US operations against both German marks and Japanese yen were split equally between the Federal Reserve's and the Treasury's accounts, but the Federal Reserve warehoused $3.0 billion worth of German marks for the Treasury's exchange stabilization fund in June 1989, thereby helping to finance its interventions. By September 1989, the authorization for warehousing had reached $10 billion. It would soon climb higher (see figure 6.18).

The real federal funds rate remained high during this time, suggesting that the FOMC kept a relatively tight monetary-policy stance. Consequently these huge Treasury directed intervention purchases of foreign exchange once again appeared inconsistent with the design of monetary policy. The operations also flew in the face of the Jurgensen Report's conclusions, which found that if domestic policies were incompatible with exchange-rate objectives, sterilized intervention was, at best, useless.

Support for the Federal Reserve's involvement with the Treasury in intervention was now clearly evaporating. At the 5–6 July 1989 FOMC meeting, those members opposed to foreign-exchange operations raised serious questions—some old, some new—about the operations. President Hoskins, for example, questioned Congress's reaction to warehousing. This was an old question. Edwin Truman, director of the board's international division, indicated that Congress had not questioned the operation, and he suggested that

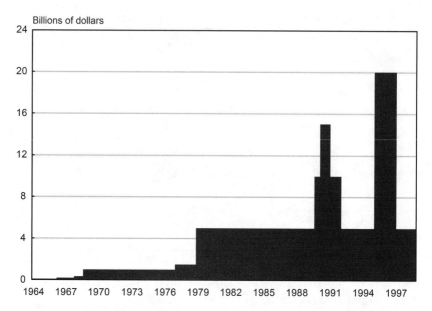

Fig. 6.18   FOMC authorizations for warehousing, January 1964–December 1998
Note: Data are from the Federal Reserve.

Congress *implicitly* approved warehousing in the late 1960s when it allowed the ESF to monetize SDRs with the Federal Reserve. Cross also noted that Congress allowed the ESF to monetize gold flows, and suggested that warehousing foreign exchange is a modern day equivalent (FOMC *Transcripts,* 5–6 July 1989, 2). Yet, Congress *explicitly* authorized the monetization of gold and SDRs; Hoskins's point was that Congress had never *explicitly* authorized warehousing. Chairman Greenspan then suggested that warehousing might be a good thing for the central bank, since it allowed the Treasury to maintain their half of the now traditional 50/50 split on intervention (FOMC *Transcripts,* 5–6 July 1989, 2). He did not seem to appreciate that warehousing effectively left the Federal Reserve financing more than a 50 percent share, at least while the swap loan was on the central bank's books.

Cross went on to say that the recent US interventions—as well as German and Japanese operations—had largely been discrete, undertaken through a commercial bank that acted as the desk's agent.[38] He claimed that "operating visibly was not really working very effectively," and that the discrete operations had been more effective.[39] He went on to explain that when traders saw the desk attempting to support the dollar, they "hit it quickly," selling dollars (FOMC *Transcripts,* 5–6 July 1989, 4). That is, the market bet against the desk. If Cross's assessment was true, then the market no longer viewed US monetary authorities as having an information advantage. Traders could make money by doing the opposite of what the desk did.[40]

Governor Angell thought that this secrecy potentially could confuse or mislead markets, but he also raised a new concern: Did the bank that acted as the agent for the desk trade on priority information? Cross acknowledged that any bank with or through whom the desk trades could do so. Governor Angell then suggested that market participants would always act in their own self-interest, implying that they might routinely bet against the Fed if they thought it profitable (FOMC *Transcripts*, 5–6 July 1989, 5).

Governor Johnson then suggested that if the Federal Reserve stopped intervening and left intervention solely to the Treasury, it would not make any difference. If Cross were correct, if secret intervention worked better than overt operations, then the Federal Reserve could exit the program. Who would know? Greenspan seemed to agree; Cross equivocated, but Truman suggested that this would be the "worst possible world." The Federal Reserve would lose any influence that it had over the operations, and the Treasury might even stop the Federal Reserve from sterilizing the operations (FOMC *Transcripts*, 5–6 July 1989, 8).

Intervention to weaken the dollar continued until mid-October (figures 6.19 and 6.20). The desk bought $2.6 billion of German marks and $3.5 billion of Japanese yen, splitting the operations equally between the Federal Reserve's and the ESF's accounts. The FOMC raised the authorization of foreign currencies to $20 billion and the authorization for warehousing to $10 billion in late September. The Federal Reserve warehoused an additional $4 billion worth of German marks for the US Treasury, bringing the total to $7 billion by the end of October 1989. Germany sold an additional $1.6 billion.

The G7 had met in Washington DC in September 1989 and concluded that the continued appreciation of the dollar was incompatible with long-term fundamentals (Frankel 1994, 309). The FOMC began to face pressure to ease monetary policy as a means of offsetting the dollar's appreciation. This pressure only fanned the flames of concern about the conflict between intervention and monetary policy within the FOMC. In other words, the committee faced the uncomfortable choices that the fundamental trilemma of international finance presented.

At the 3 October 1989 meeting, the debate about intervention reached a crisis stage. As noted, the desk had been buying substantial amounts of German marks and Japanese yen. Governor Johnson forcefully questioned Cross about how the desk or the G7 determined the dollar's fundamental equilibrium value. It was, of course, a question that Cross could not answer. Ever since Meese and Rogoff (1981, 1982, 1983), few economists had any faith in the ability of fundamentals-based models to forecast exchange rates at anything but a very low frequency. Johnson concluded: "Well, I realize there is a resistance to a lot of the [intervention] strategy here [among Committee members], but I think we ought to step up that resistance" (FOMC *Transcripts*, 3 October 1989, 2–4).

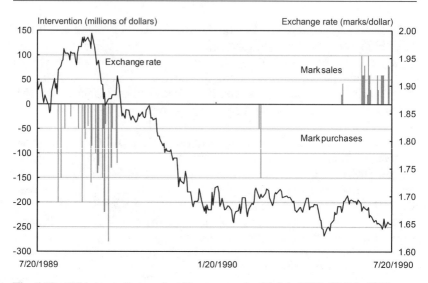

Fig. 6.19   US intervention against German marks, 20 July 1989–20 July 1990
Note: Data are from the Federal Reserve.

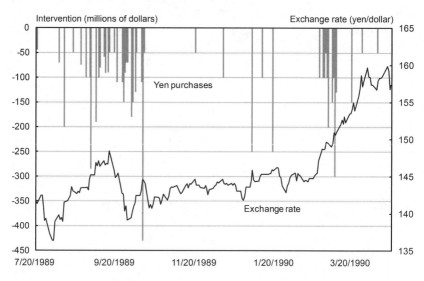

Fig. 6.20   US intervention against Japanese yen, 20 July 1989–20 April 1990
Note: Data are from the Federal Reserve.

The president of the Philadelphia Federal Reserve Bank, Edward Boehne noted that the United States and other G7 countries were selling large quantities of dollars. Apparently referring to the Jurgensen Report, he suggested that world policymakers must be contemplating some other more fundamental policy changes, since it was widely understood that intervention had only a temporary effect when not supported by other policy moves (FOMC *Transcripts*, 3 October 1989, 4). Within the context of a narrow signaling channel, which Federal Reserve staffs understood, the massive intervention implied an easing of US monetary policy.

Greenspan's subsequent comments could not have eased the committee's concern. He noted that the driving force behind recent interventions were the US Treasury and the Japanese Ministry of Finance. Greenspan seemed to imply that the Treasury wanted monetary policy conducted within the G7 framework, meaning "essentially the G-7 would start to control monetary policy." Greenspan indicated that the Japanese Ministry of Finance and Undersecretary Mulford were both in favor of intervention and a lot of it. He did not think the central bank could—or should—bring intervention to an abrupt halt, but he would try to contain the damage, and if the dollar appreciated abruptly—the dollar had been appreciating—he would then try to convince Secretary Brady that intervention was futile (FOMC *Transcripts*, 3 October 1989, 5).

Governor Johnson explicitly said that the recent sales of dollars conflicted with price stability. He noted that the public was beginning to believe the Federal Reserve's—and other central banks'—commitment to price stability. "For us to be countering that [the Federal Reserve's growing credibility] with this ridiculous approach just doesn't make sense; [it introduces] a potential doubt out there. If central banks continue to participate in this kind of strategy and show even a compromise on it, I think to some extent the markets are going to say this is a joke—in fact, they [the FOMC] are balancing the goals of the current account versus price stability" (FOMC *Transcripts*, 3 October 1989, 6). Corrigan disagreed that the G7 was trying to supplant a price stability goal with a current-account objective, but Governors Johnson and Angell seemed to dismiss him.

After October 1989, US intervention activity fell off, with the desk making occasional one-day purchases of Japanese yen. In late February and March 1990, however, the desk began a more forceful series of yen purchases. The desk bought nearly $1.5 billion worth of Japanese yen and $200 million equivalent German marks. All of this, except a small amount of Japanese yen, was for the Treasury's account, because on 2 March 1990, the Federal Reserve unilaterally suspended its participation with the Treasury's interventions. Generally since 1980, with a few exceptions, the Federal Reserve and the Treasury had split interventions operations equally. In refusing to participate, the Federal Reserve informed the Treasury that the Federal Reserve's account was near its intervention limits and that a comprehensive review of intervention was underway at the board (FOMC *Transcripts*, 27 March 1990, 1).

6.4.2   Federal Reserve Task Force

At their 22 August 1989 meeting, the FOMC formed a task force to undertake a comprehensive review of US foreign-currency operations with an emphasis on Federal Reserve participation. The objective was to provide background information to help the committee in their deliberations about intervention. The eleven Task Force papers, which the board and the Federal Reserve Bank of New York completed for the 27 March 1990 FOMC meeting, covered all aspects of the Federal Reserve's involvement: its legal authority for foreign currency operations; the Federal Reserve's objectives, tactics, and operations; cooperation between the US Treasury and the Federal Reserve System in this area; the various arrangements for financing intervention operations; its effectiveness and profitability, and intervention operations in other key developed countries. Although the papers did not espouse an overt position on intervention, Cross and Truman (1990), who summarized the work, took a firm position in favor of continued operations.

Cross and Truman saw foreign-exchange-market intervention as providing the Federal Reserve with a policy tool that could influence exchange rates independent of monetary policy, despite providing no evidence to support such a claim. They did not describe intervention as a response to a market failure, but claimed instead that policymakers "no longer can expect that exchange rates will take care of themselves . . . in ways that US policy would like or find acceptable with respect to conditions in the domestic economy" (12).[41] They asserted that monetary policy could not ignore exchange rates and that the "Federal Reserve's active participation has been constructive both in terms of US exchange rate policy and US macroeconomic policy" (13). Moreover, Cross and Truman did not find evidence that inappropriate exchange-rate considerations or international (G7) understandings on exchange rates had subverted Federal Reserve monetary policy (13), and they noted that the lack of empirical support for intervention did not mean that the operations were ineffective (14). Finally, Cross and Truman advocated holding foreign-exchange balances because they enabled the United States "to respond to exchange market developments without changes in US monetary and other policies when such changes are not deemed appropriate for domestic objectives" (18).

Yet, the emerging consensus of empirical studies offered little support for the operations. As part of the Task Force papers, Edison conducted a comprehensive review of the post-1982 intervention literature. A polished and published version appeared as Edison (1993). Edison (1993) found—once again—no new evidence in favor of a portfolio-balance channel, implying that intervention did not provide monetary policymakers with an independent instrument for affecting exchange rates. Sterilized intervention could at best have a short-run effect through an expectations channel. In addition, evidence as to whether coordinated intervention was more effective than unilateral intervention appeared disturbingly inconclusive. Bordo and Schwartz (1991), Humpage (1988), and Obstfeld (1990) concluded that the intervention episodes since 1985 were, by and large, unsuccessful in terms of their effects on dollar exchange rates.

6.4.3   Debate Renewed

If the Task Force papers were meant to assuage FOMC participants' concerns about intervention, they were a failure. Since the beginning of 1989, at a time when the FOMC maintained a tight monetary policy, the desk had purchased over $24 billion equivalent in foreign exchange, with roughly half for the Federal Reserve's account, through the largest, most protracted operations ever, and all at the Treasury's initiative. Intervention of this magnitude, as President Boehne noted, was not consistent with calming market disorder but smacked of exchange-rate manipulation (FOMC *Transcripts*, 27 March 1990, 47).

The huge volume of intervention also was affecting the quality of the Federal Reserve's balance sheet. Foreign exchange was becoming an extraordinary share of Federal Reserve assets, implying that a growing amount of an inferior form of collateral—foreign exchange rather than Treasuries—backed the central bank's reserves. To the extent that the desk held an open position, these foreign-exchange reserves exposed the Federal Reserve to valuation losses should the dollar appreciate. Federal Reserve Bank of Richmond President Robert Black suggested that there were at least two dangers associated with holding a large portfolio. One peril is that the Federal Reserve's credibility with respect to price stability would be undermined because the market might expect the central bank to ease policy to avoid a dollar appreciation and huge losses on its portfolio. The other threat is that Congress might try to persuade the Federal Reserve to ease policy to avoid big losses (FOMC *Transcripts*, 27 March 1990, 55).

Governor Johnson worried that this heavy intervention could create uncertainty in the open market, which could complicate the Federal Reserve's ability to sterilize the interventions. Johnson, who did believe that sterilized intervention could sometimes be effective in the short-to-intermediate term, wanted the FOMC to cut off the intervention at some point and to refuse to warehouse foreign exchange for the Treasury. Markets, he claimed, would understand (FOMC *Transcripts*, 27 March 1990, 49–55).

Chairman Greenspan now portrayed the Federal Reserve as the voice of reason in the whole affair. He feared that if the central bank continued to unilaterally refuse to intervene, it would lose influence over the Treasury's intervention activities; he was "quite fearful of what they might do if we weren't there to harass them toward some degree of sensibleness." He viewed the current Treasury and most previous Treasuries as "heavy interventionists" (FOMC *Transcripts*, 27 March 1990, 46–57). President Hoskins, however, turned this argument on its head, arguing that intervention gave the Treasury influence over the Federal Reserve. Hoskins agreed that the Federal Reserve could sterilize transactions, but contended that under current arrangements, the Treasury nevertheless influenced the size of the Federal Reserve's portfolio (FOMC *Transcripts*, 27 March 1990, 49).

President Corrigan, in support of the chairman, argued that not only would the Federal Reserve lose power over the Treasury, but the central bank would lose international stature, notably in the G7 (FOMC *Transcripts*, 27 March 1990, 57–59).

After a lengthy discussion, Chairman Greenspan noted that the "vast majority" of the FOMC seemed in favor of continued Federal Reserve's participation with the Treasury in intervention. He agreed to confront the Treasury about the recent size of intervention, but he noted that if the Federal Reserve confronted Treasury about intervention *in general*, it would surely lose in Congress. Greenspan then recommended that the FOMC increase the warehousing limit to $15 billion and the overall net open position to $25 billion. He agreed to Johnson's request to refuse to participate in an intervention designed to drive the dollar down (FOMC *Transcripts*, 27 March 1990, 69–70).

Some FOMC members, however, wanted to set a limit on intervention. President of the St. Louis Federal Reserve Bank Thomas Melzer then suggested that the Federal Reserve inform the Treasury that the current intervention amounts were a limit and that the FOMC did not want to see more intervention. Greenspan, however, thought that the Treasury might interpret such a warning as a threat, and he again warned that the Federal Reserve could not prevail against the Treasury in this matter (FOMC *Transcripts*, 27 March 1990, 70–71). Hoskins agreed that the Federal Reserve should participate with the Treasury to some degree, but objected to the current size of the central bank's involvement—$25 billion. He recommended a "Treasury/Fed Accord II" before the position becomes much larger (FOMC *Transcripts*, 27 March 1990, 77).

At this meeting, the FOMC voted to increase the authorization for foreign exchange from $21 billion to $25 billion effective immediately. Three members dissented: Governor Angell, President Hoskins, and Governor LaWare. The FOMC also voted to increase the authority for warehousing from $10 billion to $15 billion, and the same three individuals dissented. The Treasury's warehousing reached $9 billion in June 1990.

At roughly this same time, however, the Treasury's attitude about foreign-exchange intervention inexplicitly seemed to change. The extent to which complaints within the FOMC influenced the Treasury's perception of intervention is not clear. Nevertheless, on an 11 April 1990 conference call with FOMC participants, Chairman Greenspan reported how Treasury Secretary Brady recently told the G7 that after spending $40 billion to defend the Japanese yen, he (Brady) had concluded that, "It just doesn't work"[42] (FOMC *Transcripts*, 11 April 1990, 1). Brady would no longer offer the Japanese support for the yen. The Economic Report of the President for 1991 was the last one—at least through 1996—that mentioned foreign-exchange intervention.

The Treasury also took steps to ease the Federal Reserve's concerns about its balance sheet. Beginning on 29 May 1990, the desk began quietly selling German marks from the Treasury's account. The objective was to sell $2 billion equivalent marks by July 1990 and to use the dollar proceeds of those sales to buy back German marks that the Treasury had warehoused with the Federal Reserve. The desk sold $1 billion equivalent of these marks in the market and sold $1 billion equivalent marks off-market to a unknown central bank (*Bulletin*, October 1990, 821–22; FOMC *Transcripts*, 2–3 July 1990, Cross appendix, 2–3). The Treasury currently had $9 billion warehoused with the Federal Reserve, but by July 1990 it reduced that amount to $7 billion. The ESF also began buying back special drawing right (SDR) certificates from the Federal Reserve, and selling the SDRs to IMF members that needed them to make payments to the IMF. The ESF then used the acquired dollars to draw down warehousing commitments to the Federal Reserve. By the 13 November 1990 FOMC meeting, the amount warehoused had dropped to $2.5 billion.

As intervention abated, President Hoskins, who viewed price stability as the sole objective of monetary policy, now took aim at its ancillary mechanisms: warehousing and swap lines. He suggested lowering the warehousing authorization, now $15 billion. Hoskins also questioned why the Federal Reserve offered Mexico a swap line (see below). He noted that the other countries had AA (or better) ratings on their debt and widely convertible currencies. The swaps to Mexico were like foreign aid or a loan and did not match the traditional purpose for the swap lines. At the 18 December 1990 FOMC meeting, Hoskins questioned the renewal of the entire swap mechanism since the central bank now held a substantial portfolio of foreign-exchange reserves (FOMC *Transcripts*, 18 December 1990, 1). At the 5 February 1991 meeting, Cross recommended lowering the authorization for warehousing from $15 billion to $10 billion, noting that the Treasury never exceeded $9 billion. President Hoskins argued that if the FOMC supported this new limit—instead of letting the facility run dry—it was essentially endorsing the idea of warehousing for the Treasury. Hoskins viewed warehousing as a loan to the Treasury, which violates the principle of central bank independence. The president of the Kansas City Federal Reserve Bank, Roger Guffey, asked for a $5 billion limit (FOMC *Transcripts*, 5 February 1991, 3–4). The FOMC, however, would not lower the authorization to $5 billion for another year.

At the 26 March 1991 FOMC meeting, with many FOMC participants attempting to roll back the Federal Reserve's authorization for holding foreign exchange, and therefore its commitment to intervention, Cross championed holding a large portfolio. At that time the Federal Reserve held $17.8 billion equivalent German marks and $6.9 billion equivalent Japanese yen. A large portfolio, Cross claimed, gave the Federal Reserve more flexibility when it intervened.[43] With a portfolio of funds, the central bank need not depend on overseas sources of foreign exchange. Moreover, the market knew that the Federal Reserve had substantial funds for intervention, which reduced destabilizing speculation, and therefore lessened the chances that the central bank would have to use them. He noted that the portfolio did expose the Federal Reserve to exchange-valuation losses, but this ultimately affected only the profits that the Federal Reserve returned to the Treasury. He claimed that "if we simply adopted a conscious policy of getting rid of a substantial part of our reserves, it seems to me that that could be seen by the market and by foreign officials and by the general public as a move by the United States toward withdrawal of its role in international responsibilities and its role in helping to maintain the stability and smooth functioning of the [international financial] system" (FOMC *Transcripts*, 26 March 1991, 8–9).

Governor Mullins asked what the conceptual basis was for determining the appropriate level of reserve holdings, but Cross did not have a good reply. Chairman Greenspan noted that borrowing was an alternative. President Hoskins then recalled that in late 1987 and early 1988 when concern over intervention started, the Federal Reserve held reserves of only about $10 billion. At the time, most FOMC participants thought that intervention was of little use, but agreed that holding some reserves signaled international cooperation and "show[ed] the flag." Hoskins contended that there was no rationale for accumulating reserves since that time, and he cautioned that the exposure (the dollar was now appreciating, forcing losses on the portfolio) and continued warehousing could create problems for the Federal Reserve.

In early 1991, reducing the Federal Reserve's portfolio through sales of foreign exchange was difficult because the dollar was appreciating. On a 24 June 1991 conference call, Cross revealed that the United States had worked out a plan with the Bundesbank to reduce US holdings of German marks by DM10 billion. The transactions would be at market rates, but would be conducted off-market. The first exchange of DM4 billion was scheduled for 25 June 1991. Six more exchanges of DM1 billion each would follow over the next six months, with each priced at forward rates prevailing on 25 June 1991. Sixty percent of the marks came from the Federal Reserve's portfolio and 40 percent from the Treasury's. The transactions would exceed the daily and intermeeting limits on intervention, and were cleared with the chairman and with the subcommittee in accordance with the procedural instructions. Following a question from Hoskins, Cross indicated that this arrangement implied no future obligation to intervene. Hoskins continued to recommend lowering the authorization to hold foreign currencies (FOMC *Transcripts*, 24 June 1991, 3–6).

6.4.4   Renewed Conflicts with the Treasury

If the Treasury's views on intervention had changed it was, by and large, only a matter of degree. The United States continued to intervene after mid-1990, but the amount and frequency of these operations declined substantially. Often the United States undertook the operations largely out of a spirit of cooperation with its allies and less out of a concern for exchange rates. By and large, the FOMC seemed content with the operations until August 1992.

That summer speculative pressures within the European exchange-rate mechanism were intensifying. The dollar fell sharply against the German mark as interest rate spreads between Europe and the United States widened substantially (see figures 6.5 and 6.6). In July 1992, for example, the Bundesbank's discount rate reached 8.75 percent while the Federal Reserve's discount and federal funds target rates were lowered to 3 percent and 3.25 percent respectively. The mark moved to the top of the ERM while the Italian lira and British pound reached the bottom. Markets expected a realignment of the ERM, especially given that the Danes had rejected the Maastricht treaty.

Although the dollar fell against the German mark, the United States did not view this as a dollar problem requiring heavy concerted intervention with the Europeans. The United States did, however, intervene in concert with the Europeans on three occasions in late July and early August when the market seemed disorderly. The desk's sales of German marks were fairly large, totaling $800 million equivalent, and they seemed to surprise private-market participants. Federal Reserve Bank of New York President McDonough claimed they were successful, although the dollar continued to depreciate against the mark through August. On 11 August 1992, however, Treasury Secretary Brady called for lower interest rates, which caused the dollar to fall and appeared to sabotage the intervention (FOMC *Transcripts*, 18 August 1992, McDonough appendix, 1–7).

At the 18 August 1992 FOMC meeting, questions arose again about the purpose of the intervention and about its implication for monetary policy credibility, since it involved buying dollars when the FOMC was easing. McDonough claimed the Treasury was interested in managing an exchange rate, but that the desk was only interested in maintaining orderly markets (FOMC *Transcripts*, 18 August 1992, 2). Then Atlanta President Robert Forrestal captured the sentiment against intervention within the FOMC (FOMC *Transcripts*, 18 August 1992, 3):

> I've heard the rationale of disorderly markets, but I feel constrained to say that I was extremely surprised at this intervention, particularly the second and the third operations. Of course, I would respect the judgment of the Desk and Bill [McDonough] with regard to whether the markets were in fact disorderly. But we've had extensive discussions over the last year or so in the Committee on the effectiveness of sterilized intervention, and I thought it was the sense of this group that, unless we were going to follow intervention with some kind of substantive monetary policy move, intervention was not the policy of this committee. What really compounds the problem with respect to our credibility is having intervention and

then having that followed by the Secretary's statement that he's looking for lower interest rates. That to me made us look extremely silly, to put it lightly.

Chairman Greeenspan attempted to put the operation in a better light, noting that "we're all pretty much aware that there is very little intervention can do in and of itself to affect the average of any exchange rate over a particular period of time." But he contended that on occasion, the market breaks down and "the evidence does suggest that when that occurs we in fact can affect the market. . . . markets feed on themselves, get out of hand, and sometimes create some degree of instability" (FOMC *Transcripts*, 18 August 1992, 5).

On 21 and 24 August 1992, as the dollar moved lower against the German mark, the US Treasury asked the desk to arrange a coordinated intervention. The desk advised against the intervention, but the Treasury insisted. After consulting Chairman Greenspan, the Federal Reserve decided that it had to act in concert with the Treasury because the market might learn that the Treasury and Federal Reserve were at odds over intervention at a time when the dollar was low relative to the German mark (FOMC *Transcripts*, 6 October 1993, McDonough appendix, 1–2). Essentially the Federal Reserve had little choice in the matter, if the Treasury wanted to intervene.

The disintegration of the European monetary system had prompted these interventions. The EMS was created in 1979, but the member countries had undertaken no currency realignments since January 1987, despite substantial differences in their economic performances. After easing fiscal and monetary policy to facilitate the reunification of the country, Germany had recently been tightening to avoid the inflationary consequences of its earlier policies. German interest rates were very high, which caused difficulties for some EMS countries that were experiencing weak economic growth. Amid heavy speculation, Italy devalued the lira on 13 September 1992. On 16 September 1992, Britain and Italy pulled out of the ERM, while Ireland, Spain, and Portugal imposed exchange controls (FOMC *Transcripts*, 6 October 1992, McDonough appendix, 1–8). The Germans did not want to hold the ERM together; they wanted more flexibility to pursue domestic-policy objectives (FOMC *Transcripts*, 6 October 1992, 2).

The focus then shifted to the Japanese yen. On 27 April 1993, the United States sold $200 million equivalent yen in an operation largely designed to show cooperation with the Bank of Japan rather than a commitment to intervention. The yen was under strong upward pressure, and according to Margaret Greene, manager of the foreign desk, "market participants were doubtful that the Japanese authorities could be effective until other governments signaled they, too, were concerned about the movement in the exchange rate." The market expected that upcoming trade talks between the United States and Japan would be confrontational and the dollar depreciated sharply against the yen. At the Treasury's suggestion the desk intervened openly in several rounds, during the day. The amounts were split evenly between the Treasury's and the central bank's accounts (FOMC *Transcripts*, 18 May 1993, Greene appendix, 3–4).

Chairman Greenspan offered that the recent intervention was a response to spillover effects from the exchange market to other financial markets, which implied a lack of confidence in the dollar. The FOMC had earlier suggested that such a spillover was a necessary condition for intervention (FOMC *Transcripts*, 18 May 1993, 4–5). Further interventions against Japanese yen followed in late May, early June, and August 1993, although they remained fairly isolated events.

On 29 April and 4 May 1994, the desk sold both German marks and Japanese yen from both the Federal Reserve's and Treasury's accounts. These operations were fairly large, totaling $ 0.7 billion and $1.3 billion, respectively. Federal Reserve Bank of Cleveland President Jerry Jordan asked what the participants in the operation intended to signal through the intervention, and he noted Germany's lack of enthusiasm for the operation. (Germany bought only $250 million dollars on a single day, whereas Japan bought $1.6 billion on consecutive days between 28 April and 4 May.)[44] The object according to Peter Fisher was to communicate with both interbank traders and the broader financial markets that the dollar had gone beyond levels justified by fundamentals and to underline a change in policy (FOMC *Transcripts*, 17 May 1994, 1–4).[45]

The desk again sold $1.3 billion German marks and $1.3 billion Japanese yen in early November 1994. Japan participated, buying nearly $1.7 billion, but Germany remained out of the market. At the 15 November 1994 FOMC meeting, Federal Reserve Bank of Richmond President Broaddus argued against intervention because it must interfere with the Federal Reserve's monetary-policy independence:

As you said, Mr. Chairman, it is now widely agreed that sterilized intervention doesn't have any sustained impact on exchange rates unless it sends a signal that we are going to follow it up with a monetary policy action. This implies, for me at least, and this is really the heart of the matter, that it is not really possible for the Fed to maintain a truly independent monetary policy for an extended period of time while following the Treasury's lead on foreign exchange policy. Now, of course, in reality the way I see this is that we have maintained our independence by not making a commitment to follow interventions with monetary policy actions. But that's not a perfect situation either. (FOMC *Transcripts*, 15 November 1994, 49)

In 1995, the Federal Reserve Bank of Richmond articulated the case against intervention (Broaddus and Goodfriend 1996).[46] Although most of the core arguments were well known to FOMC participants, Richmond's perspective seemed fresh because the authors developed the exposition more completely and clearly than heretofore had been the case. They focused on the connection between intervention and monetary-policy credibility. Sterilized intervention and the institutions associated with intervention damaged the Federal Reserve's credibility with respect to price stability, they claimed, because Congress had never statutorily mandated price stability as the Fed's sole—or even chief—policy goal. The central bank's credibility with respect to price stability was purely reputation-based. Such credibility is hard to acquire and is inherently fragile. Central bank independence—keeping the Federal Reserve free of political influence—is the sine qua non of reputation-based credibility.

Although sterilized intervention had no direct impact on the monetary base, the Richmond exposition argued that economists and policymakers understood—at least since the Jurgensen Report—that such operations were ineffective unless monetary policy supported them. Participation in sterilized foreign exchange operations under the Treasury's leadership, often within G7 forums, *must* then create uncertainty about the relative weights that the central bank gave to its price and exchange-rate objectives, especially—as often was the case—when these two objectives conflicted.

Richmond also argued that the Federal Reserve's portfolio of foreign exchange—acquired through intervention, warehousing, or foreign loans—resulted in a substitution of foreign securities on the central bank's books for US Treasury securities. By holding these securities, the Federal Reserve was extending credit to foreign governments and exposing its balance sheet to market risk and sometimes to credit risk. The decision to put funds at risk by extending credit to foreign governments was a fiscal policy action that Congress—not the Federal Reserve—should undertake (Goodfriend 1994). The Federal Reserve's engagement in these fiscal operations skirted the congressional appropriations process, avoided congressionally mandated public-debt limits and, consequently, was a misuse of the central bank's off-budget status. Congress had put the Federal Reserve System outside the appropriations process to safeguard its independence. If any of these foreign-exchange operations went wrong, however, the Federal Reserve might face congressional criticism and actions that could damage the central bank's independence.

By 1994, many FOMC participants were leaning hard toward very little involvement. McDonough suggested that withdrawing from intervention or not renewing the swap lines was isolationist, and would have a big impact (FOMC *Transcripts*, 15 November 1994, 52). Governor Kelly suggested that it would signal a lack of financial management and arrogance on the part of the Federal Reserve to thumb its nose at the Treasury and the government, and it might get Congress involved (FOMC *Transcripts*, 15 November 1994, 53). In contrast, Federal Reserve Bank of Minneapolis President Stern agreed that the cost of intervention was an erosion of credibility (FOMC *Transcripts*, 15 November 1994, 54). President Broaddus then dissented on a vote to renew the swap lines.

The Federal Reserve intervened occasionally in 1995, but after August of that year, US intervention ended, except for three episodes: The United States bought $833 million worth of Japanese yen on 17 June 1998 in an isolated transaction to support the yen, but did not otherwise undertake foreign-exchange intervention in response to the Asian financial crisis. The 17 June 1998 intervention raised criticism in the FOMC that the action was incompatible with the thrust of macroeconomic policies in both Japan and the United States (FOMC *Transcripts*, 30 June—1July 1998, 5–6). Chairman Greenspan acknowledged that the administration intervened reluctantly and would probably not do so again (FOMC *Transcripts*, 30 June–1July 1998, 7). The Asian financial crisis originated in Thailand in the summer of 1997, spread to Russia a year later, and then threatened Latin America. In response to the crisis, the G7 countries and the IMF provided credit lines ($90 billion) to the affected developing countries. The Federal Reserve lowered its federal funds target rate in the fall of 1998. This action, in conjunction with similar monetary easing on the part of other key industrialized economies, increased world liquidity and reduced the prospects of global deflation. Two years later, the United States intervened again. At the administration's urging, the United States bought $1.3 billion equivalent euros on 22 September 2000 as the euro approached a record low against the dollar. This intervention—a technical fiasco—elicited a replay of the familiar complaints about intervention (FOMC *Transcripts*, 3 October 2000, 7–23).[47] The United States also bought yen following the Japanese tsunami on 18 March 2011.[48]

6.4.5   Analysis of Post-Louvre Intervention

The US interventions during the early 1990s were again largely ineffective at moving dollar exchange rates in a manner consistent with calming market disorder. Only about 64 percent of the interventions successfully altered exchange rate movements.

Between 2 May 1988 and 19 March 1997, the United States sold German marks on forty-four days and bought German marks on 111 days (see table 6.4). Twenty-two of the US sales of German marks were associated with same-day dollar appreciations, and fifty-four of the US purchases of German marks were associated with same-day dollar depreciations. In both cases, the observed number of successes was not statistically greater than the number of successes that we would expect to observe given the variable nature of day-to-day exchange-rate changes. Likewise, six of the forty-four US sales of German marks were associated with a slowing in the pace of the dollar's depreciation and seventeen of the US purchases of German marks were associated with a slowing in the pace of the dollar's appreciation. Again, however, in neither case was the success count statistically different than the number that we would randomly anticipate. United States intervention against German marks was not obviously successful at achieving common measurable outcomes consistent with calming disorderly markets.

Table 6.4   Success counts for US intervention, 2 May 1988 to 19 March 1997

German marks	Total (#)	Intervention successes (#)	(%)	Expected[a] successes (#)	Standard[a] deviation (#)
Mark sales & dollar appreciation	44	22	50.0	21	3
Mark purchases & dollar depreciation	111	54	48.5	53	5
Total	155	76	49.0		
Mark sales & smaller dollar depreciation	44	6	13.6	5	1
Mark purchases & smaller dollar appreciation	111	17	15.3	15	1
Total	155	23	14.8		
Mark sales & dollar appreciation or smaller depreciation	44	28	63.6	26	4
Mark purchases & dollar depreciation or small appreciation	111	71	64.0	67	6
Total	155	99	63.9		
Japanese yen					
Yen sales & dollar appreciation	31	15	48.4	15	3
Yen purchases & dollar depreciation	87	38	43.7	40	4
Total	118	53	44.9		
Yen sales & smaller dollar depreciation	31	8	25.8	4	1
Yen purchases & smaller dollar appreciation	87	14	16.1	11	0
Total	118	22	18.6		
Yen sales & dollar appreciation or smaller depreciation	31	23	74.2	19	4
Yen purchases & dollar depreciation or small appreciation	87	52	59.8	51	5
Total	118	75	63.6		

Note: See appendix 2 for detail.

[a] Assumes that the success count is a hypergeometric random variable.

Over the same time interval, the United States sold Japanese yen on thirty-one days and bought yen on eighty-seven days. Fifteen of the US sales of Japanese yen were associated with a same-day dollar appreciation, and thirty-eight of the US purchases of Japanese yen were associated with a same-day dollar depreciation. As with the German mark, in both cases, the observed number of successes was not statistically different than the number of successes that we randomly anticipate.

Eight of the US sales of Japanese yen were associated with a moderation in the pace of the dollar's depreciation, and fourteen of the US purchases of Japanese yen were associated with a moderation in the pace of the dollar's appreciation. Both of these success counts exceed the amount one would predict given the variable nature of daily exchange-rate movements, but only the former—eight out of thirty-one sales of yen—is statistically greater than the expected amount.

6.5   Swaps, Warehousing, and the Mexico Peso Crisis

Support for foreign-exchange-market intervention within the FOMC waned after the US stock-market collapse in 1987 because the committee increasingly viewed such operations as inconsistent with a credible commitment to price stability. As noted above, this was a fairly new concern, one that emerged as views about the role for monetary policy changed. Traditionally, FOMC participants worried that the institutions to support foreign-exchange-market intervention—warehousing foreign currencies for the Treasury and swap lines—could threaten Federal Reserve's independence if Congress came to view their use as a means of financing foreign-policy initiatives outside of the congressional appropriations process. Yet this problem had never seriously confronted the FOMC until the Mexican peso crisis of 1995. Then the import of these traditional concerns crystallized.

6.5.1   Mexican Swaps

The Bank of Mexico first joined the Federal Reserve System's swap network along with the central banks of Denmark and Norway in May 1967.[49] Mexico had maintained a reciprocal swap line with the US Treasury since 1965, which had replaced a much older agreement. During the 1960s, Mexico had experienced strong real economic growth, reasonable price stability, external balance, and ready access to international financial markets. Extending the swap line to Mexico did not seem unusual, despite Federal Reserve Bank of Cleveland President Hoskins's complaints, given the size of the Mexican economy—then larger than Austria or Denmark—and given the close economic ties between Mexico and the United States. At the time, US banks held approximately $1.3 billion in claims on Mexico (Maroni 1994b).

The FOMC expanded the Mexican swap line three times during the 1970s, bringing the regular swap line to $700 million by 1994. The growth of the regular swap line paralleled the expansion of Mexico's foreign and domestic economic activity and a sharp rise in US bank claims on Mexico. In addition, the Federal Reserve created two special temporary swap lines prior to 1994, which were associated with multilateral debt stabilization packages. The first, on 28 August 1982, gave Mexico a $325 million credit line to deal with its international debt crisis. The second, on 14 September 1989, offered Mexico $125 billion to aid in restructuring the country's foreign bank debt. In addition, in 1988 and 1993, Mexico and the United States considered additional short-term debt facilities, including an extension of the Federal Reserve's swap lines, but both parties mutually terminated these initiatives before they came to fruition (Maroni 1994b).

Between 1990 and 1994, inflation in Mexico greatly exceeded inflation in the United States, a situation that fostered a peso depreciation. Beginning in November 1991, however, Mexico maintained the peso-dollar exchange rate within moving bands that limited the pace of the peso's depreciation against the US dollar. The Mexican government had negotiated the rate of the peso's depreciation as part of a wage negotiation with local unions. This arrangement left the peso substantially overvalued relative to the dollar on a purchasing-power-parity basis and produced a large and growing current-account deficit. Foreign financial inflows associated with NAFTA helped to finance Mexico's resulting deficit, which reached 8 percent of GDP by 1994. Still, Mexican monetary authorities drew down their foreign-exchange reserves in managing the exchange rate (Maroni 1994a).

In early 1994, after concluding NAFTA and in anticipation of making the Bank of Mexico independent of the Ministry of Finance, Mexico requested a permanent increase in its swap lines with both the Federal Reserve and the US Treasury. At the time, the peso was coming under strong downward pressure in part because an uprising in Chiapas raised investors' concerns. Moreover, peso devaluations had often followed Mexican elections and an election was due in August 1994. Mexico attempted to assuage investors' concerns and avoid a peso depreciation by offering dollar-index debt (Teso-bonos) instead of peso debt (Cetes).

The proposal for an increase in the Mexican swap lines rekindled a debate about swaps at the 22 March 1994 FOMC meeting. Federal Reserve swaps were intended to finance interventions aimed at calming "disorderly markets," but Mexico presented some unusual considerations. Mexico had drawn on its regular swap lines sixteen times prior to 1994. Some of these past drawings had merely provided temporary window dressing for its foreign exchange reserves and some had offered funds in anticipation of financial-market turmoil prior to presidential elections. Moreover, Mexico currently seemed to be defending an unviable peg. Many FOMC participants—notably Alfred Broaddus, president of the Federal Reserve Bank of Richmond and Jerry Jordan, president of the Federal Reserve Bank of Cleveland—did not consider such uses as being consistent with calming disorderly markets. Chairman Greenspan, who claimed a philosophical allegiance with Broaddus and Jordan, nevertheless again argued in favor of cooperating with the Treasury (FOMC *Transcripts*, 22 March 1994, 2–15).[50]

6.5.2   Crisis and Questions about Appropriate Use

Following the 24 March 1994 assassination of Mexican presidential candidate Luis Donaldo Colosio, the United States provided a temporary increase in the Mexican swap lines to $6.0 billion, split evenly between the Federal Reserve and the Treasury.[51] Canada offered a $730 million swap line. On 26 April 1994, Canada, Mexico, and the United States made these temporary swap lines permanent as part of the North American Framework Agreement (NAFA).[52] All of the lines were reciprocal.[53] Drawings on the Mexican swap line would require FOMC approval, and Mexico must provide collateral to the Federal Reserve Bank of New York for swap drawings in excess of $1 billion. The agreement also established a formal consultative mechanism among the three countries, which helped authorities monitor economic developments in Mexico.[54]

Mexico must have thought that the mere existence of the swap lines would calm investors' fears, since the country did not immediately draw on these lines. The Bank of Mexico continued to defend the peso exchange rate out of its official reserves. Speculators, however, had a one-way bet. They knew the direction that the peso would follow; only the timing was uncertain. After the election, the Bank of Mexico committed large amounts of reserves to defending the peso and investor concerns increased. On 20 December 1994, Mexico, with its dollar reserves depleted, devalued the peso and two days later allowed the peso to float. This action precipitated a financial crisis. In response to the crisis, both the ESF and the Federal Reserve temporarily increased each of their swap lines with Mexico to $4.5 billion, bringing the total facility to $9.0 billion.

The Clinton administration asked the US Congress to provide $40 billion in loan guarantees to Mexico, but Congress refused this request. The US Treasury, however, had already made contingency plans for providing financial aid to Mexico in 1993, when it feared that Congress might defeat NAFTA and set off financial flight from Mexico. That plan envisaged offering Mexico a $12 billion credit line with $6 billion coming from the United States and $6 billion coming from Europe. Half of the US commitment would come from an increase in the Federal Reserve's swap line with Mexico from $700 million to $3 billion (Hetzel 2008, 208). This time, the ESF would provide Mexico both short-term and medium-term swaps and possibly loans and loan guarantees for a total package of up to $20 billion. The ESF currently held only $5 billion in liquid dollar assets and $19.5 billion in German marks and Japanese yen (FOMC *Transcripts*, 31 January & 1 February 1997, 59–75, 117–44). To acquire the necessary dollars, the administration asked the Federal Reserve to warehouse up to $20 billion in foreign exchange. (The FOMC had recently pared the Federal Reserve's authorization for warehousing to $5 billion.) Of that amount, the Treasury would use $6 billion to back the central bank's own swap lines with Mexico, leaving the ESF $14 billion (FOMC *Transcripts*, 31 January & 1 February 1995, 122). The Federal Reserve would warehouse German marks and Japanese yen, not Mexican pesos. Truman warned that the warehousing could extend for ten years (FOMC *Transcripts*, 31 January & 1 February 1995, 124–25).

The Federal Reserve would also provide Mexico with the regular $3 billion swap line and with an additional $3 billion special swap line. Mexico could draw on both lines for a 12 month period; the drawing would roll over every three months for up to twelve months. At the latest, final payments would be due before 31 January 1997. The Treasury, however, would have to take the central bank out of any loan after twelve months, implying that the Federal Reserve assumed no credit or market risks.[55] As the Bank of Mexico paid off each of the drawings, the special swap would disappear. While the Treasury backed up the Federal Reserve, Mexican oil revenues, acting as collateral, backed up the Treasury.

At the 31 January and 1 February 1995 FOMC meeting, Governor Melzer argued that the Federal Reserve should only participate in the swap loans to Mexico and warehousing with the Treasury if the situation represented a systemic risk to the US financial system. Otherwise, the Treasury should undertake the operations alone through the appropriations process. He worried that Congress, which was not in favor of a Mexican bailout, might view warehousing on this scale as a subversion of its will. Melzer also implied that increasing the warehousing to $20 billion might set a precedent that would continue beyond the Mexican situation when the Treasury might again be interested in intervention. Moreover, if the Federal Reserve held additional German mark and Japanese yen securities on its books and sold domestic securities to sterilize the transactions, it would violate rules about the amount of appropriate collateral to back Federal Reserve notes outstanding. Melzer recalled this being a problem when the Federal Reserve was warehousing $9 billion (FOMC *Transcripts*, 31 January & 1 February 1995, 117–45). Governors Melzer and Lindsey voted no on the measure to increase the swap line with Mexico and on the measure to increase the appropriation for warehousing with the Treasury. Presidents Broaddus and Jordan, who also opposed the action, were not then voting members of the FOMC.

On 31 January 1995, the Clinton administration announced a $47.8 billion Mexican aid package, which included $20 billion from the United States, $17.8 billion from the IMF in eighteen-month stand-by credits, and a $10 billion line of credit with the BIS. The FOMC provided $6 billion by extending the swap lines and increased its authorization for warehousing to $20 billion.

That the swap and warehousing arrangements were a fait accompli did not silence debate among FOMC participants. At the 28 March 1995 FOMC meeting, President Broaddus, after reading a board memo on the Federal Reserve's legal authority for warehousing, objected to the operation. Broaddus contended that warehousing was a fiscal operation. "By that I mean that in the end the warehousing operation has exactly the same final effect as if Congress authorized the Treasury or the ESF to purchase the foreign exchange and fund the purchase by issuing additional debt in the market. The only difference . . . is that the usual Congressional appropriations process is circumvented, and the purchase does not show up in the budget" (FOMC *Transcripts*, 28 March 1995, 4). The fiscal nature arose because in the process of sterilizing the Treasury's use of the dollars obtained from warehousing, the central bank issued Treasury securities from its portfolio. Broaddus noted that the Federal Reserve was "off-budget," and he worried that warehousing and the recent swap arrangements with Mexico suggested that the Federal Reserve was financing operations beyond the congressional budget process that the American people might not favor. He worried that this could raise congressional ire and could threaten Federal Reserve independence (Broaddus and Goodfriend 1996; Goodfriend 1994, 2013).

Greenspan responded: "On the issue of how to deal with the Treasury in this government, as fiscal agent we involve ourselves in various types of support for the Treasury and that does in some sense impinge on the independence of this institution. The trouble, unfortunately, is that we cannot be fully independent because there is only one government and there is an element here trying to draw the line. I think we are somewhat uncomfortable about the warehousing facility. I think we are all uncomfortable about our own swap line facility, and are in opposition to the initiatives of the Treasury. But we also recognize that the central bank has very broad responsibilities to ensure the safety and soundness of the financial system" (FOMC *Transcripts*, 28 March 1995, 5). The potential for spillover to US financial markets became the justification for the action.

Truman also responded to Broaddus, arguing that the Treasury could undertake warehousing with the market—that is, with banks or other financial institutions—and consequently, Federal Reserve warehousing did not represent a breach of the fiscal authority of Congress. Truman went on to say that the central bank had changed the warehousing arrangements "so that it is now very clearly an arms-length, market-related transaction." These observations, however, did not sway anyone. If the Treasury could undertake warehousing with the private sector, they should do so and leave the Federal Reserve out of the operations (FOMC *Transcripts*, 28 March 1995, 5–6).

In the end, the ESF never warehoused foreign currencies with the Federal Reserve System during the Mexican peso crisis. The warehousing authorization reverted to $5 billion in 1996 and has remained there ever since. The last time that the ESF warehoused foreign exchange with the Federal Reserve was in 1992.

Mexico drew as much as $1.5 billion on its swap lines with the Federal Reserve, but paid this amount completely down by January 1996. The Federal Reserve decided to eliminate all of its swap lines when the euro came into existence in December 1999, except for ongoing swap lines with its NAFTA partners, Canada and Mexico. During the financial crisis of 2007 and 2008 and the European debt problems of 2010, the Federal Reserve reinstated swap lines to extend dollar liquidity to foreign banks that did not otherwise have access to the Federal Reserve borrowing facilities. In October 2013, the FOMC authorized these liquidity swap lines with the Bank of Canada, the Bank of England, the European Central Bank, the Bank of Japan, and the Swiss National Bank on an ongoing basis (see epilogue).

6.6   Conclusion

The United States stopped intervening in the foreign-exchange market primarily because FOMC participants believed that intervention, and the institutional arrangements associated with it, undermined their ability to establish and to maintain a credible commitment to price stability. Intervention did not provide a method for lessening the constraints of the trilemma; instead, it interfered with the conduct of monetary policy. Absent an exploitable portfolio-balance mechanism, sterilized intervention did not offer policymakers a means for systematically determining exchange rates independent of monetary policy. By the mid-1980s, support for the portfolio-balance mechanism had evaporated. By then, most observers understood that for intervention to have anything more than a fleeting effect on exchange rates, monetary policy had to back it up, but this essentially put the cart before the horse from the FOMC's perspective. Exchange rates often responded to the overall thrust of US monetary policy, so intervening to offset them could seem to contravene the very policy that set them in motion while damaging credibility. This became a critical problem in the late 1980s and early 1990s as the FOMC attempted to bring inflation expectations— then hovering in a 3 percent to 4 percent range—to a level more consistent with their perceptions of price stability.

In addition, FOMC participants objected to many of the institutional arrangements for intervention because they threatened the central bank's independence and, in doing so, also compromised the credibility of monetary policy. The US Secretary of Treasury had primary responsibility for US foreign-exchange intervention. He often formulated intervention policy as an adjunct to macroeconomic policy coordination within the G7 framework. In doing so, he occasionally recommended changes in monetary policy. The Federal Reserve could easily fend off calls for interest rate cuts, but to refuse to undertake sterilized intervention was another matter altogether. Although the Federal Reserve had independent authority for intervention, even such strong chairmen as Paul Volcker and Alan Greenspan were extremely reluctant to exercise their autonomy for fear of appearing to undermine an administration policy. The Federal Reserve also worried that warehousing foreign exchange for the Treasury and extending swap loans at the Treasury's behest to developing countries threatened its independence because Congress might view either of these arrangements as contravening the appropriation process. The Mexican crisis brought such issues to the fore.

Because of these concerns, the United States essentially stopped intervening by the mid-1990s, but the US policymakers never dismissed intervention as completely ineffectual. Many FOMC participants accepted that the foreign-exchange market could sometimes become disorderly and that foreign-exchange intervention might offer a means of calming market disorder. Like much of the empirical literature, we have shown that intervention does sometimes affect the exchange-rate movements. Specifically, we have shown that the capacity of intervention to moderate exchange rate movements is greater than random, but at best, only about one in five interventions are successful on this score. In the late 1980s and early 1990s, the FOMC objected to the frequent and heavy interventions then underway, primarily because they threatened monetary policy credibility, not because they rarely worked.

Lessons from the Evolution of US Monetary and Intervention Policies

> There is no evidence, nor does anybody here [in the FOMC] believe that there is any evidence, to confirm that sterilized intervention does anything.
> —Alan Greenspan (FOMC *Transcripts*, 3 October 2000, 14)

7.1 Introduction

The twentieth century witnessed a transition from a gold standard to a fiat-money-cum-floating-exchange-rate regime, as policymakers in the advanced economies came to grips with the fundamental trilemma of formulating monetary policy in an open economy: Countries cannot simultaneously stabilize their exchange rates, participate fully in financial globalization, and pursue independently chosen inflation objectives. The foreign-exchange-market interventions of the floating-exchange-rate era were the tailings of this transition—a shadowy residue of the gold standard era. These interventions initially promised a way around the trilemma that promoted exchange-rate stability without restricting monetary independence. Instead, they ended up weakening the credibility of monetary policy. When that became apparent, the United States abandoned its active intervention policy.

7.2 The Trilemma and Monetary Evolution

At the start of the twentieth century, monetary authorities operated under the classical gold standard—a solution to the trilemma that eschewed independent monetary policies in favor of fixed exchange rates and free cross-border financial flows. Instead of targeting domestic objectives, they effectively focused monetary policy on maintaining fixed exchange rates. World gold stocks determined price levels. Countries merely set an official price of gold, promised to buy and sell unlimited quantities of the metal, and allowed private individuals to import or export gold freely. Official gold prices defined exchange-rate parities, and arbitrage contained exchange rates within gold export and import points. The bank notes and the national currencies that circulated were convertible into gold.

By limiting monetary authorities' discretion, the classical gold standard anchored expectations about the long-run purchasing power of money. Still, monetary authorities could exercise some discretion within the gold points to influence market exchange rates, and whenever gold movements threatened the banking sector or the domestic economy in general, authorities as far back as Nicholas Biddle undertook gold devices, proto-foreign-exchange interventions, and monetary-policy actions to affect gold flows. Although monetary authorities exercised some discretion in the short term, preserving convertibility remained their overarching, long-term objective.

World War I ended the classical gold standard and monetary authorities' near singular focus on maintaining fixed exchange rates. To be sure, the subsequent gold-exchange standard remained a strong commitment to fixed exchange rates, but not one for which countries would long sacrifice internal economic conditions. Additional policy objectives, however, required additional independent instruments. When necessary, countries sterilized gold flows, erected trade barriers, and intervened in the gold and foreign-exchange markets. Between 1924 and 1931, the Federal Reserve—in close cooperation with foreign central banks—was heavily involved in various types of exchange-market operations, including gold purchases and sales, the extension of foreign central-bank credits, and foreign-exchange interventions.

The Great Depression pushed many countries—notably the United Kingdom in 1931—off the gold standard and forced policymakers to focus on domestic policy goals. Trade restraints, competitive depreciations, and other beggar-thy-neighbor policies ran rampant. When it abandoned gold, the United Kingdom set up the Exchange Equalisation Account, a mechanism for intervening in foreign-exchange markets. Fearing that Britain might attempt to manipulate exchange rates to its competitive advantage, the United States established its own Exchange Stabilization Fund. (The United States had also devalued the dollar, but except for a brief hiatus between April 1933 and January 1934, remained committed to the gold standard.) The Exchange Stabilization Fund was the first formal US institution set up specifically for intervention. Previous arrangements, such as those undertaken during World War I, were makeshift. When a dollar exchange rate moved to a gold point, as happened relative to the French franc, or moved by a substantial amount, as happened vis-à-vis the British pound, the Exchange Stabilization Fund typically bought or sold gold instead of foreign exchange. The 1936 Tripartite Agreement between France, the United Kingdom, and the United States emphasized and promoted cooperation in these intervention operations. The Exchange Stabilization Fund remained active through 1939.

Between 1934 and the outbreak of World War II, the United States still viewed its exchange-market operations as augmenting the gold-exchange standard. The interventions over this period may have promoted short-term exchange-rate stability, but they did not address fundamental misalignments among currencies. They did not solve the trilemma. World War II, with its exchange controls and disruptions, ended the problems that the Great Depression posed for exchange markets.

The unwillingness to constrain US monetary policy to the rigors of fixed exchange rates proceeded throughout the Bretton Woods era. Under the Bretton Woods agreement, the United States pegged the dollar to gold, and other countries pegged their currencies to the dollar. Countries could, however, adjust exchange rates to fundamental disequilibria. The Federal Reserve System focused monetary policy almost exclusively on domestic economic objectives, and left other countries, which cared equally about their own domestic conditions, with the burden of defending their currencies. The Federal Reserve and the US Treasury took steps to protect the US gold stock and to help other countries defend their parities, but these actions did not address fundamental problems. In the early 1970s, countries began allowing their currencies to float against the dollar. Floating exchange rates solved the trilemma problem in favor of free cross-border financial flows and monetary-policy independence. Still, countries attempted to manipulate exchange rates through intervention. They feared that informational inefficiencies made foreign exchange rates excessively volatile and prone to substantial deviations from fundamental values. It took US policymakers another twenty years to appreciate that intervention did not provide a way around the trilemma—a way to systematically affect exchange rates independent of monetary policy.

7.3 Sterilized Intervention and Monetary Policy Credibility

The institutional arrangements and operating mechanisms adopted under the Bretton Woods system—along with attitudes about the inherent instability of the foreign-exchange markets—carried forward into the floating exchange-rate era. Initially economic theory suggested that sterilized intervention offered a mechanism through which to affect exchange rates independent of the domestic goals for monetary policy. It seemed to offer a solution to the trilemma. As time went by, however, clear evidence of sterilized intervention's independent effectiveness seemed scarce. Instead, sterilized intervention increasingly seemed a hindrance to monetary policy. Because the Federal Reserve System lacked a clear legislative mandate for price stability, its credibility with respect to that goal was fragile. Intervention and the associated institutional arrangements for intervention in the United States seemed to threaten that credibility. The problem was threefold: First, in the United States, the Federal Reserve was subservient to the US Treasury with respect to exchange-market operations. Second, to have anything other than a fleeting effect on exchange rates, an appropriate change in monetary policy needed to accompany a sterilized intervention. Could then the Treasury, by directing intervention operations, influence—or even appear to influence—monetary policy? Third, the institutional arrangements for intervention often involved the Federal Reserve in operations that appeared to contravene the congressional appropriations process. Might a jealous Congress retaliate and circumscribe the Federal Reserve's independence? These concerns, which germinated in 1961, came to full fruition thirty years later.

7.3.1 Independent within, Not of, Government

By early 1961, US dollar liabilities to the rest of the world exceeded the US gold stock, implying that the United States could not fulfill its pledge to freely exchange dollars for gold at the existing official price. This deficiency encouraged foreign central banks to convert unwanted dollar reserves into gold and raised uncertainty about the Bretton Woods parity structure. To dampen growing speculation in gold and foreign-exchange markets, the Exchange Stabilization Fund began intervening for the first time since 1939. By and large, the ESF undertook forward sales of key European currencies, hoping to lower the forward premia at which they traded against the dollar. These first few operations seemed an unmitigated—and profitable—success, but they were only the opening salvo. The fundamental flaws in the Bretton Woods system were becoming increasingly apparent.

The Exchange Stabilization Fund lacked the foreign-exchange reserves necessary to mount a protracted dollar defense and turned to the Federal Reserve System, whose participation could greatly increase the funding for such operations. To Chairman William McChesney Martin, participation was imperative. Martin hoped to reassert the FOMC's dormant influence in this area, and he may have even wanted to bring the entire function into the Federal Reserve's domain. Martin understood that the Treasury was primarily responsible for foreign-exchange operations in the United States and that the Federal Reserve must coordinate all such actions with the Treasury, but Martin did not think that the relationship threatened the central bank's independence. He viewed the Federal Reserve as independent within—not of—government. Martin's distinction implied that the Federal Reserve must cooperate with the Treasury as far as possible, particularly in governmental actions that did not directly interfere with monetary-policy decisions. At the time, intervention seemed like just such an action since the Federal Reserve could sterilize any unwanted effects on the monetary base.

While most FOMC participants accepted the chairman's direction on this matter, some were decidedly unenthusiastic. Their primary concern was Congress, whose opinion about Federal Reserve intervention in foreign-exchange markets had never been unequivocal. In 1933, Senator Glass, whom many regarded as the father of the Federal Reserve Act, admonished the Federal Reserve Bank of New York for foreign-exchange transactions that it had undertaken in the late 1920s. Glass suggested—and the Board of Governors agreed—that such "stabilization operations" were inconsistent with the Federal Reserve Act. The next year, Congress with strong direction from the Roosevelt administration, passed the Gold Reserve Act, which established the Exchange Stabilization Fund and appropriated resources to the new agency specifically for the purpose of intervening in the foreign-exchange market. Now, some FOMC participants wondered if this congressional action precluded the Federal Reserve from such operations.

In 1961, however, the Board of Governors' General Counsel, Howard Hackley, offered a new legal interpretation of the Federal Reserve Act that supported intervention. Hackley argued that various sections of the act, when considered together, did indeed authorize the Federal Reserve to hold foreign exchange, to intervene in both the spot and forward markets, to engage in swap transactions with foreign central banks, and to warehouse foreign currencies for the US Treasury.

Hackley's interpretation won the day. To be sure, a clear majority of FOMC participants have always favored the Federal Reserve's foreign-exchange operations, but two concerns surfaced immediately and would reappear over the years in various guises. First, some FOMC participants worried that the central bank's involvement would raise congressional ire. Congress had explicitly established and funded the Exchange Stabilization Fund for the purpose of intervention, and the agency also engaged in foreign lending. Congress might view the Federal Reserve's participation as a circumvention of the appropriations process. Second, some FOMC participants feared that the arrangements could threaten the central bank's independence. In 1961, their concerns focused on administration interference with their intervention decisions, but over the next twenty years, this concern morphed into a fear of losing monetary-policy credibility.

The Federal Reserve subsequently undertook direct interventions in both the spot and forward exchange markets, often in concert with the Treasury. In keeping with the key US objective of protecting the US gold stock, however, the Federal Reserve generally focused on two types of swap operations instead of direct foreign-exchange interventions. The Federal Reserve often drew on its swap lines to provide central banks in surplus countries with cover for temporary, unwanted dollar balances. Absent this cover, these central banks would quickly exchange these dollars for US gold. In addition, the Federal Reserve often used swap drawings to provide central banks in deficit countries with temporary dollar liquidity when they faced reversible shortages of foreign-exchange reserves. Ideally these liquidity providing operations raised the costs of speculation against specific currencies and neutralized potential contagion effects.

"Temporary" was the operative term for all of the Federal Reserve's operations. Because of its clearer legal authority for intervention, the Treasury undertook operations of a longer-term nature. These included backstopping the Federal Reserve when market conditions prevented the central bank from promptly reversing a swap drawing. The arrangement, however, would give the Treasury an unwanted voice in how the Federal Reserve reversed those swaps after Bretton Woods collapsed.

The swap transactions and sterilized interventions of the Bretton Woods era confronted two critical and interrelated problems: First, governments had difficulty distinguishing between temporary, reversible disturbances, against which these policies worked admirably well, and more fundamental adjustment problems, against which these policies offered no remedy. In the latter cases, these policies seemed only to delay necessary adjustments and to worsen the situation. Second, they were—along with myriad other arrangements of the period—a tactic to buy time. They did not provide governments a way around the fundamental trilemma—a way to pursue domestic policies under fixed exchange rates with free cross-border financial flows. Consequently, in August 1971, the United States closed its gold window, and in March 1973, generalized floating commenced.

7.3.2   Does Sterilized Intervention Do Anything?

The heightened speculation, large international imbalances, and excessive worldwide liquidity of early 1970s made fixed exchange rates unworkable. Few, however, believed that an international monetary system based on floating exchange rates was sustainable. Many feared that the uncertainties inherent to floating rates would discourage international trade and investment, and would provoke the same disruptive policies—protectionism and competitive depreciations—that characterized the 1930s. (Nixon, after all, imposed import surcharges when he closed the gold window.) Some even contemplated a complete breakdown of international monetary cooperation and financial order.

Although monetary authorities soon grew comfortable with floating exchange rates, they continued to view the market as inherently prone to bouts of disorder. Information imperfections could cause exchange rates to deviate from their fundamental values, create excessive volatility, and foster destabilizing speculation. Under such conditions, an official presence—particularly on the part of the United States—could help direct exchange rates along a path consistent with fundamentals and could do so with lower volatility than would otherwise be the case.

Yet, the FOMC never clearly explained how intervention might accomplish this task. In the 1970s, many economists—including the board staff— believed that intervention worked through a portfolio-balance channel, which allowed central banks to affect exchange rates independent of their domestic objectives. The foreign exchange desk, however, never described intervention in these terms. Instead the desk viewed intervention as having a psychological effect on the market that came about because the intervention expressed an official concern for exchange rates. Neither of these transmission mechanisms, however, seemed to inform their early operations. The desk, which then focused on preventing dollar depreciations, typically undertook small sales of foreign exchange executed via a commercial-bank correspondent in the brokers' market. This maintained the desk's anonymity. The desk, which was intervening without Treasury participation, favored this stealth approach because it feared that speculators might quickly bet against, and overwhelm, the operations. In all this anonymity, however, where was the official expression of concern? Moreover, because the Federal Reserve drew on swap lines to finance its sales of foreign exchange, the desk had to quickly reverse course to repay the swap. Hence, any portfolio effect quickly disappeared.

Between 1977 and 1979, market conditions changed for the worse. Monetary policy was excessively easy, confidence in the Federal Reserve quickly evaporated, and as it did, the dollar sharply depreciated. The United States began a more forceful dollar defense. The US Treasury began to intervene in the exchange market in concert with the Federal Reserve and often announced specific operations. In addition, the desk now frequently intervened directly with commercial banks, rather than through a broker. The United States, however, still relied heavily on swap drawings to finance its interventions. As an expression of displeasure with the Federal Reserve's inflationary policies, Germany threatened to attach macroeconomic conditions to further swap drawings. On 6 October 1979, with its integrity in tatters, the FOMC announced major monetary-policy changes designed to stop inflation and regain credibility.

Still the dollar did not begin a sustained appreciation—despite the sterilized intervention and the initial policy changes—until late 1980. By that time, the Federal Reserve had demonstrated its commitment to disinflation despite the onset of recession and growing unemployment. A tight monetary policy and, after 1981, a loose fiscal policy propelled the dollar on a sustained appreciation through early 1985. The heavy interventions since 1977 seemed to have had little effect, except to occasionally limit the extent of the dollar depreciation.

Consequently, by late February 1981, the United States had all but stopped intervening. The Reagan administration explained that the dollar's depreciation since 1973 had primarily reflected America's relatively high rate of inflation—a fundamental that sterilized intervention did not address. If anything, sterilized intervention may have interfered with monetary policy. Since 1979, the desk had been attempting to acquire a portfolio of foreign exchange—as protection against future imposition of conditions on swap drawings—while the FOMC was attempting to tighten policy. Such operations seemed at cross purposes. Did the market understand sterilization? Moreover, exchange markets had evolved since 1973, and the presumption that the desk possessed an information advantage over the market now seemed passé.

The Reagan administration's position on intervention—in conjunction with the dollar's persistent appreciation—culminated in the first multinational study of intervention. The resulting Jurgensen Report (1983) was by and large ineffectual, but it did reach one conclusion that would reverberate within the FOMC and that would eventually become a focal point for arguments against interventions. The report stated that, in the face of persistent market pressures, sterilized intervention was ineffective and that "supportive" domestic monetary-policy changes were necessary. By the time of the Jurgensen Report, the leading paradigm for intervention—the portfolio-balance channel—was losing ground to the signaling mechanism, whereby sterilized intervention was useful as a signal of unanticipated future changes in monetary policies. If the Jurgensen conclusion and this new transmission mechanism were true, sterilized intervention did not provide monetary authorities with a way around the trilemma.

7.3.3   Credibility and Independence

Despite the equivocal support for sterilized intervention, the United States returned to the markets in force in 1985. As the dollar appreciated, US policymakers were coming under intense pressure from businesses, academic economists, and foreign officials to intervene again in the foreign-exchange market. The Federal Reserve, concerned that the prolonged dollar appreciation might bring pressure for monetary ease and thus might undermine its ongoing inflation fight, thought that sterilized intervention might buy it some cover. The interventions that began in the mid-1980s and continued through the early 1990s were often part of an international attempt at macroeconomic policy coordination, which the US Treasury negotiated among its G5 or G7 counterparts. The evidence that these interventions—and not the monetary-policy changes that sometimes accompanied them—systematically affected exchange rates, was never compelling.

Still, most FOMC participants seemed willing to defer to the desk's opinion about the need and effectiveness of sterilized intervention until the operations started to interfere with monetary policy. In the late 1980s, the FOMC was tightening monetary policy, trying to stem a rise in inflation, and hoping to consolidate hard-won gains in its credibility. The desk, under strong pressure from the US Treasury, was buying huge amounts of German marks and Japanese yen and warehousing large positions for the Treasury. The perennial concerns about intervention arose anew, but now focused on how intervention threatened monetary-policy credibility.

The Federal Reserve Bank of Richmond articulated the fear. Sterilized intervention and the institutions associated with intervention damaged the Federal Reserve's credibility, because Congress had never statutorily mandated price stability as the Fed's sole—or even chief—policy goal. The Federal Reserve's credibility with respect to price stability was purely reputation based. Such credibility is hard to acquire and is inherently fragile. Central bank independence—keeping the Federal Reserve free of political influence—is the sine qua non of reputation-based credibility (Broaddus and Goodfriend 1996).

The FOMC's objections to intervention became threefold: First, although legally independent, the Federal Reserve had little choice but to participate with the US Treasury in major foreign-exchange operations. If it did not contribute, Congress or the administration might accuse the central bank of undermining a legitimate government operation. Second, FOMC participants—echoing the Jurgensen Report—feared that if markets interpreted sterilized intervention as a signal of future monetary-policy changes, the operations would create uncertainty about the Federal Reserve's commitment to price stability. This concern was particularly critical given the Treasury's authority over intervention in the United States, and given that the dollar often appreciated when the FOMC tightened monetary policy. Third, the operations to offset dollar appreciations and the warehousing of Treasury funds left the Federal Reserve holding foreign currency assets on its books. Foreign-exchange losses could lead Congress to accuse the central bank of mismanagement or, in the case of warehousing, of interfering with the appropriations process. Such criticisms could lead to policies that might impinge on the Federal Reserve's independence.

By 1995, these arguments and a growing uncertainty about sterilized intervention's worth had convinced US monetary authorities to revert to a minimalist approach. Since August 1995, the United States has intervened on only four occasions. Some FOMC participants now took aim at the institutional arrangements for intervention—swap lines and the warehousing facility. The Mexican financial crisis in 1995 aided their efforts.

When the Mexican crisis hit, Congress refused a Clinton administration request for Mexican loan guarantees. Then, the US Treasury embarked on an existing contingency plan that presumed heavy Federal Reserve involvement. The Federal Reserve would increase its existing swap lines with Mexico and would augment them with additional temporary swap lines to that country. To help fund any bailout, the Treasury asked the Federal Reserve to warehouse up to $20 billion in German marks and Japanese yen—a huge amount that might take a decade to unwind. The FOMC authorized the increase, but to many FOMC participants, such an involvement was a clear circumvention of Congress's appropriation process. Fortunately, in the end, the Treasury never warehoused foreign currencies with the Federal Reserve, and Mexico quickly repaid its swap drawings. Largely in response to this incident, the FOMC eliminated the then existing swap lines, lowered the limit of warehousing, and has since never warehoused funds for the US Treasury.

7.4   Lessons

This history has described the evolution of foreign-exchange operations in the United States primarily from the perspective of the Federal Reserve System. We have explained how solutions to the fundamental trilemma of international finance changed during the twentieth century and how policy-makers in the large developed economies came to favor monetary policy independence, financial globalization, and floating exchange rates. We have described exchange-market policies—from gold devices to sterilized interventions—as attempts to avoid the trilemma at least in the short run. Finally, we explained how the United States ended its active intervention policy largely because it threatened the Federal Reserve's credibility with respect to achieving price stability.

While many other key central banks followed suit, exchange-rate policy—specifically foreign-exchange-market intervention—remains a viable option for monetary authorities worldwide. In the current gloomy economic environment, with threats of "currency wars" being tossed around, the US experience with intervention suggests a few general conclusions, which may now have wider relevance.

Sterilized foreign-exchange-market intervention does not affect fundamental determinants of exchange rates, and therefore does not afford monetary authorities a means of *systematically* affecting exchange rates independent of their domestic monetary-policy objectives. Moreover, the *persistent* use of sterilized intervention may interfere with the conduct of good monetary policy if it creates uncertainty about the willingness and ability of a central bank to meet its domestic policy objectives, specifically price stability. Intervention may create uncertainty especially when it attempts to ameliorate exchange-rate movements that are themselves a response to monetary-policy initiatives, as happened in the United States during the late 1970s and often between 1987 and 1995. Such intervention may inappropriately suggest that policy will soon change, which must destroy credibility about domestic-policy objectives.

This concern about effects of intervention on central-bank credibility is especially relevant to independent central banks whose fiscal authorities have primary control over foreign-exchange intervention. The US experience shows that even central banks with well-established histories of independence find it extremely difficult to avoid participating in such operations. The public often identifies central banks with interventions, even those conducted by fiscal authorities, because central banks, acting as their governments' fiscal agents, execute the transactions and manage the countries' reserve positions. More importantly, when a central bank refuses to intervene in concert with its country's fiscal authority, it opens itself to criticism that its refusal sabotaged a legitimate government operation, should that operation fail. This may encourage officials to curtail the central bank's independence. To alleviate this problem, countries might place responsibility for foreign-exchange intervention solely within their central banks.

These concerns about the systematic use of foreign-exchange intervention do not mean that such operations are entirely ineffective or inappropriate, but their ability to affect exchange rates seems more of a hit-or-miss proposition than a sure bet. Among foreign-exchange-market participants information is costly and asymmetrically distributed. In such a market, any trader with superior information can conceivably affect price, if the market can observe his or her trades. At times, central banks may be just such traders. They have large staffs that gather and analyze data, and they maintain ongoing information relationships with major trading banks. By our estimates, however, roughly 60 percent of all US interventions between 1973 and 1997 were successful—a number that is not different than random. This overall count masked two distinctive outcomes. First, US sales or purchases of foreign exchange did not have value as a forecast that the dollar would shortly appreciate or depreciate.[1] Second, US interventions did have value as a prediction that near-term exchange-rate movements would moderate, but less than one in four operations were successful on this score. These numbers suggest that US policymakers do not *routinely* have an informational advantage over private market participants. Still, policymakers may occasionally confront periods of extreme market disorder where their actions prove successful. These should be rare events.

Moreover, a central bank might undertake such occasional interventions without damaging its credibility. As the history of the gold standard suggests, a credible central bank can occasionally deviate from its primary objective without damaging its reputation, when market participants understand that it will soon revert to its original goal. Similarly, a central bank with a sound reputation for price stability might at times intervene. As we have shown, uncertainty can arise when central banks attempt to offset exchange-rate movements that result from, or at least are consistent with, their own monetary policies, especially when fiscal authorities have primary responsibility for intervention.

The United States, to the best of our knowledge, did not employ nonsterilized intervention during the Bretton Woods period or since the inception of generalized floating.[2] When engaging in nonsterilized intervention, a central bank executes open-market operations via foreign exchange. The transactions affect bank reserves and the monetary base. Nonsterilized intervention is tantamount to introducing an exchange-rate target into a central bank's reaction function, and has the potential of introducing conflict between policy goals. If, for example, the underlying shock to the exchange market is domestic in origin and monetary in nature, no conflict exists, but nonsterilized intervention seems wholly redundant to normal open-market operations. If, however, the shock to the exchange rate is foreign in origin or nonmonetary in nature, nonsterilized intervention will interfere with the domestic objectives of policy. This conflict and the United States' primary focus on domestic policy objectives explain its reluctance to undertake nonsterilized intervention.

In the recent economic crisis, with the policy options of many central banks constrained by short-term interest rates at or near the zero bound, the purchase of foreign exchange may have provided a means of undertaking quantitative easing. Even though the effects on exchange rates of nonsterilized intervention should be similar to the effects of operations through other asset types, nonsterilized intervention in particular may evoke unjustified complaints of beggar-thy-neighbor actions. Consequently, central banks might only use this mechanism if long-term government securities are not close substitutes for short-term government securities, or if other eligible assets are in short supply.[3]

We have based these conclusions on an analysis of US exchange market policies during the twentieth century and, as noted, primarily from the perspective of the Federal Reserve System. While we offer them as lessons on intervention in general, we understand that the US experience may be unique in some undetermined manner. In that regard, historical studies of other countries' experiences with foreign-exchange intervention should be a profitable venue for further research.

Epilogue
Foreign-Exchange-Market Operations in the Twenty-First Century

E.1 Introduction

After the United States ended its activist approach to foreign-exchange-market intervention, many other advanced economies soon followed suit, but while such operations faded, they never disappeared. Among the large developed economies, Japan frequently intervened in the foreign-exchange market until early 2004, and the European Central Bank, with the Federal Reserve's participation, gave intervention a one-off try in 2001. The Great Recession seemed to pique interest in intervention again as exchange-rate volatility increased, and as threats of "currency wars" were heard. Switzerland undertook substantial foreign-exchange operations both for monetary-policy and exchange-rate objectives. The Great Recession also saw the metamorphosis of official swap lines into a mechanism for channeling foreign-currency liquidity to strapped commercial banks. Among the developing and emerging market economies, particularly in China, foreign-exchange operations have remained a mainstay of macroeconomic policy and development strategy.

In this epilogue, we briefly describe five recent developments as they relate to the Federal Reserve's history with foreign-exchange operations. First, we argue that Japan's success with intervention has been broadly similar to the United States' experience. The United States is not unique. We also suggest that Japan's continued interest in such operations occurs because the interventions have not overtly conflicted with the aims of monetary policy in that country. Such a clash contributed to the end of intervention in the United States. Second, we describe Switzerland's recent experience with foreign-exchange-market operations. Switzerland offers a comparison of sterilized and nonsterilized interventions and a modern example of the fundamental trilemma of international finance. Switzerland cannot stabilize its exchange rate, maintain an independent monetary policy, and allow free cross-border financial flows. Third, we chart the renewed use of swap lines. They continue to signal central-bank cooperation, but whereas in the past that collaboration focused on protecting the US gold stock or on frustrating speculative sales of foreign currencies, it now aims primarily at financing dollar lender-of-last-resort operations abroad. The global integration of financial markets and the reserve-currency status of the dollar may demand such a function. We speculate that this new swap mechanism could remain a key instrument of central-bank operations going forward. Fourth, we briefly discuss intervention among the developing and emerging market economies. We, like others, argue that in their pursuit of exchange-rate stability, these economies run the danger of displacing those very market mechanisms that help traders and manufacturers cope with market volatility. Fifth, we review China's exchange-rate policies. In recent years, China has sterilized part of its interventions, but should sterilized intervention work any better in China than in Switzerland or the United States? All these issues provide fodder for further research.

E.2   Japanese Intervention

Unlike most other large developed economies, Japan has undertaken fairly frequent—and at times massive—interventions. Between April 1991 and March 2004, the main period of intense Japanese activity, the Ministry of Finance bought or sold US dollars on 340 days, or approximately one out of every ten business days. Roughly 90 percent of the transactions were purchases of US dollars, and the median dollar purchase ($789 million) was more than three times as large as the median dollar sale ($223 million). Over this time period, Japan generally moved aggressively to prevent sharp appreciations of the yen, especially when Japanese macroeconomic fundamentals were weak. An exchange rate below ¥125 per dollar seemed to trigger the dollar purchases (Ito 2003, 2005, 2007; Ito and Yabu 2007). As a result of these operations, which totaled nearly $615 billion, Japan accumulated a huge portfolio of US dollar-denominated reserves.[1]

American economists find Japanese intervention particularly interesting because of institutional similarities between the two countries. The Bank of Japan—like the Federal Reserve System—conducts its monetary policy independent of governmental fiscal authorities. The Japanese Ministry of Finance, however, has sole authority for intervention; the Bank of Japan only operates as its agent. Likewise, the US Treasury has primary responsibility for US intervention, although the Federal Reserve does maintain its own portfolio. As with all official US foreign-exchange transactions, Japanese interventions are routinely sterilized. In Japan, the Ministry of Finance issues fiscal bills to obtain the yen for intervention purchases of dollars. The yen is then reinjected into the banking system when the Bank of Japan conducts the transactions. The Ministry of Finance will place any yen acquired through dollar sales on account with commercial banks, thereby sterilizing the transactions. In any event, the Bank of Japan has the capacity to sterilize any intervention operation that conflicts with its monetary-policy objectives. The institutional similarities suggest that both countries seem to view sterilized intervention as a policy instrument capable of affecting exchange rates without sacrificing the domestic objectives of their monetary policies.

Using the same methodology as we adopt in this book (see the empirical appendix), Chaboud and Humpage (2005) tested the effectiveness of Japanese intervention and found results broadly similar to those for the United States.[2] Over the entire 1991–2004 period, when the Ministry of Finance was most active, Japanese purchases or sales of US dollars demonstrated little correspondence with same-day yen depreciations or appreciations, but they were associated with more moderate movements of the yen-dollar exchange rate. This broadly similar finding suggests that the United States is not an entirely unique case, and that intervention has some modest effects.

In contrast to the consistency of the dollar's reaction to US interventions between 1973 and 1995, the yen's response to Japanese operations between 1991 and 2004 changed substantially with the Ministry of Finance's operating strategies (Ito 2003, 2005; Chaboud and Humpage 2005; Ito and Yabu 2007). During the first four years of the operations—as with the entire period—Japanese interventions were only associated with more moderate movements in the yen-dollar exchange rate. In sharp contrast to the first period, between 1995 and 2002, following the appointment of Eisuke Sakakibara as director general of the Ministry of Finance's international bureau, the typical size of a transaction increased tenfold, but interventions occurred much less frequently and persistently. Then, purchases of dollars were associated with a same-day depreciation of the yen that often represented a reversal in the yen's direction. Between late 2002 and early 2004, following the appointment of Hiroshi Watanabe as director general, the typical size of an intervention fell by about one-half, but the frequency and persistence increased substantially. All of the transactions in this last period were unilateral purchases of dollars, and the Bank of Japan often concealed its presence in the market by placing standing orders with banks that entered the market under their own names. In this last period, interventions only seemed to moderate appreciations in the yen against the dollar.

Chaboud and Humpage (2005) also found that the probability of a successful Japanese transaction increased with its size. Acting in concert with the United States, however, had little if any effect on the probability that a Japanese intervention would be successful. (The United States participated in only twenty-two of the 340 Japanese interventions between 1991 and 2004.) Likewise, Bordo, Humpage, and Schwartz (2012) found that the probability of a successful US intervention increased with its size. Coordinating a US operation with another central bank—as in the Japanese case—had little impact on the likelihood of its success.

Since March 2004, the Bank of Japan has only intervened on four occasions. On 15 September 2010, the bank bought ¥2.1 trillion worth of dollars. On 18 March 2011, shortly after a devastating earthquake and tsunami, Japan intervened in concert with the United States and other G7 countries to slow a yen appreciation (Neely 2011). The Bank of Japan bought ¥0.7 trillion worth dollars at that time. On 4 August 2011, the Bank of Japan bought ¥4.5 trillion worth of dollars—then a record amount. On 31 October 2011, however, the Bank of Japan bought ¥9.1 trillion worth of dollars—a new record amount. By summer 2011, the yen was trading at postwar highs relative to the dollar. Each of these operations has been associated with a short-lived depreciation of the yen. While the yen has not retreated from its postwar highs, it has, nevertheless, remained fairly stable since August 2011.

As documented in this book, FOMC participants frequently objected to sterilized interventions because the transactions often were at odds with US monetary-policy goals, and therefore weakened the Federal Reserve's credibility with respect to price stability. At a critical time in the late 1980s and early 1990s, the Federal Reserve bought foreign exchange when the FOMC was trying to tighten policy. In contrast, most Japanese interventions since 1991 have consisted of dollar purchases during a period of slow economic growth with very low inflation—even frequent bouts of deflation—and often with policy rates at the zero bound (McCallum 2003). Under such circumstances, Japan's frequent dollar purchases seemed broadly consistent with the needed thrust of Japanese monetary policy and probably did not damage the Bank of Japan's credibility. Still, the potential for sterilized intervention to create uncertainty about monetary policy remains a key reason that central banks in major developed countries avoid its use. Japanese monetary authorities may someday encounter the same problem.

E.3   Swiss Intervention

Prior to the recent international financial crisis, the Swiss National Bank had not intervened in the foreign-exchange market since August 1995. The bank ended its hiatus in 2009, when financial inflows—seeking safe haven against the ongoing financial crisis—moved substantial funds into Swiss francs. The appreciation of the Swiss franc threatened an already weakened Swiss economy with deflation. The Swiss National Bank's subsequent actions provided a modern example of the difficulties associated with foreign exchange operations—the topic of this book. They illustrated that sterilized intervention cannot systematically influence exchange rates independently of a country's monetary policy (Humpage 2013).

The Swiss National Bank operates with a mandate for price stability and bases current policy on a forecast of inflation. In early 2009, the

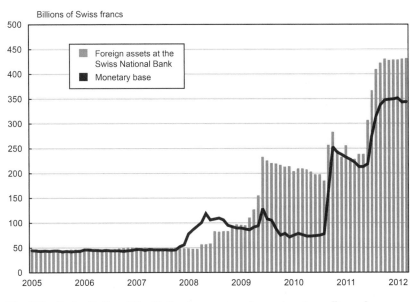

Fig. E.1   Swiss National Bank's foreign assets and monetary base, December 2005–February 2012

Note: Data are from the Swiss National Bank.

Swiss National Bank began to view monetary conditions as inappropriately restrictive despite strong money growth and recent declines in short-term interest rates, because the Swiss franc had been appreciating sharply against the euro since the fall of 2007 (Swiss National Bank 2009, 34).[3] If the franc's appreciation was indeed an indicator of a too-tight monetary policy, a broad-based deflation might ensue.

On 12 March 2009, the Swiss National Bank eased monetary policy. Its actions included a policy-rate cut, the purchase of Swiss private-sector bonds, and foreign-exchange interventions. Immediately after announcing the policy changes, the bank aggressively bought euros in the foreign-exchange market. The Swiss franc depreciated sharply from Swiss franc (SF) 1.48 per euro on 11 March 2009, to SF1.54 per euro three days later. Throughout the month, the bank's holding of foreign-exchange reserves—mostly euros, but some dollars—grew by an amount equivalent to SF9.4 billion (Swiss National Bank 2009, 72).[4] Most of these purchases appeared as an increase in the Swiss monetary base, so for the most part the operation consisted of nonsterilized interventions (see figure E.1). In April, the Swiss monetary base rose even more sharply—absent clear indication of further intervention. By then, the Swiss monetary base had doubled in just six months. Although the franc's depreciation stalled after 16 March, it did not appreciate further that year, leaving a net depreciation by year's end

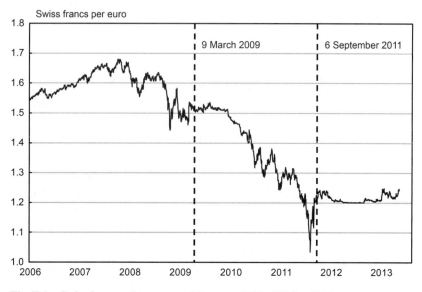

Fig. E.2   Swiss franc exchange rate, 3 January 2006–17 May 2013
Note: Data are from the Swiss National Bank.

(see figure E.2). As the year closed, the bank was projecting inflation above 2 percent in early 2012, so with the franc holding steady, the bank announced that it would henceforth only intervene against an "excessive" appreciation (Swiss National Bank 2009, 40–41).

Between April 2009 and February 2010, the Swiss monetary base contracted by 30 percent. During this period, foreign-exchange swaps, which the bank had undertaken in late 2008 and early 2009 to provide foreign banks with Swiss franc liquidity, were automatically rolling off the bank's balance sheet. The contracts were now reversing, shrinking the Swiss National Bank's balance sheet, and pulling Swiss francs from the market (Swiss National Bank 2009, 53). The Swiss National Bank took no other monetary policy actions to offset these swap reversals. In effect, the Swiss interventions were sterilized.

In early 2010, the European sovereign-debt crisis worsened, and safe-haven inflows caused the franc to appreciate sharply. Swiss foreign-exchange reserves increased by an amount equivalent to SF138 billion between January and May 2010, suggesting heavy intervention, but only about 40 percent of the acquisitions were reflected in the monetary base (Swiss National Bank 2010, 32). By and large, these operations were sterilized. Although the Swiss monetary base briefly spiked to an historical high in May 2010, the base had generally been contracting.

By mid-2010, the Swiss National Bank stopped intervening and again began operations to reduce liquidity in the banking system (Swiss National

Bank 2010, 32, 41–47). By mid-2011, the Swiss monetary base was smaller than in March 2009, despite the bank's substantial accumulation of foreign-exchange reserves. On balance since February 2009, the franc had appreciated nearly 30 percent against the euro, reaching an historic high in early August 2011. The Swiss foreign-exchange operations, which by design or by happenstance were sterilized, had failed to prevent the Swiss franc's appreciation.

During August 2011, the bank announced a series of new measures to inject liquidity into financial markets, with the objective of stemming the Swiss franc's appreciation against the euro. The bank now viewed the Swiss franc as "massively overvalued" and a renewed downside threat to price stability (Swiss National Bank 2011, 36). The bank would undertake foreign-exchange swaps, selling Swiss francs spot and repurchasing them forward. In addition, the bank would repurchase Swiss National Bank bills, which it had sold to drain liquidity from financial markets, and would undertake liquidity-providing repurchase agreements (Swiss National Bank 2011, 51). The announcements did not indicate whether or not the bank intended to purchase foreign exchange outright, but the bank's holdings of foreign-exchange reserves increased substantially in August 2011. The Swiss monetary base began to expand, indicating that the bank had not sterilized its recent foreign-exchange purchases, and the Swiss franc immediately began to depreciate against the euro.

After depreciating nearly 14 percent between 10 August and 29 August 2011, the franc underwent a stunning temporary reversal, climbing more than 6 percent in four days. In response, on 6 September 2011, the bank announced that it would "no longer tolerate" the franc exchange rate below SF1.20 per euro and that it was "prepared to buy foreign currency in unlimited quantities" to maintain this floor (Swiss National Bank 2011, 38). The Swiss National Bank then acquired SF71.5 billion worth of foreign-exchange reserves in August and an additional SF26.9 billion worth of foreign-exchange reserves in September 2011. The Swiss monetary base increased by even more in both months, indicating that the monetary authorities had not sterilized these foreign-exchange purchases, but had reinforced the interventions' monetary impact. Since September 2011, the Swiss National Bank has successfully maintained its exchange-rate floor against the euro, often through heavy nonsterilized purchases of foreign exchange (Swiss National Bank 2012, 34). In doing so, the bank has allowed its monetary base to more than double since early 2011.

The Swiss National Bank's experience since 2009 illustrates that sterilized interventions do not provide central banks with a way to systematically influence their exchange rates independent of their monetary policies. The interventions in March 2009, which increased the monetary base and therefore were nonsterilized, affected the exchange rate, as did the operations in and after August 2011, when the Swiss National Bank allowed a quadrupling of the monetary base to maintain the Swiss franc-euro floor. In contrast, the interventions after April 2009 and before August 2011, which did not raise the monetary base, failed to guide the Swiss franc lower against the euro. Instead, the franc appreciated substantially.

E.4   Swap Lines

On 12 December 2007, the FOMC reestablished swap lines with key foreign central banks as a way of channeling emergency dollar funding to foreign depository institutions that otherwise lacked access to Federal Reserve borrowing facilities.[5] Although targeted to foreign banks, the FOMC understood that these lending facilities could ease dollar funding pressures more broadly. Initially, the FOMC extended swap lines only to the European Central Bank and the Swiss National Bank, but the lines grew as the financial crisis unfolded, and by mid-2009, fourteen central banks, including some key emerging market central banks, had access to Federal Reserve System swap facilities. As the subsequent narrowing of various risk spreads suggests, the swap lines successfully calmed market uncertainty (Goldberg, Kennedy, and Miu 2010; Fleming and Klagge 2010).

After 2000, financial-market innovation and sustained globalization spurred growth in banks' foreign-currency-denominated assets.[6] European banks in particular greatly increased their holdings of dollar-denominated loans and securities. Banks funded these dollar positions largely in short-term, wholesale markets, either by borrowing dollars or—more often—by acquiring domestic currencies and converting them into dollars via foreign-exchange swaps. Although both funding routes created maturity mismatches, the latter seemed particularly risky. In 2007, according to the Bank for International Settlements, 78 percent of foreign-currency swap turnover reflected contracts with maturities of less than seven days (McGuire and von Peter 2009, 54, fn. 10). The maturity mismatch left banks vulnerable to rollover problems.

As the global financial crisis spread in late 2007, heightened financial-market credit risk dried up dollar funding. Banks not only found it increasingly difficult to fund their exposures, but many acquired additional dollar assets as they backstopped structured investment vehicles (Fleming and Klagge 2010). Maturity mismatches lengthened, and a severe dollar shortage emerged. Although US branches of foreign banks that held reserves could borrow from the Federal Reserve, most foreign banks could not.

On 12 December 2007, the Board of Governors of the Federal Reserve System established the Term Auction Facility, which offered emergency dollar loans to US depository institutions. At the same time, the Federal Open Market Committee established special liquidity swap lines with the European Central Bank and the Swiss National Bank. These swap lines essentially extended the Term Auction Facility's reach beyond US borders by financing term dollar funding facilities for foreign banks.

As with previous swap lines, the central banks involved in the new arrangements would conduct the spot and the forward legs of any transaction at the same exchange rate, thereby eliminating exchange risk. The European Central Bank and the Swiss National Bank drew on these swap lines at one- or three-month terms as they extended dollar liquidity to eligible commercial banks in their jurisdictions. The loans that the European Central Bank and the Swiss National Bank made to commercial banks were collateralized, and the interest rates on the dollar funds initially were equal to the lowest acceptable auction rate under the Federal Reserve System's Term Auction Facility. The European Central Bank and the Swiss National Bank assumed all counterparty risk. The Federal Reserve did not invest the euros or Swiss francs that it acquired when its counterparts drew on the lines. Instead, the Federal Reserve held the foreign currencies in noninterest bearing deposits with the respective foreign central bank, and the foreign central banks paid the Federal Reserve the same interest that they earned on loans to their commercial banks. According to Fleming and Klagge (2010, 2–3): "This arrangement avoided reserve-management difficulties that might arise at foreign central banks if the Fed were to invest its foreign currency holdings in the market." Initially the swap lines with the European Central Bank and the Swiss National Bank amounted to $20 million and $4 million respectively, but the amounts quickly expanded to $55 million and $12 million respectively, just prior to the Lehman Brothers collapse on 15 September 2008.

Initially, too, the Federal Reserve sterilized the swap operations by selling Treasury securities from its portfolio. The Federal Reserve's balance sheet showed little increase during 2007 and in the first half of 2008, but after the Lehman Brothers collapse, the Federal Reserve's balance sheet expanded rapidly (see figure E.3).

Dollar funding problems greatly intensified following the Lehman Brothers failure, and the Federal Open Market Committee accordingly expanded the special liquidity swap facilities in tandem with foreign central banks' dollar liquidity operations. By the end of September 2008, the Federal Reserve had offered swaps to nine central banks. The total facility had grown from $24 million to $620 million. By late October 2008, the Federal Reserve eliminated the overall limit on the facilities for the Bank of England, the Bank of Japan, the European Central Bank, the Swiss National Bank, and five more central banks—the Bank of Brazil, the Bank of Korea, the Bank of Mexico, the Bank of New Zealand, and the Monetary Authority of Singapore—obtained swap lines. Aizenman and Pasricha (2009) suggest that the Federal Reserve primarily extended swap lines to those emerging market economies in which US banks had high exposures. At the program's peak in December 2008, swaps outstanding totaled more than $580 billion and accounted for over 25 percent of the Federal Reserve System's total assets (Fleming and Klagge 2010, 5).

The swap lines allowed foreign central banks to channel dollar liquidity directly to domestic financial institutions, and the swaps expanded in size

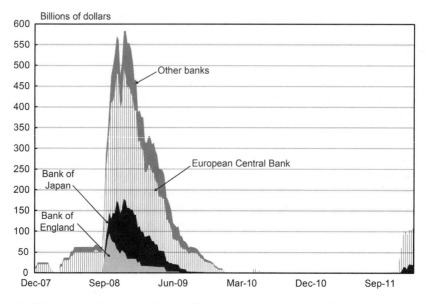

Fig. E.3   Federal Reserve dollar liquidity swaps by counterparty, 19 December 2007–3 February 2012

Note: Data are from the Federal Reserve.

and maturity structure along with the lending facilities of the foreign central banks.[7] The programs that the foreign central banks offered varied in terms of eligibility, collateral requirements, and auction types. On 13 October 2008, in the wake of the Lehman Brothers collapse, the Bank of England, the Bank of Japan, the European Central Bank, and the Swiss National Bank began offering "full allotments" of dollar liquidity—that is, as much as local commercial banks desired—at a fixed interest rate equal to 100 basis points over the overnight index swap (OIS) rate.[8] To accommodate their full allotment format, the Federal Open Market Committee removed the limits on swap drawing by these four central banks. As market turmoil calmed in 2009, and as market rates no longer exceed the OIS rate by more than 100 basis points, central-bank lending facilities were no longer advantageous to financial institutions. Swap drawings fell off in turn.

Use of the swap lines peaked in December 2008 (see figure E.3). The European Central Bank (ECB), whose outstanding drawings reached $300 billion in late 2008, was the biggest single user of the facility, followed by the Bank of Japan and the Bank of England. Although swap borrowing fell off in 2009, funding markets continued to differentiate between strong and weak financial institutions (Goldberg, Kennedy, and Miu 2010, 19–20). After a couple of extensions, the initial swap lines expired on 1 February 2010. Brazil, Canada, New Zealand, and Singapore never drew on their swap lines.

By most accounts the swaps were successful in channeling dollar liquidity and calming markets (Goldberg, Kennedy, and Miu 2010).

Unlike most previous swap agreements, the post-2007 lines were not reciprocal. The Federal Reserve did not use (or invest) the foreign exchange that it acquired through the swaps. In April 2009, the Federal Reserve established parallel swap lines with the Bank of Canada, the Bank of England, the Bank of Japan, the European Central Bank, and the Swiss National Bank that allowed the Federal Reserve to draw foreign currencies against dollars. These lines could channel emergency funding through the Federal Reserve to US banks experiencing liquidity problems in foreign currencies. The Federal Reserve never drew on these lines.

The 1 February 2010 swap-line hiatus was short-lived. On 9 May 2010, as the European debt problem roiled still-fragile financial markets, the Federal Reserve reestablished swap lines with the Bank of Canada, the Bank of England, the Bank of Japan, the European Central Bank, and the Swiss National Bank at a rate of 100 basis points over the OIS rate. With the exception of the swap line with the Bank of Canada, which maintained an overall limit of $30 billion, the other facilities were again open-ended to allow foreign central banks to auction dollar liquidity in a fixed-rate full-allotment format. On 30 November 2011, to make the facilities more attractive to commercial banks, the participating central banks lowered the interest rate on these lines to 50 basis points over the OIS rate. In addition, on 30 November 2011, the Bank of Canada, the Bank of England, the Bank of Japan, the European Central Bank, and the Swiss National Bank agreed to make temporary swap lines available to each other so that emergency liquidity was available in each of the currencies to each of the participants. All of these lines were scheduled to expire on 1 February 2014. At its October 2013 meeting, however, the FOMC made the liquidity swap lines with these five key central banks available indefinitely.

Some controversy arose over extending swap lines to countries that held substantial amounts of reserves—presumably dollar reserves. William Poole, the president of the Federal Reserve Bank of St. Louis, voted against establishing swap lines with the European Central Bank and the Swiss National Bank. He viewed the lines as unnecessary given the size of the dollar-denominated reserves held by these institutions (FOMC *Minutes*, 11 December 2007, 1, 9). In the end, however, most of the countries that received swap lines (in dollars or in other currencies) did not seem to hold sufficient reserves to meet the liquidity demands of the financial crisis (Moessner and Allen 2010; Obstfeld, Shambaugh, and Taylor 2009). Swaps can augment reserves and—what is often equally important—signal central-bank cooperation.

Besides these Federal Reserve swap lines, other central banks—notably the Bank of Japan, the European Central Bank, the Swiss National Bank, and the People's Bank of China have established swap arrangements with many emerging market economies (Moessner and Allen 2010; Aizenman, Jinjarak, and Park 2010). The ECB made euro swaps available to many European countries outside of the European Monetary Union to stem liquidity shortages, although not all countries experiencing euro liquidity problems received swap lines. Likewise, the Swiss National Bank made Swiss franc swaps available to countries experiencing Swiss franc liquidity shortages (Auer and Kraenzlin 2011). The Bank of Japan extended a yen swap line to South Korea and the Japanese Ministry of Finance extended a dollar swap line to India (Moessner and Allen 2010, 32–33).

East Asia has had an extensive swap network in place since 2000, as a means of offering financial support should a financial crisis like the one experienced in 1997 and 1998 reemerge. These swaps are designed to foster closer economic integration in the area (Moessner and Allen 2010, 32). The People's Bank of China extended new swap lines during 2008 and 2009 in part to provide a backstop against financial stress, but largely to promote the use of nondollar currencies, notably the renminbi, in regional trade and investment (Moessner and Allen 2010, 33). Besides Asian countries, the People's Bank extended swap lines to the National Bank of Belarus and the Central Bank of Argentina.

The precedent of using swaps for the emergency provision of liquidity denominated in key currencies now seems fairly well established. The dollar lines clearly enhance the currency's role as the key international reserve currency and may be necessary if that role is to continue. These swap arrangements are likely to persist.

E.5   Foreign-Exchange Operations in Developing and Emerging Market Economies

Unlike the major developed countries, which generally stopped intervening after the mid-1990s, the developing and emerging market economies continue frequent operations in their foreign-exchange markets. These small, open economies show a striking aversion to exchange-rate volatility (Calvo and Reinhart 2000). Exchange-rate volatility can often have serious macroeconomic consequences in these economies because they frequently lack hedging facilities that protect domestic firms from volatility. Ironically, the frequent interventions that developing and emerging market countries undertake, together with other policies that they pursue to increase the effectiveness of those interventions, can limit the very financial development that they so badly need.

Assessing the intervention activities in developing and emerging market economies is not straightforward. Their financial markets are underdeveloped and often tightly regulated. They often impose restrictions on cross-border financial flows. Their interventions are not always sterilized, and hence are a product of monetary policy as much as exchange-rate policy. Their motives for buying or selling foreign exchange vary widely—beyond what we have heretofore considered intervention. Still, because of their unique characteristics, these countries provide useful laboratories for understanding the behavior of exchange rates and the effectiveness of intervention.[9]

In many developing and emerging market economies, the foreign-exchange market is a—if not the—key asset market, and the local central bank is often the dominant player in that market. Almost by definition, foreign-exchange markets in these developing and emerging market countries are underdeveloped, particularly at the interbank level (Canales-Kriljenko 2004). They lack liquidity and a broad array of financial products, particularly hedging facilities. Besides attempting to stabilize exchange rates, central banks in these countries often act as a fiscal agent for the government, buying and selling foreign exchange to finance cross-border expenditures, to service foreign-currency-denominated debts, or to adjust foreign-exchange reserves. In countries where the government is a key source of foreign-exchange earnings—for example, oil-producing nations—central banks may play an important role in channeling foreign-exchange receipts to the market. Because of their familiarity with the market, central banks may also act as their governments' administrators of the foreign-exchange market. In that role, they often cast a broad web of regulations upon market participants, deciding who might trade foreign exchange, specifying the markets in which they operate, and limiting their positions and exposures. Central banks may also enforce macroeconomic controls on cross-border financial flows.

In surveys of foreign-exchange activity in developing and emerging market economies Canales-Kriljenko (2003, 2004) found that most central banks in these countries participate in the market irrespective of the underlying exchange-rate regime. They often intervene heavily in markets characterized as flexible or floating. Surprisingly, however, less foreign-exchange intervention occurs under credible fixed exchange-rate regimes. If an exchange-rate peg is credible, foreign-exchange intermediaries tend to act as stabilizing speculators, minimizing the need for official intervention (Canales-Kriljenko 2003, 6–7).

The key objective of frequent intervention in developing and emerging-market economies is to limit exchange-rate volatility. As noted, foreign-exchange markets in these countries tend to be thin, concentrated among a few traders, and generally underdeveloped, which can magnify the response of foreign-exchange rates to economic shocks or new information. Because developing and emerging market economies are often not well diversified, lack credibility with respect to their macroeconomic-policy objectives, and rely heavily on traded goods and foreign financing, exchange-rate volatility can quickly translate into macroeconomic instability. The lack of hedging facilities in particular is an important structural problem linking exchange-rate volatility to macroeconomic instability.

While exchange-rate stability is the key reason for intervention in developing and emerging market economies, acquiring foreign-exchange reserves and providing foreign exchange to market participants are often important objectives of a central bank's market operations. Developing and emerging market countries often buy foreign exchange to accumulate foreign-currency reserves. Many countries see holding substantial portfolios of foreign-exchange reserves as a means of building investor confidence by strengthening their debt-repayment capabilities, and maintaining external liquidity (Canales-Kriljenko, Guimarães, and Karacadağ 2003).[10] Moreover, buying and selling foreign exchange is necessary if the central bank is the key intermediary for foreign exchange in countries where the government is the chief foreign currency recipient.

When operating in the foreign-exchange market, only about one in five developing or emerging market economies routinely sterilizes their interventions (Canales-Kriljenko 2003, 8). Some countries simply undertake monetary policy using an exchange-rate target and dealing in foreign exchange; persistent sterilization would be antithetical to such an operation. For many others, sterilization is difficult or socially costly. They may lack financial instruments with which to quickly sterilize an operation, or the instruments may be of short duration, and therefore require frequent rolling over or management (Morano 2005 16; Mohanty and Turner 2005). Heavy persistent sterilized purchases of foreign exchange may eventually raise questions about the monetary authority's ability to service their outstanding government or central-bank securities. Likewise, frequent sterilized intervention in thin or otherwise underdeveloped money markets may also distort relative prices among asset categories. The interest cost of sterilization bonds to the monetary authority can easily exceed the interest returns on their liquid foreign-currency assets, while the return on the sterilization bonds to commercial banks can fall far short of their opportunity cost (Lardy 2008). All this fosters inefficiencies through sterilization.

Still, according to Canales-Kriljenko (2003), the interventions that emerging market economies undertake in their less-developed local markets—even when completely sterilized—are very often more effective than the interventions that advanced countries undertake in their fully developed markets. This can even be the case if the central bank in question lacks credibility with respect to its domestic-policy objectives.

Central banks in developing and emerging market economies frequently have the advantage of being big fish in little ponds. They often intervene in amounts that are large relative to the size of local foreign-exchange-market turnover, their own monetary bases, and the stock of their outstanding government bonds. Hence it is very likely that either a portfolio-balance mechanism, an order flow channel, or an expectations effect is open to them. Sometimes central banks in developing and emerging market economies achieve their relative size advantage through their regulatory powers and their use of exchange controls. Such regulations as surrender requirements, prohibitions of interbank trading, or restrictions on taking net-open positions, effectively increase the size of intervention relative to market turnover because they either reduce the size of the foreign-exchange market or concentrate foreign exchange at the central bank, or both. Foreign exchange controls in many countries require their residents to use the domestic currency—instead of a foreign currency—when making payments to other residents, and often limit their ability to hold foreign-currency deposits in banks. Some also impose controls on the use of their domestic currency by nonresidents. These all decrease the effective size of the foreign-exchange market, increasing the impact of intervention.

The key role of central banks as foreign-currency intermediaries in some local foreign-exchange markets, the important role of central banks as regulators in many local foreign-exchange markets, and the lack of an extensive interbank segment in these markets are also very likely to confer an informational advantage on the central bank. If so, a central bank might be able to successfully exploit an expectation channel through its intervention. A strict policy signaling channel, however, would be impaired if the central bank lacked policy credibility or if ongoing structural change in the economy loosened the connection between financial and real variables (Canales-Kriljenko, Guimarães, and Karacadağ 2003).

In contrast, the portfolio-balance channel does not depend on the credibility of the monetary authorities. Galati, Melick, and Micu (2005) originally speculated that the portfolio-balance effect could potentially operate in emerging market economies, even though empirical evidence generally offers little support for a portfolio-balance channel among advanced economies. As previously mentioned, emerging market countries are likely to hold larger portfolios of foreign-exchange reserves relative both to the local exchange market and to the stock of outstanding local-currency bonds than their wealthier counterparts. These are sufficient conditions, but the key necessary condition is also likely to hold: The degree of substitution between bonds denominated in their own currencies and bonds denominated in reserve currencies is very likely to be small. Hence, the risk premium is likely to be larger and more sensitive to changes in the relative stocks of assets.

A temporary order-flow mechanism may also operate better in a developing or emerging market economy than in an advanced market because of the relative size and importance of central banks in underdeveloped markets. In addition, as explained above, central banks in emerging market economies may have better information about order flow than other market participants.

Unlike their advanced-country counterparts, central banks in emerging market economies often use "oral interventions" to affect exchange rates. Because emerging market central banks often regulate their exchange markets more heavily than developed countries—that is, grant licenses, authorize individual dealers, regulate the market—they derive considerable leverage from their regulatory authority. Ideally, verbal intimidation might complement an expectations mechanism, but excessive use could clearly hamper market development (Canales-Kriljenko 2003, 24).

In the limit, as the literature clearly suggests, the relative success that developing and emerging market economies may have in conducting effective foreign-exchange-market operations can intensify the very problem that they seek to avoid. In their desire to foster stability through intervention, regulation, and control, monetary authorities in these countries often discourage private-sector financial innovation and maintain the market's immaturity. When such operations hamper financial-market development, they can actually intensify the macroeconomic consequences of exchange-rate volatility.

E.6   China's Renminbi-Dollar Peg

No country's exchange-rate practices have incited as much controversy as China's have generated. United States policymakers in particular have accused China of artificially undervaluing the renminbi relative to the dollar in order to achieve a trade advantage. China's massive accumulation of foreign-exchange reserves is, indeed, testament to such charges, but whatever trade advantage China obtains from undervaluing the renminbi should be transitory. China's control over its nominal exchange rate does not extend to its real exchange rate. Price level pressures, emanating primarily from its exchange-rate practices, must eventually induce a real renminbi appreciation and erode any competitive edge that the undervaluation provides. This process has been occurring. Although the People's Bank of China has sterilized a substantial part of the reserve accumulation since 2002, this has not prevented inflation and a real appreciation. The renminbi appreciated 30 percent against the dollar in real terms and 40 percent on a real trade-weighted basis between mid-1995 and the end of 2013.[11]

Over the past seventeen years, China's exchange-rate regime has shifted back and forth between a peg against the US dollar and, generally, a tightly controlled appreciation. In July 2005, after pegging the renminbi at ¥8.3 per dollar over the previous decade, China undertook a controlled appreciation of its currency against the US dollar.[12] The People's Bank of China interrupted the appreciation briefly with a renewed peg between July 2008 and June 2010 in response to adverse spillovers from the global financial crisis. Between June 2010 and January 2014, the renminbi again underwent a controlled appreciation against the dollar, bringing the total nominal appreciation since mid-1995 to 30 percent against the dollar. Since then the People's Bank of China has encouraged a renminbi depreciation, although the size of the depreciation has thus far been minimal.

In addition to systematically undervaluing its currency, China also discourages private financial outflows, largely by limiting the amount of foreign currencies that China's residents might hold and their ability to invest those currencies abroad in foreign assets. These controls, in conjunction with China's exchange-rate policies, have resulted in a massive accumulation of foreign exchange reserves, even during the years of renminbi appreciation. Between mid-1995 and December 2011, China's official foreign-exchange reserves rose from $250 billion (equivalent) to $3.2 trillion. Most of this foreign-exchange-reserve accumulation, however, took place after 2001 with important monetary consequences (see figure E.4).

Prior to 2003, the Chinese monetary base increased modestly relative to the country's rapid growth rate. The disparity was such that China often experienced deflation between 1997 and 2003, and the renminbi depreciated against the dollar on a real basis despite the nominal peg (see figure E.5). In 2003, however, the situation changed. Reserve accumulation picked up, as did China's monetary base and its inflation rate. Since then, China's accumulation of foreign-exchange reserves has been especially heavy. To limit the inflation consequences of its exchange-rate policies, the People's Bank started selling sterilization bonds to local commercial banks.[13] From the end of 2003 through 2009, the People's Bank offset 41 percent of its reserve

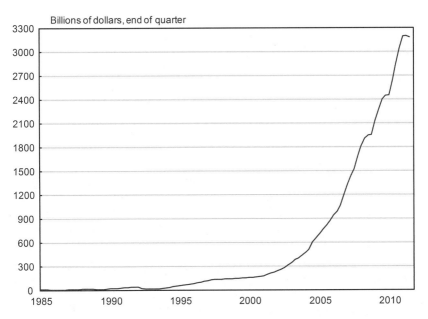

Fig. E.4   China's official foreign exchange reserves, March 1985–December 2011
Note: Data are from the International Monetary Fund.

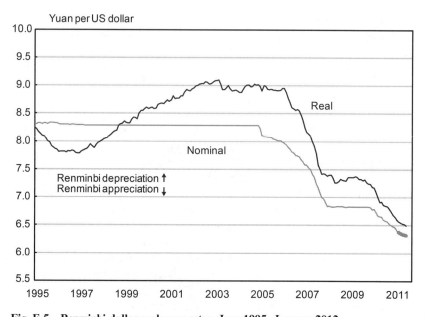

Fig. E.5   Renminbi-dollar exchange rates, June 1995–January 2012

Notes: The real exchange rate is calculated using consumer price indexes. Data are from the US Bureau of Labors Statistics, China National Bureau of Statistics, and the International Monetary Fund.

accumulation, but the monetary base continued to grow sharply (see figure E.6). In addition, the People's Bank increased reserve requirements on banks nineteen times, from 6 percent to 17.5 percent.[14]

This operation is puzzling. China's sterilized intervention could only maintain the peg or limit nominal appreciation if a portfolio-balance mechanism were at work, and as we have shown, the empirical support for such a mechanism—at least among advanced economies—seems nonexistent. Because China undervalues the renminbi, it experiences an excess demand for its currency. In defense of the peg or to limit appreciation, the People's Bank of China must buy foreign exchange and must issue sufficient renminbi base money to meet that excess demand. Effectively, this requires nonsterilized intervention—an expansion of the money supply—to prevent a renminbi appreciation. When China subsequently sterilizes the resulting monetary-base growth, the excess demand for renminbi cannot be met through a supply of renminbi. To maintain the peg or limit appreciation, the issuance of sterilization bonds must raise the nominal interest rate sufficiently—via an increased risk premium—to reduce the demand for renminbi. Has this happened? Demonstrating that the People's Bank of China sterilizes part of the reserve accumulation is necessary, but not sufficient, for explaining the renminbi's peg or its limited nominal appreciation.

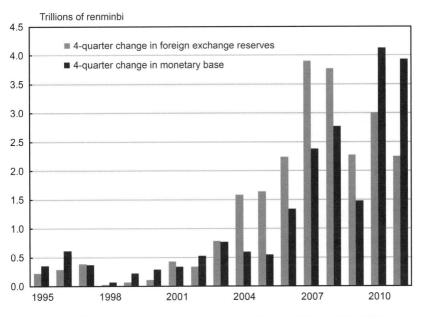

Fig. E.6   Sterilization of foreign-exchange-reserve flows in China, 1995–2011
Note: Data are from the International Monetary Fund.

Although the People's Bank of China did seem to offset part of the monetary impact from its reserve accumulation between 2004 and 2009, the monetary base nevertheless generally grew faster after 2003 than it did before that date. In 2010 and 2011, the monetary base outpaced reserve growth by nearly two to one. Although the People's Bank of China increased reserve requirements from 15.5 percent to 21.5 percent over the past two years, China has experienced a sharp run-up in its inflation rate, and a continued real renminbi appreciation.

China may undervalue its nominal exchange rate, but it has not controlled its real exchange rate, and the latter—not the former—ultimately determines equilibrium. While it is still too early to tell, the real appreciation may have restored nominal equilibrium, and China's experience may illustrate adjustment under a peg when sterilized intervention and financial restraints ultimately prove ineffective.

Appendix 1
Summaries of Bank of England Documents

This appendix provides supplemental documentation for the material found in chapter 3, section 3.4.2.

In a memorandum (possibly by Henry Clay, adviser to the governors), dated 20 November, Purchase of Gold for Account of Federal Reserve Bank Against Payment in Dollars, the text states that the price of gold in New York is perhaps $34.77, but this price is effective only in such cases when the gold is offered in the London market and the price is fixed on the dollar exchange, and of course only in such cases when there is no premium over and above the shipping parity. Today, for instance, the price was fixed at 2 1/2d. (pence) to 3d. (pence) premium on the shipping parity. This naturally excludes the shipment to New York as the outturn required on this basis would be something like $34.82. On the other hand, gold which has already been engaged for shipment to India could not under the suggested arrangement be diverted to London against payment in dollars unless the price were about $34.86.

In a note of a telephone call from Harrison to the deputy governor, on 20 November, Harrison said that with the market in its present position there was no chance of getting any gold; nor would any American commercial institution profitably buy gold for shipment. If conditions changed, however, he wished us (the Bank of England) to act on the lines agreed. The figure $34.77 he had fixed as a limit was based on talks with the New York banks that did this kind of business, and the American Treasury would prefer to stick to the limit. Harrison asked the bank to try it out; if the result was that we did not secure the gold but it was shipped to America by commercial institutions, then we could discuss altering the price. The deputy governor pointed out that it might not be possible to do anything at all by 23 November, and the amounts mentioned in the cable were much larger than was likely to come into the market. Harrison said if the limits were reached, new limits could be discussed. Gold purchases in New York on behalf of the bank with the dollar equivalent deposited for them would be available immediately. He saw no reason to expect that the market would guess that we were operating on their account. The changes in the amount of gold held by us for them would not be published since they would be acting as agents for the American Treasury, which was not required to publish its foreign gold holdings. A memorandum, dated 22 November by an unnamed writer, reports that Governor Montagu Norman wishes rules or instructions to be formulated, with respect to gold for the FRB to ensure the following:

1. That the FRB will buy here only such gold as would otherwise be shipped to New York.
2. That the FRB does not acquire any more gold than under the old arrangement.
3. That the FRB under the new arrangement does not prevent the EEA from getting gold which would have come under the old arrangement.

A note, dated 22 November by an unnamed writer, lists advantages of short-circuiting the transfer of gold: We should get a better price for our gold than we should do by selling francs and releasing gold in Paris; that the effect on the dollar-sterling exchange rate would be greater for a given expenditure than it would be if we influence it only indirectly via the franc; and that it gives us an alternative to operating through Paris.

A memorandum, Gold Purchases For Account of the FRB, dated 23 November by an unnamed writer at the Bank of England, comments that the proposed arrangement with the FRB is that the bank will buy gold for them in London and earmark it in our vaults. The object of the FRB is to prevent the shipment of gold by persons who want dollars, the FRB offering through us what they estimate to be a slightly better outturn in dollars than can be obtained by actual shipment to America. In this way the FRB hopes to put themselves in a position to acquire sterling when they want it, without shipping gold from New York, and meanwhile to conceal from the public the amount of gold moving into American hands. We have agreed, and have been authorized to act within limits of time, amount, and dollar price. The memorandum continues:

The arrangement will be effective only when the sterling price of gold is fixed upon the dollar shipping parity without any premium. If there is a premium, the dollar price which the FRB are prepared to pay will not cover the sterling price. The arrangement will not clash with bank purchases of gold for the EEA. It would clash if the bank bought gold for the FRB with sterling. The bank would buy gold for the FRB with sterling only if the bank sold dollars before or after buying gold for sterling. That would involve the bank in arbitrage risk that the arrangement does not provide for. The bank will buy gold for the EEA with sterling, paying whatever price is required to get it. FRB can get gold from two sources: (a) The big arbitrageurs who buy gold to supply a demand for dollars. They would have to be informed that the bank can give them dollars against gold at a price that would attract them. (b) The EEA when it is supporting sterling by selling gold currencies or gold. Since the United States left gold in 1933, the bank got rid of the dollars it then held and has dealt in dollars only on behalf of customers. Under the arrangement the bank would deal in dollars for the FRB. At present the bank meets the demand for dollars by selling francs or selling gold in the market. Instead the bank would sell dollars against gold for the FRB, a convenience when sterling is weak owing to a demand for dollars. Under the arrangement, it would be natural to sell gold from the EEA to the FRB, instead of the roundabout method of putting gold into the market and then buying it for the FRB. (This sentence is crossed out.) The following paragraph argues that bypassing the release of gold in Paris would get bank a better price for gold and have a bigger effect on the dollar-sterling exchange rate for a given expenditure. Ink comment on the side seems to doubt this analysis.

Cable (322/35) from Harvey to Harrison referring to Harrison's cable (283/35), dated 23 November, reports no opportunity of acquiring gold in London for the FRB.

Gold Purchases for Account of the FRB, a four-page memorandum by Henry Clay, adviser to the governors, dated 27 November. The memorandum is in four numbered sections, summarized in what follows: (1) FRB object is to provide dollars against gold in London for persons who need dollars, and gold in London for people who have payments to make in sterling (i.e., the US government for silver purchases). FRB hopes to reduce sterling-dollar rate volatility and eliminate some gold movements. FRB is offering through the bank a slightly better result in dollars than can be obtained by actual gold shipment to New York. If bank won't act on FRB behalf, it will probably employ Guaranty Trust or some other American bank in London. So far there has been no opportunity for the bank to do anything. (2) It will not be possible to make purchases under the arrangement at all times. Conditions necessary for a purchase in the bullion market include: (a) that a supply of gold is available in the market. Much gold passes through London which does not come into the market; (b) that the price of gold in London is fixed not higher than the exchange parity of the dollar; (c) that the exchange market is quiet, with no expectation of a trend that would encourage speculation; (d) that no premium on forward dollars exists In the absence of these conditions, gold could still be bought for the FRB: (i) If the EEA wishes to sell gold for dollars; (ii) If a London gold hoarder wishes to exchange gold into dollars. (3) The bank can carry out orders for the FRB by two methods: (a) One method would be for the bank to buy gold at a sterling price and sell dollars on the market. Bank could bid for gold at the fixing, up to the dollar parity, taking its share pro rata with other buyers. Simultaneously, the bank would sell dollars; if the market would absorb them at the bank's price, earmark the gold for the FRB; otherwise, the bank should take the gold for the EEA. The procedure would involve exchange speculation, but should not deter the bank. For the defense of sterling it will be advantageous to develop this type of business with the FRB. The bank should acquire gold for the FRB when sterling was weak in the region of the level at which the bank was supporting it, and for the EEA when sterling was strong or when there was a premium over the dollar shipping parity. (b) A second method would be for the bank to buy gold at a dollar price. This would be possible from two sources: (i) The big arbitrageurs who buy gold in order to supply a demand for dollars. It would be necessary to entrust someone in the market, say Rothschilds, with a standing order to buy gold for dollars, or to let the chief arbitrageurs know that we can give them dollars against gold in London, saving them the trouble of shipment; the arrangement with Rothschilds should be tried first; and (ii) the EEA, when it is supporting sterling by selling gold currencies or gold. The bank's transactions at a dollar price would not involve a clash with EEA's requirements. Experience and the EEA operators' discretion should decide when the EEA should take the initiative (selling dollars and earmarking gold for the FRB) and when it would be better to leave the initiative to the market (taking gold in exchange for dollars as it was offered). (4) The bank got rid of dollars when the US left the gold standard, and has since abstained from dealing in dollars except for the account of customers. Under the proposal, the bank would deal in dollars on behalf of the FRB. This would be a convenience when sterling is weak and the weakness is due to a demand for dollars. At present the bank meets the demand for dollars by selling francs or selling gold in the market. Instead, we would sell dollars against gold on FRB account. In these circumstances, it would be natural to sell gold from the EEA's holding to the FRB, instead of first putting gold in the market and then buying it for the FRB. We would get a better price for our gold than we do by selling francs and releasing gold in Paris. The effect on the dollar-sterling rate for a given expenditure would be greater than if we influenced the rate indirectly via the franc. Also we would have an alternative to operating through Paris.

Letter to Montagu Norman, dated 28 November, from Sir Frederic Phillips, adviser to the Chancellor of the Exchequer, comments on the Clay memorandum: (1) Unnecessary shifts of gold are frequent. Bullion is sent on long journeys and then recalled before it reaches its destination. Proposal will reduce such aimless wanderings. Savings of expense will go to the US government. (2) Phillips doubts that US Treasury will use Guaranty Trust or another American bank in London if Bank of England will not act as FRB agent. Americans won't risk holding much gold in London except in agreement with British authorities. (3) Bank should ask if FRB would give it gold for sterling, but Phillips doesn't think it worth raising the question at this point. But another question should be asked. Scheme is designed to give dollars for gold, as though FRB would always be operating to weaken the dollar and never to strengthen it. Does the FRB envisage asking the bank from time to time to sell gold for the FRB at a fixed price, say, $35.23? If not, what arrangements does the FRB envisage for selling gold if the need should arise? (4) Phillips opposes buying gold for the Fed at a sterling price. It would involve exchange risk, and why should the bank take any risk? If it buys gold for dollars, it is a mere agent. If certain countries abandon the gold standard, it would be a nuisance to be buying gold for the Americans at a sterling price. Buying gold for dollars should work smoothly. (5) Phillips believes the advantage lay with letting the big arbitrageurs into the business rather than employing Rothschilds exclusively, but says the bank knows best. (6) Phillips does not attach much importance to the question whether the arrangement will affect EEA operations. Phillips says that Sir Richard Hopkins, an adviser, reporting to the Chancellor will draw his attention to two matters: (a) Morgenthau will announce as a great triumph that he has got British authorities to cooperate in checking gold movements to the United States. That's bosh, since the plan does nothing to check acquisition of gold by the United States. (b) The plan checks physical movement of gold. There will be fewer sensational reports of enormous shipments of gold to the United States, though net movements of gold to London may appear larger. A very big new hoarder, the US government will be added to the hoarders already in London. (7) Apologizes for length of letter.

Letter from H. A. Siepmann, dated 31 March 1936 to Allan Sproul, President of FRBNY. Siepmann introduces himself as successor to Basil Catterns on the exchange department of the bank. The November 1935 order to the bank to purchase gold in London had been renewed the day of his letter, Siepmann says. He realizes that the object is not to acquire gold but to avoid its being shipped. He says, "We shall be lucky if we succeed in doing so with a bid of $34.77. Arbitrageurs who have special facilities—who can avoid, for example, the charges for interest and commission—could undercut us at the price." To be effective against all comers, Siepmann says the bid would have to be $34.78 or, when war risks are eliminated, $34.79. The prospect of a total profit of 1 percent per annum on the money during the period of shipment is enough to bring in some American banks.

We learn from a memorandum, undated (probably after 31 March 1936) from Siepmann to the deputy governor that the FRB renewed its original order (of 19 November 1935 to buy gold in London at a dollar price to prevent shipments to New York) at intervals, first of three or five working days until 11 January 1936. It resulted in two kinds of transactions: (a) a sale of 25,799 ounces by the EEA on 26 November at $34.77. This transaction, undertaken solely to open the account and so the FRB would not assume that the authorities did not care whether gold was shipped to New York or earmarked at the Bank of England, was possible only because the state of the exchanges enabled the bank to buy francs with the dollars and convert them into gold in Paris without loss. (b) two small purchases in the market of 4,000 ounces on 5 December, and 8,000 ounces on 6 December at a sterling price, and sold to the FRB at $34.77 plus 1/8 per mille brokers' commission. The resultant dollars were sold to the market. Thus, despite the British doubts that the price the FRB proposed would elicit sales of gold, sales at that price had been made. Siepmann writes, "Assuming that the FRB again renew their order from time to time, I propose that we should not repeat the first operation, that is, manufacture gold deposits in London for the FRB at the cost of a transfer of EEA gold from London to Paris, where we now have, if anything, too much. But I should like to take seriously the responsibility which, in effect or by implication, the FRB place upon us, of participating in their control operations. Their intention seems to be not merely—and not so much—to prevent arbitrage and gold shipments as such (though there may be special reasons for avoiding them at the present moment), but rather to substitute 'control' operations for 'automatic' adjustment through gold movements. If the US Exchange Fund holds gold in London, it is in a position, pro tanto, to prevent depreciation of the dollar on European currencies, but such control requires the presence of a watchful agent in London, and we are being tacitly invited to act as such."

"A dollar price of $34.77 is probably inoperative for either purpose, and I have written to [Allan] Sproul [George Harrison's successor at the FRBNY] to point this out. But it may be that even with an operative limit, our present arrangements would be ineffective. We have to carry them out through Rothschilds, to whom we simply pass the FRB limit, with instructions to report to us if occasion arises. But Rothschilds and the most active bullion brokers are themselves concerned with arbitrage, and a purely passive attitude on our part might easily lead to our missing opportunities because, instead of looking for them, we wait to have them brought to our attention. It would be a poor response to the FRB's instructions if we then had to explain that our failure to prevent shipment was due to the gold not having been offered to us."

"If the FRB order is renewed, and especially if their limit is raised, I propose that we keep actively on the lookout for any chance of doing business on their terms; that we should be ready to suggest variants to the FRB. If we can do so within their intentions, and that we should even be prepared at a later date, to extend the system, as we did, in practice, when we sold them EEA gold—to purchases based not merely upon a dollar limit but upon a price, in whatever currency, which has the effect of determining the value of the dollar."

George F. Bolton, assistant to Cameron F. Cobbold, adviser to the governors of the bank, commented that if Siepmann's idea were effectively adopted, we should encounter trouble with our European friends. The French and Dutch might complain legitimately that we, by arrangement with the FRB, were facilitating a flow of gold from Paris and Amsterdam.

Letter from Siepmann to Sproul, 2 May 1936. "You may have been surprised—I confess I was—to find that we were able to deal in gold three times this week on your terms; and you may think that I ought now to take back what I said about your price being scarcely adequate for your purposes. But I don't. On the contrary, I want to tell you once again what a tricky business it is; and I want to discourage you from believing that our present arrangements provide an effective barrage, in all circumstances, against gold movements from London to New York. I am not thinking merely of the Indian shipments with alternative destinations, of which one found its way past us—as any of them may—a week or two ago. I am thinking of the general conditions which prevail in our market here, and which require us to be uncommonly vigilant and ingenious if we are to carry out your intentions successfully. It is, of course, quite a good thing that you should keep us on our toes; and I am not pleading for a price which would make it all easy going, especially as I realize that your objective is not to accumulate gold here but to take as little as possible, or at any rate no more than you would otherwise get across the water. But let me tell you that on Thursday (30 April), when we made our second purchase for you, we had three American banks competing with us and ready to bid your price. We got there first, that time, but if you really want to achieve your object, I think you have to be prepared to outbid the market; only by a shade, maybe; but still, outbid. Shades make all the difference in a market which has become as wide and as highly competitive as the bullion market is to-day in London. The six bullion brokers have been accustomed for years to act as principals, and the hoarding demand gives them every opportunity of doing so on a fairly big scale and to their certain advantage. At times, when the market is active, they will make a two-way price, and in addition, there are about a dozen banks, English and foreign (not counting the American banks here) who have set up bullion departments, mostly in recent years, and are willing from time to time to deal in gold. This pack of hounds is pretty hot on the trail, and I don't profess to be the huntsman—because, to tell you the truth, I am quite glad to see people discover new fields of initiative and enterprise, though I am sorry that the hoarding demand should give them such regular opportunities for unloading. The immense hoards in London are not quite sedimentary; they heave and turn a little at a time, and cloud the waters of supply as well as of demand. The result is that figures and statistics have little or no relation to what is really going on at the time when they appear.

"During the past three weeks, the price of gold in London has been fixed on the dollar and, as you have seen, occasionally at par with dollar-sterling rate. What happens? Classical theory requires that arbitrageurs should get out their calculating machines, work out the profits per mille which they can make on a shipment to New York, buy their gold in London and cover their exchange, or hope to. Nothing of the kind. They just buy the gold and remain short of dollars, either spot or forward according to their individual positions. They then sit on this protected position and have a practically safe bet. Sooner or later, the London price of gold will be fixed at a substantial premium over the dollar-sterling rate, either because the dollar has weakened (and they buy their gold when it is the strongest currency in the world) or because the hoarding demand has become temporarily intensified as the result of one or the other of the scares which, nowadays, we can safely expect every week or fortnight. But if, in the meantime, finance has become a shade more costly, or patience has worn a little thin, we may suddenly see shipments of gold to your side when there is no business of the kind in the London market at all. You may then conclude that we have been less watchful than we should be!

"I have no figures at all, but it would not surprise me a bit if at the moment there were £3 or £4 million of gold now held in London but representing potential shipments to New York."

Sproul responded to Siepmann in a letter, dated 5 June 1936. "I must admit that I cannot get steamed up about our buying price for gold in London. Perhaps that is because I don't have to try to beat the market, as you do in the execution of an order, but it does deem to me to be something which can safely be the subject of experimental handling. Even if some gold does slip by, there is no great harm done.

"I am not yet convinced, of course, that our price is altogether too low to do the business under straight arbitrage conditions. One of our banks, which last month tried bringing in some gold from London, for which it paid $34.77 1/8, showed a loss of a few dollars on the transaction, and now figures that it could not hope to do better than break even at $34.77. (It had a melting loss of 1/4 per mille on the shipment it brought in.)

"The other kind of business you mentioned does not seem to me the kind of business with which we would want to compete in any case. Those fellows are just taking a flier in gold, and I shouldn't want to try to interfere with them. If, as a result of such goings on, some gold is shipped over here at times, we certainly wouldn't hold it against you.

"Our French friends seem to have put the gun to their heads again and maybe this time it will go off. Over here the market is principally interested in what will happen to the sterling dollar rate in case there is a gold embargo in France or the French try to adopt exchange control. I suppose the majority opinion in this market is that sterling will advance because of the continued pressure of French and, perhaps, other continental funds seeking to get into sterling. I personally should think, however, that sterling is quite as likely to decline in terms of dollars. If our balance of payments can't be paid off in gold, except to the extent that new or dishoarded gold comes forward, there is liable to be a pressing demand for dollars, particularly if 'investors' on your side and elsewhere, continue to think well of our securities. I gather that if this is the trend, however, you are pretty well fixed for gold which could be sold to 'moderate' the movement.

"What all this business is leading to, I am afraid, is a demonstration of the difficulties of a world of all managed currencies, or of half managed currencies and half gold currencies. I don't think we are going to get very far so long as half of us are in the boat and the other half swimming in the water, or with all of us in the water. How to get your people and our people into the same boat, on a mutually satisfactory basis, is the difficult and important problem, but the one we ought to solve, as I see it. Then we could pick up the swimmers as fast as they wanted to be taken in (without rocking the boat), and some of them could just hang on to the boat indefinitely.

"Things have come to a pretty pass when we must all spend our weekends waiting to see or hear what a Mr. Blum may do."

Appendix 2
Empirical Method for Assessing
Success Counts

A2.1 Introduction

This appendix explains the empirical methodology that we use in chapters 5 and 6 to evaluate US intervention during the floating exchange-rate period. It draws heavily on Bordo, Humpage, and Schwartz (2012). Following a methodology developed in Humpage (1999, 2000), we define three success criteria based on the correspondence between intervention and subsequent exchange-rate movements and count the number of observed successes under each criterion.[1] Then we test to see if counts exceed, or fall short of, a number that might occur randomly given the near-martingale nature of daily exchange-rate changes. A count that is statistically different from random suggests that US intervention has value as a forecast of near-term exchange-rate patterns and conveys information useful for price discovery.

Bordo, Humpage, and Schwartz (2012) also present further empirical results for this sample. They test to see if various factors, including the amount and frequency of interventions and whether the intervention was coordinated, affect the probability of success. They find that larger interventions increase the probability of success, but no other factor does so.

This appendix proceeds as follows: The next section defines our three success criteria, explains our data, and describes some key underlying assumptions. Section 3 evaluates our success counts assuming that successes are hypergeometric random variables. Table A2.1, which does not appear in the body of this book, provides results for the entire 1973 to 1995 sample period. Tables A2.2 and A2.3 provided a summary of results for intervention against German marks and Japanese yen respectively for key subperiods of our sample. Tables A2.4 through A2.9 provide the detailed results for those subperiods from which we constructed the abbreviated tables that appear in chapters five and six.

A2.2   Success Counts

We evaluate the success of US foreign-exchange operations using two specific criteria and a general criterion that incorporates the first two. In all of the definitions that follow, I_t designates US intervention on day t, with positive and negative values being sales and purchases of foreign exchange, respectively. S_t is the opening (9:00 a.m.) spot bid for foreign exchange in the New York market on day t measured in foreign-currency units per US dollar, and $\Delta S_t = S_{t+1} - S_t$. The change in the exchange rate from the opening on day t to the opening on day $t+1$ brackets US interventions on day t.[2] The target exchange rate is either German marks per dollar or Japanese yen per dollar, and I_t consists only of the corresponding intervention, that is, dollars against German marks or dollars against Japanese yen.

Our first binomial success criterion (SC_1) counts an official US sale or purchase of foreign exchange on a particular day as a success ($SC_1 = 1$) if the dollar appreciates or depreciates, as the case may be, over that same day:

$$(1) \quad SC_1 = \begin{cases} 1 & \begin{cases} \text{if } I_t > 0, \text{ and } \Delta S_t > 0, \text{ or} \\ \text{if } I_t < 0, \text{ and } \Delta S_t < 0; \end{cases} \\ 0 & \text{otherwise.} \end{cases}$$

Our second success criterion (SC_2) scores an intervention as a success ($SC_2 = 1$) if the United States sells foreign exchange and the dollar continues to depreciate, but does so by less than over the previous day. Likewise, this criterion counts intervention as a success if the United States buys foreign exchange and the dollar continues to appreciate, but does so by less than over the previous day. (For completeness, we include $\Delta S_t = 0$ in this criterion.)

$$(2) \quad SC_2 = \begin{cases} 1 & \begin{cases} \text{if } I_t > 0, \text{ and } \Delta S_{t-1} < 0, \text{ and } \Delta S_t \leq 0, \text{ and } \Delta S_t > \Delta S_{t-1}, \text{ or} \\ \text{if } I_t < 0, \text{ and } \Delta S_{t-1} > 0, \text{ and } \Delta S_t \geq 0, \text{ and } \Delta S_t < \Delta S_{t-1}; \end{cases} \\ 0 & \text{otherwise.} \end{cases}$$

Our general success criterion (SC_3) incorporates SC_1 and SC_2. Accordingly, an intervention sale of foreign exchange on a particular day is successful ($SC_3 = 1$) if the dollar appreciates or if it depreciates by less than on the previous day. A corresponding rule holds for dollar purchases of foreign exchange.

$$(3) \quad SC_3 = \begin{cases} 1 & \begin{cases} \text{if } I_t > 0, \text{ and } \Delta S_t > 0, \text{ or } \Delta S_t > \Delta S_{t-1} \text{ or} \\ \text{if } I_t < 0, \text{ and } \Delta S_t < 0, \text{ or } \Delta S_t < \Delta S_{t-1}; \end{cases} \\ 0 & \text{otherwise.} \end{cases}$$

We measure success over a single day, which some may find unduly restrictive (Goodhart and Hesse 1993; Fatum and Hutchison 2002). Despite the narrow window, the chance that we might fail to count an intervention as successful because the appropriate exchange-rate movement occurred beyond the opening on day $t + 1$ seems remote. Chang and Taylor (1998), Cheung and Chinn (2001), and Dominguez (2003), among others, suggest that exchange markets begin to respond to intervention within minutes or hours, not days. Likewise, a majority of central bank officials in Neely's (2001) survey contended that exchange rates reflect the full effects of intervention within hours. Alternatively, by keeping the window narrow, we may count an intervention as a success even though the exchange-rate change that led us to that conclusion subsequently disappears. Opening the event window beyond a single day to limit this problem, however, quickly causes overlap among interventions, making inferences about the likelihood of an intervention's success impossible.

We assume, as in Dominguez (2003, 34), that US monetary authorities base a decision to intervene on day t only on past information about exchange rates. We believe this to be an accurate characterization of how US policymakers generally reach their decision to intervene, although the desk may sometimes adjust the amount of an intervention in response to market reactions (Neely 2001; Baillie and Osterberg 1997). If exchange-rate changes and interventions are jointly determined on day t, our counts could contain a bias (Neely 2005).

Although we do not model a specific transmission mechanism for intervention, we assume that intervention operates through an expectations channel. We are testing to see if US monetary authorities have an informational advantage that they impart to the market through their interventions (Popper and Montgomery 2001). If central-bank intervention does indeed impart new information to the market, private traders will immediately incorporate it into their exchange-rate quotes. This information may be positive; that is, the market may interpret the intervention in the manner that the central bank intends. Alternatively, this information may be negative; that is, the market may react to an intervention in the opposite manner than the central bank desires. Our tests look to uncover this behavior.

A2.3   Evaluation: How to Read the Tables

Following Henriksson and Merton (1981) and Merton (1981), we evaluate our success counts under the assumption that the number of successes is a hypergeometric random variable. The hypergeometric distribution seems appropriate because it does not require individual interventions to be independent events and does not depend on a presumed probability of an individual success. To apply the Henriksson and Merton methodology, we must consider intervention sales and purchases of foreign exchange separately.

Our null hypothesis compares the actual and the expected success counts. We reject the null and conclude that intervention has positive forecast value if the success count exceeds the expected number by two standard deviations. In this case, a private dealer could profit on average by trading with the Federal Reserve. We reject the null and conclude that intervention has negative forecast value if the actual number of successes lies below the expected number by more than two standard deviations. In this case, private dealers could profit on average by trading against the Federal Reserve. If we cannot reject the null hypothesis, we conclude that the number of successes is not different than a number that could randomly occur given the near martingale nature of daily exchange-rate changes.

This approach also assumes that intervention does not change fundamental macroeconomic determinants of exchange rates. This supposition seems appropriate given that the Federal Reserve routinely sterilizes all US interventions and given the lack of evidence that sterilized intervention works through a portfolio-balance mechanism. The failure of this assumption to hold would bias our results toward finding a high number of successes in any sample.

Table A2.1, which does not correspond to any table in the body of this book, presents our results for the entire sample period, 2 March 1973 through 19 March 1997.[3] During these 6,274 business days, the United States intervened on 971 days against German marks and on 243 days against Japanese yen.[4] The first intervention against German marks took place on 10 July 1973, and the first intervention against Japanese yen followed on 24 January 1974.

The first column in table A2.1 lists the success criteria for the German marks (top section) and Japanese yen (bottom section). The second column shows official US intervention purchases and sales. Between 2 March 1973 and 19 March 1997, for example, the United States sold German marks on 469 days and bought German marks on 502 days. The next two columns of data show intervention successes. Of the 469 US sales of German marks, 136, or 29.0 percent, were successful under criterion SC_1; that is, each of these 136 interventions was associated with a same-day dollar appreciation. The next two columns show virtual successes. Virtual successes follow the respective success criteria outlined in equations 1 through 3, absent any consideration of intervention. The dollar, for example, appreciated against the German mark—whether or not the United States intervened against marks—on 2,951, or 47.0 percent, of the 6,274 business days in our sample.

The final two columns in table A2.1 refer to the hypergeometric distribution. If successes are hypergeometric random variables, then in a sample of 6,274 observations with a virtual success rate of 47.0 percent, we would expect to observe 221 successes in 469 interventions, purely by chance. The observed number of successes, 136, falls more than two standard deviations below the expected value, implying that the United States had negative fore-

Table A2.1   **Success counts for US intervention, 2 March 1973 to 19 March 1997**

Opening bid quotes

German marks	Total (#)	Intervention successes (#)	Intervention successes (%)	Virtual successes (#)	Virtual successes (%)	Expected successes (#)	Standard deviation (#)
Observations	6,274						
Criterion SC$_1$							
Sell marks	469	136	29.0	2,951	47.0	220.6	8
Buy marks	502	192	38.2	3,007	47.9	240.6	9
Total	971	328	33.8				
Criterion SC$_2$							
Sell marks	469	117	24.9	820	13.1	61.30	4
Buy marks	502	110	21.9	807	12.9	64.57	4
Total	971	227	23.4				
Criterion SC$_3$							
Sell marks	469	253	53.9	3,771	60.1	282	12
Buy marks	502	302	60.2	3,814	60.8	305	13
Total	971	555	57.2				

Japanese yen

	Total (#)	Intervention successes (#)	Intervention successes (%)	Virtual successes (#)	Virtual successes (%)	Expected successes (#)	Standard deviation (#)
Observations	6,274						
Criterion SC$_1$							
Sell yen	94	47	50.0	3,000	47.8	45	5
Buy yen	149	63	42.3	2,836	45.2	67	5
Total	243	110	45.3				
Criterion SC$_2$							
Sell yen	94	19	20.2	740	11.8	11	1
Buy yen	149	28	18.8	829	13.2	20	2
Total	243	47	19.3				
Criterion SC$_3$							
Sell yen	94	66	70.2	3,740	59.6	56	6
Buy yen	149	92	61.7	3,665	58.4	87	7
Total	243	158	65.0				

cast value. This value is so low that market participants, who knew when the United States intervened, could have bet against the United States—bought German marks on day t—and made money on average. From an expectations-channel perspective, a US sale of German marks signaled that the dollar would depreciate over the same day as the intervention. Similar results hold for purchases of German marks, implying that the United States had negative forecast value in this case too. The corresponding success counts for US official interventions against Japanese yen, however, were no different than random.

In contrast to the results under success criterion SC_1, the success counts under SC_2, for both US interventions against German marks and Japanese yen, are more than two standard deviations *above* their expected values, indicating that US interventions had positive forecast value with respect to criterion SC_2. When the dollar is depreciating and the United States sells foreign exchange, it is a good bet that the dollar will continue to depreciate, but will do so by less than on the day prior to the intervention. Likewise, when the dollar is appreciating and the United States buys foreign exchange, it is a good bet that the dollar will continue to appreciate, but will do so by less than on the day prior to the intervention.

While the successes under criterion SC_2 clearly exceed the expected number, the overall frequency of this type of success is fairly low. Only 23 percent of all US interventions against German marks and 19 percent of all US interventions against Japanese yen were successful under the SC_2 criterion.

The final, general success criterion, SC_3, combines SC_1 and SC_2. Generally, we expect that approximately 60 percent of all interventions will be successful under at least one of our success criteria purely by chance. (See the virtual counts under SC_3 in table A2.1.) The total number of actual successes under SC_3 is—in all but one case—no better than random. The exception is the total for US sales of German marks, which falls more than two standard deviations below the expected number.

A2.4   Subperiods Appearing in Chapters 5 and 6

Tables A2.2 and A2.3 provides a one-stop comparison of the results for the various subperiods that appear in chapters 5 and 6 and for some more comprehensive time periods. This overall summary informed our conclusions about intervention under floating exchange rates. In tables A2.2 and A2.3, N and P indicate whether intervention had negative or positive forecast value for a designated criterion. An R in the tables indicates that the observed number of successes was no different than the number that we expect purely by chance.

The table cautions that overall conclusions about intervention are not necessarily robust across time periods or across currencies within any time period. Nevertheless, some relatively persistent patterns stand out. First, US intervention in German marks prior to 17 April 1981 universally had negative forecast value (N) with respect to criterion SC_1 and universally had positive forecast value (P) with respect to criterion SC_2 (see table A2.2). As discussed in chapter 5, during this time period—certainly before 15 September 1977—the United States feared that private traders might interpret an intervention as a sign that the dollar was fundamentally weak and that market participants might bet against the Federal Reserve's interventions. Our results validate this concern. In addition, US policymakers usually only

Table A2.2   **A summary of the success counts across time periods, German marks**

			US intervention against German marks					
Success criterion			SC_1	SC_1	SC_2	SC_2	SC_3	SC_3
Sell/buy foreign exchange	sell	buy	sell	buy	sell	buy	sell	buy
2 March 73–19 March 97	469	502	N	N	P	P	N	R
2 March 73–17 April 81	391	348	N	N	P	P	N	R
2 March 73–14 September 77	161	176	N	N	P	P	N	R
15 September 77–5 October 79	175	58	N	N	P	P	R	N
8 October 81–17 April 81	55	114	N	N	P	P	R	R
20 April 81–19 March 97	78	154	R	R	P	P	R	R
20 April 81–29 March 85	1	24	N	N	R	P	N	R
1 April 85–29 April 88	33	19	R	R	P	P	R	R
2 May 88–19 March 97	44	111	R	R	R	R	R	R

Notes: N = negative forecast value (observed number of successes falls below the expected number of successes by more than two standard deviations). P = positive forecast value (observed number of successes exceeds the expected number of successes by more than two standard deviations). R = random (observed number of success falls within two standard deviations of the expected number of successes).

Table A2.3   **A summary of the success counts across time periods, Japanese yen**

			US intervention against Japanese yen					
Success criterion			SC_1	SC_1	SC_2	SC_2	SC_3	SC_3
Sell/buy foreign exchange	sell	buy	sell	buy	sell	buy	sell	buy
2 March 73–19 March 97	94	149	R	R	P	P	R	R
2 March 73–17 April 81	11	31	R	R	R	P	R	R
2 March 73–14 September 77	0	2	(none)	R	(none)	R	(none)	R
15 September 77–5 October 79	10	19	R	N	R	P	R	R
8 October 81–17 April 81	1	10	R	R	R	R	R	R
20 April 81–19 March 97	83	118	R	R	P	P	R	R
20 April 81–29 March 85	0	11	(none)	R	(none)	P	(none)	R
1 April 85–29 April 88	52	20	R	R	P	R	R	R
2 May 88–19 March 97	31	87	R	R	P	R	R	R

Notes: N = negative forecast value (observed number of successes falls below the expected number of successes by more than two standard deviations). P = positive forecast value (observed number of successes exceeds the expected number of successes by more than two standard deviations). R = random (observed number of success falls within two standard deviations of the expected number of successes).

hoped to smooth exchange-rate movements over this time period; that is, the United States usually cared more about SC_2 than SC_1.

Second, US interventions against Japanese yen prior to the Plaza Accord—with few exceptions—seem unsuccessful under each of our three criteria (see table A2.3). Prior to the Plaza Accord, however, the United States rarely intervened against Japanese yen. With so few observations, drawing firm conclusions about the success of US interventions against Japanese yen may be risky. (A similar caveat applies to the interventions against German marks over the 20 April 1981 through 29 March 1985 minimalist period.)

Third, the large US interventions associated with the Plaza and Louvre accords (1 April 1985 through 29 April 1988) and with the US Treasury–led interventions of the very late 1980s and early 1990s, had overall success counts that were not obviously different than previous episodes (see chapter 6). Economists have often regarded the interventions following the Plaza and Louvre accords as highly successful.

Fourth, US interventions lack positive forecast value under success criterion SC_3 during every subperiod portrayed in tables A2.2 and A2.3. Our overall finding that fewer than 60 percent of US interventions had positive forecast value seems consistent across time periods and currencies.

Tables A2.4 through A2.9, which follow, contain a complete set of results for each of the subperiods that we discussed in chapters 5 and 6 of the book following the format in table A2.1. In chapters 5 and 6 we present abridged results from these tables.

Table A2.4   **Success counts for US intervention, 2 March 1973 to 14 September 1977**

Opening bid quotes

German marks	Total (#)	Intervention successes (#)	(%)	Virtual successes (#)	(%)	Expected successes (#)	Standard deviation (#)
Observations	1184						
Criterion SC$_1$							
Sell marks	161	45	28.0	541	45.7	74	4
Buy marks	176	67	38.1	560	47.3	83	5
Total	337	112	33.2				
Criterion SC$_2$							
Sell marks	161	34	21.1	151	12.8	21	2
Buy marks	176	45	25.6	163	13.8	24	2
Total	337	79	23.4				
Criterion SC$_3$							
Sell marks	161	79	49.1	692	58.4	94	6
Buy marks	176	112	63.6	723	61.1	107	7
Total	337	191	56.7				

Japanese yen

	Total (#)	Intervention successes (#)	(%)	Virtual successes (#)	(%)	Expected successes (#)	Standard deviation (#)
Observations	1,184						
Criterion SC$_1$							
Sell yen	0	0	na	524	44.3	0	0
Buy yen	2	2	100.0	478	40.4	1	1
Total	2	2	100.0				
Criterion SC$_2$							
Sell yen	0	0	na	139	11.7	0	0
Buy yen	2	0	na	181	15.3	0	0
Total	2	0	na				
Criterion SC$_3$							
Sell yen	0	0	na	663	56.0	0	0
Buy yen	2	2	100.0	659	55.7	1	1
Total	2	2	100.0				

Note: This table corresponds to table 5.2 in chapter 5.

Table A2.5   **Success counts for US intervention, 15 September 1977 to 5 October 1979**

Opening bid quotes

German marks	Total (#)	Intervention successes (#)	(%)	Virtual successes (#)	(%)	Expected successes (#)	Standard deviation (#)
Observations	537						
Criterion SC_1							
Sell marks	175	43	24.6	222	41.3	72	4
Buy marks	58	16	27.6	284	52.9	31	3
Total	233	59	25.3				
Criterion SC_2							
Sell marks	175	49	28.0	95	17.7	31	3
Buy marks	58	12	20.7	53	9.9	6	1
Total	233	61	26.2				
Criterion SC_3							
Sell marks	175	92	52.6	317	59.0	103	6
Buy marks	58	28	48.3	337	62.8	36	4
Total	233	120	51.5				

Japanese yen

	Total (#)	Intervention successes (#)	(%)	Virtual successes (#)	(%)	Expected successes (#)	Standard deviation (#)
Observations	537						
Criterion SC_1							
Sell yen	10	6	60.0	248	46.2	5	2
Buy yen	19	5	26.3	255	47.5	9	2
Total	29	11	37.9				
Criterion SC_2							
Sell yen	10	1	10.0	72	13.4	1	0
Buy yen	19	6	31.6	68	12.7	2	1
Total	29	7	24.1				
Criterion SC_3							
Sell yen	10	7	70.0	320	59.6	6	2
Buy yen	19	11	57.9	323	60.1	11	3
Total	29	18	62.1				

Note: This table corresponds to table 5.3 in chapter 5.

Table A2.6   Success counts for US intervention, 8 October 1979 to 17 April 1981

Opening bid quotes

German marks	Total (#)	Intervention successes (#)	Intervention successes (%)	Virtual successes (#)	Virtual successes (%)	Expected successes (#)	Standard deviation (#)
Observations	400						
Criterion SC$_1$							
Sell marks	55	15	27.3	201	50.3	28	3
Buy marks	114	41	36.0	177	44.3	50	4
Total	169	56	33.1				
Criterion SC$_2$							
sell marks	55	17	30.9	50	12.5	7	1
Buy marks	114	25	21.9	60	15.0	17	2
Total	169	42	24.9				
Criterion SC$_3$							
Sell marks	55	32	58.2	251	62.8	35	4
Buy marks	114	66	57.9	237	59.3	68	5
Total	169	98	58.0				

Japanese yen

	Total (#)	Intervention successes (#)	Intervention successes (%)	Virtual successes (#)	Virtual successes (%)	Expected successes (#)	Standard deviation (#)
Observations	400						
Criterion SC$_1$							
Sell yen	1	1	100.0	204	51.0	1	1
Buy yen	10	4	40.0	177	44.3	4	1
Total	11	5	45.5				
Criterion SC$_2$							
Sell yen	1	0	0.0	44	11.0	0	0
Buy yen	10	1	10.0	49	12.3	1	0
Total	11	1	9.1				
Criterion SC$_3$							
Sell yen	1	1	100.0	248	62.0	1	0
Buy yen	10	5	50.0	226	56.5	6	2
Total	11	6	54.5				

Note: This table corresponds to table 5.4 in chapter 5.

Table A2.7 **Success counts for US intervention, 20 April 1981 to 29 March 1985**

Opening bid quotes

German marks	Total (#)	Intervention successes (#)	Intervention successes (%)	Virtual successes (#)	Virtual successes (%)	Expected successes (#)	Standard deviation (#)
Observations	1,030						
Criterion SC$_1$							
Sell marks	1	0	0.0	517	50.2	1	0
Buy marks	24	6	25.0	464	45.0	11	2
Total	25	6	24.0				
Criterion SC$_2$							
Sell marks	1	0	0.0	118	11.5	0	0
Buy marks	24	7	29.2	146	14.2	3	1
Total	25	7	28.0				
Criterion SC$_3$							
Sell marks	1	0	0.0	635	61.7	1	0
Buy marks	24	13	54.2	610	59.2	14	3
Total	25	13	52.0				

Japanese yen

	Total (#)	Intervention successes (#)	Intervention successes (%)	Virtual successes (#)	Virtual successes (%)	Expected successes (#)	Standard deviation (#)
Observations	1030						
Criterion SC$_1$							
Sell yen	0	0	na	519	50.4	0	0
Buy yen	11	4	36.4	449	43.6	5	1
Total	11	4	36.4				
Criterion SC$_2$							
Sell yen	0	0	na	102	9.9	0	0
Buy yen	11	5	45.5	142	13.8	2	1
Total	11	5	45.5				
Criterion SC$_3$							
Sell yen	0	0	na	621	60.3	0	0
Buy yen	11	9	81.8	591	57.4	6	2
Total	11	9	81.8				

Note: This table corresponds to table 6.2 in chapter 6.

Table A2.8   Success counts for US intervention, 1 April 1985 to 29 April 1988

Opening bid quotes

German marks	Total (#)	Intervention successes (#)	(%)	Virtual successes (#)	(%)	Expected successes (#)	Standard deviation (#)
Observations	805						
Criterion SC_1							
Sell marks	33	11	33.3	349	43.4	14	2
Buy marks	19	8	42.1	421	52.3	10	2
Total	52	19	36.5				
Criterion SC_2							
Sell marks	33	11	33.3	132	16.4	5	1
Buy marks	19	4	21.1	80	9.9	2	1
Total	52	15	28.8				
Criterion SC_3							
Sell marks	33	22	66.7	481	59.8	20	4
Buy marks	19	12	63.2	501	62.2	12	3
Total	52	34	65.4				

Japanese yen

	Total (#)	Intervention successes (#)	(%)	Virtual successes (#)	(%)	Expected successes (#)	Standard deviation (#)
Observations	805						
Criterion SC_1							
Sell yen	52	25	48.1	349	43.4	23	3
Buy yen	20	10	50.0	412	51.2	10	2
Total	72	35	48.6				
Criterion SC_2							
Sell yen	52	10	19.2	111	13.8	7	1
Buy yen	20	2	10.0	84	10.4	2	0
Total	72	12	16.7				
Criterion SC_3							
Sell yen	52	35	67.3	460	57.1	30	4
Buy yen	20	12	60.0	496	61.6	12	3
Total	72	47	65.3				

Note: This table corresponds to table 6.3 in chapter 6.

Table A2.9 **Success counts for US intervention, 2 May 1988 to 19 March 1997**

Opening bid quotes

German marks	Total (#)	Intervention successes (#)	(%)	Virtual successes (#)	(%)	Expected successes (#)	Standard deviation (#)
Observations	2,318						
Criterion SC_1							
Sell marks	44	22	50.0	1,121	48.4	21	3
Buy marks	111	54	48.6	1,100	47.5	53	5
Total	155	76	49.0				
Criterion SC_2							
Sell marks	44	6	13.6	274	11.8	5	1
Buy marks	111	17	15.3	305	13.2	15	1
Total	155	23	14.8				
Criterion SC_3							
Sell marks	44	28	63.6	1,395	60.2	26	4
Buy marks	111	71	64.0	1,405	60.6	67	6
Total	155	99	63.9				
Japanese yen							
Observations	2,317						
Criterion SC_1							
Sell yen	31	15	48.4	1,156	49.9	15	3
Buy yen	87	38	43.7	1,064	45.9	40	4
Total	118	53	44.9				
Criterion SC_2							
Sell yen	31	8	25.8	272	11.7	4	1
Buy yen	87	14	16.1	305	13.2	11	1
Total	118	22	18.6				
Criterion SC_3							
Sell yen	31	23	74.2	1,428	61.6	19	4
Buy yen	87	52	59.8	1,369	59.1	51	5
Total	118	75	63.6				

Note: This table corresponds to table 6.4 in chapter 6.

Notes

1. On the Evolution of US Foreign-Exchange-Market Intervention: Thesis, Theory, and Institutions

1. Useful surveys of the theoretical underpinnings and empirical effectiveness of foreign-exchange-market intervention include Dominguez and Frankel (1993b), Edison (1993), Almekinders (1995), Baillie, Humpage, and Osterberg (2000), and Sarno and Taylor (2001). Surveys of central banks' views are found in Neely (2001, 2007) and LeCourt and Raymond (2006), and surveys of market participants' views are found in Chueng and Chinn (2001). Neely (2005) also considers some econometric issues. Almekinders and Eijffinger (1994, 1996) and Baillie and Osterberg (1997) focus on reaction functions. While for the most part this book does not consider intervention among emerging and developing countries, Canales-Kriljenko (2003, 2004), the BIS (2005), and Ishii et al. (2006) contain surveys of that topic.

2. For a basic statement of the trilemma see Feenstra and Taylor (2008, 585–87).

3. The Federal Reserve Act requires the Federal Reserve to "promote effectively the goals of maximum employment, stable prices, and moderate long-term interest rates." This three-part object is generally expressed as the Federal Reserve's "dual mandate"—price stability and maximum employment—assuming that moderate interest rates result from achieving the "dual mandate." Most policymakers accept long-term price stability as a precondition for achieving both high employment and moderate long-term interest rates (see *Board* 2005).

4. Central banks will occasionally time these transactions to maximize or minimize their influence on exchange rates. In such circumstances, these commercial or customer transactions constitute a type of "passive intervention," as Adams and Henderson (1983) first described.

5. As O'Rourke and Taylor (2013) have recently pointed out, the trilemma is a simplification, but still a useful organizing mechanism. Historical evidence—as shown in this book—support its predictions. Also see Obstfeld, Shambaugh, and Taylor (2005).

6. Wages and prices were more flexible during the classical gold-standard era than today, but they were becoming less flexible after 1890 (Hanes 1993, 2000). In addi-

tion, banks and governments issued notes and currency on fractional-reserve bases, which gave rise to runs during uncertain times.

7. By "real" we mean an event that affects relative prices, such as terms-of-trade shocks, changes in productivity growth, or commodity price shocks.

8. This is an issue that deserves further study.

9. For small, advanced countries with relatively thin domestic securities markets, like Switzerland, the purchase of foreign exchange might offer a mechanism through which to conduct a quantitative-easing type of monetary policy. See our epilogue.

10. The portfolio balance mechanism also assumes that no restrictions exist on cross-border financial flows and that Ricardian equivalence does not hold.

11. Many models and empirical applications assume that relative changes in the stock of securities leave interest rates unaffected because monetary policy determines interest rates. Nevertheless, interest rates can be part of the adjustment process.

12. Consider also the voluminous literature on Taylor Rules.

13. This issue becomes critical to our story in chapters 5 and 6.

14. See chapter 5.

15. See Taylor (2005), Reitz and Taylor (2008), and Sarno and Taylor (2001).

16. Cheung and Chinn (2001, 462–64) report that traders are about evenly split on their assessment of intervention's effectiveness. Traders also suggest that intervention increases exchange-rate volatility, but a higher volatility can be consistent with market efficiency. Neely (2001, 2007) and LeCourt and Raymond (2006) report that central banks believe that intervention is effective.

17. The effect of the size of an intervention for the probability of success seems fairly robust across samples. The effect of coordinated intervention on the probability of success seems less robust. Humpage (1999) found support for coordination over the 1987 through 1990 period. Bordo, Humpage, and Schwartz (2012) find little support of coordination over the entire US experience. Still most research finds that coordination increases the effectiveness of intervention.

18. What constitutes coordination may be a trickier concept than often imagined. Most studies define coordinated intervention as occurring when the two central banks, whose currencies define the exchange rate, intervene in the same direction on the same day. Often, however, central banks will intervene for a long string of days. Over these periods, a bank may intervene on consecutive days in concert with the other central bank. Sometimes, however, one bank will skip a day or a few days, while the other bank intervenes on those days. Should these events be considered coodinated? What about the actions of third party central banks?

19. This section draws on Schwartz (1997). See also Henning (1999, 2008) and Osterberg and Thomson (1999).

20. In 1988 and 1990, for example, the ESF made temporary stabilization loans to Yugoslavia and to Hungary, respectively, whose currencies were of little economic importance to the United States, but the loans fostered foreign-policy objectives.

21. Since the late 1970s, Congress has imposed some oversight on operations and on the financing of the ESF, but these are largely after-the-fact reporting requirements. Fund operations remain squarely within the purview of the Treasury (Henning 2008).

22. Leahy (1995) and Task Force (1990e, Paper no. 10) calculate profits using an alternative formula. Their profit estimates, unlike the official calculations, take explicit account of the opportunity costs of holding foreign exchange. These calculations show that the United States has earned an overall cumulative profit on its accounts, that the United States has sometimes incurred losses on the accounts, and that the variability of the returns on the portfolio has risen with the portfolio's size.

23. Friedman's criterion considers only valuation gains and losses; it also abstracts from any net interest earnings.

24. Osler (1998) suggests that more elaborate trading rules, specifically head-and-shoulders rules, largely mimic much simpler rules.

25. The relationships among intervention, profits, and the private sector factor into our narrative several times in chapters 4, 5, and 6. Also, see the empirical appendix.

2. Exchange Market Policy in the United States: Precedents and Antecedents

1. Also after 1901, the bank would make sure that it had adequate supplies of gold by offering an above market price for gold from South Africa (Moggridge 1972, 8).

2. Although Austria-Hungary adopted a gold currency after decades of being on a paper standard, it never obligated the banks to redeem its notes in terms of gold. See also Yeager (1976).

3. According to Flandreau and Komlos (2002), the Austrian National Bank operated as if it were bound by a target zone as Bordo and MacDonald (2005) claim was the case for the core countries.

4. Although we focus mainly on the Bank of England, the Banque de France also engaged in extensive exchange market policies including gold policy, spot and forward market interventions, and swaps. See (Clarke 1967).

5. Reflecting higher eastbound Atlantic freight rates and higher interest costs of shipping gold from New York (Moggridge 1972 171).

6. It kept its operations secret by, for example, operating through the Anglo-International Bank and through numbered accounts at the New York Fed (Moggridge 1972, 184).

7. However, according to Howson (1980, 10), offsetting wasn't completely automatic because the supply of Treasury bills was determined not only by the operations of the EEA but by the Treasury's funding operations.

8. According to Rousseau and Sylla (2004), the financial system of the Northeast, especially the stock market and commercial paper market, was as advanced as England's by the 1830s.

9. See Temin (1969).

10. Rolnick and Weber (1986).

11. Throughout the nineteenth century the foreign exchange market was dominated by sterling bills. There was never a market outside the United States for bills in dollars.

12. See Perkins (1975) and Officer (1996).

13. According to Knodell (2003) the profit earned by the Second Bank's foreign exchange business completely covered the losses it suffered by serving as the Treasury's fiscal agent in paying and receiving taxes and servicing and managing the national debt.

14. In the fall of 1837, after the Second Bank of the United States lost its federal charter, Biddle, now head of the United States Bank of Pennsylvania, arranged a successful corner of the cotton market for the purpose of both reviving it and reducing the discount on sterling. A similar operation in 1839 failed and led to the bankruptcy of the bank (Redlich 1951, 133). We do not regard this manipulation as legitimate exchange market policy.

15. However, existing data on real GDP (Berry 1988) and Industrial Production (Davis 2002) do not indicate any decline in these years.

16. Indeed it may have served as a precedent for the gold (and silver) purchase policies followed by the Roosevelt administration in the 1930s, when the Treasury set a (daily) target from March 1933 to January 1934 for the price of gold with the objective of devaluing the dollar and raising the domestic price level.

17. The act also removed the aggregate limit on national bank notes and limited the retirement of greenbacks to the expansion of national bank notes.

18. Indeed they argue that the gold purchase policy was counterproductive since it raised the premium on gold, the opposite of what was required.

19. Timberlake (1975) disagrees with Friedman and Schwartz on the role of Treasury policy. He argues that the Resumption Act allowed the secretary of the Treasury to retire greenbacks equal to the gross amount of national bank notes issued without accounting for voluntary retirement of national bank notes by the commercial banks. Successive secretaries of the Treasury took advantage of this provision to reduce high-powered money.

20. See Friedman and Schwartz (1963, chapter 3).

21. Other policies followed included paying the interest on government debt early and acceptance of security other than government bonds as collateral for government deposits in national banks, hence allowing the government bonds to serve as national bank collateral (Friedman and Schwartz 1963, 151; Timberlake 1978, 176).

22. A similar device was used during a stringency in September/October 1906.

23. Also, by paying out gold certificates in place of Federal Reserve notes (Chandler 1958).

24. See Bordo and Eichengreen (1998) who demonstrate, based on a model of the gold exchange standard, that absent the Great Depression, the system could have survived for at least another thirty years.

25. Also see Wheelock (1991, 99). At the time Miller and the Board did approve the policies. See Meltzer (2003), chapter 4.

26. According to Schlesinger (1957, 466–67), "But by early January [1933] Roosevelt could assure William Randolph Hearst that it [his cabinet] would be a 'radical' cabinet; there would be no one in it who knows his way to 23 Wall Street. No one who is linked in any way with the power trust or with international bankers . . . the Secretary of the Treasury would not be a banker."

3. Introducing the Exchange Stabilization Fund, 1934–1961

1. The suggestion that Congress might be requested to appropriate additional funds to be used by the ESF was made on one occasion only. On 14 January 1948, in testimony before the Senate Foreign Relations Committee on financing the European Recovery Program, Treasury Secretary John W. Snyder proposed extending stabilization loans to European countries, adding, "At the appropriate time, Congress may then be requested to appropriate additional funds to be used by the United States Stabilization Fund to make those loans" (Treasury Annual Report 1948, 300).

2. The Republican minority of the House Committee on Coinage, Weights, and Measures (HR 6976, 1934, Report no. 202, pt. 2, 3–5) in its report on the Gold Reserve Act objected to section ten that created the ESF because "it places autocratic and dictatorial power in the hands of one man directly over the control of the value of money and credit and indirectly over prices. . . We believe it is too great a power to place in the hands of any one man."

3. The secrecy in which the two funds were designed to operate was subsequently modified.

4. The Morgenthau Papers (reel 12, book 42, 163–64) describes a case of funds transfer in which shipping gold rather than a direct foreign exchange transaction was possible. On 30 October 1936, Charles Cariguel, director of the Bank of France foreign exchange department telephoned Werner Knoke, manager of the FRBNY foreign exchange desk, to inform him that the bank had to repay £40 million sterling to the Bank of England that it had borrowed originally for three months and had

renewed three times. He intended to accumulate sterling if possible, and "it would help him greatly if the dollar-sterling rate could be kept steady at the present level." Knoke replied that "there was a very definite desire here to keep the sterling rate upon an even keel. I inquired guardedly whether 4.89 was the top price for his calculations." Cariguel answered that "over 4.89 would throw my calculations out of gear." He pointed out that if the market learned that he intended to pay off the loan, it was likely to speculate on the rise and try to push the rate higher. "This he did not want to happen." Knoke inquired "what he would do if he found that the rate, as a result of his operations, went up, also whether it was his preference to operate in sterling rather than repay in gold. Cariguel replied that he would operate in sterling if the market permitted, that probably the chance of his being able to do so was small, and that quite possibly the bulk of the operation would have to be done in gold." Cariguel said he wanted Knoke's reaction before going to London to discuss the repayment with his counterpart at the Bank of England.

5. It is ironic that the FRBNY became the fulcrum of foreign exchange intervention. A year earlier, the Banking Act of 1933 had stripped it of any discretionary power in foreign exchange matters.

6. The FRBNY was permitted to cooperate with foreign central banks to prevent the exchange rates of gold standard countries from actually reaching the gold export point, thus denying gold arbitrageurs a profit opportunity. The FRBNY could obtain gold from the Treasury for this purpose without redeeming gold certificates.

7. In a handwritten letter, dated 20 April 1936, Allan Sproul of the FRBNY remarked to H. A. Siepmann of the Bank of England, "I should think that you would be putting in a lot of time these days considering what you are going to do if France—in one way or another—leaves the gold standard and, incidentally, deprives you of the opportunity of buying and selling sterling against francs. In that event, there is going to be an immediate job of minimizing disturbances in the foreign exchange market which will bother us all, leaving out of consideration, for the moment, the longer range questions of policy which such an event would create. I haven't gone in for forecasting what is going to happen to the franc, but the next two or three weeks look critical, and I hope you will keep in touch with us" (Bank of England archives).

8. Nevertheless, commenting in a letter to Allan Sproul in May 1936, H. A. Siepmann of the Bank of England wrote, "I hope that we remain personally in touch like this, in spite of taboos."

9. A private dinner party at the home of the acting undersecretary of the US Treasury, which Morgenthau and the representative of the British Treasury attended, was the occasion on 7 May 1936 for the latter's writing to his superior in London (principal assistant secretary, overseas finance division of HM Treasury) that Morgenthau said to him, that "he would like, and it might be useful for the two treasuries, to have the channel of communication through myself open." The letter continues: "Since the United States Treasury has taken over the direct control of currency matters, the channel of communication between the Bank of England, the Reserve Bank of New York, and the United States Treasury, has been disused, if not entirely blocked, and Mr. Morgenthau, no doubt feels himself somewhat in the dark. Thus the position presumably is that the United States Treasury is expecting France to go off gold before long, that they are afraid this may be followed by a new round of currency unsettlement, that they do not themselves at all want to devalue the dollar further, but that they do not know British intentions and are somewhat nervous that if sterling were to follow the franc any distance an outcry for corresponding dollar depreciation would be raised here, and that they would accordingly be glad of information or of any measure of cooperation which they can get from His Majesty's Government (assuming I suppose in practice that they are anxious for the pound to

be held as steady as possible and would welcome any statement or action that can be made or taken to this end.) I don't know whether there is any answering gesture that we can usefully make, but you ought to know of this matter" (letter by T. K. Bewley, Archives, Bank of England).

10. Fears of inflation delayed adoption of a cheap money policy by the Bank of England until the spring of 1932 (Sayers 1976 II, 416, 430).

11. In Bank of England Archives there is a confidential note of a telephone conversation 28 January 1935 initiated by Jay Crane, deputy governor of the FRBNY, with B. G. Catterns, chief cashier (later deputy governor). Crane reported that, under US Treasury instructions, the FRB during the previous week had bought gold in Paris and London and some silver. On the twenty-sixth and twenty-eighth, the FRB had bought sterling. (On 30 April, Crane resigned his position at the FRB for a job at the Standard Oil Company).

12. Note that the calculation of the New York-London shipping parity differs, as the cost of an ounce of gold in New York is $35 plus the charges incurred in shipping to London, so the sterling equivalent price of gold is not the same as in the case of the London-New York shipping parity.

13. The significance of the description "fine troy ounce" of gold bars was revealed in a letter, dated 20 April 1937, from Allan Sproul (Harrison's successor at the FRBNY) to G. L. F. Bolton, principal, foreign exchange section, Bank of England. Sproul inquired whether fine bars assaying .995 or over, according to a sheet he thought Rothschilds might have published, were acceptable on the London gold market, and that bars less than .995 fine were not acceptable. Sproul complained that in the bank's shipment to the FRB of 11 March 1937 per steamship *Manhattan*, consisting of 766 bars, there were 288 bars (mutilated United States Assay Office bars), the fineness of which had ranged from .993 to .9948. When the bars were turned in to the United States Assay Office in New York, the FRB had to pay a parting and refining charge of a little over $2,000 on all those bars which assayed below .995. It turned out that the bars in question had been received by HM Treasury from Paris, and would not have been acceptable on the London market. The bars were sold to the FRB at a time when the bank was shipping gold to New York, and it seemed only reasonable to the bank's bullion office to give the FRB bars which had been minted at the United States Assay Office.

14. The text of the American declaration is available on reel 9, book 33, 258–60 of the Morgenthau Papers.

15. His announcement, however, of the change from the 31 January 1934 policy was not issued until 12 October after the technical details, described below, had been arranged with the Bank of England and the Bank of France.

A further step the secretary took to implement the new policy of reciprocal gold dealings with other countries and mutual consultation concerning the level of exchange rates was that he requested and obtained the president's approval on 5 November for purchase from and sales of gold to the general fund of the US Treasury by the ESF at a flat price of $35 per ounce.

16. The BIS (1937–38, 19) commented: "The first effect of the devaluation of the gold bloc at the end of September 1936 was a reflux of funds from the London market to France, the Netherlands, and Switzerland. The movement towards France, however, was reversed after about two months. Discussion at a BIS meeting on 11 and 12 October in Basle concluded that the return flow of capital to France would have been much larger had the government not penalized private gold hoarders who did not give up their gold to the Treasury, as the devaluation statute required, and had no tax been imposed on alleged profits from speculation" (Morgenthau Papers, letter dated 28 December 1936 from Cochran to Morgenthau, reel 12, book 43, 17).

The return flow of capital continued in the direction of the Dutch and Swiss markets. In the last quarter of 1936 and the first quarter of 1937, however, there was a flow of funds from London to the United States, sustained by large shipments of gold. Against the dollar the low point of $4.88 to the pound was reached at the beginning of March 1937.

17. On 1 December 1936, Cariguel of the Bank of France told Merle Cochran, first secretary of the US Embassy in Paris, that the handling charge was too expensive for him to deal in gold in the New York market. Even to earmark gold at New York would cost about ten centimes on the dollar, while to ship it, the one-quarter of 1 percent charge made a difference of about 32 centimes on the dollar; Cariguel said that it was necessary to hold the franc at a very fixed rate for the present. He could not afford variations which would permit payment of these charges (Morgenthau Papers, reel 12, book 43, 76).

18. On 12 December 1936, the governors of four Scandinavian central banks (Sweden, Norway, Finland, Denmark) met at Helsingfors in regard to the tripartite declaration and the supplements implementing it. They saw little immediate prospect that any one of the four would adhere to the arrangement for three reasons: (1) They wanted to stand together on monetary questions, and none of them was inclined to act unless the others acted similarly; (2) Denmark had exchange controls and was not eligible to join; (3) Sweden was satisfied with the facilities granted by London for gold transactions on that market (Morgenthau Papers, letter of 28 December 1936, from Cochran in Paris to Morgenthau, reel 12, book 43, 82–83).

19. On 26 September 1936, a Saturday following the declaration on Friday by the three tripartite governments, when it was deemed important for foreign exchange markets to be quiet pending devaluation of the French franc, Morgenthau was disturbed to learn that the price of sterling was falling. Werner Knoke, the FRBNY foreign exchange desk manager, reported that the Russian State Bank gave Chase an order to sell 1 million pounds sterling at any price for dollars. Morgenthau misinterpreted this order that weakened sterling as a communist attack on the tripartite program, and held a press conference to denounce the Russian government and crow that he had foiled that action by buying the 1 million pounds sterling that "they had ordered dumped on our market." He was then informed that the Russian sale of sterling was commercial, to repay Sweden for a loan (Morgenthau Papers, reel 10, book 34, 291–301, 354–57). Governor Harrison told Morgenthau that he had reacted before he had all the facts, but the latter continued to blame the Soviets for disturbing the foreign exchange market.

20. According to Sayers (1976 II index, 666), "Money Employed" was a customers' account. He describes it as follows: "The Bank of England was prepared to accept London balances for other central banks, and to employ these balances remuneratively for their owners. From this point the bank went on, in a purely technical way, to develop its standard practices in handling Money Employed (interest-bearing deposits, though avoiding the form), Treasury Bills and Fine Bank Bills for other central banks" (ibid., I, 158).

21. Brown (1942, 171) notes that the fluctuations in the no. 2 sterling account and the "Money Employed" account were closely related to special exchange transactions with the Central Bank of Argentina.

22. Why did sterling appreciate and arouse the Treasury's concern? The EEA had been accumulating gold from the time the franc was weak in the period leading up to the 1 October 1936 French law. The franc strengthened after its devaluation until the start of November, when it again lost repute. It was the flow of gold from France, principally to London, as confidence in the franc waned, that led to sterling appreciation. Gold also flowed from France to Holland, Switzerland, and the United States.

23. Della Paolera and Taylor (1999, 596, and 2001, 196, n. 21) emphasize that Argentina was scrupulous in servicing its large external debt in the 1930s but do not identify the creditor countries.

24. These currencies appreciated as a result of a reflux of funds from the London market to the Netherlands and Switzerland that followed the devaluation by the gold bloc at the end of September 1936. The movement of funds continued through the first quarter of 1937 (BIS 1938, 19).

25. Various suggestions to use the ESF for gold sterilization were not approved. One proposal would have directed the fund to acquire gold abroad by converting its foreign exchange into bullion. This gold would be sold to the general treasurer who would not deposit gold certificates with the gold certificate fund, as he usually did, but would issue securities to obtain funds.

According to another proposal, the ESF would purchase all imported gold on its arrival which would then be sold to the general treasurer. The ESF under this proposal would have operated in the same way as the EEA, which purchased all incoming gold with sterling obtained from the sale of Treasury bills.

Letters of instruction covering these two procedures were to be sent to the FRBNY, the Superintendent of the New York Assay Office, and the Philadelphia Mint.

In a memorandum to the secretary, Jacob Viner proposed that ESF be involved in only two classes of gold transactions: purchases of foreign gold or sales of gold abroad, whether or not sterilized, or purchases of domestic gold if sterilized. None of these proposals was put into effect.

26. The BIS (1937–38, 19–20) discussed second quarter 1937: "In the following months . . . when it was thought there might be a cut in the price of gold in the United States (followed perhaps in other centres), the markets came under the influence of the 'gold scare'. The demand for dollars was intensified and a wave of gold selling occurred, more than £60 million being dishoarded on the London market alone, a fact not unconnected with the appearance of a 'discount' on the price of gold in London as compared with New York. . . . This tendency to purchase dollars continued throughout the summer but was offset to a large extent by the influx to London of French funds, particularly in May and June, and later, in September." The report (20–21) added: "During the period of the gold scare from April to June 1937 the gold price in London fell below this parity; in the parlance of the market, there developed a 'discount,' an altogether abnormal situation. This was due to the fact that the American banks which usually made arbitrage purchases were reluctant to work under conditions that might have led to a considerable loss if the price of gold had been reduced in the United States, and thus gold in transit could be sold only at a price lower than $35 per fine ounce. As soon as these fears subsided, the 'discount' disappeared. Gold then moved to the United States at the shipping parity, showing that arbitrage was again working effectively. From the end of September the gold price in London rose above the shipping parity, and gold could therefore no longer be profitably shipped from London to the United States."

27. "[O]n 7 April 1937 a spate of rumour swept through financial and commodity markets on both sides of the Atlantic, alleging that the Roosevelt Administration had determined to reduce the price. On the following day, representatives of the discount market came into the Bank for their regular weekly talk with the Governor, who told them that 'the rumour of reduction in the U.S.A. gold price was not based on fact but was based on truth, it must come sooner or later'" (Sayers 1976, 484).

28. The EEA was funded with £175 million at its start; the amount was increased to £375 million in 1933, £435 million in 1936, and £635 million in 1937 (Sayers 1976, 488).

29. The BIS (1937–38, 20) commented: "In the second half of the year, when stock prices fell on Wall Street and a recession in American business set in, the trend turned against the dollar. In November this tendency was sharply intensified by the 'dollar scare' when it was feared in some quarters that there might be a further devaluation of that currency. Although this scare passed, the dollar rate in London remained around $5 to the pound in the following months. In the second half of 1937 a strong export surplus developed in the United States while in the United Kingdom the balance of trade became increasingly adverse."

30. Georges Bonnet, minister of finance, in the 1937 government of Camille Chautemps, floated the franc in June of that year, when budget deficits plagued the Treasury, and capital flight drove the depreciation of the franc.

31. Chautemps was followed by Leon Blum in 1938. Edouard Daladier succeeded Blum. He presided over the deliberate depreciation of the franc below market level and kept it there. He obtained prior consent of neither the Bank of France nor the Treasury for this measure.

32. It repurchased most of the gold sold to Mexico, and purchased a small amount from the Central Bank of Chile.

33. Desterilization began in September 1937, when the Board of Governors of the Federal Reserve requested the Treasury to release $300 million from the inactive gold account. The Treasury released the amount requested, but continued to sterilize all further gold purchases, which amounted to $174 million in that month, so that inactive gold held by the Treasury fell only $126 million in September 1937, with a corresponding decline in Treasury cash and deposits at the FRB. As of 1 January 1938, the Treasury limited the addition to the inactive account in any one quarter to the amount by which total gold purchases exceeded $100 million, and on 19 April 1938 discontinued the inactive gold account, which then amounted to $1.2 billion. Gold sterilization involved Treasury sale of bonds to pay for gold purchases, offsetting an increase in the monetary base that would have arisen from a gold inflow. Desterilization reversed the process. The Treasury instead of selling bonds printed gold certificates, which it deposited at the Federal Reserve banks.

34. From 27 April to 5 May the ESF bought 37 million francs and sold only 3.5 million francs for the account of the Bank of France. The bank was a steady buyer of gold amounting to $45 million from the ESF until 23 May, the greater part by 5 May.

35. Sayers (1976, 563) reports an untrue story that circulated in November to the effect that an American-Anglo agreement had been reached on a $4.50 rate for sterling. He comments that the Americans at that time would never have accepted that degree of sterling depreciation, and that the British would have had no confidence in their ability to maintain that rate in the conditions confronting them.

36. As Alfred Hayes, then president of the FRBNY, remarked at a 5 December 1961 Federal Open Market Committee (FOMC) meeting, "The Stabilization Fund has been used for a number of purposes, such as shoring up weaker countries—which is almost a State Department activity." See the (FOMC *Minutes*, 5 December 1961, 1054).

37. The 1936 Treasury annual report contains no reference to the agreement with Mexico.

38. Mecatta and Goldsmid and the National Provincial Bank, Ltd., were selected as depositories of silver in London, with the approval of Morgenthau, and the London branch of the Guaranty Trust Company was chosen as depository for the sterling proceeds of gold sold. The FRBNY chose seven New York silver depositories, all safe deposit companies.

39. Chase Bank and National City Bank of New York were appointed as agents. According to Brown (1942, 35), the number of London depositories of silver was

increased to seven, with the addition "of the remaining five bullion brokers," but he mentions only four: Samuel Montagu & Son, Pixley and Abell, Sharp and Wilkins, and N. M. Rothschild & Son.

40. The Silver Purchase Act specified that no more than 50 cents an ounce be paid for silver in the country on 1 May 1934. A purchase price of 64.5 cents for newly mined silver had previously been decreed. There was no limit on the price paid for foreign silver. In 1934 the average market price of silver in New York was under 60 cents (Census 1975, Series M-270).

41. The delay in shipment was occasioned by the rise of the sterling price in London from 24 to 32 pence per ounce. As a result the Central Bank of China could not obtain silver in Shanghai on the terms of the contract with the Chase Bank.

42. The program destabilized the Chinese silver standard and ultimately led to its abandonment for a fiat monetary system in 1935. China had been a large importer of silver and had benefited from the 46 percent decline in the US silver price in 1929–31. The silver lobby argued for an increase in silver prices to help China, when in fact a low silver price had obtained a relative advantage for China over gold standard countries in terms of the deflation they experienced. China suffered less thanks to the fall in silver prices. The silver purchase program that raised silver prices harmed not only China but also Mexico and other countries on a silver standard (Jastram 1981, 98–99).

43. In his chapter 6, Meltzer (2003, 456–576) exaggerates the importance of the ESF as the means by which Morgenthau asserted his ability to control monetary policy. For two of many explicit statements by Meltzer, see pp. 457–58 and 574–75. Two facts undermine this view. First, the ESF had limited resources, not the $2 billion in capital the statute allocated to it from the devaluation profit, but only the $200 million the Treasury assigned to it for operating. Second, the ESF balance sheets before 1940 show the small amounts of its holdings of government securities (Schwartz 1997, table 1, 144). Morgenthau, as Meltzer is well aware, wanted low interest rates, not control of open-market operations. If he had attempted to supersede the Federal Reserve, its officials would have expressed their opposition in the many forums available to them. There is no record of such action by Morgenthau and of Federal Reserve dissent. No one disputes that the Federal Reserve was dominated by the Treasury during the New Deal, but it was passive not because of threats by Morgenthau but because of its own beliefs that low interest rates and excess reserves proved that monetary policy was accommodative and needed no further attention.

4. US Intervention during the Bretton Woods Era, 1962–1973

1. For an overview of Bretton Woods see Meltzer (1991, 2009a, b), Bordo (1993), and James (1996). Previous discussions of US intervention during the period include Coombs (1976), Pauls (1990), Todd (1992), and Hetzel (1996).

2. Article VI of the IMF Articles of Agreement authorized restrictions on financial flows.

3. In contrast, Germany and the Netherlands revalued in 1961.

4. To construct the real price of gold, we deflate the official price using the non-seasonally adjusted consumer price index, 1982–84 = 100.

5. All US balance-of-payments data are from the US Commerce Department as reported in the CEA (1969).

6. Coombs (1976, 48) notes: "By the late fifties Washington officials were already dropping hints of government concern over the erosion of our gold stock, which further sensitized the qualms already felt by many European officials."

7. Triffin (1960) suggested creating a source of nondollar international reserves through the IMF. The IMF first issues special drawing rights in January 1970.

8. Unless otherwise indicated, data on gold in this section are from Board of Governors (1976) tables 14.1 and 14.3.

9. These figures include a $344 million payment (gold subscription) to the IMF in 1959.

10. Until 1968, US law mandated a 25 percent gold reserve requirement on outstanding notes and deposit liabilities of the Federal Reserve banks. On 3 March 1965, the Congress dropped the gold reserve requirement on deposit liabilities, and on 18 March 1968, Congress eliminated the gold reserve requirements on notes. This further limited the amount of gold freely available to meet foreign central bank claims.

11. See Darby et al. (1983).

12. Bordo and Eichengreen (2013) show that most FOMC dissents between 1961 and 1966 were for tighter monetary policy and that dissenters justified their actions, at least in part, on balance-of-payments concerns.

13. Meltzer (1991), Hetzel (1996), and Pauls (1990) also discuss the issues raised in this section. See also James (1996).

14. Hetzel (1996, 22) notes that most key European currencies were undervalued relative to the dollar.

15. Budget deficit data are from the CEA (2005), table B-78, and include on-budget and off-budget balances.

16. The data in this section appear in Bordo and Eichengreen (2013), appendix 2.

17. See the discussions of FOMC decisions in Bordo and Eichengreen (2013).

18. This program became known initially as "Operation Nudge" and eventually as "Operation Twist."

19. Congress established the Exchange Stabilization Fund under the Gold Reserve Act of 1934 for the purpose of foreign-exchange-market intervention. We discuss the ESF in chapter 3.

20. Unless otherwise indicated, the information and data in section 4.4 about Treasury interventions come from "Treasury Experience in the Foreign-Exchange Market," and is hereafter referred to as "US Treasury, *Experience.*" See References. See also *Bulletin,* (September 1962, 1138–53).

21. US Treasury *Experience* (1962a, 721).

22. This statement, of course, ignores the cost of financing and covering the transactions.

23. Debt prepayments stemmed from negotiations between the Eisenhower administration and Germany over the cost of troop deployment.

24. We report data from the *Desk Report* (1963, 7, B-23), which differ from the *Bulletin,* (September 1962, 1144).

25. The Treasury swaps were on an ad hoc basis. Unlike the Federal Reserve System, which we discuss below, the Treasury did not maintain formal reciprocal swap lines that reverted to a standby basis when not drawn down.

26. The analysis in this section draws on the Federal Open Market Committee *Minutes* (12 September 1961, 19 December 1961). See also Hetzel (1996), Todd (1992), and Task Force (1990d, Paper no. 1).

27. These data on the ESF are discussed in US Treasury *Memorandum* (1962b, 2). US Treasury *Experience* (1962a) also contains a table showing foreign currency holdings.

28. Whether the impetus for the Federal Reserve's participation in US foreign-exchange operations originated with the Treasury or with the Federal Reserve System is not entirely clear. The Treasury's website suggests that the Treasury "invited" the Federal Reserve to participate in the interventions in 1962, and this is the conventional view (see www.ustreas.gov/offices/international-affairs/esf/history). Coombs

(1976, 71) and FOMC *Minutes* (9 January 1962, 66–67) suggest a different view that we subsequently develop.

29. Todd (1992, 134–35), who once served on the legal staffs at the Federal Reserve Banks of New York and Cleveland, argues that Hackley set out to interpret the Federal Reserve Act in a way that would support intervention, rather than to provide an objective interpretation of the statute.

30. Although open-market operations, including foreign-exchange interventions, fell under the purview of the FOMC, these associated activities fell under the Board of Governor's jurisdiction.

31. In the 1920s and 1930s, however, the Federal Reserve Bank of New York was providing stabilization funds to foreign central banks; it was not directly defending the dollar's exchange value.

32. Warehousing refers to a swap transaction between the Federal Reserve System and the US Treasury in which the Treasury sells foreign currency to the central bank for dollars spot and buys it back forward at a specific rate and settlement date. See chapter 5 on warehousing.

33. Hackley (1961, 19–20), however, did not believe that the Federal Reserve could deal directly with the IMF in any way other than in its capacity as an agent of the Treasury.

34. Why the Treasury did not seek to increase the ESF's appropriation is unclear. The Treasury may have feared that Congress would only increase the ESF's appropriation if the Treasury would agree to some type of congressional oversight. The ESF is unusual in that only the president and the secretary of the Treasury can review its actions (Schwartz 1997).

35. A copy of this letter is found in Task Force (1990a, Paper no. 2, appendix A).

36. Robert H. Knight, general counsel of the Treasury, had warned Hackley that the Federal Reseve should move forward without legislation in part because "there was a range of ideas on the Hill with regard to the Federal Reserve System, including varying views with respect to the operation and organization of the Federal Reserve. Legislation, if sought, might become a vehicle for adding various amendments the nature of which could not be foretold." (See FOMC *Minutes*, 9 January 1962, 61).

37. Governor Robertson expressed the reasons for his dissent at the 5 December 1961 FOMC meeting. See FOMC *Minutes* (5 December 1962, 57–62). See also Task Force (1990a, Paper no. 2, 3–4).

38. In 1982, with the onset of developing-country-debt problems, some members of Congress expressed concern that the Fed might use its authority to invest in foreign securities as a means of providing financial assistance to debtor countries (FOMC Task Force 1990d, Paper no. 1, 23–24).

39. This section is based on the discussion that appears in the FOMC *Minutes* (13 February 1962, 82–95). See also *Bulletin* (September 1962, 1150–53), and Task Force (1990a, Paper no. 2).

40. The Federal Reserve had maintained very small balances in accounts with the Bank of Canada, the Bank of England, the Bank of France, and the Bank for International Settlements since before the Second World War.

41. The Treasury also has maintained swap lines, but typically on an ad hoc basis. With the exception of a Mexican swap line, Treasury swaps were not reciprocal. Often the Treasury established swap with developing countries to provide those countries with temporary loans. The Treasury's first swap line was with Mexico in 1936.

42. Moreover, the liquidity that swap drawings provided did not add to the US balance-of-payments deficit.

43. The Federal Reserve sometimes undertook "third party swaps" in which it would swap one foreign currency for another. These were typically used to pay down an outstanding balance on swap line.

44. In the late 1970s, as discussed in chapter 5, conditionality with respect to swap drawings became a problem and encouraged the United States to accumulate a large portfolio of foreign exchange.

45. "All this may seem to be an excessively roundabout way for the Federal to borrow foreign currencies. But apparently when the Federal Reserve Act was drafted, no one had contemplated such a need, and no explicit statutory provision for such borrowing was made. The swap technique, on the other hand, was clearly authorized and yielded precisely the same results as a direct borrowing from a foreign central bank" (Coombs 1976, 77).

46. Coombs (1976, 75–76) reprints the original swap agreement with the Bank of France.

47. The European central banks include those of Austria, Belgium, England, France, Germany, Italy, the Netherlands, and Switzerland.

48. In 1967, the FOMC did not accept a proposal to extend a swap line to Venezuela because that country did not meet IMF Article VIII requirements (FOMC *Minutes*, 4 April 1967, 10–13; Holland 1967). In 1969, the FOMC did not accept a proposal to extend a swap line to Ireland because of its relatively small size (Reynolds 1969).

49. A general chronology of events is found in *Bulletin* (various issues) and *Desk Reports* (various issues).

50. The Federal Reserve established a Swiss franc swap line with the BIS in 1962 to supplement its line with the SNB, which faced statutory limits on loans to non-Swiss banks (Task Force 1990f, Paper no. 9, 11).

51. See the previous discussion of the "Guidelines For System Foreign Currency Operations."

52. The data in this paragraph come from Solomon (1971, 3–4). We do not have comparable data for the entire 1962 through 1971 period.

53. For background see Bordo, Dib, and Schembri (2010) and Yeager (1966).

54. Much of the information in this section is from MacLaury (1969) and pertains to operations prior to 1968. We have no information on such operations after 1968.

55. Although US monetary authorities did not undertake very many spot market transactions with the objective of affecting the exchange rate, they frequently made spot market purchases and sales of foreign exchange in conjunction with other activities. They might, for example, buy foreign currency in the spot market to repay a swap or to meet forward exchange commitments.

56. A general chronology of events is found in *Bulletin* (various issues) and *Desk Reports* (various issues).

57. Actually, the Bundesbank sold marks against dollars in Germany and the Federal Reserve "took over" the Bundesbank transactions.

58. At this time the Netherlands bank, which maintained a fairly rigid limit on dollar accumulation, was also selling dollars spot into the market, so these transaction amounted to a market swap with the dollars reverting to the United States.

59. The Treasury undertook similar transactions in 1962 or 1963.

60. The G10 were: Belgium, Canada, France, Germany, Italy, Japan, the Netherlands, the United Kingdom, the United States, Sweden. Switzerland joined the General Arrangements to Borrow in 1964.

61. A negative net forward position indicated that the agency had more outstanding foreign currency liabilities that foreign currency assets.

62. Modern warehousing involves a spot purchase of foreign exchange from the Treasury coupled with a forward sale back to the Treasury. Chapter 5 discusses warehousing.

63. The narrative in this section draws on *Bulletin* (1963 through 1968).

64. In fact, the UK pound experienced several crises between 1945 and 1962. Bordo, MacDonald, and Oliver (2010) offers a brief discussion and references.

65. In early January 1963, the Federal Reserve drew $25 million equivalent British pounds from its swap line with the Bank of England and sold $5.6 million equivalent of this drawing to support the dollar.

66. The Federal Reserve used its holdings of sterling to obtain other currencies during the year. On 31 March 1964, the Federal Reserve sold $10 million equivalent sterling to the US Treasury, which used these funds to acquire Swiss francs through a sterling-Swiss franc swap with the BIS. In September and December, both the Federal Reserve and the US Treasury swapped sterling for Dutch guilder. Federal Reserve and Treasury swaps of sterling for Swiss francs were reversed in December.

67. The banks lent dollar reserves.

68. See chapter 5 for a discussion of intervention tactics.

69. As discussed below, France would not participate in a scheme that it equated with maintaining the reserve status of a specific currency, but would offer a general line of credit to the United Kingdom (Coombs 1976, 134).

70. After some cantankerous negotiation, other central banks reluctantly agreed to $400 million in credits (Coombs 1976, 143).

71. Estimates of the gold points appear in the *Desk Report* (1964) and Coombs (1976, 47).

72. On the collapse of the Gold Pool, see Coombs (1976, 152–73).

73. "Mr. Coombs said that the swap line with the French was useless. The only purpose in continuing the swap line was to symbolize some continuing link between the Bank of France and the Federal Reserve, and to avoid an overt disruption of relationships which might lead to market disturbances" (FOMC *Minutes*, 23 August 1966, 21).

74. The Netherlands Bank also sold $30 million in gold to the US Treasury (FOMC *Memoranda*, 18 June 1968, 3).

75. The controls actually required French banks to break outstanding forward contracts with their customers and turn over to the Bank of France the spot foreign exchange held as cover for those contracts.

76. The Bank of France also repaid $45 million of its swap debt in February and $12 million in March.

77. The Treasury swapped nearly its entire mark portfolio for Swiss francs during the Cuban missile crisis.

78. See Coombs et al. (1963, 114–21).

79. The possibility of an imminent mark revaluation left the Treasury, with outstanding forward commitments to sell marks, exposed. On 18 November, the Federal Reserve sold the Treasury $52.3 million to provide partial cover.

80. At their Bonn meeting on 20 November 1968, the G10 countries recommended that Germany revalue the mark.

81. The narrative in this section draws on the *Bulletin* (1968–1973).

82. Following the closing of the US gold window, the French foreign exchange market closed until 23 August, when it reopened on a two-tier basis. The Bank of France would defend an official rate for trade and related transactions. All other transactions would occur at a floating market rate. Pressure continued on the official rate, and French reserves increased $1.1 billion in August 1971.

83. Germany's experience was far from unique. Other countries, including Belgium, France, Japan, the Netherlands, and the United Kingdom had similar experiences with reserve accumulations.

84. See chapter 5 on the period between the Smithsonian agreement and the advent of generalized floating.

85. In July 1973, most of the swap lines were increased to allow for renewed US

foreign exchange interventions, see chapter 5. At this time the line with the Swiss National Bank increased from $1.0 billion to $1.4 billion and the Swiss franc line with the BIS rose from $1.0 billion to $1.25 billion.

5. US Intervention and the Early Dollar Float, 1973–1981

1. Most of the liquidity entered Germany. See Hetzel (2002) for brief history and useful references.

2. Greene (no. 127, August 1984a; no. 128, October 1984b; no. 129, August 1984c) provides detailed surveys of US interventions over select intervals between January 1975 and September 1981. Greene was an assistant vice president in charge of the foreign exchange desk over these years.

3. This paragraph follows Bordo and Eichengreen (2013). See also Romer and Romer (2002, 57), and Hetzel (2008, 68).

4. Orphanides (2002, 118) estimated a Taylor rule for the period, and found that the coefficient on the unemployment gap was substantially greater than the coefficient on the inflation term. This result suggests that policymakers gave more weight to the former than the latter in their policy decisions.

5. Barsky and Kilian (2004, 126) argue that OPEC's actions in late 1973 were a reaction to high US inflation rates in the late 1960s and early 1970s. The resulting dollar depreciation eroded the real purchasing power of the cartel's revenues and strengthened OPEC by increasing the demand for oil outside of the United States. Similarly, the growing lack of confidence in US monetary policy and the fear of inflation that emerged over the 1970s may have distorted economic decisions in ways that further eroded growth in the nation's potential to produce.

6. The United States increased the official gold price from $35 per ounce to $38 per ounce. Chapter 4 discusses the collapse of Bretton Woods.

7. These financial controls included the interest equalization tax, controls imposed through the office of foreign direct investment, and the Federal Reserve's voluntary credit restraint program.

8. The Smithsonian Agreement allowed for wider (2 1/4 percent) bands on either side of the new dollar parities. This change conceivably permitted European currencies to fluctuate as much as 4 1/2 percent against each other. At their 7 March 1972 Basle conference, the six EEC members agreed to limit fluctuations in their currencies to 2 1/4 percent. See also chapter 4.

9. Treasury Secretary Connally did not want reform discussions to take place within the G10 because he believed that the G10 was stacked against US interests (Solomon 1982, 219).

10. In early 1973, Germany, the United Kingdom, and the United States favored a temporary float, while Belgium, France, Japan, the Netherlands, and the developing countries most strongly opposed floating (de Vries 1985, 187–97).

11. We discuss the Jurgenson Report in chapter 6.

12. The FOMC *Memoranda* (19–20 March 1973, 49–71) contain a discussion of this meeting, which Chairman Burns, Governors Daane and Bryant, and Special Manager Coombs attended. This paragraph draws on that discussion.

13. Chapter 4 discusses this problem and its resolution.

14. Under Bretton Woods, except for the case of revaluation, the borrower assumed any exchange risk associated with exchange-rate movements within intervention bands.

15. The FOMC had authorized Coombs to negotiate an increase in the swap lines on 20 March 1973 (FOMC *Memoranda*, 19–20 March 1973, 87).

16. After December 1980, any country drawing on the swap lines agreed to take the full exchange risk in exchange for changes in the interest rates (Task Force 1990f, Paper no. 9, 7).

17. The official US intervention data does not draw a distinction between active and passive interventions.

18. The remainder of this section draws heavily on Hooper (1977) and Pardee (1973).

19. In 1981, the Federal Reserve placed simultaneous bid and offer rates in the market. "In all, the Trading Desk at the Federal Reserve Bank of New York operated in the market as *a net buyer* of marks on nine of fourteen trading days between February 2 and 23." [emphasis added] (*Bulletin*, June 1981, 486–87).

20. Greene (no. 127, 1984a) analyzes the US interventions from January through March 1975. We do not analyze these individual cases separately because outside of the motivating factors, the operations were all broadly similar in size and frequency.

21. The US Treasury purchased German marks from the market in October 1973 and January 1974 and used these funds to retire outstanding mark-denominated securities with the private sector and to repay mark obligations with the IMF. The Treasury also paid marks to a foreign central bank. The Treasury added a small amount to its balances in January 1974, but sold this in the market during February 1974.

22. Evidence suggests that large interventions increase the chances for "success." See Bordo, Humpage, and Schwartz (2012).

23. This paragraph draws on Greene (no. 128, 1984b, 10–12).

24. Burns had expressed uncertainty about intervention at least as early as July 1977 (see FOMC *Transcripts*, 19 July 1977, 3).

25. Burns' views are found in the FOMC *Transcripts* (5 January 1978, 8; 17 January 1978, 5–15).

26. Burns chaired the 28 February 1978 FOMC meeting because Miller, who was to have taken over at this point, was still testifying to Congress.

27. Our data also indicate that between November 1976 and January 1979, the Federal Reserve continuously sold marks off-market to some other official entity for Swiss francs to retire outstanding debt obligations. These sales totaled $353 billion and were largely financed out of swap borrowings and transactions with the market (see chapter 4).

28. In January 1974, the desk bought $4.6 million worth of Japanese yen for the Treasury's account (*Bulletin* 1974, 205).

29. The Federal Reserve also drew nearly $152 billion on its Japanese yen swap line, and the desk sold $194 million yen by late November. The Treasury accounted for approximately 15 percent of the Japanese yen sales. Likewise the Federal Reserve drew $707 million on its Swiss swap line in November and December and sold these funds in the market. The Treasury did not intervene in Swiss francs.

30. Truman (2005, 354) reports that the "Bundesbank would not agree to the [1 November 1978] package . . . until the Federal Reserve agreed to a decisive monetary policy move."

31. We explain warehousing below.

32. Volcker (January 1976, 8) already expressed a similar assessment of earlier interventions: "intervention is a tactic—sometimes useful, sometimes not. By itself, it will accomplish little if not accompanied by appropriate domestic policies, by internal stability, and by some willingness to take account of international considerations in policymaking."

33. Truman (2005, 354) indicates that Volcker "received a harangue from the German authorities about getting the US economic house in order."

34. This section draws on Axilrod and Holmes (1979), Greene (no. 129, 1984c), Holmes and Pardee (1979), Morton and Truman (1979), and Task Force (1990h, Paper no. 8).

35. In late 1978, the Federal Reserve temporarily acquired a balance of $1.5 billion equivalent German marks through a warehousing-type operation with the US Treasury. Since warehousing operations are swaps, these funds did not increase the Federal Reserve's net open position in German marks, as holding reserves outright would have.

36. This, of course, was not the first time that the issue came up. In 1975, for example, Pardee recommended increasing the amount of working balances in German marks to avoid having to buy marks when the mark was trading at the top of the snake (FOMC *Memoranda*, 15 July 1975, 4).

37. Ironically, as Morton and Truman (1979, 5) warned, as the United States increased its own holdings of foreign exchange, it might *have* to undertake a greater amount of intervention. Other countries—particularly the smaller ones—might diversify their portfolios to hold fewer dollars. When the dollar subsequently depreciated, these foreign countries might be less inclined to intervene in dollars.

38. The Treasury issued an additional $1.1 billion equivalent German mark denominated Carter bonds in 1980.

39. The net open position equals foreign currency balances plus any net forward position less foreign currency liabilities.

40. Greene (no. 129, 1984c, 12–13) describes the desk's perception of market disorder: "In making judgments about conditions in the exchange market and the need for orderly market intervention, US authorities considered many dimensions of trading. They evaluated the variability of the exchange rate itself as indicated, for example, by the magnitude and speed of rate changes within a day, day to day, cumulatively over several days or longer, and relative to perceived or known changes in the underlying economic fundamentals. They also evaluated market participants' perceptions of the risk of dealing as indicated, for instance, by the width of bid-asked spreads, the existence of large gaps between successive rate quotations, or an unwillingness on the part of market professionals to take currency into position even temporarily and thereby cushion the impact on the market of their customers' currency needs."

41. Greene (no. 129, 1984c, 12) also notes that no institution that sold foreign exchange to the desk had enough information to deduce the overall size of the operation on a given day.

42. As Holmes and Pardee (1979, 9–10) note, central banks invest the funds that other central banks deposit with them in bills of their domestic governments.

43. As explained in chapter 4, the FOMC is authorized to buy foreign exchange from the "open-market," which includes the US Treasury.

44. "In order that the [Federal Reserve] System's weekly statement would not reflect too large an increase in its 'other assets,' the System at the end of its statement week of July 27 [1966] swapped $88.2 million [equivalent] pounds for one day with the U.S. Treasury." (*Desk Report* 1967, 10) Why the Board did this is unclear, but it may have taken the action so that speculators would remain uncertain about the degree of support being offered to the pound.

45. On Coomb's desire to give the Federal Reserve a bigger say in the policy decisions, see (FOMC *Memoranda*, 14 November 1967, 31). As we show in chapters 4, 5, and 6, this was a frequent motive for maintaining and expanding the Federal Reserve's involvement in intervention.

46. During the last half of 1976, the Treasury undertook two swap drawings with England totaling $300 million. These were repaid by the end of the year.

47. Exactly why the Federal Reserve began warehousing directly with the Treasury instead of the ESF remains unclear, since foreign currencies obtained from the sale of Carter bonds could easily be transferred from the Treasury to the ESF. Indeed, subsequent to the authorization, this may have been how the transactions were actually handled: "In the case [1978–79], the German marks and Swiss francs obtained from Carter bond sales were credited to the Treasury's General Fund Special Accounts at the Bundesbank and the Swiss National Bank, but then were immediately sold to the ESF. Since the ESF's resources were insufficient at the time to handle the transactions . . . the ability to warehouse the foreign currencies with the [Federal Reserve] System enabled the ESF to acquire these bond proceeds from the General Fund" (Task Force 1990h, Paper no. 8, 25).

48. Carter bonds allowed the Treasury to acquire foreign exchange without expanding the foreign money supply when the foreign exchange was sold for dollars.

49. The United States intervened on 30 March 1981, following an assassination attempt on President Reagan. See Greene (no. 129 1984c, 29) for a detailed account.

6. US Foreign-Exchange-Market Intervention during the Volcker-Greenspan Era, 1981–1997

1. The Reagan administration seemed to begin its minimalist intervention strategy in late February or early March of 1981. United States intervention was very heavy in January 1981, but tapered off in February with a final heavy intervention on 22 February 1981, when President Reagan was shot. Treasury Secretary Donald Regan formally announced the new policy on 17 April 1981 (see chapter 5).

2. Chapter 5 discusses the inauguration of Chairman Volcker's monetary-policy initiatives.

3. The FOMC adopted monetary targets in 1970 and began making these targets public in early 1975.

4. In October 1982, the FOMC formally abandoned monetary targets for a federal funds rate target. On this episode, see Silber 2012.

5. During most of the Reagan years, the Republican Party maintained a small majority in the US Senate, but the Democrats had a substantially larger majority in the House of Representatives.

6. "Although I accept that [a higher real return on investment] could in principle help explain the dollar's strength, my judgment was that the magnitude of the decline in national saving was substantially greater than the increased demand for investment" (Feldstein 1994, 67).

7. As chapter 4 explains, Sprinkel contended that because sterilized intervention did not alter fundamental macroeconomic determinants of exchange rates, it could exert only a temporary influence on the market at best. He also maintained that intervention—even when sterilized—could interfere with domestic monetary policy.

8. This was the most enduring conclusion from the report. As we will show, FOMC participants referred to it, often noting that to be effective, monetary policy had to back up intervention. The desk and the Treasury seemed to forget the finding. This conclusion ultimately became the focal point for arguments against intervention within the FOMC.

9. Solomon (1983, 7–8) also discussed this problem.

10. Rogoff (1984) provides a thorough survey of the empirical tests of the portfolio-balance model, especially of those papers important for the study of foreign-exchange intervention. Rogoff's paper circulated as a memo in early 1983 and was undoubtedly part of the background research for the Jurgensen Report.

11. We consider here only high-frequency empirical studies of the effects of intervention. Empirical studies of intervention profits appear in chapter 1, and early studies of intervention appear in chapter 5.

12. In 1984, the Treasury removed the withholding tax on interest paid to foreigners, which would have increased foreign demand for US financial assets and would have encouraged a real dollar appreciation.

13. See the collection of papers that appear in Federal Reserve Bank of Kansas (1985).

14. These congressional inquires eventually produced the Omnibus and Trade Competitiveness Act of 1988, which encouraged the president to pursue macroeconomic-policy coordination and exchange-market intervention and instructed the Treasury secretary to analyze the exchange-rate policies of other countries for exchange-rate manipulation.

15. These were not the only interventions during the minimalist, or pre-Plaza period, but the intervention that began in January 1985 marked a change in the administration's attitudes toward intervention. An analysis of all pre-Plaza interventions follows in the next section.

16. Japanese intervention data for the period are not available.

17. We do not know the exact day of this intervention because it does not appear in the Board's official daily data on US foreign exchange operations.

18. We did not include the earlier interventions of the minimalist period in figure 7 because they were largely one-off actions. We also do not consider the single US interventions against Japanese yen on 1 February 1985, which was not successful by our criteria.

19. Bagshaw and Humpage (1986) studied volatility using the moments of a stable-Paretian distribution.

20. Volcker had this assessment of exchange markets: "I was pretty well convinced by then [August 1985] as a matter of market judgment that the basic direction of the dollar was lower. Certainly, the growth of the U.S. economy seemed to be losing momentum, and if there was to be any change in monetary policy it would likely be toward greater ease and lower interest rates. But the prospects for a lower dollar were not so clear to others and the dollar rebounded." (Volcker and Gyohten 1992, 242–43).

21. The G5 (Group of Five) consisted of France, Germany, Japan, the United Kingdom, and the United States. The G6 consisted of the G5 plus Italy. The G7 consisted of the G6 plus Canada.

22. A reprint of the Plaza communiqué can be found in Funabashi (1988, 261–66). The text references paragraph 18.

23. Volcker and Gyohten (1992, 244) also indicate that the United States proposed a 10 to 12 percent appreciation of foreign currencies relative to the dollar.

24. We are not sure to which market—Singapore, Hong Kong, Tokyo, or all three—the term "Far East" refers.

25. A further statistical analysis of success under our criteria appears below in table 3.

26. Feldstein (1986) does find a somewhat faster yen depreciation after the Plaza, but attributes it to shift in policy rather that the intervention.

27. On 27 January 1987, the United States sold $50 million equivalent yen to demonstrate cooperation with Japanese authorities who had recently been buying dollars (*Bulletin*, May 1987, 333). On 11 March 1987, the United States made a unilateral $30 million purchase of German marks.

28. Funabashi (1988, 45–49) and Destler and Henning (1989, 51–52) discuss this episode. These two accounts differ on whether Volcker had worked out an agreement with Pöhl before or after the Board's vote and his threat to resign. The text follows

Destler and Henning, which is consistent with Volcker and Gyohten (1992, 274), and with Silber (2012, 254–56).

29. The G6 communiqué is reprinted in Funabashi (1988, 279–80).

30. Funabashi's book is based on anonymous interviews with individuals associated with the G5, G6, or G7 meetings.

31. Frankel (1994, 307) notes: "Most knowledgeable observers surmised that probably no explicit quantitative range had in fact been agreed on."

32. See also Kahn and Jacobson (1989) and, for a somewhat different opinion, Obstfeld (1983).

33. See chapter 1 on the transmission mechanisms of sterilized intervention.

34. See Klein and Rosengren (1991), Dominguez (1992), and Kaminsky and Lewis (1996).

35. One of the Jurgensen Report's conclusions maintained that monetary authorities needed to back their sterilized interventions with appropriate monetary policies, if such operations were to have anything other than a fleeting effect on exchange rates.

36. Eleven of the eighteen US interventions against German marks (or 61 percent) proved successful according to our criteria since 27 June 1988. This percentage is not obviously greater than the amount typically observed by chance (see table A2.1 in appendix 2). Moreover, the dollar generally appreciated during this period despite the repeated sales of dollars.

37. The view that intervention increases exchange-rate volatility has considerable empirical support.

38. Cross discusses discrete intervention as a tactical choice (see chapter 4). He did not discuss it as a means for avoiding a conflict between monetary policy and intervention.

39. Cross explained discrete intervention: "That is to say, we operated through a bank acting as an agent so they—although the word does get around in some way and people who are following these markets closely can often tell a lot of what's going on—we did not go in openly buying foreign currencies" (FOMC *Transcripts*, 5 and 6 July 1989, 3).

40. Cross's assessment is not generally true. As discussed in appendix 2, US intervention did not have negative forecast value after March 1985, implying that traders could not on average expect to profit by betting against US interventions. Traders could profit on average by betting against US interventions during the early float period; see chapter 5.

41. The page numbers in this paragraph refer to Cross and Truman (1990).

42. The transcripts do not explain how Brady determined this amount. The Board redacted part of the transcripts. The amount may include foreign intervention amounts against yen. Since 1 January 1989, the United States had purchased $13 billion equivalent Japanese yen.

43. Congressman Gonzales was currently threatening to hold hearings on the Federal Reserve System's portfolio of foreign exchange.

44. This and subsequent Japanese interventions are from published official Japanese Ministry of Finance data, which we converted to dollars at prevailing exchange rates.

45. See also (Goodfriend 2013, 345–47).

46. The article initially appeared in the Federal Reserve Bank of Richmond's 1995 Annual Report.

47. On these last interventions see also Goodfriend (2013, 347–49).

48. FOMC *Transcripts* are not yet publically available for 2011.

49. Much of the background on Mexico's swap lines comes from Maroni (1994a, b).

50. Goodfriend (2013, 341–45) also provides a detailed account of this episode.

51. Federal Reserve Bank of Richmond President Broaddus dissented.

52. NAFA is a financial agreement among the participants of NAFTA, the North American Free Trade Agreement, to provide swap lines.

53. The United States also set up a $2 billion swap line with Canada.

54. Texas Congressman Henry Gonzalez was highly critical of the swap lines, claiming that Congress never granted the Federal Reserve explicit legal authority for swap lines, and that they exposed US taxpayers to default risk.

55. On the "take-out" see (Goodfriend 2013, 343–44).

7. Lessons from the Evolution of US Monetary and Intervention Policies

1. If a central bank routinely had better information about pricing than the market, then its trades should serve as a forecast of subsequent exchange-rate movements. See our empirical appendix.

2. That said, the Federal Reserve has occasionally considered balance of payments or exchange rate objectives in its monetary-policy decisions.

3. See McCallum (2003).

Epilogue: Foreign-Exchange-Market Operations in the Twenty-First Century

1. Dollar amounts of Japanese intervention are from Chaboud and Humpage (2005).

2. Studies of Japanese intervention include Fatum and Hutchison (2003), Frenkel, Pierdzioch, and Stadtmann (2005), Galati, Melick, and Micu (2005). Humpage and Ragnartz (2005) apply the same methodology as Chaboud and Humpage (2005) to Swedish intervention.

3. Rich (1987, 2000) explains that in the late 1970s and in the mid-1990s when financial inflows appreciated the franc, the Swiss National Bank modified its strict adherence to monetary and price targets to account for exchange-rate movements.

4. We did not have access to official Swiss intervention data, but inferred intervention activity from changes in Swiss foreign-currency reserves, official (but general) statements about intervention, and data on components of the Swiss monetary base.

5. Following the 11 September 2001 terrorist attacks, the Federal Reserve also instituted similar swap lines with the European Central Bank ($50 billion) and the Bank of England ($30 billion). At that time, the Federal Reserve expanded its existing swap with the Bank of Canada to $10 billion. The lines expired after thirty days. The European Central Bank drew $23.4 billion on its line and repaid the amount on 17 September 2001. The Bank of Canada and the Bank of England did not draw on the lines. See *Bulletin* (December 2001, 761).

6. Our discussion of foreign banks' balance sheets draws on: McGuire and von Peter (2009), and Moessner and Allen (2010). See also Fleming and Klagge (2010), and Goldberg, Kennedy, and Miu (2010).

7. On this aspect of the swap lines, see especially Goldberg, Kennedy, and Miu (2010).

8. An overnight index swap (OIS) is an interest-rate swap where the period floating rate in the swap is equal to a geometric average of the federal funds rate. The OIS rate refers to the floating rate portion of the swap. Hence the OIS rate is related to the average federal funds rate over the period of the obligation.

9. A very good introduction to exchange-market operations in developing and emerging market economies is Canales-Kriljenko (2003, 2004) and Canales-Kriljenko, Guimarães, and Karacadağ (2003). This section drew heavily on these

articles. See also the papers in Bank for International Settlements (2005). These sources also provide many useful references.

10. As noted in chapter 5, the United States bought foreign exchange to build a portfolio of foreign-exchange reserves in the late 1970s and early 1980s.

11. We calculated the trade-weighted appreciation using J. P. Morgan's real, broad, effective exchange-rate index.

12. China's currency is the renminbi, but its currency unit is the yuan, whose symbol is ¥.

13. The People's Bank also raised reserve requirements and imposed direct controls on bank lending to control inflation.

14. On sterilization, see also Ouyang, Rajan, and Willett (2010) and references therein.

Appendix 2: Empirical Method for Assessing Success Counts

1. Chaboud and Humpage (2005) and Humpage and Ragnartz (2005) apply this same methodology to Japanese intervention (1991–2004) and Swedish intervention (1993–2002), respectively.

2. The United States conducts most US interventions by far in the New York market, but has occasionally placed orders through correspondents in both the European and Far Eastern markets. We cannot isolate these few transactions.

3. The United States did not abruptly end its intervention on 19 March 1997. United States interventions began to taper off in the early 1990s. After August 1995, the United States intervened against Japanese yen on 17 June 1998, against euros on 22 September 2000, and again against Japanese yen on 18 March 2011. These last three interventions are the only instances of US intervention during the floating exchange rate era not included in our analysis. Our exchange-rate data determined our sample, which ends on 19 March 1997.

4. The United States intervened against some other European currencies during the 1970s and early 1980s, but data on these currencies are not available.

References

Abbreviations use in text for references:

BIS: Bank for International Settlements
Board: Board of Governors of the Federal Reserve System
Bulletin: *Treasury and Federal Reserve Foreign Exchange Operations, or Treasury and Federal Reserve Foreign Exchange Operations: Interim Report*
CEA: Council of Economic Advisors
Desk Report: *Federal Reserve Bank of New York, Annual Report on Operations in Foreign Currencies*
FOMC *Memoranda*: *Federal Open Market Committee, Memoranda of Discussion*
FOMC *Minutes*: *Federal Open Market Committee, Minutes of the Federal Open Market Committee*
FOMC *Transcripts*: *Federal Open Market Committee, Transcripts of Federal Open Market Committee*
IMF: International Monetary Fund
Task Force: *Task Force on System Foreign Currency Operations*

Adams, D., and D. Henderson. 1983. "Definition and Measurement of Exchange Market Intervention. Board of Governors of the Federal Reserve System." Staff Studies no. 126.
Aguilar, J., and S. Nydahl. 2000. "Central Bank Intervention and Exchange Rates: The Case of Sweden." *Journal of International Financial Markets, Institutions and Money* 10 (3–4): 303–22.
Aizenman, J., Y. Jinjarak, and D. Park. 2010. "International Reserves and

Swap Lines: Substitutes or Compliments?" National Bureau of Economic Research Working Paper no. 15804, Cambridge, MA.

Aizenman, J., and G. K. Pasricha. 2009. "Selective Swap Arrangements and the Global Financial Crisis: Analysis and Interpretation." National Bureau of Economic Research Working Paper no. 14821, Cambridge, MA.

Almekinders, G. J. 1995. *Foreign Exchange Intervention, Theory and Evidence*. Hants, United Kingdom: Edward Elgar Publishing.

Almekinders, G. J., and S. C. W. Eijffinger. 1994. "Daily Bundesbank and Federal Reserve Bank Intervention— Are they a Reaction to Changes in the Level and Volatility of the DM/$ Rate?" *Empirical Economics* 19 (1): 111–30.

———. 1996. "A Friction Model of Daily Bundesbank and Federal Reserve Intervention." *Journal of Banking and Finance* 20 (8): 1365–80.

Auer, R. and S. Kraenzlin. 2011. "International Liquidity Provision during the Financial Crisis: A View from Switzerland." Federal Reserve Bank of St. Louis, *Review* 93 (6): 409–17.

Axilrod, S. and A. R. Holmes. 1979. "Holding of Foreign Currency Balances." Memorandum to the Federal Open Market Committee, April.

Bagshaw, M., and O. Humpage. 1986. "Intervention, Exchange-Rate Volatility, and the Stable Paretian Distribution." Federal Reserve Bank of Cleveland Working Paper no. 8608, July.

Baillie, R., O. Humpage, and W. Osterberg. 2000. "Intervention from an Information Perspective." *Journal of International Financial Markets, Institutions and Money* 10 (3–4): 407–21.

Baillie, R., and W. Osterberg. 1997. "Why Do Central Banks Intervene?" *Journal of International Money and Finance* 16 (6): 909–19.

Bank for International Settlements. 1938. Eighth Annual Report. Basle, Switzerland. http://www.bis.org/publ/arpdf/archive/ar1938_en.pdf.

———. 1983. Fifty-Third Annual Report. Basle, Switzerland.

———. 2005. Foreign Exchange Market Intervention in Emerging Markets: Motives, Techniques and Implications. BIS Paper no. 24, May.

———. 2010. Triennial Central Bank Survey, Report of Global Foreign Exchange Market Activity in 2010, December. http://www.bis.org/publ /rpfxf10t.pdf.

Bank of England. 1964. "The London Gold Market." *Quarterly Review* 4 (1): 16–21.

———. 1968. "The Exchange Equalisation Account: Its Origins and Development." *Quarterly Bulletin* 8 (4): 377–90.

Bank of England. Archives miscellaneous unpublished materials.

Barsky, R. B., and L. Kilian. 2004. "Oil and the Macroeconomy." *Journal of Economic Perspectives* 18 (4): 115–34.

Beckhart, B. H., J. G. Smith, and W. A. Brown Jr. 1932. *The New York Money Market, vol. IV: External and Internal Relations*. New York: Columbia University Press.

Beine, M., and O. Bernal. 2007. "Why Do Central Banks Intervene Secretly? Preliminary Evidence from the Bank of Japan." *Journal of International Financial Markets, Institutions, and Money* 17 (3): 291–306.

Berry, T. S. 1988. *Production and Population Since 1789: Revised GNP Series in Constant Dollars.* Richmond, VA: Bostwick Press.

Bhattacharya, U., and P. Weller. 1997. "The Advantage to Hiding One's Hand: Speculation and Central Bank Intervention in the Foreign Exchange Market." *Journal of Monetary Economics* 39 (2): 251–77.

Bloomfield, A. 1959. *Monetary Policy under the International Gold Standard, 1880–1914.* New York: Federal Reserve Bank of New York.

———. 1963. "Short-Term Capital Movements under the Pre-1914 Gold Standard." Princeton Studies in International Finance no. 11, International Finance Section, Princeton University.

Board of Governors of the Federal Reserve System. 1934–61. *Federal Reserve Bulletin.* Washington, DC.

———. 1963. "Financing the US Payments Deficit." *Federal Reserve Bulletin* (April):421–42.

———. 1966. "Federal Reserve Operations in Foreign Exchange, 1962–1966." Unpublished memorandum, March 21.

———. 1976. *Banking and Monetary Statistics 1941–1970.* Washington, DC: Board of Governors of the Federal Reserve System.

———. 2005. "The Federal Reserve System, Purposes and Functions" Washington, DC: Board of Governors of the Federal Reserve System. http://www.federalreserve.gov/pf/pdf/pf_complete.pdf.

Bodner, D. E. 1970. "Proposed Modification of Procedures to Be Employed in Transactions under Certain Swap Lines." Unpublished Memorandum, Board of Governors of the Federal Reserve System, 3 December.

Bonser-Neal, C., V. V. Roley, and G. H. Sellon Jr. 1998. "Monetary Policy Actions, Intervention, and Exchange Rates: A Reexamination of the Empirical Relationships Using Federal Funds Rate Target Data." *Journal of Business* 71 (2): 147–77.

Bordo, M. D. 1984. "The Gold Standard: The Traditional Approach." In *A Retrospective on the Classical Gold Standard, 1821–1931*, edited by M. D. Bordo and A. J. Schwartz. Chicago: University of Chicago Press.

———. 1993. "The Bretton Woods International Monetary System: A Historical Overview." In *A Retrospective on the Bretton Woods System, Lessons for International Monetary Reform*, edited by M. Bordo and B. Eichengreen. Chicago: University of Chicago Press.

Bordo, M., A. Dib, and L. Schembri. 2010. "Canada's Pioneering Experience with a Flexible Exchange Rate in the 1950s: (Hard) Lessons Learned for Monetary Policy in a Small Open Economy." *International Journal of Central Banking* 6 (3): 51–99.

Bordo, M., and B. Eichengreen. 1998. "Implications of the Great Depression for the Development of the International System." In *The Defining*

Moment: The Great Depression and the American Economy in the Twentieth Century, edited by M. D. Bordo, C. Goldin, and E. N. White. Chicago: University of Chicago Press.

———. 2013. "Bretton Woods and the Great Inflation." In *The Great Inflation, The Rebirth of Modern Central Banking*, edited by M. D. Bordo and A. Orphanides. Chicago: University of Chicago Press.

Bordo, M. D., O. F. Humpage, and A. J. Schwartz. 2012. "The Federal Reserve as an Informed Foreign Exchange Trader: 1973–1995." *International Journal and Central Banking* 8 (1): 1–29.

Bordo, M. D., and R. MacDonald. 2005. "Interest Rate Interaction in the Classical Gold Standard, 1880–1914: Was There Monetary Independence?" *Journal of Monetary Economics* 52 (2): 307–27.

Bordo, M. D., R. MacDonald, and M. J. Oliver. 2010. "Sterling in Crisis: 1964–1967." *European Review of Economic History* 13 (3): 437–59.

Bordo, M., and A. Schwartz. 1989. "Transmission of Real and Monetary Disturbances under Fixed and Floating Exchange Rates." In *Dollars, Deficits, and Trade*, edited by J. Dorn and W. Niskanen. Boston: Academic Publishers.

———. 1991. "What Has Foreign Exchange Market Intervention Since the Plaza Agreement Accomplished?" *Open Economies Review* 2 (1): 39–64.

———. 1999. "Under What Circumstances, Past and Present, Have International Rescues of Countries in Financial Distress Been Successful?" *Journal of International Money and Finance* 18 (4): 683–708.

———. 2001. "From the Exchange Stabilization Fund to the International Monetary Fund." NBER Working Paper no. 8100, Cambridge, MA.

Bordo, M., D. Simard, E. White. 1996. "France and the Bretton Woods Monetary System: 1960–1968. NBER Working Paper no. 4642, Cambridge, MA.

Bremner, Robert P. 2004. *Chairman of the Fed: William McChesney Martin Jr. and the Creation of the Modern American Financial System*. New Haven: Yale University Press.

Broaddus, J. A., and M. Goodfriend. 1996. "Foreign Exchange Operations and the Federal Reserve." Federal Reserve Bank of Richmond *Economic Quarterly*, 82 (1): 1–20.

Brown, W. A. Jr. 1942. "Operations of the Exchange Stabilization Fund, 1934–1939." Unpublished draft, National Bureau of Economic Research, July.

Burns, A. F. 1973. "Statement to the Subcommittee on International Economics of the Joint Economic Committee, June 27, 1973." *Federal Reserve Bulletin* 59 (7): 508–12.

Cairncross, A., and B. Eichengreen. 2003. *Sterling in Decline: The Devaluations of 1931, 1949, and 1967*. New York: Palgrave Macmillan.

Calvo, G. A., and C. M. Reinhart. 2000. "Fear of Floating." NBER Working Paper no. 7993, Cambridge, MA.

Canales-Kriljenko, J. I. 2003. "Foreign Exchange Intervention in Developing and Transition Economies: Results of a Survey." International Monetary Fund Working Paper WP/03/99.

———. 2004. "Foreign Exchange Market Organization in Selected Developing and Transition Economies: Evidence from a Survey." International Monetary Fund Working Paper WP/04/4.

Canales-Kriljenko, J. I., R. Guimarães, and C. Karacadağ. 2003. "Official Intervention in the Foreign Exchange Market: Elements of Best Practice." International Monetary Fund Working Paper WP/03/152.

Carlson, J. B., J. M. McIntire, and J. B. Thomson. 1995. "Federal Funds Futures as an Indicator of Future Monetary Policy: A Primer." Federal Reserve Bank of Cleveland, *Economic Review* (Quarter 1):20–30.

Carlson, M. 2006. "A Brief History of the 1987 Stock Market Crash with a Discussion of the Federal Reserve Response." Finance and Economics Discussion Series no. 2007-13, Board of Governors of the Federal Reserve System, November.

Chaboud, A. P., and O. F. Humpage. 2005. "An Assessment of the Impact of Japanese Foreign-Exchange Intervention: 1991–2004." International Finance Discussion Papers no. 824, Board of Governors of the Federal Reserve System.

Chandler, L. V. 1958. *Benjamin Strong, Central Banker.* Washington, DC: The Brookings Institution.

Chang, Y., and S. Taylor. 1998. "Intraday Effects of Foreign-Exchange Intervention by the Bank of Japan." *Journal of International Money and Finance* 17 (1): 191–210.

Chari, V., L. J. Christiano, and M. Eichenbaum. 1998. "Expectations, Traps and Discretion." *Journal of Economic Theory* 81 (2): 462–92.

Cheung, Y-W., and M. D. Chinn. 2001. "Currency Traders and Exchange Rate Dynamics: A Survey of the US Market." *Journal of International Money and Finance* 20 (4): 439–71.

Chiu, P. 2003. "Transparency versus Constructive Ambiguity in Foreign Exchange Intervention." BIS Working Paper no. 144, Bank of International Settlements.

Christiano, L. J., and C. Gust. 2000. "The Expectations Trap." Federal Reserve Bank of Chicago *Economic Perspectives* 24 (2): 21–39.

Clarida, R., J. Gali, and M. Gertler. 2000. "Monetary Policy Rules and Macroeconomic Stability: Evidence and Some Theory." *Quarterly Journal of Economics* 115 (1): 147–80.

Clarke, S. V. O. 1967. *Central Bank Cooperation 1924–31.* New York: Federal Reserve Bank of New York.

———. 1977. "Exchange Rate Stabilization in the Mid-1930s: Negotiating the Tripartite Agreement." Princeton Studies in International Finance no. 41, International Finance Section, Department of Economics, Princeton University.

Coombs, C. A. 1976. *The Arena of International Finance.* John Wiley & Sons: New York.

———. 1971. "System Operations in Forward Markets." Unpublished memorandum. May.

Coombs, C. A., M. Ikle, E. Ranalli, and J. Tungeler. 1963. "Conversation on International Finance, Federal Reserve Bank of New York." *Monthly Review*, August , 114–21; cited in *Bulletin*, September 1964, 1125.

Craig, B., and O. Humpage. 2003. "The Myth of the Strong Dollar Policy." *Cato Journal* 22 (3): 417–29.

Cross, S. Y., and E. M. Truman. 1990. "Task Force on System Foreign Currency Operations." Memorandum to the Federal Open Market Committee, March.

Council of Economic Advisors. 1969. "Economic Report of the President." Transmitted to Congress February 1969, Washington DC, Government Printing Office.

———. 1984. "Economic Report of the President." Transmitted to Congress February 1984, Washington DC, Government Printing Office.

———. 2005. "Economic Report of the President." Transmitted to Congress February 2005, Washington DC, Government Printing Office.

Darby, M. R., A. E. Gandolfi, A. J. Schwartz, and A. C. Stockman. 1983. *The International Transmission of Inflation.* Chicago: University of Chicago Press.

Davatyan, N. and W. R. Parke. 1995. "The Operations of the Bank of England, 1890–1908: A Dynamic Probit Approach." *Journal of Money, Credit and Banking* 27 (4): 1099–112.

Davis, J. 2002. "A Quantity Based Annual Index of US Industrial Production, 1790–1915: An Empirical Appraisal of Historical Business Cycle Fluctuations." Unpublished PhD diss., Duke University.

Della Paolera, G., and A. M. Taylor. 1999. "Economic Recovery from the Argentine Great Depression: Institutions, Expectations, and the Change of Macroeconomic Regime." *Journal of Economic History* 59 (3): 567–99.

———. 2001. *Straining at the Anchor.* Chicago: University of Chicago Press.

Destler, I. M., and C. R. Henning. 1989. *Dollar Politics: Exchange Rate Policymaking in the United States.* Washington, DC: Institute for International Economics.

de Vries, M. G. 1976. *The International Monetary Fund 1966 – 1971, The System under Stress*, vol. 1. International Monetary Fund: Washington, D.C.

de Vries, M. G. 1985. *The International Monetary Fund 1972–1978, Cooperation on Trial*, vol. 1. International Monetary Fund: Washington, DC.

Dobson, W. 1991. "Economic Policy Coordination: Requiem of First Step? Policy Analysis in International Economics." Paper no. 30, Institute for International Economics, Washington, DC, May.

Dominguez, K. M. 1992. "The Informational Role of Official Foreign Exchange Intervention Operations: The Signaling Hypothesis." In

Exchange Rate Efficiency and the Behavior of International Asset Markets, edited by K. M. Dominguez, 41–80. New York: Garland Publishing Company.

———. 2003. "The Market Microstructure of Central Bank Intervention." *Journal of International Economics* 59 (1): 25–45.

Dominguez, K. M., and J. A. Frankel. 1993a. "Does Foreign Exchange Intervention Matter? The Portfolio Effect." *American Economic Review* 83 (5): 1356–69.

———. 1993b. *Does Foreign Exchange Intervention Work?* Washington, DC: Institute for International Economics.

Dooley, M. P., and J. R. Shafer. 1983. "Analysis of Short-Run Exchange Rate Behavior: March 1973 to November 1981." In *Floating Exchange Rates and the State of World Trade Payments*, edited by D. Bigman and T. Taya. Cambridge, MA: Ballinger.

Dornbusch, R. 1976. "Expectations and Exchange Rate Dynamics." *Journal of Political Economics* 84 (6): 1161–76.

Drummond, I. M. 1981. *The Floating Pound and the Sterling Area, 1931–39.* Cambridge: Cambridge University Press.

Dutton, J. 1984. "The Bank of England and the Rules of the Game under the International Gold Standard: New Evidence." In *A Retrospective on the Classical Gold Standard, 1821–1931*, edited by M. D. Bordo and A. J. Schwartz. Chicago: University of Chicago Press.

Edison, H. 1993. "The Effectiveness of Central Bank Intervention: A Survey of the Literature after 1982." Special Papers in International Economics no. 18, Princeton University.

Eichengreen, B. 1992. *Golden Fetters: The Gold Standard and the Great Depression, 1919–1939.* New York: Oxford University Press.

Einzig, P. 1931. *International Gold Movements*, 2nd ed. London: MacMillan.

Evans, M. D., and R. K. Lyons. 2001. "Portfolio Balance, Price Impact and Secret Intervention." NBER Working Paper no. 8356, Cambridge, MA.

———. 2005. "Are Different-Currency Assets Imperfect Substitutes?" In *Exchange Rate Economics: Where Do We Stand?*, edited by P. DeGrauwe. Cambridge, MA: MIT Press.

Fatum, R., and M. Hutchison. 1999. "Is Intervention a Signal of Future Monetary Policy? Evidence from the Federal Funds Futures Market." *Journal of Money, Credit, and Banking* 31 (1): 54–69.

———. 2002. "ECB Foreign-Exchange Intervention and the EURO: Institutional Framework, News and Intervention." *Open Economies Review* 13 (4): 413–25.

———. 2003. "Effectiveness of Official Daily Foreign Exchange Market Intervention Operations in Japan." NBER Working Paper no. 9648, Cambridge, MA.

Federal Open Market Committee. *Memoranda of Discussion*, (various issues). Board of Governors of the Federal Reserve System: Washington, DC. http://www.federalreserve.gov/monetarypolicy/fomc_historical.htm.

Federal Open Market Committee. *Minutes of the Federal Open Market Committee*, (various issues). Board of Governors of the Federal Reserve System: Washington, DC. http://www.federalreserve.gov/monetarypolicy /fomc_historical.htm.

Federal Open Market Committee. 1962. "Scope and Character of Initial Foreign Currency Operations of the System and Proposed Short-Term Program for Coordinated Treasury and System Operations in Foreign Currencies." Unpublished documents distributed to the FOMC by Messrs. Coombs and Young on 6 February 1962.

Federal Open Market Committee. *Transcripts of the Federal Open Market Committee*, (various issues). Washington, DC: Board of Governors of the Federal Reserve System. http://www.federalreserve.gov/monetary policy/fomc_historical.htm.

Federal Reserve Bank of Kansas City. 1985. *The US Dollar—Recent Developments, Outlook, and Policy Options.* A Symposium Sponsored by the Federal Reserve Bank of Kansas City, Jackson Hole, Wyoming, August 21–23.

Federal Reserve Bank of New York, "Annual Report on Operations in Foreign Currencies." Unpublished report submitted by the Special Manager of the System Open Market Account for Foreign Currency Operations to the Federal Open Market Committee, various issues, 1962–1997.

Feenstra, R. C., and A. M. Taylor. 2008. *International Economics.* New York: Worth Publishers.

Feldstein, M. 1986. "New Evidence on the Effects of Exchange Rate Interventions." NBER Working Paper no. 2052 , Cambridge, MA. October.

———. 1994. "American Economic Policy in the 1980s: A Personal View." In *American Economic Policy in the 1980s*, edited by M. Feldstein. Chicago: University of Chicago Press.

Flandreau, M., and J. Komlos. 2002. "Core or Periphery? The Credibility of the Austro-Hungarian Currency 1867–1913." *Journal of European Economic History* 31 (2): 293–320.

Fleming, M. J., and N. J. Klagge. 2010. "The Federal Reserve's Foreign Exchange Swap Lines, Federal Reserve Bank of New York." *Current Issues in Economics and Finance* 16 (4): April.

Frankel, J. 1994. "Exchange Rate Policy." In *American Economic Policy in the 1980s*, edited by M. Feldstein. Chicago: University of Chicago Press.

Frankel, J., and K. E. Rockett. 1988. "International Macroeconomic Policy Coordination When Policymakers Do Not Agree on the True Model." *American Economic Review* 78 (3): 318–40.

Fratianni, M., and F. Spinelli. 1984. "Italy in the Gold Standard Period, 1861–1914." In *A Retrospective on the Classical Gold Standard, 1821–1931*, edited by M. D. Bordo and A. J. Schwartz. Chicago: University of Chicago Press.

Frenkel, M., M. Pierdzioch, and G. Stadtmann. 2005. "The Effects of Japanese Foreign Exchange Market Interventions on the Yen/US Dollar

Exchange Rate Volatility." *International Review of Economics and Finance* 14 (1): 27–39.

Friedman, M. 1953. *Essays in Positive Economics*. Chicago: University of Chicago Press.

Friedman, M., and A. Schwartz. 1963. *A Monetary History of the United States 1867–1960*. Princeton, NJ: Princeton University Press.

Funabashi, Y. 1988. *Managing the Dollar: From the Plaza to the Louvre*, Washington, DC: Institute for International Economics.

Galati, G., W. Melick, and M. Micu. 2005. "Foreign Exchange Market Intervention and Expectations: The Dollar/Yen Exchange Rate." *Journal of International Money and Finance* 24 (6): 982–1011.

Gavin, F. J. 2004. *Gold, Dollars, and Power, the Politics of International Monetary Relations, 1958–1971*. Chapel Hill: University of North Carolina Press.

Genberg, H. 1981. "On the Effects of Central Bank Intervention in the Foreign Exchange Market." Unpublished paper of the International Monetary Fund Research Department, April.

Ghosh, A. R., and P. R. Masson. 1988. "International Policy Coordination in a World with Model Uncertainty." *International Monetary Fund Staff Papers* 35 (2): 230–58.

Giovannini, A. 1986. "Rules of the Game During the International Gold Standard: England and Germany." *Journal of International Money and Finance* 5 (4): 467–83.

Goldberg, L. S., C. Kennedy, and J. Miu. 2010. "Central Bank Dollar Swap Lines and Overseas Dollar Funding Costs." Federal Reserve Bank of New York Staff Report no. 429, February.

Goodfriend, M. 1994. "Why We Need an 'Accord' for Federal Reserve Credit Policy: A Note." *Journal of Money, Credit, and Banking* 26 (3): 572–80.

———. 2013. "Policy Debates at the Federal Open Market Committee: 1993–2002." In *The Origins, History, and Future of the Federal Reserve System, A Return to Jekyll Island*, edited by M. D. Bordo and W. Roberds. Cambridge: Cambridge University Press.

Goodhart, C. A. E., and T. Hesse. 1993. "Central Bank Forex Intervention Assessed in Continuous Time." *Journal of International Money and Finance* 12 (4): 368–89.

Greene, M. L. 1984a. "US Experience with Exchange Market Intervention: January–March 1975." Board of Governors of the Federal Reserve System, Staff Studies no. 127, August.

———. 1984b. "US Experience with Exchange Market Intervention: September 1977–December 1979." Board of Governors of the Federal Reserve System, Staff Studies no.128, October.

———. 1984c. "US Experience with Exchange Market Intervention: October 1980–September 1981–December 1979." Board of Governors of the Federal Reserve System, Staff Studies no. 129, August.

Hackley, H. 1961. "Legal Aspects of Proposed Plan for Federal Reserve

Operations in Foreign Currencies." Board of Governors Internal Memorandum, November.

———. 1969. "Legal Aspects of Proposals for Assisting Treasury in Connection with Cash and Debt Ceiling Problems." Board of Governors Internal Memorandum, January.

Hagen, J. von. 1989. "Monetary Targeting with Exchange Rate Constraints: The Bundesbank in the 1980s." *Federal Reserve Bank of St. Louis Review* (September/October):53–69.

Hall, N. F. 1935. *The Exchange Equalisation Account.* London: Macmillan.

Hamada, K., and M. Kawai. 1997. "International Economic Policy Coordination: Theory and Policy Implications." In *Macroeconomic Policy in Open Economies*, edited by M. U. Fratianni, D. Salvatore, and J. von Hagen. Westport, CT: Greenwood Press.

Hammond, B. 1957. *Banks and Politics in America.* Princeton, NJ: Princeton University Press.

Hanes, C. 1993. "The Development of Nominal Wage Rigidity in the Late 19th Century." *American Economic Review* 83 (4): 732–56.

———. 2000. "Nominal Wage Rigidity and Industrial Characteristics in the Downturns of 1893, 1929, and 1981." *American Economic Review* 90 (5): 1432–46.

Henderson, D., and S. Sampson. 1983. "Intervention in Foreign Exchange Markets: A Summary of Ten Staff Studies." *Federal Reserve Bulletin* 69 (11): 830–36.

Henning, C. R. 1999. *The Exchange Stabilization Fund: Slush Money or War Chest?* Policy Analyses in International Economics (57). Washington, DC: Institute for International Economics.

———. 2008. *Accountability and Oversight of US Exchange Rate Policy.* Washington, DC: Peterson Institute for International Economics.

Henriksson, R. D., and R. C. Merton. 1981. "On Market Timing and Investment Performance. II. Statistical Procedures for Evaluating Forecasting Skills." *Journal of Business* 54 (4): 513–33.

Hetzel, R. L. 1996. "Sterilized Foreign-Exchange Intervention: The Fed Debate in the 1960s." Federal Reserve Bank of Richmond, *Economic Quarterly* 82 (2): 21–46.

———. 2002. "German Monetary History in the Second Half of the Twentieth Century: From the Deutsche Mark to the Euro." Federal Reserve Bank of Richmond, *Economic Quarterly*, 88 (2): 29–64.

———. 2008. *The Monetary Policy of the Federal Reserve, A History*. Cambridge: Cambridge University Press.

Holland, R. C. 1967. "Criteria for Increasing Membership in the Federal Reserve Network of Reciprocal Currency Arrangements." Unpublished Memorandum, February.

Holmes, A. R., and S. E. Pardee. 1979. "Holdings of Foreign Currency Balances by the Federal Reserve." Memorandum to the FOMC, April.

Holthan, G., and A. H. Hallet. 1987. "International Policy Cooperation and Model Uncertainty." In *Global Macroeconomics: Policy Conflict and Cooperation*, edited by R. C. Bryant and R. Portes. New York: St. Martin's Press.

Hooper, P. 1977. "Procedures for Federal Reserve System Foreign Currency Operations." Internal memorandum of the Board of Governors, April.

Howson, S. 1980. "Sterling's Managed Float: The Operations of the Exchange Equalisation Account, 1932–39." Princeton Studies in International Finance no. 46, International Finance Section, Department of Economics, Princeton University.

Humpage, O. F. 1984. "Dollar Intervention and the Deutchemark-Dollar Exchange Rate." Federal Reserve Bank of Cleveland Working Paper no. 8404.

———. 1988. "Intervention and the Dollar's Decline." Federal Reserve Bank of Cleveland, *Economic Review* 24 (2): 2–16.

———. 1990. "A Hitchhiker's Guide to International Macroeconomic Policy Coordination." Federal Reserve Bank of Cleveland, *Economic Review* 26 (1): 1–14.

———. 1991. "Central-Bank Intervention: Recent Literature, Continuing Controversy." Federal Reserve Bank of Cleveland, *Economic Review* 27 (2): 13–26.

———. 1999. "US Intervention: Assessing the Probability of Success." *Journal of Money Credit and Banking* 31 (4): 731–47.

———. 2000. "The United States as an Informed Foreign-Exchange Speculator." *Journal of International Financial Markets, Institutions, and Money* 10 (3–4): 287–302.

———. 2013. "The Limitations of Foreign-Exchange Intervention: Lessons from Switzerland." Federal Reserve Bank of Cleveland, Economic Commentary, no. 2013-13.

Humpage, O. F., and W. P. Osterberg. 1992. "Intervention and the Foreign Exchange Risk Premium: An Empirical Investigation of Daily Effects." *Global Finance Journal* 3 (4): 23–50.

Humpage, O., and J. Ragnartz. 2005. "Swedish Intervention and the Krona Float, 1993–2002." Federal Reserve Bank of Cleveland, Working Paper no. 05-14.

Hung, J. H. 1997. "Intervention Strategies and Exchange Rate Volatility: A Noise Trading Perspective." *Journal of International Money and Finance* 16 (5): 779–93.

Hutchison, M. 1984. "Intervention, Deficit Finance and Real Exchange Rates: The Case of Japan." Federal Reserve Bank of San Francisco, *Economic Review* (Winter):27–44.

International Monetary Fund. 1972. "Annual Report of the Executive Directors for the Fiscal Year Ended April 30, 1972." Washington, DC, IMF.

Irwin, D. A. 1997. "From Smoot-Hawley to Reciprocal Trade Agreements: Changing the Course of US Trade Policy in the 1930s." NBER Working Paper no. 5895, Cambridge, MA.

Ishii, S., J. I. Canales-Kriljenko, R. P. Guimarães, and C. Karacadağ. 2006. "Official Foreign Exchange Intervention." International Monetary Fund Occasional Paper no. 249.

Ito, T. 2003. "Is Foreign Exchange Intervention Effective?: The Japanese Experiences in the 1990s." In *Monetary History, Exchange Rates, and Financial Markets, Essays in Honour of Charles Goodhart*, vol. 2, edited by P. Mizen. Cheltenhan, United Kingdom: Edward Elgar.

———. 2005. "Interventions and Japanese Economic Recovery." *International Economics and Economic Policy* 2 (2–3): 219–39.

———. 2007. "Myths and Reality of Foreign Exchange Interventions: An Application to Japan." *International Journal of Finance and Economics* 12 (2): 133–54.

Ito, T., and T. Yabu. 2007. "What Prompts Japan to Intervene in the Forex Market? A New Approach to a Reaction Function." *Journal of International Money and Finance* 26 (2): 193–212.

James, H. 1996. *International Monetary Cooperation Since Bretton Woods.* New York: Oxford University Press.

Jastram, R. W. 1981. *Silver, the Restless Metal.* New York: John Wiley.

Jeanne, O. 1995. "Monetary Policy in England 1893–1914: A Structural VAR Analysis." *Explorations in Economic History* 32 (3): 302–26.

Johnson, G. G. Jr. 1939. *The Treasury and Monetary Policy 1933–1938.* Cambridge, MA: Harvard University Press.

Jonung, L. 1984. "Swedish Experience Under the Classical Gold Standard, 1973–1914." In *A Retrospective on the Classical Gold Standard, 1821–1931*, edited by M. D. Bordo and A. J. Schwartz. Chicago: University of Chicago Press.

Jurgensen, P. (Chairman). 1983. "Report of the Working Group on Exchange Market Intervention." Washington DC, US Treasury Department, March.

Kahn, G. A., and K. Jacobson. 1989. "Lessons from West German Monetary Policy." Federal Reserve Bank of Kansas City, *Economic Review* 74 (4): 18–35.

Kaminsky, G. L., and K. K. Lewis. 1996. "Does Foreign Exchange Intervention Signal Future Monetary Policy?" *Journal of Monetary Economics* 37:285–312.

Keynes, J. M. 1925. "The Economic Consequences of Mr. Churchill." Reprinted in Keynes, *Collected Writings*, vol. 9. London: Macmillan.

———. 1930. *A Treatise on Money, Vol. 2: The Applied Theory of Money.* London: Macmillan.

Klein, M. W., and E. Rosengren. 1991. "Foreign Exchange Intervention as a Signal of Monetary Policy." Federal Reserve Bank of Boston New England, *Economic Review* (May/June):39–50.

Knodell, J. 2003. "Profit and Duty in the Second Bank of the United States' Exchange Operations." *Financial History Review* 10 (1): 5–30.

Kole, L. S., and E. E. Meade. 1995. "German Monetary Targeting: A Retrospective View." *Federal Reserve Bulletin* 81 (10): 917–31.

Lardy, N. 2008. "Financial Repression in China." Peterson Institution Policy Brief no. PB08-8.

League of Nations. 1944. *International Currency Experience.* Geneva, Switzerland: League of Nations.

Leahy, M. P. 1995. "The Profitability of US Intervention in the Foreign Exchange Markets." *Journal of International Money and Finance* 14 (6): 823–44.

LeBaron, B. 1999. "Technical Trading Rule Profitability and Foreign Exchange Intervention." *Journal of International Economics* 49 (1): 125–43.

LeCourt, C., and H. Raymond. 2006. "Central Bank Interventions in Industrialized Countries: A Characterization Based on Survey Results." *International Journal of Finance and Economics* 11 (2): 123–38.

Loopesko, B. 1984. "Relationships among Exchange Rates, Intervention and Interest Rates: An Empirical Investigation." *Journal of International Money and Finance* 3 (3): 257–77.

Lyons, R. K. 2001. *The Microstructure Approach to Exchange Rates.* Cambridge, MA: MIT Press.

MacLaury, B. K. 1969. "Discussion of Questions Raised by Governor Maisel Concerning System Foreign Currency Operations." Unpublished Memorandum, January.

Maroni, Y. 1994a. "Mexican Exchange Rate Policy over the Past Forty Years." Unpublished memorandum, March.

———. 1994b. "History of the Reciprocal Currency (Swap) Agreement between the Bank of Mexico and the Federal Reserve System." Unpublished Memorandum, March.

Martin, W. McC. Jr. 1961. "Federal Reserve Operations in Perspective." *Federal Reserve Bulletin*, 272–81. Board of Governors of the Federal Reserve System, Washington, DC, February. (Reprint of a statement before the Joint Economic Committee on 7 March 1961.)

Mayer, T. 1999. *Monetary Policy and the Great Inflation in the United States, The Federal Reserve and the Failure of Macroeconomic Policy, 1965–79.* Cheltenham, United Kingdom: Edward Elgar.

McCallum, B. T. 2003. "Japanese Monetary Policy, 1991–2001." Federal Reserve Bank of Richmond, *Economic Quarterly* 89 (1): 1–31.

McGouldrick, P. 1984. "Operations of the German Central Bank and Then Rules of the Game 1879–1913." In *A Retrospective on the Classical Gold Standard, 1821–1931,* edited by M. D. Bordo and A. J. Schwartz. Chicago: University of Chicago Press.

McGuire, P., and G. von Peter. 2009. "The US Dollar Shortage in Global

Banking." *Bank for International Settlements Quarterly Review* (March):47–63.

McKibbin, W. J. 1997. "Empirical Evidence on International Economic Policy Coordination." In *Macroeconomic Policy in Open Economies*, edited by M. U. Fratianni, D. Salvatore, and J. von Hagen. Westport, CT: Greenwood Press.

McKinnon, R. I. 1976. "Floating Foreign Exchange Rates 1973–74: The Emperor's New Clothes." In *Carnegie-Rochester Conference Series on Public Policy*, edited by K. Brunner and A. Meltzer, 79–114. Amsterdam: North-Holland.

Meese, R., and K. Rogoff. 1981. "Empirical Exchange Rate Models of the Seventies: Are Any Fit to Survive?" International Finance Discussion Paper no. 184, Board of Governors of the Federal Reserve System.

———. 1982. "The Out-of-Sample Failure of Empirical Exchange Rate Models: Sampling Error or Misspecification?" International Finance Discussion Paper no. 204, Board of Governors of the Federal Reserve System.

———. 1983. "Empirical Exchange Rate Models of the Seventies: Do They Fit Out of Sample?" *Journal of International Economics* 14 (1–2): 3–24.

Meltzer, A. H. 1991. "US Policy in the Bretton Woods Era." *Federal Reserve Bank of St. Louis Review* 73 (3): 54–83.

———. 2003. *A History of the Federal Reserve, Vol. 1: 1913–1951*. Chicago: University of Chicago Press.

———. 2005. "Origins of the Great Inflation." *Federal Reserve Bank of St. Louis Review* 87 (2, part 2): 145–75.

———. 2009a. *A History of the Federal Reserve, Vol. 2, Book One, 1951–1969*. Chicago: University of Chicago Press.

———. 2009b. *A History of the Federal Reserve, Vol. 2, Book Two, 1970–1986*. Chicago: University of Chicago Press.

Merton, R. C. 1981. "On Market Timing and Investment Performance. I. An Equilibrium Theory of Value For Market Forecasts." *Journal of Business* 5 (3): 363–406.

Micossi, S., and S. Rebecchini. 1984. "A Case Study on the Effectiveness of Foreign Exchange Intervention: The Italian Lira (September 1975–March 1977)." *Journal of Banking and Finance* 8 (4): 535–55.

Miller, A. C. 1935. "Responsibility for Federal Reserve Policies: 1927–29." *American Economic Review*, 26 (3): 442–56.

Mitchell, W. C. [1908] 1966. *Gold, Prices and Wages under the Greenback Standard*. New York: Augustus M. Kelley Publishers.

Moessner, R., and W. A. Allen. 2010. "Central Bank Co-Operation and International Liquidity in the Financial Crisis of 2008–9." Bank for International Settlements Working Paper no. 310, May.

Moggridge, D. E. 1972. *British Monetary Policy 1924–1931: The Norman Conquest of $4.86*. Cambridge: Cambridge University Press.

Mohanty, M. S., and P. Turner. 2005. "Intervention: What Are The Domestic Consequences?" Bank for International Settlements Paper no. 24, May.

Morano, R. 2005. "Motives for Intervention." Bank for International Settlements Paper no. 24, May.

Morgenthau, H. Jr. Morgenthau Papers on microfilm (60 reels). Franklin D. Roosevelt Presidential Library and Museum, Hyde Park, New York.

Morton, J. E. 1977. "Background Information on System 'Warehousing' of Foreign Currency." Internal Memorandum to Governor Wallich, Board of Governors of the Federal Reserve System, January.

Morton, J. E., and E. M. Truman. 1979. "US Holdings of Foreign Currency Balances." Memorandum to the FOMC April.

Mouré, K. 1991. *Managing the Franc Poincaré: Economic Understanding and Political Constraint in French Monetary Policy, 1928–1936.* Cambridge: Cambridge University Press.

Mussa, M. 1981. "The Role of Official Intervention." Occasional Paper no. 6, Group of Thirty, New York.

Myers, M. G. 1931. *The New York Money Market, Vol. I: Origins and Development.* New York: Columbia University Press.

———. 1970. *A Financial History of the United States.* New York: Columbia University Press.

Neely, C. J. 1998. "Technical Analysis and the Profitability of US Foreign Exchange Intervention." *Federal Reserve Bank of St. Louis Review* 80 (4): 3–18.

———. 2001. "The Practice of Central Bank Intervention: Looking Under the Hood." *Central Banking* 11 (2): 24–37.

———. 2005. "An Analysis of Recent Studies of the Effects of Foreign Exchange Intervention." *Federal Reserve Bank of St. Louis Review* 87 (6): 685–718.

———. 2007. "Central Bank Authorities Beliefs about Foreign Exchange Intervention." *Journal of International Money and Finance* 27 (1): 1–25.

———. 2011. "A Foreign Exchange Intervention in an Era of Restraint." *Federal Reserve Bank of St. Louis Review* 93 (5): 303–24.

Neely, C. J., and P. Weller. 1997. "Technical Analysis and Central Bank Intervention." *Journal of International Money and Finance* 20 (7): 949–70.

Neely, C., P. Weller, and R. Dittmar. 1997. "Is Technical Analysis Profitable in the Foreign Exchange Market? A Genetic Programming Approach." *Journal of Financial and Quantitative Analysis* 32 (4): 405–26.

Neumann, M. J. M., and J. von Hagen. 1991. "Monetary Policy in Germany." In *Handbook on Monetary Policy*, edited by M. Fratianni and D. Salvatore. Westport, CT: Greenwood Press.

Nurkse, R. 1944. *International Currency Experience.* Geneva, Switzerland: League of Nations.

Obstfeld, M. 1983. "Exchange Rates, Inflation, and the Sterilization Problem." *European Economic Review* 21 (1–2): 161–89.

—————. 1990. "The Effectiveness of Foreign-Exchange Intervention: Recent Experience, 1985–1988." In *International Policy Coordination and Exchange Rate Fluctuations*, edited by W. H. Branson. Chicago: University of Chicago Press.

Obstfeld, M., and K. Rogoff. 1997. *Foundations of International Macroeconomics.* Cambridge, MA: MIT Press.

Obstfeld, M., J. C. Shambaugh, and A. M. Taylor. 2005. "The Trilemma in History: Tradeoffs among Exchange Rates, Monetary Policies, and Capital Mobility." *Review of Economics and Statistics* 87 (3): 423–38.

Obstfeld, M., J. C. Shambaugh, and A. M. Taylor. 2009. "Financial Instability, Reserves, and Central Bank Swap Lines in the Panic of 2008." National Bureau of Economic Research Working Paper no. 14826, Cambridge, MA. March.

Officer, L. H. 1996. *Between the Dollar-Sterling Gold Points: Exchange Rates, Parity and Market Behavior.* Cambridge: Cambridge University Press.

O'Rourke, K. H., and A. M. Taylor. 2013. "Cross of Euros." *Journal of Economic Perspectives* 27 (3): 167–92.

Orphanides, A. 2002. "Monetary-Policy Rules and the Great Inflation." *American Economic Review Papers and Proceedings* 92 (2): 115–20.

—————. 2003. "Historical Monetary Policy Analysis and the Taylor Rule." Board of Governors Finance and Economic Discussion Series no. 2003-36, July.

Osler, C. L. 1998. "Short-Term Speculators and the Puzzling Behavior of Exchange Rates." *Journal of International Economics* 45 (1): 37–57.

Osterberg, W. P., and J. B. Thomson. 1999. "The Exchange Stabilization Fund: How It Works." Federal Reserve Bank of Cleveland Economic Commentary, December.

Ouyang, A.Y., R. S. Rajan, and T. D. Willett. 2010. "China as a Reserve Sink: The Evidence from Offset and Sterilization Coefficients." *Journal of International Money and Finance* 29 (5): 951–72.

Pardee, S. E. 1973. "Review of Techniques for Intervention in the New York Exchange Market." Unpublished Federal Reserve Bank of New York office correspondence to Mr. Coombs, 17 September.

Pauls, B. D. 1990. "US Exchange-Rate Policy: Bretton Woods to Present." *Federal Reserve Bulletin* 76 (11): 891–908.

Perkins, E. J. 1975. *Financing Anglo-American Trade: The House of Brown 1800–1880.* Cambridge, MA: Harvard University Press.

Popper, H., and J. Montgomery. 2001. "Information Sharing and Central Bank Intervention in the Foreign Exchange Market." *Journal of International Economics* 55:295–316.

Powell, James. 2005. *A History of the Canadian Dollar.* Bank of Canada. http://www.bankofcanada.ca/en/dollar_book/dollar_book.pdf.

Redlich, F. 1951. *The Molding of American Banking: Man and Ideas.* New York: Hafner Publishers.

Redmond, J. 1984. "The Sterling Overvaluation in 1925: A Multilateral Approach." *Economic History Review* 37 (4): 520–32.

Reeves, S. F. 1997. "Exchange Rate Management when Sterilized Interventions Represent Signals of Monetary Policy." *International Review of Economics and Finance* 6 (4): 339–60.

Reitz, S., and M. P. Taylor. 2008. "The Coordination Channel of Foreign Exchange Intervention: A Nonlinear Microstructural Analysis." *European Economic Review* 52 (1): 55–76.

Reynolds, J. E. 1969, "Ireland as a Candidate for a Reciprocal Currency Arrangement with the Federal Reserves," Unpublished Memorandum, 16 December.

Rich, G. 1987. "Swiss and United States Monetary Policy: Has Monetarism Failed?" Federal Reserve Bank of Richmond, *Economic Review* (May/June):3–16.

———. 2000. "Monetary Policy without Central Bank Money: A Swiss Perspective." *International Finance* 3 (3): 439–69.

Richardson, J. D. 1994. "US Trade Policy in the 1980s: Turns—and Roads Not Taken." In *American Economic Policy in the 1980s*, edited by M. Feldstein, 627–58. Chicago: University of Chicago Press.

Rogoff, K. 1984. "On the Effects of Sterilized Intervention: An Analysis of Weekly Data." *Journal of Monetary Economics* 14 (2): 133–50.

———. 1985. "Can International Monetary Policy Cooperation Be Counterproductive?" *Journal of International Economics* 18 (3–4): 199–217.

Rolnick, A. J. and W. E. Webber. 1986. Gresham's Law or Gresham's Fallacy? Journal of Political Economy 94(1): 185 – 199.

Romer, C. D., and D. H. Romer. 2002. "The Evolution of Economic Understanding and Postwar Stabilization Policy." In *Rethinking Stabilization Policy*, A Symposium Sponsored by The Federal Reserve Bank of Kansas. Jackson Hole, Wyoming, 29–31 August.

Rousseau, P. L., and R. Sylla. 2005. "Emerging Financial Markets and Early US Growth." *Explorations in Economic History* 42 (1): 1–26.

Sarno, L., and M. P. Taylor. 2001. "The Official Intervention in the Foreign-Exchange Market: Is It Effective and, If So, How Does It Work?" *Journal of Economic Literature* 39 (3): 839–68.

Sayers, R. S. 1936. *Bank of England Operations 1890–1914*. London: P. S. King and Son Ltd.

———. 1957. *Central Banking after Bagehot*. Oxford: Clarendon Press.

———. 1976. *The Bank of England 1891–1944*, 2 vols. Cambridge: Cambridge University Press.

Schlesinger, A. M. Jr. 1957. *The Crisis of the Old Order, 1919–1933, Volume I: The Age of Roosevelt.* Boston: Houghton Mifflin.

Schreft, S. L. 1990. "Credit Controls: 1980." Federal Reserve Bank of Richmond, *Economic Review* (November/ December):25–55.

Schwartz, A. J. 1983. "The Postwar Institutional Evolution of the International Monetary System." In *The International Transmission of*

Inflation, edited by M. Darby, J. Lothian, A. Gandolfi, A. Schwartz, and A. Stockman. Chicago: University of Chicago Press.

————. 1997. "From Obscurity to Notoriety: A Biography of the Exchange Stabilization Fund." *Journal of Money, Credit, and Banking* 29 (2): 135–53.

Sharkey, R. P. 1959. *Money Class and Party*. Baltimore: Johns Hopkins University Press.

————. 2012. *Volcker: The Triumph of Persistence*. New York: Bloomsbury Press.

Smith, W. B. 1953. *Economic Aspects of the Second Bank of the United States*. Cambridge, MA: Harvard University Press.

Solomon, R. 1968. "The Two-Market System for Gold." Unpublished Memorandum, Federal Reserve System, March.

————. 1971. "Use of Swap Network." Unpublished Memorandum, August.

————. 1982. *The International Monetary System, 1945–1981*. New York: Harper & Row Publishers.

————. 1983. "Official Intervention in Foreign Exchange Markets: A Survey." Unpublished Brookings discussion paper, revised version, March.

Sprinkel, B. W. 1981. "Testimony before the Joint Economic Committee, Congress of the United States (Ninety-Seventh Congress; First Session) May 4, 1981." Washington, DC: US Government Printing Office.

Stevens, E. 1989. "Monetary Impacts of US Dollar Sales in the Foreign Exchange Market." Federal Reserve Bank of Cleveland, Unpublished Internal Memorandum, July.

Swiss National Bank. 2009. *Annual Report*. Zurich, Switzerland. http://www .snb.ch/en/iabout/pub/annrep/id/pub_annrep_2009.

————. 2010. *Annual Report*. Zurich, Switzerland. http://www.snb.ch/en /iabout/pub/annrep/id/pub_annrep_2010.

————. 2011. *Annual Report*. Zurich, Switzerland. http://www.snb.ch/en /iabout/pub/annrep/id/pub_annrep_2011.

————. 2012. *Annual Report*. Zurich, Switzerland. http://www.snb.ch/en /iabout/pub/annrep/id/pub_annrep_2012.

Takagi, S. 1991. "Foreign Exchange Market Intervention and Domestic Monetary Control in Japan, 1973–1989." *Japan and the World Economy* 3 (2): 147–80.

Task Force on System Foreign Currency Operations. 1990a. "Evolution of Formal Procedures for FOMC Oversight of System Foreign Exchange Operations." Unpublished Paper no. 2, January.

————. 1990b. "Evolution of US Exchange Rate Policy." Unpublished Paper no. 3, January.

————. 1990c. "Federal Reserve-Treasury Coordination." Unpublished Paper no. 6, January.

————. 1990d. "Legal Basis for Foreign-Exchange Operations." Unpublished Paper no.1, January.

————. 1990e. "Profits and Losses in US Foreign Currency Operations." Unpublished Paper no. 10, January.

————. 1990f. "Reciprocal Currency Arrangements (The 'Swap' Network)." Unpublished Paper no. 9, January.

————. 1990g. "Review of Approaches and Tactics of Intervention in the Context of Changing Market Conditions Policy and Objectives." Unpublished Paper no. 5, January.

————. 1990h. "US Official Holdings of Foreign Currencies." Unpublished Paper no. 8, Foreign Exchange Department, Federal Reserve Bank of New York, January.

Taylor, M. P. 2005. "Official Foreign Exchange Intervention as a Coordinating Signal in the Dollar-Yen Market." *Pacific Economic Review* 10 (1): 73–82.

Temin, P. 1969. *The Jacksonian Economy*. New York: W. W. Norton.

Thornton, H. [1802] 1978. *An Inquiry into the Nature and Effects of the Paper Credit of Great Britain*. Fairfield, NJ: Augustus M. Kelley.

Timberlake, R. 1975. "The Resumption Act and the Money Supply." *Journal of Economic History* 43 (3): 729–39.

————. 1978. *The Origins of Central Banking in the United States*. Cambridge, MA: Harvard University Press.

Todd, W. F. 1992. "Disorderly Markets: The Law, History, and Economics of the Exchange Stabilization Fund and US Foreign-Exchange Market Intervention." In: *Research in Financial Services: Private and Public Policy*, vol. 4, edited by G. G. Kaufman, 111–79. Greenwich, CT: JAI Press.

Treasury and Federal Reserve Foreign Exchange Operations.(various issues). *Federal Reserve Bulletin*, Board of Governors of the Federal Reserve System, Washington, DC.

Treasury and Federal Reserve Foreign Exchange Operations: Interim Report. (various issues). *Federal Reserve Bulletin*, Board of Governors of the Federal Reserve System, Washington, DC.

Triffin, R. 1960. *Gold and the Dollar Crisis, The Future of Convertibility*. New Haven, CT: Yale University Press.

Truman, E. M. 1980. "Background Material on System Foreign Currency Operations." Memorandum to the FOMC, December.

————. 2005. "Reflections." *Federal Reserve Bank of St. Louis Review* 87 (2, part 2): 353–57.

Unger, I. 1964. *The Greenback Era: A Social and Political History of American Finance, 1865–1879*. Princeton, NJ: Princeton University Press.

United Kingdom (Parliament). [1918] 1979. *First Interim Report of the Committee on Currency and Foreign Exchanges after the War*. Papers by Command, Series no. 9182. Reprint. New York: Arno Press.

US Bureau of the Census. 1975. *Historical Statistics of the United States, Colonial Times to 1970, Bicentennial Edition*. Washington, DC: US Government Printing Office.

US Senate. 1931. Hearings before a Subcommittee on Banking and Currency on The Operation of the National and Federal Reserve Banking System. Seventy-First Congress, Third Session.

US Senate. 1941 Hearing before the Committee on Banking and Currency on "Dollar Devaluation and the Stabilization Fund. Seventy-Seventh Congress, First Session.

US Treasury Department. *Annual Report, 1934–61.* Washington, DC: US Government Printing Office.

US Treasury. 1962a. "Treasury Experience in the Foreign Exchange Market." Transmitted by Robert H. Knight, Treasury general counsel to Ralph A. Young, adviser to the Board of Governors of the Federal Reserve System, (12 pages with 5 tables). (9 February). Recorded in Records Section on 12 February.

US Treasury. 1962b. "Treasury Memorandum on Treasury and Federal Reserve Foreign Currency Operations and Policies—Relationships and Coordination (As Amended to Meet Federal Reserve Suggestions)." (draft copy, 6 pages). (6 February). Recorded in Records Section on 12 February.

Vitale, P. 1999. "Sterilized Central Bank Intervention in the Foreign Exchange Market." *Journal of International Economics* 49:689–712.

Volcker, P. A. 1976. "Priorities for the International Monetary System." Federal Reserve Bank of New York, *Monthly Review* 58 (1): 3–9.

Volcker, P. A., and T. Gyohten. 1992. *Changing Fortunes, The World's Money and the Threat to American Leadership.* New York: Times Books.

Waight, L. 1939. *The History and Mechanism of the Exchange Stabilisation Account.* Cambridge: Cambridge University Press.

Wheelock, D. C. 1991. *The Strategy and Consistency of Federal Reserve Monetary Policy 1929–1933.* Cambridge: Cambridge University Press.

Willis, H. P., and J. H. Chapman. 1934. *The Banking Situation: American Post-War Problems and Developments.* New York: Columbia University Press.

Yeager, L. B. 1966. *International Monetary Relations: Theory, History, and Policy.* New York: Harper & Row.

———. 1976. *International Monetary Relations: Theory, History, Policy, Second edition.* New York: Harper & Row.

Index

Page numbers followed by the letter *f* or *t* refer to figures or tables, respectively.

Federal Reserve Bank of Richmond, 268, 315, 321, 326, 339
Federal Reserve Bank of St. Louis, 245, 345
Federal Reserve Task Force (1989), 313–18
Federal Reserve–Treasury Accord, 14–22, 119
First Bank of the United States, 40–42
Flandin, P.-E., 70, 72, 73
floating rates, 24, 54, 219; advent of, 217–21; Bretton Woods and, 208, 226; Canada and, 201; efficacy of, 279; intervention and, 210–66, 378–88 (*see also specific currencies, topics*); sterilization and, 221–22; swap lines and, 226 (*see also* swap lines); trilemma and, 24, 334 (*see also* trilemma); US dollar and, 210–67. *See also specific currencies, topics*
FOMC. *See* Federal Open Market Committee
Forrestal, R., 319
forward transactions, 22, 28, 158–60, 391n4; appropriate use, 147; Austro-Hungarian Bank and, 32; BIS and, 156; Bretton Woods and, 160; cable transfers, 140; covers and (*see* cover operations); dollar and, 134, 186, 287, 367; ESF and, 69–70, 133, 135, 136, 335 (*see also* Exchange Stabilization Fund); Federal Reserve Act and, 336; FRBNY and, 147 (*see also* Federal Reserve Bank of New York); French francs and, 182, 186, 187; gold and, 78, 103, 111, 146; interest on, 151; Italian lira and, 159–60, 163, 259; marks and, 107, 135, 160, 186, 188, 193–204, 207, 257, 261, 318; SDRs and, 16; spot market, 28, 36, 133, 140, 149, 160, 164, 336, 353, 401n55, 402n75 (*see also* spot transactions); sterling and, 80, 102, 160, 171–74, 176, 207, 260; swap lines, 18, 137, 140, 147, 151, 159, 160, 170, 186, 353 (*see also* swap lines); Swiss francs and, 135, 136, 152; warehousing and, 401n62 (*see also* warehousing). *See also specific institutions, currencies, topics*
franc, Belgian, 23, 50, 69, 83, 227, 231
franc, French, 65, 67–74, 148, 183f, 185f; Bank of England and, 36; Bank of France and, 36, 50–52, 58, 151, 181–87; Bretton Woods (*see* Bretton Woods period); crisis of 1936, 74; devaluation of, 72, 74, 176, 181–87, 395n19; dollar and, 67–76, 81; EEA and, 37, 75; ESF

and, 23, 67–76, 261, 333; Gold Pool, 164, 181–87; Great Depression, 52; IMF and, 162; interventions and, 66, 67–74, 181–87, 231, 251, 255 (*see also specific institutions, topics*); Smithsonian Agreement (*see* Smithsonian Agreement); Tripartite Agreement (*see* Tripartite Agreement); WWI and, 47–48, 50, 333
franc, Swiss: BIS and, 156, 208, 402n66, 402n85; cover operations, 151–56, 259; Cuban missile crisis and, 158, 402n77; devaluation of, 86; dollar depreciation, 238–51, 255; ESF and, 104–7, 134–36, 148 (*see also* Exchange Stabilization Fund); G10 and, 206; gold and, 20, 86, 93, 137, 206; marks and, 134; Roosa bonds and, 163; SNB (*see* Swiss National Bank); swaps, 151–55, 206–8, 226–27, 231, 353, 356, 401n50; Tripartite Agreement, 85, 86, 93, 104; warehousing and, 259–62, 406n47
France, Bank of: de Gaulle and, 187; dollar and, 67, 184–86, 219; EEA and, 75; ESF and, 69–73, 93–105, 397n34; Federal Reserve and, 48, 71, 148, 151, 186, 251, 402n73; franc and, 72, 184, 186–87 (*see also* franc, French); French financial crisis of 1936, 74; gold and, 67, 72, 74, 76, 86–88, 180, 182, 187, 392n4, 395n17, 402n82; IMF and, 187; monetary policy and, 68, 184, 186–87, 402n82; Tripartite Agreement, 86; US Treasury and, 68, 69, 72, 86, 187
Franklin National Bank failure, 222–23
FRBNY. *See* Federal Reserve Bank of New York
Friedman, M., 21

G5. *See* Group of Five
G6. *See* Group of Six
G7. *See* Group of Seven
G10. *See* Group of Ten
General Agreement on Tariffs and Trade (GATT), 200
Genoa Conference (1922), 33
Glass, C., 53, 139, 335, 336
Glass-Steagall Act (1933), 53
gold exchange standard: abandonment of, 34; classical standard, 4, 54 (*see also* gold standard, classical); European banks and, 32; exchange rates and, 27, 29, 32, 333–34; Great Depression